DATE DUE			

RIDING HIGH

America in the Cold War

RIDING HIGH

America in the Cold War

CARL SOLBERG

 Mason & Lipscomb PUBLISHERS   NEW YORK

Grateful acknowledgment is made for permission to quote from the following:

Two lines from "Blowin' in the Wind" by Bob Dylan, which appear on page 125. © 1962 M. Witmark & Sons. All rights reserved. Used by permission of Warner Bros. Music.

Lines from Robert Lowell's poem, "Inaugural Day, January 1953," which appear on page 271. Reprinted by permission of Farrar, Straus & Giroux, Inc. from *Life Studies* by Robert Lowell. © 1953 by Robert Lowell.

Lines from Lorraine Hansberry's play, *Raisin in the Sun*, which appear on page 299. © 1958, 1969 by Robert Nemiroff as Executor of the Estate of Lorraine Hansberry. Used by permission of Random House.

Quotation from page 336 of *Beckoning Frontiers* by Marriner S. Eccles (edited by Sidney Hyman), which appears on pp. 370–371.© 1950, 1951 by Marriner S. Eccles. Reprinted by permission of Alfred A. Knopf, Inc.

To T.R., B.S. *and* H.F.G.

CONTENTS

INTRODUCTION   1

1. The Year of the Ruptured Duck
    THE COLD WAR BEGINS   7

2. The Hardening of the American Position
    THE REMOLDING OF THE AMERICAN MIND   32

3. The Hidden Cost of the Marshall Plan
    and the Taming of American Labor   65

4. The Paradox of the Peacetime Draft
    THE BERLIN BLOCKADE   96

5. A Communist China, a Communist Bomb
    THE SEARCH FOR A SCAPEGOAT   126

6. Last Stand
    THE KOREAN WAR AND McCARTHYISM   166

7. The Liberator in the White House
    THE GOSPEL OF MASSIVE RETALIATION   205

8. Retreat From Sacrifice
    THE CONSUMER SOCIETY AND
    THE END OF STALINISM   245

9. The Disintegration of White Supremacy
    THE SUEZ CRISIS AND THE EMERGENCE
    OF THE THIRD WORLD   292

10. Sputnik and the Illusion of the Primacy
    of American Education   335

11. The U-2
    THE SPLIT-LEVEL STYLE IN GOVERNMENT
    AND SOCIETY   377

CONTENTS

12. The Cuban Missile Crisis and the Rise of the Military-Industrial Complex   425

13. The Nuclear Test Ban Treaty, the End of the Cold War, and the Strange Sequel in America and Vietnam   466

SUMMATION   491

BIBLIOGRAPHICAL ESSAY   513

NOTES   531

INDEX   606

Introduction

T HE UNITED STATES was at the zenith of its power. The
Depression that Stalin expected did not happen. Young people with
babies in their arms were rapping on the doors of suburban real-estate
agents. Returning from World War II, GI's found jobs with big corporations, took on twenty-five-year mortgages, and threw themselves unquestioningly into corporate careers. The cars in which their wives chauffeured
them and their children had fins on them. The children swung hula hoops,
boys ran around with propellers whirling on their heads. The favorite
reading of college students, by Gallup poll, was *Mad* magazine. The
favorite music, by count of 45 r.p.m. record sales, was rock-and-roll, Elvis
Presley moaning "Houn' Dog." All the time, blacks were passed by, left
out even of the crumbs and shavings.

It was also a time when one of the greatest living American writers
said in Stockholm: "There is only one question—when will I be blown
up?" While Eisenhower put off summits, John Foster Dulles walked the
brink of Asia. The engineer in Trenton and the accountant in Sac-
ramento, who had killed krauts in the Huertgen Forest a few years before,
tried to get used to their country's new German allies. Charlie Chaplin
was refused a visa to reenter the United States, Paul Robeson denied a
passport to leave, and the voice of McCarthy was loud in the land: "I have
here in my hand. . . ." Later a young President stood up and said: "We

are going to the moon," Martin Luther King cried: "I have a dream," ghetto-dwellers burned the cities and the pain of the Kennedy assassination was felt in millions of homes. All Americans were marked by these years.

This was the time of the Cold War.

The Cold War came about after 1945 when the United States and Communist Russia were left as the only two big nations to emerge strong and expansive out of six years of world war. The Americans half wished to withdraw, half to work with their wartime ally. But when the Russians shouldered unheeding into the places left by the destruction of German and Japanese power, fear that Stalin sought world revolution united Americans in implacable hostility to any Russian advance. The showdown quickly turned into a bipolar confrontation between superpowers, capitalist America against Communist Russia, with their attending auxiliaries and satellites grouped around them in antipodal camps, West and East. It lasted from 1945 to 1963. All through these years, the world knew neither war nor peace. The technology of war rose to such levels that only the two superpowers could compete, and yet neither saw a way to make nuclear war without itself being destroyed. Though both sides mounted mighty mobilizations of arms, materiel and men, there were never armed hostilities between the United States and Russia. To the end their fix, defined by the chief technologist of the age, Robert Oppenheimer, remained that of "two scorpions in a bottle."[1]

There has been a spate of writing about the Cold War. From Churchill and Truman to Johnson and Robert Kennedy, the principals of the West (but not the East) have marshaled their documents and memoirs. Their biographers and aides have produced large tomes stressing containment as "realistic" responses to Soviet aggressiveness. Later the "revisionists" countered that the United States did as much as the Soviets to bring about the collapse of their wartime alliance and the deadlock of terror that followed.

This book takes another tack. Its subject is the relationship of the Cold War to American society at home. The book undertakes to show that the events of the Cold War marked the society and people of the United States, searing flesh and spirit, and leaving scars that will affect us as long as we live. It focuses attention on a dozen high points of these years—the Truman Doctrine, the Berlin Blockade, the Cuban Missile Crisis and so on—and pairs or juxtaposes with each such crisis certain important developments that took place on the home front—such as the silencing of the young, the enactment of the peacetime draft, and the rise of the military to a leading place in American life.

In the larger movements of human history, social conjunctures are so numerous, varied and complex that it becomes impossible to call any event of the Cold War a "sufficient" cause for what followed in American society. Signal contributions have been made by the authors of the New Left in showing the influence of economic considerations in American diplomacy since 1945; but these interpretations locate the sources of Cold War policy within too narrow a focus. This book restricts itself to no kind of conspiratorial theory of history to account for outcomes. If the young people of America, for example, were kept in classrooms in these years to the highest average school-leaving age in history, there is no imputation here that corporation heads, union leaders or others planned it that way. Nor is there any assumption, when it is suggested that the Cold War had something to do with the widespread desire for family security, consumer goods and "privatism" after 1945, that the rush to the suburbs which expressed these urges was due solely to impulses set in motion by the Cold War.

This book is about the *unintended* consequences to America of the Cold War. It proceeds from the almost ironic assumption that all the great decisions of these years and, above all, those early decisions which got the United States into the Cold War, were made with every intention of doing what was perceived at the time to be in the best interest of the nation and its people. They were based upon a calculation of immediate interests and immediate consequences that seemed overwhelmingly to call for such action at the time. But these decisions had other, less immediate results that were not foreseen at the time. Things happened that changed everything, changed us, and changed our lives.

Why, it must be asked, do nations and their leaders take actions that turn out to have effects that depart so far from what they confidently and righteously expect? Error, personal traits, received information, beliefs, institutional forms, and the sheer limits of knowledge account for much of the trouble. Such is the nature of action that a President cannot wait to assimilate all of the considerations that specialist advisers can put before him. Even then, in human affairs such reasons will always be contingent: for any action a whole range of consequences may follow, so that experience itself is a treacherous guide. Long ago Robert Merton, the theorist of social action, put his finger on the inherent weakness in the concerted efforts of mankind and called it "the imperious immediacy of interest."[2] It means that the overriding concern in most human actions will be with the immediate consequences, to the exclusion of considering any other consequences of the same act. "When compulsive ardor gives the charge," Hamlet said, "reason panders the will."

There is an important corollary to this proposition, which Merton has called the "self-fulfilling prophecy." Concern with immediate consequences may be utterly rational in the circumstances, upheld beyond cavil by common sense and supported by the most objective analysis of the situation that self-interest seems to call for. But it is just as true that intense interest often precludes this kind of analysis precisely because the dominating concern with satisfying that interest generates an emotional bias on its behalf. This factor, built into (and unique to) human behavior, leads inexorably to the "self-fulfilling prophecy."[3]

Having made their assessment of a situation, men respond to the meaning the situation has for them. The way they have defined the situation becomes an integral part of the situation and thus affects the future. What they do later, and what others do, is determined by the original assessment. In this way, Americans and their leaders in the aftermath of the Second World War identified the Russians as Communists bent on aggressive expansion. After all, Moscow's propaganda said this was so. But the American judgment owed a great deal to recent experience with the aggressive behavior of Nazi Germany. It was fresh in everybody's mind that the Western nations had failed to size up Hitler's Germany as aggressive at Munich in 1938, when firm action could have checked its expansion. Watching the Russians set up Communist puppet regimes throughout eastern Europe after 1945, it was easy to equate Russian expansiveness with German expansiveness, which had ended in war. From this assessment, made with an immediacy of interest so imperative as to obliterate thought of remoter consequences back home, everything else followed.

For in conformity with the principle of the self-fulfilling prophecy, the assessment that the Russians presented the sort of military threat that Nazi Germany did, operated to bring about the situation it had defined. The representatives of the United States and Russia became progressively alienated, each apprehensively responding to an "offensive" move of the other with a "defensive" move of its own, and escalating their reactive hostility again and again to the brink of oblivion.

The ultimate irony of this history is that probably both the Americans and the Russians were wrong in their original assessment of each other. The devastating absurdity of the self-fulfilling prophecy, Merton says, is that its "specious validity . . . perpetuates a reign of error."[4] It is not the province of this book to follow the consequences in Russia, where Stalin's successors found it necessary to denounce him and split Communism itself to break the chain of error. The United States, mobilized as if for war, persisted in seeing itself beleaguered in a polar world, with a Moscow-managed "international Communism" arrayed monolithically against it. The defection of Yugoslavia from the Eastern camp in 1947 did little to shake this view. Not even the strain caused in the Eastern camp after 1949 by the victory of Mao Tse-tung's brand of Communism in China shook the catatonic American conviction that the United States was up against a single world foe commanded from Moscow.

After nearly two decades, however, the Russians in 1963 signed with the United States what Americans told themselves was an innocuous limited nuclear test ban treaty—and that did it. The Chinese thereupon publicly denounced the Russians for doing so, thus disclosing to Washington that it was not up against a monolithic "international Communism," shattering the illusion of a bipolar confrontation of two superpowers, and ending the Cold War. But it is not to be supposed, when an entire society has shaped its values to fear and hatred of Communism, that the expectations of the American public and its elected representatives could swing around at once. For almost a decade after the collapse of Cold War polarity, anti-Communism remained the currency of public discourse and even policy in the United States, justifying a colonial-type war in Southeast Asia and ever-higher expenditures on the arms industry and the military establishment. Not until President Nixon made his visits to Peking and Moscow in 1972 was America ready to acknowledge that the Cold War was over and it was indeed a new world, not bipolar at all, but a configuration of four and perhaps five big powers, moving into a new kind of balance.

This book grew out of my reflections on a period I have lived through and written about as a journalist for *Time* magazine. It could not have been written without the steadfast support and critical encouragement of Professor Henry F. Graff, a diplomatic historian with the vision to insist that in the Cold War domestic, not diplomatic, affairs were the thing to concentrate on. Professor Graff, who read all early drafts of the manuscript, Professor Eugene Rice, department chairman, who made the author welcome as Visiting Scholar, and the entire membership of the Columbia University history department, lent immeasurable support. The following made suggestions or comments, or criticized parts of the manuscript: Professors Zbigniew Brzezinski, Lawrence Cremin, Sigmund Diamond, Phillips Davison, James Marston Fitch, Eric Foner, William T. R. Fox, Herbert Gans, John Garraty, Percival Goodman, Roger Hilsman, Kenneth Jackson, Bela Kiraly, Leonard Krieger, William Leuchtenburg, Seymour Melman, Robert Merton, James William Morley, Peter Passell, Joseph Rothschild, James Shenton, Marshall Shulman, Fritz Stern, B. J. Widick, C. Martin Wilbur and Howard Wriggins.

Others who lent help were: Professors Thomas C. Davis, James Flick, Eric Goldman, William Griffith, Gabriel Kolko, T. A. Larson, C. Eric Lincoln, M. L. Nieburg, Robert Perry, Lee Rainwater, Arthur Schlesinger Jr., Roger Shinn, Gaddis Smith, Richard W. Solberg and Chilton

Williamson; also Elie Abel, Herbert Alexander, Marvin Barrett, Roy Bennett, Hugh Borton, Gurney Breckenfeld, Edward L. R. Elson, Rick Fried, Mark Gelfand, James A. Hagerty, Louis Halle, Douglas Haskell, James Hester, Walter McQuade, Willis Player, Margaret Quimby, Alan Walker Read, Herbert I. Smith, John Steele, Michael Sumichrast, and Sam Welles. William F. Forbis read the entire manuscript. Thomas Michaels and Sara Solberg helped greatly in research. Sgt. Carl Solberg did research on the draft. The Butler Library provided houseroom and superb professional support, notably through the reference staff headed by Eugene Sheehy.

Port Chester, New York
June, 1973

CHAPTER 1

The Year of the Ruptured Duck

THE COLD WAR BEGINS

THE FIRST IRONY of the Cold War was the man who predicted it. In the last days of the Second World War one of the most terrifying and compelling human beings of all time was sputtering toward extinction. Adolf Hitler had shown the world how appallingly far a leader could go by harnessing the twin forces of the twentieth century—mass manipulation of men's minds and high technology. In one short lifetime he had devised, made, and carried through from start to finish a revolution such as no single man—neither Napoleon, Marx nor Lenin—had ever done before. So well had he understood, so ruthlessly had he exploited, the forces of human violence and hatred that he had inflamed and then subdued all Europe. And by the end he had been brought low only by the combined forces of the forty-two nations he had roused against him.

In his bunker under Berlin, Hitler was an old man at fifty-six. He shuffled and he stooped. His entire left side shook uncontrollably. He had to have a chair pushed beneath him when he wished to sit down. His face was white, rigid. Broken and half-paralyzed, the lord of the Thousand Year Reich began to dictate his last testament. The crude hatred, contempt and rancor that were the deepest forces in his character were vomited up. The monologues guttered off into rantings and ravings against all who had stood in his way—above all, against the Jews.

Yet, even in terminal dissolution and self-destruction, there hovered more than a semblance of the mental power that had charged Hitler with such explosive force. One day Forster, Gauleiter of Danzig, entered the bunker to tell Hitler that his situation had become impossible. He came out of Hitler's presence a changed man, asserting that the Fuehrer had promised to find him more defenders and vowing that he would fight on.[1] It was then that Hitler decided to dictate a final chapter of his testament. The date was April 2, 1945, when Roosevelt, Churchill and Stalin were exchanging their messages on how they would organize the postwar world.

The pages of the testament were duly typed and each sheet authenticated by the large, loose, formless signature of Martin Bormann, Hitler's henchman to the last. Unearthed a decade later in southern Germany where they had been sent for safekeeping, these fragments caught the last glint of the dark forces which Hitler had conjured. In a burst of prophetic power the doomed dictator foretold the future that would follow from the destruction he had brought down on the political world:

> With the defeat of the Reich and pending the emergence of the Asiatic, the African and perhaps the South American nationalisms, there will remain in the world only two great powers capable of confronting each other—the United States and the USSR. The laws of both history and geography will compel these two powers to a trial of strength; either military or in the fields of economics and ideology. These same laws make it inevitable that both powers shall become enemies in Europe. And it is equally certain that both of these powers will sooner or later find it desirable to seek the support of the sole surviving great nation in Europe—the German people.[2]

A SECOND IRONY of the Cold War was the euphoria that preceded it.

Less than three weeks after Hitler dictated his testament, two great armies that had marched and fought on the beaches of Normandy and the streets of Stalingrad smashed through the last narrow corridor of German resistance to meet at the Elbe River. Lieutenant Albert L. Kotzebue, leading a twenty-five-man patrol of the American 69th Division, wheeled his jeep into a Saxon courtyard and spotted a strange-looking man in an unusual uniform astride a pony. A Russian! The scouts next raced on to the Elbe River two miles beyond, leaped into a rowboat, and using their rifles as oars, paddled to the eastern side. There they met a group of Russians and exchanged salutes. Farther north, Lieutenant William D. Robinson led a patrol of four men to the Elbe at Torgau, where he started crawling out across the twisted girders of a wrecked bridge. A Russian soldier climbed out from the eastern side. They met above the waters of the Elbe, grinned and pounded each other exuberantly. At another point Russians clad in blue shorts swam the river to greet the "Tovarichi Amerikanski." At Torgau there was a feast with a main dish of fried eggs, dancing in the streets, and toasts in wine and vodka.[3]

The great event was announced simultaneously in Moscow and Washington. The Russians had come 1500 miles from the foothills of the Caucasus, the Americans 800 miles through the Atlantic Wall, the West Wall and the Rhine defenses. Pesident Harry S. Truman proclaimed jubilantly that the men—from General Courtney Hodge's 1st Army and Marshal Ivan Konev's 1st Ukrainian Army—met "where they intended to meet—in the heart of Nazi Germany." "We well know what a fighting partnership is," said the Moscow newspaper *Red Star*. "In the Red Army and the armies of the Allies there will always remain the word 'Torgau' —the funeral salute fired over the grave of Hitlerite Germany." The *Chicago Sun* captioned its cartoon of American and British soldiers lifting high a Russian tanker on their shoulders with: "The Gang's All here."[4]

A THIRD IRONY of the Cold War was the popular rush back to peace that led up to it.

During the winter of 1945-46, the United States lived in a fever of "reconversion." The greatest war in history had been won; Hitler had been exterminated in his bunker, and the Japanese, much sooner than expected, had been compelled to surrender by the obliterating force of the atomic bomb. From five continents 11,000,000 American fighting men were converging on home. All they seemed to want to talk about was how many "points" they had in the Army's system for determining who would get home first. The streets of the country were filled with men in ill-fitting civilian clothes, sporting on their lapels the little gold "ruptured duck" pin that identified veterans returned to civilian life.

The hard times of the 1930s were gone; people were loaded up with uncashed war bonds, and savings accounts bulged. A rash of strikes broke out—a war-denied luxury—among coalminers, steelworkers, dockhands and even Long Island gravediggers, and spread until 1,400,000 were idled. A daffy little book about a lady chicken rancher called *The Egg and I* was the popular reading of the day. Newspapers front-paged the story of a crowd of teenage boys and girls in Los Angeles storming a department store sale of blue jeans. And from Miami a newsman reported:

An enormous amount of money is being spent here these days—a million and a quarter through the mutual machines at Hialeah every

afternoon, plus another half million at the dog tracks and Jai Alai, but
doormen, maids, waiters and such people who depend on tips are getting
little of it.

The explanation seemed to be that thousands vacationing in Miami had
made real money for the first time in their lives during the war, and since
they were paying prices as high as $30 a day for their hotel rooms, they
were now holding on tightly to their change.[5]

President Charles Wilson of General Motors journeyed to Washington to find out whether some manpower could be shifted from military
to civilian production at his plants, and was told he was too impatient.
("You engineers and mechanics don't understand politicians," Bernard
Baruch told him.) He did not have to wait much longer. In practically no
time at all American industry obtained repeal of the wartime excess-profits
tax and made the switch to peacetime output smoothly enough to keep
on all but the most elderly pinch-hitters, the lady welders, and the girls
who married returning soldiers at a record rate. Housing, not jobs, was
suddenly the nation's number one postwar problem.[6]

Jobs were certainly easier to get than homes. Living space was in such
short supply that Benny Goodman's band played for a benefit in Cleveland at which people pledged rooms-for-rent instead of money. Of the
nation's 33,500,000 married couples, no fewer than 3,000,000 shared
somebody else's quarters, usually their parents'. The federal government's
short-term response to these pressures was an improvisational shambles.
At first, still thinking that creating jobs was of greatest urgency, the
government lifted all controls on industrial construction—and held back
on residential housing. Then, reversing itself, it launched a Veterans
Emergency Housing Program to build 950,000 units in 1946. Not even
half that number got built, chiefly for lack of materials, and the program
had to be scrapped.[7]

Improvisation and confusion were the characterizing marks of the
American government as it struggled to position itself amidst the pent-up
forces that began to flow as war ended. Didn't Americans—or at least
their government—know that war brings change? The first convulsive
reflex of the nation and of the administration was to lunge right back
toward a way of life as it had been perceived before Hitler took Paris and
the Japanese attacked Pearl Harbor. Just four days after the surrender of
Germany, America's new President, Harry S. Truman, took the advice of
administration officials for whom the issues of reconversion of the nation
were uppermost. Abruptly, Truman canceled the entire program of lend-
lease credits to Britain and Russia. The tremendous program of procurement for the armed forces (having long since delivered the impossible

numbers of planes and tanks that President Roosevelt had called for after Pearl Harbor) had already been cut back; the war plants had stopped making small arms in 1943. At the command of the administration, the Congress and the country, the men and women of the Army, Navy and Air Force were streaming home from all continents. If America was on the road to change in 1945, the change it first sought was in the direction of its old peacetime pursuits.

A FOURTH IRONY of the Cold War was the man who ordained it.

The humble American President who led the way was in office almost by accident. The country, shucking its uniforms and shaking off its war regime with such compulsive single-mindedness, found it hard to get used to the idea of President Truman at the White House. Truman took office just before V-E Day, and many people felt that a very little man was filling in for a very big man as the nation's Chief Executive. A good many had never known any other President than Roosevelt. Indelibly printed in everyone's mind were scenes that belonged to April 12, 1945; every American could remember where he had been and how he had heard the news of President Roosevelt's sudden death.

Shock had been followed by a kind of appalled wonder. People told of the moment in Sam Rayburn's Capitol office when Truman, about to have a drink with the speaker, took up the telephone, went pale and muttered "Holy General Jackson," as he heard Steve Early's odd, strangled voice from the White House, "Please come right away."

The next moment was recalled with awe. The Vice President was greeted at the White House by Mrs. Roosevelt, who put her arm on his shoulder and said, "The President is dead." Vice President Truman choked and asked if there was anything he could do for her. She answered: "Is there anything *we* can do for *you*? For you are the one in trouble now." The next day President Truman told reporters:

> Boys, if you ever pray, pray for me now. I don't know whether you fellows ever had a load of hay fall on you, but when they told me yesterday what had happened, I felt like the moon, the stars and all the planets had fallen on me.

That same week the nervous new President, upon entering Congress for his first speech in office, forgot himself and immediately started speaking. Rayburn growled, the nation overhearing it all on the microphones, "Just a minute, Harry, let me introduce you, will you?"[8]

What sort of a man was this new President who was to lead America away from the traditional back-home preoccupations of two centuries and into global Cold War? Harry Truman's knowledge of foreign policy issues was pitifully weak, partly because President Roosevelt had not bothered to ask his opinion on international problems. An Allied ambassador, trying to provide his government in London or Moscow or Rio with some background on the views of the new leader in Washington, could hardly avoid cabling the one widely printed remark of the Missouri senator made after Hitler invaded Russia in 1941: "If we see that Germany is winning we ought to help Russia, and if Russia is winning, we ought to help Germany, and that way let them kill as many as possible."

Millions of Americans concurred with that opinion during the summer before Pearl Harbor swept them all, including the junior senator from a state with strong isolationist traditions, into the Second World War. Harry Truman was often called the little man become Senator. For all his great gifts of courage and decision, this was fundamentally true. Acutely aware of his limitations, he carried himself with the jauntiness of a gamecock—"a gutsy little fighter," his contemporaries said. Lacking much formal education, he read widely and accumulated a quite remarkable fund of information about American history. But he distrusted ideas and lacked historical perspective. In 1948, when he made pivotal decisions about the Cold War with the Soviet Union, he cited a discredited old forgery as basis for dismissing the Russian leaders as men who "have fixed ideas and those ideas were set out by Peter the Great in his will. . . ."

Because he wore thick, prismatic lenses to compensate for his poor sight, Truman gave the impression of seeing more than he did, of looking owlishly wise when his grasp of affairs was not always complete. Though he appointed a number of extremely able men, he enjoyed the close company of small minds. His political opinions, sniffed a professor, "sound like my barber's." He was a product of small-town America, his wife Bess gloriously so. Asked how it felt to be the nation's first lady, she replied, "So-so."[9]

Simplicity was a source of strength for Truman, and the bond between him and his countrymen. Though he made no excessive appraisal of his capabilities, he was determined to live up to his responsibilities. To his mother—the same border-bred Martha Truman who refused to sleep in the Lincoln bed when she visited the White House—he wrote "Dear Mama" letters until her death at ninety-four in 1947. They were filled with a beguiling, small-boy pride over meeting Stalin ("I like Old Joe") and firing cabinet officers ("Well, I had to fire Henry today.") that sounded for all the world like a schoolboy's report that classes were hard but he was working resolutely and doing his best. In the full consciousness of duty discharged, he could write the day after he relieved General Douglas MacArthur of his command in 1951:

> I could do nothing else and still be President of the United States. Even the Chiefs of Staff came to the conclusion that the civilian control of the military was at stake, and I didn't let it stay at stake very long.[10]

Something of the same spirit shone though when, preparing to leave the White House two years later, he delivered his farewell address:

> I felt that there must be a million men better qualified than I to take up the presidential task. But the work was mine to do and I had to do it. And I have tried to give it everything that was in me.[11]

Born in Missouri in 1884, Truman owed his rise to the highest office to the fact that he came from a border state. It tells much about changing America that he was picked for the vice presidential nomination in 1944 because he stood somewhere between the South and the North, and that when he sought reelection as President four years later, he could be tabbed as the man from Independence, starting point of the Oregon Trail, and hailed as mediating leader from a newer American border "a little West of center." The significance of this swing for the nation's politics was not lost on the ambitious Lyndon B. Johnson of Texas, who was in the process of discovering that his origins in the ranch country uplands at the western edge of the Gulf coastal plain made him not just a Southerner, but a man of the rising West.

Harry Truman grew up near Kansas City in the heartland America of white frame houses, elm-shaded streets, Masonic lodge meetings, and Baptist preaching. Having run the family farm at Grandview for more than ten years, he knew what it was to drive a gang-plow pulled by four mules. But for him the shaping experience was going off to the Army in the First World War. It brought out in Harry Truman the kind of patriotism that many other Americans shared. First, he ran the canteen at Camp Doniphan, along with another artilleryman, Eddie Jacobsen. Then he was sent to France in command of his company. "Everything I am," said Truman later, "I owe to Battery D." His very walking pace, a brisk 120 steps a minute, was learned marching with the Army along French roads. The esteem that he carried away from his military life contributed to the high regard he had for such men as General George Marshall and General MacArthur. He never pinned the Congressional

Medal of Honor on a GI without saying that he would rather have the Medal than be President.

After the armistice ending the First World War Truman opened a haberdashery with his friend Eddie Jacobsen in Kansas City. The venture failed, however, in the business depression that followed the war, and Truman went into politics. He became a minor cog in the political machine of Tom Pendergast. In 1934 he was elected to the United States Senate, where he proved to be a loyal but obscure New Dealer. During a railroad investigation Senator Truman worked with a young counsel Max Lowenthal, who had been Justice Louis Brandeis' law clerk. Brandeis was then over eighty and one of the great judges of America's liberal tradition. Lowenthal invited Truman to go with him to one of Brandeis' Sunday afternoon get-togethers at his California Street apartment. The conversation was spirited and wide-ranging. "I'm not used to meeting people like that," Truman said, and went again.

In the Second World War, Truman's "watchdog" committee on defense spending dug fearlessly and saved the government billions. It also made a modest name for its chairman. Yet many thought, in the events that followed, that Truman emerged as an accidental Vice President as well as accidental President. Roosevelt had discovered in his third-term victory of 1940 that the big-city states provided him with his winning majorities. Four years later the big-city leaders went to Roosevelt and told him that Henry Wallace would simply not do as his running mate this time. But when the big-city leaders turned to Truman at the convention, he steadfastly refused to believe that Roosevelt wanted him. Finally someone held a receiver up to his unbelieving ear for him to hear the President's voice saying so. Fighting a wave of nausea, Truman then stopped pleading that they nominate James F. Byrnes, President Roosevelt's War Mobilizer, and he sought out Byrnes to ask for release from his pledge to make a speech for Byrnes's nomination.[12]

In 1945, both Henry Wallace and Jimmy Byrnes occupied important positions in the political life of the little man who had been, in a few short weeks, elevated past them into the White House. The day after Roosevelt's funeral, Truman asked Byrnes to become his Secretary of State, and Henry Wallace, after the other Roosevelt holdovers dropped away, stayed on in Truman's cabinet. Both acted like men who thought they, not Truman, should be President—Wallace who had missed the presidency by one hundred days, and Byrnes who had been Roosevelt's "assistant president" in the wartime White House and by his side at Yalta while Truman was playing poker with his cronies on Capitol Hill. Each man acted as if Truman were another Andrew Johnson, to be suffered in office until he, the man for the job, could secure the Democratic presidential nomination in 1948.

With this kind of company around, it took Harry Truman quite a while to impose his own stamp on his administration. He relished making decisions, and he made the big ones prescribed by his predecessor's policies: to drop the atomic bomb on Japan, to join the Allies in forming the United Nations, to support a full-employment bill that would help labor hold the jobs won in the New Deal and wartime years.

Truman bungled the job of converting the economy back to peacetime conditions. Even when he proclaimed the most liberal objectives, he often lacked the detailed grasp of problems and processes necessary for putting them over. The nation rapidly became aware that the new president had a quick temper. It was not just that Truman sometimes insulted opponents instead of convincing or conciliating them. In his scraps with such men as United Mineworkers President John L. Lewis and Republican opposition leader Robert A. Taft, he was often the winner. His battle to win reelection against great odds in 1948 gained him the admiration and votes of so many million Americans that he won that fight, too.

But Truman was never able to put over his Fair Deal program of reform, and this was largely because the leaders of Congress did not respect him. These men, the Sam Rayburns, Richard Russells and Bob Tafts, could never quite forget that the Chief Executive they were dealing with was the same back-bench Senator from Missouri with the county courthouse small-talk, who drank, played poker and voted dutifully as his leaders expected of him. One of the minor scandals of American history, the lack of any provision for pensions for former Presidents, came up for belated rectification in the Truman years. As finally passed, the benefits did not commence with Truman but only with his successor, Eisenhower. Some said that the measure was held up out of resentment at the man who squeezed in ahead of everybody else and became President.

What made the difference in the Truman succession was above all the new President's courage and rare capacity for decisions. But of great importance was his reverential regard for the office of President, and his determination to live up to its responsibilities. He loved the lore of his job, and talked much about those who had held it. Taking supper on the south porch of the White House with his wife, Bess, he was reminded by the Old Chesapeake and Ohio canal in the distance how John Quincy Adams swam there "and got his clothes stolen by an angry woman who wanted a job—the old guy did not have my guards or it would not have happened." He lectured reporters on President James K. Polk's use of his war powers. Of Franklin Pierce he said roundly, "The trouble with him was that he had no *program*."

Whatever the complexities of his ties with his old sidekicks in Congress, the President seemed to have no such difficulties with the brainy dudes he learned to rely on as he led the country into the Cold War. With these accomplished men from the world glimpsed at Justice Brandeis's on Sunday afternoons, the Achesons and McCloys and Sumner Pikes, Truman had the security of being the commander-in-chief. With Acheson in particular the relationship was one of the most complementary regard. Through the formative years of the Cold War, Acheson was a Richelieu, a great minister devising, proposing and executing policy, and Truman was his monarch, not only making the decisions but forcefully proclaiming the administration's broad purposes. At the end, preparing to step down from office, Truman could ask his secretary of state, "Dean, how should I act as ex-President?" And Acheson, arch and preachy, could respond with the words of a chief minister who was also a bishop's son, "Mr. President, you must act as the American people would wish you to act."[13]

A FIFTH IRONY of the Cold War was the man who proclaimed it.

Early in "that winter," as a best-selling novel of the 1940s was to call the harshly shifting season of 1945-46, President Franc B. McCluer of tiny Westminster College in Fulton, Missouri, had an idea. McCluer, called "Bullet" by the townspeople of Fulton (pop. 8,297), had heard that Winston Churchill, turned out of office in Britain by a sensational election upset a few months before, was coming to the United States for a holiday in Miami. Westminster College had a small endowment for bringing in speakers of "international reputation," and it was Bullet's idea to invite Churchill to speak at Fulton, thus interrupting his Florida vacation.

Hastening to Washington, Bullet looked up Brigadier General Harry H. Vaughn, star football center at Westminster in the days when Bullet was star debater, and now aide to President Truman at the White House. He confided his idea to his old classmate.

Bullet had already composed a letter to Churchill, and the two old classmates bustled in to show it to the President. Truman thought it was a good idea, and in longhand scribbled a postscript across the bottom of the letter: "This is a very fine old college out in my state. I will be glad to introduce you."

There is no evidence that at the time Truman was doing anything more than making a friendly gesture for a fellow Missourian. But Churchill already had a message very much in mind.

Even before he left office he had repeatedly urged that the Western Allies speak to Russia about their differences over Eastern Europe from a position of overwhelming strength, and events had been taking place that winter in central and eastern Europe that would make Churchill even more impatient for a showdown "settlement." By the appointed day in Fulton, Bullet's invitation to Churchill had an effect something like that of the New Jersey boy who took aim at a sparrow on a wire and blew up the arsenal behind it. At Fulton, on March 5, 1946, Winston Churchill proclaimed in one of his most powerful speeches that Cold War was descending upon the world.

News that Churchill was readying a "very important address" was conveyed to Truman by Secretary Byrnes, who flew down to Miami during the former prime minister's "rest cure," and received a preview. Admiral Leahy, the President's military adviser, endorsed the speech. Then, on the train to Missouri before he spoke, Churchill showed a copy of the speech to Truman, who voiced strong, unreserved approval. Thus when the great man spoke, the President of the United States would be physically and figuratively right behind him on the platform—in the heartland of America, in his native state.[14]

What a day it was for Fulton! From fifty miles around the country folks drove at dawn to have a look at the man whose voice was as familiar in Missouri as it was in Yorkshire. Children perched on rooftops, flags flew, loudspeakers on the courthouse blared barn-dance music. The ladies of four churches, the wives of the War Dads, and the American Legion Auxiliary buttered 30,000 sandwiches for the visitors. Young girls sold "Churchill sundaes" with English toffee ice cream. Three high school bands serenaded Churchill with the "Missouri Waltz" as he rode bareheaded and waving an unlit black cigar beside a smiling Harry Truman in an open car that bore them through the town and up to Bullet McCluer's frame house for a lunch of Callaway County ham.

Fulton being a dry town, there was a pause after lunch in an upstairs bedroom during which General Vaughn poured a slug of brandy for the prime minister. Then Churchill and Truman fell in with Bullet McCluer behind the academic procession that marched into the packed gymnasium. The organist played "How Firm a Foundation," the Presbyterian minister led in prayer, and Harry Truman made only the briefest introduction: "I know he will have something constructive to say."[15]

Six years before, when America seemed isolated and unheeding of the lightning sweep of German arms to the shores of the Atlantic, a great movement to wake the country was started in just such a small town in the American heartland. Then it was old William Allen White, the Kansas editor, who had launched in nearby Emporia his Committee to Defend America by Aiding the Allies. Now the great leader who guided British and Western democracy through those grim hours of 1940 stood at the center of traditional American isolationism and grandiloquently warned against another retreat.

A shadow has fallen upon the scene so lately lighted up by the Allied victory. From Stettin in the Baltic to Trieste in the Adriatic, an iron curtain has descended across the Continent. Behind that line lie all the capitals of the ancient states of Central and Eastern Europe. Warsaw, Berlin, Prague, Vienna, Budapest, Belgrade and Sofia, all these famous cities and the populations around them lie in what I must call the Soviet sphere, and are all subject in one form or another, not only to Soviet influence but to a very high and, in many cases, increasing measure of control from Moscow. . . . Police governments are prevailing in almost every case. . . . In front of the Iron Curtain, the very future of Italy hangs in the balance, and through the world Communist fifth columns are established and work in complete unity and absolute obedience to the directions they receive from the Communist center. . . . These are somber facts for anyone to have to recite on the morrow of victory . . . but we should be most unwise not to face them squarely while time remains.

Last time I saw it all coming and cried aloud to my fellow countrymen and to the world, but no one paid any attention. Up until the year 1933 or even 1935, Germany might have been saved from the awful fate which has overtaken her, and we might all have been spared the miseries Hitler let loose upon mankind. . . . We must surely not let that happen again.

To prevent its happening again Churchill proposed a virtual British-American military alliance. It would be "criminal madness," Churchill said, to turn over to the United Nations at that point the atomic bomb which "God has willed" into American hands. But if the United States and Britain stood together—one lesson that experience had taught Churchill about dealing with the Russians was that "there is nothing they admire so much as strength"—a "settlement" could be reached "now, in 1946."[16]

The applause in the crowded gymnasium was mild, especially for the suggestion of the Anglo-American alliance. In Washington, the reaction of Congress was mixed. Though a few thought the speech "realistic," the majority seemed cold, even shocked. American newspapers, with a few exceptions, were noncommittal, and President Truman himself refrained from any public comment as the train paused in St. Louis on the way back from Fulton and the President appeared in striped pajamas on the rear platform to greet a small crowd.

Churchill's message was far too strong for one swallow. But it had a profoundly crystallizing effect on American opinion, just as President Truman guessed it would. In calling for integration and mobilization of America's heart and treasure in a confrontation against the Russians, a man of the past was summoning the country to a radically new future. It was true that he spoke as a private citizen. Yet to all Americans who had so recently committed themselves to a great war, this was one of their heroes speaking. They were sentimental about him. They had, in the phrase of the day, "a piece of" him. Stirred by his grandiloquence, exaggeration and rhetorical bravura, they were also led by him.

For Americans, in 1946, cherished memories of Winston Churchill —his buoyant comings and goings in wartime Washington; his fierce defiance when London was on fire and the Nazis (memory savored the way he contemptuously mispronounced it "Nazzzzis") poised to leap for the Dover cliffs; his way of saying, this veteran of dimly-recalled colonial scrapes in darkest Africa and farthest-flung India, that he, himself was half-American. He lived powerfully in a shared imagination as the prophet who cried "Beware" when that other, unbearably smug umbrella-waving Englishman, Prime Minister Neville Chamberlain, was appeasing Hitler. Churchill was fondly remembered as the round figure hopping jauntily over the London debris, making the V-for-victory sign beside the bandaged London fire wardens and begrimed East End mothers in their tumbled doorways; as the "Former Naval Person" glowering like a bulldog beside F.D.R., "Uncle Joe" Stalin and all the others at the summit conferences where victory was charted for the Second World War.

Now he was old and out of office. If old, who else could summon up such fires of eloquence? If out of office, that made those still touched by the wartime rhetoric for democracy, if anything, only the prouder of him. So there was something about the old war hero that tugged at this generation of Americans, and it affected the way they perceived Europe perhaps more than all the radio bulletins and magazine stories of crises in Paris and Athens. He had been right about the coming of the war. He had been the winner. He kept alive the old fire. And the compelling thought flashed, "We should be listening to him."

A Gallup poll showed fifty-one percent unpersuaded by Churchill's reasoning. Pearl Buck, the novelist, called the speech "a catastrophe— turning our destiny a dangerous way." A reader wrote *The New York Times* to say the speech "should be required reading in every schoolroom." "Churchill exploded a bomb at Fulton," ran the Paris headline. Bernard Shaw, the playwright, told a reporter in London he thought it "nothing short of a declaration of war on Russia." The British Labour government, which had no interest in the alliance Churchill had proposed, was dismayed that the former prime minister's opinions were considered official. At the United Nations, Secretary-General Trygve Lie of Norway, who had just successfully negotiated the withdrawal of Russian troops from Norway and who looked forward to negotiation of the differences between West and East in his new organization, was fearful that "UNO," as it was still called, might not now get off the ground.[17]

The Soviet reaction came from Stalin himself. In an interview with *Pravda* the premier charged that Churchill had "sounded a call to war against the Soviet Union" and had turned the twenty-year Anglo-Russian friendship pact he had signed in 1942 into "an empty scrap of paper." Thus the speech delivered in the little Missouri town brought out into the open before all the world deep divergences between the Anglo-Americans and Russians that had been opening steadily since well before the day their forces met in triumph at the Elbe in April, 1945.[18]

These differences were rooted in history. They had been marked out for America as long ago as the outbreak of the First World War. In 1914, Colonel Edward House, confidential adviser on foreign affairs to President Woodrow Wilson, wrote a memorandum for the President that stated:

> If the Allies win, it means largely the domination of Russia on the Continent of Europe; and if Germany wins, it means the unspeakable tyranny of militarism for generations to come.[19]

The divergences with Russia were enormously enlarged in 1917 when, after America's intervention against Germany in 1917, Czarist Russia collapsed and the Bolsheviks seized power. From that moment the perceived danger of Russian expansion was transformed into something much more fearful. What Marx and Engels had predicted, Lenin now made ominously imminent, "A spectre is haunting Europe, the spectre of Communism." Not only the Bolsheviks in Moscow but rulers in other countries thought that the revolution might spread and overthrow other European governments.

Battle was joined. British, French, Japanese and American expeditions invaded Russia and fought the Communists on Russian soil in 1918; and when these forays failed, European leaders like Winston Churchill created a *cordon sanitaire* of anti-Communist states along Russia's western border to seal off the infection of revolution. Though Communism never prevailed anywhere outside Russia in those years, and though Stalin proclaimed "socialism in one country" as his program for Russia in 1927, Communists and counterrevolutionaries clashed so incessantly in Germany, Finland, Hungary, France and Spain from 1918 until 1939 that these between-the-wars years of so-called peace are better understood as a time of all-European civil war. Indeed, in the years just before the Second World War, when the government of Britain and France sought to "appease" the appetite of Nazi Germany by encouraging Hitler to devour countries on his eastern borders, they only confirmed Soviet judgments that these Western powers had never ceased to plot the overthrow of Communist rule in Russia.

Even more disruptive of future Allied unity than the hates and fears of two decades of undeclared war were the cynicism and distrust built up by the strange vicissitudes of the Second World War that broke out in 1939. The fortunes of this vast, swaying struggle, which made the Russians partners in Hitler's aggressions at the outset, abruptly transformed these invaders of Finland and Poland into allies of the West when Hitler, stopping at the English Channel, wheeled eastward and thrust at the Soviet Union.

Proclaiming that "the Russian danger is our danger," Churchill at once promised help to his old foe. "If Hitler invaded hell," he said, "I would at least make a favorable reference to the devil in the House of Commons." Between Churchill and Stalin, as they struggled desperately against the blitzkrieg, there sprang up a kind of stony banter. But Roosevelt, the president who had restored diplomatic relations between the United States and Russia when he took office, stepped in. "If I may be brutally frank," he told Churchill, "I think I can personally handle Stalin better." When Pearl Harbor catapulted America into the Grand Alliance, Hitler promptly declared war on the side of his Japanese allies. The Russians did nothing of the kind for their own allies. The Soviet Union's course of neutrality in the Pacific war was doubtless dictated by the sheer need just then to survive. Yet it fed the anger and frustration of those Americans who desired above all the defeat of Japan and who as "Asia Firsters" played their part later in splitting the Grand Alliance.

As Roosevelt shaped the American effort, the nation was fighting one enemy, the Axis, in the Atlantic and the Pacific. In shining contrast to the twisting convolutions of the early "phony war" period, America's was a righteously "straight" war of the good and democratic side against the evil dictators and militarists of Germany, Italy and Japan. When the Russians reeled back before the first Nazi onslaughts, taking enormous casualties, Roosevelt promised a billion dollars in supplies, and when America entered the war, Roosevelt decided to delay dealing with the Japanese and go after the European enemy first. By 1942 Stalin was pleading for the opening of a second front in France to relieve the excruciating pressure of the German war machine against Moscow and Leningrad. Churchill was evasive. It was at that moment that Roosevelt, in a ceremony of euphoric hope and idealism, brought the Russian, British and other Allied ambassadors together at the White House and proclaimed the birth of the United Nations. A few days later Roosevelt pledged to Foreign Minister Vyacheslav Molotov that the Russians could expect formation of a second front "this year."

Were the considerations military or political that opened the fateful gap between promise and reality? That summer and fall the Russians fought unassisted through the Battle of Stalingrad, turning point of the Second World War; the Western Allies landed and bogged down in Africa; and Roosevelt and Churchill delayed their cross-Channel invasion of Europe until June, 1944, when the Russians were rampaging toward Warsaw and Berlin. A precipitate American intervention in Europe in 1942 or 1943 would have assured, even more than in 1914, "the domination of Russia on the Continent of Europe." Faced with this utterly political choice, America preferred to find military reasons for refusing it. More than any single factor, the second-front delay roused Soviet suspicion and anger toward the United States and set the stage for the Cold War.

When at last the Western front took shape and the Allied chieftains met with Stalin at Teheran in late 1943, the question of a postwar world organization came up. As Roosevelt described it to his comrades in arms, UNO was to be a lot more muscular than the faltering old League of Nations. The United States, Russia, Britain and China, he said, would be its four policemen, enforcing order, by military intervention if need be, against any nation threatening peace. So strong and pervasive was this emphasis that at the founding conference held in San Francisco before the fighting ended, the smaller states, according to one of their ministers, felt "invited as poor relations whom rich and powerful uncles have to see from time to time." Elected its first Secretary-General, Norway's Foreign Minister Trygve Lie fully expected that the big powers would negotiate their differences at UNO's high table.

When advanced by Woodrow Wilson at Paris in 1918, the League of Nations concept conveyed "brave new world" excitement. Yet even then it was a nineteenth-century idea. With its Tennysonian vision of a "parliament of mankind, a federation of the world," the League took for granted a kind of deliberative, argumentative consensus of the liberal and conservative upper classes—what other opinions mattered? It never doubted that Europe, or at least the North Atlantic, was at the center of everything, and would of course continue to govern the world. This was more or less the selectively utopian vision that Americans, latecomers to the world organization, subscribed to when they made the United Nations so important in the 1940s and 1950s. Americans set store by open debate and majority votes, and America then had the votes. When the Third World later had the votes, the United Nations' importance waned.

Much fuss was made about the concessions that the United States supposedly had to make to entice the Russians to join the new world organization. Actually, the Russians had been members of the old League of Nations, and the United States had not. It was the Senate, repudiating the Wilsonian commitment to collective security, that had blocked United States membership in 1920. The one big concession that Roosevelt supposedly made to the Russians—the veto—was a concession made equally to the United States Senate's jealousy for American freedom of action.[20]

Here Roosevelt was not concerned about the Senate majority, who were members of his own Democratic party and would mostly vote to support him. What he needed was the backing of some of the Republican minority, who would have to provide the votes needed to make up the two-thirds majority required for any treaty ratification. The man he had his eye on was Senator Arthur Vandenberg of Michigan, top-ranking Republican on the influential Foreign Relations Committee and for two decades a leader of the midwestern nationalists of his party.

Pompous and verbose, portly and rubicund, Vandenberg was the complete Senator. Having himself written the biography of Alexander Hamilton, patron saint of his party, he gravely termed himself a Hamiltonian Republican. In his own Congressional Directory biography he had been careful to place at the head of his political achievements the chairmanship of a committee to erect a statue to Zachariah Chandler, father of his party in the state of Michigan. Long before most of his colleagues had reached the Senate, he had been in the forefront of those who believed that the basic political battle was to defend the Constitution, the dollar and the propertied way of life against those in the White House and elsewhere who were ceaselessly undermining them.

Vandenberg not only fought the League of Nations, he contributed his party's 1920 campaign slogan, "With Harding at the helm, we can sleep nights." He cast one of the two Senate votes against recognizing the Soviet Union. During the rise of Hitler he voted against repeal of the Neutrality Act, against the draft, against lend-lease. After the Nazis blitzed Poland he said, "This so-called war is nothing but about twenty-five people and propaganda." As late as 1943 he opposed the Senate resolution to commit the country to a postwar United Nations.

Yet before Vandenberg was an isolationist, he was a Hamiltonian. He opposed foreign entanglements when it seemed they might weaken America. Yet he knew that an America as strong as the land that built tanks, planes and trucks the way his state of Michigan turned them out in 1943 might require a forceful presence abroad. The Senator took a trip to London in 1944 and heard the German rockets roar over. He talked long about the new aerial strategy with his nephew Hoyt Vandenberg, a fast-rising West Point fighter pilot on his way to becoming chief of the United States Air Force. He listened intently at committee sessions to men like Secretary of State Cordell Hull, who had to deal in facts, not theories. Early in 1945, Vandenberg rose to make an important speech on the Senate floor:

> I hasten to make my own personal viewpoint clear. I have always been frankly one of those who has believed in our own self-reliance. I still believe that we can never again—regardless of collaborations—allow our national defense to deteriorate to anything like a point of impotence. But I do not believe that any nation hereafter can immunize itself by its own exclusive action. . . . Our oceans have ceased to be moats. . . . I want maximum American cooperation . . . to make the basic idea of [the United Nations] succeed. . . . I think American self-interest requires it.

The speech was hailed at the time as a conversion from isolationism, but time was to show that Vandenberg was still a Hamiltonian nationalist who had only shifted his emphasis even when he later projected intervention in Europe and the eastern Mediterranean. It would have been more accurate to say that the Senator had been converted to bipartisanism in foreign affairs. Within three weeks President Roosevelt, asking for fifty copies of the speech to take along to the Yalta conference, invited Vandenberg to become a delegate to the United Nations opening conference in San Francisco, along with Senator Tom Connally, Democrat from Texas, chairman of the Foreign Relations Committee. With the indispensable veto protection for Great Power sovereignty put in by the Russians, Vandenberg and Connally could pilot the United Nations treaty to ratification by the Senate.[21]

At this stage of transition, the Americans were unable to take the mesaure of their Russian ally as adversary. The picture of Stalin as a benevolent Uncle Joe presiding over the valiant Russian fighters seems to have almost totally blocked out any perception of the ruthless dictator. American officials in their dispatches and minutes repeatedly referred to the Soviet Politburo as a body holding opinions incalculably at variance with those expressed by the Marshal, and pictured Stalin as respecting them. At Teheran in 1943 the dictator had not yet moved his troops far enough west to want to discuss Europe's future. But when Churchill, visiting him in Moscow a year later, put before him a scheme for dividing southeastern Europe into spheres of relative Russian and British influence, Stalin read it and placed approving ticks on Churchill's proposals. Stalin approved, but the Americans, concerned about pressing their goal of free and open markets (and free and open societies) everywhere, did not. In any case Churchill had not in his proposal made mention of Poland. Even before the Allies assembled at Yalta in February, 1945, to deal with such matters, the Russians had set up their own provisional regime for Poland. Deadlock at Yalta was averted only by the flimsiest last-minute declaration that "free elections" would first be held in Poland and the other countries. The conference was hardly over before Stalin informed Churchill that it was "imperative" for Russian security to have a "friendly" government in Poland, and it was this prospect that Roosevelt was brooding over when he died.

Churchill counseled getting tough with the Russians to compel compromise. President Truman and his advisers never doubted that the way to do this was for the United States, as holder of the only major economic resources left intact by the war, to deny aid to the Russians who had lost ten percent of their population, sixty percent of their livestock and twenty-five percent of their industry in four years of fighting, unless they agreed to open up Poland and hold free elections there. When Foreign Minister Molotov passed through Washington in April 1945, on his way to the first United Nations conference in San Francisco, President Truman read him a blistering lecture. Using "blunt language unadorned by the polite verbiage of diplomacy," he warned that the course of further American-Russian collaboration would depend on how things went in Poland. "I have never been talked to like that in my life," said Molotov as he left. "Carry out your agreements and you won't get talked to like that," Truman rasped back.

All that Americans knew at the time about this exchange was that Molotov, as *The New York Times* reported, had been "impressed" by the new President. But there were plenty of indications coming back from Germany and Eastern Europe that things were going anything but smoothly between the Allies, and in San Francisco there were lengthy and open disagreements as the Russians demanded a seat for a Polish regime that contained virtually no representatives of the exiled former government in London, and sought unsuccessfully to withhold membership from an Argentine regime that had given aid and comfort in the war to Nazis. A Gallup poll indicated wide support in the United States for a proposal to bar all Communists from public office, and in November a sudden move in the House of Representatives tacked an amendment on to a war-relief appropriations bill barring further aid in any country that impeded free reporting of United Nations Relief and Rehabilitation Administration operations; that is, any country in Russian-controlled Eastern Europe. Although the Senate dropped the amendment, there was no mistaking this first clearly anti-Russian roll call in the postwar Congress.[22]

At the same time American Communist party members began deserting the party with some assertions bound to fan suspicion that the

Russians were out to subvert their wartime allies. Louis Budenz, ex-editor of the *Daily Worker*, quit with a loud shout that Communist parties outside Russia were not political parties at all but conspiracies which gave their loyalty first and last to the Soviet Union. In Canada, a Doukhobor girl testified in an Ottawa court that while working as a code clerk in the External Affairs Department she had met a Major Sokolov of the Russian embassy. Under big headlines American newspapers carried the lurid details of the Canadian spy trials. The major, said the girl, was a "hand-some man," and Mrs. Sokolov had been friendly too, inviting her to their home for "interesting" talks. She "had a feeling of love for Russia," she said in a whisper, "I wanted to help the Soviet but not to hurt Canada." After her testimony, thirteen other Canadians testified about dealings they had had with members of the Soviet embassy, including some that concerned atomic and other defense secrets.

Publicly, President Truman remained noncommittal about Winston Churchill's dire warnings of Soviet hostility. Besides, Secretary of State Byrnes, the man who had been at Yalta, had taken over the management of United States foreign policy with all his vaunted self-assurance. The main task at that stage was representing the United States at conferences of the Big Three foreign ministers called to prepare the treaties winding up the war. For this endlessly argumentative task the Secretary was required to be away from Washington for long periods of time. Byrnes went about the peacemaking job without even troubling to report back to the President.

Jimmy Byrnes was a conservative Southern Democrat, schooled in years of congressional horse-trading. At long parleys in Moscow he got all the concessions he could in the peace terms set with Rumania and Bulgaria. But the first Truman learned of these terms was when the foreign ministers' concluding communiqué was cabled back to Washington. Almost as soon as this message reached the President, Senator Vandenberg was in his office loudly protesting, on the basis of news bulletins, that the United States was permitting new regimes in the Balkan countries without the free elections that had been called for by the Yalta agreements. Shortly afterwards Byrnes flew in from Moscow, having sent word ahead that he wanted arrangements made with the radio networks so that he could broadcast to the nation what had been accomplished in Moscow.

When this information was relayed to Truman, who was sailing down the Potomac in the presidential yacht, he left word that Byrnes should first get down to the *Williamsburg* and report to him. Whatever happened next, it seems that neither Senator Vandenberg's explosion nor the Republic anti-Russian stirrings in the House were absent from the President's mind when he led Byrnes into his private cabin. As Truman recalled later, he did not hide his displeasure at the turn things had taken in Moscow. "I'm tired of babying the Russians," he said in a memorandum to Byrnes dated shortly thereafter.

Byrnes thenceforth stiffened his bargaining stance at international conferences to meet the President's wishes, but he continued to maintain toward Truman, the President said later, the attitude of the leader of the Senate toward a freshman senator. Though there was no open break, their relations cooled. Soon Byrnes, "on the advice of a physician" (he lived to be ninety-four), gave Truman his resignation and Truman, perhaps to Byrnes's surprise, accepted it effective when the peace treaties were completed. That summer the President asked Army chief of staff General Eisenhower, who was leaving for an inspection trip of the Far East, to ask General Marshall, Truman's special envoy to China, whether he would be willing to take Byrnes' place after completing his mission to bring the contending Nationalist and Communist forces in China together. Eisenhower duly brought back Marshall's acceptance.[23]

Thus matters stood when Henry Wallace made his bid to set the Truman administration's foreign policy. For some time, in cabinet and out, Wallace had been saying that "getting tough" with the Russians would get America nowhere: "The tougher we get, the tougher the Russians will get." Although this sort of talk made the President uneasy, Wallace regarded himself as the true heir of the New Deal, and Truman himself had the notion that Wallace represented the views of a large segment of Americans. One day in September, the Secretary of Commerce showed Truman a speech he was to make in New York asserting that the United States was not trying to meet the Russians halfway. If it did, the argument went, America would find cooperation toward peace. The speech at one point contained this sentence: "When President Truman read these words, he said that they represented the policy of the Administration."

A reporter got an advance copy of the speech and read the sentence to Truman at his press conference. The President replied, "That is correct."

"Does that apply just to that paragraph, or to the whole speech?" the reporter pressed.

"I approved the whole speech," said Truman.

Another reporter asked, "Mr. President, do you regard Wallace's speech a departure from Byrnes's policy?"

"I do not," the President shot back.

"Towards Russia?"

Said the President, "They are exactly in line."

After Wallace delivered the speech, Secretary Byrnes sent a teletype message from Paris to the White House: "If it is not completely clear in your mind that Mr. Wallace should be asked to refrain from criticizing the foreign policy of the United States while he is a member of your cabinet, I must ask you to accept my resignation."

Senator Vandenberg, chief symbol of bipartisan foreign policy, told reporters, "We can cooperate with only one Secretary of State at a time."[24]

Within a week Henry Wallace was fired—and the Republicans made the most of the disarray around the President. "To err is Truman," was the jibe of the day.

Truman's difficulties in keeping order in his political household were matched by his troubles in coping with the economic and social pressures that seemed to be closing in all around him. The President fumbled his efforts to hold prices down. When his veto of a bill scuttling consumer price controls left the nation with none at all, the index of twenty-five basic commodities shot up twenty-five per cent in sixteen wild days. When he then obtained power to roll back meat prices, stockmen held back their cattle from the market until angry housewives could not find hamburger in stores at any price. Labor also gave the President a hard time. He had tangled with John L. Lewis, and had used wartime powers to send 72,000 striking anthracite miners back to work under government control. Lewis had ordered still another miners' walkout. When President Truman, after a nationwide rail stoppage, forced a settlement by threatening government seizure of the railroads, Alexander Whitney, boss of the trainmen's union, vowed that Truman had "signed his political death warrant." In Detroit and Chicago, there were ugly race riots, in the South six lynchings. In Atlanta violence against blacks and black-owned homes mounted; Jews were being threatened. "All the advances which minorities made under the New Deal and the war seem to be in question," said the Cleveland *Plain Dealer.*[25]

Was this getting back to normal? It was the Republicans who captured the mood as the fall congressional campaign hit its peak. "Had enough?" they asked on thousands of billboards, on lapel buttons, in newspaper ads, on platforms in villages, courthouse towns and cities. The war over, it was time to cut taxes, head off inflation, curb strikes and end shortages. The nation had had quite enough, and that fall elected the first Republican Congress since the days of Herbert Hoover.

Even more than the stalwarts of small-town America who gave the nation the administrations of Harding, Coolidge and Hoover, these men harked back to the old rural values and social ethics. But much had passed in the intervening years, above all in the way of extending to the consumer and even more to the urban dweller the benefits of a government paternalism. Many feared that America had been rolling, as the title of Friedrich Hayek's widely read and even more widely quoted book had it, *The Road to Serfdom.*[26]

A nationwide rancor supported the Republicans. All kinds of Americans harbored grievances, spite, resentments. Of such pent-up ill feelings no section, no group, no class held a monopoly. Democrats hunkering on their heels in Deep South country stores spat out their hate for "what the Negroes are getting away with." Republican businessmen at Chamber of Commerce luncheons in Oregon and Ohio choked on their fried chicken at mention of the latest "insolence" of the labor unions. Stenographers, paperhangers and shoe salesmen hit the ceiling every time they saw the size of the withholding tax on their paychecks. But the loudest cries of rage came from near the top of this terrain of discontent, from the upper levels occupied by men and women who called themselves conservative and did not want to conserve the *new* status quo.

Many were possessors of high-bracket incomes who, in Heywood Broun's phrase, had been "bitten by the income-tax bug." Such people saw the New Deal years as one long process of separating them from their wealth and doling it out to others. Abroad as well as at home, the whole thrust of government in Washington seemed to them directed toward but one outcome—the spending of increasingly large sums of money filched mainly from their pockets. Yet the grounds of swelling disgruntlement were not only economic: many others from low and middle-income groups shared with the rich a growing displeasure about matters which had little enough to do with the pocketbook.

Ever since 1933, it seemed, the country had been in upheaval, lashing about through the turmoil of Depression and the dislocations of world war, and millions ached for just a little stability at long last. One change was particularly unhinging. For generations white, Protestant, relatively old-stock Americans had set the style and made the decisions of the nation's life. In Muncie, Indiana, as Robert and Mary Lynd recorded in their classic "Middletown" studies of that archetypical American community, the family which owned the town's leading industry had always been consulted as a matter of course about anything done in the community. Whether factory owners or small-town shopkeepers or big-city bankers, white, Anglo-Saxon Protestants were the "Best People," expecting and receiving a certain deference.

Now there was a palpable stir from below. The "Wasps" (as some upwardly mobile Jews had begun after the war to call these white, Anglo-Saxon Protestants) and German and other ethnic groups who had immigrated long enough ago to have merged with them, were having to make room for groups from the bottom. Newer elements were growing up in the cities, ethnic groups with eastern and southern European names and ways, and the established, old-stock Americans felt uncomfortable, jostled, almost displaced in an America that they had assumed belonged peculiarly to them. "What kind of a country is it?" John Hurst, an old-family, small businessman from Champaign, Illinois, asked at a druggists' convention. "I ask you what kind of a country is it that fusses over anyone who makes a big noise, and ignores Robert A. Taft?"[27]

Robert A. Taft was to an extraordinary extent the symbol and spokesman of the old-line middle Americans who in 1946 sent the first Republican majority to Congress since Hoover's time. His father, President William Howard Taft, was remembered for standing with all the weight of his portly and amiable self against the whole social reform movement of an earlier day. When the Pullman strike stopped trains in 1895, the elder Taft wrote his wife: "It will be necessary for the military to kill some of the mob before the trouble can be stayed. They have killed only six as yet. This is hardly enough to make an impression."[28]

Like his father, Robert Taft was a man of property with a respect for property. In a time of ferment and chaos, Robert Taft clung to the established values of orthodox Republicanism, isolationism, economic solvency and a strict interpretation of the Constitution. Born in Cincinnati, a member of a distinguished family of diplomats, lawmakers, judges and civic leaders, he prepared for college at Connecticut's Taft School (founded by his Uncle Horace), and was valedictorian of his class at Yale (1910) where he let his record speak for him and leaned not at all on the fact that his father was President of the United States. At Harvard Law School, he again topped his class (1913). Almost automatically young Taft left his Cincinnati law practice to enter politics against the "vain, immoral and dangerous" New Deal of Franklin Roosevelt, and, as senator from Ohio, to take over the battle which established America was waging against the tide of social reform.

The very qualities that made Taft a peculiar figure as a politican were those that traditional America liked to believe belonged especially to its way of life. His habits were as unpretentious as his baggy serge suits. Taft's idea of a good time, it was said, was a family picnic where everyone sat around munching drugstore candy bars and playing hearts. He could wear a white swingback suit utterly unaware, and uncaring, that it was twenty years out of style. He had a passion for facts and figures that brooked no venturing away from the logic of the ledger book. "Fact has neither latitude nor longitude, nor expansion," he said. "You're either right or you're wrong; you can't be nearly either." Despite his yearnings to follow his father into the White House, he remained outspoken, honest, almost unbelievably ready to make plain exactly what Robert Taft thought on any issue. "It isn't honest to be tactful," he explained. When asked what the public should do about soaring meat prices, he answered, "Eat less." If he was without oratorical flair, if he squirmed with manifest discomfort when the local party leaders slapped him on the back, if his opponents caricatured him as "often in error, but never in doubt," this only reinforced the feeling among traditionalists that Taft was the man for them. "I look at that man," said Mrs. Edith Busby of Idaho, "and I see everything which my father taught me to hold good."

Taft was unquestionably the dominating leader of the new 80th Congress, and, as first Wallace and then Byrnes left Washington and the Democrats churned about seemingly rudderless, Taft looked like the man to watch for the presidential stakes in 1948. The senator from Ohio and most other leaders took the Republican victory as a mandate to remake America at once along anti-New Deal lines. First and foremost they were going to cut spending. John Taber, the cantankerous old diehard who had succeeded to the chairmanship of the powerful House Appropriations Committee, stormed that he was going to apply a "meat-ax to government frills."

So the stage was set for reconversion, as the malcontents thought, not just from the war but from the follies of the New Deal. Yet, even as the meat-ax began to be unlimbered, the thought reportedly crossed Taft's mind: how ironical if this Congress which really had its heart set on straightening out domestic affairs would end up being besieged by foreign problems. And 1948 was an ironical year. Hardly had the Eightieth Congress assembled when news from abroad pounded on the door of every member of House and Senate.[29]

CHAPTER 2

The Hardening of
the American Position

THE REMOLDING OF THE AMERICAN MIND

"**H**OME ALIVE IN '45."
This loving scrawl, microfilmed in millions of little V-mail letters between Americans at home and in tents and quonset huts overseas, expressed a longing that seemed spectacularly fulfilled by the glorious victories that year over both Germany and Japan. Whatever filled the United States, then, with the urge so soon after this answer to the people's prayers to reverse such powerful impulses to pull back, and instead fling its commitments far and wide in the peacetime years of 1946 and 1947? What but fear—fear and its other face, a strident and assertive confidence that America could manage the world? "General and universal fear," as William Faulkner called it, was evoked by the unknown terrors of atomic destruction, and the strutting confidence, so palpably manifested by Truman in his dealings with Stalin at Potsdam and after, was also occasioned by the A-bomb.[1]

But by so much more, too. America's troops bestrode the fallen enemy not only in Berlin, where they shared occupation with allies, but in Tokyo, where General MacArthur exercised sole and godlike authority. And on the sea and in the air, if not on quite all of the earth's terrain, was not United States fiat practically law? Among the nations, Truman boasted at Waco, Texas, not long after V-J Day, the United States was "the giant of the economic world," alone unscathed by war and out to "determine the future pattern of economic relations" among nations. That pattern, he proclaimed, was "free private enterprise," and to see that pattern prevail, America demanded opened doors not only in China but in Europe—both West and East—and in all Europe's colonies. In the economic and political rebuilding of the world, the United States expected to have a say—a big say. Addressing his neighbors at Carruthersville, Missouri, shortly after the A-bombs compelled Japanese surrender, President Truman said: "We are going forward to meet our destiny— which I think Almighty God intended us to have—and we are going to be the leaders."[2]

Disagreement and distrust between the United States and the Soviet Union traced back to the day the Bolsheviks seized power in Russia. The United States sent an invasion force briefly into Siberia in 1918, and at the same time there was a violent "Red scare" in America led by Attorney General Palmer, in which thousands of foreign-born radicals were arrested. The United States did not even extend diplomatic recognition to the Soviet government until 1933. But the global confrontation that was called the Cold War took shape only when America and Russia began to emerge as the world's two superpowers at the end of the war in 1945. Even then it was not immediately clear that the other great powers could not keep their old positions and empires, and in any case the extent of polar estrangement between Washington and its wartime ally was only reluctantly admitted for some time even in private. Great, therefore, was the shock when Churchill openly proclaimed it.

Thus the Americans appeared almost to back into the leadership that Truman had asserted. On the Western side, the French and other democracies occupied by the Germans were expected all along to be economically dependent on American trade and aid. The British, who had thought they could carry on in something of the imperial style to which they were accustomed, found themselves grievously weakened by the war, more even than their leaders knew. Having borrowed $3.5 billion from the United States to put themselves right, they ran through their credit in less than a year. The Russians and the Eastern European lands they occupied had all suffered equally terrible losses and destruction, and Ambassador Averill Harriman and others counseled that they would have to open the door to United States trade and aid.

But the Russians did not play it the American way. Instead they demanded from Germany all the reparations they could get. And when the Americans resisted, they dragged away factories and practically anything movable that might fill out a few of their war-ravaged production gaps. Even more ominous in Western eyes, they stepped up pressures on their new "friendly" East European regimes to start reshaping themselves into socialist societies. In the process of reorienting their economies toward Soviet Russia's, these satellite states began closing doors to American trade, political ideas and even newsmen. All this time scarcely a word was beamed toward Washington about their need for a big American loan.

Then in February, 1946, at the same time that Churchill was in America drawing up his warning of a cold war between East and West, Stalin announced that Russia was going to go it alone. More than that, he declared that the Soviet Union was going to rebuild itself into an economic power rivaling the United States in every way. He announced a series of three five-year plans by which Russia would treble its production of steel, pig iron, coal and oil by 1961.[3]

To carry through such a program meant that the Soviet people would have to move without a letup from the exertions and exhaustions of the Great Patriotic War to yet more hardships and unending deprivations, and in Stalin's paranoid style of rule its fulfillment kept Soviet prison and labor camp populations above the 11-million mark for the rest of the dictator's lifetime. Central to this grandiose plan was an even more audacious challenge to America's vaunting omnipotence. This was the decision to throw all possible Russian resources into a long-term program of scientific research and development to offset and overcome the American preponderance in modern weapons technology. In the next Five-Year Plan, Stalin said:

> special attention will be devoted to . . . the widespread construction of all manner of scientific research institutions that can give science the opportunity to develop its potentialities. I have no doubt that if we give the scientists the proper assistance they will be able in the near future not only to overtake but to surpass the achievements of science outside the bounds of our society.[4]

The Russian purpose, well understood by the delegates who greeted this statement with "prolonged and stormy applause," was nothing less than to make the victorious Soviet state secure against any capitalist challenge. The great novelist Alexander Solzhenitsyn, who was also an electrical engineer, subsequently described in *The First Circle* the debasing rewards, the torture, the floodlit barbed wire and other "proper assistance" that Stalin lent Soviet scientists forced to labor on one crash electronic program. It may well be that the tyrant's barbarities, as Solzhenitsyn eloquently pictured them, served so far as their full force could be let loose to wreck any attempt at rational economic development. But the forces of modern technology operated with the same triumphantly impersonal thrust in communist as in capitalist society. Within little more than a year of Stalin's speech, Russian physicists put their first chain reactor into operation, new jets, submarines and cruisers were evolved comparable to those of the West and the long-range missile program, led by A. A. Blagonravov, an academician-general named director of the Academy of Artillery Sciences just as Stalin spoke, was already started on the research that was to culminate in the Sputniks of 1957.[5]

Supreme Court Justice William O. Douglas, reading Stalin's speech in Washington, termed it "the declaration of World War III." He was mistaken. Milovan Djilas, one of Yugoslav leader Tito's lieutenants, later told a different story. At a Kremlin dinner in May 1945, he said, Stalin rose from the table, "hitched up his pants as though he were about to wrestle or box, and cried out almost in a transport, 'The war will soon be over. We shall recover in fifteen or twenty years, and then we'll have another go at it.' " Stalin's postwar plan was a long-term program. Nobody in charge in Washington or London at that time believed that the Russians wanted war.

Fortuitously at this moment, in answer to a casual State Department request, there arrived in Washington from George Kennan, the American chargé d'affaires in Moscow, a long cable analyzing the motives behind Russian behavior. One of the handful of Foreign Service officers who had been stationed in Riga to study the Soviet Union during the years that the United States had no diplomatic relations with Russia, Kennan had already attracted attention during the war from Roosevelt and Hopkins for his common-sense advice. But it was his 8000-word cable of February 22, 1946, that brought Kennan into the circle of Washington authority. It caught the eye of Secretary of the Navy James Forrestal, who was obsessed with the problem of security in a postwar world dominated by a capitalist America and a Communist Russia. Forrestal, just then moving through the Washington constellation to a position as the most influential of the service secretaries (he became the first Secretary of Defense when the departments were combined in 1947), pasted the dispatch in his diary, and insisted that Truman, his advisers and "hundreds, if not thousands of higher officers in the armed services" familiarize themselves with its argument.[6]

Russia's rulers sought security, wrote Kennan, "only in patient but deadly struggle for total destruction of rival power, never in compacts and compromises with it." Viewing the world as divided into capitalist and socialist camps between which there could be no peaceful coexistence, they would do everything possible to strengthen the communist camp while working tirelessly to divide and weaken the capitalist nations. For Stalin and his lieutenants Marxist ideology simply provided the pretext:

for the dictatorship without which they did not know how to rule,
. . . for sacrifices they felt bound to demand, . . . for [forcing] their
country on to ever new heights of military power in order to guarantee
external security for their internally weak regime.

Plumbing the psychological and historical background of the Russian
character, Kennan's report forecast Soviet intransigence abroad because
of such weakness at home, and went on to spell out what was to be
adopted as the postwar United States policy for "containment" of the
Soviet Union:

Soviet pressure against the free institutions of the western world is
something that can be contained by the adroit and vigilant application
of counterforce at a series of constantly shifting geographic and political
points, corresponding to the shifts and maneuvers of Soviet policy.[7]

Kennan's report provided the intellectual framework for American action,
and as the Russians stubbornly went their own way in Eastern Europe and
the United Nations as Kennan predicted, Truman brushed aside Byrnes'
compromising and moved to apply American power to compel Moscow's
acceptance of American leadership.

As the international lines tightened and his own political base at
home crumbled in Democratic disputes followed by Republican victory
in the 1946 elections, it was time for Truman to tear a page from Roosevelt's book. Back in 1933, when FDR took office amid breadlines, closed
banks and foreclosed mortgages, he told the country: "You have to fight
a Depression the way you fight a war," and he called to his side Bernard
Baruch, America's war mobilizer in 1918, and his assistant General Hugh
Johnson, both men of war. Bellowing commands, mobilizing mimeo-
graphs and smashing bottlenecks like paper panzers, General "Iron Pants"
Johnson ran the National Recovery Administration under the emblem of
the Blue Eagle as if he were fighting for Verdun. In the late 1940s the
United States government did much the same thing.[8]

Harried by domestic disarray and convinced that there were great
American foreign policy victories to be won abroad, President Truman
now summoned the help that a great war hero could bring. If his years
in the Army had been the most prized experience of Truman's life, all of
the qualities about the Army that he most revered seemed to be embodied
in General George C. Marshall. People who worked in the White House
for Truman in these years thought that the President had more confidence in Marshall than anybody in the government and probably anybody
in the world. "Duty, honor, country"—all that was enshrined in the

professional officer's code of self-denying service—came across in the character and career of General Marshall. Grandstand fustian, quarter-deck despotism and the peremptory roar were never the trappings of his command. In the first American war fought without bands or parades, his authority was conveyed without a glint of military glamour. Yet there was an intensity about him that his speech, curiously highpitched, reinforced. Speaking and, even more, listening, he conveyed a sense of controlled calm, deriving from a self-discipline that some compared with that of General Robert E. Lee.

A Virginian born in Pennsylvania, and schooled not at West Point but at the Virginia Military Institute, Marshall had perfected his self-control in such inglorious peacetime assignments as recruiting officer in Chicago. Called to Washington by Roosevelt as war clouds gathered in the late 1930s, he created the army that fought in a dozen theaters of war, and as much as any man planned and organized the triumphant outcome. When the time had come to launch the climactic European invasion he could, as Dean Acheson said, "put aside the Supreme Command in favor of General Eisenhower because his plain duty was to stay in the Pentagon dealing with that vast complex of forces which, harnessed, meant victory." Roosevelt, who called everybody else by his first name, addressed his Army chief of staff as "General Marshall." Congress accorded him respect. Now having accomplished at an advanced age an exacting mission for the President in China, this imposing and, some said, stuffy war hero was back in Washington in mufti. For such a hero of the Republic Congress readily consented to make an exception to the law and agreed to a military man's serving as Secretary of State, the President's principal cabinet officer.[9]

Marshall had been in office barely two weeks when two messages from the British government arrived at the State Department. To Washington they were the summoning call to the world leadership that was America's manifest destiny. Their message was this: Within six weeks' time the British would be compelled to end aid to Greece and Turkey. Scarcely two years earlier Churchill had held Greece so vital to preserving the British imperial lifeline to India that he had personally gone to Athens with British troops in the middle of the war to put down a pro-Communist insurrection. As for Turkey, the British had striven successfully for 200 years to keep the Russians from getting a toehold at the Dardanelles and breaking through into the Mediterranean. Now, unable to find the means to enforce these foreign commitments any longer while its strength melted away at home, Britain was pulling out. Obviously, the British were handing over to the Americans the job of containing some 12,000 Communist antigovernment guerrillas in Greece and stemming the new Soviet pressure on Turkey to grant joint control of the Straits.

Marshall checked quickly with the State Department for the facts —what funds the Greeks and Turks had, what military forces could take the place of the British, how effective government could be organized in Greece, how much economic and military aid would cost and for how long. Beyond Turkey and Greece lay the Middle East oil fields whose assured flow was vital to the British and other West European economies and immensely profitable to the big American companies that increasingly controlled them. President Truman decided that it was vital for American interests that Greece and Turkey be strengthened and preserved in their national independence, and that only America's help could accomplish this. The tab came to $400 million, and it would have to be paid, the State Department said, or the two countries would drift into the Russian orbit.

Within two days, Truman and Marshall were laying their plans before the leaders of a Republican Congress. The general made the opening statement, and his case left the legislators unimpressed. Having just pushed through the $3.5 billion loan described as Britain's "last" request, the congressional leaders found it hard to believe that America should be asked, as Speaker Joseph Martin said, to "pull Britain's chestnuts out of the fire." Undersecretary of State Acheson whispered to Marshall for a chance to speak.

Acheson swung the argument round to the Soviet menace. For eighteen months, he said, Russian pressure on the Dardanelles, on Iran, and on northern Greece had brought the Balkans to the point where a breakthrough might open the way to Soviet penetration in Europe, in Africa and all the way across Asia to India and China. Like apples in a barrel infected by one rotten one, Acheson said, the corruption of Greece would spread through Asia Minor and Egypt, and to Europe through Italy and France, already endangered by the presence of the largest Communist parties in Western Europe. The Soviet Union, he went on, was playing one of the greatest gambles of history at minimum cost. It did not need to win all the possibilities. Even one or two offered immense gains. Only America was in a position to break up the play. These were the stakes that British withdrawal from the eastern Mediterranean offered to an aggressive and ruthless opponent.

A long silence followed. Then Arthur Vandenberg said solemnly: "Mr. President, if you say that to the Congress and the country, I will support you, and I believe that most of its members will do the same."[10]

All, Republicans and Democrats alike, were aware that a major turning point in American affairs had been reached. Hitherto, in all popular notions about the postwar world, Americans had tended to go on the general supposition that, the war over, the powers of the Old World would once again look after their own affairs. Two new and immensely disorienting perceptions had to be absorbed in order to grasp what America would have to do next. The first was the shocking realization that the British had been reduced to such a state of weakness and exhaustion that they were not now capable of safeguarding their traditional interests. For Americans this was an appalling discovery, and was to lead to a swift reappraisal of the true state of Britain and indeed of all Western Europe, with results that took shape soon afterwards in the Marshall Plan.

The second insight was even more shocking. This was the realization that not only British but American vital interests were at stake, an awareness immediately put into words by the nation's newspapers. "Suddenly," said the *St. Louis Post-Dispatch*, "the United States, which for several generations has hidden behind John Bull's coattails in matters of foreign policy, is at the forefront alone." After years of yelping about England's expecting every American to do his duty and pull its chestnuts out of the fire, wrote the St. Paul *Pioneer Press*, "we are learning that they are not British chestnuts—they are our own."

Shortly thereafter, the $400,000,000 program was ready for action, and President Truman met with congressional leaders again. Though Joe Martin was still grumbling about throwing away so much money, the most isolationist Republicans had always been viscerally anti-Communist, and Acheson had boldly internationalized the fear. This time Vandenberg advised the President that if he wanted an aid program for Greece and Turkey, he had no choice but to appear before Congress in person and "scare hell out of the country." Already many in Washington viewed the rescue operation in Greece as Secretary Forrestal described it in a cabinet meeting at the time, as "a fundamental struggle between our kind of society and the Russians," a struggle in which the Russians "would not respond to anything but power."[11]

B Y 1 : 0 0 P . M . on March 12, 1947, the House chamber was jammed. Representatives were in the rear, then senators, the diplomatic corps, the Cabinet. Among the Democratic representatives a little girl, brought along to be present at a historic occasion, grew bored and squirmed on her father's lap.

The speech had gone through many drafts. General Marshall, to whom it was cabled at the Foreign Ministers' conference in Moscow, protested that Truman was "overstating the case." Others in the White House asked Truman if he realized the implications of what he was saying for such faraway places as Finland and China. The President said that only strong and dramatic statements would move Congress to action, and went through the speech changing verbs from "should" to "must."

As delivered, it was an aggressive speech, challenging in tone and almost warlike. It was an open declaration that after two years of wrangling with the Russians over Iran, Eastern Europe and Germany, the United States was taking up the challenge to an almost limitless world contest in which the requested aid for Greece and Turkey seemed almost a small, though important, action:

> At the present moment in world history nearly every nation must choose between alternative ways of life. The choice is too often not a free one. One way of life is based upon the will of the majority, and is distinguished by free institutions, representative government, free elections, guarantees of individual liberty, freedom of speech and religion, and freedom from political oppression.

> The second way of life is based upon the will of a minority forcibly imposed upon the majority. It relies upon terror and oppression, a controlled press and radio, fixed elections, and suppression of personal freedom.

Then the President, in his flat Missouri twang, proclaimed what was to be called the Truman Doctrine:

> I believe that it must be the policy of the United States to support free people who are resisting attempted subjugation by armed minorities and outside pressures.[12]

At the end the Congress, its members looking unusually grave, rose to applaud. "An ominous situation," said Senator Walter George, Democrat of Georgia, already prepared to vote the President the requested sums. Senator Edwin Johnson, Democrat of Colorado, called the message "an attempt to extend the Monroe Doctrine to the Mediterranean," and Senator Kenneth Wherry, Republican of Nebraska, said it was "a virtual declaration of war." Representative James Van Zandt, Republican of Pennsylvania, said, "I may as well get my Navy uniform out of storage." But Vandenberg's prescription for Truman had been accurate. Soon the main complaints in Congress were vented at the bill's slighting of the United Nations, a neglect deftly remedied by Vandenberg, who inserted a reassuring clause stating that when time permitted the United States favored going through United Nations channels.[13]

Britain's Labour government was startled and taken aback at the resounding declaration with which the United States pledged cash but not men to replace the departing British forces. So blunt a challenge, the *Manchester Guardian* said, "may too easily divide Europe and the world into hostile blocs." In Paris, it was reported, the Truman message "came as a bombshell." A French cabinet crisis followed. The five Communist members of the government refused to accept its wage-freeze policy, and were ousted in early May. Almost at the same time the De Gasperi government in Italy felt strong enough to force the Communists out of the cabinet for the first time since the end of the Second World War.[14]

With the promulgation of the Truman Doctrine the United States turned decisively away from pre-World War isolationism. And what a turn! Not remotely like the precision-engineered Bismarckian shift of the nineteenth century European empire, or the dialectically razored switch of a Soviet dictatorship doubling back into a nonaggression pact with Hitler, this turn was high, wide and sweeping, almost as big and broad as a galaxy's swerve. When the United States set out to change, it changed in a big way.

In the Second World War, the turn began with the shift to cooperating with the victors in collective security, and for a nation that shunned entangling alliances that was change enough. But now the President carried his country to the other side of the world not only in the name of collective security but of American security:

> Totalitarian regimes [he said], imposed upon free people, by direct or indirect aggression, undermine the foundations of international peace and hence the security of the United States.[15]

As Truman phrased it, this was no mere assertion that the United States would intervene in Greece or Turkey, extraordinary and unprecedented though such a pledge must be. He was promising that the United States would, at its discretion, use its power to put down revolutionary movements anywhere. The President's declaration was called a Doctrine—and was meant to be doctrinaire. It was of a piece with the Monroe Doctrine, which everybody knew was a "Keep Out" sign on the Americas that had been enforced as if graven on tablets for more than a hundred years. It was a declaration of a new kind of war, fought by a kind of mobilization of the nation and all nations that resisted Soviet "pressures," and waged by all means save general armed conflict. Such a doctrine of intervention and confrontation on a global scale called for the mobilization not only of the nation's arms and legs but of its mind as well. The kind of ideological coin with which the Truman administration set out to win consent for the new doctrine was the currency of fear, and fear is a currency so easily coined and so freely circulated that it leads on, as America learned, to an inflationary debasement.

At this point the marshaling of opinion became crucial. Yet the men engaged in engineering the swing were far too preoccupied with hanging on through the turn to give much thought to the precision of their steering. By all the signs, they knew only that America must lead the world if it were to fulfill its destiny of national "greatness." But even if they believed in American freedom as the ground for this "greatness," they seemed either to see no need for explaining their commitment to freedom, or to find it easier to tell the American people what they wanted them to rally *against*. From the start of the Cold War there was a negative quality to America's ideological mobilization.

The behavioral scientists stood ready at the leaders' elbows, however, to offer their professional elucidations, and indeed prescriptions, for the shift of national opinion toward an activist and explicitly tough stance in world affairs. At the Rand Corporation, the "think tank" set up by the Air Force in Santa Monica, California, experts had been assembled to advise on psychological as well as the conventional aspects of warfare. At the universities, study groups analyzed the mass society—and how to move it. Drawing upon the findings of political and social science, and especially the insights gained since the 1930s in opinion research, Dr. Gabriel Almond of Yale advised that the public support necessary for waging the Cold War was located in three basic groups. These groups could be imagined as drawn up in three concentric cirlces that together made up the totality of American society.

At the core were the policy-making and policy-executing "elite." These were few people indeed, perhaps only a few thousand. They included the legislators, the administrators, and only the most influential leaders in business, labor, education, church and the press. So far as it extended beyond the federal government in the late 1940s, this group was almost equivalent to the membership of the Council on Foreign Relations. The Council, founded in 1921 to provide the major forum outside government where corporate leaders, bankers and government and academic experts could meet and discuss policies, reached the height of its influence as the country moved into the Cold War. A kind of superclub of some five hundred notables momentarily out of government office and in key business, academic and press positions, it maintained headquarters on New York City's Park Avenue (across from the Russian United Nations delegation) and chapters in other leading cities.

At the next circle of importance were what Almond termed the "attentive public," that group of "interested and informed" citizens, mostly college educated and well-to-do, who were keen and critical readers of newspapers and magazines and books and alertly followed the trend of international affairs. They were the audience "before whom elite discussion and controversy takes place." Numbering possibly two or three million across the country, they were regarded in the late 1940s by the

Foreign Policy Association as its natural constituency. In contrast with the CFR with its small and exclusive briefings and demanding, year-long committee studies, the Foreign Policy Association was a nationwide organization that went in for large public discussion meetings and widely disseminated background reports on world problems.

Finally there was everybody else in the body politic, the third and biggest circle identified by Almond as the "mass public." The behavioral scientists had ascertained that the vast majority of citizens did not interest themselves in national affairs, and certainly not international affairs, except in the most casual and fitful fashion. Surveys had established that the average metropolitan newspaper reader spent something like four minutes a day on the important news, or a tenth of the time he devoted to the comics, sports, local gossip and the newspaper's other service and entertainment features. Yet this was the great bulk of the electorate that must cast the ultimate vote on Cold War policy, and it had to be persuaded.[16]

In learning to think about the unprecedented kind of confrontation into which President Truman was now leading it, the country tended to fall into the attitudes of war. Yet, as the leaders explained it, it was not exactly a war; certainly nobody was talking about bloodshed. Then just what was it? On April 16, 1947, as the nation struggled to understand the new destiny to which Truman was delivering it, Bernard Baruch made a speech in Columbia, South Carolina. "Let us not be deceived," he said. "We are in the midst of a cold war." The phrase was written into the speech by Baruch's old friend Herbert Bayard Swope, former editor of the New York *World* and one of the country's highest-paid public relations men. Walter Lippmann seized on it, and used it in his nationally syndicated newspaper column.[17] The phrase suited the hour. A subsequent generation of international-affairs experts ground their teeth over its imprecision and misleading simplicity. But for millions just then groping for a way to think about America's new stance in the world, the phrase self-evidently defined the strange peace that had broken out after the greatest of all wars—and overnight became a commonplace of the American language.

In the phantasmagoric landscape of the Cold War, however, a great many Americans still had trouble getting their bearings. The topography itself shifted so dismayingly, as between enemy and ally, peace and war, totalitarianism and freedom, that it seemed to lack either fixed or familiar points of reference. "America must get used to living in a dangerous world," counseled a British visitor. "The United States is a lucky country with an almost obsessive belief in a happy ending," said a Frenchwoman. Whatever the truth of such admonitions, Americans still needed to know how they could lead the world against "international Communism" with-

out getting a clear idea of just where the danger was coming from and
when to expect it.

There was not much doubt that Americans felt vaguely threatened.
By the summer of 1948 so many people in different parts of the country
reported seeing "flying saucers" that the Air Force launched an investigation of the "sightings." Did some Americans now think that, even if the
Russians were not up to it, invaders might be descending on them from
outer space? Or were they manifesting indirectly their uneasiness about
the A-bomb? Their leaders crowed that with the A-bomb American technology had revolutionized war. The merchandisers of the new kept clamoring that Americans must learn to live with change, because American
technology would revolutionize the rest of their lives too. Could ordinary
Americans keep up with such times? Such forebodings turned people to
thinking about the future. Newspapers began to talk loudly about the new
science, "futurology."

The trouble was that though President Truman and the propagandists could whip up slogans and even programs of Cold War against
Russia, they could not make the vision of this adversary both real and
frightful for their citizenry. Russia was remote to the average American,
and what little he had learned about it from the days of wartime alliance
was that Russians gave a good account of themselves in the fighting. But
what is the enemy? How can you spot him? These, historian Allan Nevins
said, were the questions whose answers would have to be translated directly and concretely if the "dismay and anguish" of the ordinary Americans were to be overcome and they could see what they were up against.[18]
Neither government leaders nor their aides could fill the void with the
image of an adversary that people could visualize and gird against. This
was the task for an artist's imagination, and at this time just such an artist
presented America with the necessary vision. This was the Englishman
George Orwell and the vision was his futuristic novel *1984*.

In this devastatingly topical fantasy, which soared beyond his earlier
classic, *Animal Farm* (1946),[19] Orwell pictured the future as a state ruled
by an invisible but omnipotent dictator: Big Brother. The whole place was
a concentration camp. Telescreens in every apartment made privacy virtually impossible. Big Brother's Thought Police conditioned the populace
to believe that thinking is ignorance, and war is peace. This process was
called Doublethink, the language in which it was expressed Newspeak.
The Ministry of Truth busied itself with falsifying historical records
whenever policy changed. The Ministry of Love specialized in torture.
Children spied on parents. The state had negated all personal life, totally
destroyed culture.

A few years earlier Sinclair Lewis had shocked his countrymen out of their armchairs with a fantasy of American fascism called *It Can't Happen Here*. Now the readers of *1984*, their hair standing figuratively on end, thought they recognized the appalling shape of the Communist future in 1984. Orwell, cried *Time*'s reviewer, had "made Americans aware of what they might be like in thirty-five years' time." Orwell's nightmare, said Lionel Trilling in *The New Yorker*, had "magnificent circumstantiality." Overnight, Doublethink and Newspeak—used to characterize the cynical utterances of Soviet delegate Andrei Vishinsky debating at the United Nations or *Pravda*'s fawning praise of Stalin on his seventieth birthday—entered the language of the Cold War. "Big Brother is watching you," a characteristic Orwellian slogan, became a tag of everyday speech.

Armed with the powerful imagery of *1984*, many Americans felt they could visualize at last the deadly antagonist they were pitted against in the Cold War. Those who did, however, were victims of the fallacy of misplaced concreteness. The author of *1984* never meant his fantasy to be taken as a mere description of Russia. But Americans of the Cold War generation found in it what they wanted—and only what they wanted. Along with its depiction of future life in a totalitarian hell, however, Orwell's novel sketched a complete international scene. This attracted little attention at the time.

Orwell's global picture of the 1940s bore startling resemblance to the world as it actually existed in the 1970s. Oceania, Eurasia and Eastasia, three superstates easily recognizable as America, Russia and China, dominated this world. All possessed the Bomb. But none ever used it because continuous, indecisive "limited" war had proved essential to keeping their economies going. War had also turned out to be much the best way of convincing the masses of Oceania, Eurasia and Eastasia alike that only absolute dictatorship over all thought, as well as government, would preserve their lands and lives. In the canons of the Cold War, *1984* was the Book of Revelation.[20]

W H E N Americans began to mobilize ideologically for Cold War, attention turned naturally to the institutions of exhortation and instruction, to the churches and to the schools. In these years, the churches of America were notably quiescent and docile. Back in 1923, after Big Business had successfully smashed the trade unionism that had grown up during the First World War, the Federal Council of Churches had published a report on working conditions in the steel mills that effectively improved the laborers' lot. Even old Judge Elbert Gary, the Bible-quoting chairman of United States Steel, was moved to renounce the twelve-hour day. But partly because American society had grown more secularized, the influence of the old, main-line Protestant churches had since then become more and more attenuated.

After the Second World War, the wave of strikes erupting across the nation and the clashes between the established middle classes and the rising workers presented what appeared to the Federal Council to be the ugliest and most urgent source of conflict in American society. Stirred to repeat its intervention of the 1920s, the Council in 1946 elected its first lay president, Charles Phelps Taft, an Episcopalian lawyer from Cincinnati and younger son of former President William Howard Taft, and formed a high-level committee of businessmen to bring about "faith, charity and cooperation" in postwar labor-management relations.

Tall, handsome and ingratiating, Charlie Taft was a progressive Republican with a dazzling smile ("He smiled me out of court," protested an opposing Cincinnati lawyer), a photogenic family that included seven children, and impeccable credentials. Some thought he might become President. Certainly none was more favored by upbringing and background. At the age of ten he sat through his father's inaugural, reading *Treasure Island.* He had played football and captained basketball at Yale, served as a trench soldier in France, and, after building a big law practice with his brother Robert, led the most famous local-government reform of his day in Cincinnati.

Charlie Taft's progressivism, someone said, was that of "a grown-up Boy Scout looking for a good deed to do." He told the *Christian Herald:* "I can see no reason whatever for getting tight at any time for any reason." He did not serve liquor in his mansion. When he visited friends, one of them complained that "if the conversation gets trivial he just goes off in a corner and reads a book." He had no taste for gossip, no inclination for intimacy. During the Second World War he had held several moderately high offices in Washington, and in 1945 found himself defending Truman's reciprocal trade program against his brother, who led the Senate opposition to it. "The trouble with Charlie," said Robert, "is that he takes the opinions of any group of people with whom he is thrown."[21]

The trouble with the Federal Council's optimistic program for harmonizing labor and management views in 1947 was that it could not mesh ethical precepts with the conduct of worldly affairs. Arthur Flemming, later a member of President Eisenhower's cabinet, and Paul Hoffman, later administrator of the Marshall Plan, joined Taft's drive, but the Council's statement of "Christian Principles in Assumptions for Economic Life" went unheeded. It was the conservative senator's Taft-Hartley Law imposing stiff limits on unions, and not his progressive brother's high-minded pleas that labor and capital "cooperate as partners with Christian goodwill," that prevailed in 1947.[22]

Another layman had more success in steering the church into the Cold War. John Foster Dulles, as chairman of the Council's Commission for a Just and Durable Peace, brought in a key report at the Council meeting at Columbus, Ohio, in 1946 that "differences" with Russia "will never be removed by compromise or surrender." As this judgment hardened into Cold War policy, Dulles's arguments for the tough line among Protestant churchmen were powerfully supported by the intervention of the leading American theologian of the twentieth century.[23]

What the mobilization of America into Cold War needed, if it was to unite the people behind a prolonged program of sacrifice and hazard that would stand up against Communist counterattack, was ideological underpinnings. This was what Reinhold Niebuhr, more than any other American of his time, provided. Remarkably enough, this most influential voice among American Protestants spoke with almost greater persuasiveness to those outside the church than those within it. Not since Jonathan Edwards had a theologian so affected his contemporaries as Reinhold Niebuhr.

Born in Nebraska as the son of a German immigrant Evangelical pastor, Niebuhr rose out of a narrow Midwestern ethnic background to wide-ranging intellectual eminence much as Thorstein Veblen did a generation before him. Trained at Yale and in the urban ministry in Detroit, he became a professor at Union Theological Seminary in New York City in the years between the two World Wars when pacifism was a pervasive force. He was president of the pacifist Fellowship of Reconciliation in the 1920s, and vigorously involved in the Social Gospel movement that fought for social reform in faith that "the kingdom of Jesus . . . can indeed be realized [on earth]." But with the Depression and the rise of Hitler, he turned back to Jonathan Edwards' old emphasis on sin and human frailty. In lectures delivered at Edinburgh in 1939, Neibuhr declared that "a sharp distinction must be drawn between the moral and social behavior of individuals and social groups," and that:

> this distinction based upon the harsh reality that such groups as nations will always act selfishly whereas at least the possibility exists that the individual may not and certainly should not. . . . justifies and necessitates political policies [for a nation that] a purely individual ethic must always find embarrassing.

On the strength of this estimate of the collective fallibility of man, Niebuhr rounded on the "utopian idealism" of all liberalism, in church and out, that had fatuously supposed mankind was harmoniously progressing toward perfection when Western society was breaking down all over the place and Hitler was fast making ready to destroy the soft and complacent democracies. Niebuhr's powerful writings furnished a rationale, especially for young people who had grown up as campus pacifists in the 1930s, for taking arms against "the forces of darkness," as he called the Nazis, and destroying them.[24]

After the war, with scarcely a pause in his polemic, Niebuhr trained his powerful analysis on the Russians. Having made a journey through Germany and heard from old socialist friends of the repression and terror by which Stalin was spreading communism, he extended his critique of man's depravity. The trouble with the Communists was the same old bugaboo of the "sentimental" liberals—utopianism. Communism was at once the worst and most aggressive of societies because its faithful believed that they could find a more perfect union among sinful men simply by playing down the drive for property. But Communism overlooked the larger and infinitely more ineradicable factor—the will to power. Worse, Communism had always sought to get rid of the property drive by centralizing power in the top party leadership, instead of working out a balance of elements within that society as, for instance, the Founding Fathers did through America's federal constitution. Communism, making play with the concepts of science and rationality that had beguiled the liberals elsewhere, had only proved again by the ironic miscarriage of its utopian ideals in Stalin's slave-camp tyranny that science is easily put to the service of a totalitarian society.

The other big element in Niebuhr's "realism" was a pragmatic outlook that examined each changing situation in terms of what action promised, with due regard for human fallibility, to lead to positive results. In 1947, through writings in *The Nation, Life* and other journals, Niebuhr reached more unbelievers than believers with hard-hitting arguments for seeking balance of power solutions in the developing Cold War. At home, the kind of adjustments between capital and labor that the New Deal had worked out seemed about the best that could be had. But abroad, to trust world government would be a relapse into the discredited utopian liberalism of the pacifists and the Wilsonian idealists. The only cooperation with the Soviet Union must be on terms that curbed its totalitarian aggressiveness, whether in the United Nations or in plans for building up an anti-Communist Europe.[25]

The Christian "realism" of Reinhold Niebuhr laid much of the ideological pavement upon which America marched into the Cold War. It undergirded the policy of containment. It supplied the rationale for rebuilding and rearming Europe. It also provided a calculus for reckoning, by taking the inverse proportion of its utopian claims, the appalling depths of Communism's perversity and corruption.

A theologian in politics, an intellectual with a strong thrust for action, Niebuhr had become chairman of the Union for Democratic Action in 1941. When Secretary Marshall appointed George Kennan head of the State Department's new Policy Planning Staff in 1947, Niebuhr became chairman of its Advisory Committee, and in the State Department group which helped shape the Truman Doctrine, the Marshall Plan and NATO, Kennan, Paul Nitze, C.B. Marshall, Dorothy Fosdick and Louis Halle could all be counted Niebuhr's disciples. In January, 1947, when Americans for Democratic Action was organized by a group of key liberals pledged to fight "international Communism" and the Progressive Citizens of America backing Henry Wallace's anti-Cold War race against President Truman, Niebuhr was the ADA chairman.

At Union Theological Seminary, Niebuhr also saw a lot of the publisher Henry R. Luce, who was a trustee. "For peace we must risk war," wrote Niebuhr in Luce's magazine *Life* just before the 1948 elections. "Russia hopes to conquer the whole of Europe strategically or ideologically." In other *Life* articles at the time Niebuhr said: "We cannot afford any more compromises. We will have to stand at every point in our far-flung lines." It would take years, said Niebuhr, to hold out against the "egoistic corruption" of the Soviet Communists. Niebuhr's preachments carried impact. "He was the father of us all," said George Kennan, architect of the containment policy. When Niebuhr taught, said the Right Reverend Horace Donegan, Episcopal bishop of New York, "suddenly the light of revelation seemed to dawn upon us, and we began to discard the vapid and sentimental illusions that passed for Christianity." Niebuhr, an ardent Zionist, was also heard with great respect among the nation's liberal, anti-Communist Jews. He was vice chairman of the Liberal party, which carried great weight in New York State politics and enjoyed financial support from David Dubinsky's International Ladies' Garment Workers' Union.[26]

If the most influential of Protestant Cold Warriors was a theologian in politics, the strongest Catholic voice in organizing the Cold War was that of a prince of the Church with a passion for the politics of patriotism. Francis Cardinal Spellman was a figure of paradoxes. The foremost internationalist of the American hierarchy, he became its most ardent nationalist. Having led his constituency to the center of American life, he was then left behind by them. A true son of the Boston Irish community, he found, like his friend Joseph P. Kennedy, that he had to move to New York to achieve his prominence. In Kennedy's case it was because the Protestant Brahmins would not admit his family to their society; in Spellman's it was because his superior, Cardinal O'Connell, would never grant him preferment.

Born the son of a South-of-Boston Irish grocer and educated at

Fordham, Spellman was sent to Rome for higher training and in 1925 became the first American ever to enter the Vatican service as aide to Papal Secretary of State Eugenio Pacelli. After seven years the young prelate was made Auxiliary Bishop of Boston. But the Holy See neglected to clear the appointment of its young protégé with his prospective superior. When Spellman arrived in Boston, Cardinal O'Connell sent him out to be parish pastor in suburban Newton Center.

Five years went by, and just when it seemed that Spellman's exile might never end, Cardinal Pacelli decided to pay a private visit to the United States. The pastor of Newton Center met the boat, took over management of His Eminence's vacation and transformed it into a month-long transcontinental tour starting with Mass at Newton Center and dinner at his parents', and ending with luncheon at Hyde Park with the Roosevelts. At the luncheon the matter of opening American diplomatic relations with the Vatican was broached, and thereafter Roosevelt consulted the pastor of Newton Center often. There were longhand letters and White House visits. "One of those memorable experiences of my life," wrote Spellman in his diary after one visit. In 1939, when Pacelli became Pope Pius XII and promptly named his old aide archbishop of New York, Spellman wrote Roosevelt: "I wish you to be the first to know . . ." When war broke out in Europe, the White House announced appointment of Myron Taylor as special representative at the Vatican, and Pope Pius made Spellman his Military Vicar for the American armed forces.[27]

Among President Roosevelt's most influential Irish Catholic friends, some like James J. Farley had found it difficult to support the third-term candidacy. Many more, like Joseph P. Kennedy, could not bring themselves to support his policy of giving all possible aid to the British. Archbishop Spellman stood foursquare behind the President, and after America took up arms he threw himself passionately into the war. If ever a team of All-American chaplains had been named, Spellman would have been its captain. He traveled everywhere. He wrote letters to 10,000 mothers. He turned out sermons, essays, poems in praise of the war, not hesitating to invoke the reverential vision of the bloodshed of Christianity's founder to convey how inexpressibly "sweet" it could be to strive and die for the United States. The books sold more than a million copies. One of the poems brought more than $5000 from *Good Housekeeping* magazine; Metro-Goldwyn-Mayer paid $50,000 for movie rights to his book *The Risen Soldier.*[24]

For Spellman, the war never really ended. The great of the world— Adenauer, De Gasperi, Bidault—came to see him. Pope Paul VI said Mass in Yankee Stadium for 100,000 of his flock. A vast building and fund-raising program made his the richest archdiocese in the world. Yet his preoccupation with the material prosperity of the archdiocese, with bureaucratic efficiency, with finances and front-page public relations, could not stem his patriotic ardor. Every December he took off to spend Christmas with "the boys" in Germany, the South Seas, Greece and the Antarctic. When the Cold War came on, the cardinal threw everything he had into the fight.

In 1948 he brought Harry Truman to the St. Patrick's Day dinner in New York to signal his support at a moment when Henry Wallace was running for President on an end-the-Cold-War ticket. Truman responded by delivering one of his most outspoken denunciations of "international Communism." But the speech that topped the evening was Spellman's. From month to month he had been making highly publicized interventions on behalf of persecuted churchmen in Eastern Europe—Cardinals Stepinac of Yugoslavia, Mindszenty of Hungary, and Beran of Czechoslovakia. Said Spellman:

> In this hour of dreadful, desperate need we are permitting Soviet Russia to continue her policy of persecution and slaughter, dooming our neighbor nations and ourselves to reap a rotten harvest of appeasement. Once again while Rome literally and symbolically burns, the world continues to fiddle. The strings of the fiddle are committees, conferences, conversations, appeasement—to the tune of no action whatsoever.
>
> We [have] failed to face the vital, vibrant issue of fair play and peace, of foul play and war. For it is foul play for Soviet Russia to desecrate and devour the little, God-loving, free peoples of the earth even before the tears of war have dried upon the sad, scarred faces of many lands —lands that are bloody battlegrounds and fetid funeral fields for their own native sons—and ours! Fear must clutch your hearts as tightly as it grips my own, as we watch the towering glacier slide ceaselessly and mercilessly across Europe and Asia, as powerful, aggressive, ruthless forces press to a finish the issue of slavery against democracy, evil against good, might against right, Stalinism against God.
>
> I cannot believe that the Italian people will choose Stalinism against God, Soviet Russia against America—America which has done so much and stands ready and willing to do so much more, if Italy remains a free, friendly and unfettered nation.
>
> It is not alone in defense of my faith that I condemn atheistic communism, but as an American in defense of my country. We stand at the crossroads of civilization, a civilization threatened with the crucifixion of Communism.

The cardinal ended by asking his communicants, a third of whom were of Italian descent, to write to relatives in Italy to vote against Communism and for America in the next months's general elections.[29]

Spellman never abated in his zeal for the Cold War, and his thundering denunciations were echoed through the 1940s and 1950s in Roman Catholic pulpits and parish papers throughout the land. When Dulles called for the liberation of Eastern Europe, the cardinal was at his side. In 1954 Spellman went before the American Legion in Miami to denounce the partitioning of Vietnam at Geneva:

> If Geneva and what was agreed upon there means anything at all, it means . . . taps for the buried hopes of freedom in Southeast Asia. Communism has a world plan and it has been following a carefully set up timetable for the achievement of that plan, heaping infamies and agonies upon the hapless victims of Red Russia's bestial tyranny.

It was thanks to Cardinal Spellman, who sheltered him in diocesan and other seminaries through three years' exile, that Ngo Dinh Diem was able to return at this point and establish the anti-Communist regime in Saigon to which the United States lent support. But it was Joe Kennedy's son, America's first Catholic President, who withdrew American backing for Diem, and who negotiated the Treaty of Moscow in 1963 that brought the end of the Cold War. When Spellman delivered a speech of unembarrassed encouragement to United States troops in Vietnam in December 1965, he incurred the displeasure of Rome, where a new Pope was pleading for peace, and open criticism from some American Catholics. The Cold War over, the very seams of the church seemed to strain and crack under the outburst of long-suppressed opinions, and Spellman died in 1968 as a changing American Catholicism appeared to be abandoning many of the positions, and even some of the buildings, that the cardinal had so energetically erected.[30]

E V E N more than the churches of the nation, American education had swung in the course of changes set in motion by the Second World War toward the reorientation required to conform with the new ideology of the Cold War. This was first evident in the field of higher education and above all in graduate training for certain types of careers. Before the war, according to a survey made in 1938, many four-year liberal arts colleges did not offer even one course in international relations. With the end of the Second World War, there occurred a tremendous burst of international studies on American campuses as the academic community responded to the new awareness of the country's involvement in the world. Within a few years it could be said that more than half of all students enrolled at such an institution as the University of Wisconsin, or upwards of 30,000 a year, took some course in international affairs, and perhaps more significantly, professors in virtually all of the disciplines by reason of their overseas experience in military or government service or otherwise taught their students with an incomparably broadened sense of citizenship in a wider world. [31]

Even before the end of the Second World War, the need for trained personnel for the new American role in the world was seen in the universities. At Columbia the campus was virtually taken over by the Navy—a popular postwar novel, Herman Wouk's *The Caine Mutiny*, opened in a Columbia dormitory jammed with "90-day wonders." To some professors the Navy School of Military Government's crash program at Columbia suggested an important postwar service to government and business. In 1945 the Rockefeller Foundation gave Columbia $250,000 to set up an interdisciplinary Institute of Russian Affairs. The grant was a model for many others made to American universities in the Cold War. In part the aim was to train expert help for the Stimsons and Achesons and McCloys then running American policies and replacements for the Bundys and Kennans and Jessups then advising them. But beyond the manning of the international apparatus was the wider need for reorienting and educating a whole generation of citizens in the vastly expanded American involvement in the world.

In the years of the Cold War, the Rockefeller, Carnegie and (after 1950) Ford foundations provided funds to start no fewer than 191 centers for the study of international relations on university campuses. Under Dean Rusk, its president from 1953 to 1961, the Rockefeller Foundation threw the bulk of its resources into building up non-Western studies in American education. By 1966 the Ford Foundation had spent $270,-000,000 on its international program of which $155,000,000 went for "strengthening foreign area and other international studies in American universities." Knowledge of the enemy was vital to the Cold Warriors: foreign studies became the height of academic fashion, and the fat fellowships insured that much of the cream of the student crop poured into these programs through the Cold War years.

From Columbia, Harvard and nine or ten other big centers issued a stream of bright young area specialists. Some went into government (Columbia for a time provided sixty percent of the country's Soviet experts), mostly in the State Department, but also in the Pentagon and the CIA. Many became scholars, staffing the 500 area-study programs that flourished on American campuses by the 1970s, and imparting to thousands of American undergraduates an understanding of French or Brazilian affairs superior to their fathers' comprehension of American politics. At the height of the Cold War those centers regularly performed contract studies for the government. *The Dynamics of Soviet Society* (1954) and *The Prospects For Communist China* (1954), two volumes produced by Walt Rostow at Massachusetts Institute of Technology's Center for International Studies with funds provided by the Pentagon and the CIA, were widely used in classrooms. At one point, Secretary of the Navy Paul Nitze claimed that out of the universities' close collaboration with defense agencies "the outlines of an identifiable academic discipline having to do with national security affairs [has] begun to emerge." After the Cold War ended, students revolted, universities cut back their ties with the military establishments, and the foundations switched their funds from overseas to inner-city programs.[32]

If the colleges and universities swung quickly into action in the Cold War, the lower schools of the land were ready and waiting for the confrontation with "international Communism." The progressive education movement that still dominated them had somehow lost its old zest for the child-centered principles of John Dewey. Its leaders had built a professional bureaucracy, and become managers of a system for easing masses of children into the job-holding democracy of the American corporate state. In the war they had schooled a whole generation to fight in the democracy's army, and in its aftermath they took as their acculturating task the watering down of the content of education so that everybody could complete high school without strain.

Life adjustment education, as the professional educators called it, was just being introduced when the Cold War cry went up. The object, said Dr. William Prosser, founder of the movement, was to help young people lead "a more contented life." His co-chairman, Dr. Galen Jones, said the movement would make possible "perpetuation and improvement of the American way of life." To this end, the list of goals proposed by the National Association of Secondary Education said little about intellectual skills but stressed instead "salable skills" that would "meet the common and specific individual needs of youth." The Illinois Life Adjustment Program bore down on "56 real-life problems"—"acquiring the social skills of dancing, playing party games, doing parlor stunts;" the "problem of improving one's personal appearance," "the problem of selecting a family dentist," and "the problem of developing and maintaining wholesome boy-girl relationships." The first task of the schools in the Cold War, said the Illinois group, was "to reduce the tensions and meet the needs of children and youth." One of the ways suggested was to "make studies of how the last war affected the dating pattern in our culture."[33]

Such an essentially accommodating approach to the tasks of education, one which so largely derived from the assumption that the purpose of the schools was to shape young people so that they could fit with least friction into American life, was admirably suited to the engineering of the altered ideological stance deemed necessary for the Cold War. Almost as soon as President Truman proclaimed the confrontation with "international Communism," the United States Commissioner of Education, Dr. John W. Studebaker summoned the school administrators of the nation to a meeting in Denver to accept what he termed "Communism's Challenge to American Education":

> No amount of wishful thinking, no temptation to seek peace . . . should obscure the precarious world situation in which America finds itself today. The issue must be faced. Democracy and Communist dictatorship represent two antithetical systems of belief and of government. We cannot be both.

What Studebaker demanded was that the schools must not just teach arithmetic and history, they must teach democracy. J. Edgar Hoover, he said, had asked 2000 people in forty high schools what democracy meant to them—and fewer than a third "had any apparent concern about what they might do to make democracy more successful." In Tulsa the senior high school course in American history had just added a unit called the American Dream. At Roosevelt High School in Des Moines, said Studebaker, a twelfth-grade course now included eight weeks' study of "Democracy and its Competitors." Around the country schools swung into line: it was in these years that "Problems of Democracy" became a standard twelfth-grade course in American high schools. Many began to teach the evils of communism.[34]

In the reorienting of American educators to anti-Communism the example of John Dewey himself was influential. Earlier in his life he had been well disposed to the Russian experiment. But in 1937 Dewey was prevailed on, at the age of seventy-seven, to preside over a highly publicized investigation in Mexico City of the charges for which the dissident Soviet Communist leader Leon Trotsky had been tried and condemned in absentia in Moscow. The reading of the lengthy Moscow transcripts left Dewey completely disillusioned with the Soviet Union. And when the drums began to beat for the Cold War in the late 1940s, nobody on the American scene pounded louder than Dewey's disciples at Columbia Teachers College. In December 1947 Professor George S. Counts proclaimed—almost as if the recent war had gone by unnoticed—

> the supreme challenge of our American democracy's history. . . . Supported by the international network of Party agents, communism is on

the offensive everywhere, confident that it will conquer the earth. The Russians are preparing the young for war. Formal military training begins at the fourth grade. Emphasis on military games is found in the nursery school and kindergarten. Democracy to compete must develop an educational program that serves freedom as effectively.[35]

"The USA is square up against the USSR," said Dean William F. Russell.

We cannot feel complacent. We Americans should do all we can in and through and by the schools to guard our liberties and to help our children save themselves. We should bring to a high level of consciousness what America is. Let us come out of our corner fighting. They should know that God has blessed America. The first job of education for democracy at the moment is to rip the sheep's clothing off the wolf—the Bear— and to let Soviet communistic dictatorship stand revealed to the world in its true light.[36]

In December 1947 the Chief State School Officers, meeting at Los Angeles, said:

We are witnessing a worldwide struggle. We urge our members to create a climate of opinion in their respective states which will encourage the teacher to present the facts about totalitarianism in order that all may clearly see its purpose to subvert our American freedoms.[37]

By October 1949 the Educational Policies Commission of the National Educational Association was ready to face the cruncher: "Should members of the Communist party be employed as teachers?" Professor John K. Norton of Teachers College presented the answer—endorsed already, he said, by 300 newspaper editorials:

Communism is a conspiracy. It tells you what to think. You follow the party line in all respects. It regulates your economic life at every turn. Any means, no matter how it outrages the human personality, is moral under the Communist code—anything goes. Communism looks upon the school and education as especially choice means of achieving its evil end. It is the teacher's duty to destroy the loyalty of the children and youth of his country. The answer is that Communists must not teach.[38]

The strongest partisans of polarization turned out to be ex-Communists. Indeed, it was a group of Trotskyists who rallied around Dewey at the time of the 1937 Mexico City trial, and now it was Deweyite intellectuals such as Sidney Hook and George S. Counts who took the lead in forming the American Committee for Cultural Freedom. This group took quite literally the assertion of such ex-Communists as Arthur Koestler and Franz Borkenau that the Communist issue overrode conventional distinctions between right and left. In the zeal of their anti-Communism these intellectuals proclaimed the "end of ideology," all the traditional differences between conservatives, liberals and the like having paled into insignificance, irrelevance and obsolescence before the annihilating urgency of combining against "international Communism." "The words 'capitalism' and 'socialism,' 'right' and 'left' are virtually empty of meaning," said the Hungarian ex-Communist Koestler. Hook, the disciple of Dewey, looked forward to "the era when reference to right, left and center will vanish from common usage as meaningless." Members in this coalition of intellectuals, liberals and reactionary ex-Communists shared a conspiratorial view of communism and agreed moreover that the Communist conspiracy had spread through practically every level of American society.[39]

Thus Hook, like Counts, sought to distinguish between the sort of heresy whose right to speech liberalism must fight to defend, and secret movements that sought their ends "not by normal political or educational processes but by playing outside the rules of the game." On this showing, Communists were not to be accorded the same liberties as others dedicated to the American way of life. It followed that:

> a member of the Communist party has transgressed the canons of academic responsibility, has engaged his intellect to servility and is therefore professionally disqualified from performing his functions as a scholar and teacher.[40]

Thus, for the university professor quite as much as the teacher in the public schools, the answer was "Communists must not teach." The professors' lofty Committee on Academic Freedom, however, made one further distinction that the schoolteachers' commission, whose constituencies lived in the daily presence of 25,000 local school boards, did not. The expulsion of Communists should be left "in the hands of the colleges and their faculties," the professors argued, and there was no justification for the various legislative committees that were rushing to root out Communists to concern themselves with the question. Academic freedom, in this version, meant self-determination for the academic community.[41]

Among the students, the mobilizing for Cold War joined with certain other forces working for change in America to impart the stamp of passive conformity on a whole generation. In consequence of the Servicemen's Readjustment Act of 1944, by far the most comprehensive set of measures ever put together to anticipate the impact of returning soldiers upon an economy reconverting to peace, the campuses of the nation experienced a military invasion at the end of the Second World War. Education was thought of as the grand staircase of American society, and no fewer than 7.8 million of the 15 million returning GIs took advantage of the generous financial aid offered under the GI Bill of Rights for veterans who wanted to climb the ladder of educational opportunity.

Hundreds of thousands who had thought of the university as a rich man's place poured back from the theaters of war into its classrooms. The GI Bill credit of $500 a year met all or most tuition costs in 1946, and the $50 to $75 monthly living allowances were equally generous. If a few used the aid to take rumba lessons at Arthur Murray's, or like one veteran from Des Moines, to furnish himself with a first-class kit of burglar's tools, the vast majority of the veterans who took advantage of the GI Bill opted for higher education. Overnight, enrollments doubled. Clad in their old khakis, they jammed lecture halls, filled quonset-hut dormitories, and spread out into muddy, cheerless trailer towns like Shanks Village (pop. 10,000), Columbia's temporary intellectual backyard across the Hudson from New York City, while they trained to become engineers, teachers, lawyers, construction workers, mechanics.

University officials generally agreed, said Lehigh University's Dean Loren S. Hadley, that the GI's showed "a definite and noticeable maturity that cannot be attributed to chronological age." They displayed high motivation under often trying circumstances, and a clear edge on all others when it came to grades. A third were married, many had families to support, and all seemed impatient to "get into action" fast. By 1948 the tide was already ebbing, but it made its revolutionizing mark. Not only was the nation convinced that the $15 billion spent on GI education was one of the best investments America ever made, but it caused families everywhere to clamor to send their children to college too.[42]

The outcome made the progressive educators, with their feckless talk about taking the tough subjects out of the school curriculum to induce kids to stay on through high school, look silly. In giving large numbers of Americans their first push toward higher education, the GI Bill proved only a starter for what became a mighty flood. Taking themselves out of the labor market, substantially *all* young people began to stay on in high school and get their diplomas instead of quitting at sixteen, when attendance was no longer required by law. And, raising their sights, young people also began to think, in vast and swelling numbers, of going on to college for the years after high school. When contrary to expectations the economy did not collapse, thousands of parents, who had survived the Depression to make more money in the war than they ever had before, decided that the best thing they could do for their children's future was to use their savings to send the children to college.

In a few years what the GI Bill of Rights did to delay the entrance of the young into the daily working world of adult America solidified into a new, fixed pattern for the American way of life. The old, agrarian society in which the young passed straight out of puberty and the eighth grade into man's work had long vanished (though child labor was not banned until the coming of the New Deal, and lingered on even after the 1930s on the farm). The apprenticeship of the craft unions and big factories gave way so far to the new social pressures for finishing high school that young men who left school at sixteen were suddenly branded "dropouts."

In 1948 President Truman's Commission on Higher Education, taking account both of this new pattern and of the sudden and unexpected surge of the birthrate after the war, recommended that the country's colleges and universities, struggling to cope with a record population of two million students that year, be ready to take 4.6 million by 1960. On the basis of the data from the Army General Classification Test given ten million soldiers in the recent war, the commission calculated that at least 49% of the population had the mental ability for two years of college, and at least 32% were up to the full, four-year course. Many college officials threw up their hands at such a big assignment—President Robert I. Gannon of Fordham predicted it would "suffocate us with tides of mediocrity." Nevertheless, almost every college and university launched into an expansion program. By September 1960 enrollments were within 800,000 of the Commission's prediction—and by 1970 reached 6.4 million. At that point the young people of America had raised their average school-leaving age to nineteen—the highest school-leaving age ever known on earth; and 44% of all Americans of university age were enrolled in some form of higher education.[43]

Neither the consequences nor the causes of these big changes were well understood. Some saw the times as an age of maturation. On the one side children were maturing earlier—girls two years earlier than their grandmothers. On the other side, as soon became clear, the young stayed on through school and college for lengthening periods of time. Berkeley, California and Cambridge, Massachusetts, were two places with particularly large nonstudent populations, youth seemingly so well indoctrinated to stay off the labor market that by a kind of inertia built up over the years they remained around the campuses even after their schooling stopped.[44]

By the usual and more or less official explanation, such prolongation of education gave time for the increasingly specialized training required to man the ever more complex technologies of American industrial society. Yet such unnatural attenuation of the school years also worked out as a way of subsidizing people not to compete on the job market—and a more socially acceptable way than going on welfare. Whatever it did to supply the business society's sophisticated manpower requirements, the channeling of young people away from early entry into the world of work led swiftly to startling changes in American life-styles. Below the barrier erected by society emerged not only one group but two—the adolescents, still in their teens, and youth, those (of an indeterminate age) who might earlier have gone to work but now did not. A vast amount of social tension grew up, mainly between those on the two sides of the barrier, tensions that only began to be understood years later.

Thus there was a sense in which the GI Bill of Rights prepared the way for the Berkeley uprising of 1964. Maturing earlier and yet being kept on campus longer, the students inevitably grew restive at being held back from full participation in adult society and rose to break out of the system. By that time the pattern had given shape to a kind of autonomous world of youth. By 1970 this subculture had acquired along with distinctive dress, hairstyles and music, a vitality such as to make major impact on daily life in America. Older people, recoiling in confusion and frustration at the new language and new values of their children, made it a commonplace to speak of a "generation gap." What they sensed was more properly called an education gap. Thanks to the changes set in motion by the anti-Depression impulses of 1945, the proportion of young adults with college degrees almost tripled between that date and 1970—up from six percent to sixteen percent. The proportion of young people with more than one year of college had trebled—up from eleven percent to thirty-three percent. Those who had acquired high school diplomas had increased from thirty-eight percent to seventy-three percent of their age-group by 1970. If the new generation talked and behaved differently from their elders, it was mainly because they were better educated.[45]

Paradoxically, this widening cleavage had its roots in the ways in which the older generation met the end of the Second World War and the onset of the Cold War. First, the young people who flooded onto the campuses in the aftermath of the war were to some degree influenced by the job-oriented outlook of the ex-GIs in their midst. Second and more important, the security-mindedness of parents directed their children to college as the avenue for assuring them of a position in an increasingly bureaucratized, specialized society. Third and probably most important, was the larger society's need for a steady and indeed expanding supply of just such young, technically proficient recruits as Cold War demands built up.

But what of the young people themselves? The impact of these forces upon American children was profound, and utterly unforeseen. During the decades of the Cold War, when American society mobilized itself in fear—fear that the bomb might be apocalyptically turned against it, fear that "international Communism" was advancing across the world and trying to subvert the very churches, colleges, unions and political parties they belonged to—young Americans as a group had remarkably little to say.

A popular teen-age project of 1947 was the "Junior Town Meeting of the Air," at which high schoolers dutifully reminded each other "that it is important to vote and pay taxes for the Marshall Plan, and to serve in the armed forces." At seminars on "Homes of Tomorrow," teen-agers in Chicago talked about such tabby-cat topics as "What Price Popularity?," "A Sound Attitude to Sex," "Choosing Your Life Partner," "Marriage is What You Make it." The Junior Chamber of Commerce 1947 prize went to Dicksie Dillon, seventeen, of Boulder, Colorado, for an essay titled: "I Speak for Democracy." She read her winning essay on a nationwide broadcast:

Start with Sunday. You get up, that is, if you want to, and go to church.
. . .

Jan Geister, of Cuyahoga Falls, Ohio, took second prize with an essay that began:

To me democracy means a way of life. I will have a real voice in my government. And the everyday things—football games on Friday night, and things like that. . . .

When the National Association of Student Counselors brought 400 students from forty states to Washington, "not a one violated the no-smoking rule," a teacher reported, "and the night of the dance, the girls in their formals, boys in their Sunday best, sat in the dining room listening to a speaker: not a boy or girl made a move to attend the dance although the snappy dance band was already playing tentatively in the beautifully decorated gym." When 300 high school students trooped to the Columbia College Forum on Democracy in early 1949, they were so well behaved that one professor thought their questions "submissive."[46]

So little was heard from these puzzling young people through the 1950s that many older Americans began to wonder about it. Somewhere between the years 1953 and 1955 the baffled elders began calling them "the silent generation." But at a time when technology united with affluence to transistorize the rumpus rooms, dancehalls and fraternity houses of the land, that term would have been misleading if it suggested that the young quite literally fell still. Far from it, teen-agers turned up the volume. They rocked and rolled to the blare of jukeboxes and the roar of disk-jockeyed radios. In the summer of 1955, his voice oscillating between a shout and a whine, Elvis Presley starred in a western movie called *Love Me Tender* and when he appeared in person in St. Louis, pounding his pelvis against his electric guitar, the crowd tore his clothes right off him.

The sudden hero of the season was James Dean, a sullen-eyed actor in a black leather jacket who made a film *Rebel without a Cause,* in which he raced another teen-ager to the brink of a cliff to see who would leap from his stolen car first and thus show himself "chicken," or coward. The picture had hardly been released when Dean, aged twenty-four, was killed driving his silver Porsche Spyder sports car to a road race. In the following year twenty-eight of the forty-seven children born in Dean's home town of Fairmount, Indiana, were named Jimmy. An entrepreneur bought the car in which Dean was killed, built a stand at the roadside and charged thirty-five cents admission, plus thirty-five cents more to sit in the fatal seat; in six months, 780,000 paid for this privilege. Dean's death mask was placed in the collection at Princeton University, along with those of Keats, Melville, Beethoven and Mozart. "Jimmy Dean clubs" mushroomed to 3,800,000 members, a memorial book sold 1,500,000 copies, 225,000 letters addressed to Dean ("Dear Jimmy, I know you are dead. . . .") deluged his studio, more than for any living star. A teen-ager paid $75 for the belt buckle Dean wore making his last film in Texas, another paid $380 for his velvet-lined vest (raising the money by pawning jewels from her mother's dresser drawer). One young girl, who had seen Dean only on the screen, took poison. Revived with difficulty, she said: "I'll try again. I want to rejoin Jimmy in death. It's the only way to be at his side, live with him, love him, serve him."[47]

A few critics fretted at the appeal of such a youth, "rudderless, skittering on the edge of juvenile delinquency," but the Dean cult remained a phenomenon without visible links to what seemed to be going on. To a reporter sent out by *Newsweek* to find out what the class of 1953 worried about, a Vassar girl confided: "We're a cautious generation." A Princeton senior said over his beer: "The world doesn't owe me a living —but it owes me a job." "You want to be popular," explained a Northwestern coed, "so naturally you don't express any screwy ideas. To be popular you have to conform." What did the collegians want out of life? *Newsweek*'s conclusion was that mostly they wanted to be contented, to have a home and family, and to make a success in their chosen field. "Men preferred jobs with big corporations. Women were prepared to help."[48]

"Security is the theme of the students who come into my office to discuss their vocations," said Professor Leland Miles of Hanover College, Indiana, in a widely quoted speech in 1954. By 1957, when *The Nation* invited sixteen noted teachers across the land to submit their reading of the students' outlook, the cultural characteristics had grown so sharp as to be unmistakable. "They are more conservative than a comparable group would have been twenty-five years ago," reported Professor Carlos Baker from Princeton. "One of them asked in class, 'Why should we go out on a limb?' "

Passivity, absence of political passion of the sort that gave people a mission in the 1930s, caution—these were the traits singled out. "Something in the climate of opinion and action in which these young people have grown up," wrote novelist Wallace Stegner from Stanford,

> has made many of them what I can only call 'goal-keepers.' They lie at the mouths of their private barrows, watchful and suspicious and they warn potential intruders away from their privacy.

What was it in the atmosphere in which these students had grown up that made them such careful young men? To Allan Seager at Michigan there was no question that the "something" in the air that damped down passions was fear.

> [The student] seems to take this fear so much for granted that it is hard for him to be articulate about it. 'War' and 'the bomb' are the words that eventually come out in any discussion, and he says he wants to get some living done before anything happens.[49]

Twenty years later the futile stasis and deadlock of the young people of the 1940s and 1950s had vanished with the Cold War that produced it. In 1970 the Scranton Commission, President Nixon's Commission on Campus Unrest, prefaced its findings on the Kent State University and Jackson State College killings with a brief retrospect over the record of student discontent in America:

> The history of American colleges is filled with incidents of turmoil, disorder and riot. . . . It is not so much the unrest of the past half-dozen years that is exceptional as it is the quiet of the twenty years that preceded them.

The Commission then added:

> From the early 1940s to the early 1960s American colleges and universities were uncharacteristically calm, radical student movements were almost nonexistent, and disruptions were rare. The existence of this 'silent generation' was in part a reflection of the Cold War. But as the Cold War lessened, students felt less obliged to defend Western democ-

racy and more free to take a critical look at their own society. Once again the American campus became a center of protest.[50]

From the day the Truman Doctrine was proclaimed, the United States committed its heart, mind and treasure in steadily increasing confrontation against Russia and the perceived menace of "international Communism." American power spread throughout the world as Truman had foretold, in the twentieth-century version of manifest destiny. This required that America became and for years remained a mobilized society. To be mobilized for so long and in such fashion is to be immobilized. The effect upon the young was unnaturally and inordinately stultifying. Among the consequences of the Cold War, foreseen and unforeseen, none was more fateful than the impact it had upon the young through two decades. Even when the Commission on Campus Unrest cast up its accounts the results had only begun to come in. For this silenced generation had yet to assume the direction of the country's political, cultural and industrial destinies. This is a recurring theme of Cold War times; it comes up again in Chapter Ten, which deals with further influences of East-West rivalry in the schools during the Eisenhower and Kennedy years.

CHAPTER 3

The Hidden Cost of the Marshall Plan
and the Taming of American Labor

THE HEROES of the Second World War lasted longer than the heroes of the First World War. They lasted a quarter of a century longer, with great consequences for America and the world. After 1918 not only Wilson but Clemenceau, and before long Lloyd George, disappeared, and when a dozen years later the supreme war commander Marshal Foch was given a hero's burial at the Arc de Triomphe, it was for most people an occasion suddenly and momentarily recalling a bygone past. America had turned against Wilson and his world policies, and Harding and Coolidge had carried the nation into another age. America and the whole world, it seemed, had turned against war. Spirits like Remarque and Keynes, Eliot and Hemingway, E. E. Cummings and Jules Romains, led a whole generation to curse the senseless slaughter and to tap new springs of life. In American literature, the 1920s became the Golden Age.

But after the Second World War the men who had led the way to victory remained. Lesser figures came on stage briefly—an Attlee to start the Third World on its way to independence, a Paul Ramadier to swing France to America's side in the Cold War. But the great heroes who had held the supreme power still loomed large, and the millions who had followed them in battle (Truman was one) seemed to feel the need of their continued presence. Winston Churchill, who was already sixty-eight when called to be prime minister at the start of the war, stayed on as Britain's Tory leader until in 1955, at eighty-four, after a series of incapacitating strokes, he handed over his office to Anthony Eden. Eisenhower, for Americans the ultimate embodiment of this era of long-lived war heroes, had become the oldest man ever to occupy the White House when he finally retired in 1961 at sixty-nine. The extraordinary gerontocracy of the heroes of the Second World War was not brought to its final conclusion until, twenty-five years after the liberation of Paris, De Gaulle gave up the presidency of France in 1969, at the age of seventy-nine.

That old men held the highest office through so many of these years did not only give a sober and conservative tone to the times, it colored the backward looks too. As long as the Churchills and Eisenhowers remained onstage, the widespread and unquestioning acceptance of the Second World War as a crusade for democracy and freedom was maintained. Only after their departure did scholars begin to reexamine the way the Cold War grew out of it. The reinterpretation of the Second World War itself had not really started a quarter of a century later. When the cast of principal characters did not change the same way after 1945 as after 1918, the very loyalties thus prolonged began to determine the course of events. The attachment that Americans carried for Churchill tended to illuminate the way they viewed Europe more than, say, their fitful approbation for the specific anti-Communist policies chosen by Premier Ramadier in a 1947 French cabinet shakeout that might have been crucial to the Cold War.

It was said of the Civil War that it lifted up and ennobled the men who were in it, that it did more for them than they for it—and that after Appomattox the Americans who had been exalted by the experience felt adrift in "slackwater" times. If for large numbers of Americans the supernal exertions of the Second World War provided that sort of uplifting experience, the Cold War provided escape from a similar slackwater letdown.

There was a great awareness in such people that they could continue the great experience of the Second World War in the Cold War. It was visible in Eisenhower's pulling out of the presidency of Columbia University and summoning the old campaigners to go back to Europe with him to set up an Allied headquarters just like before, but this time called SHAPE instead of SHAEF. It was to be seen in General Mark Clark's being summoned during the Cold War to go back to Italy, not to command troops, but to hold the fort for America at the Vatican. With General MacArthur on the front in Asia and General Clay brought back to lead in Europe, the Lovetts and McCloys and Claytons who had served so stalwartly in the Washington war effort returned to yet more commanding service in the new contest against Russia. When General Eisenhower was brought to the White House to hold back the hands of time, it was the grandest act of prolonging what millions had thought was their finest hour.

Thus the Cold War operated to prevent the return to normalcy, to keep alive what had been perceived as a "good" war, to keep a number of people from slipping off into slackwater existence. Almost the first of the old heroes called back was General Marshall. He was brought in by Truman to carry out a mission of high importance to bring about peace between the warring forces in China. The need for his presence seemed even more urgent when he was summoned next to run the State Department and organize the Cold War. Up to that moment President Truman had been losing so many fights on the political front that the country had begun to take him for an interim president. After his party lost its majority in both houses of Congress for the first time in sixteen years, the new Democratic senator from Arkansas, J. William Fulbright, had called upon him to resign. With his war hero's prestige, and with the bipartisan support that he could evoke in Congress and nation for a costly and risky program of large-scale foreign commitments, Marshall fairly saved Truman. Taking his place as the President's senior minister, General Marshall gave him the chance to seize the political offensive and to hold it against all comers.

The transformation was swift. The first result was the Truman Doctrine. And as the President went before Congress to deliver his message that America must oppose the Communist threat everywhere, General Marshall went to Moscow to negotiate the preliminaries of a German peace treaty at a foreign ministers' conference. His big moment did not come during the tiresome, drawn-out green-table sessions. It came at a private session with Stalin. The meeting was stormy. Marshall emerged convinced that the Russians were stalling while Western Europe slid toward chaos. "While the physicians disagree, the patient is sinking," he told the country upon his return.[1]

Even while the Administration was delivering its Greek-Turkish aid program to Congress, Walter Lippmann wrote: "Everyone recognized that what is called the Greek crisis is only a first installment." James Reston, after attending a briefing by Undersecretary Acheson, wrote in *The New York Times:* "What is needed after this is not just two isolated loans but a kind of peacetime lend-lease to defend America by aiding its allies. . . . The Soviet Union would then be confronted by the thing it respects most—American power." Marshall had already created inside the State Department what it had never had in the past—a small policy planning staff. Its head was none other than George Kennan, brought home from Moscow for the purpose as the author of the celebrated "containment" cable. Now Marshall called in Kennan, and gave him the assignment of preparing a scheme for what the United States could and should do. "Avoid trivia," he said.[2]

Not the sort of man to get lost in details, Kennan turned urgently to the task. There was not a day to lose. As Truman's chief ministers saw it, "the skiff was approaching the waterfall." The United States, Undersecretary of State Acheson said in a speech to Mississippi cotton growers in May of 1947, "would push ahead" with the reconstruction of Germany and Japan without waiting for the Big Four agreement. If the countries of Western Europe were to escape chaos, he said, they would need shipments worth $16 billion from the United States in 1947; yet they could not expect to send back exports to the United States worth more than half that sum in payment. The difference would have to be made up from what little extra Americans could import from them—and from "new methods of financing."[3]

When Senator Vandenberg read these figures in the newspapers, he nearly hit the roof. No sooner, he told Marshall, had he sweet-talked his budget-chopping Republican colleagues into accepting the big emergency bill for Greece and Turkey than he was now to be asked to open the Treasury to just about every country in the world. As he stormed on, Marshall called in Acheson, and, as Acheson later recounted, they let Vandenberg continue on for a few minutes to cool off. Then they assured him that the Truman Administration had no intention of asking any further appropriations—not at that particular session of Congress. At this Vandenberg heaved a great sigh of relief, and Marshall spoke. The Administration, he said, wanted to share with the leaders of Congress and later with public groups:

> one of the greatest problems our people had ever faced. Now as never before national unity depended upon a truly nonpartisan policy in the year of a presidential election. Who would carry out an agreed policy no one was bold enough to predict. . . . The security of the country was the supreme consideration.[4]

That was the first fact of political life Marshall and Kennan had to accept as they drew up their scheme—that the Republicans might win office and run it. The second fact, made plain enough soon after the war but fairly screamed from the rooftops by the 1946 election results: Congress would accept no further nonsense about administering large-scale American relief funds through the United Nations. Though run by Americans, UNRRA—the United Nations Relief and Rehabilitation

Agency—had been subjected to certain constraints by such states as Poland, Bulgaria and Yugoslavia while operating within their borders. To be denied freedom to dispense American food and aid (totaling $2.6 billion) with the sovereign authority Herbert Hoover and his staff exercised in the same mission after the First World War, and this by the same states that were pressing socialization and oppressing all who hindered it —this was more than members of Congress could abide.

The third fact, as the planners saw it, was that in Western Europe, where the Americans had the upper hand, the need was not only for food but for all the materials needed to build up the economies so that they could be self-sufficient and resist Communism. Britain had achieved its prewar levels of income and output by 1946 and exceeded them by 8% by 1947, and French production, no more than half its prewar size in 1946, attained 95% of prewar levels by 1947. Italy and the Netherlands were both still below prewar levels too in 1947, but it was Germany that was in direst straits. Income and output there stood at 33% of 1938 levels in 1946, and at only 40% in 1947, and the 1500 calories a day doled out in the American Zone were perhaps enough to sustain a person in bed but certainly not enough to nourish someone at work on any sort of job.[5]

Within three weeks Kennan brought in his scheme, which stressed not the menace of Communist actions as such, but Europe's economic dislocation and need to work out a plan for overcoming this. Assistant Secretary of State Will Clayton flew in from Geneva with a powerful memo that began: "It is now obvious that we have greatly underestimated the destruction of the European economy by war," and went on to report that millions were starving in the cities, that communication between cities and the food-growing countryside had broken down, and that French farmers were feeding grain to cattle. To survive, he said, Europe needed swift help from America—something like $6 to $7 billion worth of coal, cotton, food and shipping services a year for three years. The Europeans should draw up a joint plan for all this, and all other nations could help with certain raw materials—but "the United States must run this show."[6]

With the understanding that the scheme would be left open for the Russians to join in, Marshall now decided that he was ready to unveil it. Scarcely a dozen weeks had elapsed since the big plunge for Greece and Turkey had been taken, and already the Administration was poised to spring its huge program for going into the rest of Europe. If ever there might have seemed a moment for eloquence in the Cold War, this was it. Certainly in the subsequent enactment and execution of the Marshall Plan, there was plenty of talk, not all of it by the European beneficiaries, about the grandeur of the undertaking. But General Marshall was a very understated man, and besides it is not apparent that either he or his aides thought of their plan as an act of international generosity without precedent in the annals of statecraft. So on June 4, 1947, invited to receive an honorary degree at Harvard's commencement, the general made a short speech:

> Our policy is directed not against any country or doctrine but against hunger, poverty, desperation and chaos. Its purpose should be the revival of a working economy . . . so as to permit the emergence of political and social conditions in which free institutions can exist. . . . Any government that is willing to assist in the task of recovery will find full cooperation, I am sure, on the part of the American government.

Then in six sentences he spelled out his plan:

> It is already evident that, before the United States government can proceed much further in its efforts to alleviate the situation and help start the European world on its way to recovery, there must be some agreement among the countries of Europe as to the requirements of the situation and the part these countries themselves will take in order to give proper effect to whatever action might be undertaken by this government.
>
> It would be neither fitting nor efficacious for this government to undertake to draw up unilaterally a program designed to place Europe on its feet economically.
>
> That is the business of Europeans.
>
> The initiative, I think, should come from Europe.
>
> The program should be a joint one, agreed to by a number of, but not all, European countries.
>
> The role of this country should consist of friendly aid in the drafting of a European program and of later support of such a program so far as it may be practical for us to do so.[7]

Quite simply, this speech was the most important act of America's postwar foreign policy. It gave definition and substance to the wide-sweeping rhetoric of President Truman's declaration before Congress three months earlier. It affirmed the broad American determination to intervene in concrete terms, without assigning to the Russians responsibility for stirring up crises everywhere in the world, as Truman did so roundly later on. At the time therefore, Marshall's speech served as an all-purpose weapon for the Administration's new aggressively internationalist foreign policy. To start with, it offered an assurance of expanding American sales overseas when many in both America and Europe believed that their prosperity hinged on a big American flow of exports. It also appealed to those who, like certain former New Deal liberals grown disenchanted with the Allied deadlock in the United Nations, were looking for way to contain Russian Communism but were not ready to consider more than economic measures.

As delivered, the Marshall speech was aimed not at the public, which pays little heed in any case to what is said at commencement ceremonies. It was not even aimed at Congress, which could hardly have been expected to line up for any scheme that seemed at this point to offer financial assistance to the Russians. It was directed to governments. Beforehand, Undersecretary Acheson had met with three British correspondents, explained the speech's purposes, and asked them to cable or telephone the full text and have their editors send a copy to Foreign Minister Bevin along with Acheson's estimate of its importance. This was done. Bevin, getting the word after he was already in bed, leaped out, elephantine frame and all, and put his office to work with the cry: "This is the turning point." Georges Bidault, foreign minister in a French government that had just shed its Communist members for the first time since the war, was almost as fast. Within two weeks they met with Molotov in Paris to discuss how Europeans might devise a European recovery plan, what the economic requirements might be, and what part they would all play in it.[8]

Though Molotov arrived with eighty-nine aides, the Russians were suspicious of the private French-British meeting beforehand, the French-British proposal that Europe's economies be integrated so that Eastern Europe would provide raw materials for factories in the West, and the prospects of the United States' "decisive hold" on the whole program. As Bevin later recounted, he had noticed that Molotov had a bump on his jutting brow that swelled when he was under emotional strain. The Soviet foreign minister was discussing the plan on the third day when an assistant handed him a telegram from Moscow. He turned pale, and the bump on his forehead swelled. His whole manner changed, he became much more harsh. "I suspect," said Bevin, "that Molotov must have thought that the instruction sent him from Moscow was stupid." It was an order for Russian withdrawal which, Bevin added, "made operations much more simple."[9]

Next day Bidault and Bevin invited twenty-two other European nations to join in drawing up a plan for European recovery and within a fortnight representatives of sixteen nations were at work in Paris. Czechoslovakia, after agreeing to attend, withdrew its acceptance after a visit to

Moscow by Premier Klement Gottwald and Foreign Minister Jan Masaryk.

Acting just as quickly, the Russians negotiated trade agreements in July with all the states of Eastern Europe then occupied by Russian armies. The effect was to divert eastward a large trade that until then had flowed to Western Europe: from that point on at least seventy percent of Eastern Europe's trade was with Russia and its satellites. At the same time Moscow announced establishment of the Cominform, or International Communist Information Bureau, representing the Communist parties of nine countries (Russia, Yugoslavia, Poland, Bulgaria, Czechoslovakia, Hungary, Rumania, France, Italy). In the West this was seen as a reconstituting of the old Comintern, Moscow's instrument of international propaganda between the wars. Until the German invasion of Russia in 1941 made its chief targets into his allies, the Comintern had tirelessly repeated Stalin's dogma of the 1920s which divided the world into a Moscow-centered "Socialist camp" and a hostile "Imperialist camp."

In these latest moves the figure of Andrei Zhdanov, the party chief in Leningrad, loomed large. Described by a Yugoslav visitor as "short, with a brownish, clipped mustache, high forehead, pointed nose and sickly red face," Zhdanov was a major force for the hard line in the Soviet leadership. He had led the ferocious purges in Leningrad in the 1930s. When Stalin signed his pact with Hitler in 1939 and proceeded to take over the Baltic states, Zhdanov was in the forefront of the attack on Finland. As the man who had organized the successful defense of Leningrad through the longest and bitterest siege of the Second World War, he was quick after the war to assert that "the decisive role played by the Soviet Union" in "the military defeat of the fascist states . . . altered the alignment of forces between the two systems—the Socialist and the capitalist—in favor of Socialism."[10] When Stalin informed the Soviet peope in early 1946 that they must themselves rebuild and immensely expand their country's industrial strength, it was Zhdanov who led the campaign to purge the Soviet Union of Western influence, purify and propagate Stalinist dogma, and deify Stalin himself. Zhdanov, the unrelenting Zhdanov, it was thought, was the likeliest to succeed Stalin.[11]

If the bundle of hastily signed trade agreements with its Eastern European satellites (culminating in the COMECON regional pact of 1949) was Moscow's reply to the Marshall Plan initiative, the slashing attack that Zhdanov delivered at the first meeting of the Cominform in Warsaw may be seen as Russia's ideological counterthrust to the Truman Doctrine announced a few months earlier. Loosing against the United States for the first time the "imperialist" epithets the old Bolsheviks had hurled against the colonial overlords of London and Paris in the 1920s and

1930s, the Zhdanov speech further polarized the contending hates and fears of the two new superpowers.

Where Truman had drawn a picture of "two alternative ways of life" and Winston Churchill had rung down a metaphoric iron curtain between two halves of Europe, now Zhdanov saw the world as divided into two camps:

> The more the war recedes into the past, the more distinct [is] the division . . . : the imperialist camp on the one hand and the democratic camp on the other. The cardinal principle of the imperialist camp is to strengthen imperialism, hatch a new imperialist war, combat Socialism and democracy, and support reactionary and antidemocratic profascist regimes and movements everywhere.

The Marshall Plan, he said, was an instrument of "world domination by American imperialism," and Russia would "bend every effort that this plan be doomed to failure." The Socialist camp

> have proved they are a mighty force standing guard over the independence of all European nations. . . . If they [European nations such as France and Italy] display the will and determination, they can foil this plan of enslavement. All that is needed is the determination and readiness to resist. . . .[12]

When the Administration proposed its Marshall Plan in 1947, it was doubtful that Congress would ever have approved a European recovery program that opened the Treasury to the Russians. But once the Russians walked out of the first meetings in Paris, and began to fight the Marshall Plan as American "enslavement," Senator Vandenberg was soon saying: "I do not see how we can avoid the necessity of keeping ourselves insulated against world Communism by maintaining these sixteen nations of the Western Union and helping them to rebuild an anticommunist, self-supporting society." He also insisted that "it be effectively demonstrated to the American people" that the Marshall Plan would "serve their own intelligent self-interest."[13]

Both of these points counted heavily in putting across the Marshall Plan to Congress and country. If, as his contemporaries noted, Arthur Vandenberg was no great shakes in thinking up policies, he was exquisitely equipped as a political sensor and was strategically placed in time and station to get policies carried out. "Without Vandenberg in the Senate," said Dean Acheson later, "the history of the postwar might have been very different." Not only was Vandenberg the solid, reliable sort of Republican, signed by birth and bearing and sealed by his every speech and vote, that most authentic isolationists would have recognized and wished to follow as true bearer of their tradition. He also happened to represent the state, Midwestern of course, that harbored America's most dynamic businessmen, the leaders of the automotive industry. The big automakers of Detroit had indeed thrown themselves into the prodigious war production efforts of the Second World War as they never did in the First. Without them, in fact, Franklin Roosevelt's heroic targets of 50,000 warplanes a year could never have been achieved.

Now, though the motormakers of Detroit were also in the van of postwar reconversion, it was Michigan's converted isolationist senator who insisted that those who managed the arsenal of democracy to victory should get the job of starting Europe's factories going again. He wrote to the investment banker Marshall had summoned to Washington as his chief aide, Undersecretary of State Robert M. Lovett, that "four or five top-level business executives" be called as "aggressive witnesses" before the Senate Foreign Relations Committee hearings. The European Recovery Program, he said, was to be essentially a "business" program.[14]

In the widest perspective one can see that American corporations had been getting ready for this moment for nearly a hundred years, and that many of the biggest of them had already gained some experience of operating abroad. One can also see that it was the Second World War that had already projected America into the wider world. Yet there was an impulse to pull back in 1945 and 1946, after the exertions of worldwide war, and it took a rare conjuncture of bipartisan pressure-group mediation and a skillful manipulation of often contending influences by the Trumans and Marshalls and Vandenbergs to turn the tide. To take only one example, those liberal, free-trading, export-oriented forces that had been assembled in the State Department by former Secretary Cordell Hull and that had had much to do with shaping policies up to the Marshall Plan, were not now to be allowed to put the plan into action. Members of the new Republican majority in Congress wanted no part of commitments that might bring unwelcome new competition for their constituents' industries. So when Vandenberg heard that Assistant Secretary Clayton had said the United States was "morally committed . . . to a reciprocal tariff reduction, as we could impose upon the European nations what we were not willing to do for ourselves," Vandenberg commented: "This is an excellent demonstration why Mr. Clayton would not be acceptable to Congress as the ERP Administrator." And within the Administration it was the new Undersecretary of State Robert Lovett, the Wall Street investment banker sensitively attuned to the desires and potentialities of the more protectionist-minded Republicans and their industrialist allies, who on Marshall and Truman's behalf now carried through the conversations with Vandenberg and others that established the terms of bipartisan action.[15]

In the drafting of the Marshall Plan legislation, Vandenberg insisted on the program's being administered separately from the State Department as a "business administration." His committee unanimously and the Senate overwhelmingly supported him. "That the business side of this essentially business enterprise shall be under effective control of adequate business brains recruited specially for the purpose," had been Vandenberg's purpose all along. Having canvassed, he said, a hundred-odd businessmen and hearing one name reeled off first on almost every list, Vandenberg proposed to Truman the name of Paul Hoffman, president of the Studebaker Corporation and top-drawer automobile executive. "I found him to be the common denominator of the thought of the nation," intoned Vandenberg as he won swift confirmation of Hoffman as director of the new Economic Cooperation Administration charged with carrying out the European Recovery Program.

To man ECA Hoffman pulled one topflight man after another out of private enterprise. "The key figures were pretty solidly from business ranks," said *Time* magazine. "Investment bankers, corporation lawyers, steelmen, paper and pulp men, and so on, through a miniature Who's Who of management and ownership."[16]

"No. 1 ECAmerican abroad," as *Time* called him, was W. Averill Harriman, once the New Deal's tame millionaire and now the graying wheelhorse of the new diplomacy. In a bipartisan tit-for-tat, he was the Democratic businessman given the top job in Europe in return for Republican industrialist Hoffman's being named head man in Washington. Mission chief in France was David Bruce, former son-in-law of industrial magnate Andrew Mellon, former director of twenty-five corporations including Westinghouse, Union Pacific, and the Rockingham, Massachusetts, raceway, son of a multimillionaire former senator from Maryland and brother of James Bruce, the latter a director of thirteen corporations. Norman Collisson, former chief engineer for the huge American Gas and Electric combine and wartime manager of sixty oil refineries, was the hard-driving boss of ECA's mission in Frankfurt. Thomas Finletter, partner in a leading Wall Street law firm, served as ECA's chief in Britain. Alan Valentine, director of Freeport Sulphur and Bausch & Lomb as well as president on leave from the University of Rochester, ran the ECA mission in The Hague. James Zellerbach, Pacific Coast paper and pulp man (Crown Zellerbach) directed ECA work in Italy.

Men like Bruce and Finletter fit in so effectively that they stayed on for leading careers in government. The rough-and-ready Zellerbach found his hands full at first. Leftwing Italian newsmen heckled and flustered him. Government ministers, explaining land redistribution, stared when he cut them short with: "I'm not interested in politics—I want facts. It's strictly a business proposition." By telling them that land reform was bad because it would decrease production, he antagonized a lot of Italians. But after eight trips into the dusty hinterland Zellerbach was ready to say: "It's more of a challenge than ever," and survived to serve as Eisenhower's ambassador in Rome a decade later.[17]

In its four-year span, Paul Hoffman proclaimed, the Marshall Plan set the European economy back on its feet and the aggressive Soviet state back on its heels. When it began governments were falling, workers were jobless, families were hungry. In the bitter early winter of 1947 the American mission members saw a Socialist, Interior Minister Jules Moch, faced by a Communist-led strike that blacked out the coal-burning power plants of Paris, send tanks into the coalfields to break up the strike. And in two or three years these Americans saw a new crop of European businessmen not only turn out steel and plastics and radios and even automobiles in brand-new, Marshall Plan-financed plants, but also begin to compete successfully in American markets. Manufactured imports never had and did not then play an important role in America's foreign trade. But when the Korean War came along, United States defense buying touched off a tremendous demand for materials that European traders knew how to supply. Europe began to close the huge dollar gap that the ECA men had thought could not be closed for generations. As the Second World War made a success of the New Deal recovery program for America, the Korean conflict made the Marshall Plan for Europe's recovery a winner.[18]

THE MARSHALL PLAN was proposed at a time when the results could be as desirable for the economic health of the United States as they were necessary for that of Western Europe. Though the Second World War was followed by what even a Soviet economist, Eugene Varga, termed "perhaps the largest boom the United States has ever known," a deep-rooted dread of another Depression lay close beneath the consciousness of the citizenry and their leaders for many years. The President's Council of Economic Advisers had predicted a big decline in exports unless there were a new foreign aid program. Many businessmen and others were apprehensive in the spring of 1947 of a recession. Under the chairmanship of Secretary of the Interior Julius Krug, a second Marshall Plan committee investigated the United States' resources and capabilities and concluded that a large foreign-aid program, far from straining the economy, would be an admirable engine for driving the economy toward the goals of domestic as well as foreign policy.[19]

At the time many Americans readily accepted the praise of Western Europeans for their generous spirit in making available the emergency economic help by which the stricken nations were able to pull themselves back onto their feet.

In later years it was often said that Marshall Plan aid enabled the countries of Western Europe to recreate their industrial structure in such basic industries as steel, cement and machine tools with such up-to-the-minute plants and with such a high degree of mechanization that the new efficiency thus obtained enabled them to take markets away from American enterprises equipped with older machinery and methods. All this overlooks the fact that practically all of the $13 billion Marshall Plan money was in fact spent inside the United States for goods and commodities needed under the Europeans' program for rehabilitation. Indeed, the sums spent inside the United States stimulated American industries themselves to invest in equipment and methods that not only made them more competitive but in some cases revolutionized their technology. Such outcomes were sometimes foreseen and even expected. But as so often happened in the Cold War, some phases of the Marshall Plan set in motion or speeded up processes that had important and quite unintended effects upon American society.

A good example of such unintended consequences was the result of the heavy European demand for shipments of American cotton in these years. Traditionally the bulk of the cotton that Europe needed had come from the American South, and in fact the Houston cotton-exporting firm of Anderson, Clayton long headed by Undersecretary of State Clayton (one of the principal architects of the Marshall Plan) was the largest in the world. After the First World War cotton prices had plunged when America pulled out of Europe. Southern cotton never really recovered until the Second World War revived the export business. After 1945, the disastrous experience that befell Southern cotton farmers might well have been repeated, but it was not, thanks to the Marshall Plan. Largely on the strength of Marshall Plan orders, American cotton exports shot up 4300% in the five postwar years over the preceding five-year level, and continued to rise to a peak in 1960 when half the entire American cotton crop of 14 billion bales was sold overseas.[20]

The impetus to expand exports under the Marshall Plan and other postwar emergency programs coincided with, and powerfully boosted, a revolutionary trend taking shape in the 1940s. This was the invasion and conquest of the Southern cotton plantation by machines, long after the rest of American agriculture. Ever since slaveholding days the backbone of Southern cotton-growing had remained the sharecropper system. During the long growing season needed for cotton to mature in the warm, humid Delta climate, lots of hard labor was needed. Black sharecroppers and their families, living in houses on the white owner's land, provided the intensive, ever-available stoop labor on a fixed proportion of that land in return for the value of half the crop they produced. Under that system the black population stayed almost exactly where it had lived in slavery times—down on the old plantation.[21]

In 1943, at a time when both black and white rural Southerners were being drawn off in large numbers to the armed forces and to nearby cities and Northern industrial centers to work in war plants, the mechanical cotton picker was introduced commercially in the South. The tractor had already made its appearance in the cotton fields but its adoption, because of the total labor requirements of Southern cotton-growing, had been slow except in the new irrigated lands of West Texas and California. There followed the introduction of chemical weed-killers that literally cleared the way for the lumbering cotton-picking machines.

As the Marshall Plan orders flowed into the Southern cotton country, the big cotton growers in the Delta obtained the means to invest in the machines, and as the tractors, the pickers and the insecticides took over, the black fieldhands were pushed off the land ("Who needs the Negro?" was the title of a magazine article of the day). Between 1945 and 1960 the number of black tenant farmers in the rural South plummeted from 482,000 to 181,000; between 1940 and 1960 2,700,000 blacks left the South for the cities of the North and West. Thus, by what Charles Silberman in *Fortune* magazine described as "one of the great population changes in history," black rural poverty was transferred in a few short years to the ghettos of the urban North. This fateful movement traced in important part to the Marshall Plan purchases that financed the South's belated agricultural revolution.[22]

Such socially unmanageable consequences appear to have been totally unforeseen when America put through its humanitarian program to save the peoples of Europe. Yet the mass transfers of rural blacks from the South created huge problems for northern cities by the 1960s. They were the last and most painful uprootings in a vast displacement of country people as a consequence of the mechanization of American agriculture. Starting with the New Deal in the 1930s, the United States government fought by subsidies to farm owners to cushion and slow down the impact upon human beings threatened with being torn from their land by the revolution of technology. Doubtless some small owners were helped. But neither black nor white tenants ever saw these payments, which went increasingly to the agricultural industrialists who controlled more and more of the best land. By the end of the Cold War this process left scarcely three million farmers producing roughly twice as much food from substantially the same acreage as was produced by the combined efforts of a third of the nation's manpower in 1900. By any standards, such productivity was a prodigious achievement, rivaling if not surpassing the gains scored by American industry. But the uprooting of millions was only part of the price. The farmer who survived bore small resemblance to the stalwart tiller of the soil in whom Jefferson placed such faith. He was a large-scale commercialist engaged in something called "agribusiness." Farming, along with oil and mining, had become one of the country's chief three extractive industries and like the others had become what the economists called a labor-scarce industry.[23] Like all such extractive industries, it was also winning a name for polluting the human environment. During the Cold War the consumption of farm fertilizers nearly tripled, from 13.2 million tons to 33 million tons. Phosphate fertilizers that helped set productivity records for the new factory-farms leached out of the tilled land and feedlots into rivers and streams—and wrought ecological havoc in the Great Lakes region and other once-favored places.[24]

I N A L L the direct and indirect ways in which the United States after the Second World War lurched to avoid another Big Depression, organized labor manifested a powerful new presence and, in political decisions at the highest levels, a major new influence. The ideology of political democracy proclaimed in the Truman Doctrine and affirmed in the presuppositions of the Marshall Plan may have been fundamentally that which the middle classes made dominant in the nineteenth century. But everywhere in the modern world society was experiencing the rise of the working class. In Europe, where the old order had fragmented, big labor emerged strongest after 1945. In America, though no labor party took shape there, the ruling Democratic party had entered into coalition with the forces of labor by the end of the Second World War.

All this came about because workers organizing to win a larger share of the fruits of their output mounted the biggest change in the America of the 1930s. In the depth of the Depression they fought bloody battles for the company towns of western Pennsylvania. They broke heads and slugged goons at the steel-mill gates of South Chicago. They sat in through tense and hungry weeks at the automobile plants of Flint and Detroit. Their impelling motive was hunger in their homes, their resort was to organize in a body, and their first goal was to hold on to their jobs. By means of collective bargaining provisions put through in the NRA and Wagner acts, the Roosevelt Administration succeeded in edging and gentling the most unruly and potentially disruptive elements of the new Congress of Industrial Organizations, or CIO, into the larger American community.

But even after pitching in and making good money in the big war effort against Hirohito, Mussolini and Hitler, these forces retained their trade-union militancy. Their unions were raucously democratic. Leaders rose fast and fell hard. Rank and file bellowed their say. They were so high-spirited that John L. Lewis, the old mine-union leader who formed the CIO, did not care that they were also full of Communists, Socialists and strife. It was Trotskyists whose smart, fast-pivoting tactics in the 1934 Minneapolis strike first put the Teamsters on the high road to power. Communists provided the winning spark among the Electrical Workers. Socialists of the Central European school stitched the organizing line for the two big needleworkers' unions of New York City. Young, feisty, shirtsleeved, quick with their fists, the new unions of the CIO came out of the big war brawling ferociously among themselves for leadership in the peacetime struggle against the bosses.[25]

Though America remained a business society and industry its leading institutionalized power, the principal new economic, political and social force to emerge from the New Deal years was organized labor. Fifteen million strong, this powerful body of citizens lined up for the most part behind the party of Franklin Roosevelt and Harry Truman. The Truman Administration, reflecting this new alignment of forces, was anxious to avoid another Depression and made a considerable effort to protect the workers' jobs.

To this end the 1946 Employment Act was passed and the GI Bill of Rights put through to cushion and delay the return of veterans to the job market. Yet none of these measures could alter the reality that the end of the Second World War, bringing with it violent readjustments in goals and rewards, compelled a renegotiation of labor-management relations. In this stormy passage the unconcluded struggle for leadership of organized labor broke out anew, and in the thick of the battle the Cold War supervened to sway the outcome, with fateful consequences for the historical evolution of the American labor movement.

Even before the Second World War erupted, John L. Lewis had broken with Roosevelt, and taken his miners out of the CIO. But his old sidekick Phil Murray, strong-willed head of the United Steel Workers' 600,000 dues-paying members, succeeded to the leadership of the CIO and though the craft-oriented America Federation of Labor remained strong as ever among the construction and other old-line trades, there was no telling how far the dynamic CIO, organized along the same mass-industry lines as big business itself, might go. Strikes were exploding across the country like firecrackers. More man-hours were lost in work stoppages in the twelve months after V-J Day than in any year in American history. Detroit, heart of the automobile industry, was hot as a stove lid. The men were jumpy. Rival leaders jockeyed for a place in the showdown. The United Auto Workers' West Side Local 174 struck the Kelsey-Hayes Wheel Co. for firing its union delegates in the post-V-J Day lull, and the meeting hall was jammed with members. "We fought for democracy," shouted Chester (Moon) Mullins, the local chairman. "Down with the brasshats and porkchoppers. They've lost touch." A soft tenor Negro accent wafted from the rear: "But you're the biggest one." In this no-nonsense atmosphere, "The Redhead," as his fellow tool-and-die-makers called Walter Reuther, the UAW's young vice president for General Motors, led the union out on strike against the world's biggest manufacturing company. His demand: the same pay for a peacetime forty-hour week that members had earned for forty-eight during the war. This was a 20% pay boost.[26]

In the new kind of world created by a dozen years of New Deal reform and all-out war, the pattern-making negotiation was bargained out on the picket line. The place was Detroit. The parties were the biggest corporation and the biggest union in the biggest business. In terms of leadership no union man had such excellent credentials as Walter Reuther. He was the kind of labor leader who called himself a socialist. He had grown up in Wheeling, West Virginia, where his father, an old German Social Democrat, had drilled into his sons ideals of social justice to be achieved by working-class solidarity. With his brother Victor he had traveled and worked for a year in the Soviet Union. Back in UAW ranks in Detroit he had sung the leftwing assembly-line song:

> When they tie the can to a union man,
> Sit down! Sit down!

He had fought in the "Battle of Bulls' Run" and reeled bloody with leftwinger Dick Frankensteen out of the "Battle of the Overpass" at Henry Ford's River Rouge plant. At the head of 600 strikers and a brass band he had marched out of a GM plant to win union recognition. In 1939 he had joined forces with the national CIO and the Communist Party to defeat UAW President Homer Martin's bid to impose an iron grip over the auto workers. He had always coupled pay demands with programs for social action. In the war he had taken the lead in demanding the automobile industry's conversion to the war effort, and got into a wrangle with GM President Charles E. Wilson for it. But his campaign for building 500 planes a day in the auto plants had gained national backing.

When Reuther led the way into the GM strike after V-J Day, the hierarchs of his union, the elders of organized labor in Washington and the Truman Administration all tried to head him off. But such were the stakes of the confrontation that all the factions of the UAW had to fall in behind the rambunctious young redhead. The strike went on all winter from Thanksgiving, 1945 to Easter, 1946. It ended with an eighteen-and-one-half cents hourly pay rise for 500,000. The issue, not really reducible to arithmetic though expressive of labor's emergence as a major institution of American life, was that "hunger must no longer be an issue at the bargaining table." Literally hundreds of other strikes followed in the nation, and labor unions emerged big and strong. A pattern had been set not only for all American industry but for all the postwar years.[27]

On the strength of this "moral victory," Reuther aimed for the presidency of his union, which was held by R. J. Thomas with the support of CIO President Murray and various elements among the auto workers including Communists. Seizing upon anti-Communism as the grappling hook for his climb to the top, Reuther ran against Thomas and narrowly won. When Truman then proclaimed the Cold War, Reuther took the President's side.

In Washington's eyes the Cold War meant war without quarter on Communists. In France and Italy, for instance, where Communists were strongly entrenched in the unions, the operating American view, expressed by Major General William J. Donovan, wartime United States intelligence chief, was that the fight was:

> essentially a labor fight—a fight to gain control of the labor unions. As strength has been given to those members of the labor unions that are anti-Communists, there has been a little slow-up both in Italy and in France.[28]

In the stress of the international fight, Reuther shelved working-class solidarity and, like the AFL's business-unionist leaders, channeled funds from the Central Intelligence Agency to anti-Communist factions in Italy and France that helped split the trade union organizations of those countries. He was among those who welcomed Secretary Marshall to the CIO convention in the midst of the wave of anti-Marshall Plan strikes in France. Within his own union he was fighting to keep his office. His slogan against Communists and other leftwingers was: "Against Outside Interference." His goal was to purge from the UAW leadership all, including Communists, who had opposed him. In this fight, the help afforded by the arch-conservative authors of the Taft-Hartley Law was crucial. Enacted by a Republican Congress over Truman's veto in mid-1947, this law was intended by its sponsors—and opposed by all organized labor—as a check on union power. As such, it was moderately effective. But the law also contained a proviso demanding labor's conformity to the new ideology of Cold War. This was the requirement that all unions, if they wanted government sanction for representing their workers, obtain affidavits from their officers affirming that they were not Communists.

Only John L. Lewis's United Mine Workers (and the equally entrenched International Typographers Union) successfully defied this prescription. But in all other unions the leadership was forced to face the issue: if they did not comply, then any other union was free to move in and take the union's members. Within the UAW Reuther's slate, ready to a man to comply, carried the election, and out went not only the Communists but all their allies as well. On the wider front American labor, forced to choose between institutional survival and working-class solidarity, opted for organization—and the casualty was trade-union militancy.

CIO President Phil Murray called in Len De Caux, the longtime editor of the *CIO News* and told him he would have to go. At the CIO convention in Atlantic City a Murray-named committee brought in an amendment inserting in the CIO constitution the Taft-Hartley prohibition against any Communist serving as officer in any member union. It was passed. Later Reuther, as head of the Resolutions committee, charged the United Electrical, Radio and Machine Workers, the Mine, Mill and Smelter Workers, the Farm Equipment Workers and eight other leftwing unions defying this amendment with "blind and selfish willingness to act as puppets for the Soviet dictatorship and its foreign policy with all its twists and turns." Thereupon the eleven unions—a third of the CIO's strength—were expelled.[29]

The consequences of labor's joining in the Cold War were many and far-reaching. After the CIO's expulsion of the eleven dissident unions, there was general rejoicing that American labor had purged itself of its left. It was just what Congress had hoped for. But the outcome went beyond even what happened in Italy and France, where the forces of the Cold War succeeded in splitting the labor movement. In America the price of the Cold War was the destruction and disappearance of the left, as signified by the rout of Henry Wallace's third-party candidacy in the 1948 elections. To many this seemed, in the mood of the day, good riddance. The further consequence, however, was that the normal balance of political forces was upset, making possible an inordinate preponderance of conservative and reactionary elements that was to be felt at every level of the nation's life. In the absence of regenerative militancy on the left through two decades, America swung to extremes of Cold War excess that ended in the national disarray, malaise and military disaster that followed when the Cold War finally dissolved in the 1960s.

For labor, the consequence of following Truman into the Cold War was that the fire went out of its belly. Under Murray's successor as president of the United Steel Workers, David J. McDonald, who looked and lived like a big-time business executive, the union was run like Alcoa, Koppers, United States Steel or any other of Pittsburgh's giant corporations. Within the United Auto Workers the brawling, the catcalls, the rowdy songs faded away. Meetings ceased to be boisterous or indeed well attended. When the leftist remnant persisted in straight-out demands for higher wages, Reuther ignored them. As president of the UAW and, after 1951, of the CIO, Reuther led the way toward a new kind of solidarity never dreamed of during the sit-ins of the 1930s.

Under the pattern established by General Motors' strike settlement with Reuther's militants in the spring of 1946, Big Labor became something of a partner of Big Business in the growth of American economic prosperity. Automobiles were the country's top manufacturing business, and General Motors was far and away the top automobile company. As president of General Motors, Charles E. Wilson entered into a kind of undeclared coalition with Reuther and the auto workers. During the years after 1946, Wilson conceded to the auto workers successive rounds of wage increases to induce increased production. Starting in 1947 by an agreement that few other corporations were big or rich enough to emulate, he agreed to tie wage boosts to the national cost-of-living index. By the time he left to become Eisenhower's Defense Secretary, he had entertained the union's demands (though Ford was the first to grant them) for a guaranteed annual wage. Between 1947 and 1961 the 700,000 UAW members doubled their pay, a pattern roughly followed by management-union bargaining in other industries.

The significance of this pattern-setting partnership lay in what Big Business and Big Labor were able to accomplish together. With increasing pay went increased mechanization of industry, and with the greater automation went greater productivity per worker. The name of the pattern was growth. Growth for his country as the way to his corporate goal of maximizing profits—that was what Charles Wilson meant when he blurted that "what was good for our country was good for General Motors and vice versa." Growth for his country by the greater buying power of well-paid unionists—that was what Walter Reuther harped on when he pressed the companies to hand over to the workers their share of productivity gains. With all his ebullience Reuther asserted that the nation's goal must be the elimination of poverty. But the implication of his argument was that the nation would achieve the goal without any forced redistribution of wealth, simply by applying itself to the growth of productivity. Thus Big Labor, increasingly the undeclared partner of Big Business, looked to economic growth as the ticket for both enhanced security and painless reform. And no matter how earnestly Reuther encased each annual package of union demands in social objectives, militancy faded. For labor, a politics of consensus supplanted the politics of upheaval by which it had battled upwards in the 1930s.[30]

The ranks of organized labor continued to grow through the Eisenhower years until 1956, when they reached their peak of 18,500,000. Thereafter they declined. When recession followed in 1957 and 6,000,-000 Americans lost their jobs, neither wages nor prices retreated. In fact General Motors, having spent a billion dollars on automating in 1956, agreed to Reuther's call for another wage hike and then raised prices once again. This provoked a congressional inquiry by Senator Estes Kefauver, Democrat of Tennessee, into charges that in the automobile and other large industries "administered prices" set by a few supercorporations after bargaining with their unions had tended to supplant prices governed by the marketplace.[31]

Yet for Reuther and the CIO there were consequences of joining the Cold War that were utterly different from what they bargained for. After the gains of the New Deal and the Second World War, the CIO was the strongest and most modern organization of the American working class and seemingly destined to become a major and enduring force in the national life. Why, indeed, should not the growth of its kind of industrial unionism lead on in postwar America, as it had in every other Western democracy, to formation of a major political party? And who but Reuther would lead it?

The unforeseen consequence for Murray and Reuther of striking down the militant left in their big campaign against "international Communism," was that they let the steam out of their own movement, and left themselves weakened and ill prepared to overcome those elements which were both anti-Communist and antiliberal in the Cold War years. The CIO lost its dynamic, and far from expanding to lead the American labor movement, was itself taken over by the AFL in the merger of 1955. Reuther was made vice president, but already organized labor had ceased to grow. Reuther, the shorn liberal, symbolized its failures. In 1945 he had been a man of international importance, widely mentioned as a future president of the United States. When he died in 1966 he was lonely and isolated. "Business unionism," narrow, standpat and shot through with corruption, was labor's legacy from the Cold War.[32]

THE FEAR of another Depression and determination to maintain full employment that helped rally labor to join the Cold War and back the Marshall Plan were strong and pervasive forces that worked unforeseen changes in the patterns of American life. First the enactment of the GI Bill of Rights and the tremendous expansion in numbers of young people who completed high school and went on to college after 1945, served to build up a large body of adolescents and youth who remained for an unprecedented length of time students outside the adult world of work. Then, driven along by persistent anxieties about the Depression and the return of unemployment, a second major social change broke through to the surface at just about the time that the Marshall Plan was being enacted in 1948.

This was what might be called, by contrast with the earlier drive to subsidize youth for staying off the job market, the movement within the American society to separate its older citizens from the working force by underwriting their early retirement. The emergence of this long-developing movement, again with outcomes unforeseen by those advocating the various steps along the way, was signaled by a quite sudden shift in the late 1940s in what workingmen said they wanted.

For more than a century American trade unionism had demanded, along with higher pay, shorter working hours. After the end of the Second World War American labor, strong in its collective bargaining power, had exchanged the overtime pay of the war years for a series of hefty wage increases and the assurance, through a kind of labor-management consensus ratified in countless contracts by 1948, of a forty-hour week. Though old New Dealers and some of the more flamboyant rhetoricians of industry still kept talking about the coming thirty-hour week, it rapidly became evident around bargaining tables that with the forty-hour week the American industrial worker of the day had attained substantially the working hours he wanted. Thus was established what at once became a feature unique to the American scene, something Western Europe had not gained a quarter of a century later: the universal two-day weekend.[33]

"Weekend" was an English word, and the British weekend, with its nineteenth century connotations of lordly and leisurely withdrawal whatever the crises in Commons or Khartoum, was part of the trappings of imperial rule. In a Cold War America which abjured imperialism but had an empire, a universal two-day weekend arrived as just such an appurtenance of power. Though nobody quite said it, the power that kept American oil rigs pumping uninterruptedly in the troubled Middle East not only fattened capitalist fortunes but also fueled the union member's motor trip to the beach or the ballgame. The streets and sidewalks of America filled with beefy males self-consciously outfitted in loud-patterned "sport shirts" merchandised specially for wear in the idle hours of the weekend. (The loudest of these garments were called "Truman shirts," after the noisy-colored ones the President wore vacationing at his favorite getaway spot in Key West.) Skilled in the use of their hands, these men by the thousands used their new days off rebuilding an old car, repainting an apartment or, when the chance finally came to buy a house of their own, picking the economy model with only the ground floor completed. Then, trotting back and forth to lumberyard and hardware store, they carpentered, wired, and fit the plumbing in the second-floor "expansion attic" as their mortgages grew smaller and their families larger.[34]

The twin of such domesticity was security, and in a season when security was the watchword at every level of the nation's life, the leaders of American labor came forward with a new collective-bargaining demand. Now that the working man had won his two-day weekend, the new objective proclaimed was financial independence for the worker when he retired. In the midst of these currents of change, the National Labor Relations Board handed down a ruling that pensions were a fit subject for collective bargaining.

Under the scowling leadership of John L. Lewis, the soft-coal miners went on strike for the fourth consecutive year since the war. Once again the nation's coal stocks shrank. Once again the newspaper columnists cried havoc. Prodded by Senator Taft the government got an injunction against Lewis under the new Taft-Hartley Law. Then one morning the nation read in the headlines that Lewis had ordered the 200,000 strikers back to work. The mine owners had agreed to a settlement. A pension fund—what unheard-of creampuff coddling was this for the smudge-faced miners?—had been set up. The owners had promised to pay retirement benefits of $100 a month at age 62. To ensure that everything was on the up-and-up, Senator Styles Bridges, ranking arch-conservative Republican of the Senate, had consented to act as "public" trustee of the fund. Senator Taft had been outfoxed, and once again John L. led the way for labor.

Other pension plans were quickly sealed in the steel, electrical and automobile industries. Union and management representatives wrote many of the new plans in such a way as to tie them to the level of Social Security pension payments. If federal payments were to increase, the private benefits might be reduced by that amount. Early in 1949, when President Truman announced his postelection list of proposed reforms, fatter Social Security benefits topped his program for Congress. That summer, as the first postwar recession deepened and union after union struck for retirement-pay benefits, Congress stirred to action. The Social Security amendments, first to be adopted since New Deal days, extended coverage to eleven million more workers and boosted pension payments by seventy-seven percent.[35]

The action of Congress in expanding pensions constituted the single most notable legislative step to offset the recession, although once again as in 1945 federal unemployment insurance played its cushioning part as nearly 7,500,000 workers drew benefits for nearly 90,000,000 weeks of unemployment during 1949. The cry for security keynoted the pension campaign—security in retirement for the individual, security in its labor procurement policies for industry, security against mass unemployment for government. In the technological march of America, Social Security Commissioner Charles Schottland explained, "the mechanization of industry" was "ruling people out of work at an earlier age." The United Auto Workers in Detroit ran lunch-hour seminars on "early retirement" at the plant. Industry saw the federal-private pension system as a way of increasing productivity of the labor force, trade unions saw it as an instrument for extracting higher wages. For society at large, the pension system became a device for taking a large and significant segment of the population off the labor market.[36]

At first there was no denying that John L. Lewis, the giant who had made the miners' union both the backbone and vanguard of organized labor, had scored again. For those miners who kept their jobs hourly wages rose from $1.49 in 1949 to $3.25 in 1959—the highest hourly pay in industry. Fringe benefits won included complete medical care for union members at ten union-owned hospitals plus the pensions—all financed by a forty cents royalty on every ton of coal mined. By 1960 the United Mine Workers had grown into a wealthy financial institution, holding assets of nearly $50 million, and Lewis, investing the union's money in the stock of two Washington banks and then merging them into one $235-million institution, was the second biggest banker in the nation's capital.

But the price Lewis paid for his pensions deal proved calamitously high for the miners. Taking advantage of the favorable prices paid for coal exported to Europe under the Marshall Plan, the mine operators proceeded to invest in labor-saving machinery underground and expand strip-mining on the surface with the help of huge mechanical shovels. By the end of the Cold War strip-mining had taken over thirty percent of the entire industry, and eighty-five percent of the coal mined underground was either machine-cut, mechanically loaded, or both. While prices of almost everything else soared, the cost of a ton of coal at the mine declined from $4.89 in 1949 to $4.77 in 1959, almost solely because productivity per worker man-hour rose eighty-five percent in the intervening years as machines took over almost all the work. Overnight coal miners were obsolete: membership of the union sagged below 300,000—and in 1960 the number of miners actually working sank to 42,922. As of June, 1961, the total number of miners who had retired on $100 a month pensions from the union welfare fund stood at 66,759—but thousands of others had been laid off before attaining eligibility for the pension, and under the plan members who had been out of work for a year forfeited their rights to hospital and medical benefits. When Lewis died in 1969, the once all-powerful miners' union was a hollow shell.[37]

Yet the movement for paying older people to quit work continued to spread fast and far. In 1934 half of the aged population of America depended on relatives and friends for support; by 1954 four-fifths of all retired people over sixty-five lived on federal pensions, and an estimated thirteen percent more supplemented their Treasury Department checks with benefits from private funds. By 1963 private pension funds had mushroomed to such mammoth size that they constituted one-third of all personal savings—and ninety percent of all new savings added in the United States that year.[38]

Undoubtedly the move to expand retirement pensions during the 1949 recession, quite as much as the drive begun by the 1944 GI Bill of Rights to give the young more years of schooling, amounted to actions by the society to stabilize employment and wages and avert another Depression by removing millions of possible competitors from the job market. Just as the earlier move led to the rise of a kind of subculture of youth, the shift toward the earlier retirement of American workers opened a generation gap at the other end of the age spectrum and brought about the emergence of a new world of the retired.

Americans over sixty-five nearly doubled in numbers between 1940 and 1960; and as an enlarging proportion of the population through the Cold War years hardly constituted a force for political change. But during these same years they were increasingly severed from the rest of society. Personnel offices in the corporations told them to go away. The dynamics of the changing family that all but eliminated the three-generation household cut them loose physically and emotionally from the nourishing bonds of kinship. Rejected by a society that reversed the ancient tradition of respect for old age, the old in America lived increasingly to themselves. The number of Primary Unrelated Individuals, the Census Bureau category that included widows and widowers who live alone, rose seventy-eight percent, and the scandalous refusal until 1965 to provide federal medical care for pensioners might well have persuaded old people that the society wished to be quits of them.

But the 1950s saw Florida, Arizona and California emerge as the three fastest-growing states, at least in part because of the number of older Americans settling there upon retirement. In 1963, 106,899 "senior citizens" cashed their green Treasury pension checks each month in St. Petersburg, Florida (pop. 181,698). "Leisure Worlds," "Heritage Villages" and other retirement communities consisting entirely of old people sprang up as a phenomenon of the 1960s to meet the shared needs of those who had left the labor force and embarked upon a new and different existence. A new medical specialty—geriatrics—began to be practiced in their midst. They carried on their own community activities, subscribed to their own magazines, belonged to their own year-round travel clubs, drove their own cars and trailers on their own motor tours, and, inevitably, maintained their own lobbyists in Washington. Whether in such groups or in involuntary solitude, the retired people on the farther side of the life-cycle lived as far apart from the mass of workers in the middle as the young in their autonomous world on the nearer side in this economically enforced panorama of social segregation.[39]

J U D G E D in material terms, the problem of the American labor movement as it settled into its place as a leading institution in the Cold War society was not that it had failed, but that it had been too successful. The partnership of Big Labor and Big Business was profitable to the union men, and with every passing year this seemed more self-evidently so: average weekly earnings in manufacturing grew from $44 in 1945 to $97 in 1963, and even after making allowance for the inflation of the period this was a fifty percent rise. Undeniably, as Walter Reuther liked to say, America's union movement was "the richest in the world." [40]

Yet, once the basic industries were unionized and union membership within them became mandatory, the ardor of worker participation in his local cooled fast and the movement ceased to grow. In these changed circumstances the trend toward decentralization within many mass-production enterprises contributed to the erosion of the big industrial unions that had dominated the CIO. At the same time, a strong movement away from unskilled to semiskilled and skilled labor as more and more machines were introduced, operated to enlarge the ranks of the AFL-oriented craft unions. Historically unions, like churches, had been exempted from certain taxes and regulations because they were presumably dedicated to a cause higher than pecuniary profit. But now hierarchies ruled them and rank-and-file democracy atrophied. Leaders and members alike took over from the business world middle-class standards and values of success. Many moved to the suburbs. And inside the factory, blue-collar workers demanded conditions associated with middle-class occupations: coffee breaks, no time-cards, longer vacations and a shorter work week with much higher pay. "To a distressing degree," wrote The New York Times' labor editor, A. H. Raskin, "there has been on both the management and labor sides a tendency to yield to that curse of comfortable living and settled relationships—middle-aged spread."[41]

What kind of championing of the underdog was this? As business unionism took command within both the AFL and CIO groups, and leaders increasingly substituted cash values for human values as the standard of union achievement, the way was opened wide to corruption of the union movement.

For years there had been evidence of racketeering and penetration of underworld influences into the ranks of certain unions, particularly within the AFL. In 1952 for instance, the New York State Crime Commission established that bosses of the International Longshoremen's Association, by reason of their control over the point at which ships' cargoes were shifted to trucks at New York City piers, operated like medieval robber-barons, erecting their sluice-gates and exacting tolls on whatever passed through. But it was the mushrooming of union welfare funds after the mine operators struck their bargain with John L. Lewis in 1948, and the unwillingness of the AFL-CIO to do much of anything about restraining the free and easy way in which many union officials were handling the huge sums of money flowing into these funds, that finally led, in 1957, to intervention by a Senate committee.[42]

Chairman of the investigating committee was Senator John McClellan, a conservative Arkansas Democrat and stern inquisitor. Chief counsel was Robert F. Kennedy, then thirty-one. Chief target—although the committee found plenty of malfeasance among officials of the bakery, distillery and laundry workers' unions too—was the International Brotherhood of Teamsters, by then the largest and richest of all American unions. Starting at the top the committee went after Dave Beck, the fat and florid former brewery-horse driver from Seattle who had ascended to the presidency in 1952. Armed with piles of documents, affidavits and depositions, Bobby Kennedy brought out that a year after his election Beck had "borrowed" $250,000 from the union's Western Conference. Neither the conference president nor its auditor could explain how Beck acquired the money, but the committee was satisfied that a major share of it went to build a swimming pool at Beck's Seattle home, and new houses for various relatives and friends in a Seattle suburb. Kennedy went on to establish that huge trucking firms that had every reason to fear costly labor tieups showered Dave Beck and his family with "loans," lucrative business franchises, plane rides and chauffeured automobile trips through Europe. (At the Anheuser Busch brewery, which gave distribution contracts to a company headed by his son, Beck was known as "His Majesty, the Wheel.") In all, the committee concluded, Beck "took, not borrowed" $370,000 in union funds. This included a profit of $11,585.04 pocketed from a fund Beck raised when a ranking Teamster official died in 1956 and Beck called upon his union brothers to send in money to help buy off the widow's remaining mortgages. In words that fairly rang with the outraged disgust of its youthful counsel, the committee said:

> If all points elicited against Mr. Beck were written off the record, his handling of the trust fund of his best friend, Ray Leheney, would damn him in the eyes of all decent people. Even in the handling of a sacred trust from a lifelong friend Beck saw the chance for a profit and took it . . . The man . . . was motivated by an uncontrollable greed.[43]

As Beck—bellowing that "God never created me in the crucible of infallibility"—was retired as Teamster president on a $50,000-a-year life pension (he was subsequently sent to jail for five years for embezzlement), James Hoffa came on in his place. As chairman of the Teamsters' powerful Central States Conference, Hoffa was already running the show in fact, and Kennedy was hot on his heels too. Son of an Indiana coal-miner, without formal education beyond the fourth grade, Hoffa was a product of the same Detroit labor "jungle" of the depressed 1930s that gave Walter Reuther, Emil Mazey and Leonard Woodcock to the American labor movement. But there was a world of difference between these men. The social idealism of the New Deal passed Hoffa by. Five-feet-five, 170 pounds of mostly muscle, he was a no-holds-barred street scrapper who led his first strike (of strawberry loaders) at eighteen. Hoffa fought to survive —and then dominate. "Whatever you can do to me I can do to you only more," he boasted. "I know where I'm going . . . I'm no damn angel." Reuther and his men only made the trucks; Hoffa organized the men who drove them, and brawling, browbeating, blustering, bribing, he built up in time more raw power. "I will tell you something about politics," he said. "There are just two ways to play it. You either make speeches or else you spend dough. We spend lots of dough."[44]

Bobby Kennedy demanded to know what Hoffa did with the "dough." In his rise to Teamster power, Hoffa won wage rises and improvements in working conditions that gained the lasting loyalty of truck-drivers. Over and over he used the leverage of his union's strength in one place to outbargain employers in another, making deals and building quid-pro-quo relationships with owners and operators that tightened his control of trucking, increased his clout and opened investment opportunities for the union and for those in his sphere of influence. Back in 1946 Hoffa had been convicted and fined for forcing small shopkeepers to buy union "permits" to run their own trucks between the wholesale markets and their stores. Thereafter, as Hoffa's influence spread to St. Louis, New York, Philadelphia and Chicago amid a welter of slippery deals and odorous coverups, the admiring comment around the trucking terminals of Detroit was: "Jimmy always beats the rap."

Sparring day after day with Bobby Kennedy before the nation's fascinated eyes, Hoffa never fell back, as Beck had, on the Fifth Amendment plea that he could not answer lest he incriminate himself. But the acknowledged master of local, regional and national wage-rate bargaining displayed a failure of memory on every one of the eighty-one counts of wrongdoing the committee eventually charged him with. The record showed how Hoffa set up one lieutenant, Allen Dorfman, to write the insurance for the union's welfare fund, and then went into a lucrative motel deal on the side with Dorfman and the president of the insurance company that got the business. A timely union loan of $800,000 to one of the welfare fund's employer trustees, never repaid, helped make sure that another Hoffa deal went through. Repeatedly union and welfare fund money was lent to trucking firms that had to negotiate contracts with Hoffa. Tracing the many ways the Teamster boss spent union money, the committee listed the names of 107 racketeers whose doings on the fringes of his union Hoffa protected. "The perplexing skein of Hoffa's peculiar financial manipulations," as the committee described certain side dealings, led through Florida real-estate promotions financed from Teamster funds to uniform jackets sold to Michigan unionists to the acquisition of trotting horses and racetrack shares.[45]

Highballing twelve-wheel, twenty-ton trucks over the road was wearing labor, and between 1950 and 1965 Hoffa bargained a dozen increases that more than doubled his men's pay. He got them $200-a-month pensions starting at the age of fifty-seven. He cut Teamster officials in on his deals. When Hoffa stood for Beck's place in the teeth of the national uproar over the McClellan Committee hearings in 1957, a Chicago teamster named Thomas Hagerty thought to run against him on a cleanup ticket. "We've got a new slogan," delegates whooped. "Hagerty for Integrity, Hoffa for president." Amid the outcry, the AFL-CIO expelled the Teamsters, but members stood by their leader. When Bobby Kennedy brought in a seemingly airtight case against Hoffa for trying to bribe one of the Senate committee staff, Jimmy wriggled out of it, winning acquittal from a Washington jury, and again the saying went round the Detroit truckers' cafe counters: "Jimmy is the greatest little bastard who ever put on shoes."[46]

But the nation had heard enough about the abuses exposed in the McClellan Committee hearings, and in 1959 Congress enacted the Landrum-Griffin Act. The law imposed regulative restraints for the first time on the labor movement which unions, with one or two exceptions, had been unwilling to initiate themselves. Regular union elections became mandatory. Individual members gained more legal protection for their rights. And the power of union officials to make free with union funds was curbed. In 1964 Hoffa was finally convicted with seven others of conspiracy and fraud in handling more than $20,000,000 in Teamster pension fund loans, and sentenced to five years in prison.[47]

The trade union movement accepted, if it did not welcome, the new regulations. Labor had become one of America's vested interests, an established institution. Its members sat in the Senate, in state houses across the land, in city halls. No fewer than 75,000 union members served on local health and welfare boards, pillars of their communities. Some forty-six percent of all members had moved into income brackets that had to be classified as middle-income. These men lived in suburbs, watched TV nightly and supported the welfare state. It would have been absurd to call them militant. When the United Department Store Workers in New York pressed an organization drive in the 1960s, officials got the idea of seeking a little help from the International Brotherhood of Electrical Workers and asked Harry Van Arsdale of Local Three about the possibilities of fraternal support. After all, many electricians' wives and daughters had taken jobs in department stores when their families found living in the suburbs something of a struggle. When Van Arsdale consulted his men, they gave him this answer: "One dues-payer in the family is enough."[48]

The inheritors of the labor movement found their spokesman in George Meany, president of the AFL-CIO after the 1955 merger. A gruff, stumpy Irish Catholic from the Bronx, Meany lacked ties of any sort with the all-but-forgotten militancy of labor's past, and even boasted that "I never went on strike in my life, never ran a strike, never ordered anyone else to run a strike and never had anything to do with a picket line." For all his crusty manner and advanced years (he was sixty-one when elected president in 1955), such a leader was in spirit with the generation that manned the building trades and factories in the booming Cold War years. Having left his plumber's union local in 1922, he had risen through the bureaucracy to front-office slots as treasurer and then president of the old AFL. Now he was a kind of power broker in the corporate state, and much more like a bigtime Washington lobbyist than a leader of any working-class crusade.

He rode each day in a chauffeur-driven Cadillac to a sleek office overlooking the White House. He lived in a spacious home in suburban Bethesda, and golfed at his country club with cabinet ministers. His suits were tailormade; his colorful waistcoats came from London. He was a connoisseur of French wines and dined in fancy restaurants.

Unions dedicated "simply to get higher wages for their members," wrote sociologist Daniel Bell in 1956, "only become a partner in a collusive enterprise that strongarms the rest of the community." In this atmosphere of Big Business-Big Labor partnership, Meany's role was to reflect the stance and outlook of the aging middle-class union hierarchy, and this he did with such heavy-footed force that by the closing years of the Cold War people began to amend General Eisenhower's identification of the "military-industrial complex" at the center of America's arms race as the "military-industrial-labor complex." On behalf of a constituency that had come to hold vested interests in Department of Defense contracts—a third of all factory jobs in Southern California, perhaps a fourth of those in the Seattle area, depended on military spending—Meany was warning by 1963 against practically any relaxation in Cold War attitudes and expenditures.

This was the measure of the American trade union movement's transformation in sixteen years. When General Marshall was invited in 1947 to address the CIO convention on his plan for saving Europe—the first Secretary of State ever to appear before a CIO assemblage—the movement was young, rowdy and on the rise. By the time the Cold War ended, the American labor movement had grown rich, rigid, entrenched; and it was stagnating. Defending labor's big stake in an economy in which defense was the leading industry, its leadership had become locked into an obsessive preoccupation with the threat of monolithic "international Communism." In Marshall Plan days Meany plunged into the Cold War by helping the CIA foment rival labor organizations against Communist-led unions in France and Italy. By the 1960s he was committing the AFL-CIO against a nuclear test-ban treaty, supporting the blundering CIA attempt to invade Cuba, and upholding the Diem dictatorship in South Vietnam. Such was the rigidity of AFL-CIO opposition to any gesture of East-West détente by this time that President Meany opposed some steps, such as the removal of trade barriers with Russia, that even the United States Chamber of Commerce supported.[49]

America's labor movement, in short, having lost its fire in the Cold War, then lost its way.

CHAPTER **4**

The Paradox of the Peacetime Draft

THE BERLIN BLOCKADE

F̲O̲R̲ ̲T̲H̲E̲ hard, cold men who led America into the sudden and deadly confrontation with Russia, the obsessive doctrine was that power respects only power. The tough style had been forecast in Truman's 1941 statement that if the United States saw Germany winning the war it should help Russia, and if Russia gained the upper hand it should help Germany—so that Russia and Germany would eliminate each other as far as possible.

The tough stance was enormously advanced by the strength the United States had amassed by 1945. In stopping Germany twice in a lifetime, America had built the greatest fleet, the greatest air force and one of the two greatest armies in the world. If such might was not enough, Truman, becoming President at this moment, discovered a matchless ace in the hole—the atom bomb. Suddenly the little man who had pled for prayers as he was worn in was talking to Molotov "in a way I've never been talked to before," and winding up a summit with Stalin at Potsdam with the determination never to hold another. He then played his big card— and after Hiroshima the United States could beat all its other swords into ploughshares. After that, Truman crowed at Carruthersville, America would lead the world.

In the canceling of lend-lease, in their no-nonsense postwar loan negotiations with the exhausted British, in the diplomatic byplay with

Stalin that ended with the hasty Russian pullback from Iran, Truman and his associates confirmed for themselves their country's seemingly limitless power. They were not disposed to ride along with Roosevelt's Teheran and Yalta compromises conceding Russia's dominant position in Eastern Europe. Yet the Russians kept resisting American leadership. They showed themselves aggressively hostile. They began to sovietize the lands they occupied. To this, the Truman administration's response was to flex its power.

The late 1940s was a time of American power. The Russians were invited to Eniwetok and Bikini to witness the A-bomb's destructiveness. The United States Air Force was then the spread-eagler of the world. By then the B-29s that had dropped the A-bombs on Hiroshima and Nagasaki were giving way to a new behemoth of the skies. The twenty-ton monster bomber B-36, with its ten engines, four of them jets, could fly more than 10,000 miles without refueling. In 1948 the Strategic Air Command, newly created for the mission of delivering the A-bomb, established its headquarters at Offutt Field in Nebraska. Cranking up for the new kind of warfare that vaulted across both land and sea, SAC thus took up a position commanding the whole world from the continental heartland of North America. This was the time of SAC's dry runs to Wake Island, which just happened to be the same distance from certain United States bomber bases as Leningrad, except that it was over water all the way. The whole world knew what these trips were meant to say. The message was further underlined by front-page photographs of smaller B-29s and B-50s practicing refueling in midflight over the Atlantic and Pacific.[1]

The thought that there would soon be a world in which the atom bomb was America's hope would have shocked nine out of ten citizens in the victorious days of 1945. Late that year the National Opinion Research Center asked a cross-section of Americans whether they expected a new world war in twenty-five years, and obtained an affirmative answer from just thirty-two per cent. The proportion rose in 1946 when Stalin proclaimed Russia's determination to go it alone and Churchill proclaimed the Cold War. By the end of 1947, after Truman himself took up the Cold War cry, the number who expected the country to be at war within ten years' time had climbed to fifty-four per cent. The doctrine of wielding power to contain a power only recently America's wartime ally, which had seemed crude and unbearably brusque even when proclaimed by so eloquent a phrasemaker as Winston Churchill, was beginning to take hold outside the Truman Administration itself. The great, rearing, plunging, galaxy-swirling shift of the American nation from withdrawal to worldwide anti-Communist activism was under way. Yet even after promulgation of the Truman Doctrine and announcement of the Marshall

Plan, popular opinion had a long way to go to catch up with Truman, Forrestal and the new B-36s.[2]

From the moment that Stalin pulled Russia and its satellites out of the Marshall Plan talks in Paris in the summer of 1947, the Truman administration openly ranged itself against "international Communism" on all fronts. At a time when the schools of America organized to teach "zeal for democracy," and when union members at mass meetings were being told to root out all "leftwingers," no institution of the society was quicker to take up the Cold War cry than the press. The great majority of newspaper publishers who had been trying for years to undo the works of Roosevelt's New Deal now saw that things were swinging their way at last. Having done their bit to unseat price controls in 1946 and rooted home the Taft-Hartley Act in the summer of 1947, a substantial portion of the press played up the antics of the House Un-American Activities Committee and helped blackmail Hollywood later that year into a submissive conformity. When the Committee summoned Adolphe Menjou, Robert Taylor and some 350 other movie stars, producers, directors and writers to testify on industry ideology, the papers had a field day. Rupert Hughes, otherwise unable to identify Communists, was quoted as saying: "You can't help smelling them." The famous German playwright Bertholt Brecht, hauled in by the Committee for a minor bit he had written years before, came across in newspaper headlines as some sort of hack scripter spooning Communist ideology into American cinematic romances.[3]

At this time, the *New York Mirror*'s Broadway columnist, Walter Winchell, held the same kind of ascendancy on Sunday-night radio that the *Daily News* columnist, Ed Sullivan, later gained on TV. Having won a huge audience during the war by lacing his gossip bits with patriotic excoriations of the Nazis, Winchell kept the formula but began blasting "Communazis" and "Redvermin" when the Cold War broke out. That fall he got into a slanging match with Andrei Vishinsky, the vituperative Soviet delegate to the United Nations who had been chief prosecutor for Stalin in the trumped-up trial of purged Soviet leaders in Moscow back in 1937-38. When Vishinsky dared Winchell to visit Russia and report what he saw, Winchell shouted: "I will go only if the Russian government extends to me and the men I pick to go with me the same courtesies that [the Communists] get over here—the right to go wherever they please and write whatever they please." Though Winchell's next column nominated forty-one newsmen, mainly fellow employees of the Hearst organization, for the trip, the Cold War had already grown too bitter for such exchanges. On September 20, 1947, the State Department acknowledged that it had itself adopted one of the most regressive aspects of Russian policy. Pierre Courtade, correspondent of the French Communist news-paper *L'Humanité* at the United Nations, had been given a visa that restricted him from traveling more than twenty miles outside New York City and expressly forbade him from "propaganda work."[4]

The press, news magazines and the radio carried the government's ball on play after play, spreading well beyond the "attentive public" such phrases as "iron curtain," "cold war," and "international Communism."

I N   T H E   contest of power after the Second World War, the big prize up for grabs was Germany. Almost the first result when West and East rushed in was that the contending forces, to gain advantage, dropped revenge as a policy and encouraged the Germans to start up their ruined factories and trade with their recent enemies. Very quickly the line be-tween the contending forces, a line drawn across Germany during the war and intended to separate the occupying forces in the interval before a peace treaty was signed, became Winston Churchill's "Iron Curtain."

To the West were the American and British zones (out of which a zone was carved for French occupation): these contained perhaps 45,-000,000 Germans and, in the Ruhr district within the British Zone, what had long been the industrial heart of Germany and all Europe. To the east was that part of prewar Germany that had not already been annexed by Russia or handed over to the reconstituted state of Poland. This was the Russian Zone, containing perhaps 18,000,000 Germans, a highly devel-oped economy (but without anything like the concentrated heavy industry of the Ruhr), and the once-proud but now frightfully battered city of Berlin.

Berlin was a special case, however. In the last days of the war Ameri-can and British forces might have captured it. A fortnight before the end Stalin summoned Marshals Zhukov and Konev from the front expressly to read them a report that the Western Allies were preparing to do so. "Well," said Stalin, "who is going to Berlin, we or the Allies?" General Eisenhower, against the wishes of Winston Churchill, ordered his forces to pull back out of the territory marked for Russian occupation. After fighting in which the Russians suffered heavy casualties, Marshal Zhukov took Berlin. Then, under the wartime agreements that carved out the German occupation zones, Zhukov stood aside to permit contingents of Americans, British and later French soldiers to occupy assigned sectors of Berlin in the brief interval until a peace treaty should be signed.[5]

No peace treaty was signed, of course. The foreign ministers of the United States, Britain and Russia met repeatedly, always to disagree. They disagreed about Eastern Europe, where Russia was imposing its will; about

Western Europe, where the United States was not prepared to lose what it had gone to war twice to save; about Iran, China, Korea. About Germany itself, after the first war-crimes trials, purges of Nazi officials and dismantling of war plants, they disagreed totally. They were particularly far apart on reparations, which the Russians who had suffered heavy war losses wanted much more urgently than the Americans, who had not.

Yet it was the Russians, intent on getting more goods for their economy, who first openly dropped the policy of revenge. They abruptly announced that no more factories would be dismantled and shipped to Russia; instead, the factories would be left where they were, and the Germans would produce the goods. Secretary Byrnes took a very serious view of this Russian announcement. The Americans had clearly been easing up on the Germans, but had been reluctant to say so outright. Convinced that the Russians were stealing a march to build up pro-Soviet sentiment among the Germans, especially among the socialists who were the largest surviving democratic element in the country, Byrnes decided that an immediate American response was called for.[6]

Taking counsel with Senators Vandenberg and Connally, members of his delegation at the foreign ministers' conference in Paris, Byrnes flew to Berlin to talk with his old associate General Lucius D. Clay. Deputy American military governor in Germany at the time, Clay was no ordinary Army bureaucrat. Bushy-browed, hawk-nosed, autocratic, with booming voice, Southern accent and quick smile, he was politician, industrialist and top-flight professional officer rolled into one. He was in fact a charter member of the military-industrial complex.

His father had been senator from Georgia, his great-granduncle was none other than Henry Clay. He himself had been a Senate page, and grew up on politics. Trained as an engineer, he had spent the war dealing with supply and production problems at the highest level, much of the time as a civilian aide and close coworker with Byrnes in the Office of War Mobilization. He was a driving mobilizer, credited with having put through the wartime ban on racing, the prohibition against display lighting, and the midnight curfew for certain cities. His close friend and West Point classmate Dwight Eisenhower always insisted it was Clay, on brief assignment from Washington, who cracked the monumental supply jam at Cherbourg in 1944 that until then had stalled his drive across France. Specifically requested by Eisenhower for the German job, Clay lost no time ditching the official scheme for pastoralizing postwar Germany and now had all the plans ready for Byrnes to make the Western occupation zones self-supporting.

In company with Clay and the senators, Byrnes traveled to Stuttgart in Hitler's armored train. On September 6, 1946, in the city's only unbombed hall, he made America's countering bid to the Germans. To a hastily assembled audience of German notables he announced not only that the United States favored getting the German economy going again but also regarded the country's eastern boundaries—*i.e.*, the Oder-Neisse border with Poland that Russia demanded—as "not fixed." On his own responsibility when he was unable to get through to the White House by telephone, Byrnes also pledged that American troops would stay as long as there were occupation troops in Germany. Foreign Secretary Bevin followed through by affirming that Britain favored a merger of the Western occupation zones as well. Soon Marshall, Clay and others were saying that the recovery of Europe required the recovery of Germany.[7]

Here was a development that called for a tremendous wrench in the way Americans thought about the world. Little more than a year before, shaken to startled attention by Harry Truman's hard, cold bid to "scare hell out of the American people," they had gone along with his call for resisting Russian Communism with dollars, but not with troops. Then they had been rallied for the Marshall Plan. That, too, was mostly emergency dollar aid to wartime allies, and besides the whole thing sounded good for American business and farmers. The involvement with Germany, which seemed to demand that Americans junk or rethink a good many of the leading ideas they had held throughout the Second World War, called for an enlargement of the American world outlook by a whole order of magnitude.

This, in the circumstances, was asking too much of the American people.

The state of Europe, amid the wreckage of two world wars, was catastrophic—a condition far from unknown to the long memories of Europe. But only once in their national experience, when brother was pitted against brother in Civil War, had Americans known catastrophic change as a collective as well as personal experience. For a century and a half, facing for the mostpart only the challenges of harsh nature as they spread westward, they had moved steadily through triumph after triumph on what the geographers termed their "island continent."

Some island, some continent. Its heartland so huge that Midwesterners grew up without sight or even thought of the sea, this island had coasts so remote from each other that inhabitants long tended, depending on whether they were New Yorkers or San Franciscans, from Newport News or Newport Beach, to live in Atlantic and Pacific worlds. Formed out of individuals who had fled the corrupt Old World for the unspoiled New, unified by the shared convictions that white-skin freedom, democracy and honest toil had accomplished its triumph, island America came to exceed even island Britain in the righteous distaste with which it viewed venal, decadent, quarrelsome, doom-ridden Europe. And there was no denying that by the time America intervened to save Europe in its second world war, it had grown rich and strong while keeping intact the same system of democratic, republican government for longer than any other country worth mentioning.

Now destiny was calling this nation of innocents to its first full exposure to the World, Old and New, as it really was. America as a society was being brought up suddenly against such catastrophic changes as other societies had long known. Even in 1948 Americans had not yet grasped, however, that being spared such exploding, wrenching dislocations had been due to the geographical and historical factors that were by then, in C. Wright Mills' phrase "merely history." The experience was only beginning. It was not until two decades later, when their perceptions had been sharpened by the lacerating experiences of two painful and extremely unpopular wars, that something everybody else seemed to know began to come clear to Americans: their lives, collective and individual, were embedded in a wider history. Americans are still learning that they can cope no more than other mortals with their troubles in such a way as to control those vast dislocations that engulf all men.[8]

T H U S suddenly in early 1948, caught up and swept along by the necessities of its successive actions, the United States found itself propelled into a scene in which humanity itself seemed to lie nakedly exposed to the iron vicissitudes of history. It was springtime in Berlin. Under the sweet-smelling lindens, 3,000,000 Berliners breathed the dust of their ruin-city. Behind the roofless walls, fear grew like weeds. Hope was carted off like rubble. From the poles of the postwar world, the two supernations marshaled their immense and coordinated energies, thrust out their probing vanguards, and converged for showdown over the broken body of Berlin.

As they lurched closer, rattling their tanks and reaching for their bombs in a terrifying series of feints and parries, a marvelous irony was disclosed: the United States and Russia were seen to be vying for the good opinion of the same beaten Berliners on whom they had rained 26,000 tons of high explosive bombs and uncounted rounds of artillery shells barely two years before.[9]

At the burned-out Reichstag building the only life to be seen were crows flapping around the beheaded statues on the roof. On the shuttered Reichschancellery balcony was chalked the bitter beatitude: "Blessed are the dead, for their hands do not freeze." At dusk a lone policeman patrolling his rounds waved a stick at a fourteen-year-old prostitute who had strayed from her normal beat. As he came to a tree at the corner, he tore off little slips of paper that had been pinned to it. "Want bread, offer German cigarettes," read one. "Will sell linen tablecloth and curtains for money or food," read another. "Discharged PW wants pair of pants, gives money or potatoes," read a third.

This was illegal barter, but in the spring of 1948 every Berlin neighborhood had its *Brotbaum*, or bread tree. A city official, the bite of the east wind in his voice, said: "Berlin is on Moscow's shopping list. If the price is cheap enough, the Russians will snap it up and take it." At a moment when two pounds of bread cost $15 and a pound of coffee $100 on the black market, the question was how much the city was worth. The answer, it turned out, was plenty.[10]

The struggle for Berlin was the struggle for Germany. It was true that Berlin lay a hundred miles inside the Russian occupation zone, and that neither the Yalta nor Potsdam agreements spelled out the details of access by the Western Powers to their occupation sectors in Berlin. But like the Russians, the Americans, British and French were in Berlin by right of conquest, and road, rail and air corridors of access—temporary as the occupation zones themselves—would be and were arranged by the Russians. In 1945 Marshal Zhukov agreed to access by rail along two routes, by road along the Autobahn from Kassel, and by three air corridors.[11]

As differences over Germany's future turned into deadlock, all the fine talk about treating the occupied country as a unity grew ever more hollow. Each side demanded as its price for German unity the application in all zones of its particular policies. As a result the zone borders soon hardened into territorial frontiers, those between the American, British and French zones no less than those marking the limits of Red Army occupation.

It was the catastrophic state of Western Europe, quite as much as the perceived danger of aggressive Russian designs on Central Europe, that drew the three Western occupation zones together. General Clay and others were already arguing that countries such as Belguim, the Netherlands and France would never be able to recover their economic health without access to the coal and industrial output of the German Ruhr. The British were painfully aware that their occupation zone could be nothing but a burden on their own hard-pressed Treasury unless the dismantling for reparations was finally stopped and its output exported in quantities sufficient to make it self-supporting. On January 1, 1947, therefore, the economies of the British and American zones were fused in an entity called Bizonia.

It is from this event, some have said, that the Russians might date the start of the Cold War. Thenceforth the Americans made large dollar infusions into the economies of Western Europe, including that of West Germany. Closer economic integration was followed before long by closer political integration. The West Germans sided with the Western world.[12]

By 1948 West German industrial regions were producing twenty-five percent more coal than in 1938, and making a significant contribution toward the recovery of Western Europe. Yet the domestic economies of the three western zones still languished. Even with emergency food shipments that Clay obtained from the United States, food was rationed at a subsistence level of 1550 calories a day, workers could not produce a full day's work, and apathy was alarming. The Reichsmark was depreciating fast. When cigarettes, the recognized currency of postwar Germany, went for a thousand marks each, it began to look like the bad old inflationary days of 1922 all over again. Convinced that the spiral would never stop so long as the Russians were free to print Reichsmarks as fast as they pleased, Clay and his colleagues determined to put through a drastic currency reform. Their plan: replace the old mark with a new one valid only in the West, and encourage German officials in the West at the same time to end price controls and introduce a free market economy.[13]

As the Americans and their allies moved toward the crucial decision to emplace an economic wall along the Iron Curtain, the Russians were readying their countermoves in the East. If this was the moment for showdown, for drawing the line in Central Europe, there were several that Stalin could make. First, he could make sure by driving a bargain while Russian troops still occupied key posts there, that Finland would always have a regime "friendly" to the Soviet Union. Second, he could consolidate Russia's hold on its own zone of Germany, which had been impaired by the persisting presence within it of American, British and French forces in Berlin. Third, he could consolidate Russian power over the non-German countries east of the Iron Curtain.

Czechoslovakia was the one country east of the Iron Curtain from which Russian troops had been withdrawn. Under the leadership of President Eduard Benes and Foreign Minister Jan Masaryk, two of the foremost democratic diplomatists of Europe, the country had managed somehow to keep a sort of balance between East and West. In the first postwar elections Communists had obtained thirty-eight percent of the vote, and under Premier Klement Gottwald they held a strong position. But in 1948 new elections were due, and in anticipation of them Benes proposed weakening the Communist-controlled police. Gottwald refused, and a Soviet mission flew into Prague and forced Benes to back down. In a midnight coup on February 26, Gottwald's forces seized control and Czechoslovakia was consolidated into the Russian bloc. A few days later Masaryk plunged to his death from a third-story Foreign Office window

—a suicide, the Communists said; defenestrated, his friends in the West firmly believed.[14]

The Czech coup was a shocker. It rocked official Washington, already on tenterhooks over the perils of getting the Marshall Plan through with West Germany included. On March 5 a telegram arrived from General Clay in Berlin, reporting a shift in Soviet mood which led him to feel that war might come with "dramatic suddenness." The British advised Marshall there was reason to believe the Russians, after pressuring the Finns into a treaty of "friendship," might demand another from Norway. As President Truman called on the new CIA to assess the chances of war, Marshall told the press that the nation had arrived at a "fateful hour" in its affairs. On March 17 Joseph and Stewart Alsop wrote in their syndicated column: "The atmosphere in Washington today is no longer a postwar atmosphere. It is a prewar atmosphere."[15]

Following the overthrow in Prague, American apprehensions leaped to Italy, where the Communists were threatening to win the April elections. Food shipments were stepped up, loans were announced. Proclaiming that "the constant advance of the Iron Curtain across Europe has created a great crisis," Speaker of the House Joseph Martin urged "people of Italian descent to send an airmail letter to their relatives in Italy pointing out the peril and urging defeat of the Communist party in the balloting. "A twenty-five cent stamp might turn the tide for peace," cried Martin.[16]

Washington's "March crisis" had two important results. In the hue and cry over the fall of Czechoslovakia, Congress stopped delaying and voted the necessary credits to start the Marshall Plan. Secondly, the slow rise of popular apprehension needed to accomplish mobilization for the Cold War gave way to a swift burst of alarm. In March, 1947, the Gallup poll reported that a record seventy-three percent of the American people believed that a third world war was inevitable.[17]

For a brief time, however, the crisis eased. Anti-Communist forces won the Italian elections handily by a three-to-two margin. Dean Rusk, director of the State Department's Office of Special Political Affairs, had predicted that the Russians would land troops in the Middle East to enforce a United Nations partition plan for Palestine, but instead they joined the United States in extending swift recognition to the new state of Israel. As it happened, trouble flared up, all right, in the spring of 1948, but it broke out just where the Americans were not looking for it—on Russia's side of the Iron Curtain. In Yugoslavia, in fact.

If Westerners thought of Eastern European countries as satellites orbiting around the Russian sun, Yugoslavia might even then have been seen as the most distant of these lesser bodies and the one least subject to Moscow's enslaving gravity. Marshal Tito, the country's chieftain, was like no other follower of Stalin in Eastern Europe. A wartime guerrilla leader, he had liberated his country without help from the Red Army, and in doing so had built up a base of broad popular support such as no other Communist leader had. His country did not border on the Soviet Union and indeed, with its access to the Mediterranean, had been courted by the British and Americans during the Second World War and after.

There was no doubt about Tito's Communism; he was the only leader in the bloc who stood solidly with Stalin and Zhdanov in the creation of the Cominform, and had taken the lead in criticizing the French and Italian parties for being overcautious. But there was no doubt about Tito's nationalism either. When Stalin began demanding full Yugoslav cooperation in the economic and military aid agreements the Russians began to draw up after they turned their backs on the Marshall Plan, Tito balked. He went right on signing deals with non-Communist countries to acquire the machines he needed to build up basic industries. The Russians thereupon cut back on trade, and in the same kind of punitive action carried out against the Chinese fourteen years later, withdrew their technical aid personnel from Yugoslavia. The kind of consolidation that overtook Benes and Masaryk was intended for Tito. "I will shake my little finger," said Stalin, "and there will be no more Tito."

It did not work out that way. Surviving a Stalinist attempt to overthrow him from within, Tito in April dismissed two pro-Soviet Yugoslavs from high office. Still unbeknownst to the Cold Warriors west of the Iron Curtain, Cominform headquarters were unceremoniously removed from Belgrade to Bucharest. Then on June 28, just as the Russians were making the move on Berlin that was to consolidate their grip on East Germany, a stunning piece of news was broadcast from behind the Iron Curtain: Yugoslavia was being expelled from the Cominform for "nationalism."[18]

Although the threat of a Praguelike coup, not to mention a Red Army invasion, hung over the Yugoslavs from that moment onward, Tito's police proved more effective than those the Russians sent in. Stalin, ever cautious, held back from war. But Tito became his mortal enemy. To stamp out any chance that Titoism might spread within the bloc Stalin ordered bloody purges in all other countries of Eastern Europe. Traicho Kostov, second-ranking Bulgarian Communist, was sent to the gallows. In Albania, General Kochi Xoxo was executed for the crime of Titoism. Laszlo Rajk, former Interior Minister, was brought to trial and hanged in Hungary. Wladislaw Gomulka was ousted from party leadership and arrested in Poland. Ana Pauker, oldtime Comintern official and general in the Red Army, was turned out of office in Rumania. In a span of two years, it has been estimated, one out of every four Communist party members in Eastern Europe fell from power. Inside the Kremlin, there were changes. Zhdanov, blamed for the Yugoslav breakaway, lost favor. He died later in 1948, aged 52.

The defection of Tito was the most significant single political event of the Cold War in Stalin's time in Eastern Europe. Coming on the heels of the coup in Czechoslovakia it might well have defused the crisis in the Cold War, but it did not. Washington, George Kennan said later, "over-acted in a most deplorable way." For the defection of Tito effectively liquidated the very Greek uprising that had been the occasion of the Truman Doctrine and America's mobilization for Europe a year earlier: now Tito, who had largely supplied the rebels across his southern border, was obliged to close the border and pull back to defend himself against Stalin. Moreover, in defying Stalin, Tito had both disproved Stalin's dogma that the world was divided into "two camps" and refuted the Western notion that Communism was monolithic behind its Iron Curtain. In fact, he had fractured the Iron Curtain.[19]

Yet that was not how the West saw it—at least the hardy metaphor, used by Hitler's propaganda minister, Goebbels, before Churchill hung it out again as the Cold War front-line, kept appearing in American propaganda long after Congress, finding Tito alive and well in Belgrade and still resisting Stalin, belatedly voted to send military and economic help to the heretical Communists of Yugoslavia. In the spring of 1948, whatever the outcome of Stalin's efforts to consolidate elsewhere, the showdown for America loomed in Berlin. It was on the Russian moves to consolidate their hold on their part of Germany in the face of Allied moves in the West, that American attention was riveted. On March 20, Marshal Soko-lovsky, Russian commandant in Berlin, after being refused information concerning meetings in London to put through currency reform in the three Western zones of Germany, rose and walked out of a meeting of the Allied Control Council. General Clay watched and later wrote: "The stage had been set for the imposition of the Soviet blockade of Berlin.[20]

THE BERLIN BLOCKADE did not begin all at once. After Sokolovsky stalked out there was silence for several days. Then on April 1 the Russians, denying that the Allies had any right in Berlin, forbade American, British and French road and rail traffic in and out of Berlin without prior Russian inspection.

It was not yet viewed as a showdown when General Clay dispatched a test train with a few armed guards aboard to see if the Russians meant business. "The train," Clay learned, "progressed some distance into the Soviet zone but was finally shunted off the main line by electrical switching to a siding, where it remained for a few days until it withdrew rather ignominiously." So the Russians were not fooling. Cabling Washington, Clay began a small airlift to supply the 4000 Western occupation troops in Berlin.[21]

Rail and road traffic resumed. On June 7 the Western occupying powers put out word from London that they were not fooling either: agreement had been reached to set up a unified West Germany with "minimum requirements of occupation and control." This was to be the decisive announcement concerning postwar Germany. It had been arrived at without any consultation with the Russians, and the Russians who had long seen it coming, did not let the challenge pass unanswered. On June 11 all rail traffic to Berlin was stopped for two days. On June 12 all road traffic was stopped for bridge "repairs," and on June 16 the Soviet representative walked out of the joint Allied body governing Berlin. On June 18, implementing their big decision, the Allies announced their currency reform for West Germany.[22]

This was the act that triggered the final split with the Russians in Germany and brought on the blockade of Berlin. Five days later the Russians ordered a new, separate currency system for their own occupation zone, including Berlin, and on June 24 they stopped all rail traffic with the West because of "technical difficulties." Hours later other "technical difficulties" blocked all canal and road movements as well. The blockade of all the conventional avenues of military and civilian supply was complete.

The first reaction of General Clay and his political adviser, Robert D. Murphy, was to propose putting an armored column on the road into Berlin at once. President Truman said that if the Joint Chiefs of Staff would put their approval in writing, he would approve the idea too. But neither they nor the Secretary of State nor the governments of Britain and France would approve. Against the small number of undermanned divisions the Western powers had in Germany, the Russians had thirty in their occupation zone surrounding the city, and these were backed by many more nearby in Poland and Czechoslovakia.[23]

Yet the President had already said—and Forrestal had recorded it in his diary—"We are going to stay, period."

There was nothing to do but take to the air. Supplying the troops stationed in Berlin by air was no great problem, as Clay had cannily made sure by the little airlift started in March. But what about the civilian population of the Allied sectors? Could an airlift provide the 2,250,000 people of West Berlin with enough to live on? Such a thing had never been done before. Possibly food could be flown in, but what about coal —coal for light and power, coal to keep the city going, coal to give warmth, if it came to that, in winter?

General Clay put in a phone call to General Curtis LeMay at United States Air Force headquarters in Wiesbaden. LeMay was an oldstyle, seat-of-the-pants flier who was never happier than when leading combat missions. He was also famous as organizer and commander of the B-29 "saturation" raids that leveled Tokyo. "Curt," said Clay, "have you any planes that can carry coal?"

"Carry what?" asked LeMay.

"Coal," repeated Clay.

"We must have a bad phone connection," said LeMay. "It sounds as if you are asking if we have planes for carrying coal."

"Yes, that's what I said—coal."

"Sure," said LeMay, rallying quickly. "The Air Force can haul anything. How much coal do you want us to haul?"

"All you can haul."

"Eventually," LeMay recalled later, "it dawned on me what he was talking about. He was going to buckle down and supply the city of Berlin entirely by air. I told him we'd have to get some help from home."[24]

Thereupon began one of those miracles of organizational improvisation that brings out the qualities with which Americans are uncommonly well provided. At its center, animating, organizing and directing an operation that mobilized all Berlin, West Germany and much of America, was Clay.

The Cold War gave a lot of American military men a second fling at the exhilarating challenge of crisis command. In the years after the Second World War, the armed forces were full of high-ranking officers destined to serve out the rest of their careers in honorific posts who were summoned instead to lead new campaigns against the Russians. Thus it was that the Army's prize troubleshooter of the Second World War, the same General Clay who had broken the bottleneck at Cherbourg, the same Assistant War Mobilizer who Jimmy Byrnes said could run anything, chanced to be in Berlin when a military challenge was to be met by a feat of peaceable logistics. Thus it was that Curtis LeMay, the terror of Tokyo, was soon copiloting a grimy transport through the murk over Berlin and pinning medals on young airmen who carried the most coal. And thus it was that General William H. Tunner, the man who won fame by supplying beleaguered China over the Himalayan "Hump," was summoned to Europe to surpass his wartime triumphs by organizing the airlift that broke the Berlin blockade.[25]

As the operation got under way there were just two airfields in the Western sectors of Berlin. Twin-engine Douglas C-47s, flying in one of the three airlanes from the West, each twenty miles wide, that had been agreed to by Marshal Zhukov in 1945, began landing and discharging coal packed in GI dufflebags. Within two weeks four-engine Douglas C-54

Globemasters arrived, reinforced by RAF Dakotas and Yorks. Navy cargo planes joined in. German civilians worked frenziedly to extend and strengthen the runways.

The unceasing roar of the planes filled every ear in Berlin. It echoed off the stone walls of hollow, bombed-out houses. Less than three years before the same terrible and typical twentieth century sound had driven the inhabitants underground in dread. Now this sound, the voice of cold, mechanized anger, dinned into Berliners' ears with a message of life.

At Tempelhof, the Air Force transports lumbered in at the rate of one plane evey three minutes. Scores of ten-ton trucks rolled out to meet them. German civilians—famous plane designers and decorated pilots among them—labored twenty-four hours a day to get them unloaded. In the orange and white control tower were GIs wearing headphones and surrounded by Coke bottles, cigarette stubs and the chaotic chorusing of tense voices:

> Give me an ETA on EC-84 . . . That's flour coming on EC-12. . . . Roger. . . . Ease her down. . . . Where the hell has 85 gone? Oh yeah, overhead. . . . Wind is now north-northwest. . . . The next stupid Charlie 47 has nothing on his manifest. . . . Are you in charge of putting deicing fluid in aircraft? Well, who the hell is?[26]

With these voices in the unwarlike Battle of Berlin mingled others. In the House of Commons Foreign Minister Bevin said: "None of us can surrender." In Washington General Marshall said: "We intend to stay." At his command post, General Clay said: "The American troops under my command will use force of arms if necessary. I will not be bluffed." "There is a cruel spirit ready to act in Berlin tomorrow the way it acted in Prague today," cried Socialist Annadore Leber in the West Berlin Assembly. At a mass meeting of 80,000 Berliners at the Schoeneberg courthouse, Socialist Mayor Ernst Reuter shouted defiance: "We will build a dam against which the red tide will beat in vain."[27]

Only Cold War could have given rise to so curious a confrontation. Shortly after the airlift began General Clay and his Western fellow commanders found themselves chatting with General Sokolovsky in his office. The technical difficulties, the Russian said, would continue to impede ground traffic until the Western Powers abandoned their plans for West German government. "He was confident we would be forced to leave," said Clay afterward. "He was enjoying the situation." The airmen flew on —"Clay's Pigeons," they called themselves—knowing as all knew from Clay and Sokolovsky on down that the Russians could shoot them down any time they so decided. Once a Russian fighter plane crashed into a

British transport sending both down in flames, and there was an anxious time before the Allies could be sure it was an accident. Clay, a visitor reported, was drawn tight as a steel spring. There were innumerable scrapes and snafus in the German fog. One evening the tower at Tempelhof was hushed as controllers tried to make contact with a C-54 lost for a quarter of an hour over Berlin. Finally the plane landed. "Here they got the fifth largest city in the world," growled a radioman, "and they miss it."[28]

Until 1949 it had been stated American policy to outlaw the A-bomb, though endless talks with the Russians about controlling it through the United Nations had come to naught. In the tension of the March crisis and the Berlin blockade it was suggested that B-29s, the only planes at that moment in operational squadrons that could deliver the A-bomb, be flown to Britain and to Marshall's surprise the British Labour government agreed. On July 18 two B-29 groups were flown to British bases. Two months later the President told Forrestal "he prayed that he would never have to make such a decision, but that if it became necessary, no one need have a misgiving that he would do so. . . ." The evening after Truman made this declaration, some twenty publishers assembled by Forrestal agreed that if war came over Berlin, the American people would expect the bomb to be used.[29]

By then all America was being drawn into a kind of human chain that joined hands in the air bridge to Berlin. Radios broadcast the daily tonnages like Dow-Jones averages. Newspapers played up the name that GIs gave their airlift: "Operation Vittles," and reporters rode atop heaps of coal sacks to relate the instrument-flying and cargo-handling feats of "LeMay's Coal and Feed Company." Mayor Reuter, invited to America, was greeted as a hero wherever he went. At a Washington conference Clay won a pledge of enough help to step up the airlift to 4,500 tons daily through winter. It was expensive but as an officer said: "One week's supply of Berlin would be cheap compared to a day of war." President Truman's stand on Berlin took the issue of foreign affairs right out of the 1948 presidential campaign. After conferring with Senators Vandenberg and Dulles, Republican presidential candidate Thomas E. Dewey said:

> The present duty of Americans is not to be divided by past lapses, but to unite to surmount present dangers. . . . In Berlin, we must not surrender our rights under duress.[30]

More than any other factor, the Russian blockade of Berlin in the summer of 1948 ruined Henry Wallace's chances of rolling up a big third-party presidential vote that fall.

As winter came on, the airlift was stepped up as promised. New radar techniques were worked out that permitted landings under conditions hitherto thought impossible. It was at Berlin that the Ground Control Approach (GCA) system was perfected that was later adopted for bad-weather landings throughout the world. That winter a third airfield was built, and steel mats were laid on runways to take the new, bigger C-74 transports. The foundation beneath them, packed in place by gangs of Germans, as many as 17,000 at a time, consisted of brick rubble—"the scraps of the city," LeMay noted, "that we had pounded to pieces" a few years before. Berliners, permitted electric power for only two hours in every twenty-four on a staggered schedule, often did their day's cooking when power came on in the middle of the night. It was precisely in this ordeal that the Berliners established their ties with Americans. "During the blockade," said Ambassador Robert Murphy, "they became for all practical purposes our allies."[31]

THE MANNER in which the blockade was ended is one of the most instructive stories from an era of goldfish-bowl diplomacy. In January, 1949, after the Western Allies had been successfully supplying Berlin by air for nine months, Kingsbury Smith, European General Manager for Hearst's International News Service, submitted to the Russian Foreign Office four questions addressed to Stalin. This was a gambit often tried by correspondents in those days. Once in a while, if it suited Stalin's purposes, the questions were answered, and the correspondent had a front-page story. This time Stalin answered, and his statements, besides making a splash in the papers, caught the eye of the new Secretary of State, Dean Acheson.

"We judged the episode to be a cautious signal from Moscow," Acheson said later. "In answering a question on ending the blockade, Stalin had not mentioned the stated Russian reason for it—the new West German currency." To Acheson this meant that Moscow was ready to raise the blockade for a price. The question, of course, was the price. If, for example, the Russians really wanted the Western governments to abandon their plans for a West German government, he thought that would be too much.

At his regular press conference Acheson was asked, as expected, about Stalin's answers. Blandly he ran through them all until he came to the one about raising the blockade, and then said:

There are many ways in which a serious proposal by the Soviet Government . . . could be made. . . . I hope you [the press] will not take it amiss if I point out that if I on my part were seeking to give assurance of seriousness of purpose I would choose some other channel than a press interview.

A few days later Ambassador Philip Jessup, the United States representative to the United Nations Security Council, visited Washington to talk with Acheson and State Department Counselor Charles E. Bohlen. It was agreed that Jessup, when he next saw his opposite number, Russian Ambassador Jacob Malik, should ask Malik "as a matter of personal curiosity, whether the omission of any reference to the monetary reform in Stalin's answer was significant." The chance to pop the question came as the two men walked into a Security Council meeting on February 15. Malik said he did not know the answer. Jessup suggested that if Malik learned anything about the matter, Jessup would be interested to know.

A month later Malik asked Jessup to call at his New York office, and told him that the omission was not accidental. The currency question was important, he said, but could be discussed at a meeting of the Council of Foreign Ministers. Did that mean, asked Jessup, after the lifting of the blockade? Malik replied that he had not been asked to ask that question. Jessup replied: "Why don't you ask now?" Less than a week later, on March 21, the answer came back that if a definitive date for the foreign ministers' meeting could be set, the blockade could be lifted before the meeting took place. It was now Malik's turn to ask a question: would the Americans and others hold up preparations for a West German government until after the meeting? As instructed, Jessup answered that he expected the preparations would be continued but since they could not be completed for some time, they would not be important—that is, if the Russians really wanted to get on with the Council of Foreign Ministers meeting.

It took a while to get the British and French agreement, and the Russians tried vainly to get a pledge that no West German government would be established either during or before the Council of Foreign Ministers. On May 4 unconditional agreement was reached. All restrictions on Berlin traffic would be lifted on May 10, and eleven days later the Council of Foreign Ministers would meet in Paris—for the first time in two years—to discuss problems in Berlin and Germany, including the currency reform.[32]

The day was proclaimed a legal holiday in Berlin, and was of course hailed in the West as a victory. The military challenge had indeed been met—and met by peaceful means. The Russian squeeze had not worked. The Russians proceeded to carry out consolidation in their part of Europe by creating an East German regime as counterpart to the West German state established that summer by the Western Allies at Bonn. Western access to Berlin, however, remained to trouble the security of the East German state. It also remained subject to Russian military power, as the Western Allies and Berliners were to be uncomfortably reminded a decade later when Nikita Khrushchev brought pressure to get the Allies out. Two decades after the victory of the airlift, Berlin had not yet ceased to be a dangerous and explosive position in the heart of Europe.[33]

Out of this long and dogged confrontation, moreover, the emotional solidarity emerged that enabled the Americans to accept as allies the Germans upon whom they had made war only four years before. In the shock and fright of further Soviet aggressiveness that followed the Czech coup in early 1948, much more than Marshall Plan financing was rushed through Congress. Senator Vandenberg, working with Undersecretary of State Lovett, introduced a resolution declaring it the sense of the Senate that the government should promote:

> association of the United States, by constitutional process, with such regional and other collective arrangements as are based on continuous and effective self-defense and mutual aid.[34]

On the basis of this seemingly delphic declaration, which Vandenberg guided through to passage June 11, 1948 by a vote of sixty-four-to-four, Lovett met repeatedly with the ambassadors of Britain, France, Belgium, the Netherlands, Luxemburg, and Canada and drafts were prepared of a North Atlantic regional treaty that would add political unity and military strength to the economic recovery that the United States was working for in Western Europe. The American, British and French moves to give political form to the West German occupation zones that had become central to the Marshall Plan recovery program of course fitted integrally together with the North Atlantic Treaty plans. By spring, when Dean Acheson succeeded Lovett as the State Department's man in these talks with senators on one side and ambassadors on the other, a NATO pact was whipped into shape. The idea that an attack on one should be considered as an attack on all came from the Rio Treaty of 1942, which Senators Vandenberg and Connally had sponsored, and the idea of allies jointly taking measures to restore peace and security came from the Vandenberg-authored Article 51 of the United Nations treaty.

Applying these ideas to Europe was new, but authorization to do so had been provided by the Vandenberg Resolution. Accordingly, on April 4, 1949, in the presence of President Truman, Secretary Acheson and eleven other foreign ministers signed the NATO treaty—just a month before the Berlin airlift came to an end. In some sense, then, NATO, the first military alliance the United States had ever entered into with Europe in time of peace, was also a result of the Berlin Blockade.[35]

I F   T H E   Berlin Blockade converted Americans to alliance with the people on whom they had made war four years before, there were consequences of the "March crisis" of 1948 on the home front that were far less discernible at the time and that ultimately proved of gravest importance for the well-being of the American society. Of these, by far the most significant was enactment, amid the 1948 war scare, of the peacetime draft. No decision made then for what seemed good Cold War reasons had a sequel more fateful for the generational solidarity and continuity that bound together the community of Americans.

At the end of the Second World War the United States had reduced the strength of its armed forces in eighteen months from 12,000,000 men to no more than 1,500,000, and in March, 1947, at President Truman's recommendation, Congress had allowed Selective Service, the system under which 15,000,000 men had been called to arms in the recent war, to lapse. This was in line with deep-rooted national traditions that went back to the declaration of the Continental Congress in 1787:

> Standing Armies in time of Peace are inconsistent with the principles of republican Governments, dangerous to the liberties of a free people, and generally converted into a destructive engine for establishing despotism.

These traditions, characteristic of the most simple agrarian peoples, but shaped also by a tremendous revolutionary experience, set absolute store by a militia of citizens that would rally to the Republic's defense in times of dire peril. In this order of democracy, the corollary of "One Man, One Vote," was "One Man, One Musket," and citizens who defended their liberties ordinarily by their votes would, in emergencies, defend them by their guns. By contrast a standing army was what the British Crown had sent to fight against them, and was anathema to all good Americans. Keeping their powder dry, such Americans held that *no* government, not even a government of their own elected officials, could be trusted *not* to infringe on their liberties.[36]

Geography and history lent aid to the embattled farmers. In the War of 1812 Congress kept calling for volunteers even after the British landed and burned the national capital; a year later Thomas Jefferson could write that he was happy the United States had "so few of the desperate characters who compose modern regular armies." Well after the Civil War broke out, the government put through the first limited draft law. Though the draft provided only two percent of the Union army's strength, it was fiercely resisted. It applied only to communities that did not produce a predetermined quota of volunteers. The well-heeled could get off by paying the government $300 or hiring a substitute. In New York and Boston nearly a thousand men died in riots protesting the draft, and in the midst of the Gettysburg campaign 10,000 troops had to be detached to quell them. There were other riots in Rutland, Vermont, Portsmouth, New Hampshire, Wooster, Ohio.

With the end of the Civil War conscription lapsed, and the nation went back to its ingrained habits of voluntary military service. As before, local police forces, National Guard units commanded by state governors and the widespread possession of firearms in the revolutionary and frontier traditions, served to ensure that no centralized monopoly of armed force existed within the United States. At the same time a strong tradition grew up within the American officers corps against involvement in politics, and the civilian government, though prone to take this restraint for granted, did not outrageously offend the corporate interest and pride of the officers. For this the United States was uncommonly well served by its officers' corps through two world wars.

In April, 1917, when Congress declared war on Germany and the nation moved to carry the war to the enemy overseas, the draft was proposed as a means of providing the troops. A fierce debate broke out. Thundered Senator James A. Reed, Democrat of Missouri, "The draft is not democratic, it is autocratic . . . despotic . . . Prussian. Its essential feature is that of involuntary servitude." "In my state they have a feeling that a conscript is a slave," cried Representative John Nicholls, Democrat of North Carolina. "Conscription is state slavery," said George Huddleston, Democrat of Alabama. Representative James F. Byrnes of South Carolina—the same Jimmy Byrnes who later held the office of War Mobilizer—asked: "Must we Prussianize ourselves in order to win democracy for the people of the world?" "Much as I dislike to believe it," objected Representative Carl Hayden, Democrat of Arizona, "yet I am convinced that most of the propaganda in favor of selective conscription is founded not so much upon a desire to win a war as it is to accustom the people to this method of raising an army and thereby to establish it as a permanent system in this country."

Woodrow Wilson called the draft, as enacted, "selection from a nation that has volunteered." But of those called in the first draft, half asked exemption, and no fewer than 252,294 failed to appear for induction. Many others left the country or failed to register, and so many had teeth extracted to disqualify themselves physically that the War Department threatened to prosecute dentists who thus helped draft evaders. No sooner was the fighting ended than the United States went back to voluntary military service. Indeed, never until the eve of Pearl Harbor had Congress enacted any form of peacetime draft and even then, when France had fallen and Hitler was on the point of invading the British Isles, the bill had squeaked through the House of Representatives by one vote.

Thus, letting the draft lapse again after the Second World War was in the oldest traditions of the American Republic. It also reflected a sense in Congress that the United States, having acquired the atomic bomb, could not expect ever again to fight a war requiring massed armies like those of the First and Second World Wars. Yet after the Second World War the armed forces were never allowed to slip into such a condition of dismantling as after the First World War, when the professional army of the United States numbered less than 100,000 in a population of 120,000,000. Defense, even in the years of the most headlong "reconversion," continued to be the largest item in the federal budget at a level something like eight times that of 1939. And military men continued to be heard, indeed were among the most influential voices, in government.[37]

Not only had General Marshall been recalled to take over the State Department, and American interests in Germany and Japan placed under Generals Clay and MacArthur. The effect of the Military Security Act of 1948, which was seen and debated at the time as a measure for bringing together the Army, Navy and Air Force in a single, unified department, was to create the basis for the large and permanent military establishment that had been feared and forbidden from the foundation of the Republic. From the day the new law gave statutory standing to the Joint Chiefs of Staff, they were constantly and increasingly consulted by President Truman. Security, planning, mobilization, code-cracking, research—all were institutionalized within the military framework, manned and indeed managed, by military men. The Central Intelligence Agency, brought into being by the new law, was placed under a military man, Admiral Roscoe Hillenkoetter. Military men headed American diplomatic missions in four countries, General Walter Bedell Smith, Eisenhower's wartime chief of staff, in the most sensitive post of all, the ambassadorship to the Soviet Union.

Although the new law explicitly forbade creation of a General Staff under a single military commander on the Prussian model, the Chairman of the Joint Chiefs was soon given voice in the National Security Council, the small group of high presidential advisers set up at the peak of the new edifice. As Samuel Huntington wrote a decade later: "Military men and institutions acquired an authority and influence far surpassing that ever previously possessed by the military profession on the American scene."[38] To this should be added that, insofar as the business of the National Security Council was determination of the posture and actions of the United States in relation to its interests in the world, the establishment of this body tended to give the Secretary of Defense a position practically coequal with that of the Secretary of State in the shaping of foreign policy.

The business of the National Security Council was precisely the nation's security, and at its first meetings in early 1948 President Truman was urged by the Secretaries of State and Defense, both men of the Pentagon, that the tide of demobilization must be reversed in America. "We are playing with fire while we have nothing with which to put it out," warned General Marshall. Forrestal argued insistently for a bigger military budget. Profoundly disquieting to the chief members of the National Security Council was the sudden, midnight overthrow of democratic government in Czechoslovakia, and shortly thereafter came the cable from General Clay, facing the Russians in Berlin, that he now sensed that war might be near.[39]

At this new crisis in the Cold War, Marshall urged revival of the plans for instituting universal military training that had been waved aside at the end of the Second World War. Universal military training was a permanent program similar to that of Switzerland and other European countries. Under this system every fit man would undergo six months' training when he attained the age of eighteen, and it was backed by members of a presidential Advisory Commission who argued that such a program was the only way for a democratic society to maintain a state of preparedness. For Americans to adopt universal military training at this hour, said Marshall, would be an act of dedication,

> . . . clear evidence to the world that we do not propose to abdicate our responsibilities in Europe or anywhere else in combatting the rising and spreading tide of Communism.

Truman was persuaded. But when he proposed to deliver his appeal to the country at a St. Patrick's Day dinner in New York City, Marshall thought this unsuitable. He urged the President instead to go before a joint session of Congress to underline the solemnity of his message. In Congress as well as in the Administration, talk of war abounded. When, therefore, Truman took the rostrum on March 17, 1948, expectations were quite as great as when a year before he went before the Congress to proclaim the Truman Doctrine.[40]

This time Harry Truman did not need Senator Vandenberg to tell him to "scare hell out of the American people." In one of the fiercest addresses ever delivered by a President, Truman identified the enemy in his opening words:

> The Soviet Union and its agents have destroyed the independence and democratic character of a whole series of nations in Eastern and Central Europe. It is this ruthless course of action and the clear design to extend it to the remaining free nations of Europe that have brought the critical situation in Europe today.
>
> The tragic death of Czechoslovakia has sent a shock through the civilized world. Now pressure is being brought to bear on Finland to the hazard of the entire Scandinavian peninsula. Greece is under direct military attack from the rebels actively supported by her Communist-dominated neighbors. In Italy a determined and aggressive effort is being made by a Communist party to take over control of the country. The methods vary but the pattern is clear.

Such a sinister design must be opposed, said Truman. "The will for peace must be backed by the strength for peace." Thereupon he called upon Congress as quickly as possible to enact Universal Military Training for all Americans. And to revive the draft.[41]

"An American Legion speech," exulted National Legion Commander Edward F. Neil. "Undoubtedly the strongest speech ever made by a President of the United States against another country with whom we are at peace." Up shot the stock market by five points, the biggest rise in two years. "The only answer left," said *Time*. "A direct threat of war," cried the *Christian Century*. "Stalin's march across Europe parallels in every detail Hitler's brutal strategy in 1938-39," said the Catholic weekly *America* in an approving editorial. The Moscow *Literary Gazette* scoffed at Truman's "hysterical screams." But in Berlin the following day Marshal Sokolovsky walked out of the Allied Control Council meeting—the beginning of Russia's military challenge for Berlin.[42]

Congress, speeding the Marshall Plan to quick passage after Truman's appeal, heard a long series of distinguished witnesses testify for the proposed conscription measure. Elder statesman Henry Stimson raised his respected voice for coercion as the only way to save the United States from the condition of military unpreparedness in which it found itself just before the Second World War. Justice Owen J. Roberts, who had led the inquiry into Pearl Harbor, testified that universal military training might have averted such a disaster. Dwight Eisenhower called UMT the only "insurance against extinction."[43]

To rouse opinion to the urgency for adopting coercion to build up the country's armed forces, military men for the first time drew pictures for Congress and the public of what the Third World War would be like. In the first five hours of attack, said Lt. General Leslie Groves, director of the Manhattan Project, 40,000,000 Americans would be killed. What the country faced, said Lt. General Raymond S. MacLean, chief of the division for UMT of the Joint Chiefs of Staff, was "lightning" war. Destruction might arrive in the form of mass air assaults over the North Pole, said Lt. General Carl Spaatz, chief of the Air Force. "The enemy would try to eliminate the United States at the outset," testified Lieut. J. Lawton Collins, deputy chief of staff. "We would have chaos . . . civil disorder and sabotage." Airborne troops would drop on the countryside, new types of submarines would surface and bombard the coastal cities.[44]

Despite the big campaign Congress rejected "universal training," as Truman preferred to call it, out of hand. But under the mounting crisis of Cold War, Selective Service was reinstated as an emergency measure limited to two years' duration. Even so, proponents such as Senator J. Chandler Gurney, Republican of South Dakota, found themselves assuring colleagues that they did "not permanently wish to saddle a selective service system on the youth of our nation." "What we propose," said Representative Leory Johnson, Republican of California,

> is, under ordinary circumstances, contrary to our traditions—it is contrary to our democratic way of life. [But] we are living in a world of fear, of chaos. . . . You cannot have liberty unless you have security. This bill will bring about world security. . . .[45]

Within two years of the March crisis and the enactment of the peacetime draft in June, 1948, America found itself embroiled in the "police action" that came to be known as the Korean War. This was a new and bigger crisis of the Cold War: a new military manpower law was put through.

In the Korean crisis, the necessity of a large standing army, even in peacetime, ceased virtually to be questioned. "True peace," said Congressman Melvin Price, Republican of Illinois, "is something living generations may dream about and remember, but may never know again." In this mood Senator Edward Martin, Republican of Pennsylvania, told his colleagues: "America must move forward with the atomic bomb in one hand and the cross in the other." "There is nothing controversial about selective service," intoned Senator Edwin Johnson, Democrat of Colorado. It is "an equitable and democratic manner of mobilizing our manpower."

The rhetoric of traditional voluntarism, in short, had all but vanished. What was left of it rang with lamentation, but not with contrition:

the fault was not America's but that of Russia, an "implacable adversary" that forced the atom-carrying, cross-bearing democracy to distasteful lengths. Said Representative Edmund Radwan, Republican of New York:

> Of course the idea of compulsion is distasteful. There is no moral satisfaction that by law we shall compel the youth of our land to learn how to kill as well as to keep from being killed. There is no moral satisfaction that for the first time in our history we must resort to compulsory conscription, but we do not live in a world of our own choice, of our own comfort. We are faced today with an implacable adversary who does not and will not understand our honorable intentions unless these intentions are backed by unquestionable might.[46]

The new law bore the title: "Universal Military Training and Service Act of 1951." But that did not mean that the proponents had got their way at last. Part of the law spelled out all the details of the UMT program that Stimson, Grenville Clark and Julius Ochs Adler and others had advocated ever since they opened their demonstration citizens'-army camp at Plattsburgh, New York in 1917 and 1940. These men, former Bull Moose Republicans, had imbibed deeply of the "strenuous life" ideals of Theodore Roosevelt and the martial ideas of his old shooting companion, Dr. Leonard Wood. A Harvard Medical School graduate who left his post as President McKinley's White House physician to help organize the Rough Riders in the Spanish-American War, Wood went on to serve as military governor of Cuba and the Philippines. General Wood favored a citizen army over a professional one: in 1915, with the enthusiastic support of Stimson, Clark and Adler, he founded a summer training camp for businessmen at Plattsburgh, New York, to demonstrate the benefits of fulfilling the "military obligation of citizenship." Stimson had just finished delivering a plea to Yale alumni for a new generation of Plattsburghers in 1940 when FDR telephoned him in New Haven to serve again as Secretary of War. But for the behind-the-scenes work of corporation lawyer Grenville Clark, it has been said, there might have been no draft law in 1940. Major Julius Ochs Adler, part owner of *The New York Times,* and Judge Robert Patterson, Stimson's top aide and successor at the War Department, also crusaded for UMT in peace and war. There was something of the boy scout about these men. Stimson regretted all his life that the Spanish-American War "caught me napping"—he volunteered too late to see action in Cuba. He sternly barred his house to all divorced persons. With TR and Elihu Root, he belonged to the Boone and Crockett Club, a society of New York City bear-hunters.[47]

But the part of the law establishing universal military training remained a dead letter. Congress declined to authorize funds for it. UMT in the words of Lt. General Lewis B. Hershey, Selective Service Director since 1939, "has not been put into effect because public opinion has not accepted it, as it has accepted Selective Service." By terms of the new law, the draft age was lowered from nineteen to eighteen, the term of active service was lengthened from twenty-one months to two years, and the time of active and reserve service was stretched to eight years in all.[48]

What made Selective Service supportable to public opinion and preferable to Congress was precisely that it was selective, and some people said that the callups for the Korean War were so selective as to amount to a national scandal. Among the 5,720,000 Americans summoned to service in the Korean "police action" were between 600,000 and 700,000 veterans of the Second World War. Yet through the variances made possible by reason of student deferments, job classifications, physical disabilities and others exemptions subject to local administrative determinations, some 1,600,000 qualified younger men of draft age were not called.[49]

After the end of the Korean War, General Hershey's sensitivity to opinion transmitted through Congress kept the draft calls low. But the "temporary" system kept being extended without change. At the same time most legislators remained dead set against spending the sums necessary to make a military career attractive, leading John Kenneth Galbraith to say: "The draft survives principally as a device by which we use compulsion to get young men to serve at less than the market rate of pay." In such terms voluntarism seemed banished to the dustbin of history, and it was possible for Richard Russell, Democrat of Georgia, during a brief debate on extending the law in 1955 to say: "The regular draft is the keystone of the arch of our national defense." So far had the nation moved in a few Cold War years.

The end was not yet, however. Several of the crises of the Eisenhower and Kennedy years were met by calling Reservists to active duty, and once again there were many complaints about the inequities of the sacrifices made. In the Berlin crisis of 1960, some 150,000 Reservists were called, at least a third of whom had served active duty stints whereas hundreds of thousands of others had not served and were not called. Then and later, college student deferments remained the most glaring of all the inequities of the draft. One college professor who had served two years as a draftee was called back for emergency duty as a radio operator. He was not even allowed to delay until the end of the school year, "although," he pointed out wryly, "most of my students were deferred in order to attend my classes."[50]

By the time of the 1951 law, however, the draft had become an integral part of the enormous military structure being reared among the ever-mounting urgencies of the Cold War. Senior congressional commit-teemen like Senator Russell, university adminstrators, employers, trade union leaders and 4,000 local draft boards increasingly shared with the military a vested interest in resisting change. However unequally it bore down on some of the young they belonged to a silenced generation. The system was more than serviceable to the military establishment: the basic policies of procuring manpower for the military came to be shaped more and more round the so-called Selective Service System.

This was swiftly made plain when the Kennedy administration came into office. Its new strategy of "flexible response" emphasized the need to develop conventional military forces and thereby reduce dependence on nuclear weapons. That took men. As Secretary of Defense Robert McNamara set out to build a military force capable of fighting local wars in Asia, the draftee achieved the unsought distinction of being America's indispensable man for war.

Volunteers, the military had long been convinced, could never pro-vide the numbers of men required. Military technology, on the other hand, was advancing at such a fearsome clip that only those most recently trained could adequately perform the functions of a modern soldier. The more heavily the Adminstration became committed to "flexible re-sponse," and the more swiftly the cost of this infinitely expensive new policy shot up, the greater became McNamara's disinclination to entrust his ever more complex "weapons-systems" to weekend Reservists and middle-aged National Guardsmen. The draftee, by contrast, was the Ar-my's man for two uninterrupted years, and for longer if he "extended," that is, volunteered to stay on for another three-year hitch. It took six months to a year to give him basic and advanced technical training in the weaponry of modern war, but after that he was ready for a full twelve months with an operational outfit, usually Army and increasingly infantry, usually overseas and increasingly in Asia. The draftee, in short, was so much more trainable, serviceable and, it could almost be said, disposable, that in 1964 McNamara called for outright abandonment of the National Guard.[51]

Thus it came about that when the United States became involved in Vietnam much of the backbone of the conventional forces that the Pentagon had trained up for the job was provided by the American draftee. Even the British, when they ruled most imperiously over palm and pine, never conscripted their citizens to serve overseas in time of peace. Even the Boer War of 1898, the climactic campaign of British colonial conquest, was fought only by professionals and volunteers. But the United States proceeded to do in the 1960s what the British Empire in its prime never thought to do. By a series of unprogrammed decisions beginning all the way back in the National Security Act of 1948, the United States found itself after 1965 fighting a war in Vietnam for which the Boer War seems an unwitting but not unfitting precedent—and fighting this war with a largely conscript army.[52]

The results of carrying Cold War policies to such an extreme were themselves extreme. For a long time the fact that the Selective Service System permitted so many exemptions and deferments had been building up to an attitude among the young of cynicism and contempt for its workings. Barely half of those registered ever served. By the 1960s most of those who were inducted under the system considered thmselves"suckers," and so did the estimated four in ten who volunteered for other forms of military service under stimulus of a prospective draft call. Then around the middle of the 1960s young Americans began to revolt against the draft. College, with its automatic student deferments, had always been a privileged sanctuary for middle-class sons. Now, when Washington was going to great lengths to avoid calling reservists to active duty, the sons of the working class who had always rallied to the Reserve and National Guard outfits, began to look upon their units as privileged sanctuaries too.[53] Large numbers of young people burned their draft cards. Some invaded Selective Service offices and poured blood on draft records. Many openly defied the Army authorities, and took part in demonstrations against Army induction centers. An estimated 30,000 fled to Canada, thousands more to Sweden and other countries. Unquestionably resistance to the draft played a large part in the student demonstrations that closed 130 universities in the spring of 1970.[54]

As this resistance mounted, the tactics of the young tended to move from evasion to defiance. Conscientious objectors in the past had been few in number (before 1962, the proportion was 1 in 600 registrants), and had given only religious scruples as reason for refusing to serve. But between 1966 and 1969 the number of cases filed by federal attorneys against resisters to the Selective Security Act shot up 600 percent, and after the Supreme Court upheld a young man's right to plead moral and philosophical objections to war, local draft boards had to wrestle with many more such cases. Draft counseling centers soon outnumbered draft boards in large cities. Meanwhile, according to Curtis Tarr, Selective Service Director, in 1970 more than seventy percent of those called were beating the draft on physical, mental and other grounds in the nation's more affluent areas, and among those inducted the Army was reporting some 30,000 deserters and 160,000 absent without leave by late 1969.[55]

By this time it was fully apparent that the younger generation was to be silenced no longer. But the tensions so long built up and suppressed through the Cold War years now burst out in generational conflicts of all sorts—over the abuse of the natural environment, over materialism in the consumer society, over sex, over religion. On no question was the conflict stormier than between those now rebelling at the draft and the older people who had been unconcerned with and unsympathetic to youth so long as they were kept off the job market and out of competition with themselves. "How many roads must a man walk down before you call him a man?" sang Bob Dylan.[56] By this time a large proportion of the young had come to feel that the draft was being used by their elders not only to deprive them of their fundamental choice about how their life was to be spent, but also to send them overseas to kill or be killed. As the prospective draftee now saw his predicament, Brooklyn College Professor Edgar Z. Friedenberg reported, "the adults who run things in the country propose to use him as an expendable object," and "the only value they attribute to him is the value he may possess in serving *their* purposes, which they assume to be the National Purpose."

In what appeared to be a generalized reaction against the insubordination of the young, Congress voted in 1968 to extend the Selective Service law virtually without change. The American Legion called on the government to send the draftees to Vietnam—and it was a fact that whereas one in seven in the armed forces was a draftee, one in three GIs killed in Vietnam was a draftee. "Forget the First Amendment," shouted Representative F. Edward Hebert, Democrat of Louisiana, urging the Justice Department to "clean up this rat-infested area" of youthful draft resistance. Student demonstrators responded by flaunting Viet Cong flags, and many state legislatures cut student scholarships in angry reprisal. In families, in schools, in churches, in the commonest of American social encounters, alienation of young and old was marked. Thus long after the Cold War passed, its unforeseen consequences persisted and exacerbated the strains of the national life. None was more painfully unsettling than the generational conflict let loose in the 1960s and 1970s by the insistence in 1948 that America adopt the military draft in time of peace.[57]

CHAPTER 5

A Communist China, a Communist Bomb

THE SEARCH FOR A SCAPEGOAT

T HE American people emerged from the era of Franklin Roosevelt carrying two consuming, obsessive fears that colored some of their most basic attitudes. One, already mentioned in Chapter 3, was the dread of another Great Depression. The second was the dread of another Pearl Harbor.

Every nation, it is said, is haunted by its own special nightmare, its own uniquely perceived danger, felt down in the very pit of the national stomach, known to the national memory from the bitterest and often oldest national experience. For the French it was a powerful state across the Rhine, for the English any challenger on the sea, for the Germans having to fight on two fronts at once. For the Russians, whether czars or commissars, it was the *cordon sanitaire* of hostile states that distant adversaries forever tried to throw around them to seal them off from the rest of the world. For the Americans, after their ocean-given security was so traumatically shattered in December, 1941, it was another Pearl Harbor sneak attack.

When in 1945 the country turned from victory to the sweet pastimes of peace Americans still remembered Pearl Harbor. They could never forget it. Almost without exception, people talked a good deal in the first postwar weeks about the atom bomb; many had it on their minds even more than they talked about it. Somewhere in the Tennessee Valley, they learned, in a couple of university labs in Chicago and New York, in the remote deserts of the Southwest, teams of scientists, engineers and technicians had labored in utmost secrecy to bring forth a terrible weapon of destruction. No question about it, as people understood from the government's carefully prepared statements, this was not just the biggest bomb in the biggest of all wars. It was a weapon of a wholly different order. It killed not only by the surpassing force of its detonation and shock waves, *it also killed by the rays it emitted.* The unbelievable mushroom burst it made was somehow not an explosion but an implosion, its obliterating light was somehow the same light as the light of the sun. It harnessed the power of the universe, it was said, and so prodigiously, the newspapers recounted, that its makers could not be sure until they first tested it whether their device might start a "chain reaction" and blow up the world. The harness held, and when reporters looked up Otto Hahn, the German physicist whose 1939 experiment with uranium had shown that it might conceivably be done, he told them that he marveled at the fantastic ingenuity of the Americans who could bring the reaction under control.[1]

Most fabulous of all was being told that Dr. Albert Einstein was at the bottom of it all. The utterly incomprehensible and manifestly unwordly ideas about relativity and curved space of this dreamy-eyed Jewish refugee genius at Princeton had been the subject of good-natured and condescending bafflement for Sunday-supplement readers for years. Now grown-ups laboriously spelled their way through chart-filled newspaper and magazine explanations. The other-wordly Dr. Einstein, it seemed, had written the legend for the atomic age back in 1905 in a single reductive equation that old and young would henceforth unblinkingly recite: $E = mc^2$.

Devised just in time, the appalling new weapon had ended the war —and it was America's. Though many outsiders had helped in the making, it was America's. Should not something be done to control it through some international agreement now that the war was over? The general idea got no further than the first primitive reflex of greed and terror: the unkeepable secret of the bomb should be kept.

On September 11, 1945, Henry Stimson, who had been Taft's Secretary of War and Hoover's Secretary of State before serving as Roosevelt's Secretary of War from 1940 to 1945, relinquished his office at the age of seventy-nine. That same day he wrote this word of advice to President Truman:

> Relations [of mutual trust and confidence] may be perhaps irretrievably embittered by the way in which we approach the solution of the bomb

with Russia. For if we . . . merely continue to negotiate with them, having this weapon rather ostentatiously on the hip, their suspicions and their distrust of our purposes will increase. My idea of an approach to the Soviets would be a direct proposal after discussion with the British (action of any international group of nations would not in my opinion be taken seriously by the Soviets): to control and limit the use of the atomic bomb as an instrument of war.[2]

This was not done; the primitive reflex prevailed.

"Now more than ever," said President Truman voicing the prevailing mood, it was "necessary to guard and maintain the secrecy of the bomb." Other ways to postwar security—the Rooseveltian way of cooperation with Russia, Stimson's way of compromise by direct negotiation—were abruptly rejected. Atomic controls of a general sort were sought through the United Nations. These were for years the subject of endless palaver, of harmless platitudinizing and aggrieved vituperation, with only negative results. But the ultimate atom-bomb secret—"the know-how of putting it together," as President Truman phrased it in a speech in October, 1945, at the county fair at Carruthersville—that must never be shared with the Russians. To reporters the next day he added the second and gratuitous judgment:

I don't think it would do any good to let them in on the know-how because I don't think they could do it, anyway.[3]

Security, then, was the name of America's game after the Second World War. The word was on every high official's lips, on every plain citizen's mind. The very Department of War was renamed the Department of Defense. The supreme seat of government decision became the National Security Council. And the foundation of national security became the knowledge, the uneasy knowledge, that America alone possessed the A-bomb.

Even more than in the days of Wilson and Roosevelt, it became necessary for America's security to keep the adversary as far away as possible. Weeks and weeks of congressional hearings in 1945 laid bare the scandalous negligence before the Japanese attack on Pearl Harbor; and God knew, the Republicans cried, that the same Democrats were still in office and showing nothing like the required alertness against new perils. In such times there were those who said that the atomic weapons, if secretly made by an enemy, could be carried into the country by suitcase. The press printed stories of how a single bomb exploded in the waters of San Francisco or New York harbor could not only pulverize the city but by poisoning the waters with radioactivity render the place almost forever uninhabitable. In such terms an enemy would not even need an air force: just a few infiltrators might make their way ashore and destroy the vitals of the nation.

Early in 1946, just before Winston Churchill's momentous speech at Fulton, a dozen Canadian Communist party leaders and others were convicted in Ottawa of operating a wartime Russian espionage ring. The Canadian Royal Commission's scrupulously objective report showed many indications that the Russians had been looking for atomic intelligence. American newspapers played up the atom-spying angle. They also reported jarring tales of America's own Communists. Amid rowdy scenes Kansas-born Earl Browder, longtime chief of the tiny party,[4] was expelled for having followed a line too friendly to the American war effort. Louis Budenz, having quit as editor of the *Daily Worker* and joined the Catholic Church, went on the air in Detroit with sensational charges. Communist parties were "not political parties at all," he asserted. They were conspiracies that gave their loyalty first and last to Russia. So saying, he proceeded to identify a German emigré, Gerhard Eisler, as the Russian secret agent who gave American Communists their orders.[5]

A few days later, the Republicans captured both houses of Congress in the first postwar elections. President Truman read the returns and swung right. Not only did he launch a militantly anti-Communist foreign policy; domestically one of his first acts after the election was to name a special committee on security. On the basis of its report he proceeded to appoint a Loyalty Board with powers to check into the life and thoughts of every government employee. Thus it was Truman who first began "ferreting out" Communists in the United States government, and it was his attorney general, Tom Clark, who ran the show from the first blacklisting of "subversive" organizations in 1946 to the launching of the loyalty-oath drive that soon had milkmen, wrestlers and beauticians swearing fealty to the United States government.

If they were not the intellectual authors of the shrill and sinister passage of political history that Richard Hofstadter called "the Grand Inquisition of the 1950's," Truman and his attorneys general had at least started it. Their program, which grew with each new turn of the Cold War, both spread fear and responded to it amid the public pilloryings staged by the Republican heresy-hunters in Congress. Thus creation of the Temporary Commission on Loyalty was followed in March, 1947 by Executive Order 9835. This presidential directive laid down a program that incorporated all the major premises of the demagogic witch-hunters of the next six years—the existence of a Communist threat inside America, the likelihood that employes could subvert policy as well as pass secrets, the supposition that the menace could be better combatted by a security program than by counterespionage. The Truman plan was to "screen" all federal employes for Communist ties by prying into the privacy of their minds and consciences. It was a security program concerned with "loyalty"—ideological purity. "That," said Truman, "should take the Communist smear off the Democratic party."[6]

During the next few years under Executive Order 9835, some six million Americans faced Truman's inquisitors. Every present and prospective federal employe and every member of the armed forces was compelled under oath to declare whether he now or at any earlier time harbored any thoughts that could be construed as disloyal to the United States government. Each was compelled to disclose any and all memberships he held then or previously in societies or parties or organizations, and the answers were then scrutinized alongside the list of eighty organizations certified by the Attorney General as subversive, that is, controlled directly, or indirectly as "fronts," by the Communist party. That was not all. The individual was also directed to provide under oath the same detailed information about members of his family. The truth of any and all declarations was then checked by inquisitors who spoke to neighbors, coworkers or others whose comments, rich in hearsay, were duly entered in the subject's dossier.

In the years after 1947, taking account of the turnover in jobs, some nine to thirteen million Americans appear to have been subjected to the Grand Inquisition. The number of fulltime federal investigators required to conduct the inquisitorial tasks was 20,000, in addition to whom a great many others engaged in surveillance activities but did not work directly for government agencies. It may well be that a fair proportion of the American population was engaged at this time in watching or being watched. There can be little doubt that the security investigations of the Cold War period were felt widely and deeply throughout the American society. On the calculation that there were about 40,000,000 families in the early 1950s, each with an average of two to three adult members, it seems likely that one in four American famiilies knew at first hand the experience of the Grand Inquisition, and that most families must have known somebody who had been through the experience. Out of this number, an estimated 11,500 government and private employes were finally dismissed, denied clearance and otherwise excluded from jobs.[7]

The Republicans, assuming command of Congress in early 1947, took it from there. Amid the most extravagant publicity they launched a whole series of congressional "security probes" into the ideological purity not only of government employes but of people from the movies, the press, the professions and other sectors of society. For sheer recklessness and publicity-mongering mendacity, the House Committee on Un-American Activities under J. Parnell Thomas of New Jersey led the pack. Surrounded by ex-Communist listmakers and ex-FBI gumshoes, Thomas led expeditions to expose movie stars like Charlie Chaplin and writers like Howard Fast for subverting Hollywood; to pillory prominent citizens like President Frank Graham of the University of North Carolina for lending their names to Communist-backed causes; to hound scientists like Dr. Edward U. Condon of the U.S. Bureau of Standards for having opposed his efforts to bring the new Atomic Energy Commission under military rule.

A serious-faced young California Republican with an intensely lawyerlike way about him brought some new purposefulness to the committee's scatter-shot antics. Richard Nixon's maiden speech in Congress, though taking liberties with the facts to tie Eisler to the Canadian spy ring, succeeded in winning a citation against the evasive Eisler for contempt of Congress. Nixon also brought in a bill "to curb or control the Communist party" by compelling it and its front-organizations to register with the attorney general. To advance his cause Nixon outdid the President himself in his expressions of alarm at the Communist coup in Czechoslovakia. What happened in Prague could happen in America, he cried, unless the country took the security measures his bill called for. "The security of this nation," thundered another House debater, "demands that all Communists within our borders be rendered politically and economically impotent." In the rising excitement, the Truman administration brought the eleven top American Communists to trial in 1947 for conspiring to overthrow the government.[8]

Early that summer congressional investigators happened upon a Vassar graduate named Elizabeth Bentley. Miss Bentley had been the paramour of a Russian agent in wartime Washington. "Beautiful Blonde Spy Queen," screeched the *New York World-Telegram* when the investigators slipped it the story in advance. The House Committee on Un-American Activities, inviting her to repeat her lurid tales, was told that a certain Whittaker Chambers had been giving evidence corroborating her stories to the grand jury that had indicated the Communist leaders in New York. Escorted by a pack of reporters and photographers, the committee brought in Chambers, a senior editor of *Time* magazine.

To Americans habituated to the old, often prejudiced hostility against socialism and communism that had been so widespread in the 1920s and was still a mainstay of the McCormick-Hearst press and the Republican opposition through the Roosevelt years, Chambers was a devastatingly new kind of anti-Communist. A figure out of the underworld of ideological warfare ("I went to school to Lenin," he said),

Chambers was an ex-Communist intellectual who needed a new ideology to explain and reliably foretell the course of history as Marxism no longer did. For him as for such European ex-Communist ideologues as Arthur Koestler and Franz Borkenau, Marxism was "the God That Failed," and like them he was looking for a new one. From his viewpoint the petty, middle-class differentiations of Republicans and Democrats, fought out with tolerant regard for the right to hold differing opinions, were not ludicrously inadequate, they were tragically wrong. Once, even while America and Russia fought as allies, Chambers had edited a magazine essay on what happened to well-meaning people who got in the path of "international Communism." He had pictured the pitiful family of the czar, huddled in abject confinement before their murder by the Bolsheviks —"ghosts on a roof." To deliver the world from monolithic Communism ruled by Stalin from Moscow and from the fatal danger of the slightest gesture of reconciliation with it, a far more comprehensive anti-Communist doctrine must be shaped and inculcated.[9]

A man of literary gifts, who wrote plays and short stories and had translated modern German classics, Chambers looked and talked like a witness out of a Dostoevski novel. Born in Philadelphia the son of a newspaper artist, he grew up moody and morose in Brooklyn. His only brother committed suicide. At Columbia, where he joined the Communist party, he was expelled for stealing books. Later he gravitated to the secret side of Communist party life—the furtive meetings, secret hideaways, phony names. In 1938, disillusioned at last, he broke with the party and, though fearful that Stalin would have him murdered, got a job with *Time* magazine. Now a short and rather fat man in his forties, with heavy-lidded eyes, he felt called upon by history to bear witness and rouse the nation against international Communism and all its devilishly subversive works and ways. In low, portentous tones Chambers testified:

> I served in the Communist underground, chiefly in Washington, D.C. I knew at its top level a group of seven or so men. One member of the group was Alger Hiss who, as a member of the State Department, helped to organize the United Nations at San Francisco and was in the United States delegation at the Yalta conference.
>
> The original purpose of this apparatus was the Communist infiltration of the American government, but espionage was certainly one of its original objectives. Let no one be surprised at this statement. Disloyalty is a matter of principle with every member of the Communist party.[10]

Chambers's witness indeed widened the Cold War. It was also dynamite in American politics. Nixon and his fellow committeemen could hardly contain themselves. The man Chambers had boldly named was no obscure clerk in the Commerce Department. Hiss was a high New Dealer who had been pictured prominently at international conferences and had been a party to FDR's "giveaway" to the Russians at Yalta. Chambers readily said he had met Hiss in 1934, when Hiss was a young investigator for Senator Nye's Munitions Committee inquiry, and had known him as a fellow Communist until 1938. At that point Chambers had broken with the party and vainly tried to get Hiss to. "He cried when I left," said Chambers.

Though Chambers had much else to say, it was the name of Alger Hiss on which the committee fixed its attention. Why, members wanted to know, was Chambers so positive that Hiss was a Communist?

> NIXON: Do you have any evidence?
> CHAMBERS: Nothing beyond the fact that he submitted himself for the two or three years that I knew him as a dedicated and disciplined Communist. I collected his dues.[11]

Alger Hiss, who had left the government in 1946 to become president of the Carnegie Endowment for International Peace in New York, promptly issued a denial of Chambers' charges and asked the committee for an opportunity to deny them under oath. At forty-four, the lean and handsome Hiss was in every way, as the *New York Herald Tribune's* Washington correspondent Bert Andrews wrote, "a young man on his way up." Member of an upper-class Baltimore family of socially impeccable background, he had graduated with highest marks from Johns Hopkins, gone to Harvard Law School, and done so well that he earned a coveted clerkship after graduation in 1929 with Supreme Court Justice Oliver Wendell Holmes himself.

After his service with the Nye committee, Hiss and a number of other recent law school graduates had been Young Turks in the legal department of the Agricultural Adjustment Administration during the earliest days of the New Deal. After a year or so they lost out to more conservative forces in one of the interdepartmental battles, and went their separate ways. Hiss became Assistant Solicitor General, then joined the State Department as aide to Francis Sayre, Assistant Secretary of State for Trade Agreements and son-in-law of Woodrow Wilson. Thereafter he rose within the State Department to high responsibilities in government. Toward the end he had been given the honor for his services of carrying the Charter of the United Nations from San Francisco to Washington, and then been practically handpicked by John Foster Dulles for the Carnegie Endowment presidency, a stepping stone no doubt to yet higher things in Washington. President Truman, at his press conference the day Hiss appeared before the committee, blasted its noisy probe into Communist activities as a "red herring" to distract the public from the Republican Congress' failure to act against inflation.

Hiss made an impressive witness, appearing forthright, clear-spoken, urbane. Of his accuser he said: "The name means absolutely nothing to me. So far as I know, I have never met him." Bitingly, he added: "I should like to have opportunity to do so." When the committee counsel showed him a photograph, Hiss said: "That's not an unusual-looking person. It might be anybody—it might even be the chairman of this committee." Representative Karl Mundt, presiding, reddened as the spectators laughed. When Hiss left, the committee went into a huddle. The majority were persuaded that Hiss had carried the day. "Let's wash our hands of the whole mess," said one. "We've been had," said another. "We've been ruined. The press will believe Hiss." Only Nixon persisted. He remembered that when Hiss had been asked whether he had ever seen Chambers he had answered: "The name means absolutely nothing to me. . . . " Thus under oath he had avoided a categorical statement that he did not know his accuser.

Nixon and one or two others went to New York to see Chambers secretly. Even if it might not be possible to prove that Hiss had been a Communist, it should be possible to prove that he and Chambers had known each other if Chambers could supply details of Hiss's private life in the years 1934 to 1938. Chambers proceeded to tell of the Hiss family nicknames, their homes, their furniture. He recalled that Hiss was a birdwatcher who had once seen a rare prothonotary warbler, so named for its resemblance to a purple-gowned English law court officer. He said that Hiss had turned over a 1929 car to a party member. He also mentioned what he had failed to mention at his first appearance—that Hiss had known him not as Whittaker Chambers, but as "Carl."

Armed with this ammunition, Nixon and the others met Hiss again in private. This time Hiss hedged more in his answers and, wary though he was, unknowingly confirmed many of the details which Chambers had provided. Midway through the sessions he gave the committee a name, George Crosley. This, he said, was the name of a magazine writer, a free-lancer who had hung around him at the Nye committee hearings. The name had not been brought to mind by the photographs of Chambers, he said, but by a newspaper report stating that Chambers had displayed considerable knowledge of the Hiss household. The committee interpreted this to mean that Hiss now realized that he could not get away with a flat denial. "To save time," Nixon suggested a confrontation.

This took place the very next day, in a private session held in Room

1400 of the Hotel Commodore in New York City. After Hiss was sworn in, Chambers entered. Nixon asked both to stand, then asked Hiss if he had ever known Chambers before. Hiss walked up to Chambers and asked to look at his teeth. Then he asked Chambers to keep talking. Still Hiss said he could not positively identify Chambers as "George Crosley." He began asking Chambers questions. After a few answers, Hiss broke in: "Mr. Chairman, I don't need to ask Whittaker Chambers any more questions. I am perfectly willing to identify this man as George Crosley." Chambers then made positive identification of Alger Hiss, whereupon Hiss walked up to him, shook his fist in his face and challenged him to repeat the charges "out of the presence of this committee" so that he could sue for libel. "I challenge you to do it, and I hope you do it damned quickly." A quarter of a century later, the evidence supports Chambers' comment that "Alger Hiss was acting from start to finish. "[12]

Two weeks later, just as the 1948 presidential campaign got under way, the committee staged the public confrontation in Washington before massed cameramen and reporters. Hiss testified for six hours, Chambers for three. In his best prosecuting-attorney manner Nixon pressed Hiss hard about details of his household in the 1930s that Chambers had provided. Hiss was extravagantly careful, prefacing some two hundred answers with "to the best of my recollection." It was lawyer against lawyer, Nixon trying to prove Hiss' guilt by association with Chambers, Hiss rebutting with a list of thirty-four such eminent associates as Byrnes, Dulles and Acheson to prove what Nixon termed innocence by association.

The grimmest drama, feral in intensity and now throat for throat, lay between Hiss and Chambers. Why had not Hiss simply acknowledged, as many other witnesses did, that he had a youthful brush with Communism back in the Depression but had long since left it behind? "Alger must still be a Communist," Chambers told friends. Chambers accepted Hiss's challenge and stated on *Meet the Press* that Alger Hiss was a Communist. In September Hiss sued him for libel in Baltimore.[13]

"One of these men is lying!" screamed the Washington *Daily News.* In the near-hysterical uproar that attended the hearings, it was impossible to get an answer. Few who followed the hearings and argued themselves hoarse over the dinner table those hot summer evenings seemed ready to make the simple judgments that in other times they made of other men.

On Hiss's side two different groups, impelled alike by seemingly uncontrollable passions, accepted what they saw as symbolic combat. Because Hiss chose to wrap gentility around himself and deny utterly that he had ever had truck with such a scruffy radical as Chambers, members of established America, impressive numbers of socialites and corporation executives who hated the New Deal, not to speak of Communism, fiercely defended the hyperrespectable image of Alger Hiss—Hiss the old-stock American, Hiss the sedate Episcopalian, Hiss the faultlessly correct State Department official—against what they saw as the image of his upstart accuser.

Liberals frothed with cocktail-party fury. Loudly contemptuous of the buffoonery of the Committee on Un-American Activities, they raged at the attempts made to use the accusations against Hiss as proof that the New Deal and the Rooseveltian legacy at the United Nations were tainted with treason. For old New Dealers it had been a lifetime's faith that the united forces of social amelioration, working and warring aginst the common foe, had saved America in the 1930s and the world in the 1940s. Now this progressive America was being torn apart by foreign and domestic strife, in danger of being ground to pieces in the shifting gears of international ideologies.

When the committee asked what motives he might have for trying to ruin Hiss, Chambers answered:

> We were close friends. But we got caught in the tragedy of history. Mr. Hiss represents the concealed enemy we are all fighting. I am testifying against him with remorse and pity. But in this moment of historic jeopardy in which this nation now stands, so help me God, I could not do otherwise.

Later, even more apocalyptically, Chambers wrote:

> The two irreconcilable faiths of our time came to grips in the persons of two conscious and resolute men. With dark certitude both knew, almost from the beginning, that the Great Case could end only in the destruction of one or the other contending figure; just as the history of our times . . . can end only in the destruction of one or both of the contending forces.[14]

The anti-Communism of the ex-Communists was to prevail in America, but for Chambers history saved the Dostoievskian denouement that he seemed almost to anticipate. On the evidence placed on the record at that point, it was far from certain that Chambers could make his word alone stand up in court against that of his adversary. Still, heartened by the support of Nixon and the Republicans, and buoyed up by the rising tide of anti-Communist sentiment, Chambers could look to the Republican election victory promised in all the polls. With Dewey in the White House and Republican anti-Communists taking over the Justice Department and long-suppressed FBI files, the balance must tip in Chambers's favor.

But the Red-scare frenzy that seized Washington had not yet caught up the country. In the century's most stunning upset, Truman won reelection. Chambers, at his Maryland farm, was despondent. Now it looked as if Hiss might win his libel suit and, in pretrial examinations in Baltimore, Hiss' lawyers aggressively challenged Chambers to provide evidence other than his own unsupported assertions. Chambers saw, as he wrote later, "I might well lose the suit."

Trapped and despairing, Chambers made the move that was to destroy not only Hiss but himself. He journeyed to New York to see his nephew, Nathan Levine. Together they went to the bathroom of the Levine apartment in Brooklyn and from a recess in a disused dumbwaiter shaft Chambers pulled out a dust-covered envelope that he had entrusted to Levine at the time he broke with the party eleven years before. In it were sixty-five typed pages, copies or summaries of State Department documents; three memos in the handwriting of Alger Hiss; a long memo in the handwriting of Harry Dexter White, an Assistant Secretary of State who had since died; two strips of developed microfilm and three cylinders of undeveloped microfilm.

The pile of papers and developed microfilm were turned in at Baltimore, where the lawyers took one horrified look and handed them over to the Justice Department. Chambers kept the three containers of microfilm—in case the Justice Department should yet suppress the papers. Amid a roar of publicity, Chambers led investigators for the Committee on Un-American Activities into his Maryland pumpkin patch, reached into a pumpkin that had been hollowed out and carefully put back in place, and pulled forth the three packs of microfilm. They proved to contain photographs of some fifty documents from the office of the Assistant Secretary for Trade Agreements dating from 1936 and 1937. Nixon, who was photographed hurrying back from a holiday in the Caribbean, charged on arrival in Washington that the government was trying to figure out a way to "place the blame for possession of these documents on Mr. Chambers."

The next day Hiss was indicted by the New York grand jury for perjury—the statute of limitations made it impossible to bring an indictment for espionage. His career in ruins, Hiss resigned from the Carnegie Endowment, and the publishers of *Time* hastily accepted Chambers' resignation. Hiss's lawyers, through two long and bitter trials (the first ended with a hung jury, eight-to-four for conviction), fought to prove that since Chambers had so completely changed his story after the election, all of his allegations against their client must alike be lies. In the end the documents from the dumbwaiter were incontrovertible and Hiss, found guilty, served the maximum five years in federal prison.[15]

By that time the anti-Communist doctrine of the ex-Communists and anti-Communists expanded into the official American ideology of the Cold War. From Truman and Forrestal to Johnson and Rusk, it animated all the "theories" in Washington. Founded upon an uncritical examination of lessons of the past, it shielded successive Administrations and their "problem-solvers" from the impact of changing reality through two decades. If the Cold Warriors believed in monolithic Communism, it was because Stalin was supposed to rule all Communist parties. Every reconciling gesture constituted a "second Munich" because they knew that Hitler's totalitarianism started world war after Munich. For the habit of the time, encouraged by such books as Hannah Arendt's *Origins of Totalitarianism*, was to equate German fascism with Russian Communism as "two essentially identical systems," and predict the conduct of the existing totalitarianism from the record of the vanquished one. Yet the dreaded totalitarianism of National Socialism had been defeated, and from captured documents and other testimony people now began to see what an inefficient system Nazism had really been. The totalitarianism of Soviet Communsim, having triumphed, loomed more monolithically menacing than ever. Professor Arendt, quoting copiously from such first-hand witnesses as the ex-Communist Victor Kravchenko's *I Chose Freedom* (1946), drew a picture of a "gigantic apparatus of terror" whose end was the "total domination of man."

These perceptions, once fixed, were not to be shaken. Russian propaganda ceaselessly reinforced them. Pertinent facts, such as Russian demobilization in the crucial years after 1945, and major developments, such as the radical split between Stalin and Mao Tse-tung's Communism, were simply ignored. America's leaders, armed with a "theory," needed no facts, no information.[16]

C H A N G E , many Americans would have boasted as the United States swung in a few postwar years from isolation to world leadership, was the all-American word. The official name for it was progress. Another was growth. Americans gloried in change as the life and breath of their country, as the ground of its greatness, the stuff of subduing frontiers, building skyscrapers, waging and winning two world wars. Change led on to the New World from the Old, to republics after kings, to democracy after feudalism and fascism.

As the leading principle of the free private enterprise system by which America achieved such wealth, change shaped the American way of life. Dynamically restless, Americans liked to change jobs, addresses, cars, spouses. If there was inconvenience and occasionally sacrifice in living for change, the torn-up streets, the closed textile mills, the pockets of unemployment added up to a small and momentary price paid for progressing from wool to synthetic fibers, metal to plastics, steam engines to diesels, pistons to jets. Much of the American sense of omnipotence after 1945 rested on the belief that change was not only good but manageably so: businessmen especially liked to talk about "the engineering of change."

For all who shared the faith that change was the American way 1949 was, as historian Eric Goldman called it, a "year of shocks." It was a disconcerting time also for a government that had just won reelection on an overall Cold War program that had kept the country prosperous and out of war for four years. The biggest of the shocks of 1949 were the loss of America's A-bomb monopoly and the loss of China to Communism. So great were the shocks that more than two decades later America had not got over them.

Early in 1948 the Air Force issued a report assuring the nation that it could expect to keep its A-bomb monopoly for at least four more years. But in Congress, where Republicans were looking for signs of Communist infiltration from Hollywood to Harvard, such assurances were received with suspicion. The Atomic Energy Commission, the civilian agency set up in 1946 to safeguard and develop the bomb, was an obvious target. Its chairman was David Lilienthal, former head of the Tenneseee Valley Authority and an ultra-New Dealer.

In May, 1949, when newspapers reported that thirty grams of uranium had disappeared from an AEC laboratory, Senator Bourke Hickenlooper, Republican of Iowa, charged Lilienthal with "incredible mismanagement," and demanded a congressional investigation. Though the missing uranium had already been found, a full-scale inquiry got under way. Members of the Joint Congressional Committee on Atomic Energy grilled Lilienthal about the AEC program for training young scientists. Under the program, panels of professors awarded the fellowships for university study. One young man so selected refused to say whether he had been a Communist. Rather than interfere, Lilienthal said stoutly, he would back the decision of the scholars. "Much too loose when it comes to national security," was Senator Vandenberg's verdict. "No one can make any sort of argument for educating young Communists at government expense—and least of all in atomic physics." Though cleared of Hickenlooper's scattershot charges, Lilienthal concluded that he would probably have to resign and went off to Martha's Vineyard to think about it.[17]

At this point the bad news arrived. Lilienthal, driving up to his cottage after a late party, saw a hatless, gesturing man by the gate. It was General James McCormack, the AEC's Director of Military Applications. Inside, Lilienthal lighted a kerosene lamp. "Then," said Lilienthal later, "he gave it to me—the feeling in the abdomen—here it is: what we'd feared ever since January 1, 1946, in our first meeting." Samplings made in Japan of particles carried in the air from Russia indicated that the Russians had exploded an atomic bomb.

Rushing back to Washington, Lilienthal looked up the experts. He found Oppenheimer, wartime chief of the atomic scientists and now chairman of the Scientific Advisory Commission, "frantic, drawn," Robert Bacher, the AEC's scientific member, "deeply worried." Then he spoke to President Truman, who thought "German scientists in Russia did it, probably." Three days later Presidential Press Secretary Charles Ross summoned reporters to his White House desk. "Close the doors," said Ross. "Nobody is leaving here until everybody has this statement." Then he passed out mimeographed sheets. A reporter read and whistled. In a moment all the reporters tore through the lobby, smashing the nose of a stuffed deer on their dash to the pressroom telephones. The President of the United States had announced: "We have evidence that within recent weeks an atomic explosion occurred in the USSR."[18]

With "things too near panic," as Lilienthal noted, Secretary Acheson announced soothingly that "the eventual development of this new force by other nations was to be expected." General Bradley, chairman of the joint chiefs of staff, said: "It calls for no change in our defense plans." But in Chicago Harold C. Urey, eminent Nobel Prize atomic researcher, said what many Americans felt. He was "flattened" by the announcement, he told a reporter. "There is only one thing worse than one nation having the atomic bomb—that's two nations having it." "We have been deluded," cried Republican leader Tom Dewey. "There has been treason in the State Department," said Senator Pat McCarran, Democrat of Nevada. "Laxity in safeguarding against Communist espionage has permitted what was once the secret of the atomic bomb to fall into the hands of America's only potential enemy," declared Senator Karl Mundt, Republican of South Dakota. "The Russian achievement in advance of any foreseeable timetable evidences obvious leaks of information," said Senator Styles Bridges, Republican of New Hampshire. Senator Alexander Wiley, Republican of Wisconsin, urged the President to get key government personnel out of Washington as soon as possible. "We would be a sucker for a solar-plexus atomic blow which could knock our country out a few months before an atomic war starts," he said.[19]

At the first meeting of the AEC commissioners after the President's announcement, Lewis Strauss of the Republican minority proposed: "We should now make an intensive effort to get ahead with the Super"— meaning the hydrogren bomb. Lilienthal demurred. Then on November 1 Senator Edwin (Big Ed) Johnson, Democrat of Colorado, and a member of the Joint Congressional Committee on Atomic Energy, blew the situation wide open. On a nationwide *Meet the Press* broadcast he blurted what he called the "top secret" fact that the United States was at work on a superbomb that might develop "1000 times" the power of the Nagasaki bomb.

Thereafter the pressure built up fast. The probability of developing a workable H-bomb, dismissed in 1945 as out of the question, had risen by 1949 to fifty-fifty. But men like Robert Oppenheimer and James Conant, almost all of the scientific experts who had developed the bomb and advised the civilian AEC commissioners, thought the first bomb had brought such evil on the world ("We built one Frankenstein," exclaimed an advisory committee member.) that they felt only distaste for the idea of adding the superhorror of thermonuclear weapons. Defense Secretary Louis Johnson was all for launching a crash program. Lilienthal, leaving office, pleaded for a review first. Acheson, sure that "delaying research would not delay Soviet research," proposed to start on the H-bomb and start the strategic review too. On January 30, 1950, President Truman made the fateful decision—to go ahead with the "Super," and to "undertake a reexamination of our objectives."[20]

I F   T H E   end of its A-bomb monopoly shook America's sense of omnipotence, the fall of China to the Communists late in 1949, bursting with delayed suddenness on the American consciousness, baffled and frightened the nation. John Foster Dulles called the establishment of Communist government in China "the worst defeat the United States has suffered in its history." Senator Taft said that the State Department "with its pro-Communist Allies" had been following a plan for liquidating Chiang Kai-shek's forces in favor of the Communists. The Young Republican Federation charged that the United States government had "actually aided" the Communists to gain power. General MacArthur said that the United States ought to have backed Chiang "though he were the devil incarnate." Governor Dewey, the Republican leader, said the government had "allowed 400 million more in China to be conquered by Soviet agents," and now stood to "lose" all Asia. People kept repeating that phrase—the "loss" of China. That said China was America's to lose. Why?

When Winston Churchill returned from his early Second World

War consultations in Washington, he told his colleagues in London: "I learned one thing in Washington: *China!*" Making proper allowance for exaggeration, the fact is that a certain runaway quality in America's conception of itself entered into what Americans thought about China. What some scholars have called the American aberration about China was not simply a momentary flareup of postwar American politics. From the time America came to consciousness of itself in the eighteenth and nineteenth centuries, it knew itself as the vanguard, continuator and conquering embodiment of the West. Westward lay the course of empire, and America was its frontier. Was not the West the future? By an impulse as old as "civilization," meaning white civilization, from Greek and Phoenician colonizers to the Europeans exploring and dividing the New World, west was the way.

Americans grew up knowing that they *were* the Northwest Passage to Asia, that all lying to their west was, by manifest destiny, "ours to engross." They hacked out the Central National Road, then the transcontinental railroad, not only to gird America's East and West but also to bring America nearer to the marts of China. "The flight of the eagle is toward the West," trumpted the *New York Herald* in 1845. For the successive governments of nineteenth century America, the goal was the Pacific and the object was the commercial empire beyond. The gorgeous bay of San Francisco was seen as the golden gate to trade between Pacific America and Asia, the one possessing gold and cornucopias of food, the other, traditionally rich in luxurious commodities.

Whatever Commodore Perry's success in breaking down the isolation of Japan, it was Secretary of State John Hay's proclamation of the Open Door to China in 1901 that represented the ultimate expression of the American expansive spirit. In tones of moral exaltation, Hay's doctrine upheld poor, put-upon China's "unity and administrative integrity" against the territorial designs of the wicked imperialists in Europe and Japan. In plainer terms, it was America's passport for letting itself into twentieth century China. The Open Door was, as Walter Lippmann said, America's quintessential foreign policy, "almost a policy for the export of the American way of life." As such it was enough to give China an excessively favored spot in the landscape of American regard.

Though American businessmen talked long and loudly about "400 million customers," British and Japanese stakes in China remained far larger. And though American missionaries seem not to have had much influence on China, they certainly had a lot of influence on America, where two of the first presidents of the Chinese republic were approvingly identified as Christian converts and where Generalissimo Chiang Kai-shek's handsome wife, educated at mission schools and at Wellesley, was a frequent and enthusiastically welcomed visitor.

But the truth was that the American policy for the first four decades of the century contained two contradictory elements—the principle of the Open Door so loftily affirmed on the one hand, and the persistent refusal to go to China's aid with military force on the other. American pronouncements gave the impression that the United States had important stakes in China; but the concrete acts of American governments down to Pearl Harbor betrayed a low estimate of American interests in China. Republican Administrations, from the first Roosevelt and Taft to Harding, Coolidge and Hoover, all professed concern for the "unity and administrative integrity" of China, but all clung tenaciously to the hope that somehow, even when the Japanese detached Manchuria by force in the 1930s, American interests and purposes in China could be promoted without use of American force. Down to Cold War times Democratic Administrations, assigning top priority to Europe in two successive world wars, gave less attention to China than the Republicans. (Even Franklin Roosevelt's belated pressure against Japan, which had its outcome at Pearl Harbor, was applied after the Japanese had seized the entire Chinese coast and destroyed the cream of Chiang Kai-shek's armies, and was exerted primarily to stay Japan's further expansion southward to pick up French, British and Dutch possessions made vulnerable to aggression by events in Europe.)[21]

From the time of John Hay, the Republicans were America's China party, and it was no accident that after first trying to get the China-born Republican publisher Henry Luce for the job, Roosevelt in 1944 made General Patrick Hurley, Hoover's Secretary of War, his special emissary to China. Even in the Pacific phase of the Second World War China was a minor factor, and considering that the Japanese occupied the entire East Asian coast it would hardly have been otherwise. Roosevelt's policy was to pat China on the back to keep it in the war while talking grandly about making China a great power after Japan's defeat.

As American ambassador in 1944, Hurley hoped to achieve both these goals by uniting the contending forces in China's civil war in a single coalition government. If, as Hurley believed, China was to be made politically, militarily and economically strong, it was necessary to draw the Chinese Communists into the regime. This required negotiating with the Communist leader, Mao Tse-tung, in his mountain fastness in northwestern China. The Comanche warwhoop with which Hurley, a son of the Oklahoma frontier, greeted Mao as he climbed down from his plane in Yenan in November, 1944, may well have been the farthest cry of America's westward movement.[22]

Mao Tse-tung was no conventional Communist leader. Indeed, Stalin and Molotov had told Hurley that he was not a "real" Communist. Unlike all other major Communist leaders, he had never been to Moscow.

And the strategy and tactics he had developed for Chinese Communism were strangely unlike anything advertised out of Moscow.

Tall, strong, pungent, and earthy in speech, Mao was born in 1893, the son of a Hunanese peasant, in the agricultural heartland of China. Having learned the classics and enrolled in a teachers college, he came to political consciousness at precisely the moment the Chinese Revolution overthrew the last of the Manchu emperors and proclaimed the Republic in 1911. Like other students in Changsha he cut off his pigtail and joined the revolution. The first published work of Mao was a call to his country-men to engage in physical exercise to gain strength and will to resist foreign pressures and build up an independent China.

After the Russian Revolution Mao, then an assistant librarian in Peking, helped start a Chinese Communist party. For several years he loyally followed Moscow's directives to work closely with the first President, Sun Yat-sen, and then with Generalissimo Chiang Kai-shek. But when the party's efforts to stir the urban proletariat of Shanghai and Canton to insurrection failed, Mao decided that the hope of Chinese Communism was the peasants in the countryside. At the same time he put into practice his belief that the party could not move forward without creating its own army. This brought him into sharp dispute with Moscow; it provoked four years of war with Generalissimo Chiang.

The climax was the epic, 7,000-mile Long March by which Mao and the Chinese Communists turned their back on the great coastal centers that Chiang and everybody regarded as crucial to the country's control and ended by establishing a new capital at Yenan in the northwest. Here Mao had Mongolia and the Russian border at his back, and more impor-tant the Japanese, whose encroachments into Manchuria and North China Mao denounced as China's greatest peril, were within striking distance of his guerrilla forces. In the northwest Mao began to build up his base in the peasantry. The Communists worked through a somewhat reformed "United Front" rule that left the populace no worse off than before, and gave some, through limits on rents and redistributing of land, a stake in the new economic order. They kept inflation under control and fought corruption, purifying and improving leadership through "rectifica-tion" campaigns. In such surroundings, Mao worked out his ideas about recruiting and training guerrillas ("The guerrilla army moves among the peasants like a fish in water"), and though the Communists could not manage positional warfare against the Japanese at this point, they mobil-ized almost the entire rural population in their areas through their guer-rilla activity against the hated Japanese. Soon, under the popular slogan "Unite to expel the foreign aggressors," Mao's forces even papered over their split with the Generalissimo.[23]

When Hurley urged the Communists to enter a coalition government under Chiang, Chou En-lai became Yenan's negotiator in Chiang's capital in Chungking, and Mao, traveling in Hurley's plane, and wearing a blue handkerchief around his neck and "plain blue overalls and jacket that might have come out of any country store in America," took part in the talks. All military aid to the Communists would have to be channeled through Chiang, and Mao's troops, limited by earlier agreement with Chiang to 45,000 men, had multiplied to ten times that number by 1945. Rather than fight the invader head-on, they infiltrated, worked their way around the cities and the lines of communication into the countryside which the Japanese could not occupy, and, though split up into units of 1,000 or 2,000 men, controlled vast areas once ruled by Chiang.[24]

In the end, neither the Communists nor Chiang's National Government in Chungking turned the tide of China's war against Japan. This was accomplished by the Americans, who bypassed China almost completely and struck directly for the Japanese homeland. The Russians, once Hitler was defeated, were free to join the final onslaught. The price they exacted for their participation was the return of old Czarist holdings in East Asia, including the return of Japanese-held Sakhalin and the Kurile islands; naval bases at Dairen and Port Arthur; control of the Chinese Eastern railroad across Manchuria and certain commercial rights along the railroad; and acknowledgment of the independence of the Russian satellite Outer Mongolia.[25]

In August, 1945, the Americans knocked Japan out of the war with atomic bombs. At the same time the Russians attacked the Japanese army in Manchuria and overran it. From their stronghold in the northwest Mao's Communists at once fanned out across Shansi and Jehol provinces into north China and Manchuria. Though by Allied agreement the Japanese were supposed to surrender to Chiang's forces, the Russians did nothing to stop Chinese Communist "civilians" from entering Manchuria, helping themselves to abandoned Japanese arms and regrouping as "soldiers." Later the Russians, formally honoring Chiang's claims to sovereignty over all China, pulled back from Manchuria, but Mao's forces under Lin Piao had already gained their foothold there.

As the major victor in the Pacific, the United States fully expected that its interests, expressed in the Open Door idea, would prevail as never before in China. But there were limits on American power in Asia, above all manpower limits. United States insistence that only American troops would carry out the occupation of Japan worked out in practice as America's major Asian commitment. While its forces were still deployed for the war effort, the United States in a tremendous operation airlifted half a million of Chiang's troops to disarm the Japanese and reoccupy the big cities along the coast. The United States also brought in vast supplies for Chiang and put 50,000 Marines ashore to back him up. At this point, intent on using its leverage of power to restore unity in China, the United States again sought to bring the Communists into a coalition regime before their race with Chiang's forces to occupy Japanese-held areas brought back the old state of civil war. After Ambassador Hurley's resignation, President Truman sent General George C. Marshall, who had just resigned as chief of staff in America's greatest war, to work out a peaceful solution. [26]

Despite prodigious efforts, the Marshall mission failed. To Chiang the Americans were allies who had helped him back to Nanking, enabled him to gain the upper hand in the race for territory, and must now back him all the way even if, against Marshall's advice, he wanted to go into Manchuria without pausing first to consolidate his position in North China. For his part Mao scorned the United States as a "paper tiger" unable to fight in China, and if he acquiesced in a truce or two his opposition hardened as the contest intensified for control of Manchuria. In early 1947 Marshall returned to become Secretary of State and lead America into sweeping Cold War involvements on the other side of the world. Then, at the moment Chiang told the new American ambassador that victory was six months away, the strength of Mao's Communists began slowly to emerge.

What made this so difficult for Westerners to see was that they knew mainly the cities, and the cities thronged with Chiang's troops. But in the Shantung countryside, where Chiang had a half million men deployed between Peking and Shanghai, the mobile Communists evaded battle and kept up hit-and-run tactics. As a *North China Daily News* correspondent reported in 1947:

> The larger part of the railway system north of the Yangtse has been disrupted. Many workers in the repair gangs have been killed, and there has been an enormous wastage of materials. No sooner has a section been repaired than, owing either to lack of sufficient troops or the carelessness of government commanders, the Communists break in and destroy the line. The farmers are unable to send their produce to the large towns which have always been dependent on the surrounding agricultural districts for their food supplies.

> The morale of the Communist forces is higher than that of their opponents. Many of the arms supplied by the United States end up in Communist hands. If loyalty and effectiveness of the government armies are dubious, it is because the government itself has lost prestige and no longer inspires confidence in the country. [27]

In Manchuria unexpected Communist winter offensives shook up the large forces Chiang sent north to take Harbin. By May the Communists drove southward in five columns. By July they turned the tables, not only wrecking the railroad but isolating Chiang's troops in the other big Manchurian cities. On May 30, 1947, the American consul general described the slippage at Mukden:

> In past two months morale of Nationalist forces has deteriorated at rapidly accelerating pace. . . . It is reflected in jumpy nerves of military garrison, efforts to evade conscription, and panicky building of trench systems everywhere with only "Maginot" defense strategy in mind. . . . Apathy, resentment and defeatism are spreading fast in Nationalist ranks causing surrenders and desertions. Main factors contributing to this are Communists' ever-mounting numerical superiority, Nationalist soldiers' discouragement over prospects of getting reinforcements, better solidarity and fighting spirit of Communists, losses and exhaustion of Nationalists, their growing indignation over disparity between officers' enrichment and soldiers' low pay, hard life and their lack of interest in fighting far away from home among 'alien' unfriendly populace (whereas Communists being largely natives are in position of fighting for native soil). There is the possibility of a sudden debacle laying all Manchuria open to the Communists.[28]

By the end of summer all possibility of Nationalist victory in Manchuria had vanished, and as new Communist thrusts cut rail links between central China and Peking, it began to look as if all of China's Northeast could become, as Marshall and others had warned, a gigantic trap for Chiang's forces.

In the countryside Mao's Communists by 1947 had handed out land to from forty-three to sixty million peasants and thereby bound much of the rural population to his "peasant revolution." In the cities, Chiang's regime showed strain. In a series of actions by the secret police, it seized control of the universities. On October 28, 1947, it outlawed the Democratic League, thus alienating the liberal elements to whom Marshall had looked for a moderate alternative to the Communists and Chiang's rightwingers. Nationalist China was being devoured from within. Incessant currency manipulation and shameless siphoning off of American aid to corrupt ends led even the long-suffering merchant class to mutter "nothing could be worse." On payday in Shanghai government clerks sprinted to get rid of their Chinese dollars before they grew more worthless; even little children and beggars carried the stuff around in bales. American officials reported that the economy was "disintegrating."[29]

In March 1947 Undersecretary of State Acheson told a Senate committee:

> The Chinese government is not approaching collapse, it is not threatened by defeat by the Communists. The war with the Communists is going to go on much as it has for 20 years.

But as the summer wore on the Republican majority in Congress, long subdued by Marshall's great prestige, began to grow restive. "Our Far Eastern policy," rumbled Senator Vandenberg, "might well shift its emphasis." In October 1947, Henry Luce's *Life* magazine published an impassioned demand for the United States to carry the Cold War to the Communists in Asia by rushing new, large-scale aid to Chiang Kai-shek.

Life's "Report on China," authored by former Ambassador William C. Bullitt, was the opening gun. Thenceforth Luce, son of a missionary to China and militant anti-Communist, kept his magazines on the firing line shooting broadsides at the Administration for not aiding Chiang. His influence in the Republican party in the East was considerable. Roy Howard brought the guns of the Scripps-Howard newspaper chain to bear. *The New York Times* took pot-shots. Here was a loudly anti-Communist issue in which Republicans were not inhibited from taking Administration targets under fire for fear of hitting hostages they had given for European policy (such as ECA Chief Paul Hoffman and U.N. Ambassador Warren Austin) in the name of "bipartisanship."[30]

When Truman summoned Congress that fall to pass emergency aid for Europe, Representative Walter Judd, Republican of Minnesota and former medical missionary to China, introduced a demand for "interim aid" for China too. At the same time, Senator Taft proclaimed himself "absolutely opposed to aid to Europe." Marshall got it, but only by promising a big credit for China at the following session. Yet the Republicans differed from the Democrats only in wanting to vote more aid to Chiang. Even Judd, who liked to propose sending General MacArthur to China to supervise the use of American military supplies, insisted: "Not for one moment has anybody contemplated sending a single combat soldier in."[31]

By 1948, when for the first time in Chiang's long rule a National Assembly convened, Mukden lay under siege and Communist guerrillas raided right up to the walls of Peking every night. Mao's Communists claimed they ruled a quarter of China and a third of its people. At the end of March the American ambassador reported:

> Demoralization and deterioration . . . an increased sense of helplessness in government circles . . . an increasing realization, shared even by the

Generalissimo, that military victory over Communists is impossible and that some other solution must be reached. . . .[32]

Chiang now looked for the Third World War to break out and bring America again to his side; and by autumn of 1948 members of his regime were betting on the election of Thomas E. Dewey as President to deliver the money and arms, and if possible the men, that could hold China against the Communist tide.

In October, when Chiang landed an armored division for one more fling in his fatal gamble for Manchuria, the Communists surrounded it and won its surrender. The Mukden garrison marched out a few miles and gave up. Within weeks Chiang lost 500,000 men, very few of them killed. Then in November the Communists closed in at Hsuchow in central China in a great battle for Chiang's capital at Nanking. Half a million men fought on each side. The battle lasted twenty days. Mao's men killed Chiang's two principal commanders, and wiped out their force including the last of Chiang's thirty-nine American-equipped divisions. Of 550,000 Nationalists lost, the Communists claimed 327,000 surrendered. With not even a remnant to oppose them the Communists reached the Yangtse River. On October 1, 1949, Mao proclaimed the People's Republic of China. In January, as Nanking and Peking fell, Chiang resigned.[33]

In the United States the realization that Communists had taken over the world's largest country at last sank in. At once the recriminations began. After Secretary Acheson met with a group of embittered Republican members of Congress, they charged he had said America's policy was to "wait until the dust settled." The Emergency Committee for Aid to Anti-Communist China asserted that "most of the $125 million" worth of arms aid voted earlier by Congress, failed because the State Department assigned it a shipping priority too low, to arrive in time for the crucial battles of late 1948. In what was to become the standard Republican line, Walter Judd proclaimed that Americans in office had delivered to Generalissimo Chiang the stab in the back that delivered China to the Communists:

A handful of Communists, fellow-travelers and misguided liberals in what has become widely known as the 'Red cell' in the State Department, the Far Eastern office, have consistently followed the Party line with respect to the Chinese Communists [and] caused one of the most amazing reversals in history.[34]

Such were the fulminations of the Asia-First Republicans when a new China rose and slammed shut the Open Door on what Americans knew was Manifest Destiny. The event was as *The New York Times* called it a "catastrophe" for American policy. In the atmosphere of suspicion and fear generated by the Cold War the impact of this bewildering setback in Asia scarcely four years after a triumphant V-J Day far exceeded the customary bounds of American political outrage. The nation was in no mood to hear the Administration's excuses, and when the State Department went to the length of publishing 1076 pages of documents and dispatches from China leading up to the fall, senators dismissed the White Paper unread as a "whitewash" and others called it "face-saving explanations of past failures." America was riding into a political nightmare.

But they all, Democrats and Republicans alike, said it was international Communism that took over China. As Secretary Acheson phrased it, Mao and his forces were "attempting to establish a totalitarian dominance over the Chinese people in the interests of a foreign power." At once overwrought and overconfident, America simply did not hear the meaning of what Mao said on taking over in Peking: "China has stood up." Mao's revolution was a Communist revolution, there could be no mistaking that. But it was also, as he saw it, China's assertion at last of the proud and independent selfhood toward which the bound and prostrated giant had begun to struggle with the revolution of 1912.

As certain of their dispatches printed in the White Paper showed, there were American Foreign Service officers who clearly described the Chinese brand of Communism in practice long before it mastered the country. The reports and recommendations of John Paton Davies, John Stewart Service, Ray Ludden and others went unheeded. These specialists were transferred out of the field, then driven from the government as "security risks." Their reports did not fit into Washington's "theory." In all conscience, it was difficult then to penetrate the extent of relations between Soviet Russia and the Chinese Communist party and the true attitudes of each toward the other. But America, wrathful and fearful, had its eye fixed on Moscow, and missed what was new. For the China that stood up was not only a new force in American and Asian history, it was a new force in Communist history.[35]

ALL OF the hates and fears that had been building up in America since the Second World War flashed in the thunderheads that rose over the land with the Russian bomb and the Communist capture of China. Out of these charged clouds of frustrated emotions poured a politics of hysteria that flowed over America and merged into the "Grand Inquisition of the '50s."

What funneled these sour moods and enormously increased the

Korean War tensions in the nation was a simultaneous malfunctioning of the nation's political system that was itself traceable in no small part to the onset of the Cold War. The pendular alterations in office of the two big American political parties, indispensable to the healthy functioning of the country's system of government, had somehow stopped happening in the 1940s. Such swings over the past century had made possible the rise of America's free-enterprise economy in the nineteenth century and its modification by welfarism in the twentieth. From Lincoln to Hoover, Republicans, the party of business, held the inherent majority and wrought the country's industrial revolution; while the Democratic "outs" periodically mustered enough discontent for them to take over for a few years and put through ameliorating reforms. Then in one of those rare tidal changes—what V.O. Key called a "realignment" election—Franklin Roosevelt forged in Depression days a powerful coalition of the unemployed, farmers and small businessmen that transformed the Democrats into the "permanent" majority. The coalition achieved huge electoral successes in the 1930s and then, when a new crisis arose, not domestic but foreign, the country put tradition aside and gave its support to a third and even fourth term of office for the Democratic president.[36]

In 1946 the political pendulum seemed free to swing at last, and when it swung it catapulted the Republican "outs" back into control of Congress for the first time in twenty years. No Republican doubted that the party would reclaim the White House in 1948. Leading Democrats were resigned to it. Truman's top cabinet officers, Marshall and Forrestal, fully expected it. But the Roosevelt coalition proved too durable. The Republicans and their candidate, Governor Dewey, awaited victory too complacently. The author of the Truman Doctrine put on a terrific campaign, ostensibly staking all on a long list of post-New Deal domestic issues while actually playing both sides of the street on the larger but supposedly proscribed, because bipartisan, questions of foreign policy. By his tough stand against Russian Communism Truman completely took the Cold War issue away from the Republicans without losing too many votes, as it turned out, to the fading appeal of the third-party peace candidate, former Vice President Wallace. Winning a stunningly unexpected reelection, the Democratic President disrupted the pendulum's swing and doomed the Republicans to four more years of what was already the longest exile from national office of either party since Civil War times.[37]

For the Republican stalwarts in Congress and country, the outcome was a crusher. For Dewey's moderate Eastern wing of the party, whose members had come so close to the fruits of office that they could practically taste them, the result was flattening enough. Yet their shock and disappointment was tempered by the fact that under Truman they had been halfway "ins" already, helping Truman devise and run the "bipartisan" Cold War in Europe. In the annals of Republican despair, then, the calamity of deprivation was not at all so total for the Eastern internationalists as for the hardshell Middle Westerners led by Senator Taft and the *Chicago Tribune*. For these people, only change abroad as well as at home could save America. In their view, the New Deal program had daily debauched, demoralized and bankrupted the American Way of Life for twenty years, and they believed that the Democrats were now on their way to internationalizing the New Deal by vast giveaway schemes for the benefit of foreigners. They had never wanted any part of "Me-Too Tom" Dewey's campaign chatter about keeping the New Deal but administering it less wastefully and inefficiently. For Robert Taft, the solid Establishment figure from the banks of the Ohio, the sober and upright senator venerated as "Mr. Republican," the aftermath of 1948 was, said his biographer William S. White, "the sad, worst period." Believing that "the Democrats were literally destroying the country," said White, "he began, if unconsciously, to adopt the notion that almost *any* way to defeat or discredit the Truman plans was acceptable."[38]

If this was the mental state of such a paragon of respectability, of a man who never for a moment forgot that his father had been President of the United States and that the White House was his own destination, what of the more untrammeled of his followers among the conservative Midwesterners and Westerners who dominated the Republican opposition in Congress? Narrowly outpointed in what they regarded as a "freak" election (Truman had failed to win an absolute majority), they now set their face against any form of cooperation with the government. Forming a parliamentary coalition with conservative Democrats, they quickly smashed the Fair Deal program that President Truman proposed in his inaugural address. In the absence of Senator Vandenberg, who fell ill at the time, they broke up the bipartisan accord that had supported the Administration's foreign policy since 1945. They bludgeoned the Administration for its failures in the Far East. And with the defeat of Dewey, who had campaigned against the outlawing of the Communist party, the congressional diehards threw themselves into a kind of parliamentary pogrom against any Communist influence anywhere in America. By yet more committee investigations (thirty-five in 1949), by ceaseless parliamentary infighting, and by attacks in the press, they seized on every chance to attack the "ins" as "soft on Communism." The wildness of these attacks reflected the frustration of the Republicans at finding themselves still in the wilderness after 1948.[39]

He was a black Irishman with a five-o'clock-shadow no TV makeup man could efface. He was bony, angular, hulking, of medium height. His arms were short and hairy, his hands huge as a third baseman's mitt. His mouth was wide, his teeth bad, eyes dark yellow and darting, nose ski-shaped but bent like a boxer's. His voice was strong and nasal, and could carry far even when delivered full blast through what seemed like clenched teeth. It could slide up and down his throat and, emerging from a barrel chest, blatt like a trombone. He was not a good speaker. Disconcertingly, he often interrupted himself to say, courtroom fashion: "Strike that."

Fierce intensity and clumsy energy surged out in his every movement. Seated, he carried his chin in, which made him appear to look up at anyone who faced him. Speaking, he threw his voice like an uppercut. Walking, he lunged forward as if launching a blow. Crude and shouldering, contemptuous of graces, he exuded a relentless and even forced competitiveness. "I never saw him when he seemed to be taking it easy," said a friend.

Senator Joseph Raymond McCarthy, Republican of Wisconsin, was a loner, with few intimates. It is true that he liked having people around, and would throw an arm over a constituent's shoulder. He ate and drank in often strident conviviality. "Incinerate it," he invariably said when ordering his steak. But though he seemed to listen, he fidgeted while others talked, and when he spoke it was often not to answer but to talk of something else. And what would he talk about? About Joe and his plans, what he was going to do. He joked, but his joking was aggressive horseplay. He laughed, but without mirth. His smile was gloating. When, however, people bridled at his schemes, he grinned and even giggled. Always he surprised by the sheer cheek of his aspirations. He never did a thing by halves. He was a plunger who plunged for more than others expected him to—and got it.

In Grand Chute, Wisconsin, it seemed excessive that the fourth son of Timothy and Bridget McCarthy, the fearful and gawky boy who had grown up on one of the lumbered-out pine country's poorest farms, finished high school at twenty-one, and then trucked chickens to Milwaukee to pay for his night courses at Marquette University law school, should at once measure himself for a judgeship. And then it seemed too much that an uncombed county judge, a Democrat freshly elected on the Republican ticket, and still learning to ride circuit among the North Woods Indian-reservation towns, should take instant aim on the United States Senate. It also seemed unlikely that, commissioned a lieutenant in Marine air intelligence and packed off to the South Pacific, he could walk out of his tent beside a Bougainville airstrip, speak a few words to a Marine general locked in combat for Rabaul, and a few days later receive orders to fly home and tour Wisconsin as a Senate candidate in defiance of the prohibition against members of the armed forces engaging in political campaigns.[40]

It seemed even unlikelier after losing his 1944 primary race that he would run again in 1946 and beat Bob LaFollette, bearer of the state's most famous name. And who, then—after watching this obscure, back-row senator run errands for four years for prefab housing promoters and soft-drink companies in Washington—who then would have supposed that overnight Joseph R. McCarthy would make himself into the most feared and powerful demagogue of his time?

So, as he conferred with friends at the Colony Restaurant in Washington in January, 1950, this rough-and-tumble backwoods brawler was looking for a dramatic issue with which to assure himself reelection. Of the three others at the table, one suggested championing the St. Lawrence Seaway. McCarthy said he didn't think that would do. Then Father Edmund Walsh, regent of the School of Foreign Service at Georgetown University, suggested Communism and its capacity for subversion. "That's it," said McCarthy. "The government is full of Communists. We can hammer away at them."[41]

Anti-Communism was an old issue for Republicans, and had loomed in American politics for thirty years. Throughout the New Deal and Fair Deal years, anti-Communist conservatives freely charged Democratic Administrations with "selling the country down the road" to collectivism at home and with "selling out" Eastern Europe and China to "the Kremlin" abroad. Nor was "Communists-in-government" a new accusation when McCarthy came along to hurl it. It was the pet issue for years of Republicans and Democrats alike in the House Un-American Activities Committee.

Anti-Communism was already a Republican cry when the party took control of Congress in 1946 and a House Appropriations subcommittee under Karl Stefan, Republican of Nebraska, set out to probe the State Department. Under heavy congressional pressure the State Department permitted a team of investigators led by Robert E. Lee, a former FBI agent, to examine the department's loyalty files. Drawing on all the raw information he found in the files, including unconfirmed statements and allegations collected by a half dozen agencies, Lee put together a list of data on some 108 department employees. Thereafter the "Lee list," as it came to be called, was used by several committees investigating expenditures, and in early 1948 the department informed one such committee that of the 108 "cases" on the Lee list, only some 57 were still employed.[42]

So matters stood in early 1950 when the Republican National Committee arranged some speaking dates for McCarthy. He was to go to

Wheeling, West Virginia, to address the County Women's Republican Club, and then to Salt Lake City and Reno for other meetings. McCarthy at this point asked a *Chicago Tribune* staffer, Willard Edwards, for some help on his speeches. The *Tribune* man handed him the Lee list. There was also a copy of an old letter from Secretary of State Byrnes to a congressman, dated July 26, 1946. In this letter Byrnes explained that of some 3,000 wartime federal employees transferred into the State Department, a screening committee had recommended that permanent employment be denied in 284 cases—and of these 284 cases, seventy-nine had been terminated by that date.[43]

In Wheeling on February 9, McCarthy waved aloft the letter in a gesture that was to become his trademark:

> I have here in my hand a list of 205 men in the State department that were known to the Secretary of State as being State Department members and who nevertheless are still working and shaping the policy of the government.[44]

Two nights later in Reno, brandishing his other document, McCarthy shouted:

> I have here in my hand 57 names of [State Department] individuals who would appear to be either card-carrying members or certainly loyal to the Communist party but who nevertheless are still helping to shape our foreign policy.[45]

McCarthy himself was not prepared for the national storm touched off by his charges. Yet only two weeks before, Alger Hiss had been convicted of falsely denying that he had passed State Department documents to the Communists, and a few days later Dean Acheson, the head of the State Department, had declared that he would "not turn his back on Hiss." And only two days before McCarthy spoke, came the shocking confession of the British scientist, Klaus Fuchs, that he had handed over the secret of the A-bomb to the Communists in 1945 and 1946 while working in New Mexico. After such unsettling disclosures the sight of a United States senator waving evidence in his hand that he said proved the State Department was honeycombed with Communists made headlines in the press and a stir in the nation. The charges rang like an alarm bell in the night.[46]

McCarthy himself said that he got action by changing the cry from "treason" to "traitors." But he also turned a conventional political issue into a political nightmare by his own unconventional personal qualities—

a flair for self-dramatization, a breathtaking indifference to facts (his slogan when he first ran for office was "Justice is Truth in Action"), and a stubborn unwillingness to back down.

Called upon by Majority Leader Scott Lucas to explain himself, McCarthy in six wild hours on the Senate floor roared that the loyalty of eighty-one State Department employees was "questionable" but declined to name any names. The *Washington Post* condemned his speech as "irresponsible"; Senator Taft termed it a "reckless performance." But McCarthy's hammering had struck right on a national nerve and Taft was soon urging that McCarthy "should keep talking, and if one case doesn't work out he should proceed with another."[47]

When Alfred Kohlberg, a New York Chinese-lace importer and leader of the so-called China Lobby, got in touch with McCarthy, the Senator's charges began to focus on State Department "traitors" who had "sold out" Chiang Kai-shek to the Communists. Brought before a special investigating committee headed by one of the Senate's most senior Democrats, Millard Tydings of Maryland, McCarthy began to name some names. He asserted that Dorothy Kenyon, a New York City judge who had been a delegate to the United Nations, belonged to "at least eighteen Communist-front organizations." He then turned on Ambassador-at-Large Philip Jessup, who had prepared the State Department White Paper defending its China policy, and charged him with "an unusual affinity for Communist causes." Badgered by Democratic senators about the number of people he was accusing, which changed from two hundred eight to fifty-seven, then eighty-one and now ten, McCarthy roared: "Let us be done with this silly numbers game," and reduced his number to just one. The man was Owen Lattimore, a specialist on Far Eastern studies at Johns Hopkins University who had been an occasional adviser, but had never worked for the State Department at all. On Lattimore's conviction as "the top Soviet agent in America," McCarthy said, he would "stand or fall."[48]

It didn't work out that way at all. The Tydings Committee cleared Lattimore and everybody else named by McCarthy. But it also made the mistake of asserting that there were no subversives in the State Department, a statement never capable of absolute proof, and after the Hiss case a statement widely doubted by the public at large. By then the Washington *Times-Herald* was denouncing the investigation as a political "whitewash," McCarthy was receiving Americanism awards in New Jersey, and the Young Republicans in Chicago were proclaiming: "The Midwest can be proud of Representatives like McCarthy." About this time the Washington *Post* cartoonist, Herblock, sketched a big Republican elephant being pushed by Senators Taft, Wherry, Bridges and party chairman Guy

Gabrielson toward a stack of mud buckets, with one extra big bucket of mud on top. On the biggest bucket he printed the label: MC CARTHY-ISM. Then and there the word passed into the language. The surge of anti-Communist revolt that climaxed the rising fears of the 1940s and raged on to challenge the established order of the 1950s had its name, and the expression of its most violent, reckless mood.[49]

To Herblock and others at the time, McCarthyism was a smear, a mad spy-chase, a huntdown of dissenters. It was all of these and much more. It was the shadow cast over the United States government by the most unabashedly flannel-mouthed demagogue to appear in Washington since the days of Huey Long. It was, at times sweeping along the whole government with it, the total assertion of anti-Communism as a way of life. It was also an instrument for attacking the presidency, whether held by Truman or Eisenhower. In the sudden range of support and the intense emotional heat generated by McCarthy, it was the almost volcanic out-burst of those rightwing Republican forces centered in the Middle West, whose quarrel was with the twentieth century and its demanding respon-sibilities, whose program was for standing pat in the hometown but changing everything in Washington and foreign affairs, and whose gospel of social, economic and political reaction was printed daily in the *Chicago Tribune.*[50]

Back of the McCarthyism of the Midwestern heartland was a craving for revenge upon the perpetrators of world and national change, and a bid by rightwing Republican leaders to regain the controlling position their forces had once held in American life. For twenty years, while the world was largely made over, they had been denied any hand on the levers of national political power. Once they had constituted the "natural" majority, secure in their continental isolation, their elm-shaded small towns, their white-spired Protestant churches, their flourishing family-owned factories. Then two World Wars shattered the protected remote-ness of their landscape. Powerful new technologies bypassed their court-house squares, drained their people away to the cities, and robbed their pulpits of their once commanding authority. The anti-Depression mea-sures enacted by the New Deal diminished the old dependencies upon local factory owners, merchants and mortgage holders. In all of these once self-sufficient small towns the federal reforms instituted a new reliance upon what had been a hitherto remote and alien source—monthly green checks showered down by a centralized welfare state in faroff Washington for social security, unemployment insurance and acreage allotments. On top of these deeply resented changes, this older America was called upon to pay still higher taxes and endure still more curbs on personal freedom to carry on the Cold War in outlandish places like Iran and Greece, and to see American blood shed in ignominious catastrophes like the Korean War.[51]

For grievances as deep and long-standing as these, Communism was hardly a target so much as a weapon, and this doubtless helps explain why McCarthy never cared much about how many Communists be unearthed or whether the hapless individual he publicly tortured was or was not a Russian espionage agent. Scores were being settled, and those on whom vengeance was wreaked were liberals, New Dealers, internationalists and even Republicans—anybody who had responsibility for what had gone on in Washington and the world during what McCarthy was soon calling "twenty years of treason." In this view of the midcentury predicament, the New Deal was indistinguishable from the Welfare State, the Welfare State was mixed up with Socialism, and Socialism was another name for Communism. Accordingly, real, live, card-carrying Communists, when found (as they almost never were), signified nothing much to McCarthyism. The target was really all those liberals and progressives and internationalists who had manned the high places of power while the Old America was being destroyed.[52]

In this sense Joe McCarthy was a throwback—a farm boy who rose in the classic nineteenth century trajectory to the peak of national politics as the striking-hammer of conservative Midwestern Republicans. As it happened, this Wisconsin backwoods from which McCarthy sprang was not the steady-beating heart of the American nation. It was a frontier in retreat, of farms closing down, of villages drying up, of small businesses watching their trade and even their children riding off down the highways to the cities. Polls revealed that the most earnest supporters of the Wisconsin senator were the small-town businessmen who felt squeezed between the big unions and the big corporations. This Joe McCarthy, tractored off the land and circuit-riding and tailgunning his way into the United States Senate, symbolized and spoke for an older America in retreat from and revolt against modernity.[53]

But another Joe McCarthy, escaping from the boondocks to the streetcorners of Milwaukee, and kneeing, kicking and gouging his way to the Senate, symbolized other and much less clearly defined elements in American society. Support for McCarthy came from the new-wealth groups, such as oil wildcatters, shopping center developers and plastics manufacturers. Two of the wealthiest men in America, the Texas oil speculators Sid Richardson and H. R. Hunt lined up with McCarthy. Even more significantly, the fact that McCarthy was a practicing Catholic also stirred support in some Democratic strongholds. Along with his readiness to flout Marquess of Queensberry rules in any fight, this was a factor that made him widely feared by his fellow Senators. "How do people feel about McCarthy these days?" asked Senator Henry Cabot Lodge, Republican of Massachusetts, of his state's Democratic governor, Paul A. Dever. "Your people don't think much of him," said Dever, "but mine do."[54]

McCarthyism received accessions from ethnic groups like the Irish and Germans who may have felt a need after the Second World War to prove their patriotism by an excess of anti-Communist zeal. In the senator's home state of Wisconsin, ethnically German counties gave strong support to his version of patriotism that vented its wrath at the dessicated and adulterated brand attributed to the Establishment. Many of these voters were economically on the rise as they moved with McCarthy into the Republican party, and proclaimed these flag-waving values so loudly because they believed them appropriate to the social station they strove to confirm. Whether for the Germans on the fat farmlands of southeastern Wisconsin or for the Irish tied to their tenements in south Boston, angry anti-Communism of the vituperative sort that McCarthy let loose could bring out some of the rising agony of white ethnic America. The nation was moving into a new order of social conduct.[55]

In an uncompleted country like the United States the word "American" does not stand by itself. As Nathan Glazer has pointed out, it carries an additional meaning of patriot or authentic American, and critic and opponent of foreign ideologies. In the pluralist society "old Americans," or "old-stock Americans"—white, of British origin, and Protestant—had long ceased to constitute a majority. But other elements in the pluralist society, while preserving an identity imposed by history, family and fellow feeling, still felt a burden to establish the Americanness of this identity. In New York City, for example, this was accomplished by a further extension of interest—the Jews ran the garment industry, the Irish dominated politics and civil service, the Italians concentrated in trucking and contracting and the vegetable business.

In the amalgam of the Pacific Coast, people came closest perhaps to registering the abstraction of the "American." But the pressures were severe, and some found inchoate expression in McCarthy's outpourings. The "Old America" assimilated no more than its ethnic cousins—the old Dutch of New York, the Pennsylvania Germans, the Scotch-Irish of Virginia. The Irish and Italian immigrants had both at different times competed directly with black labor. The blacks were at the bottom of the society, and that had always been important. The others could always jump on them. But now it was not acceptable to kick them any more, and the strains were already being felt.[56]

Yet McCarthyism was never organized, and it never connected with a broad public in such a way as to become a mass movement. It lifted the senator to a place where he could launch destructive attacks upon several institutions of established America, including the presidency itself. It furnished the driving force with which the conservative Middle Western wing of the Republican party fought first the Democrats and then the Eastern Republicans for control of the Cold War.

In the course of this bitter battle, which was immensely exacerbated after June, 1950, by the frustrations of the Korean conflict, the established policy of waging Cold War primarily against the Russians in Europe was upheld. Yet the victory was not won without great cost. Richard Rovere did not much exaggerate when he said that from early 1950 to late 1954 McCarthy "held two presidents captive," and that during this period Truman and Eisenhower:

> could never act without weighing the impact of their plans upon McCarthy and the forces he led, and in consequence, there were times when because of this man they could not act at all.[57]

In the atmosphere created by such bushwhacking at home and a war without victory overseas, America was impelled to new excesses. When in the summer of 1950 a San Francisco judge permitted Harry Bridges, the Australian-born leftist West Coast dock union leader, to be freed on bail, Joseph Donohue, the United States attorney prosecuting the perjury case, declared: "I am going to resign tomorrow. God help America." In New Rochelle, New York, the city council passed an ordinance requiring every Communist living in or "regularly passing through" to register. One man, somewhat confused, climbed off his morning train for New York at New Rochelle and presented himself at city hall—where he was told the list was for Communists, not commuters. By the last week of August, when newspapers blossomed with ads for "Country Properties for the Atomic Age," and "Safe Country Living," what might have seemed like the ultimate scream of national frustration and rage shrilled around the world.[58] A member of the President's cabinet called for "preventive war." "I would be willing to pay any price to achieve a world at peace, even the price of instituting a war," declared Secretary of the Navy Francis Matthews, an Omaha millionaire and leading Catholic layman, in a Boston speech. Forces opposed, said Matthews,

> would brand our program as imperialist aggression. We could accept that slander with complacency, for in the implementation of a strong, affirmative peace-seeking policy, though it cast us in a character new to a true democracy—an initiator in a war of aggression—it would win for us a proud and popular title—we would the first aggressors for peace.[59]

It is no light matter to recall that James Forrestal, the first Defense Secretary to preside at the Pentagon in the Cold War had to be placed under a psychiatrist's care and threw himself to death two months after relinquishing office. Whatever the circumstances that produced the Matthews outburst, Truman repudiated it within days. Within two weeks he fired his top man at the Pentagon, Defense Secretary Louis Johnson, and as he had done in the big crisis of his first term, brought in General Marshall to reestablish control of the situation. His action pulled the Pentagon back into line (Matthews was sent to be ambassador in Ireland, and General Orville Anderson, the Air War College commandant who bugled that the Air Force was poised and only waiting orders to drop the bomb on Moscow, was retired). The price, as it turned out, was a partisan onslaught against General Marshall that fated the old hero to a retirement and death amid plaudits as grim as those poured out for his unfortunate predecessors.[60]

At the moment there was no mistaking the mood of the country. Congress was bent on such extremes that it made Truman, who compared it with the time of the Alien and Sedition Acts of 150 years before, seem libertarian by contrast. When he tried to slow the anti-Communist stampede by sending up his own subversives-control bill, he found "a lot of people on the Hill . . . running with their tails between their legs." Republican Senators Nixon and Mundt saw their chance at last to put through their bills for registering all Communist party members and all Communist-front organizations and their officers. But the man who led the way to the reactionary heights at this hour was a Democrat. Silverhaired Pat McCarran, seventy-four, of Nevada, was chairman of the Senate Judiciary Committee, and by his control over judicial appointments swung a big stick over both his fellow members and the Administration. McCarran took charge of the coalition of conservative Democrats and Republicans who demanded new and drastic antisubversive legislation. An Irish Catholic virulently opposed to immigration of either people or ideas, he brought in an omnibus bill that wrapped up the Republican proposals with a lot of his own pet devices for curbing aliens and the foreign born.[61]

Enactment was a foregone conclusion but at the last minute liberal Democrats joined the frenzy. Partly to co-opt the extremist drive and partly to show the voters that their anti-Communism was not only real but even more hardhitting, they decided to go the conservatives one better. Led by Paul Douglas of Illinois and Harley Kilgore of West Virginia, they brought in an alternative antisubversion measure that appalled libertarians. Based on the unhappy precedent set in the Second World War when the government rounded up 72,000 West Coast Japa-

nese-Americans and "detained" them at inland camps for the war's duration, their "concentration camp bill," as other senators promptly labeled
it, provided that all persons thought to be subversive would be locked up
as a menace to security the moment the President declared a national
"emergency." Rising in almost solitary opposition Senator Estes Kefauver,
Democrat of Tennessee, pointed out that the country was already fighting
an undeclared war that could be designated as such an "emergency."[62]

Rather than choose between the two measures, the Senate simply
tacked the concentration camp bill onto McCarran's, and whooped the
whole weird package through over a Truman veto and a lame, late try by
Senator Humphrey and one or two other concentration-camp proponents
who had changed their minds and now wished to stop what they had
started. Thus along with a Subversive Activities Control Board charged
with registering Communists and Communist-front outfits, there came
into being at the center of the "free world," a network of "concentration
camps." With Justice Department funds earmarked by Congress in
1951-2 for the purpose, the Federal Bureau of Prisons refurbished six
former World War installations. These six camps (located at Allenwood,
Pennsylvania; Avon Park, Florida; El Reno, Oklahoma; Florence,
Arizona; Wickenburg, Arizona; Tule Lake, California and "needing only
about as much work as would be required to make the beds and light the
fires," stood ready, *The New York Times* reported in 1955, "to receive
those deemed dangerous to security if a national emergency should arise."
For twenty-one years until, long after the Cold War, Congress repealed
it, this legacy of concentration-camp legislation remained in the law of the
land.[63]

McCarthy crested during the Korean War years. From the early days
he attacked the conduct of the war, blaming the deaths of Americans in
battle on "a group in the State Department that make Benedict Arnold
look like a piker," and railed at "egg-sucking, phony liberals" who sold
China into "atheistic slavery." Acheson and Jessup he called "dilettante
diplomats" who "whined" and "whimpered" and "cringed" before Communists. "It all fits into a pattern," said McCarthyite Senator George
("Molly") Malone, Republican of Nevada. "We deliberately lose Manchuria, China, Korea and Berlin. We follow the pattern in sometimes
apparently unrelated events but it all adds up to losing strategic areas
throughout the world."[64]

As Congress rushed to pass anti-Communist legislation before the
1950 elections, McCarthy received 2,000 invitations to speak—more than
all other senators put together. He picked his spots. In Maryland, where
his enemy Tydings was opposed by an unknown named John Marshall

Butler, McCarthy led the attack. Ruth McCormick Miller, the niece of Colonel Robert R. McCormick of the Chicago *Tribune* and editor of the McCormick-owned Washington *Times-Herald*, brought in a Chicago PR man named Jon Jonkel. A faked photograph showing Tydings in apparently intimate conversation with ex-Communist party chief Earl Browder was circulated, while Jonkel devised the campaign strategy:

> Let's not get into the business of proving whether or not [Tydings'] inquiry was a whitewash. Let's say in the business that a doubt exists. The Democratic party has to resolve the issue of Communism. It is a big issue. Doubt exists. All we have to do is to go out against it.[65]

Doubts—doubts about Korea, about China, about Communist A-bombs—swirled everywhere in the November, 1950, congressional elections, and McCarthyism thickened them. Thousands of postcards sent out asking: "Do you want Communism?" helped topple the dignified Tydings of Maryland. Daubing Helen Gahagan Douglas "the pink lady" helped Richard Nixon into the Senate in California. The "soft on Communism" line helped replace another foe, Majority Leader Lucas, with Everett McKinley Dirksen, in Illinois. McCarthy, with several fresh senatorial scalps dangling from his belt, was a feared man in Washington.[66] Although his party fell just short of a majority in Congress, the Republican-Dixiecrat combination now held the whip hand.

Look out for McCarthy, was the Senate watchword. "Joe will go that extra mile to destroy you," warned the new Majority leader, Lyndon B. Johnson of Texas. Nobody in the Senate raised a remonstrating word any more. McCarthy upset a lot of people; he barked a lot of shins that had never been barked before. He had always aimed the biggest and wildest of his kicks at the most respectable, most genteel, most socially secure people in the nation and little men, whether old Americans or new, liked that. Back on the first night at Wheeling, when Americans had not yet quite grasped that one of the most immaculate of the State Department's officers had actually been trafficking secrets to the Communists, McCarthy had lunged straight at the ruling Establishment and laid America's troubles to:

> the traitorous actions of those who have been treated so well by this nation. It has not been the less fortunate or members of minority groups who have been selling this Nation out, but rather those who have had all the benefits that the wealthiest nation on earth has to offer—the finest homes, the finest college educations, and the finest jobs that the Government can give. This is glaringly true in the State Department.

There the bright young men who are born with silver spoons in their mouths are the ones who have been the worst.[67]

The most dangerous of all, he insisted, was Secretary Acheson, whom he called variously "the Red Dean," and "that pompous diplomat in striped pants with the phony British accent."[68]

After the elections Arthur Krock wrote in *The New York Times* that the real loser in the voting had been the State Department. "I state it as a fact," wrote the old New Dealer James Rowe, "that no Democratic politician in the Senate or House will undertake to defend the Department of State in the next session." It did not even help that the Administration had just browbeaten Secretary General Trygve Lie into accepting FBI investigation of United States citizens employed by the United Nations—a casual Cold War action that had the effect of forcing the international organization launched with such high hopes only four years before into a crippling subservience to United States national interest. When Ambassador Jessup's name was submitted to a Senate subcommittee for delegate to the UN, McCarthy had only to repeat his old charge that Jessup had worked in the Institute of Pacific Relations with Communists. Though Jessup had been confirmed five times before by the Senate, after the 1950 election the nomination was tabled. A few weeks later, when the Chinese Communists overran American defenses in Korea, forty-six Republican senators voted, "Secretary Acheson does not command the support of the American people," and only the stubborn defiance of President Truman kept Acheson on the job. When not much later the President dismissed General MacArthur, McCarthy called it "the greatest victory the Communists have ever won."[69]

After the President's advisers got the best of the argument in the subsequent Senate inquiry, McCarthy decided to attack and destroy the most eminent of them. This was General Marshall, the one man in public life who had been for years beyond the reach of anyone's criticism but had now been drafted again from Virginia retirement to fill a big gap as Defense Secretary. Marshall may have been Henry Stimson's idea of the greatest American soldier since Washington. He may have been a figure of whose dignity and character politicians like Truman and commanders like Eisenhower stood in awe. But Mr. Integrity, as certain newspapers called him, had "lost" China. With Alger Hiss whispering to FDR at Yalta, Lattimore passing notes to State Department career diplomats in Chungking, Chou En-lai swaying Marshall in Nanking, and John Carter Vincent of the China Desk in Washington sabotaging aid shipments for Chiang Kai-shek—it was easy to see how it had all happened. Respectable Marshall may have seemed. But there were more EMs in America than generals, and enlisted men never thought much of generals—generals gaudy with medals, generals pompous with cars and drivers, generals issuing impossible orders.

So McCarthy told the Senate one day, Mr. Integrity was part of "a conspiracy so immense and an infamy so black as to dwarf any previous such venture in the history of man." Only Senator Langer, Republican of North Dakota, interrupted McCarthy—and that was to praise him. To arraign a man of such eminence, McCarthy had arranged to have his staff document his accusations with an entire book. *(America's Retreat from Victory: the Story of George Catlett Marshall)*. This book was his speech and the senator soon stopped reading and left the rest to be entered in the *Congressional Record*. He himself may never have read the book through; if he did, he found little to substantiate his charge that Marshall had sold China, sold Korea, and sold America all to the end "that we shall be contained and frustrated and finally fall victim to Soviet intrigue from within and Russian military might from without." It was the technique of the "multiple lie"—an accusation so long and containing so many untruths that no one could ever pin down all the lies at one time.

Shortly afterwards, without being called down for it, the Senator asserted in a Senate defense of his speech that Marshall "would sell his own grandmother for any advantage." Three months later, the Communists having asked for ceasefire negotiations in Korea, Marshall retired from office and returned to Virginia. It is unlikely that his nomination to any job thereafter would have commanded swift senatorial approval. The general had been soiled beyond further use to his country. He died in 1959.[70]

CHAPTER 6

Last Stand

THE KOREAN WAR AND McCARTHYISM

AT THE THIRTY-SECOND anniversary celebration of the Bolshevik Revolution in November, 1949, the Russian leaders in Moscow looked at the world from their platform atop Lenin's tomb and were well pleased. The fabulous Communist victory in China, proclaimed Georgei Malenkov with Stalin at his side, was the decisive action in the takeover of all Asia. He proudly announced that Chairman Mao Tse-tung would shortly lead a triumphal mission to the Kremlin. In the high expectancy of the greatest revolutionary hour since the Bolsheviks gained power, other Asian delegations hastened to Moscow to join in the talks. One of these was led by Kim Il Sung, president of the People's Republic of North Korea.

Korea was a pretty remote place in the consciousness of America in the winter of 1949–50. This little country lying on the Asian shores between China and Japan had not been fought over in the Second World War. It had not even been quarreled over when the Americans and Russians fell out after the war. By quite casual decisions made in 1944 and 1945 the two big powers had agreed to occupy roughly equal halves of the country on either sides of a line suggested by Colonel Dean Rusk, an American army officer who had seen wartime service in Asia. The line was the 38th parallel.[1]

The two zones of Korea were in fact quite different. The part the Russians occupied in the north was dry-farming country, planted in wheat and millet; in 1945 its farms were bigger than those of the South, with a larger proportion owned by those who tilled them. It was also more industrialized, but the population was only 6,000,000 compared to 20,-000,000 in the South. The part the Americans occupied in the South was predominantly a region of irrigated rice cultivation, its economy basically one of tenant farming along with extensive fisheries.[2]

The Koreans were the Poles of Northeast Asia. Their position between the powerful Chinese, Japanese and Russians doomed them to uncertain national existence, and they were all the more fiercely nationalist because of it. Nationalists and Communists alike, all the oldline Korean leaders flocked to the traditional capital of Seoul in the American zone following the Japanese surrender in 1945. Their one thought, now that the Japanese overlords had been brought low, was to construct a united and independent Korea. But the American authorities refused to have anything to do with them. Pending establishment of a five-year joint trusteeship with the Russians that had been tentatively agreed upon at the 1945 Foreign Ministers' Conference in Moscow, everything was held up.[3]

While the frustrated Korean chieftains milled about in Seoul and the rift widened between the Americans and Russians, a youthful Korean guerrilla fighter who had returned to the country with the Russian army was busily organizing local governments around his native city of Pyongyang in the North. This was Kim Il Sung. To the older generation of Koreans he was totally unknown. Yet at thirty-three he had already spent a lifetime fighting in the shadowy and pseudonymous underground of international Communism. Born Kim Su Ju in a peasant household just outside Pyongyang, Kim was taken by his father at an early age to Manchuria. While attending a Chinese school in Kirin, he joined the Communist party at the age of fourteen, and when the Japanese invaded Manchuria in 1931 he took to the countryside. For ten years he operated as a partisan leader against the Japanese troops, rising to command a division in the Chinese Communist First Army. It was not a very large division, but it gave the Japanese trouble. [4]

Some of Kim's exploits of these breakneck years carried him across the border into his native Korea. On June 4, 1937, as recorded in old Japanese police records in Tokyo, he led a band of fifty to one hundred men in a midnight raid on the town of Poch'imbo. The attackers killed the Japanese police officers and burned their command post as well as the houses of pro-Japanese Koreans before retreating to Manchuria. To curb his depredations the Japanese mounted a special army detachment commanded by a Korean colonel, the same Kim Sok Won who as a general led the South Korean army against him at the outbreak of the Korean War in 1950.

From 1941 to 1945 Kim is said to have fought with the Russian army, and this was presumably the time he began calling himself Kim Il Sung, after a legendary early hero of Korean national resistance to Japan. At all events it was with Russian help and a name roughly equivalent to George Washington that this strapping and durable international Communist who had never belonged to any Korean party at all presented himself as the organizer of the New Korea. Bargaining, purging, assassinating, he laid claim to "absolute power" in what became the Democratic People's Republic of North Korea. This was well before Syngman Rhee, beating the old Nationalists and Communists of Seoul in a scarcely less savage round of purges and assassinations, emerged as President of the Republic of Korea south of the 38th parallel.[5]

Considering that the Russians had placed advisors in every sector of government from the cabinet to the police, and that certain parts of the economy such as oil and shipping were directly controlled by the Russians through joint-stock companies, it seems fair enough to call Kim's North Korea a Soviet satellite. Though the same term could not quite be used to describe United States influence over Syngman Rhee's regime after the American troops withdrew in mid-1949, the army had 400 American advisors and the United States was quite substantially committed to supporting the South Korean economy. Still, Secretary Acheson had seemed quite clearly to imply otherwise in a major speech he delivered in Washington in January, 1950. In those Cold War days the press had not yet begun to talk about "brinkmanship" in its Secretaries of State. Yet Acheson's National Press Club address, though less aggressive in tone, was as calamity-courting a piece of international cliff-walking as any attempted later by John Foster Dulles.[6]

After having won a negotiated end to the Berlin Blockade Truman and Acheson may have thought they had taken the measure of Stalin's caution. Yet they had little enough to guide them as to the Kremlin's assessment of Communism's prospects in the Far East after Mao's victory in China. In words carefully cleared with both Pentagon and White House, Acheson outlined the American position in Asia following the Communist takeover of mainland China. This was a position of withdrawal. The boundary of American defenses in the Pacific, said Acheson, now ran from the Aleutians through Japan to the Philippines. Nowhere did it touch on the Asian mainland. But because the line also ran to the east of Formosa, a tremendous roar went up in Washington. Chiang Kai-shek, taking the country's gold supply with him, had come to roost on Taiwan, or as the West called it, Formosa. Senator Bridges, ranking Republican in the upper chamber, moved at once to cut off funds for the State Department unless Acheson stood by Chiang Kai-shek. Senator William Knowland, sometimes called the Senator from Formosa, demanded the Secretary's resignation.[7]

More than anyone, Knowland's voice sounded the historic call of the Republican party to look west across the Pacific rather than east over the Atlantic. He was born in Alameda, California, member of a family that had owned the rock-ribbed Oakland *Tribune* and upheld California Republicanism for most of the century. He was a staunch member of the order of Native Sons of the Golden West. In the Senate he held the seat long occupied by Hiram Johnson, bitter foe of Woodrow Wilson's war on Germany and lifelong proponent of American power in the Pacific. He was the spokesman for the shipping industry of Pacific ports that looked to the Far East as the only area for expanding its trade. As an undergraduate at Berkeley, his wife used to say, "Billy came across Lenin's sentence, 'the road to Paris is through Peking,' and most everything he has done since has been intended to block that road." Although there is no record of Lenin's having said just that, Knowland used it in almost every foreign-policy speech, and in 1950 alone he spoke 115 times in the Senate on Far Eastern questions. Strapping, mirthlessly intent, with something of Senator Taft's faith in a certain rudimentary logic as the highest form of intelligence, Knowland thundered:

> The Munich men in the State department are setting the groundwork of an appeasement of Mao Tse-tung which will make the betrayal of the Czechoslovak republic to Hitler twelve years ago fade into insignificance.[8]

For Democrat Acheson, breaking an utterly fresh trail across the blasted political landscape of the Western Pacific, such partisan dangers, while perilous enough to life, limb and eardrum, were well known. What carried Acheson to the teetering brink was that the defense line he drew in his speech also left out South Korea.

The fall of China transformed the way the United States looked upon Japan, and this in turn was bound to affect the way America viewed a state less than fifty miles from Japan's coast. After the Second World War America had treated Japan strictly as conquered territory, perhaps useful as a defense outpost and staging area. As the Cold War intensified in Europe, this dismissive attitude came under review. Now, by the same Cold War urgencies that reversed American attitudes toward Germany, Japan was seen as a major bastion against Communist China and Russia and indeed as a potential partner in offsetting the loss of China in that part of the world. In mid-May, in a move of vital concern to Russia and China, President Truman announced that the United States was preparing to negotiate a peace treaty with Japan that would grant independence to the enemy of the Second World War and implant on its soil, by long-term agreements, American military bases. To the Russians these

American moves were second in importance only to the American steps taken in early 1948 to reform the German currency and sponsor creation of the anti-Communist West German state, a move to which the Russians had responded by blockading Berlin. Nor could the Chinese, invaded repeatedly by Japan in the last seventy-five years, remain indifferent to initiatives that threatened to build up Japanese power again.[9]

When Kim Il Sung visited Moscow in the flush of Communism's great victory in Asia, Nikita Khrushchev said in *Khrushchev Remembers*, Kim told the Russians that "he wanted to prod South Korea with the point of a bayonet." At the first poke, he explained, an internal explosion would go off in South Korea, and the people would rally to his regime. This was revolutionary talk suitable to the hour of Communism's triumph in Asia, and besides:

> the struggle would be an internal matter which the Koreans would be settling among themselves.

Stalin told Kim to figure out just what he would need, and come back with a concrete plan. As Khrushchev tells it, Kim was soon back with "everything worked out."

The authenticity of this account, drawn from one of thirty chapters pulled together from taped interviews, is questioned by some scholars. The account of Korean events at least seems reasonable, all the more so because here Khrushchev did not make out the best case for the Communists. He said he still thought Stalin was wrong when after saying, "Well, why not?" and giving Kim the arms he asked for to invade South Korea, Stalin pulled out all the Russian advisers and line-of-supply people as soon as the Americans' counterattack at Inchon made things rough. Criticizing this decision, Khrushchev still seemed unable to understand the eminently sound reason he says Stalin gave him: "If the Americans pull it off I don't want any Russians in PW camps."

Presumably this exchange took place during Mao Tse-tung's Moscow visit, and Stalin, still doubtful and "worried that the Americans would jump in," put the matter to Chairman Mao. Mao approved the scheme and "put forward the opinion that the USA would not intervene." The "requisite" tanks, artillery, rifles, machine guns, engineering equipment and antiaircraft weapons were readied. Russian MIG-15s were stationed in North Korea. Then at two in the morning on June 25, 1950, eight North Korean divisions led by 150 Soviet-made tanks, surged into South Korea. In a shrill radio appeal Kim Il Sung summoned all South Koreans to help "unify the country." Workers should strike, farmers withhold food, guerrillas blow up highways and bridges, intellectuals should agitate for a mass rising, and soldiers should throw down their rifles and join the invaders. Said Khrushchev:

> Kim believed that South Korea was blanketed with party organizations and that the people would rise up in revolt when the Party gave the signal. But this never happened.[10]

But Kim's bayonet prod did touch off an explosion on the other side of the world. For the Cold Warriors of the Truman administration, edging up to a tremendous new round of peacetime rearmament against the Communists, the invasion of South Korea had blasted the ground from beneath their feet. "International Communism" had suddenly and brutally swung into a second and deadlier phase of the world conflict—the use of armed force.

These men in Washington were startled. Their policy had been to wield America's power without resort to armed force. Now that policy had come a cropper. The rules that had worked so well in the first five years in Europe and the Middle East—of giving peaceful aid to non-Communist countries menaced by subversion from within, of building up the economic strength of such countries as Greece and Turkey, France and Italy, of flexing American might in Berlin while withholding armed force—these rules did not apply in Asia. No sooner had Communism gained the victory in China than Stalin had pulled away from the European side of the world to strike in Asia.

America's visceral response, from start of the Cold War to finish, was to apply its power as if it were omnipotent. The men in Washington never doubted that it was "international Communism" that had so abruptly raised the stakes in Korea. They saw the enemy as indivisible, as sleeplessly aggressive in the same war-bent certitude of historical inevitability as the other totalitarianism of the Nazis had been, and they saw it as Kremlin-directed. They did not then often identify this enemy as "Stalinism." There was still a certain ambivalence about Stalin as the wartime ally. Even Truman, when it suited his purposes, could say from the rear of a presidential train in Spokane in 1948, "I like Old Joe."

Yet there was an important sense in which Stalinism permeated and shaped the reflexive obsessiveness and rigidity of their own Cold War outlook. For two such ruthless, nonmoral figures as Hitler and Stalin, the one a madman and the other paranoid by all the evidence, to rise in quick succession to world dominance, back to back as it were, is unusual in history. The experience of having to deal one after the other with two such monstrous dictators had something to do with the excess of zeal that the men in Washington for their part displayed toward power in these years.

Dealing with such types in Berlin and the Kremlin almost without a break for two decades greatly damaged the American capacity for getting on with the more usual sort of human beings in the world—and this would include Stalin's successors. It certainly damaged the American ability to negotiate with the rest of the world, for instance with the North Vietnamese. How, a younger generation was to ask, could Johnson and Rusk believe that Ho Chi Minh was a Hitler—*Uncle* Ho?

If the world's greatest power were to pick up the challenge thrown down by "international Communism" in Asia, however, it would not only have to draw up rules for the new, armed-force phase of the Cold War, it would also have to reconsider its policies for Asia. However much America had persisted in asserting its westward destiny as manifested in the doctrine of the Open Door to China, its policymakers for years had drawn back from Asian commitment. This was true even of the Republicans with their historic Pacific propensity. At no time had the Open Door doctrine contained a military component for America. In the years between the two World Wars the Harding, Coolidge and Hoover administrations, by agreement with the Japanese, withdrew American power from the western Pacific, basing the fleet in Hawaii. In the postwar years General Marshall as Democratic Secretary of State in 1947 had conspicuously placed American interests in Europe over Asia when he returned from his mission in China to propose the Marshall Plan to save Europe.

Just how powerful was America? Had this country, drawn into the Second World War by the Japanese attack in the Pacific, not fought to save China too? Did not the might that turned the Pacific into an American lake extend to upholding the "free world" on its Asian shores as well? The dilemma of America was that of the island continent which faced two ways, and there were those like Walter Lippmann who kept dinning into the country's ears that it must choose between Atlantic and Pacific and, indeed, *had* made the transatlantic choice. But this was not how the world looked to millions of Americans five years after their greatest military triumph, it was not how it looked to many Republicans in Congress or to their favorite general in Tokyo, and it was probably not how it looked to the President in Independence, Missouri.[11]

The first pivotal days in June, 1950, was the time of what President Truman, who made many important decisions, called "the most important decision I ever made." In subsequent years much came to be made of the difficulty a President faced at such times in obtaining information and advice that enabled him to act after taking all major factors into consideration. Neither the old-fashioned cabinet nor the new-fangled National Security Council, though the latter brought together the President's topmost advisers, came to be thought apt for the crises of Cold

War. To sit with him during the Cuban Missile Crisis of 1962 President Kennedy formed his Excom, or Executive Committee of fifteen. When later President Johnson brooded on his intervention in Vietnam, he summoned his "Tuesday Cabinet" of seven. President Nixon, in his first-term overtures to Peking and Moscow, relied on the advice of Henry Kissinger within the White House itself.[12]

In making his Korean decision and the array of related decisions that went with it, Truman found his Kissinger in the State Department. Secretary Acheson, stepping in at a moment when the Defense Department confessed itself to be without any plans for such an eventuality as the attack in Korea, provided in effect the kind of overviewing plan out of which the President could act.

When news of the invasion hit Washington, Secretary Acheson telephoned President Truman at his home in Independence. Truman immediately approved a move to call the United Nations Security Council into session. In the absence of the Soviet delegate, who was boycotting the meetings over the Council's refusal to seat a Communist as representative of the new government of China, the Council voted seven-to-zero to ask North Korea to withdraw and agree to a ceasefire. Then as the President flew back to Washington, the new breed of "crisis managers" came into their own. These were the technicians of Cold War, the élite group of Washington insiders who helped the President make his decisions. They had their forerunners in the Forrestals and Kings, the Lovetts and McCloys, who were privileged to enter Admiral Leahy's Map Room in President Roosevelt's wartime White House. They had their successors in the Bundys and Rostows, the Max Taylors and Earle Wheelers, who appeared at each successive Southeast Asia crisis. Now at Blair House, where the President lived while the White House underwent extensive structural repairs, the lights burned late in the night. Black limousines rolled through the dusk bearing the twelve top diplomatic and military advisers to a late dinner and the first of many night meetings with the President. In a Washington still quivering from Pearl Harbor, these experts, more self-conscious than their forerunners and including a high proportion of Yale men among them, produced their cabled and classified reports. [13]

President Truman valued the "cool courage and steadfast judgment" of Secretary Acheson whose "suggestions," read from notes at the first night's meeting the President adopted almost intact. Again and again throughout the Truman administration there was a persisting sense, after the bold leadership of Franklin Roosevelt, of a smaller man making tremendous decisions, and never, not even after the dropping of the A-bomb and the proclamation of the Truman Doctrine, was this impression more palpable than when Truman decided to resist the Communist aggression in Korea.

He said that he was going to hit them hard, and he did. On Acheson's advice he directed General MacArthur in Tokyo to give the retreating South Koreans air and naval support at once. Yet he did not ask Congress for a declaration of war, and indeed he soon insisted that the forces he sent into Korea were conducting a "police action." The lurch of power between Atlantic and Pacific, the sway of politics between defenders of Europe and Asia-Firsters, the equipoise between West and East—all entered bewilderingly into the balance. In the lack of trust engendered by such omissions and mystifying utterances, however, the credibility gap that plagued America a decade later began to open in the summer of 1950. Senator Taft, righteously convinced that his own father would never have made free with the inherent powers of the Presidency to take the country into war by such "complete usurpation" of Congressional authority, bitterly resisted Truman's way of going into Korea.[14]

A second part of Truman's decision also had far-reaching consequences. "To keep the conflict from spreading," the President ordered the Seventh Fleet into the Formosa Strait where it could prevent the Communists on the mainland and Chiang-Kai-shek's Nationalists on Taiwan from attacking each other. The first result of this action was to prevent Mao, who had been deriding the United States as a "paper tiger," from invading and subduing the last bit of China left outside his control. The second and spectacular consequence of Truman's directive to the Seventh Fleet, because it gave Chiang a new lease on life, was to give new hope to those Republicans and others who believed that an omnipotent America had somehow "lost" China—rather like an outfielder who drops a fly when he almost has it in his hands. Having "lost" China, such people could now tell themselves: "We can make it all up in Korea." All of a sudden, thanks to the political brief drawn up for him by Acheson, President Truman found himself praised by his old critic, Senator Knowland, for having "drawn a line" against Asian Communism. Taking note that Truman had not after all abandoned Chiang, Knowland said:

> I believe that in this very important step which the President of the United States has taken in order to uphold the free peoples of the world, he should have the overwhelming support of all Americans regardless of their partisan affiliation.[15]

This was not all. As yet another part of his Korean action President Truman ordered a substantial increase in American aid to the Philippines and to the French in Indochina. In the latter decision, prompted by

Acheson, the overriding consideration was sustaining French strength and anti-Communist resolve in Europe. Nobody noticed at the time, but it was the beginning of an American involvement in Indochina that would keep the "crisis managers" occupied for much of the next twenty years.[16]

The very day after Truman's decision, a second American-originated United Nations resolution endorsed it by directing members to assist the South Koreans. When MacArthur then asked authority to send in ground forces, Truman promptly agreed. One week later MacArthur was designated United Nations Supreme Commander in the first military action in support of collective security since the end of the Second World War.

When a bipartisan group of congressional leaders trooped in to hear the news from the President, not a single voice opposed the American commitment. Many called Truman's decision "courageous." Invoking United Nations sanctions promptly against an aggressor, the President had done precisely what democracy's leaders had signally failed to do in the appeasing years leading up to the Second World War. Congressional Democrats hailed Truman's action as a stand against Moscow-engineered aggression; Senator Hubert Humphrey of Minnesota praised it as quite possibly "the greatest move for peace of the twentieth century."

Of greatest importance for the President's decision was the support that liberals gave him encouraging him to rely on the inherent powers of the Presidency under the constitution in going into Korea. On the advice of Acheson, who feared the effect on troop morale of a drawn-out debate and attacks by such extremists as Senator Jenner of Indiana, the President did not ask Congress for a joint resolution backing his step. What was missing in the whole swift sequel of events was an expression of the sixty-eight percent opinion recorded in a Gallup poll as favoring peace negotiations with the Communists. Those who might have spoken were cowed into silence and kept out of office by the bristling belligerence of a majority roused to fierce anti-Communism by the Cold War. The stock market rallied, and the number of his countrymen who according to opinion polls thought President Truman was doing a good job rose from thirty-three percent to fifty percent. Only Senator Taft, charging that Acheson's January speech had amounted to an "invitation to attack" from the North Koreans, and condemning the President for acting without getting Congress's prior approval, struck a strong dissenting note in Cold War America. Abroad, Truman's decision was seen not at all as a trigger-happy American reaction in Asia but as a well-judged riposte to aggression. No fewer than eleven of America's allies, nine of them in Europe, rallied to the United Nations and arranged to send fighting contingents to Korea.[17]

Meanwhile the Americans, rushing from Japan to stop the Soviet-armored blitz, were outnumbered, outgunned, outtanked. Major General William Dean, the field commander, was captured. Sergeant Raymond Kemp of Pittsburgh told of the rout:

> We ran across six of them mountain tops and killed four guys. We were out of ammo . . . I can't stand it—seeing friends get it and not be able to help them drives you crazy. I thought the Huertgen Forest was bad and Normandy but they were nothing like this . . . I'm not hit. But . . . oh God, what it did to me.

In many ways, in men and leaders and the very weapons they fought with, the war in Korea was for America the last battle of the Second World War. In September, a sudden shift turned the tide abruptly in America's favor. By a bold amphibious assault far up the coast at Inchon, General MacArthur sent the North Koreans flying, their tanks and artillery abandoned behind them, across the 38th parallel. It was the last big American triumph of the Second World War, accomplished indeed with leftover landing craft from MacArthur's island-hopping campaigns of 1944 and 1945. The press hailed it as brilliant, but it was really a last hurrah.[18]

Ceremoniously handing back his capital to Syngman Rhee, MacArthur sought and got Washington's authorization to send American and South Korean forces north across the 38th parallel to accomplish the "destruction" of Kim's remaining forces. This did not at once alarm America's allies. But on the Communist side the chagrin at the failure of the South Koreans to rally quickly to Kim and the surprise at the vigor of America's response now gave way to apprehensions. It began to look as if the Americans might finish off the war by establishing an independent Korea and building up Japan as a major new anti-Communist ally in the Far East the way they were building up an anti-Communist European center in Germany. Stalin, as cautious in the face of American power in Asia as in Europe, pulled out all Russian advisers with Kim's army. But Chou En-lai, according to Khrushchev, suddenly appeared in Moscow to propose that Chinese forces now move into North Korea to stem the American advance.[19]

After President Truman's decision to intervene in Korea, Chou had issued a statement so blistering that Secretary Acheson called it tantamount to a declaration of war. Presumably Chou was furious because the stationing of the Seventh Fleet in the Formosa strait blocked an imminent Communist move to seize Taiwan, almost the last bit of Chinese territory not under their rule. Soon after, thousands of Chinese troops, including many destined for Taiwan, moved north from the Formosa Strait area to Manchuria and the Korean border. When the Allies crossed the 38th parallel in late October, the Chinese warned the Indian ambassador that China would not "sit back with folded hands and let the Americans come up to the border."[20]

The Allies thought the Chinese were bluffing. The United Nations passed a resolution prepared by Assistant Secretary of State Dean Rusk declaring that the aim was now to unify Korea by force, and on October 15 at a meeting with President Truman at Wake Island, General MacArthur assured the President, "We are no longer fearful of Chinese intervention." At that very moment, Stalin and Mao having agreed, the Chinese had crossed the Yalu River.

At first they came stealthily and in small "volunteer" units. By this covert and gradual infiltration Mao could of course achieve maximum surprise and reduce the risks of a sharp American counterblow. The strategy also left the Chinese free to pull back if the Americans heeded China's diplomatic warnings and kept away from the Yalu River border. But the Americans plunged right on.[21]

On Thanksgiving Day General MacArthur fed his troops turkey dinner with all the trimmings. Then, proclaiming "they will eat Christmas dinner at home," he sent them off to the border in his final, win-the-war offensive. Two days later, when his troops were at their most exposed and overextended, 200,000 Chinese Communists under command of General Peng Teh-huai, the scourge of Shansi, struck south with crushing force. They wiped out the South Korean II Corps. They overran the American Second Infantry Division. They cut off the First Marine Division near Changjon Reservoir a few miles from the Manchurian line.[22]

The Americans had to retreat as fast as they could. They clawed southward through snow and narrow gorges, between rocky ridges filled with Chinese machine-gunners. Much of the fighting was at night, and in close quarters. Two-thousand-six-hundred-fifty-one wounded were flown out in four days; once 117 bodies were buried in a single grave and a bulldozer used to push a covering over them—there was no time for anything else when a grave had to be blasted from ground frozen to eighteen inches. The rout was not stopped until they were back behind the 38th parallel 200 miles to the south. It was a major American defeat, though total casualties were relatively light by Second World War comparisons—13,000 as against 80,000 for the Battle of the Bulge. For Chinese arms it was the first major victory, the first gained by Chinese over forces of a great power since the Opium War of 1838–40.[23]

Proclaiming an "entirely new war," MacArthur now demanded that the United States carry the war to China proper. He urged that American bombers strike at Manchuria supply bases and that Nationalist troops invade the mainland from Taiwan. President Truman rejected MacArthur's proposals. But when he told reporters he would not rule out the use of the atomic bomb under certain circumstances, Prime Minister Clement Attlee hurried over from England to urge restraint.[24]

For a time after Seoul fell to the Chinese, it looked as if the Americans were going to be pushed right off the peninsula. Then General Matthew Ridgway who had arrived in Korea at Christmas to take command of the Eighth Army, rallied the dispirited GIs. At his shoulder he wore a grenade, just as when he commanded the parachute landings in Normandy. He set up a new line of resistance along the Han River south of Seoul and announced that there would be no more "bugouts." He called upon his commander as at the St. Lo breakthrough to keep three precepts always in view—coordination, maximum punishment and intact maintenance of major units. His phrase for it was "good footwork combined with firepower." GI's termed it the "meat-grinder":

> You began with the longrange artillery from ten miles away enveloping the hills in tall columns of dust flung up by tons of high explosive, followed by the quicker shellbursts from the more accurate lighter guns, at a shorter range. You bombarded the positions further with tank guns while swooping aircraft plastered them with napalm and rockets, and the infantrymen secure in their foxholes let loose a murderous hail of staccato fire with rifles, machine guns and mortars. This lasted for the morning. In the afternoon the infantry crept up the slopes of the hills to find if anyone was left there.[25]

Now it was the Chinese whose rapid advance had overtaken their supply line, and while General Ridgway turned the Normandy meat-grinder along the front, the Air Force pounded roads, bridges and railways. The rout was halted. But this was all-out combat, and the callup of fighting men, some 1,400,000 in three years, exceeded the number drafted later during any comparable period in the Vietnam war. A regimental commander said:

> They're fighting now because the platoon leader is leading them, and the platoon leader is fighting because of the command, and so on right to the top.[26]

It could also be said that the American Army, fighting for its life on a nonwhite continent, changed its attitude toward race. Ridgway, backed by Army Chief Lawton J. Collins, broke up all-black units under fire and integrated blacks into line outfits at the front with results felt at once by the Chinese on the front. They were also felt soon in integrated training camps back in the United States, and before long in all America. The Americans began to shove the Chinese back. Within four months Ridgeway's soldiers retook Seoul and battered their way back to where it all started—the 38th parallel. In Washington leaders agreed that aggression against this frontier after all was what the United States had gone to war to stop. Now President Truman prepared an offer of a standstill compromise on or near the 38th parallel.[27]

At this delicate moment General MacArthur, without even bothering to tell Washington, issued his own call for a Chinese surrender. This, in Truman's view, was clear insubordination. When at almost the same time Representative Joseph Martin Jr., leader of the Republican opposition, rose in the House and read a letter from MacArthur praising Martin's criticism of the President's policy and asserting "there is no substitute for victory," Truman dismissed MacArthur from all his commands in the Far East and replaced him with General Ridgway.[28]

The popular response in America was the most vehement in modern American history. Within days, 26,636 denunciatory letters and telegrams rained down on the White House. "Impeach the little war-politician stupidity from Kansas City," said one. "Impeach the Judas in the White House who sold us down the river to leftwingers and the UN" read another. The President was burned in effigy in many towns, booed at the opening of the Washinton baseball season, and publicly denounced as a "son of a bitch" and "agent of the Soviet Union" by two Republican senators. Honolulu, San Francisco and New York greeted MacArthur as a conquering hero. Speaker Martin arranged for the general to address a joint session of Congress. The whole country tuned in on TV and radio. The cadences they heard, the countenance they saw, were of an earlier America, somewhat reminiscent in fact of William Jennings Bryan. MacArthur presented his program for ending the war in Korea by bombing China. At the end he quoted the old barrack-room ballad: "Old soldiers never die; they just fade away."

> Like the soldier of that ballad, I now close my military career and just fade away, an old soldier who tried to do his duty as God gave him the light to see that duty.[29]

At least one Administration supporter feared for a few moments that the general's listeners might march right out the door on the White House. Two members of Congress buttonholed reporters to insist it was the greatest speech ever delivered. Dewey Short, Republican of Missouri, said in so many words: "We have heard God speak today." Three weeks later a sizable proportion of the Senate met in joint committee to review the dismissal of the man their chairman, Richard Russell of Georgia, greeted as "one of the great captains of history."[30]

In the course of these hearings America at last got its chance to find out not only why Truman had relieved MacArthur but also why the United States had failed for the first time to fight a war to victory. MacArthur had to answer questions, and the Administration's spokesmen had to spell out their Korea and Far Eastern policies, and before they were done, their whole strategy for the Cold War. MacArthur was heard saying that the United States should accept all risks to win the victory that had eluded him in Korea, and Truman's advisers were heard replying, in the words of General Omar Bradley, that the Korean war was the "wrong war" in which to accept ultimate risks. It was—a distasteful word for Americans, and difficult to understand or accept—a "limited" war.

Ranged against America, as the men around Truman saw the world, was a vast, contiguous Eurasian landmass of peoples managed by "distant and shadowy figures in the Kremlin." The old sense of omnipotence which Truman so exuberantly expressed after V-J Day had somehow faded. After Changjon Reservoir the nation was to hear less of such boasts. In the world Administration spokesmen now talked about, a world in which America looked to both Europe and Asia, both the Atlantic and Pacific, the Korean fighting must be kept strictly limited. This, Acheson said, was because the takeover of Europe and its industrial base was the Kremlin's main objective. If all-out war over China's intervention in Korea brought the Russians in on the side of what he termed their "largest and most important satellite," the result must be "explosive not only for the Far East but for the rest of the world as well." Acheson pleaded for time to build up "positions of strength" for the expected showdown in Europe. MacArthur countered that there would never be a better time to risk general war than at that very moment, when the Russian A-bomb was little developed.[31]

As the weeks of debate raged on it became apparent that MacArthur had lost the argument. Yet the kind of patriotism he represented was not too different from that of Truman himself, who had been badly used by MacArthur. MacArthur had patronized him. He had ignored Truman's orders and played up to the Republican opposition. When MacArthur deigned to receive Truman at Wake Island, his conduct was such as to make Truman look "like an insurance salesman who had just signed up an important client," as The New York Times Reporter Anthony Leveiro observed, at the very time MacArthur was mismanaging his campaign in Korea. Truman was in truth slow to fire MacArthur, and the reason was that with his old Battery D reverence for serving his country in khaki, he worshipped that kind of man.[32]

In any event the other side flashed their first signals for a negotiated end to the Korean stalemate, and the American public plainly wanted an end to the affair. At the same time the Truman administration pressed boldly ahead with the huge military buildup it had planned—and simultaneously with the Korean War carried out—to meet the anticipated Russian armed thrust in Europe. In a sense then, the war in Korea might have been viewed as a war waged for Europe, and it was certainly claimed that President Truman's decision to stand and fight in Korea restrained the Russians from following up with another aggressive move in Europe, perhaps through a satellite state like Czechoslovakia or Hungary. But the 150,000 American casualties in Korea were not to be counted solely as the price of keeping Russia back of the Iron Curtain on the other side of the world. The war in Korea had also been waged for Asia.[33]

There, after all the racing to the Yalu and back, the United States had successfully defended the Republic of Korea against Communist assault. It had also become embroiled in war with China, with consequences that extended long past the Cold War. But nothing said at the MacArthur hearings could blot out the inexorable limits laid upon American omnipotence: the United States could not at the same time hold the line in Europe and impose its will on the Asian mainland. That had been the lesson of the Communist victory in China after 1945. The lesson was now taught a second time in the effort to wind up the Korean conflict.

The Americans duly obtained their peace treaty with the Japanese in September, 1951. Their defeat in the Second World War had left the Japanese with a deep aversion to war. But after the Chinese intervened in Korea to inflict a crushing defeat upon the general who had been their supreme lawgiver for five years, the Japanese redoubled their devotion to their new constitutional clause outlawing war—and the United States was never able to arrange with Japan the same kind of military alliance that it made with the Germans in Europe.[34]

For America the political price of the Korean War was a high one, and the Chinese found a way to raise it still higher. Toward the end of the last offensive in Korea, Secretary Marshall told the senators at the MacArthur hearings that in one two-week period American soldiers had "disposed of the fighting power" of twenty-six Chinese divisions. That was April, 1951, and the Chinese were clearly hurting more than the Americans at that point. Yet when the Russians proposed peace negotiations, Mao at once shifted to a strategy of protracted conflict. Sitting and stalling at the conference table, his representatives gradually wore away the psychological edge that Ridgway's comeback campaign had achieved. Over the next interminable twenty-six months it was the American people who were hurting more. The Korean war, dismally stalemated by Mao's strategy of will-sapping delay, dragged on long after the peace talks began.

Long before then patience had run out in America, the old arguments against limited war found new voices, and McCarthyism was riding high in the land.[35]

THE ELECTION of General Eisenhower as President in 1952 might have been expected to put an end to the disease called McCarthyism. Instead the infection reached new peaks of virulence, spread yet more widely through the national bloodstream and wrought outright destruction within the organs of government itself. Effective power in the new Congress was wielded by those who had opposed Eisenhower's nomination and these Conservative Republicans were of no mind to separate themselves from the burning appeal of the Communism-in-government issues with which McCarthy had made himself synonymous. It was President Eisenhower's "passion" his aide C. D. Jackson remarked "not to offend anyone in Congress," an attitude shared by the new Secretary of State, John Foster Dulles.

Eisenhower's reluctance to curb McCarthy gave the senator every chance to wield the power he acquired as chairman of the new Congress's Government Operations committee. McCarthy remarked that he thought there were still Communists in the State Department, and that Dulles could do something to root them out by naming a good security officer. The Secretary named the very man McCarthy mentioned, Senator Bridges's former administrative assistant, Scott McLeod. Then McCarthy on his own hook announced that he had "negotiated" with Greek shipping magnates to stop trading with Communist China and North Korea. Harold Stassen, the new Mutual Security Director, angrily condemned this as "undermining" the administration's conduct of foreign affairs. Dulles hurried to arrange a lunch with McCarthy, and all Eisenhower would say was that Stassen might have meant "infringement" rather than "undermining."[36]

Exploiting the delicate political balance between the Administration and congressional conservatives, McCarthy opened up an investigation of the State Department's overseas information program that filled the nation's headlines. Roy Cohn, twenty-seven, his subcommittee's new chief counsel, and his friend, G. David Schine, also twenty-seven, spun through Europe on an eighteen-day whirl and returned to report "appalling infiltration" of the department's overseas information libraries. The State Department dismissed officials and ordered librarians to remove "books of . . . any Communists, fellow-travelers, etcetera from their shelves." All sorts of books were removed, including some by the cousin of the secretary, Foster Rhea Dulles. Some librarians, taking no chances, burned them. Finally even Eisenhower was compelled to acknowledge the scandal. About to receive an honorary degree at Dartmouth, he blurted: "Don't join the book burners."[37]

Three months after taking office Eisenhower said under insistent press-conference questioning that he would intervene if congressional inquiries threatened the international relations of the United States. When McCarthy announced his displeasure with the selection of Charles Bohlen, Roosevelt's adviser at Yalta, as Eisenhower's ambassador to Russia, the Administration got Senator Taft in person to persuade McCarthy not to block the nomination. Taft did so, but afterwards warned that there must be "no more Bohlens." Within the Senate six of the men elected in 1952 were thought to owe their seats largely to McCarthy's campaigning. It was a rare moment that year when a senator spoke up after McCarthy openly called upon the State Department to pass classified information to him. "Then you are advocating government by individual as against government by law?" rasped John McClellan, Democrat of Arkansas, senior minority member of the Government Operations Committee. McCarthy replied, "The issue is whether the people are entitled to the facts." At rallies the popular song was, "Nobody Loves McCarthy But the People."[38]

From time to time Vice President Nixon, as the Administration's liaison man with McCarthy, would get the senator to let up and deliver a tough speech instead of a "real dirty" one, or hold off on one of his investigations—of the Central Intelligence Agency, the Atomic Energy Commission, the security status of J. Robert Oppenheimer. But McCarthy took for his targets the inner citadels of the ruling Establishment, and this was the source of much of his popularity and power. The State Department had been his first target, taken under fire the moment the conviction of Alger Hiss conferred on his wildest charges the monstrous possibility of truth. The second of the citadels attacked by McCarthy was the Army, and he did not hesitate to victimize its most distinguished generals or tonguelash its entire leadership.

The deed of headlong recklessness that brought McCarthy to the beginning of his decline and fall was an attack on the ultimate pillar of the American establishment—the church. He had humiliated the Army, humbled the State Department, and now he leaped on the National Council of Churches of Christ in America. In the summer of 1953, as McCarthy took aim, the preacher at Riverside Church in New York City and the evangelist in his tent at Little Rock had one theme. In America, the evangelist said, "everyone is scared to death."[39]

Already Congressman Harold Velde, the former FBI agent who now headed the House Committee on Un-American Activities, had had wealthy Bishop G. Bromley Oxnam, the presiding bishop of the Methodist Church of the United States, before his committee to ask about his membership in the wartime Council of Soviet-American Friendship. Already Representative Donald Jackson, Republican of California and great friend of Vice President Nixon, had charged that Oxnam "served God on Sunday and the Communist front for the balance of the week." But when McCarthy went after the Protestant Establishment he finally overreached himself.[40]

In the July 1953 issue of the rightwing *American Mercury* J. B. Matthews, just hired by McCarthy as a committee consultant, charged that the largest single group in the nation backing the Communists was the Protestant clergy. A few days before, Lyndon Johnson had proposed to the new Majority Leader William Knowland that a bipartisan select committee be appointed to make a study of McCarthy and report to the Senate. Knowland, deeply conservative, was skeptical and while he knew that McCarthy was "a Republican problem," many Republicans thought McCarthy could help the party in the 1954 elections in the Midwest and West. Then the news ticker in the Senate cloakroom tapped out the new McCarthy charge. Lyndon Johnson read it and called across to Senator Harry Byrd. "Here, see this," said Johnson. "Joe's gone too far this time."

Matthews' attack was a broadside charge that "at least 7000" Protestant clergymen supported Communism as "party members, fellow travelers, espionage agents, party-line adherents and unwitting dupes." Enraged, Senator McClellan demanded on behalf of Democratic committee members that its author be fired and its charges repudiated as "a shocking and unwarranted attack on the American clergy." As calls and telegrams poured in from concerned ministers across the nation a Republican member, Charles Potter of Michigan, also announced his "present" opinion that Matthews be dismissed.[41]

When McCarthy refused to act, the four Democrats resigned in a body. Even the White House stirred to action. Deputy Attorney General William P. Rogers arranged for the cochairmen of the National Council of Christians and Jews to send the President a telegram protesting the attack as "deplorable and unjustifiable." Actually, the Rogers staff wrote the telegram and then ransacked the country to locate the signers. The minute the wire arrived at the White House Eisenhower issued a statement, also prepared by the Rogers staff, denouncing "generalized and irresponsible attacks that sweepingly condemn the whole of any group" as "alien to America." Said Eisenhower:

Such attacks betray contempt for the principles of freedom and decency. When such attacks condemn such a vast portion of the churches or clergy as to create doubt in the loyalty of all, the damage to our nation is multiplied.

The churches of America are citadels of our faith in individual freedom and human dignity. This faith is the living source of all our spiritual strength. And this strength is our matchless armor in our worldwide struggle in the face of godless tyranny and oppression.

McCarthy, the rough-and-tumble fighter, had given his opponents a wide and irresistible opening, and they jumped in. Two days later McCarthy fired Matthews, and abandoned his assault on the Protestant Establishment. It was, said *Time*, "the first such clubbing that he had taken in 6½ years in the Senate," and though at the beginning of 1954 a Gallup poll recorded a majority (fifty percent of the American public) convinced that McCarthy was doing a good job, it was downhill for McCarthy from this point on.[42]

Early in 1954, egged on by Cohn, McCarthy returned to his attack on the Army. Cohn was trying to help his friend Schine who, despite the best efforts of McCarthy and Cohn, had been drafted into the Army. Sent to Fort Dix, New Jersey, Schine found that he did not care for the rigor of basic training, and appealed to Cohn for rescue.

Cohn tried. He bombarded the Army with demands that Schine be given special privileges. He suggested to Secretary of the Army Robert Stevens that Schine be made his aide for sleuthing out disloyal soldiers. When the Secretary seemed cool to that idea, Cohn urged that Schine be transferred to West Point to study military textbooks for signs of Communist propaganda. When that scheme failed, Cohn used McCarthy's clout to press for a civilian-clothes job for Schine in New York. Again he was refused.

It was at this point that McCarthy's "Loyal American Underground" sent him a tip: look into the Army's handling of the investigation into the loyalty of Dr. Irving Peress. Peress was an obscure New York City dentist and member of the leftwing American Labor party who had been inducted into the service and stationed at Camp Kilmer in New Jersey. While the investigation was going on a routine promotion had come through for Peress from captain to major. But the result of the investigation led the Army to discharge the dentist within ninety days. When McCarthy heard of this he summoned Peress before his subcommittee, where the dentist took the Fifth Amendment. Three days later, discharged by the Army, Peress was safely beyond the reach of the military law.

With his usual extravagance, McCarthy roared that the Peress case was "the key to the deliberate Communist infiltration of our armed

forces." Three days later, as headlines blared: W H O P R O M O T E D
P E R E S S ? he called another hearing. One of the witnesses was General
Ralph Zwicker, hero of the Battle of the Bulge and now commander at
Fort Monmouth. When Zwicker refused on the advice of Army counsel
John Adams to provide the names of all officers involved in Peress's
discharge, McCarthy boiled over. "You are a disgrace to the uniform" he
shouted. "You're shielding Communist conspirators. You're not fit to be
an officer. You don't have the brains of a five-year-old." When Adams
tried to intervene on Zwicker's behalf, McCarthy ordered him from the
hearing room. "You're going to be put on display next Tuesday,"
McCarthy told Zwicker.[43]

Secretary Stevens ordered the general not to appear again before the
committee, but then, after a meeting with McCarthy, appeared to yield.
Later he repudiated the agreement with McCarthy, and McCarthy re-
torted through the press: "The Army is holding Schine hostage to get me
to lay off" a spy ring at Fort Monmouth that—the senator said—had been
set up in wartime by Julius Rosenberg and was still in operation. By now
Adlai Stevenson was calling the Republican Party "half Eisenhower and
half McCarthy," and Senator Ralph Flanders, Republican of Vermont,
took the Senate floor with anger and scorn.

> He dons his war paint [said Flanders]. He goes into his war dance. He
> emits his war whoops. He goes forth to battle and proudly returns with
> the scalp of a pink Army dentist. We may assume that this represents
> the depth of Communist penetration at this time.[44]

That night Edward R. Murrow's *See It Now* TV program focused on
Senator McCarthy. The show presented the senator in his own words and
gestures but at the end Murrow said:

> We cannot defend freedom abroad by deserting it at home. The actions
> of the junior Senator from Wisconsin have caused alarm and dismay
> among our allies abroad and given considerable comfort to our enemies,
> and whose fault is this? Not really his. He didn't create the situation of
> fear, he merely exploited it, and rather successfully. Cassius was right.
> The fault, dear Brutus, is not in our stars but in ourselves.[45]

From the day the unfortunate Stevens had been trapped in his agreement
with McCarthy, the Administration also began to move against
McCarthy. Yet even now, the matter was deemed one for Congress to
deal with. The White House wanted the Armed Services Committee to
take on the inquiry, but Chairman Leverett Saltonstall, Republican of

Massachusetts, was up for reelection and would have none of it. So McCarthy's own subcommittee voted to investigate the McCarthy-Army quarrel, with television cameras in the room and McCarthy temporarily vacating his chair to his friend Senator Karl Mundt of South Dakota, next ranking Republican.[46]

The atmospherics surrounding these hearings were nightmarish. The spring of 1954 was probably the high point of the Cold War for America. On January 12 Secretary Dulles hurled hellfire and brimstone at the Kremlin in a speech threatening "massive retaliation" against any hostile Communist move anywhere. In Washington after McCarthy threatened to investigate the Communist ties of Robert Oppenheimer, the head of the wartime atomic bomb project, President Eisenhower ordered a "blank wall" placed between the scientist and all Cold War programs while a special board grilled him in secret about whether he had passed any blueprints to the Russians. On April 3 Secretary Dulles asked the leaders of Congress for a resolution endorsing American armed intervention in Indochina to save the French army surrounded by Communists at Dienbienphu. Day after day the Secretary laid down a deafening propaganda barrage against the Guatemalan government for "openly playing the Communist game" while plotting in secret with his brother Allen at the Central Intelligence Agency to overthrow the Central American government's leftist regime. On April 13 *The New York Times* broke the sensational story that the "father of the atomic bomb" himself had been stripped of his government privileges and denounced as disloyal: "O P - P E N H E I M E R ' S   S E C U R I T Y   S U S P E N D E D :   H E A R I N G S   I N   P R O G R E S S . [47]

Amid such events, shortly after 10:00 A.M. on April 22, 1954, a TV spectacular began playing in the Senate caucus room on Capitol Hill. There were many actors in the drama that was played out in the thirty-six daily installments, but the key figure was McCarthy. This was McCarthy in the life, as the Democrats had insisted when they pressed for televising the hearings. This was McCarthy the brawler whose forensic biting, kicking and rabbit-punching had gained him such power over rivals in the political infighting in Washington. "A point of order," the senator was saying before the first announcement was ended. "Mr. Chairman, may I raise a point of order."

He rode contemptuously over what his fellow senators tried to say. He seized the floor from opponents by physical force, repeating in his strong, singsong voice until the opponent wearily gave way. He smeared right and left, and then accused others of smearing. He sidetracked, and then bewailed diversion. He tried to introduce a cropped photograph of Schine and Stevens, and then charged deception in the Army. It was

Republican officeholders who were now the targets, and in hitting at them McCarthy was striking at the President. From the White House came a complaint that McCarthy's demands violated the rights of the Executive, and that these rights "cannot be usurped by any individual who may seek to set himself above the law of the land." McCarthy's retort was to talk again about "the evidence of treason that has been growing over the past twenty"—and, pausing to bear down heavily on the altered number— "twenty-one years."

"If you are going to play with McCarthy," said Senator Stuart Symington, one of the committee's minority members, "you have to forget about any of those Marquess of Queensberry rules." McCarthy's office had prepared dossiers on all the participants, not excepting his fellow senators. One dossier held unspecified charges against McClellan gathered from his enemies in Arkansas. Another folder, labeled "Jackson's record," was waved threatingly aloft by Roy Cohn after Senator Henry Jackson, Democrat of Washington, interfered with a McCarthy move. The dossier on Symington contained an old 1952 campaign blast about a teenage joyride that Symington and two other boys had taken in a neighbor's car back in 1930. McCarthy's style was to barge into the committee room, toss an arm over Symington's shoulder and leer, "Stole any cars lately, Stu?"[48]

If the thunder of the Cold War reverberated all around the McCarthy-Army TV hearings, lightning bolts from the fierce partisan campaign being fought for control of the Senate also bounced close round the caucus room. The 1954 elections were coming up, Senate Republicans stood 48–47 against the Democrats with Wayne Morse of Oregon Independent, and the Republicans were looking for gains. Styles Bridges, Everett Dirksen and other McCarthy supporters intervened repeatedly behind the scenes on behalf of the senator, whom they credited with having retired five Senate Democrats in 1950 and 1952 elections. In their eyes McCarthy's anti-Communism was the weapon for winning.

One place where Republicans saw a chance to pick up a seat was Wyoming. There the seat was held by Lester C. Hunt, sixty-one. A mild-mannered dentist, Hunt was the man who as a state official had put the bucking bronco on Wyoming's license plates. After a term as governor he had moved on to the Senate, where he established a liberal voting record. Senator Hunt had already announced for reelection and because he was personally popular it was thought he would win; if however any other Democrat were running, the Republicans could probably take the seat.

On June 9 lightning flashed in the United States Senate, momentarily illuminating the unhappy features of Lester Hunt. Ever since October, 1953, when his only son had been convicted on a police charge of homosexual conduct in Washington's Rock Creek Park, Hunt had lived in private anguish. He brooded over the tragedy in his family and over the unfeeling way some hinted it would be exploited. Early in 1954 he entered the hospital for a kidney condition. Then, to the Democratic chairman of his state he dispatched a startling message:

> I shall never be a candidate for elective office again. I am compelled to withdraw my announcement as a candidate for reelection.

Reason given was his health. Newspapers now said that Wyoming, one of the "battleground states" in the 1954 elections, looked like going Republican.[49]

Three weeks later the lightning flashed over Washington, and again the victim was Hunt. Early on Saturday, June 19, 1954, at the height of the McCarthy-Army uproar and four days after the government published the Oppenheimer hearing transcript, the Senator from Wyoming sat down at his desk in the Senate Office Building, and blew out his brains.

Everybody in Washington issued shocked statements, including Senator Mundt, chairman of McCarthy's committee during the TV hearings. Hunt, said Mundt, was *not* the unnamed Senator that McCarthy had said the night before on TV he was going to expose for "just plain wrongdoing." But as one Democratic senator remarked shortly before Hunt shot himself:

> Every man in public life lives in a glass house. There are few if any people who haven't done something in the past that could be used against them in a political fight by an opponent willing to bar no holds.[50]

Hunt, who was only the second senator ever to take his own life, was as vulnerable as any man. He was not in good health; two years earlier his brother had committed suicide in Colorado. Ten years later Allen Drury, a member of *The New York Times* Washington staff, wrote a fictional account of McCarthyite Washington entitled *Advise And Consent*. In Drury's bestseller, later made into a popular movie, a senator commits suicide in his Senate office one Saturday after a Senate opponent confronts him with photographic evidence of a homosexual episode in his past. At the time Marquis Childs wrote in the *Washington Post* that Hunt's Senate foes let him know that "the facts . . . would find their way into every mailbox in Wyoming if Hunt should run for reelection this fall." There is no evidence that McCarthy was personally connected with the Hunt tragedy. But the miasma of intimidation and slander that

McCarthyism spread over Washington in the spring of 1954 had everything to do with Hunt's death. The Grand Inquisition had reached into the Senate and claimed a victim.[51]

Meanwhile the appearance that McCarthy was making on TV was beginning to cost him heavily in support. The movie star Rod Steiger, watching the hearings with his family, heard his mother turn to his grandmother and say, "Ooh, I think he's mean." Yet the same confirmed minority cast him as a dauntless fighter, chipping away at the forces of conspiracy and ignorance. The senator would probably have come through without disastrous change if he had been willing to play it safe. But he was still the street-fighter who vowed that

> if one was ever approached by another person in a not completely friendly fashion, one should start kicking at the other person as far as possible below the belt until the other person was rendered helpless.[52]

Kicking and swinging, McCarthy finally missed once too often, left himself wide open, and wound up on the mat, knocked out for good.

The moment of climax came on June 10, just after Oppenheimer's public disgrace and just before Hunt took his life. By this time Joseph M. Welch, the chief Army counsel and a member of the proper Boston law firm of Hale and Dorr, had become almost as familiar a figure to TV watchers as the Senate committee members. An Iowa-born graduate of Harvard Law School given to wearing bow ties (he had 150 of them), Welch was a lawyer of the old school who worked at a stand-up desk in his paneled State street office and liked will cases best "because they have all the elements of human passion." He lived in a 150-year-old gabled house amid fireplaces and carved reliefs of sailboat hulls. McCarthy, ready to mix it up with almost anybody as the hearings went on, gave Welch a wide berth.[53]

By the thirtieth day of the hearings everybody in the caucus room including McCarthy knew that when this big man with the bay window and the butter-won't melt-in-his-mouth manner said "I'm just a small-town lawyer," it was time to sit up. Among TV watchers Welch had established himself as a comfortable and decent man with a courtly and affable way of asking nettling questions and then looking surprised when his little sallies were greeted with laughter. On this afternoon Welch was shooting mocking questions at Cohn about whether the subcommittee exposed Communists as fast as it discovered them. McCarthy listened in rising anger. Then he was on his feet, interrupting and suddenly injecting the name of Frederick G. Fisher, a young member of Welch's law firm who had once been a member of the Lawyers' Guild. Fisher, McCarthy charged:

> has been for a number of years a member of an organization which was named, oh, years and years ago as the legal bulwark of the Communist party.

From the witness chair Roy Cohn grimaced toward McCarthy, shaking his head and mouthing what seemed to be the words: "No, no." McCarthy slammed onward:

> I am not asking you at this time why you tried to foist him on this committee. Whether you know he was a member of that Communist organization or not, I don't know. I assume you did not, Mr. Welch, because I got the impression that, while you are quite an actor, you play for a laugh. I don't think you have any conception of the danger of the Communist party. I don't think you yourself would ever knowingly aid the Communist cause. I think you are unknowingly aiding it when you try to burlesque this hearing in which we are attempting to bring out the facts, however.

As McCarthy finished, he grinned across the table at Welch. The facts were known—that Welch's assistant, James D. St. Clair, had brought Fisher to Washington to help on the case, but Welch, learning from Fisher that at law school he had joined the Lawyers' Guild, had decided to send him back to Boston—and Cohn and others had prevailed on McCarthy not to drag Fisher into the hearing.

Once McCarthy brought the matter up before the cameras, however, Welch was ready for him. As McCarthy finished, he stared at him pale and disbelieving. His face had gone white with anger. The puckish look was gone. "Until this moment," he said, "I think I never really gauged your cruelty or your recklessness."

McCarthy turned unheeding to ask an aide for a newspaper clipping about Fisher so that he could put it in the record. Welch, on his feet, said: "You won't need anything in the record when I have finished telling you this."

He explained Fisher's background, his position in Hale and Dorr, his brief membership in the Lawyers' Guild, his present work for the Young Republicans. Then he turned toward McCarthy again:

> Little did I dream that you could be so reckless and so cruel as to do an injury to this lad . . . I fear he shall always bear a scar needlessly inflicted by you.

Still McCarthy pursued his point and once again Roy Cohn tried
vainly to shush him. Again Welch cut him short:

> Let us not assassinate this lad further, Senator. You have done enough.
> Have you no sense of decency, sir, at long last? Have you left no sense
> of decency?

Millions of people sitting transfixed before their TV screens saw
Welch, tears in his eyes, walk from the room, saw the snarl that McCarthy
turned toward the camera. And they heard, after a moment, a roll of loud
applause from spectators and cameramen in the caucus room. They saw
McCarthy stare in bleak surprise, and saw people avoiding him as they
left the room. McCarthy was talking. Spreading out his hands in a gesture
of puzzlement he asked: "What did I do wrong?"[54]

McCarthy never recovered from his TV exposure. The very next day
Senator Flanders rose in the Senate to move a vote of censure. This time
it led to appointment of a Select Committee inquiring into McCarthy's
behavior. From this point McCarthy never again commanded the same
headlines in newspapers, spread the same terror on Capitol Hill or, as the
1954 elections showed, packed the same lethal wallop in congressional
contests. On December 22, 1954, the Senate voted 67-to-22 to "condemn" McCarthy's conduct as a senator. Isolated and ignored thereafter,
McCarthy drank a good deal and died of a liver ailment, aged 47, in
1957.[55]

The case of Robert Oppenheimer also came to final judgment in the
fevered summer of 1954. It was a case without parallel in the Cold War.
Not only was Oppenheimer the wizard who presided over the building of
the bomb, he was also the brilliant preceptor who had tutored the leaders
of government and Congress in the new verities of the atomic age. But
the man was an intellectual and America had always had a hard time
understanding intellectuals, especially those as complex as Oppenheimer.

Before joining the Manhattan Project, Oppenheimer consorted with
radicals. His two wives were both Communists. To help the Lincoln
Brigade and other leftwing outfits fight fascism in Spain, he gave money
to the Communists. As boss of the Manhattan Project, General Leslie R.
Groves never quite said of Oppenheimer's radical affinities as Lincoln said
of Grant's drinking—that he wanted the name of the whisky so he could
give it to his other generals—but he was convinced that from the time
Hitler declared war on the United States Oppenheimer put all radicalism
aside to beat the Germans to the bomb.

When the scientists saw their invention used against the people of
Hiroshima and Nagasaki, many expressed bitter remorse. Oppenheimer

absented himself from the Los Alamos laboratories and returned to private life as head of the Institute of Advanced Study at Princeton. Yet he was constantly called in, as chairman of the Atomic Energy Commission's Scientific Advisory Committee, to put government and Congress in the picture about the new weaponry. He was no friend of the arms race. Often he stepped on toes. He publicly ridiculed Lewis Strauss of the Atomic Energy Commission for expressing fear that isotopes shipped abroad for peaceful uses of atomic energy might end up in Communist hands. At a time when the Air Force fought tooth and claw for defense dollars, Oppenheimer coolly suggested diverting funds from the Strategic Air Command to create an Arctic early warning system that might save civilian lives in an atomic war. After the Russians exploded their A-bomb in 1949, Oppenheimer angered the more avid Cold Warriors by resisting a crash H-bomb program until Washington should first try negotiating an understanding with the Russians. He infuriated the Air Force even more by urging a diversion of the atomic stockpile from bombers to develop small tactical nuclear weapons that troops could use in ground warfare.

Under fire Oppenheimer demanded a hearing. André Malraux has observed that he should simply have put as his case: *"Je suis la bombe atomique."* Instead the great physicist was led through days and weeks of examinations about discrepant statements out of his past until he ended in the abject admission: "I was an idiot."

On June 29, 1954 the AEC under Strauss as chairman upheld the special panel's two-to-one condemnation, and Oppenheimer was thenceforth barred as a "security risk" from all further part in matters affecting the national interest. He remained director of the Institute at Princeton to his death in 1967. In December, 1963, a few months after the Cold War ended, President Johnson, following through on an initiative begun by President Kennedy, presented Oppenheimer with the Enrico Fermi Award, the highest honor the United States can bestow upon a scientist. But his security clearance was never restored.[56]

O F A L L the linkages to be seen between an overenergetic foreign policy and developments at home after the Second World War, perhaps the most basic were those which occurred when the fear of another Depression acted in a way to reinforce the dread of another Pearl Harbor. Thus the relationship of the American economy to the Cold War is historically of the greatest importance.

Notwithstanding the prolonged boom that followed the Second World War, this deep-rooted dread of another Depression lay close beneath the consciousness of the citizenry and their leaders for many years. It lingered on through even the second decade of unbroken prosperity; it colored the country's thinking all through the Cold War. As late as 1961 President John F. Kennedy said of the $20 billion space program he was about to lay before Congress: "We've got to make this thing the most glamorous WPA you ever saw."

Such apprehensions became the engine of policy, from the Servicemen's Readjustment Act of 1944 and the Employment Act of 1946 to the Marshall Plan in 1948 and Point Four in 1949 down to President Kennedy's ten percent depreciation allowance for business in 1962. The Korean War, a turning point in the Cold War in so many ways, offered an economic as well as military challenge to the power of the United States.

The outcome, since it had been decided to meet the challenge by waging war without disturbing the flooding tide of business as usual, was inflation. Two months after the war broke out, employment attained a record level of 62,000,000 jobs—well beyond the 60,000,000 jobs Henry Wallace had been scoffed at for predicting only a few years before—and the paychecks outraced the supply of goods. A new breed of salesman elbowed his way into the company of fast-talking buttonholers—the mutual fund salesman. His pitch was that you didn't have to live on Park Avenue to become an owner of American business—and getting a piece of the action was the best way to hedge against rising prices. Before the Korean War was six months old, more than a million American neo-capitalists bought mutual fund shares.[57]

Inflation was the inseparable companion of the Cold War. Late in 1950 the administration was forced to announce that the dollar bought only 59.5 cents worth compared to what it fetched at the end of the Second World War. The rise in prices was the sharpest in five years. The President's Council of Economic Advisers acknowledged that the country was "in the grip of inflation." The Council put the rise at 15%—and that seemed low to most people. Everything cost more—a car, up 20%; a new house, up 15%; a pair of shoes, up 11%; a haircut, up 25%. The price of a call from a coin telephone doubled from 5¢ to 10¢.[58]

In the face of pleas to "buy nothing from fear," department store sales shot up twenty-five percent. As the government moved to freeze prices and wages, traders nearly cornered the coffee market, making a swift killing as prices doubled overnight. Even before the Korean War broke out, a subcommittee of the Senate Committee on Executive Expenditures had begun to expose the "five percenters" who sold actual or pretended influence with government officials. Testimony before the senators showed that these five percenters were often bigtime operators working with leading officers in the procurement sections of the armed forces. It came out that some of these influence-peddlers had found their way into the White House, where indeed certain offices adjoining the President's were filled with red-faced men who smoked long cigars and kept their hats on, as if they were still in the courthouse where Harry Truman had once presided in Kansas City. The committee learned that shortly after the Second World War a perfume company impatient to import some essential oils through the remaining wartime regulations, had presented a $520 deep-freeze to Harry Vaughn, who sat in the office next to the President's and could expedite such matters.[59]

At a time when cruel dispatches about heavy American casualties in Korean fighting filled the front pages, a Senate subcommittee investigating Reconstruction Finance Corporation loans brought out some stories of less than sacrificial valor at home. One involved a group of prominent former government officials including ex-Secretary of State Edward R. Stettinius and a sweetheart deal for surplus property. With the help of expeditious stamping of papers at the Maritime Commission and the even timelier approval of an RFC credit, the group was able to put in just $100,000 of their own money to buy five surplus tankers that they then promptly resold for a profit of $2,800,000.[60]

The same committee went over the sorry affairs of a Columbus, Ohio, manufacturer of prefabricated housing, Charles Strandlund, who ran up $38 million in uncollectable debts at the RFC. Not even a $15,000 fee to Senator Joe McCarthy for writing a puff pamphlet for Strandlund's Lustron Company saved it from bankruptcy. This committee's investigators came upon a mink coat that quickly became as notorious as the deep-freeze in the lexicon of Washington's free and easy ways. Ever since the 1920s, when appreciative industrialists used to give them to Ziegeld Follies dancers, mink coats had occasioned stories, and this one was no exception. "Some people think girls get mink coats the same way minks do," wrote one commentator. The mink of which he told was a $6,540 beauty worn by the wife of a former RFC examiner of loans named E. Merl Young. The investigators presented evidence that it had been acquired with the financial help of a New York lawyer. The lawyer's firm, it was shown, had represented a company in its application for a $150,000 loan that was later approved. Another committee found enough evidence of high-level "tax-fixing" for delinquents willing to pay the price, to send nine of the men who frequented the President's outer office to jail a few years later. They included T. Lamar Caudle, Assistant Attorney General in charge of the Tax Division and the President's appointments secretary, Matthew H. Connelly.[61]

Other scandals burst to the surface at this time, and the corruption they betrayed touched some of the most sensitive sources of national pride. One of the most shocking concerned the United States Military Academy at West Point. If there was an institution in the country that America looked upon as dedicated to the highest traditions of the nation it was the Point. Under its austere grey towers, character was built; out of its ranks of faultlessly groomed, magnificiently drilled young men marched the officers who would lead everybody's sons in battle. Now the Academy disclosed that it was dismissing ninety cadets for cheating in examinations. One was Robert Blaik, son of the West Point football coach and an All-American quarterback. Eight others were members of the Army's starting eleven, one of the outstanding teams in the country.

Even more bewilderingly, a great many of those dismissed turned out not even to be contrite, and insisted it was the "honest" students who had owned up to what they were doing and the "liars" the ones who were still cadets. Coach Blaik defended the dismissed athletes as "men of character" and told reporters there was "no moral reason" why they should be regarded as anything else. "Stop knocking football," said Blaik. "God help this country if we didn't play football. . . . General Eisenhower came to West Point with his greatest desire to play football."[62]

Along about this time came another shocker. The most brilliant basketball team in the United States was the City College five of New York City. They had won the national championship several years running. They were lions wherever they went. Now the district attorney's office abruptly announced that three of the five members of the first team admitted taking bribes of up to $1500 for rigging scores. Within days other players at Long Island University, New York University, Bradley University, the University of Kentucky and Toledo University were brought to trial for "shaving points" for bribes paid by gamblers betting on the scores. Were not games supposed to say something to the young about Triumph and Defeat? Were not games supposed to be games, and business separately business?[63]

To Senator J. William Fulbright, who had presided over the University of Arkansas before presiding over the committee's mink-coat and surplus-tanker disclosures, all these signs evinced a wider corruption. Reviewing the committee's findings alongside the "shocking" decay in collegiate sports standards, the senator pronounced them a "mirror" of attitudes that were being shaped by and were shaping the atmosphere of Cold War:

> The question of the moral strength of our people [he said in a Senate speech] is not just an internal domestic matter. It has grave possibilities in our international relations. A democracy can recover quickly from physical or economic disaster, but when its moral convictions weaken it

becomes prey for the demagogue and the charlatan. Tyranny and oppression then become the order of the day.

Among so many influential people morality has become identical with
legality. We certainly are in a tragic plight if the accepted standard by
which we measure the integrity of a man in public life is that he keep
within the letter of the law. What seems to be new about these scandals
is the moral blindness or callowness which allows those in responsible
positions to accept the practices which the facts reveal.[64]

What made the disclosure about the basketball players so disconcerting for millions of Americans was that they had seen these lads repeatedly
in action—on television. Along with the other big changes of the Korean
War years, television arrived in a big way when coaxial cables and mi-
crowave relays first spanned the country in 1951 and the Federal Communications Commission granted large numbers of station licenses in
1952. Coming along when it did, TV abetted the Cold War psychology
by its power of instantaneity, its distortion of perspective, the selectivity
of its programming and the conforming cowardice of the commercialists
who controlled it. By 1951 there were 7,200,000 TV sets in America's
homes and bars, and already countless people had experienced the sensational immediacy of watching athletes in exciting action while sitting in
their own living rooms. Television's electronic eye, which had opened to
the wider dimensions of a sixteen-inch screen by 1950, was terrific for
bringing sporting events to the viewer, and the introduction of the Zoomar lens in 1948 thrust the eye so close up that the householder in the
living room could watch every twist and turn of a basketball game, every
blink and grimace of a presidential nominating speech, while it happened.

Did Americans love change? Nothing since the automobile had such
a wide impact in the everyday life of ordinary people. Of the three big
technological innovations that swept into American life during the Cold
War decades (the jetliner and the computer were the other two), television had by far the biggest effect. A Westinghouse report soon found that
Americans spent more time on the average before their TV screens than
they did at work. As a universal instrument of home entertainment, the
new machine changed family life, habits and households, and rivaled the
hearth itself as the prime acculturating force in the society.

Like the jetliner and the computer, which pared days into hours and
minutes into nanoseconds, TV subtly harnessed the mass society to the
speeded-up tempo of modern times. It enormously heightened everybody's sense of immediacy. In great part because of the imperatives of
commercial priority, this may have been illusory: of the 3,285 evening
hours of prime-time programming that the networks began providing each

year, ninety-nine percent was simply entertainment and was produced, before long, on film for later broadcast. The most exciting things on TV were what you—and millions like you—*did* see as it happened on the football field sometimes thousands of miles away. Thus, instant play led to instant replay, and the same kind of technological imperative demanded, and got, instant coffee, instant oatmeal, and instant soup. As good a symbol as any of this compulsive instantaneousness was probably the aspirin tablet dissolving before your eyes on the TV commercial in six—count them—seconds.

When so much of the day was programmed to happen so fast, a pervasive impatience prodded the tempo of all living. Attention span shortened, and not only in children. The length and complexity of all messages shrank, and not only those given over to trivia. When President Martin Van Buren had wished to present his views about rechartering the National Bank at the time of the panic of 1837, he published them in a ten-page letter to the Speaker of the House of Representatives. By the later Cold War years members of the United States Senate queued patiently at times for hours to enter the Capitol's sole TV room and utter before Bob Trout or Roger Mudd's camera the abbreviated statement that might win one minute on the evening's newscast. Instant America, habituated to the blink-and-think pace of TV, expected—and received— one-minute solutions to its problems.[65]

Physical proximity with millions, if only for a minute, was what the senators (and the sponsors) wanted. Such physical proximity was stunningly new, and such unprecedented shrinking of the "aesthetic distance of the image," was bound to hit the viewing eye with startling impact when the TV camera was turned loose in other areas than sports. This happened in early 1951 when television cameras were admitted to the hearings of the Special Senate Committee to Investigate Organized Crime in Interstate Commerce. After warmups in three other cities the committee, with Senator Estes Kefauver as chairman and Rudolph Halley as counsel, held televised hearings in New York City. Offices emptied, men jammed bars and restaurants and housewives' electric irons burned untended through their ironing boards as an estimated 30,000,000 Americans—by far the largest TV audience ever assembled up to then—stared in rapt fascination at what *The New York Times* called "perhaps the most absorbing and instructive day of video ever presented."

The show had everything. On the side of virtue were the senators with their sharp, relentless counsel. Opposed to them were a sullen lot of superbly tailored racketeers, gimlet-eyed gamblers, dumb cops, molls, venal politicians, and slick lawyers who looked as though they had been sent over by Hollywood's Central Casting Bureau. "It was difficult at times to believe that it was real," said the *Times*.

Up stepped pudgy Frank Erickson, a professional gambler who never got beyond fourth grade ("I refuse to answer because it might criminate me," he said), then came Joe Adonis, boss of the New Jersey underworld, dark and seething with menace, but saying little about the committee's evidence of his close ties with New York City officials. The show had sex. In flung Virginia Hill, "soignée in a platinum stole," and wide-brimmed hat. She was also annoyed. She pointed to a cameraman and screamed, "Make those goddam fools stop. I'll throw something at them in a minute." She told a simple tale about how a seventeen-year-old waitress from Alabama met a friend of bigtime bookies named Joe Epstein and got to know fellows like Joe Adonis and Charlie Fischetti and Bugsy Siegel. The committee had a shrewd idea that Virginia Hill had been a bank courier for the gamblers, but Virginia did not admit much. She explained her unlimited income in short bursts of her Alabama drawl: "I went with fellows. Like a lot of girls they got, giving me things and bought everything I wanted. . . . Whatever I had, outside of betting on horses, was given me."

Then on came Frank Costello, the "prime minister of the underworld." His face was heavily lined, his eyes hard and arrogant. A graduate bootlegger of the Prohibition school, Costello had given the Horatio Alger story a new twist: he had risen from rum to riches. When he demanded that the TV cameras be taken off his face, the Committee agreed—so the cameramen turned instead to Costello's hands. Viewers saw the hands twitch nervously over papers or pour water into a glass while Halley drove hard to pin down evidence that Costello was what the Committee was perfectly sure he was—head of one of the two big crime syndicates operating across many states and master wirepuller of New York City politics. The show came to a perfect climax when Costello, refusing to answer the Committee's questions, stalked from the hearings in an exit that Hollywood could not have bettered as the arrogant underworld boss.

During the eight days the cameras were trained on the hearings, the research firm Videodex reported, 69.7% of all New York City sets tuned in—more than twice the number that turned on for the Yankees' World Series games the year before. Merchants complained to the committee that their businesses were paralyzed. Movie halls emptied during the hours of the proceedings. Housewives fed their babies in front of the set. In many cities across the country business and home life were noticeably affected. One Chicago movie manager took a look at the number of customers in his aisles and ran an ad: "Ten Per Cent Off During Kefauver Hours."

The Kefauver show was television's first big spectacular. It sent the Senator to the Democratic National Convention the following year with 340 delegates pledged to him for the presidential nomination. But it never sent Costello up the river. In fact, when the whole episode passed, it was more difficult than ever to assess the effect of this powerful new invention on the course of events. It was not at all clear that an all but saturating experience of eight days of the most compelling TV-watching had in any detectable way altered the conduct of either licit or illicit affairs in America.[66]

But where else could politicians assemble such a number of voters as at any hour turned their faces toward the TV screen? The mesmeric machine in the living room presented itself as a formidable new tool for swaying people—and as such a revolutionary advance in the technology of political persuasion. Once the new tool for influencing voters had been the telegraph: William H. Seward, Lincoln's rival for the presidential nomination before 1860, scored by ensuring that his oration "The Irrepressible Conflict" went out on the wires, to be reported as no such address had ever been reported before. In 1886 the linotype machine came along, and spread the speeches of Grover Cleveland more widely than any before. In the 1930s Franklin Roosevelt, a man of many media, seized upon radio. By ingratiatingly informal "fireside chats'" heard in millions of homes (he spoke on radio twenty times in his first ten months), he persuaded his countrymen to follow him through the greatest movement of social advance in American history. In the Second World War, when radio girdled the globe, Winston Churchill stirred yet wider audiences. Then, as John F. Kennedy said in bestowing honorary American citizenship upon him in 1963, he "mobilized the English language and sent it into battle."[67]

The last major figure not known to television was General Marshall. Truman, owlishly wise behind prismatic lenses, Acheson suave in guardsman's mustache, McCarthy holding up the document in his hand—they all came on thenceforth on TV. The cameras made their appearance at the 1948 Republican and Democratic nominating conventions—both held in Philadelphia for the reason that it was on the coaxial cable between New York and Washington and linked to fourteen stations reaching audiences in thirteen states with 167 electoral votes. Many people that summer visited friends who had sets (there were 400,000 sets on the Eastern seaboard in 1948), to catch unforgettable glimpses of Truman, the feistiest underdog in American history, bringing the dejected delegates to their feet with the shout: "Senator Barkley and I will win this election and make these Republicans like it, don't you forget that!" In those untutored days it was still possible to see politicians on the floor drinking from hip flasks.[68]

The networks broadcast the conventions, the great occasions of the Presidency, Cold War UN debates; and in the nightly newscasts offered brief tidbits of public affairs. Beyond that politics on television had to be bought and paid for, like everything else on the air. In 1948 the advertising men urged Governor Dewey to film some spot announcements for use on TV during the last weeks of the race. Dewey refused, and in 1952 the men from Madison Avenue hardly had to remind Dwight Eisenhower of what had happened to the candidate before him. Not without disgusted snorts "that an old soldier should come to this," Eisenhower submitted to the experts and filmed the answers for some fifty twenty-second spots at a New York City studio specializing in commercials. Late in October 40 million American TV-watchers were peppered with question-and-answer bursts like this:

ANNOUNCER: Eisenhower answers the nation!
CITIZEN: What about the cost of living, General?
EISENHOWER: My wife Mamie worried about the same thing. I tell her it's our job to change that on Novemer 4.[69]

It was the start of a sharp escalation in the cost of American political campaigning. Eisenhower's first campaign cost $7,374,900 and $2,046,-000 of it was spent for television. In 1958 Clarence Long, an economics professor at Johns Hopkins, ran an outsider's race for the Senate against Baltimore Mayor Thomas D'Alesandro. Backed by only one precinct leader in the entire city, Long had no money. But sixteen inches of snow had fallen on the city when Long wangled a couple of minutes on TV to answer a D'Alesandro boast about taxes. Long wasted no time discussing the Middle East, Asia, Korea, but tore into his opponent. "D'Alesandro?" cried Long. "He can't even get the snow off the street!" He was heard behind every blocked doorway in the stranded city. Long, showered with letters, was a political personage overnight, and in due course was elected to Congress. "I had to make a noise and make it fast," said Long. "If you have a lot of money like a Kennedy, you can take the high road."[70]

No other medium rivaled TV for size of audience, and the candidates vied to buy TV time. In 1960 the Democrats spent $10,000,000 to elect Kennedy, $6,204,986 for television and radio. Television outlays for both parties rose from $34,600,000 in 1964 to $59,200,000 in 1968. Something like seventy-five percent of candidates' outlays in 1968 went for spot announcements on local stations of less than five minutes' duration. By 1970 the cost of political campaigning, due almost entirely to television, was a national scandal. When the parties spent $60,000,000 on TV, as they did in that nonpresidential year, they had virtually to sell themselves to the big contributors to pay their bills. The burden of financing campaigns imposed by TV opened the way to major corruption, since contributions of $500,000 were such as to leave any officeholder helplessly beholden. It was Sir Denis Brogan who observed that when senators began in the first part of the century to be elected directly instead of by state legislatures the entrance fee to the Senate only rose higher, and what had been called a "millionaire's club" became a multimillionaire's club. With television, it might almost have been said to have become a billionaire's club.[71]

Richard Nixon, running for Vice President in the autumn of 1952, found himself under pressure to withdraw from the race because of charges that California supporters had put together an $18,000 fund for his support after his election to Congress. After feverish consultation with his advisers, he went on TV with a plea that made scant reference to the fund but pulled out all the stops in defense of a campaign gift that no one had ever heard of before—a black and white spotted dog that his six-year-old daughter Tricia had promptly named Checkers. The show brought a deluge of supporting telephone calls, telegrams and campaign contributions, and saved Nixon's political life.[72]

Considering himself a master of the medium after the Checkers coup, Nixon accepted John F. Kennedy's campaign challenge eight years later to debate on TV, and came off badly. This was only partly because Kennedy spoke more persuasively than Nixon, who argued points lawyer-fashion and lost sight of the audience. In large part it was due to the fact that Nixon had a light skin and that the orthicon-image television camera looked right through such a skin, X-ray fashion, and brought out the tiniest hairs growing beneath the surface. Since the "Lazy Shave" makeup that Nixon wore in the first debate was ineffective in such conditions, he came out looking haggard and heavy-bearded in unfavorable contrast with the fair and cleancut Kennedy.[73]

The cosmetic lapse of the 1960 campaign was a rare setback in the rush of the politicians and their handlers to dominate and exploit such a powerful new means of communication. "Image-building" was as old as the campaign photograph, the myth of log-cabin origins, the "front-porch" campaign of William McKinley in 1896. In the age of radio, William Leuchtenburg relates, most Americans did not know that FDR was crippled. With the arrival of TV, candidates walked as it seemed right into the voter's living room, looked him straight in the eye, and talked easily as if speaking to no one else in the whole world. Since this identical "image" loomed in some twenty million living rooms, candidates crowded in every artifice to appear with every hair in place, every pear-shaped tone rounded to pear-shaped perfection, every sentence faultlessly read from the teleprompter hidden out of sight of the camera ("You have the most remarkable memory in history," said a woman to Walter Cronkite, after twenty years of nightly teleprompting.)

So annihilatingly close was the proximity television achieved that it also destroyed the need for middlemen between the leading politicians and the general public. The candidates of the television age owed less and less to the state-centered, city-bounded power bases of traditional party organization. With the help of their financial patrons, they carried their appeals and promises straight to the TV-watchers. Yet by the time an Eisenhower or a Kennedy had come into the home on TV, a vaguely troubling ambiguity settled over the seeming intimacy of the encounter. A kind of tipoff was provided as to the unreality of the reality when the pitchman on commercial after commercial sauntered forward on the tube and presumed to identify himself to those watching in the living room as their self-invited "guest." Of course the watchers knew Eisenhower or Kennedy well, as they thought: they had "seen" him in earlier encounters. They knew his look, his tone, his small mannerisms. They knew—and heard—him closeup.

But no more than to Seward on the telegraph, McKinley on the porch, or Roosevelt on the radio, could they talk back to him.

Television, miraculously collapsing all intervening time and space, brought the political leader and the led face to face—only to limit them to a one-way conversation. The individual, for all the enveloping proximity of the encounter, could not talk back. And this was such a colossal abridgment after all of the sensory intimacy of the relationship that it might well have had something to do with the alienation that overtook the society in the television age of the 1950s.

How, asked President Eisenhower of his Cold Warriors, how could we teach the great public beyond the metropolitan centers that do not have the masses of printed information available in the large cities, about what the government is doing? In the 1950s, as TV sets multiplied into ninety percent of America's homes, as transcontinental TV was inaugurated with the televising of the Japanese Peace Treaty signing in San Francisco in 1951, the answer to Eisenhower's cry was delivered to the hilt. The saturation of the nation by TV was the answer. In those days it was said that communication was a cure for conflict. When the Toronto English professor, Marshall McLuhan came forward to say that TV, unlike print, was a "cool" new medium that brought people together, corporation executives lionized him and talked about communications, specifically TV, pacifying workers and dissenters in a society of consensus. These same years were the time of the "lonely crowd," of the "silent generation,"—of young people listening without the chance to talk back to the yak-yak of Cold War. It was a time of frustration of a whole society.

With all the other changes by which television helped draw Americans more and more into a shell of unreality, there occurred the loss of certain kinds of dignity in the nation. The surest use for television as a political instrument was in leading a lofty cause, but there was not much in either Korea or Vietnam to kindle a rhetoric like Churchill's. Though the instrument carried momentary power for Kennedy on a frosty inaugural morning when he said: "Ask rather what you can do for your country," Lyndon Johnson came to find that it was hard to get people stirred up over the soil bank, or a new immigration law, or cleaning up the slums.

In a larger, and troubling, sense the symbols of power were undraped for the first time with television. During these years, for example, the President had moved across the street to live in Blair House while the Executive Mansion, weakened by the ravages of time and burned by the British in 1812, underwent extensive reconstruction. Then in 1952 President Truman moved back in, and one evening on television took the nation over the refurbished mansion. What Americans had known only from the outside and through museumlike tours of a few ground-floor rooms they now saw inside, a family home where, Mr. Truman told them, the clocks were wound every Friday. So seen, it ceased to be the same beautiful, two-dimensional facade familiar to and revered by all. This was the beginning of the end of the mystery of certain symbols. Television took you to the Capitol where Eisenhower, awkward in his civilian's homburg, prepared to take his inaugural oath. It let you in backstage at the FBI and at the Pentagon. A year or two later, when McCarthy hauled the chiefs of the Department of the Army before the cameras and grilled them until the very habiliments of office seemed ripped off their backs, it could almost be said that Government itself had ceased to be mysterious.[74]

CHAPTER 7

The Liberator

in the White House

THE GOSPEL OF MASSIVE RETALIATION

A MERICA'S Cold War reached its peak after the Republicans took command in the 1950s. Already, as the earth shrank, the United States had abandoned isolation for global involvement and under the impact of technological and scientific advance had, like other modern industrial nations, become a mass society. But along with such transformations, and in some respects underlying them, two powerful forces peculiar to America that had long been gathering strength emerged to dominate the national life as the Republicans captured the White House in 1953. The first was an all-encompassing expansiveness that, given the nature and values of American society, swept the country into an uninhibited drive for business growth. The second was an extreme antiradicalism—an anti-Communism—that had been growing since early in the century and in America's Cold War years came to fruition, so to speak, not at home but abroad.

For a nation that was born in insurrection and reared with radicalism in its bones, the turning point was not hard to see. Up to the Bolshevik Revolution of 1917 America's radicals, loosely joined in a Progressive movement and fed up with the inertia and corruption of the capitalist parties, had edged steadily to the left. Yet the telltale signal was that these radicals, political leaders and popular writers alike, shrank from taking the next step and embracing Marxism. Charles Beard, the Indiana-born historian, read Marx as well as Madison in order to rewrite the history of the Republic's origins in a fundamental work of 1913—*The Economic Interpretation of the Constitution.* Yet when the First World War broke out many of the Progressives pitched in, persuaded that they could do more to accomplish radical change from within the war effort.

Then the Bolshevik Revolution burst upon the American consciousness—and paralysis followed. The United States sent an invasion force into Siberia briefly in 1920. At the same time a violent "Red scare" spread through the land. Attorney General A. Mitchell Palmer, in raids organized by the youthful Justice Department official J. Edgar Hoover, rounded up some 6,000 foreign-born radicals, ransacked their homes (almost always without warrants), and otherwise rode roughshod over many people's rights. Congress, setting its face against any foreign-born bearers of revolutionary tradition now abjured as alien, voted in 1924 and 1929 to stop all further open immigration from abroad.

Excepting such few men as Upton Sinclair and Thorstein Veblen, the thunderous old American left was scared stiff. The debacle of Robert LaFollette's third-party candidacy in 1924 proved what happened to radicals in the 1920s. The Bull Moosers of the 1912 Progressive party breakaway ceased their snorting and pawing and became "safe." Walter Brown took his place in Hoover's cabinet, Ickes and Wallace found their way into Roosevelt's, and Alfred M. Landon, the fiery populist who bolted the hegemony of bankers as a Bull Mooser for Theodore Roosevelt in 1912, ran as the Republican mainstay against the other Roosevelt in 1936. Donald Richberg, reduced to writing pamphlets, finally got to Washington in time to help save the old system by running the NRA.

In such straits the republic of Washington, Jefferson and Tom Paine needed fifteen years before it could recognize the Russian revolution. At the height of the New Deal the antiradicalism rooted in Congress formally designated those who did not love God and property as "Un-American," and with noisy help from the *Chicago Tribune* and Hearst press set out to expose them. Far from being obliterated by the Second World War drive for collective security and "one world," this force fed on wartime frustrations and fears. After 1945 it rose swiftly as the belligerently nationalist component in the bipartisan "internationalism" that was thought to have prevailed. Truman first seized upon and led it, and the "bold" decisions by which he exported America's antiradicalism assured that he became, upon reelection, President in his own right. The effect of these decisions was to enforce a renewed and enlarged anti-Communist consensus. Such former radicals as John Dewey, Reinhold Niebuhr and Walter Reuther rallied to prove themselves "good Americans" and to lead the world confrontation while programs of social change withered in hostility and neglect at home. Once historians said of such old-style European monarchies as the France of Louis Napoleon, that they embarked on adventures abroad to distract their people from ills at home. At this time the United States, with a hand from Stalin, went to Cold War against "international Communism," rather than attend to problems at home.[1]

The other force that seized on America in the 1950s was the surging impulse to expand the economy beyond all known limits. The whole climate of America since 1945 had conspired for the growth of big enterprise. The population exploded. National power burst its continental limits and spread over the whole world. Technology, not only in the form of machines but even more in the mechanics of large-scale organization, both enabled and enforced headlong growth. The very size of modern government, contrary to old business fears, operated to facilitate corporate growth.

Thus, as soon as the Second World War ended, the government canceled all its wartime contracts with industry, paying huge cash indemnities for immediate termination in many cases. Corporations, having expanded mightily to perform the prodigies of wartime output, now faced the challenge of large-scale reconversion to peacetime production with huge cash reserves in their coffers.

Here even the New Deal's restrictive legislation favored growth of the corporations. Income taxes passed under the Roosevelt administration stood so high and remained so high after the war that many big stockholders in the higher brackets were not at all eager for corporations to pay them fat dividends just then. Since they would only have to pay top rates to the Internal Revenue Service on such income, they preferred to see profits on their money reinvested by the corporation. In that way they might eventually take capital gains instead, which would be taxed at much lower rates.

The very prospect of government intervention, which had formerly been viewed as a threat by business, now became a force for corporate growth. The knowledge that Washington stood ready to act, under the Employment Act of 1946, to ensure full employment in the economy if necessary became a potent addition to what Keynes called "inducements to invest." Influencing private investors to buy more common stock and business exeuctives to anticipate higher levels of construction and installation costs as well as a steadier rate of consumer demand, big government thus provided a prod to expansiveness in corporate decision-making.

Under the force of these powerful convergences, the old hostility between business and government grew insensibly more perfunctory during the Truman administration. Like it or not, after the collaborations of all-out war, they now found themselves jointly involved in the multi-billion-dollar overseas expansions for the Cold War. Thus when American commodity exports to Europe plunged from $15 billion to $3 billion in 1947 as government contracts for emergency relief shipments tapered off after the war, the Marshall Plan came to the rescue of exporters. Its enactment in 1948 committed the government to a four-year plan to advance $13 billion in aid to Western Europe, the first $400 million being made available on an emergency basis already in the winter of 1947–48. When the long feared and foreseen recession finally struck the country in July, 1949, Marshall Plan purchases helped cushion the shock to American business.[2]

"The international situation," as the President's Council of Economic Advisers reported, "exerted an important influence" in that recession year "through high national defense expenditures and through a renewed expansion of government expenditures to aid foreign countries." During 1949, such aid "reached a postwar record of $5.9 billion." Since total American exports dropped at this point as Latin American and other countries used up their war-accumulated credits in the United States, "the effect of increased [Marshal Plan] aid was to limit the decline of exports" and thus to soften the impact of the economic downturn in America.

As more and more stress was laid on cooperative measures to assure growth in the economy, much of the steam went out of the old trust-busting spirit in Washington: when the government's long-drawn-out antitrust cases against the telephone giant, AT&T, and against the leading Wall Street investment bankers were lost in the early 1950s, the few who seemed to care approved of the decision. By then old New Dealers like Adolf Berle and David Lilienthal were delighting the moneybags by writing that "bigness" in modern business was not only inevitable but a good thing.[3]

The doctrine, as it emerged from the analysis of liberal economists like Robert Nathan and Leon Keyserling, and in the expansive preachments of publicists like Eric Johnston and Elliot Bell, was that everybody would gain by growth. As such, it was just about the most optimistic proclamation to come out of America since Mary Baker Eddy stated that pain was a figment of human fancy. But, said Keyserling, a remarkable change had come over the United States. When he and other young reformers went to Washington in the early days of the New Deal, people thought that the satisfying of everybody's economic wants was an unattainable goal.

But now! Now the exertions of a great war had enormously expanded the economy, and the legislation of the New Deal had equipped it with built-in stabilizers. As a consequence, the United States had passed from an economy of scarcity to an economy of abundance. The rich were still rich—in the 1950s as in the 1930s one percent of the population owned twenty-eight percent of the national wealth—but for most Americans this wealth had lost its social sting. This, said the old radical writer Granville Hicks, "is because almost all of us are better off than we were, and therefore aren't so bitter against those who are still better off." There were still 11,000,000 families with incomes of less than $3000 a year. But the great mass of the population led by organized labor had experienced a marked rise in real income, and the abundance of consumer goods had effaced the more glaring differences in living standards between them. Growth made all this possible.

Instead of slicing the pie differently, then, said Keyserling, President Truman's chief economic adviser, let the pie grow bigger, and there would be plenty for all.[4]

In the perspective of history, the booming years after the Second World War were no more than a prelude to the mighty expansion of the American economy that took hold after 1950. This expansion also grew out of the Cold War. To get the better of international Communism, more than the Marshall Plan was needed. To save the Europeans from the domination of Soviet Russia, unifying the Atlantic community in NATO was also deemed insufficient. Under the prevailing view in the United States government, expressed by Secretary of State Acheson, military power was also needed. Dealing with the Soviet government, Acheson said, was:

> like trying to deal with a force of nature. You can't argue with a river, it is going to flow. You can dam it up, you can put it to useful purposes, you can deflect it, but you can't argue with it.

Negotiating with Russia was futile, in his judgment, and even the fruits of economic recovery and the political cohesion that the Marshall Plan and NATO were producing would be swept away unless the West mobilized military power to dam the outward flow of Russian force. That was Acheson's conviction even before the Soviet Union exploded its atomic bomb.[5]

From the moment in late 1949 when America learned of that event, the lid was off, and the nation launched upon the tremendous military expansion that touched off the arms race of the next twenty years. At the State Department Acheson pushed out George Kennan, who viewed the containment policy as a fundamentally diplomatic doctrine calculated, with only relatively small and flexible military forces supporting it, to bring the Russians to the negotiating table. When President Truman ordered the big policy review after getting word of the Russian A-bomb, Acheson and his new chief planner, Paul Nitze, urged the Pentagon to forget about budgetary constraints and figure out all that America would need to build up "positions of strength" against an aggressively A-armed Communism. Instead of the five percent of its total GNP that the United States had spent on its military effort between 1947 and 1950, Nitze wrote, such a rich nation could well expend up to twenty percent of its peacetime Gross National Product on national security without bankruptcy.[6]

This was the new doctrine adopted, in the National Security Council paper NSC-68, on the eve of the Korean War, and it underlay the big changes that America experienced as a result of the Korean conflict. Under this drastically revised and enlarged plan for America's Cold War, only a fraction of the hugely increased Defense Department funds voted in the next years went to prosecute the Korean war. The vast bulk of the money went for two far broader purposes: to expand the national economy in anticipation of general war with the Communists, and to build up the military dam of overseas bases that alone, the Cold Warriors said, could stem the tide of Russian expansion.

On the military front, the result was to enlarge American forces to six divisions in Europe, to underwrite Washington's costly blueprints for a 100-division NATO army that General Eisenhower was to lead in Europe, and to create a 143-wing Air Force three times the size of the pre-Korean Air Force and so powerfully manned and widely based as to throw international Communism back anywhere in the world. At the end of the so-called "Great Debate" during which Senator Taft demanded a choice between arming in Asia and arming in Europe, Congress voted to build up the army, navy, and air force until it should be possible to do both at once. Even while cries for impeachment of Administration leaders were being heard, Congress was approving their program for a $50 billion defense budget that raised America's expenditures for military purposes to a peacetime record of fourteen percent of the nation's total output. Overnight the military-industrial complex, the subject of Chapter XII, became America's biggest business.[7]

On the economic side, the new goals served to globalize the doctrine of growth, and the results were if possible still more transforming. So vast and sudden was the American economy's expansion that its stepped-up demand for imports at just about any price filled the pockets of the raw-material-exporting nations, closed the supposedly permanent "dollar gap" of Europe, put the Marshall Plan over the top and emancipated Europe from America for good. Such was the American economy's performance in spite of its inflationary fevers that the United States kept up its regular peacetime flow of foreign aid and continued to send private investment abroad at a rate of nearly a billion dollars a year. Finally, the expansion increased the size of the economy by a whole order of magnitude. By 1956 the gross national product was one quarter larger than before the Korean War. The surge was to be measured by such yardsticks as the growth of electric power (up seventy-five percent in six years), aluminum (doubled between 1950 and 1955), and steel (up from 86,-460,000 tons in 1950 to 102,872,000 tons in 1956). The United States economy grew so big that none on earth could compare with it. Growth —many worried that it was inflationary, but none yet called it cancerous —became synonymous with business prosperity.[8]

The 1952 elections put businessmen explicitly in charge of the American economy, and again it was Michigan, center of the Middle Western heartland and seat of the country's biggest and most dynamic business, that led in the management of national change. Eight years earlier Senator Arthur Vandenberg of Michigan had reached out a hand to President Roosevelt and pulled the Republican senators after him out of their traditional isolationism and into the new internationalism that led on into a bipartisan Cold War. Then Vandenberg as chairman of the Senate Foreign Relations committee helped put across the Marshall Plan, exacting as his price that businessmen should run it and that a good Republican automobile-maker, Paul Hoffman of Studebaker, should be in charge. But by 1952 it was time for political change, and for this the Republican party needed a basis for a wider appeal than either a Dewey or Taft could make. In 1949 Michigan's Vandenberg, ill with cancer, had looked ahead to 1952 and glimpsed General Dwight D. Eisenhower as the party's unbeatable candidate. A year after that Dewey, the unsuccessful candiate of 1948, had come out for the general as the man to lead the Republican party back to the White House.

When therefore the Democratic administration bogged down in Korea after 1950, America's military hero came forward, bright and untarnished, to reunite the nation by a Great Crusade. His was a motorized bandwagon. The story goes that not long before the Republican National Convention in 1952, Senator Robert Taft grew worried that his old friend Arthur Summerfield, the national committeeman from Michigan, might not be able to deliver the state's delegation to him at the Chicago convention. The senator paid a visit to Charles E. Wilson, president of General Motors, in Detroit, and according to the story this conversation took place:

TAFT: Charlie, I'd like to ask you a favor. I'd like to ask you not to put pressure on Arthur Summerfield.

WILSON: I'm sorry. I can't do it. Our international business is too important to us.

Not only Wilson and his top executives at General Motors, Harlow Curtice and Arnold Anderson, but Paul Hoffman of Studebaker and Henry Ford II and Ernest Breech of Ford, were on hand in Chicago as Arthur Summerfield—whose Chevrolet agency at Flint was said to be the world's largest—duly delivered Michigan's delegation for Eisenhower to assure the general's first-ballot victory over Senator Taft.[9]

Eisenhower's victory, said Reinhold Niebuhr, was "significantly engineered by eminent proconsuls of the budding American imperium, partly drawn from the Army and partly from business." Representative of the Army men was General Lucius Clay, former commander in Germany and now chairman of Continental Can. Clay brought Eisenhower together with Dewey, with Dulles and half the others who entered his cabinet. It was he who conveyed to Henry Cabot Lodge, later Eisenhower's convention manager, the message that the general, though he had never cast a vote in his life before 1948, was a Republican. The businessmen crusaders who had the general's ear oftenest were those who had been his golfing and bridge-playing companions after the war—men such as Clifford Roberts, a New York City investment banker, George Allen, a Washingtonian who held large oil properties, and Alton (Pete) Jones, president of Cities Service Oil Company, who had grown up in a little Missouri border town much like the Abilene in Kansas to which the general returned to start his race in 1952.[10]

The occupation of Washington by the businessmen, however, was not accomplished without important constraints laid down along the way. The most important of these arose by the inability of the hero-President to carry with him more than the barest of Republican majorities in the two houses of Congress. But there were other limits dictated by the singular character of the general they had designated as their leader and the quite special set of circumstances that brought him to the Presidency.

A B O V E and beyond all the other heroes of the Second World War, Eisenhower was the kind of general Americans could like for their president. He was democratic, friendly, warm, modest. He had pooh-poohed —and this was exactly to the taste of millions of his countrymen—all of the many suggestions made during his military triumphs that he return to America to run for office. Then, in what turned out to be a master political stroke, President Truman appointed Eisenhower supreme commander of the NATO forces in Europe. This ended the general's brief civilian career as president of Columbia University, and brought him back to the center of the public scene as more than ever the embodiment of the European commitment in the struggle against Communism. Liberator of Nazi-occupied Europe, and now restorer of its defenses against the shadow of Stalin, Eisenhower stood as shining symbol of America's victorious and united purpose at a time when the national consensus was fracturing amid the ugly surge of McCarthyism, and when a seamy growth of corruption was being laid bare in the Democratic administration in Washington.

Truman later asserted that Eisenhower thought he might receive both parties' nomination in 1952 and be elected, like Washington, by acclamation. Certainly some told the general that standing for the Presidency would only mean carrying out his NATO assignment another way, making sure by accepting the country's highest office that America would keep the faith with collective security against "international Communism." But the clinching argument, Eisenhower said later, was provided during the visit of Senator Lodge to his Paris headquarters in September, 1951. Quite obviously Lodge had talked with Dewey, Dulles and Clay back home, and Eisenhower was pleased later to summarize the points as his own:

> The Republican party [he said] must now seek to nominate one who, supporting basic Republican convictions—which had come down to us from Lincoln and Theodore Roosevelt—could be elected, and achieve at least a partial reversal of the trend toward centralization in government, irresponsible spending, and catering to pressure groups—and at the same time avoid the fatal error of isolationism.[11]

In retrospect such pleas and promises perhaps sound somewhat contrived and consensual. But in calling a great military hero to lead party and people in a country that still thought of itself as profoundly civilian, it was necessary to avoid any appearance of a draft. Whatever the general may have expected, there was a brisk fight. Lodge entered Eisenhower's name in the New Hampshire primary, where the general handily defeated Taft, the isolationist stalwart. In Minnesota, where it was too late to enter his name, Eisenhower's backers organized a write-in campaign that came within a few votes of knocking former-Governor Harold Stassen out of the running in his home state. Nonetheless Taft went to Chicago with 500 of the 1200 delegates pledged to support him to the end. Boldly contesting Taft delegations from Texas, Louisiana and Georgia and unseating the Taft regulars in a bruising floor fight, the crusaders from the Army, from business and from the party's internationalist wing put together a majority that nominated their hero on the first ballot.[12]

At this point, as the Democrats came to life and nominated Governor Stevenson of Illinois, the Great Crusade regrouped. While Eisenhower beckoned the nation to follow him on "the straight road down the middle," the Lodges, Deweys and Rockefellers stepped to the rear. Arthur Summerfield, the Taftite who had delivered Michigan to Eisenhower, was appointed chairman of the Republican National Committee and Sherman Adams, governor of New Hampshire and one of Eisenhower's few eastern backers not tied to the Deweyite internationalist camp, was put in charge of the campaign. The motorized bandwagon shifted to the most volatile antiradical fuel and soon found itself on the same track as the Grand Inquisition.

After a conference with the general in New York City, Senator Taft issued a statement that any differences between them on matters of domestic and foreign policy were "differences of degree." When the Eisenhower train shortly afterward rolled into Wisconsin, Senator McCarthy climbed aboard and won the general's endorsement. In his Milwaukee speech Eisenhower, at Adams's prompting, left out the passage he had prepared repudiating McCarthy's attack on his friend and benefactor, General Marshall. McCarthy went on the air and called, unrepudiated, for an end to "twenty years of treason" in government. After General MacArthur called for carrying the war by A-bomb, if necessary, to China, Senators Knowland, Bridges and McCarthy toasted "Back to the Mainland" at Chiang Kai-shek's Washington embassy. The candidate of unity and reconciliation found himself telling an American Legion convention in September:

> We are threatened with a great tyranny, a tyranny that has brought thousands, millions of people into slave camps and is attempting to make all humankind its chattel. . . . Dare we rest while these millions of kinsmen remain in slavery? The American conscience will never rest until these people are restored again to be masters of their own fate.[13]

If business expansiveness and virulent antiradicalism were forces in Eisenhower's victory, it was above all the general's popularity that won the Presidency in 1952. To have competed for this prize was essential—anything else would have been contrary to the American way. This was no strutting Patton or posturing MacArthur but a "democratic" general. There could be nothing snobbish about a five-star general known as "Ike." Not to have seemed modest would have been contrary to the image of the military hero America could honor as it was honoring this man at midcentury.

Yet in insisting upon his modesty, popular sentimentality imposed a falsity upon its hero that was to flaw his presidency and rob it of much of its effectiveness. America, be it said, thinks of the presidency for its generals as a place to retire to. The Presidency, whether for Washington or Grant or Eisenhower, is a sort of reward from the Republic. It is the biggest salute a general can get. Eisenhower accepted and agreed with the country's appraisal of himself as a hero who had won its greatest military victories in history, and his air of modesty should not be allowed to obscure the fact that he ultimately accepted the Presidency because "it was coming to him."

This assumption, or presumption, carried the profoundest implications for his conduct of the office. Undeniably, Eisenhower was relatively old, hence possibly tired, when he assumed office. Elected at sixty-one, he lived to be the oldest man ever to occupy the White House. But discounting implications of age, it was ultimately Eisenhower's acceptance of his place as hero in war and peace that helps account for the notable lack of energy and zest that marked his eight years in power.

By contrast a Roosevelt or Kennedy fought to get the office. Each battled up through the contending ranks of men impelled by like ambitions—the very same politicians for whom Eisenhower repeatedly expressed detestation and contempt. And each, having gained power, wielded it almost joyfully. Truman and Johnson, though each succeeded to the presidency without first winning it, both turned at once and fought to keep and use the power in their own right. Even when the power landed on Truman so abruptly that he spoke of a "load of hay" falling on him, he leaped up and grasped the powers of office.

To say that Eisenhower, who had already made formidable decisions in his career, responded less than eagerly to the opportunities of the presidency, is not to say that he lacked ambition. Dr. Ethel Alpenfels, a New York University anthropologist who met the general in his days at Columbia, was startled once to hear him say, "Suppose another fellow and I traveling together on the same plane were the only two men who could be promoted to the same job—I might throw him out of the airplane." That sort of fantasizing did not suggest a lesser ego-drive than that which more flamboyant rivals expressed in pearl-handled revolvers or assembled ranks of yea-saying courtiers. Eisenhower wanted the Presidency, but more for itself than for what he could do with it.[14]

As President, Eisenhower saw himself as a sort of institutional figure looming benignly above all others in the moiling scene below. And surely the country tended to share this view. For millions of Americans there was something deeply reassuring about the confidence, warmth and almost transfiguring smile of this plain, good man. Unlike almost all the other generals, he was liked by those who fought under him. Now, almost inevitably, there gathered about him—it was what happened with heroes, but it was typically Republican too—a thick aura of respectability. To this he seemed willing to contribute himself.

He had grown up in Abilene, Kansas, where his father had failed in business and gone to work for the rest of his life as a creamery hand. "We were very poor," he said. "The glory of America is that we didn't know it." He had been reared in the pacifist River Brethren sect of Mennonites, and named it is said by his mother, who later became a Jehovah's Witness, for the famous prairie evangelist Dwight L. Moody. But he had gone away to become a professional soldier and many other things his Dunkard minister-grandfather would never have approved of. Among other things Eisenhower became one of the world's keenest bridge players. This skill obtruded artlessly when the general returned forty years later to pay tribute at Abilene to his sturdy origins:

> Their Bible . . . was a lively and lusty influence in their lives. They believed in it with a happiness and contentment that all would be well if a man would take the cards that had been dealt him in this world and play them with the best of his ability.[15]

As a high-minded leader summoning his people back to their founding values in an hour of the most extensive revival of religious interest since the First World War, Eisenhower for the first time in his adult life showed a concern about establishing a tie with a church. The President made known that he would like to become a member of the National Presbyterian Church—his wife had been reared a Presbyterian—in Washington.

The Reverend Dr. Edward L. R. Elson, as pastor, expressed himself delighted but pointed out that certain steps were required to become a member of any Presbyterian church. In consequence Eisenhower became the first President ever to have been baptized in the White House and then, instructed in the rudiments of doctrine, he was formally welcomed as a member. James Hagerty, the President's press secretary, related that the general, pointing to Dr. Elson's public boast in the *Washington Post* that his was the church of the Presidents, growled, "You go and tell that goddam minister that if he gives out one more story about my religious faith I won't join his goddam church." Eisenhower not only went regularly to worship but handed out copies of Dr. Elson's sermons to his staff. He began each of his cabinet meetings with silent prayer, and helped launch a series of national "prayer breakfasts" by attending the first one. But the impression lingered among those close around him that these commitments were casual. Disarmingly he told the cabinet one morning:

> Saw a really fine film on Luther last night. I suppose some Catholics might resent it—but—what the devil—it was all 400 years ago, wasn't it?[16]

The cloak of respectability that went with Eisenhower's lofty presidential comportment covered some of the most engaging of the general's traits and foibles. This "man of peace" had a fearsome temper, bawled out aides in parade-ground bellows and in sudden, blind, frustrated rages could hurl across the Oval Room a large volume of federal statutes fetched by an aide to answer a question. But he also showed unvarying consideration to those around him, never dressed them down in the presence of others, asked about their wives and always knew what their children were doing. He could walk straight across a roomful of personages and salute by name a junior faculty member with whom he had had a few social evenings twenty years before. But when a Hagerty balked at saying something that would only cause him to "catch hell" from the newsmen waiting outside, Eisenhower could grin coolly and say: "Better you than me, boy."[17]

Even for such prosy men as Truman and Nixon the majesty of office invested their goings and comings with a good deal of drama. In the case of Eisenhower, the aura of Olympian respectability surrounding a hero-president generated at times a jarring discrepancy between image and actuality. In the summer of 1957 Eisenhower was at Newport on one of his frequent golfing holidays when events forced upon him the necessity of ordering troops into Little Rock to enforce a federal court order integrating the city's schools. To take so grave a step required that the President go on the air and explain his action to the country. To broadcast from a golf club, his staff thought, was hardly appropriate, and at Providence there were not then facilities for a nationwide hookup. "You could bring him into Boston," said one, "but if you were to bring him into Boston you might as well bring him into Washington." Even some of the jaded newsmen who had reported the President absenting himself for golf 120 days in a year were startled when he delivered the address hastily drafted to fit the change from clubhouse to White House. "I felt," said the general, "that in speaking from the house of Lincoln, of Jackson, of Wilson, my words would better convey . . . the firmness with which I intend to pursue this course."[18]

It was as natural as his smile that the hero-President, finding his aptest precedents in his own long soldiering experience, should place himself as Chief Executive atop an Armylike chain of command. To the general's way of thinking, the trouble with Truman, for whom he had little respect, was that as President he was always wading into fights. To the five-star general's eye, this was an offense to rank and order, a departure from station. When Senator McCarthy succeeded in putting his tarbucket smear on the government during Eisenhower's first year in office, the general blazed away in private—but he shied from any kind of public confrontation. "I will not get into the gutter with that guy," he told his staff.

To his way of thinking, the trouble with Roosevelt as President was that "he was a cruel man." Roosevelt, as Eisenhower had ample opportunity to observe, would go to any lengths, including assigning the same job to two different men, unbeknownst to them, to ensure that he got the information that would enable him to stay on top of *his* job and make the decisions about the man's task that he knew he would ultimately have to make. "Cruel" may seem an inadequate word to characterize so robust and yet astute an exercise of presidential powers, yet it should not be thought that Eisenhower, in standing clear of all such involvements, deliberately placed himself in the position of a limited monarch, a do-nothing President who reigned but did not rule. Quite the contrary. Eisenhower had obtained efficiency in his military career and came into the Presidency knowing just how to do it. He created around his office a kind of general staff, and put the machinery of the cabinet, the National Security Council and the Executive Office to work as never before.

His system was so organized that almost all the affairs of government were dealt with on their way up through the chain of command. A thoroughgoing "general staff man," he prided himself on his ability to "delegate," in the sense of delegating both work and responsibility. Sherman Adams, having managed Eisenhower's campaign, became his manager for domestic affairs, and was soon a wonder to behold. He was on top of innumerable matters large and small. He was in touch with everybody. He made up to 200 telephone calls a day. Undersecretary of Labor Arthur Larson, pinchhitting for Secretary James Mitchell, fielded one. The voice came through from the White House flat and crisp. "Where's Jim?" "In San Francisco seeing Harry Bridges," said Larson. The receiver clicked, and Adams was hurrying on to what might next have been an invitation to Robert Frost to stop by and see the President. "Poor Ike," said Harry Truman, "he'll sit there, and he'll say, Do this! Do that! And nothing will happen. Poor Ike—it won't be a bit like the Army. He'll find it very frustrating."[19]

While Eisenhower saw himself in his institutional role as above the melee, in what he called his operational sense he thought of himself as just one among equals—the head of the executive branch and no more. As such, he felt bound to stay out of the affairs of all other branches of government, federal, state and local, and especially the federal legislative branch. This self-restricting conception of the Presidency accorded with the modesty befitting the most affectionately regarded hero of a democratic and ineradicably civilian-minded republic. It accorded also with the self-concept of a President whose mission at this particular moment in history was to unite the people by reconciliation and consolidation. Time, task, temper and heroic station all combined to impel Eisenhower to turn away from the strong, driving Executive developed by Roosevelt and Truman to a style of constraint not seen around the White House for more than a generation. Such a turn may have been healing. But for a nation hurtling into the second half of the twentieth century as proclaimed leader of the world, it was a backward-looking turn.[20]

Many said that Senator Barry Goldwater, after being soundly thrashed in the 1964 presidential elections, had the satisfaction of seeing the man who beat him, Lyndon Johnson, take over and carry out the very policy of intervention in Vietnam that the loser had advocated. In much the same way, some of the basic ideas put forward by Senator Taft in 1951 when he thought he was headed for the White House, were adopted by the hero brought in at the last moment by the Eastern internationalists to head off the threat of Taft's neo-isolationism.

Neither the modesty of the general or his decent regard for the opinion of others, neither his deference to the legislative branch or his notorious distaste for the grubby details of politicking, not even the "better you than me, boy" style of his conduct of the presidential office sufficed to account for the headway that Taft and his conservative ideas gained on practically every domestic issue. Eisenhower's own prejudices were all against expanding the role of the federal government in social and business affairs. He believed in the absolute primacy of thrift, he wanted to return government functions to the states, he spoke scornfully of "creeping socialism," he thought that deficit financing was "sin," and he was strongly convinced that high taxes and deficit financing were "stifling free enterprise." This was the Eisenhower who came from the heart of the nation, the man from Abilene.

W H E N the American people elected General Eisenhower President in 1952, they looked to him as an experienced military man to apply the nation's immense strength in such fashion as to avoid falling into another such disabling deadlock as Korea. Everything that Eisenhower had learned from the Second World War and his experience as commander of NATO forces confirmed his view that security depended on collective security. He had no intention of abandoning internationalism. Still, he shared the feeling of those who voted for him that the United States ought to change the tactics by which it sought its world goals. He agreed with the congressional conservatives who wanted less aggressive presidential policy-making, and he was exceedingly aware of the strength of the McCarthyites. It was his nature—and a basic component in his popular appeal—to look sharp for the opinion of others, and his military training predisposed him to rely upon subordinates once he had determined policy.

John Foster Dulles had been the party's acknowledged exponent in the field of foreign affairs since 1944, backed by Dewey and the Eastern internationalist wing on the one hand, yet holding the view on the other, especially after a brief term in the Senate in 1949–50, that policy must keep in line with the views of neo-isolationists in Congress. All this made it natural and even inevitable that Dulles should become Eisenhower's Secretary of State and for six years one of the most powerful figures ever to hold that office.

If Truman and Acheson had made a forceful Cold War team that was because Acheson made the plans, Truman made the decisions and the Administration, with only minor modifications by Congress, carried them out. With Eisenhower and Dulles the division of labor was imposingly different. Eisenhower decided strategy and left everything else to Dulles. But what was the strategy? To all intents and purposes it was an anti-Communism even more rigid than that of Truman and Acheson and now enforced by a conservative and often McCarthyite Congress. On the other hand the tactics seemed to take in so much strategy that Dulles appeared to everybody including statesmen in other capitals to carry United States foreign policy around with him in his hat. Only in times of catastrophe like the Suez crisis of 1956—and then only because the Secretary was suddenly stricken with cancer—did the President emerge as decision-maker. Eisenhower had a strategy, all right, negative, reactive and pursued entirely behind scenes through mild and invisible restraints laid upon his formidable Secretary of State. The strategy, which followed the election returns, was "no more Koreas."

The combination of a monarchical presidency and a thoroughgoing delegation of ministerial power found its modern example in the relationship between Eisenhower and his principal minister. Born in Watertown in upstate New York in 1888 and educated at Princeton and George Washington University Law School John Foster Dulles was, as he did not hesitate to say, a man of uncommon abilities. From his Presbyterian minister father he learned the rigors of a Calvinist piety and from his maternal grandfather, who had been briefly Secretary of State in President Harrison's administration and took him along to The Hague conference in 1908, he acquired a passion for diplomacy. Later when his uncle Robert Lansing became Woodrow Wilson's Secretary of State, he attended the Versailles Conference as a minor member of the American delegation.

In the next two decades Dulles rose to be perhaps America's premier lawyer. He played a leading part in the floating of German bonds and corporate stock on American markets that enabled the Germans to make reparation payments after the First World War under the Dawes and Young plans. He had a hand in the pyramiding of holding companies by which Wall Streeters exploited public utility franchises up to the crash of 1929. Ironically, considering his later involvement in the Suez crisis, the firm of Sullivan and Cromwell, which he headed, rose to wealth and power representing stockholder interests in Theodore Roosevelt's 1902 coup by which Panama was detached from Colombia and the United States agreed to pay $30,000,000 for the rights of these interests to build the Panama Canal. The United Fruit Company, whose Central American plantations Washington sent gunboats and Marines to protect time and again in the heyday of dollar diplomacy, was a Sullivan and Cromwell client in the 1950s when a leftist Guatemalan government seized 400,000 acres of its land and the CIA, headed by another Sullivan and Cromwell partner, his brother Allen, staged an anti-Communist uprising that restored the banana lands to United Fruit.[21]

Through the 1930s Dulles was an isolationist, but in 1938 he attended the Oxford Conference of Faith and Order as a delegate of the Federal Council of Churches, and had what he called a religious experience. "There is no way to solve the great perplexing international problems except by bringing to bear on them the force of Christianity," he concluded. In this way Dulles moved not only to support intervention overseas to crush the iniquities of Hitler but later to stem the worldwide onslaughts of a godless Communism. As the Cold War intensified he became a leading Republican foreign policy expert, and after Vandenberg fell ill of cancer he carried through a dextrous bit of bipartisanship by negotiating the Japanese peace treaty for the Democratic administration without compromising the congressional Republicans' insistence on keeping free to denounce Democratic failures in Asia. Taking office he assured Eisenhower: "With my understanding of the intricate relationships between the peoples of the world and your sensitiveness to the political considerations involved, we will make the most successful team in history."[22]

As Secretary, Dulles traveled nearly half a million miles and visited forty-five countries. As he told the British:

> He wrote most of the President's statements himself. When they had to be tough, they were made by the Secretary of State from the State Department. When they were idealistic, they were made by the President but written by the Secretary of State.[23]

The nature of the Cold War as conducted in the Dulles years left little scope for the President's "idealism." The Eisenhower-Dulles team hewed to the line of the anti-Communists in Congress, and truckled to McCarthy in the management of the State Department.

No sooner had Eisenhower assumed office with all the prestige of a great hero and all the authority of a sweeping electoral triumph, than there occurred the very event for which a watchful providence might have brought such a personage to the Presidency. This was a fateful death on the other side of the Cold War. For two decades Josef Stalin had occupied the position of a god in Russia. He was absolute ruler, a tyrant to rank with Ivan the Terrible or Genghis Khan. Defending his dominance he had murdered thousands; imposing his programs he had executed millions. He had built Russia's industrial might, preserved it in a frightful war at a cost of twenty million lives, and expanded its power and influence across Europe, Asia, the world. Now he was dead of a cerebral hemorrhage at seventy-three. To hear such news Eisenhower was wakened in the night for almost the only time of his Presidency.

But the providential moment for action was not seized. Whatever a Theodore Roosevelt or a Franklin Roosevelt might have done in this hour, Eisenhower made no slightest move to capitalize on the event by proposing an end to the Cold War. "Well, what do you think about this?" he said to Dulles next morning, and Dulles was already so pinned down by the McCarthyites in Congress that he had no action to recommend. Intelligence experts told the President that the new Soviet premier would have to consolidate his internal control, and consequently would undertake no new departures in foreign policy anyway.[24]

The new premier to nobody's surprise was the same Georgi Malenkov who had made the principal speeches at the 1952 Russian Communist Party Congress with Stalin at his side. But Americans, as rigid in their ideological as in their diplomatic expectations of Moscow, were sure that they were up against "totalitarianism" and that the Russians could never solve the problem of the succession without an orgy of bloodletting. Soviet Communism, Dulles told the Senate as he took office,

> believes that human beings are nothing more than somewhat superior animals—and as long as it does I do not see how there can be any permanent reconciliation.[25]

Within days after Stalin's death the new Russian government ended a long deadlock at the United Nations that brought election of Dag Hammarskjold of Sweden as the new Secretary General. Moscow next issued a proclamation giving up all its old claims to Turkish territory. The Russians also extended the olive branch to the French, obviously in hopes of further delaying ratification of the European Defense Treaty and the rearming of Germany. On March 30, following his return from Stalin's funeral, Chou En-lai issued a conciliatory statement about repatriation of prisoners that opened the way for resuming talks to end the Korean War. Later in the year the new government in Moscow made even more striking gestures for relaxing international tensions.[26]

Yet the "thaw" that set in in 1953 never affected the temperatures of the Cold War. Though coincidence brought new governments to power in West and East that year, the opportunity was lost. In both camps rightwing forces bent on preserving the status quo succeeded in killing off moves toward abating or terminating the Cold War. In Russia, as recounted in the next chapter, they overthrew Malenkov. In the United States, as already related, they held the Eisenhower administration captive.

Eloquently indicative of the power of these forces was the way in which Winston Churchill, who was again prime minister of Great Britain, was brushed off by Washington. Seven years earlier, calling for Western solidarity against Stalin's postwar power buildup, Churchill had proclaimed the Cold War at Fulton, Missouri, and now, with an old man's impatience, he demanded its end. "It would be a mistake," he told the House of Commons, "to assume that nothing could be settled with the Soviet Union until or unless everything is settled." He urged:

> a summit-meeting of the smallest number of powers and persons possible
> —not overhung by a ponderous rigid agenda or led into mazes and
> jungles of technical details by hordes of experts and officials drawn up
> in vast and cumbrous array.[27]

The response of Americans seemed to be that they had not become the world's leaders to preside over the liquidation of the Cold War. Senator Knowland, in a singular misapplication of Churchillian history, accused the old man of "urging a Far Eastern Munich." Senator Paul Douglas, Democrat of Illinois, accused Churchill of "nudging the United States into a position where we will have to acquiesce in the main features of Communist proposals." When Churchill sent a personal appeal to the White House it was "neither welcome nor successful." From Eisenhower it elicited a very cold public reply prepared by Dulles. At a press conference the President said that the dignity and self-respect of the United States demanded some evidence on Russia's part that a meeting such as Churchill proposed would be worthwhile. First on the long list of preconditions that Eisenhower reeled off was a truce in Korea.[28]

Korea was the one place where the two sides got together. Upon his return from a frontline visit after the election, Eisenhower had warned in Dullesian language that unless the war ended quickly the United States might retaliate "under circumstances of our own choosing." In May Dulles passed word to the Chinese through Indian diplomats that this could mean the United States might use small "tactical" atomic bombs in Korea. On July 27, 1953, the Communists signed an armistice that left Korea divided roughly as before along the 38th parallel. Eisenhower later said that "danger of atomic war" induced the Communists to make peace.[29]

Though the death of the dictator five months before may also have played its part, Dulles was confident that the new Administration's policy, at once broader, more idealistic and more aggressive than Truman's, was paying off. "What we need to do," he had said, "is to recapture the kind of crusading spirit of the early days of the Republic," and it was remarked that the Secretary himself, with his eagle's beak and stern-jawed severity, had the look of a founding father.[30]

Instead of waiting for the Communists to attack, he said, and then "containing" them by fighting costly "brushfire" wars in remote places like Korea, the United States should concentrate on warning the Kremlin that nuclear blows at the solar plexus of "international Communism" would be the consequence of any aggression. Since, the argument went, "international Communism" was a conspiracy controlled from Moscow and Peking, such an explicit threat would keep the peace.

The new approach, moreover, would save money. Although Dulles had been working it up for years, and had put it to Eisenhower in a memorandum in Paris in early 1952, it was in fact tailored to suit a Congress run by Majority Leader Taft and dominated by conservatives and McCarthyites. The very name the new Administration gave to its Cold War program was borrowed from Senator Taft. The "New Look" as it emerged in 1953 and 1954 reshaped the American military establishment by putting the emphasis on the nuclear weapon and the bombers that delivered it while cutting back on the rest of the armed forces from 3,200,000 to 2,800,000 men. In achieving a lower military minimum than Truman had set, the New Look cleared the track for the fullest development of what Republicans felt was the true source of the nation's power —the American business economy.[31]

The doctrine rested on three ideas—that America now confronted Communism in Asia as much as in Europe; that America relied nakedly on nuclear retaliation to deter Communist advance; and that America's armed forces, instead of being committed piecemeal in Korea and in other places, would be held as a kind of strategic reserve at the center and deployed as America, not its enemies, desired. These were Taftian, not to say neo-isolationist, ideas, and they were meant to save money. When

Dulles in the next few years flew tirelessly round the globe signing up Asian countries in the Southeast Asia Treaty Organization (SEATO) and Middle Eastern nations in the Central Treaty Organization (CENTO), the clinching argument to Congress for these paper alliances was that it would cost far less to arm and maintain local armed forces than to station American units in such places.[32]

To save big sums, said George Humphrey, Eisenhower's Secretary of the Treasury, it was first necessary to "get Korea out of the way." But Joseph Dodge, the Detroit banker who became budget director, then found that most federal welfare outlays were mandated and hence not susceptible to much cutting. Soon Charles Wilson, the "business brains" that Eisenhower had installed to rationalize the Defense Establishment, set up a wail: most of the $10 billion reduction the new team sought to balance the budget was being demanded—while war still rumbled on in Korea—of the Pentagon. One day that summer Senator Taft learned at a White House meeting that Eisenhower could not bring the budget into balance in his first year or even before the 1954 congressional elections. He exploded, pounded the table and shouted: "You're taking us right down the same road Truman traveled. It's a repudiation of everything we promised."[33]

Under driving pressure from Humphrey, who turned out to be just about the most effective operator in the new Administration, the Pentagon scaled down its requests by $6 billion. It was still not enough. Late in 1953 Wilson took a hand and imposed a flat ten percent additional reduction on each of the services. Thus the Army and Navy shrank in size and the Air Force, now the official bearer of death and lord of battles, emerged with half of the nation's defense allotment.[34]

Since only the more "idealistic" utterances of the Eisenhower administration came from the President, it devolved upon John Foster Dulles to explain to the public a new program that was at once more fearsome and less costly. This he did in an address to the Council of Foreign Relations at New York City in January 1954 that has often been called the peak of America's Cold War. With the air of a stern lawgiver bearing the commandments down amid lightning flashes from the mountaintop, the Secretary proclaimed that the United States would no longer permit the Communists to pick time, place and method of war. Henceforth, to deter the armies of Communism, the United States would "depend primarily upon a great capacity"—embodied in America's airatomic power—for instant "massive retaliation." The American government would choose when and where to strike, and because it was "normal that at some times and some places there may be setbacks to the cause of freedom," the spectacle of Uncle Sam in the scowling person of John

Foster Dulles pacing vigilantly up and down the embattled brinks of freedom and occasionally pausing to rattle the bomb carried ostentatiously on his hip, would keep the adversary at bay and the world at peace.[35]

For all his determination, energy and relentless brink-walking Dulles failed to make the United States a more effective force in world affairs. Time soon demonstrated the impracticality of his innovations. Massive retaliation made little sense when the Russians possessed nuclear weapons as powerful as those of the United States. Adlai Stevenson said that Dulles' doctrine presented the United States with the grim choice of inaction or a thermonuclear holocaust. For America's allies Canada's Foreign Minister Lester Pearson asked an anxious question about Dulles' "instant retaliation with means of our own choosing"—what was meant by "instant," "means" and "our"? Members of Congress at once pointed out that if "instant" meant what the dictionary said, the administration's plan was unconstitutional because it conveyed an intent to make war before asking Congress to declare it. If "our" meant America alone, then NATO and other allies could hardly stand supinely by while American A-bombers took off from their airfields. Indeed the British lost no time informing Washington that no American A-bombers would take off from Britain for Moscow without express British consent.[36]

As for the "means" that Dulles spoke of, other events of early 1954 intensified the restiveness and fear stirred up among America's allies. In February a member of the Joint Congressional Atomic Energy Committee disclosed devastating details of the first American thermonuclear test at Eniwetok eighteen months before. The device of 10.4 megatons "erased from Pacific charts the island of Elugelab," tearing a mile-wide crater in the ocean floor and spreading "complete devastation" in a six-mile-wide area. Winston Churchill told the House of Commons that these reports filled his mind "out of all comparison with anything else" for days,[37] when still more appalling reports began arriving from the Pacific testing grounds. On March 1, 1954, a slight rain of white ashes began sifting down onto the deck of the Japanese fishing boat *Fortunate Dragon*. Two hours before the crew members had seen a great flash in the direction of Bikini atoll eighty miles to the northeast. Nobody had told them that the Americans were exploding a hydrogen bomb there.

By the time the boat reached Japan two weeks later the crew showed symptoms of radiation poisoning that some on shore recognized from the days of Hiroshima and Nagasaki. The upsurge of fear and anger in Japan brought the fall of a government and a marked cooling in relations with the United States. The death of the *Fortunate Dragon*'s wireless operator and the hospitalization of a half dozen others suffering from radiation burns and blisters sent a groundswell of uneasiness round the world, stirring the Pope to a new plea for peace, leading Nehru to demand a moratorium on all tests, and prompting candidates in New Zealand elections to charge that the United States was secretly preparing to test hydrogen bombs in Antarctica. It helped not at all that one American said with some sense of pride that "the explosion went so far beyond what was predicted that you might say it had gotten out of control," and still less that others suggested that the fishermen were "spying."[38]

Yet the most serious defect of Dulles' massive retaliation speech was the discrepancy between its fulminating rhetoric and the emerging reality that already threatened to turn such boasts back on themselves. In 1954 and in successive crises thereafter Dulles was to make repeated noises about American nuclear power, and these exercises were later, in a *Life* magazine article in January, 1956, called "brinkmanship." What was *not* reflected in Dulles' speech was the new factor that more than any other had arisen to destroy the Administration's hope of balancing the new budget: the explosion of the first Russian hydrogen bomb on August 18, 1953.[39]

The Russian feat took place fully two years before American experts expected it. It also occurred only eleven months after the first American hydrogen bomb success, whereas the Russians had not been able to explode their first A-bomb until four years after the first American one. This alone might have told Washington planners that the American lead in nuclear weapons no longer provided the sure basis upon which to found a Cold War strategy. That the American margin of technical superiority was small and getting smaller was made still plainer when the experts examined the airborne product of the Russian explosion. This disclosed that the Russian device was made by other and better means. The original American hydrogen device employed two heavy isotopes of hydrogen— deuterium and tritium. The tritium cost millions of dollars a pound to make, and required the use of quantities of costly plutonium that might otherwise have gone into atomic bombs. The end product, finally, was bulky. The Russian bomb, on the other hand, used a relatively cheap substance, lithium-6-deuteride, and used an atomic bomb as a trigger. The American hydrogen bomb exploded eight months later at Bikini adopted this more efficient and inexpensive process.[40]

If massive retaliation made little sense when Russia had nuclear arms to offset America's, Dulles' other schemes were equally unrealistic. At his suggestion the President announced in his first State of the Union message that the American Seventh Fleet would "no longer be employed to shield Communist China." Thereafter the Secretary talked much about "unleashing Chiang Kai-shek" against the mainland. The slogan was calculated to please Asia-Firsters in Congress who had supported MacArthur's proposal that Chinese Nationalist troops join the United Nations Forces fighting Communism in Korea. But it was a hollow slogan because Chiang could not even have held Taiwan without the protection of the American fleet.[41]

In a campaign speech at Buffalo in 1952 Dulles promised that the new Administration would use "all means to secure the liberation of Eastern Europe." He was responsible for Republican platform promises to "repudiate all [secret] commitments such as those of Yalta which aid Communist enslavements" in Eastern Europe. As Secretary of State in January 1953 he told the peoples of Eastern Europe in a radio address that America would support their efforts to free themselves. Only a few months later the new Russian leaders loosened political controls in East Germany and at the same time demanded higher output from workers for the same pay. The workers' reaction was to stage the first real protest against any Communist government since the Russians took over in Eastern Europe in 1945.

On June 16 they marched waving flags and posters down Stalinallee in East Berlin. The following day they started a general strike, tore down Communist flags and demanded free elections. Echoing Dulles' talk of "liberation" and "rollbacks," the American radio in West Berlin broadcast encouragement to the strikers. Then suddenly Russian tanks appeared in Berlin, Dresden, Leipzig, Magdeburg, and Jena. As the armor smashed the demonstrations, Dulles made no move. It was not lost on the people of Europe that "liberation" had proved an empty word for the East Germans.[42]

Every one of these disappointments derived from the new administration's determination to outdo the Democrats and wrest the Cold War initiative from the Communists. In no part of the world were the Republicans in Congress more impatient for such action than in the Far East. Shortly after Dulles' massive retaliation speech, the Eisenhower administration's resounding affirmation that the same threat of nuclear retaliation would meet Communist aggression in Asia as in Europe was put to the test.

Franklin Roosevelt wanted no part of helping to restore French colonial rule in Indochina after the defeat and expulsion of the Japanese. But the onset of the Cold War and the American judgment that France must be saved at all cost from Communism had their consequences in Southeast Asia. After receiving American help for his underground forces during the Japanese occupation, Ho Chi Minh vainly wrote seeking President Truman's support for "the same status as the Philippines" for his country; eight such letters went unanswered. By the late 1940s the United States took the French side against Ho's long fight to win independence, and when the United States went to war in 1950 to stop the Communist invasion of Korea it sharply increased its aid to French forces fighting Communist insurrection in Indochina. This move, determined almost solely by America's desire to overcome French resistance to the rearmament of Germany in the new forces under General Eisenhower's command, was fateful in the history of American commitments in Southeast Asia. The price of rearming Germany was following the French into Vietnam.[43]

By 1954 the United States was providing seventy percent of the cost of French military effort in Indochina, and insensibly the Americans had swung round to seeing their stake in the fighting as greater than that of the French. This was because in the meantime the American "police action" in Korea had transformed itself into a three-year war fought, from the time of Mao's intervention in November, 1950, mainly against Communist China. To Secretary Dulles Korea and Indochina were "two flanks [and Taiwan the central front] in a single Asian conflict being fought by the United States and its allies with Communist China."[44]

Thus, said Dulles, when the Chinese agreed to the Korean armistice in May, 1953, they at once turned southward and began actively assisting the Communists pressing the French forces in Indochina. This was also the standard Asia-First view. When General MacArthur was informed of the Korean armistice, his biographer relates, he exclaimed: "This is the death warrant for Indochina." In June 1954 Joseph Alsop wrote: "The free world would not now be menaced with a catastrophe in Indochina if MacArthur had won his fight against the artificial limits of the Korean war."[45]

The disaster of which Alsop spoke was the fall of Dienbienphu on May 7. Ground down by the guerrilla tactics of Ho and the continuing cabinet crises of Paris, the dispirited French army had decided to make its stand at this inland town situated not far from the Chinese border and at the bottom of a valley easily commanded by Communists from surrounding mountain ridges. It was an odd choice, but the French had picked the spot as a likely place to draw Ho into the open and fight. As the weeks and months went by, the fortunes of the opposing sides were reversed. The Vietnamese forces grew. They cut the French supply lines. They inflicted prohibitive casualties on French patrols. Then, to the consternation of the French, they brought up heavy artillery and began systematically shelling the isolated Foreign Legionnaires.

On March 20 General Paul Ely, the French chief of staff, flew to Washington to ask American intervention. A debate broke out in the Administration and among Western Allies. Dulles, Nixon and Admiral Arthur Radford, the new chairman of the Joint Chiefs of Staff, all urged an American air strike to save the French. General Nathan Twining, chief of the Air Force, later told how it would have been done:

> I still think it would have been a good idea [to have taken] three small tactical A-bombs—it's a fairly isolated area, Dienbienphu—no great town around there, only Communists and their supplies. You could take all day to drop a bomb, make sure you put it in the right place. No opposition. And clean those Commies out of there and the band could play the Marseillaise and the French could march out of Dienbienphu in fine shape. And those Commies would say, "Well, those guys might do this again to us. We'd better be careful." And we might not have had this problem we're facing in Vietnam now if we'd dropped those small A-weapons.[46]

Eisenhower appeared to waver. Within the Administration General Matthew Ridgway, the Army chief of staff, weighed in forcefully against intervention. As the man who pulled the bacon out of the fire in Korea, he was not without prestige. As Army chief he was in a position to send a dozen staff officers to take a hard look at the actual scene. They reported problems of logistics and supply that argued a single American bombing attack could not accomplish much. Saving the French would require six American divisions and a total of 600,000 men—just about what General Westmoreland said he needed to win twelve years later. Ridgway made sure these reports reached Eisenhower, the one man best qualified to assess their weight.[47]

On April 3 Dulles nonetheless informed congressional leaders that the Administration wanted a resolution passed authorizing commitment of American forces. The representatives and senators said that first the French must grant Indochinese independence. But when they learned that the Joint Chiefs were split and that the Allies had not been consulted, they held off. Tentatively therefore Eisenhower ruled against American intervention. But to meet the objection that the Allies had not given approval, a message went out to Churchill from Eisenhower next day comparing the threat in Indochina with the dangers of "Hirohito, Mussolini and Hitler," and urging the British to join in a coalition to prevent a catastrophe in Asia.[48]

"The United States," Dulles informed the American ambassador to France, "is doing everything possible to prepare public, congressional and constitutional basis for united action in Indochina." To this end Eisenhower flashed the same kind of signal to the American people that the Truman administration had sent out seven years before in urging support for Greece and Turkey. That time it was Acheson, pulling out all the stops, who drowned out doubts by describing local rescue as a fight against world Communism. If Communism moved into Greece, said Acheson, it would be "like apples in a barrel infected by a rotten one," spreading to "infect Iran and all the East, Africa through Turkey and Egypt, and Europe through Italy and France."[49]

Now Eisenhower at a press conference provided an even scarier and more simplifying metaphor for what he called America's stake in Indochina. The struggle for Indochina was crucial, he said, because Southeast Asia was full of tin, tungsten and rubber that America and its allies could hardly get anywhere else. And if France lost, "many human beings would pass under [Communist] dictatorship" by:

> what you would call the 'falling domino' principle. You have a row of dominos set up, you knock over the first one, and what will happen to the last one is the certainty that it will go over very quickly.[50]

If Indochina fell, the rest would presumably topple into the Communist bloc, Thailand, Burma, India, Malaya, Singapore, and even Indonesia— all Southeast Asia and possibly Japan too. Common sense could have replied that these were ancient and different peoples, separated by language, culture, impenetrable mountains and wide seas, never in all history subjugated by any single force military or otherwise. It did not matter. The image, adumbrated by fears, struck and stuck in popular awareness, and for years afterward helped shape the way America perceived Southeast Asia.

On May 7 Dienbienphu fell to the Vietnamese Communists, and again Eisenhower considered intervening. If certain conditions were met, the Administration "as a last resort to save Indochina" would "go to Congress for authority to intervene with combat forces." The requirement that the British join in was dropped. The only remaining conditions were that the French grant "genuine freedom" to the Indochina states —Vietnam, Cambodia and Laos. On May 10 Eisenhower told Dulles to prepare a resolution that he would take before Congress asking authority to commit American troops in Indochina.[51]

It was too late. The French had had enough. In Paris a new government took office under Pierre Mendès-France determined to cut French losses and get out of the Indochina fighting. Though British Foreign Secretary Anthony Eden was by now trying to make peace in Indochina, this did not stop Dulles from flying to London to seek Churchill's assent in case Congress should ask for it. Churchill declined to go along—all the more so because within the week the interested parties were to sit down together at Geneva to discuss the Indochina question.[52]

Thus massive retaliation came to its first showdown, and was found wanting. As the Geneva conference got under way the French hastily granted independence to Laos, Cambodia and Vietnam, while Eden put forward a compromise scheme for splitting Vietnam at the middle and letting Ho Chi Minh take the northern half. With Senators Knowland and McCarthy roaring retribution on his congressional flank, Dulles was of no mind to make himself a party to any transaction that deeded real estate to Communists. He ostentatiously absented himself from the Geneva proceedings.

At the time of the Korean invasion America had stepped up aid to the French in Southeast Asia, as it thought, to get French assent to German rearmament within the proposed European Defense Community. Now the French, abandoning Indochina, turned around and voted down the EDC. Undoubtedly the prospect of such a French turnabout in Europe was enough to induce the Russians to exert pressure on the Vietnamese comrades to accept terms.

Though Dulles sent Undersecretary of State Bedell Smith to the Geneva meeting, the United States, he said, would only "take note" of the agreements signed there and in Washington the National Security Council decided they were a "disaster." Most other governments expected that France would remain a presence in Vietnam, keep a strong influence over the newly constituted regime of President Ngo Dinh Diem, train its army, and insure that the elections specified for 1956 by the Geneva Accords were carried out. But Washington decided to "work with France only so far as necessary to build up the indigenous forces able to provide internal security, and in economic and political affairs to bypass the French and work directly with President Diem."[53]

When the Geneva agreements were negotiated, Eisenhower acknowledged later, no informed observer would have doubted that Ho Chi Minh would have won any fair election in Vietnam. The United States then proceeded to frustrate the Geneva program for elections, insure the extension of the country's eight-year-old civil war, and pave the way for the intervention in the 1960s of the kind that was so narrowly averted by the Geneva Accords in 1954.[54]

W H E N the Republicans came back to power in 1953, a good many of them felt that the country, after a painful lapse of twenty years, was again being run by those who owned it. Campaigning in Cleveland Eisenhower had told a group of supporters:

> It is high time that we bring into the Pentagon the businessmen of the United States. Until we get business brains in a sixty-billion-dollar busi-

ness, men such as K. T. Keller [of Chrysler] or Charles Wilson [of General Motors] we are not going to save the money we can.[55]

Wilson, president of the nations' biggest corporation since 1941, was Eisenhower's nominee for Defense Secretary. According to the Securities and Exchange Commission lists, he was the country's "highest paid citizen" receiving an income of $626,000 in 1951 not to mention 39,470 shares of General Motors stock. In 1950 he told stockholders that about twenty percent of the company's production volume was going to defense, and by 1952 the company was the nation's leading defense contractor, holding 7.8% (or $5.5 billion worth) of all defense contracts. Yet when Wilson appeared before a Senate committee for routine confirmation hearings, he not only assumed that the company would go on being top supplier to the Pentagon but he said that he intended to handle General Motors contract negotiations himself.

> I would like to tell you men . . . that there is a change in the country. The people are not afraid of big businessmen like me now. What is good for the country is good for General Motors, and what is good for General Motors is good for the country.[56]

Although Americans had not heard much about a "military industrial complex" at this point in the Cold War, there was a superconfident ring about that last phrase—"what is good for General Motors is good for the country"—that jarred the ears of both the nation and Congress. The Senators began asking questions. "The issue," said Chairman Leverett Saltonstall, Republican of Massachusetts,

> is whether a man can be holder of stock in an organization that does business with the government, when he is the government officer that may be concerned with that business.

The issue was posed by a law passed in 1948 by a Republican-dominated Congress, and Wilson's position appeared contrary to the law. Richard Russell of Georgia, ranking minority member of the committee, served notice that the new administration could expect little cooperation for its projected legislation in Congress unless Wilson changed his tune. Wilson was not confirmed and sworn in until he had satisfied the Senators that he would divest himself of his General Motors stock and thereby his conflict of interest.[57]

Editorialists hailed this as fair warning from Congress that the businessmen could not expect to manage government operations with the same high hand they were used to in corporate life. Yet the slap on the wrist administered to Charles Wilson did not prevent the rise of the military-industrial complex to great power in the years that followed. More significantly, the incident seems to have had an important effect on the role of General Motors and, because the company was something of a bellwether for the rest of the nation's business, on the evolution of the American economy during these years.

An enterprise strong in capital, management and research capabilities, General Motors held $12 billion in government contracts during the Second World War and, suspending all output of cars for the duration, entered into production of no fewer than 377 new items. After 1945 the company showed itself able and willing to execute defense contracts while blanketing the automobile and truck markets. But from the moment of Wilson's brush with the senators over conflict of interest, his company pulled away from war work and concentrated its enormous resources as never before on the expansion of its consumer market. From a postwar peak of $1.9 billion in fiscal 1953, General Motors' volume of defense production fell away to $347 million in President Eisenhower's last year in office. Accepting the political signals from Washington, so to speak, to stay away from major defense contracting, the world's biggest manufacturing enterprise threw the full force of its commercial dynamic instead into greatest possible aggrandizement of a consumer economy.[58]

It was anything but a self-denying choice. These were the fat years after the Korean War when Big Business finally had its free run, when the corporations were in a position to exploit prosperity. This was the time when it almost seemed as if there were a sign across the entry to the country: "No admission except on business."

In these years the value of General Motors stock quadrupled; in 1955 the company sold $325,000,000 worth of stock to the public and in 1956 $700,000,000 worth of Ford shares were snapped up when the company went public. There were also stock splits. By the mid-1950s General Motors was a supercorporation with assets greater than Argentina's, revenues eight times bigger than New York's, and half the car-and-truck market of the United States. By then General Motors was so programmed for growth that Wilson's successor, President Harlow Curtice, stopped talking in terms of percentages of the car market for his company's prospects. Instead he measured them in terms of the country's Gross National Product. "We have three percent of the GNP now," he exulted, "and we won't have any less than five percent next year." Indeed, *only* growth made such goals attainable. At that stage General Motors could have lowered prices and driven Ford and the rest to the wall but refrained because of fears of antitrust action.

But after selling a record 8,000,000 cars in 1955 General Motors sold only 7,000,000 the following year. In the face of the decline the momentum for growth in Detroit did not flag. The automobile companies granted Reuther another rise in the UAW's annual "package." General Motors spent a billion dollars on automating in 1956, and then raised prices. It was a way of achieving growth in companies' and workers' income, while staying out of trouble with the Justice Department's antitrust lawyers. But it provoked a congressional inquiry by Senator Kefauver into charges that in the automobile and other large industries "administered prices" set by a few supercorporations after bargaining with their unions had tended to supplant prices governed by the marketplace.[59]

In the Washington of the 1950s businessmen did not have to pay much heed to such charges. Of the nine cabinet members chosen by Eisenhower, three were General Motors men—Wilson, Summerfield and Douglas McKay, who had been governor of Oregon and owner of a Chevrolet agency in Salem before being named Secretary of the Interior. The cabinet as a whole had such a strongly business cast that T.R.B., the *New Republic*'s commentator, described it as "nine millionaires and a plumber." (Martin Durkin, president of the Steamfitters Union, a Democrat and Stevenson supporter, had been named Labor Secretary in an apparent effort to show Eisenhower's determination to rise above labor-management conflicts; but Taft called the appointment "incredible" and Durkin was out within five weeks.) Undersecretary of the Treasury W. Randolph Burgess, formerly of the National City Bank, expressed the general feeling in a talk to the Bankers Club of New York: "They're our kind of people now." After twenty years of New Deal and Fair Deal, said McKay, "we're here in the saddle as an administration representing business and industry."[60]

Of these businessmen no more pristine specimen was to be found than George Humphrey, the new Secretary of the Treasury. Humphrey was an Ohioan who saw things the way Taft did. He had spent all his life in the M. A. Hanna Company of Cleveland, a huge combine of manufacturing, mining and banking interests. He saw simple answers for complicated political questions, and with disarming directness, said so. When he accepted his new job, he extracted a promise from Eisenhower: "If anyone asks you about money, I want you to tell them to go and see George." The great thing was to get the government back, he said, on a "sound, businesslike basis."[61]

So it went. Budget Director Joseph Dodge, moving in from Detroit's Security National Bank, looked at the books. Debts were four times bigger than annual income, current bills were mountainous, cash in the till was nowhere near enough to pay them when they fell due. Like a good businessman, he demanded spending cuts. Treasury Secretary Humphrey looked at Dodge's figures, then looked at the humming dynamo of American industry he had helped build and run. Even though there was a war on he called for lifting all controls so that business could speed up and generate wealth enough to fill both private and government tills. Defense Secretary Wilson looked at Dodge's and Humphrey's recommendations and affirmed that national security depended on a sound economy. The best way to assure prosperity, Eisenhower cheerfully agreed, was to rid the economy of price and wage controls. There should be tax cuts too.[62]

As these marketplace magnates went confidently about unleashing the enterprises of America, the future of the President's Council of Economic Advisers came up for discussion. Taft and other people in Congress wanted to abolish them. The nabobs from Detroit and Cleveland thought it a waste to get economic guidance from men who had never met a payroll. But others in the White House warned the President that the first Republican administration since Hoover was to be judged by its capacity to avoid another Depression. So it was that they brought in Arthur Burns.[63]

In an administration filled with figures like Eisenhower, the All-American hero from the Kansas plains, and Dulles, the austere Presbyterian who looked and even sounded like an author of the Federalist papers, an Arthur Burns was a new kind of American. He had been born Arthur Bernstein in Stanislau, Austria, and brought as an infant to America where he grew up, the son of a Passaic, New Jersey housepainter. He waited on tables in Asbury Park summer hotels in the 1920s, never thinking twice about turning over all his earnings to his father. A smart kid, he studied under Wesley Clair Mitchell, the Columbia economist, and later held the Wesley Clair Mitchell chair in economics at the university. When all the liberal academics, social workers, lawyers and businessmen flocked to New Deal Washington, Burns stayed behind and delved long into the business cycle. He learned the ropes of the expanding American economy, and then described them to the old Wasp society in such works as *The Frontiers of Economic Knowledge*.

The message was this: we can manipulate society. It was possible, in the systems-engineering language of the more freewheeling trade-cyclists of the day, to "fine-tune" the economy. In human terms, fiddling with dials and nudging index needles could work out at full prosperity—or 9,000,000 unemployed. To an Eisenhower who had proclaimed "never another depression," such a man had to be listened to.

Intently serious, a man who found little humor in the things that came before his thick-lensed scrutiny, Arthur Burns wore a high collar, and parted his hair in the middle with the air of earlier times. But he was soon the only official with a fixed weekly appointment with the President

(Mondays at 11:00 A.M.), and making policy with men whose clubs he could not, as a new American of Jewish origin, belong to. He was the nation's chief social scientist. His specialty was the management of human affairs.

Shortly after the high-powered administration businessmen had "freed" the economy, Dr. Burns brought the cabinet to startled attention. He had looked at the indicators, he said quietly between puffs at his curved-stem pipe, at the Federal Reserve Board industrial production index, at the stock market, at inventories. They told him that five months after the Republicans had taken office a recession was under way. There was a flap among White House officials. Some scurried to pull together public works projects. The President brought up his pet idea—highway construction. Then Dr. Burns spoke again. The marketplace magnates wheeled to listen.

It was going to be a recession, said Burns, but not a very severe one, perhaps not so severe as the last one in 1949 when 6,000,000 men had been thrown out of work. To break out the public-works programs, he said firmly, would not be warranted. The downturn would diminish the Treasury's intake by a billion dollars, but the billion would stay in private pockets and be spent by consumers, and the proposed income-tax cut would give the economy another $7 billion shot in the arm. Another $2 billion would probably flow into the economy through its built-in stabilizers, social security and unemployment-benefit payments. All this, if the government would shift to an easy-credit policy for a bit, should moderate the decline and bring the economy back to a vigorous climbing angle in 1954. Since a phenomenal population rise was also taking place in these years, with the effect of impelling all consumer and other expenditures upward, the nation hurtled across the roller-coaster dip in Eisenhower's first years with all the élan Burns said it would.[64]

Meanwhile, well before the cabinet businessmen brought the government's spending accounts under control, the Republican Congress and administration cut corporate and individual taxes. The consequence of the tax concessions voted in 1953 was to divert $7.4 billion from public to private channels, and, in the specific case of the tax-form dividend exclusions that benefited the 6,000,000 out of 57,000,000 income-tax payers who held common stocks, $300,000,000 remained in the nation's best-lined private pockets instead of going into the federal Treasury—a reward far in excess of the $11,098,046.49 contributed by essentially this same group of citizens to the Republican *and* Democratic campaign chests in the 1952 election campaigns.[65]

Generals do not get much money. When Eisenhower drove up to Morningside Heights to take over the presidency of Columbia in September, 1949, he remarked that the Cadillac he stepped out of represented the sum total of his liquid assets at that point. As between the politicians and the businessmen, the general greatly preferred the company of the businessmen, and stood in some awe of the richest ones. These men had so much more money than he did. There was nothing new about this. As President, General Grant appointed Adolph E. Borie of Pennsylvania to his cabinet simply because Borie bought him a house. He also tried to nominate Alexander T. Stewart, leading department store magnate of his day, as Secretary of the Treasury in a passage reminiscent of the Charles E. Wilson episode. Congress refused to vote confirmation on grounds that the appointment contravened a 1789 law—since repealed—that barred a man of commerce in that post.[66]

The Eisenhower administration's ties with members of the oil industry were particularly close. One of the first measures shepherded through Congress by Senator Taft, before he was felled by cancer, was the "tidelands" oil bill, by which the federal government relinquished to the states the rights to oil-bearing lands lying offshore but within the three-mile limit. For years oil-business friends of the general such as Pete Jones, George Allen and Sid Richardson had pressed for this measure, which involved what the *Oil and Gas Journal* termed "the richest drilling prize in history" and *The New York Times* "one of the greatest and surely most unjustified giveaway programs in history." No sooner had the Eisenhower administration taken over, moreover, than it moved to kill a Justice Department suit against the country's seven big international oil companies that charged them with operating a cartel for controlling Middle Eastern oil output. Then, on the recommendations of a special four-man expert panel, the government instituted oil-import quotas that brought about a forty percent boost in domestic oil prices. Afterwards one of the panel members joined Cities Service, the big company run by the general's friend, Pete Jones, as president and Jones' number two man. Much later it came out that Jones, along with George Allen and a third oilman, B. B. Byers of Tyler, Texas, paid all the expenses of the 190-acre farm that General Eisenhower acquired at Gettysburg in 1950, a sum eventually exceeding $500,000.[67]

THE WEALTH and power of America's oil companies, increasingly derived as they were from all around the world, raised a perplexing question for Americans in the years after the Second World War: what does a superstate do when inperialism has become a disreputable word but the nation obviously has an empire? The great leap of American business abroad in the Eisenhower years, in the midst of an obsessive Cold War preoccupation with providing a policing presence throughout the "free world" to hold back an aggressive "international Communism," eventually disclosed some unwitting answers.

Having made its start at old-fashioned empire-building in 1898, the United States appeared for a while to be following in the path of the British. The acquisition in 1940 of the string of lend-lease bases stretching along the Atlantic from Newfoundland to Bermuda to Trinidad bore marked similarities to the way the British picked up outlying places at the Congress of Vienna in 1815—Helgoland, Capetown, Zanzibar, Trinidad and Tobago. And Truman, Stimson and Forrestal seemed to be operating in the same classic fashion when at the end of the Second World War they insisted on gathering in for the United States all the Japanese-held islands in the Western and Central Pacific, refusing to bargain or even discuss their action with their Russian, British and Chinese allies.

But after 1945 this kind of imperialism went out of style. America recoiled from taking up the burden in such out-and-out political fashion. The Philippines were set free, and the lend-lease bases swiftly became military fossils comparable in every way to the forts guarding the entrances to New York and San Francisco harbors. In an age of dissolving empires, empire-building had to find new and wholly unforeseen forms.

Seldom if ever had the world witnessed such a grand-scale demonstration as the Marshall Plan of the business adage: "You can only prosper as much as your customers prosper." As Europe sprang to life, the enticing prospect of profit possibilities in a Europe shielded and stabilized by American military might internationalized the appetite of United States corporations for growth. After the recovery sparked by the Marshall Plan's $13 billion and fired by the Korean War came the boom in West Germany, the reassuring return of Conservative government in Britain, and energetic modernization in France. The climate was right. American corporations had accumulated solid experience by branching first into Canada and Latin America. Now Europe was brought suddenly near by airliners so that American executives could explore and discover opportunities in two weeks instead of six. Improvements in transoceanic and cable connections had a reinforcing effect. It became not much more difficult for a New York headquarters to run a plant in Amsterdam than in Atlanta. The American enterprisers flooded into Europe.

Undoubtedly the wave was given impetus by the efforts at uniting Europe started by the Marshall Plan, advanced by the European Coal and Steel Community of 1952, and brought near to completion in a European Common Market in 1957 rivaling the American continental market in size and attractiveness. Between 1950 and 1967 the United States' capital stake in European business increased by more than tenfold, and by the beginning of the 1970s stood at more than $15 billion. Practically none of it was the kind of foreign investment by individual rentiers in railroad and other company shares favored by British, French and Dutch capital in the nineteenth century heyday of imperialism and copied in the United States by Wall Street promoters of Latin American bonds and stocks for a few years after the First World War. In terms of ownership and control, this new kind of economic imperialism was more forthright. Overwhelmingly, it consisted of American corporations buying or building their way into Europe by direct investment in manufacturing plants there.

The rush was led by the biggest American companies. Of the country's top hundred firms, sixty-two acquired facilities in Europe. By 1965 700 of the top 1000 had branches or subsidiaries in Europe. Even more than back home, the trend among the invaders was very strongly toward oligopoly—the modern, more precise term for what Theodore Roosevelt and his trustbusters meant by monopoly. Only twenty American firms accounted for two-thirds of the American investment in Europe. In the three biggest European markets—West Germany, Britain and France—forty percent of the direct United States investment was accounted for by three companies—Standard Oil of New Jersey, General Motors and Ford.[68]

Even so, this growth of American business in their midst might not have been so unsettling to Europeans, since the total American-owned share of their overall economy did not exceed six percent. But what led such an intelligent European as the Frenchman Jean-Jacques Servan-Schreiber to write a book called *The American Challenge* in 1967 was that the American growth was centered in the fastest-growing sector of the European economy. This had everything to do with America's lead in technological innovation.[69]

Along with all its other advantages, the United States had built a dominant position in world science: between 1951 and 1969 Americans took twenty-one of thirty-eight Nobel prizes in physics, nine out of twenty-seven in chemistry, twenty-three of forty in medicine and physiology. America had surpassed Europe in development and application of scientific discoveries: in the mid-1960s United States gross expenditures on research and development were sixteen times those of Germany, ten times Britain's, and three times those of all Western Europe put together. Since about two-thirds of the American outlays for R&D were financed with public money—largely as will be seen in Chapter 11 for the Cold War arms race—the technological edge held by American corporations was attributable to official United States policy. Scientific discoveries were usually made in universities, often outside the United States, and freely accessible to all. American R&D excelled at industrializing these discoveries, bringing innovation to the point of commercial application, by virtue of superior teamwork within large and complex organizations. At IBM, for example, R&D teams shortened by several years the time-span for bringing in the so-called third generation of computers in the 1960s, and the company was said to have spent several billion dollars doing it.[70]

As early as 1963 American firms in France controlled forty percent of the country's oil market, sixty-eight percent of its photographic film business, sixty-five percent of its telecommunications supply industry. By 1967, American corporations controlled fifteen percent of Europe's consumer-appliance market, fifty percent of the market for semiconductors, ninety percent of the computer business, and ninety-five percent of the "new market for integrated circuits—miniature units crucial to guided missiles and the new generation of computers." The threat to the nation-state imposed by this kind of dominance was made starkly clear in the 1960s when the United States State Department, at odds with General De Gaulle over his efforts to build up his own *force de frappe*, or nuclear missile system, refused export permits to Control Data Corporation for essential computer parts ordered from the United States for the French missiles' computer controls. General De Gaulle's crash-program for building up Compagnie Bull as a French computer-maker was unavailing, and for a time another American company, General Electric, had to be brought in as its partner.[71]

By that time it was apparent that the international growth of these enormous companies was confronting not only Europe but the rest of the world, not excepting the United States, with a new and powerful kind of institution: the multinational corporation. Big as these enterprises loomed in Europe, they were big everywhere else in the trading world, and getting bigger. Not all were based in the United States: quite a number were based in Europe, and indeed after the European comeback of the 1950s the European supercorporations grew and spread faster on the average than the Americans.

Archetypically, the multinational corporations had a deep impact wherever they moved in. For every dollar they transferred back to their home countries, they put an average of four dollars into circulation locally in the routine conduct of business. This alone could have profound social and economic effects in small countries. General Motors, largest of the multinationals operating in Europe, had an annual income bigger than that of half the world's nations, a payroll bigger than the population of Luxembourg. Standard Oil of New Jersey, the second largest, did a bigger business outside the United States than in its home country.[72]

By their very existence, plan, purpose, such enterprises were supernational. They were owned by persons all over the globe. Their managers

might be drawn from wherever competence could be found; their technical personnel and labor force could be, and often were, completely international. Whether airlines, banks, telecommunication combines or oil
companies, such corporations existed, grew and multiplied because they
performed needed functions. Their rise was thus perfectly natural. Their
vitality and expansiveness were formidable, and they kept exhibiting more
multinational characteristics.

At first they had spread, the economists said, because they made a
product that sold well at home and, wishing to preempt competition and
make the most of a good thing, simply took their experience and expertise
into new markets abroad. By the late 1960s the multinationals had progressed well beyond such primitive modes of thought. A few had even
grown ambivalent about where their headquarters were—like Royal
Dutch/Shell, based in both the Netherlands and Britain. The biggest
American multinationals—almost the same thing as saying the biggest
American companies—now had a fifth of all their assets abroad, and were
well launched on new ways of doing nearly a third of all their business
outside the United States.[73]

"Global scanning," the new style of looking at all their far-flung
facilities and opportunities, had led them boldly to mesh complex logistical networks among their affiliates all over the world. IBM produced one
type of integrated circuit in France, another in Germany, and a hybrid
in a third country. British-controlled Unilever tested detergents and synthetic soaps in the American market before putting them into production
in Britain and elsewhere. Bendix went to Taiwan's cheap labor supply to
make automobile radio assemblies for many different world markets. Ford
made fender steel in the Netherlands for car production in other European countries, and tractor components in Germany and motors in Britain to be used in United States assembly plants. Singer cross-hauled many
makes of sewing machines between Scotland, Canada, Japan and the
United States, concentrating production of different types wherever
"scanning" of markets and costs suggested. By the late 1960s United
States-based multinational corporations alone handled an international
trade in manufactured and partly-manufactured goods of impressive proportions—$9 billion in exports from the United States, $6 billion from
Europe, $1.4 billion from the less developed parts of the world. By 1970
the gross value of the overseas production of American multinational
enterprises had risen to $110 billion a year—more than twelve percent of
the Gross National Product of the United States.[74]

The rise of the multinational corporations raised many questions.
"How can a national government," asked former Undersecretary of State
George Ball, "make an economic plan with any confidence if a board of

directors sitting 5,000 miles away can by altering its pattern of purchasing and production affect in a major way the country's economic life?" And what was to be said when an international oil company, opening up a new oil field in an undeveloped country like Venezuela, exercises authority equal to, and in some cases greater than, the local government, building roads and schools, bringing in a variety of skills which are gradually passed on to the local population, and practically changes the social structure of the body politic? And a labor union in Pittsburgh or Detroit, seeing branch plants being build abroad—what can it ask but whether jobs are not being lost for American men? The vitality and growth of the multinational corporation could frighten De Gaulle. It also gave pause to every President from Eisenhower to Nixon, all of whom battled to control America's international balance of payments while executives of the multinationals shifted billions of dollars around seemingly beyond their reach.[75]

In the past United States foreign policy toward Latin America and the Middle East could have been said to have been practiced for American business. As United States Marine Corps General Smedley D. Butler bragged long ago:

> I helped make Mexico safe for American oil interests in 1914. I helped make Haiti and Cuba a decent place for the National City Bank boys to collect revenue in. . . . I helped make Honduras "right" for American fruit companies.

During the 1950s United States industry was blocked by the State Department in attempts to increase investments in both Indonesia and Liberia; and it must also be said that American Zionists managed to neutralize anti-Israeli sentiment in the oil-oriented State Department. On occasion during the 1940s and 1950s federal antitrust actions thwarted practices designed to raise businessmen's export prices in the oil, chemical, ball-bearing and coated-abrasive industries. But the multinationals were not to be denied. When Middle Eastern oil states later joined forces, the international oil companies admitted them as partners in their world-scanning confederation as a preliminary to marketing a larger share of Middle Eastern oil in the United States and, in consequence, intensifying the United States' international balance of payments problem.[76]

Such contradictions reflected the conflicting economic and political interests struggling for control of aspects of foreign policy in the aftermath of the Cold War. Two-thirds of the way through the twentieth century these struggles were increasingly dominated by the new kind of imperialism embodied in the multinational corporation. The drives of this imperialism often did not coincide with the interests of any state, just as it endeavored often to carry out, for better or for worse, things that not any state seemed at the time to get done.

The emergence of the international corporation as a new and important entity with many of the characteristics of the sovereign state was a significant and unexpected event. It was as natural, Professor Frank Tannenbaum said, as the slow rise of a trading and commercial community that finally created the European nation-state as a substitute for medieval order.[77] Whatever its ultimate import, this startling development was an unplanned outcome of America's Cold War, as well as a phenomenon of the twentieth century march of mass organization. It was a globalizing of an imperative more powerful than the old drive for empire—the imperative of corporate growth.

CHAPTER 8

Retreat From Sacrifice

THE CONSUMER SOCIETY AND THE END OF STALINISM

T HAT ANY and all peoples should be liberated from foreign yokes was a truth that Americans had held self-evident since 1776. Though often honored in the breach, this principle remained prominent among American war aims through the first and second World Wars. In a Cold War waged to ideological extremes, but under most brutal nuclear constraints, the good old American notion of "liberation" was bound sooner or later to let the general public in for cruel disappointments and land its official proponents in some preposterous predicaments. This finally happened in 1956, in events discussed in this and the following chapter. In that year the United States, having called at the top of its voice since the Cold War began for the liberation of Eastern Europe, offered no help whatsoever when the people of Hungary rose in insurrection against the Russian occupiers—who had the capability of making nuclear war against America. At the very same moment the United States found itself intervening to frustrate the colonialist reoccupation of Suez by its British and French allies—who had not this capability.

Like the discovery that the United States could not "win" the Korean War, these events delivered yet another blow to what Sir Denis Brogan called "the illusion of American omnipotence." This was above all true in the case of the paralysis of United States policy toward the Hungarian uprising. From the time of Winston Churchill's Iron Curtain speech in 1946, Americans had grown to expect the liberation of what were called the "captive nations" or "slave states" of Eastern Europe. Their leaders had condemned Stalin for making a mockery of his Yalta pledges of "free elections." Their government, their press, their most respected spokesmen, voiced rising national anger at the tragedies in the East—mass arrests in Yugoslavia in 1946, the jailing and apparent torture of the patriot-prelate Cardinal Mindszenty in Hungary in 1947, the crushing of Czech democracy in a night in Prague in 1948.

The America that had freed Western Europe, it was supposed, would put an end to Eastern enslavement. Was not the United States training men in North Carolina to jump into Yugoslavia? The West had a Chiang Kai-shek for every East European country. Long after the Soviet Union absorbed the Baltic states, the Latvians, Lithuanians and Estonians maintained phantom embassies in Washington. Organizations of anti-Communist exiles operated in London, Paris, Munich from every Iron Curtain nation, along with outfits purporting to represent Byelorussia, the Ukraine, and even "Cossackia" and "Udel-Ural."[1] Radio Liberation and Radio Free Europe, both more or less openly supported by the United States government, beamed broadcasts and floated balloons laden with pamphlets and food packages eastward across the Iron Curtain.

"To help liberate all European people enslaved by the Communist tyranny," Representative Charles Kersten, a McCarthyite Republican from Wisconsin, secured adoption of an amendment to the Mutual Security Act of 1951 allocating $100 million of foreign aid funds for organizing military units composed of anti-Communist exiles in Europe. In 1952 the American Liberation Center opened its doors on New York's Fifth Avenue, presided over by Robert Vogeler, an International Telephone and Telegraph executive released by the Hungarian government after eighteen months' imprisonment for spying for the Central Intelligence Agency. The liberators, said Kersten, one of five members of Congress on hand to give the center a send-off, would encourage Czech workers to sabotage their country's five-year plan, offer rewards to Russian pilots to fly West, and lead to liberation without major wars. [2] In 1952 the Republicans nominated the liberator of Europe for President, labeled Truman's containment policy "negative and passive," and proclaimed "liberation" as their program. "Rollback" was the popular slogan, proclaimed by Richard Nixon before the Business Advisory Council. "The only way to stop a head-on collision with the Soviet Union is to break it up within," proclaimed John Foster Dulles before a Polish-American rally in Buffalo. On taking office his first speech was a radio pledge to Eastern Europe: "You can count on us." President Eisenhower, Senator Taft, Cardinal Spellman, labor leaders George Meany and Walter Reuther, were only a few of those who spoke for the cause on radio and TV.[3]

Then in the summer of 1956 all that the Cold War seemed to be leading up to exploded in the lands that Stalin had so long ground under his heel. With breathtaking bravery the people of Poland rose against their Russian overlords and won concessions. Then the Hungarians took to the streets against the Stalinists. Day followed day while the freedom fighters threw themselves in reckless heroism against the Russian tanks in Budapest. But the United States government remained inert. Americans went around asking: "Aren't we going to do something? Are we going to let these people die?" They asked about the Seventh Army, poised and ready in West Germany through many a Cold War crisis and massed, as they thought, for just this moment. And NATO—was it not primed to march against Communism? What was all this Cold War rhetoric about? Americans really *thought* the Poles and Hungarians and Czechs were captive nations. All those years it had been dinned into them through newspaper stories, radio and TV newscasts, speeches by their leaders, through the society-page benevolence balls for "Captive Poland," through the very postage stamps on their letters that flaunted the flags of the "captive nations." But after all, the United States did nothing for them.

Such were some of the components of the United States public response to the tremendous international events that broke in on the nation in 1956 precisely at the moment General Eisenhower stood before the people as a candidate for reelection on a platform of "peace and prosperity."

What the slogan-makers meant by peace had been there for all to see and feel: the vast relief still felt in the nation at the end of a bitter Asian war that had guttered on for three harrowing, frustrating years. But Americans were learning to live with another, more ambivalent kind of peace in the 1950s. The expectations voiced by people in polls through the late 1940s and early 1950s that a third World War was inevitable had somehow not been fulfilled. Amidst all the fear and unspoken forebodings, against all common expectations, the nation eked out from year to year, this strange condition that was neither war nor peace.

Was it possible that when East as well as West possessed the bomb the culminating blowup might by some strange and unknowable series of changes simply not take place? With Russian passing nonviolently to new leadership, with the West's greatest hero in reassuring charge of its security, the eerie state of neither war nor peace seemed almost to stabilize. The two sides kept piling on more terrifying technologies, waging subversion and sabotage against each other in Guatemala, Iran, Indochina. Among their respective citizenries, each kept ideological combat-readiness at a pitch hitherto attempted only in times of armed conflict.

And yet, for the private individual if not the state, for the common citizen if not the seer brooding on man's fate, this was peace, and peace of a kind where more than ever it seemed to make sense for a man to look out for his own private well-being.

All kinds of things conspired to turn Americans to privatism in the 1950s. The mobilized peace of the Cold War poured billions through defense plant and military base payrolls, and the mood was to take and use it while it lasted. The demobilized peace after Korea removed controls, brought reductions in personal and corporate income taxes. By 1956 a record splurge in consumer spending and endlessly flowing prosperity made even a lot of Democrats insist on General Eisenhower's reelection.

In the mass media, whether it was Arthur Godfrey selling Buicks on the tube, or the editors of *Life* saluting the American Way in their 200 ad-packed pages, little but complacency was to be heard. The big postwar boom seemed just then to be running on into an indefinite future. "Nothing less than the elimination of poverty as a fact of life was in sight," said *Time* at the end of 1956. "The breadth of the land, the untapped riches of its resources, the growth of its population, the optimism of its people, all suggested that American capitalism was approaching this age-old goal."[4]

At the heart of the business boom, said the *Federal Reserve Bulletin*, was private spending, and at the heart of the spending, added *Fortune*, was the rise of "the great mass" of Americans into a new, moneyed middle-income group disposing of fantastic quantities of "discretionary" funds that they spent for goods as fast as the American economy could provide them. Before the crash of 1929, though the nation boomed, 80% of all American families dwelt near the bottom of the economic ladder, doomed to incomes below $4000 in 1950 dollars and permitted notwithstanding their numbers no more than a 46% hunk of the nation's economic pie. Now all that had changed.[5]

By 1953—and largely as the result of gains registered in the years after the Cold War began—millions upon millions of working-class Americans had climbed higher on the economic ladder and joined members of the old middle class in the middle-income brackets. In consequence no fewer than 18,000,000 families—more than a third of all Americans—could now be counted in the group of citizens receiving between $4000 and $7500 a year in 1950 dollars. To this hugely expanded middle-income group now went something like 42% of all the money earned by Americans. When to this "great mass" were added the next higher income group—those receiving between $7500 and $10,000 per year—who had in the same period increased from two to three million families, the big bulge at the middle of American society grew to overpowering proportions. In all, well over half of all American familes (58%) now had a real income measured in constant dollars of from $4000 to $10,000 —as compared to a mere 31% of the nation in 1931. This was the development, of course, that caused many to say that America was becoming one vast middle class.[6]

The signs of middle-bracket spending were to be seen everywhere. They could hardly be missed at the beaches where throngs in bathing trunks and bikinis disgorged from ranks of pastel station-wagons bearing sun lotion, cameras, parasols, portable radios, portable iceboxes and food enough for an army platoon. They were formidably evident in the drive-ins, in the Howard Johnson and Hot Shoppe restaurants along the highways, where the multitudes spilled out for their casual refreshment stops. But most of all this new superprosperity was visible in the suburbs.

When the boom in housebuilding began to roll in the Cold War years, its takeoff helped lift America past the first postwar recession in 1949. So powerful were the forces pushing people to build and own homes that they swept upwards of one-fifth of the nation out of the cities and into the suburbs. The homebuilding drive wrought perhaps the most visible of all postwar changes on the face of the nation, and enabled some 60 million urban Americans to live in surroundings of grass, trees and fresh air. But the headlong rush to the suburbs had other, unforeseen consequences. It tore gaps in the fabric of local communities everywhere. And by developing something of the same obsessive preoccupation with the values of security exhibited in America's national and international life in these same Cold War years, it ended by seriously straining and weakening the larger unity of American society.[7]

By the late 1940s irresistible forces converged from every quarter to whip up the lateral explosion of Americans out of the cities and into the suburbs. Some of the most powerful forces were demographic. Was there a biological response to the threat posed by the A-bomb that reversed the plunging birthrate against all forecasts and filled postwar America with babies? As 12 million servicemen returned from the war the birthrate— which had shrunk as low as 77 per thousand females in the Depression year of 1935—shot up to 113 in 1946. What newspapers called the "population explosion" produced a crop of 3.8 million babies in 1947, and rolled on to a peak in 1957 of 122 live births per thousand females in childbearing years. At the same time the proportion of Americans over 25, those in the age group likeliest to form families and need new dwellings, increased.[8]

As if the population spurt was not enough, a vast backlog of unfilled needs for housing had built up in the Depression and war years: in 1945 the National Housing Administration had calculated that the country needed 12.6 million new units after the war; as late as 1945 there were still 2.5 million couples quartered with their relatives. On top of all this Americans had been accumulating personal savings at an annual rate of more than 20% of their income from 1942 to 1945. By V-J Day war prosperity and higher incomes had created a large body of consumers able and thirsting to fulfill the old American ambition to own a private home.[9]

The impulse of the American to live with some room around him was as old as Daniel Boone. The idea that he should own his own place was enshrined in the Constitution, the Homestead Act and the "Our Town" iconography of *Saturday Evening Post* covers with their white Anglo-Saxons in white colonial cottages behind white picket fences. Immigrants streaming in from countries where land ownership was denied to all but a select few were imbued with the desire to take title to land and a home of their own. As never before, people after the war seemed to want a place where they could have children and bring up a family. Overwhelmingly they were young, and so optimistic about their prospects of promotions and increased incomes as to be willing to accept long-term financial obligations to do so. At the same time they did not mind saying that they wanted to enjoy life as much as possible. [10]

Over and above all such forces, more important even than the Niagara of babies and the floodtide of savings, the big shove that sent the suburban housing boom crashing through the American landscape came through the home-loan insurance and guarantee program of the Federal Housing Administration and, through the GI Bill of Rights, the Veterans Administration. Before the Federal Housing Act of 1934 and other New Deal changes, only people who could put down something like half the purchase price in cash could buy new homes. Even with such a hefty down-payment the buyer had to make up the rest of the purchase price by committing himself to not one but two and even three high-interest mortgages and accepting the necessity of paying them off in no more than six or eight years. When householders could not keep up payments in the Depression, they lost their homes by foreclosure—at the rate of 250,000 a year.

The FHA and VA changed all that by offering to back mortgages that covered substantially the whole purchase price of inexpensive homes and provided for amortized repayment over twenty and even thirty-year periods at such low interest rates as four and five per cent. This unconditional forward commitment on the part of the federal agencies made all the rest possible. First, it emboldened those less than fearless enterprisers, the bankers, to provide large-scale credit to builders. This in turn enabled builders to mass-produce enough homes in one place to begin using modern industrial technology instead of horse-and-buggy methods.[11]

Up to that point the average contractor built two or three houses a year; sixty percent of them built only one in 1939. In 1946 the quaint old way of putting up homes was laughed out of court by Eric Hodgins's expertly grim bestseller *Mr. Blandings Builds His Dreamhouse.* Hodgins's book, which was promptly turned into a popular movie, pictured in gruesome detail the financial and psychic tortures he went through in getting his house built by the usual army of contractors, carpenters and assorted pipefitting clumsies. It was no accident that Hodgins was also an editor of *Fortune.* The Luce magazines, beating the drum for the American Way of Life, were then proclaiming the glorious inevitability of change in the direction of mass-marketing all consumer products—including shelter and including social and political opinions too. On the home front, the way to mass-marketing was to buy up a large and inexpensive tract of land—almost invariably outside city limits—and, "using industrial methods," as the new Luce magazine *House and Home* explained, build 300 to 500 houses at a time.[12]

The most spectacular builders of the new sort of dreamhouse were Abraham Levitt of Long Island and his two sons. At the end of the Second World War they bought 1,800 acres of potato fields some thirty-five miles east of New York City and named the tract Levittown. Backed by guarantees from FHA and the VA, they ran in bulldozers and trenching machines that took only 27 minutes to strip and ditch each 60 by 100 foot lot. In a few minutes more crews poured the concrete slab. Meanwhile at a single big assembly center other Levitt crews knocked the precut walls together (Levitt carpenters hammered but did not saw). As fast as the little houses were set on their slabs, some 50 subcontractors swarmed in to fit windows, string wires and connect bathtubs. Soon the Levitts were putting up 400 1-1/2-story, 4-1/2-room houses a week, as alike as Fords.

"A dream house is a house the buyer and his family will want to live in for a long time," said the Levitt ads. The first to throng into Levittown with their cribs and diaper pails were the veterans—from the top of a waiting list of 10,000. Having faced reentry into civilian life squashed in with their in-laws or in tiny apartments where landlords frowned on children, they considered their two-bedroom Cape Cods and their muddy, treeless lawns as seventh heaven. When the town of Hempstead held up approval of Levitt's plans, 800 GIs demonstrated for the cellarless variance. At first Levitt rented the houses (for $65 a month), but soon began selling them at $7900—$1500 less than competitors' prices. While the rest of the economy slumped in 1949, Levittown sold 17,447 houses and welcomed 60,000 settlers. Abraham Levitt was hailed as the Henry Ford of mass housing. As new Levittowns rose around Trenton and Philadelphia, the pattern of mass-produced suburban expansion was set.[13]

The pattern, shaped ultimately by the preference of Americans for the free-standing house, drastically favored new houses over old and single-family dwellings over city apartments. Under FHA legislation, loans for repairing old houses were difficult to get and loans to contractors for apartment buildings carried higher rates. But for the cookie-cutter houses being stamped out in thousands around the fringes of the cities, key provisions of the law prescribed easy terms and maximum credit. As if the law itself did not give the single-family detached house all the breaks, guidelines not in the legislation but established by the FHA bureaucracy and the real estate industry further broadened and accelerated the thrust toward suburban proliferation. The agency was run as if it were a private business. To minimize its investment risks, the FHA's staff rated all neighborhoods according to prior experience of repayments. Setting up four categories in order of preference, they assigned each of the categories a color. On secret office maps FHA officials marked out the entire United States, allotting to every neighborhood—every block—its rated color. Lowest was red, and any community that contained such "adverse influences" as smoke, odor or "inharmonious racial or national groups," as the FHA *Underwriters' Manual* bluntly phrased it, was inked out in red. If an area included older properties and slums, its rating sank to the point where it became virtually ineligible for federal funds. Thus, fostering blight by avoiding blight in the cities, the FHA channeled an ever larger share of the government's money toward the new and homogeneous suburban neighborhoods at a safe distance from the problems of the city.

For the private homeowner the best chance of gaining an FHA-approved loan was to select a house in a white, middle-class neighborhood. Accordingly, Levittown, Long Island, became upon its completion the largest community in the United States without a single black resident. To communities with "enforced zoning, subdivision regulations and suitable restrictive covenants," the FHA accorded its highest ratings. Covenants to keep out "inharmonious racial groups" received official endorsement until 1949, when the Supreme Court struck them down as contrary to the equal-rights provisions of the Fourteenth Amendment. Even then, such was the spirit in which national housing law and credit were administered, that fewer than 2 percent of government-insured houses constructed between 1946 and 1959 went to blacks.[14]

Because Congress so consistently supported the public's desire for private, one-family homes, the subsidizing of the suburbs did not stop with the funneling of cheap government credit in their direction. Discriminatory tax policies added substantially to the attractiveness of home ownership to middle and upper-income groups. Under the system of computing personal income taxes, homeowners obtained a tax-free return, in the form of a deduction allowance for interest paid, on the sum they had invested in their dwelling. At the same time they were allowed, as renters were not, to deduct important items of their housing cost. The result was that in the 1950s the typical homeowner got a direct federal subsidy in the form of tax savings that offset about fifteen percent of his annual housing costs. By the late 1950s Washington's tax-form subsidy to private householders, in the shape of deductions permitted for property tax and home mortgage interest payments, was estimated at from $2 to $2.6 billion a year. In the Cold War years this suburban giveaway may well have topped $30 billion—a sum ten times larger than what the government spent in the same period to house the urban poor.[15]

With such inducements Americans plunged for home ownership as never before. Between 1947 and 1970 their mortgage debt rose from $34.8 billion to $337.5 billion, and made the residential mortgage industry the fastest-growing sector of American business. Of the 15 million private homes built between 1945 and 1965 nearly half were financed by the FHA and VA. The long decline in home ownership that set in when Americans began congregating in vast cities had been reversed, and in the teeth of continuing urbanization the proportion of Americans who owned their homes advanced by 1970 to a record of 63%.[16]

One more overwhelming force powered the mass exodus to the suburbs: the private passenger car. Having emptied rural America in the first part of the century, the automobile helped redistribute the country's urban population in the second. Without the family car the private, free-standing house could never have prevailed. The millions of mass-produced homes in the metropolitan outer rings rose on empty land beyond the trolley terminals and railroad stations. The automobile made them accessible.

In the most pervasive fashion the two-tone tailfinned car was the symbol of what was taking place in the 1950s. Necessity, convenience, luxury—the automobile was many things. But for Americans it spelled privacy and freedom—freedom to be alone, to travel, to move, to explore —and in a society dedicated to the gratification of private desires the automobile, after the private house, was the possession prized above all others. By the middle 1950s three out of five families owned cars, one in five owned two cars and about two-and-one-half percent owned three cars. Allowing for all the urban household of the aged and infirm, the young unmarried in the cities and the city apartment dwellers and others who had no special reason to need or want a car, it was likely that just about every family in America that wanted an automibile had one.[17]

During the 1950s, when the country bought a record 58 million new cars, the private automobile replaced the passenger train as the principal means of conveying people between cities. Between 1946 and 1954 automobile registrations doubled; in the same years the number of mass-transit riders fell by fifty-five percent. Life in the suburbs was in good part life on wheels—driving to work, to school, to shop. Shopping centers sprang up—every one of which had to have six square feet of parking space for one square foot of selling area, and within less than two decades metropolitan America had 20,000 of them. One in every six Americans gained his livelihood out of the automobile business in these years. A fifth of all steel, two-thirds of all rubber produced, went into the manufacture of cars, and cars consumed half the nation's oil output.[18]

Invented in the nineteenth century, the automobile evolved by the 1930's into essentially the vehicle it remained thereafter. Throughout these decades, years of unparalleled production and profits, American automobile manufacturing remained, in the words of economist Lawrence White, "a technologically stagnant industry." This was a consequence more than anything else of the overpowering domination attained in the industry by General Motors. By the 1950s only two or three rivals remained in the American automobile business and these, large as they were, had to be described as "satellites" because they existed only by sufferance of a supercorporation whose sales in 1966 stood at $20.2 billion, surpassing the income of half the governments in the world.[19]

Throughout these years, while General Motors kept a carefully measured half of the motor market, a tight little oligopoly, convinced that they and they alone knew what kind of cars the American public wanted, held the steering wheel of the nation's biggest business. Not surprisingly the cars they produced seemed also to be those most profitable for them to produce. By the Eisenhower years utility and comfort in cars had given way to styling and luxury. Safety, as exemplified in shatter-proof windshields, resisted by the manufacturers for years, was pushed aside as a drag on profits. The emphasis was on sales, and styling, the oligopolists said, was what sold cars.

The master lines of policy were laid down by General Motors Chairman Alfred N. Sloan, an engineer whose talents were greatest in management and sales. By changing models every year and playing on the desire of motorists for "bigger and better cars," General Motors and its imitators (which even included, before his death in 1947, Henry Ford) made the customers somehow dissatisfied with the cars they had and put them in mind to "trade up" for costlier new ones. Although the main elements of cars remained unaltered after the introduction of Ford's V-8 engine in the 1930s, the annual face-liftings required by the Sloan system had by the late 1950s cost an average $4,843,000 per year, or $800 for each new car.[20]

The stylists of Detroit influenced far more than the sales of cars. The low silhouette that drew out the afterlines of cars in tailfins in the 1950s was pronounced by William M. Schmidt, executive stylist for Chrysler "the universal key to contemporary design." It was picked up in the long, low lines of the ubiquitous ranchhouse, in the sharply rectilinear edges of the electrical appliances from refrigerators to waffle irons that filled American kitchens in record numbers in the same years. Some even said that Detroit's decision to lower first the freeboard and then the headroom of automobiles after the Second World War induced Americans to accept lower ceilings in all their living spaces and thus permitted builders to crowd apartment and office floor-levels closer than ever before.[21]

Between 1949 and 1955 cars grew half a foot wider and two feet longer. In the same years the horsepower of the three basic makes of cars rose from 90–100 to 120–160, and the fancier Cadillacs had 250 horsepower by 1955, 375 by 1957. "This year the hot one's even hotter," bugled the Chevrolet advertisements of 1956. Other ads urged "billing yourself as a Human Cannonball," and driving a 400-plus horsepower model "like *you hate it*—it's cheaper than psychiatry." Buyers could choose cars named Stingray, Tiger, Cutlass, Cobra, Cougar, Marauder, Fury, Charger, Barracuda.[22]

Cars multiplied not only in number, size, speed, but also in maiming power; by 1959 Daniel P. Moynihan calculated that one out of three cars built in Detroit wound up with blood on it. To ease the crush, the nation spent $2 billion on new roads in 1949, $3 billion in 1953, $4 billion in 1955. It was clear that something would have to be done—and for the one and only time in his eight years in office General Eisenhower marched out in front of his country and seized the lead. The President proposed a vast, ten-year, $27 billion program of highway-building. Existing highways were unsafe, he said, full of traffic snarls and a costly impost on the conduct of business. Better roads were also needed for the conduct of the Cold War. Modern highways would be highly useful for swift military movements across the country, and "in case of atomic attack on our cities the road net must permit quick evacuation of target areas." He therefore gave to his "grand plan" the name of "Interstate Highway and Defense System."[23]

The politicians leaped to salute what turned out to be the largest public works project ever undertaken by man—an enterprise to dwarf the pyramids of Egypt and the Great Wall of China. The Eisenhower years, cried Senator Francis Case, Republican of South Dakota, would go down in history as the years of "Ike, the Builder." Said the practical-minded

Representative Charles Buckley, Democrat of New York: "If we have good thruways and good highways, people will buy more cars." The plan was ecstastically hailed by the highway lobby, a phenomenally broad pressure group that numbered oil, rubber, automobile, asphalt and construction industries; car dealers and renters; trucking and bus concerns; banks and advertising agencies that depended on companies involved; the American Automobile Association; state and local officials who wanted the federal government to pay for new highways in their areas; and labor unions. "Highways and motor vehicles," declaimed the president of the American Association of State Highway Officials, "are truly the keystone of the American way of life."[24]

In the spirit of the times, some members of the highway lobby underlined the advantages of superhighways in enabling people to move away from areas under nuclear attack. Dr. Howard Wilcox of General Motors foresaw a market for air-conditioned cars equipped with filters that could remove decontaminants from the air along the expressways. "These automobiles," explained Wilcox, "might become mobile bomb shelters able to give adequate protection to one's family while they move to a safer location in the event of enemy attack." Dr. Wilcox also touted horsepower for these defense speedways: "We need an auto capable of providing safe, sustained speeds of 150 to 200 miles per hour for the average driver" during "the short-haul trip of 100 to 200 miles."[25]

Under such urgent considerations the President's old friend General Clay, named head of the planning committee, rushed out a report in January, 1955. The President's scheme, as Senator Case's enthusiasm suggested, had been started to help rural districts, and proposed making the grants to the states on a fifty-fifty basis. The Clay panel decided instead that the federal government must take "principal responsibility" and furnish ninety percent of the funds. After a long wrangle about the method of financing, Congress in 1956 voted a special federal gasoline tax and directed that all proceeds be paid into a Federal Highway Fund out of which the Bureau of Public Roads would then dispense funds to the states for freeway construction.

Clay's committee sold the Interstate system to Congress as the carrier of long-haul traffic, bypassing downtown areas with only a limited number of feeder highways to link the high-speed cross-country network with the central cities. Yet of the $27 billion spent in the next decade, $15 billion went for urban areas. The Interstate Highway and Defense system was transformed from a high-speed, long-distance network into a blunt instrument for chopping huge gashes through central cities and their environs for concrete spillways carrying the floods of local commuter traffic in and out of the burgeoning suburbs. This traffic, far more than the long-haul traffic, generated the gas-tax revenue that enabled the engineers to build highways. There was no provision for, and little thought of, social planning. Since Washington had agreed to the 90–10 split in cost apportionment, the cities could not resist the temptation to get as many miles as they could out of their state highway departments. The states were happy to join in because inner-city expressways built up the gas-tax receipts that enabled them to build the rural portions of the system.

The result, unintended of course, was that the interstate routes soon cut massive concrete strips into the downtown areas of every big American city. Far from solving the cities' traffic problems, the new roads only created new ones. Besides engulfing downtown areas with commuter automobiles, they devoured living quarters, jammed those displaced into other habitations, and sealed off carless ghetto dwellers in a new and frustrating kind of urban isolation. Thousands were uprooted, whole neighborhoods were blighted. By 1959 General Eisenhower himself questioned the cost of these urban welts, which ran up to $40 million a mile, and warned the road-builders that running the interstate system into the cities contravened the law. "The national interest," he said, extended only to long-distance travel.[26]

But the general had gone to a lot of trouble to avoid overcentralization in framing the law, and in the confusion of contending authorities and pressure groups the single-minded highway engineers in the state capitals paid no heed to Eisenhower's guidelines. Building went on as scheduled. In this the bulldozing roadbuilders simply represented the dominant mood of the society. In the United States of the 1950s privatist values held sway. The desire of the car owner to take his car wherever he went no matter what the social cost drove the Interstate Highway System, with all the force and lethal effect of a dagger, into the heart of the American city.

THE MAINSPRING of the suburban rush was the headlong drive of millions of Americans to fulfill their individual desires for a bit of private living in the country. Out of the distant past Americans had inherited the dream, the idea of dwelling in a park or garden, an idea doubtless derived from England and some sort of folkish, peasant, biblically-colored memory, expressing an urban wish for contact with nature—an idea centering in a domesticated landscape of social peace.[27] The large-scale builders who took advantage of the federal subsidies, bought up the open land around the cities, and multiplied their ticky-tacky houses into every last corner of the metropolitan areas, left precious little room in their preassembled, tightly-packed, hastily-paved landscapes for social peace. Yet suburbia, the real-estate promotion, was also paradise gained.

Late in 1947 *Better Homes and Gardens* magazine reported a new "phenomenon—the way ranch houses have captured the fancy of American families." The new style of house had spread almost overnight across the country, and the builders sold them as fast as they put them up from Orange County, California, to Nassau County, New York. Within months the ranchhouse emerged as the single most popular design, and the suburban developers swiftly made it the standardized American dreamhouse.

In 1950, when 1,908,000 new, single-family houses were started, more than in any other year in the nation's history, eighty-six percent of them were "ranch-type" houses.[28]

In its original form, with its long, low outlines and its gently-sloping, peaked roof, the ranchhouse was a structure indigenous to the American West. Its windows opened on wide vistas, its doors on acres of buffalo grass. The ranchhouse that the mass-builders produced (scarcely one in ten of all postwar houses were architect-designed), was a one-story dwelling with a slightly-peaked roof, and a rambling appearance of ground-hugging horizontality. "The California ranchhouse of the Eastern seaboard," sniffed *Harper's* magazine, "has no architectural style but it has a romantic name, and an aroma of barbecued spareribs, and that evidently is the secret of its success."[29]

"Low and outside," was one critic's call, and the mass-produced "ranch" of the tract-developers came close enough to home plate to give America a whiff of its dream. It had a picture window, which meant that it let in lots more light than the porch-covered bungalows that were popular in the 1920s. Having everything on one level made for ease for the elderly and informal living for the young, and the house opened effortlessly to the breezes and the outdoors. In place of the porch there was a patio, which became the very meeting-place of the new indoor-outdoor cult of privatized family comfort. The children played in the patio where mothers could keep simultaneous watch on them and the television set, and fathers cooked the hamburgers on the patio grill in the long summer evenings.[30]

Without basement, corridors or formalized dining rooms and entry halls, the ranchhouse was cheap to build, and just about the smallest dwelling that could hold the postwar family. Later, when the cult of comfort sprawled unbuttoned over the land, ranchhouses sometimes bent round kidney-shaped swimming pools and, especially in the South and West where land was less dear, rambled on to lengths of up to 200 feet. But the vast majority of single-family houses built in the suburbs after the war were small, one-story structures called ranchers, ranchburgers or simply ranch-type houses, and they never went out of style even after the drive for the dreamhouse flagged in the closing Cold War years. Of the 27.5 million single-family, free-standing houses constructed between 1945 and 1970, possibly something like 22 million were one-story, ranch-type dwellings.[31]

The oldest dilemma that has afflicted American society from its founding in the New World has been the ceaseless conflict between its often unbridled individualism and its fitful and inadequate sense of community. By an exquisite irony of history, the transformation of America into a twentieth century mass society presented the nation with this dilemma anew. In a vast, urbanized culture, the individual could not but count for less. Yet in this environment of accelerating anonymity for the individual and aggrandizing power for the giant corporation, an economic doctrine took hold which impelled Americans to conduct their lives as if they were sovereign consumer-units in a market-society given overwhelmingly to the consumption of material goods, and to make their daily economic and social choices in privatistic, self-regarding terms oblivious to larger, i.e., community considerations.

After the exertions of the Second World War roused them to a peak of community effort, Americans deeply desired to return to their own individual pursuits. At the same time the explosion of the atomic bomb in 1945 and of the Russian A-bomb in 1949, bore out the conscious and unconscious apprehensions that Americans had lost their "free security," as the historian Vann Woodward phrased it, and inflamed the desire to look to private concerns in new and unsettling ways. After the A-bomb destroyed Hiroshima and Nagasaki, a Tennessee Valley Authority official demanded "decentralization of this country's concentrated urban centers," and a Philadelphia planning expert urged Americans to spread out into "rural cities—otherwise destruction is our domicile."[32]

It would be hard to say what impelled Americans to withdraw into such privatism as was manifested in their flight to the suburbs in the postwar years. Latent fear, fear of a more terrible Depression and of a more dreadful Pearl Harbor, underlay and obscurely reinforced the more visible drives that brought about the biggest shift of population in the country's history. At the height of what newspapers called the "war scare" of March, 1948, one John Barogni, an ex-infantryman who had served in the European campaign, announced to friends as he left his Chicago office: "This thing has decided one thing for me. I was thinking about getting a house out in the suburbs. Now I know I'm going to get it. At least the wife and kids will be safe."

People snapped up a new government pamphlet "Survival Under Atomic Attack," joined the Sky Watchers (4,000,000 volunteers) keeping twenty-four-hour vigil on suburban hilltops and city towers), ducked into basements during the first nationwide air-raid drills, and marked the numbers 640 and 1240 on their radio dials. The latter were the numbers householders were to turn to when the Russians attacked and "Conelrad" went into effect. Conelrad—Control of Electromagnetic Radiation—was the scheme announced by Washington in 1952 for keeping some channels open for emergency communication while minimizing the chance for Russian bombers to use broadcast beams to home on their targets. Before the scare ended, large signs were placed along roads leading from large cities to the suburbs:

"NOTICE.
IN CASE OF ENEMY ATTACK,
THIS HIGHWAY WILL BE CLOSED."[33]

"Escape to Scarborough Manor," suggested a real estate ad of the day. "Escape from cities too big, too polluted, too crowded." What many sought as they rushed to their suburban ranchhouses was privacy, and a good many did not even want to discuss politics. They wanted to get off by themselves, to do as they pleased in the privacy of their family, and to find within it the nuclear bond that was possibly to be had, say, when husband and wife shared the joys of cooking.

Not all suburbs were alike, but they were a lot more alike than different. The central fact was that this huge middle mass of 40 million people, settling for the most part in the vast ring of housing developments mushrooming around the cities, were spending record sums of money on themselves. To the passing eye they were look-alikes living in row on row of ranch-type houses, facing the same winding streets, the same neat lawns, the same front walks cluttered with tricycles and bicycles. What was less obvious was that these people turned inward rather than outward, and were alike chiefly in their voracious privatism.

In the sense of the mutuality of rooted, knitted societies, they were anything but community-minded. Three preoccupations filled their lives. First was their jobs, usually as remote as Hudson Bay from their home communities. Second was their cars. On these they lavished loving care, fitting them out with lights, liquor, tape-players, medicine chests and all the tiny gewgaws of private indulgence that a man liked to have by where he spent, privately of course, a sizable portion of his daily life. Third was their homes, managed by the wives, overrun by the children, and main- tained by the husbands. The feathering of these usually unfinished nests was nothing less than obsessive. A whole new technology of easy-to-apply, quick-to-dry, water-based paints sprang into existence to permit young mothers to spatter their walls and kitchen cupboards while the children were off at kindergarten. The young men spent their nights nailing up plasterboard to turn the "expansion attic" into cubicles for the growing offspring.

Television was a major force in their lives. Nearly all who owned sets in 1951 had them in their living rooms, and they almost always had them on. Eleanor Maccoby, making a careful study of television's impact in homes near Cambridge, Massachusetts, reported "no tendency to cut down when the novelty ceases. Favorite programs become a firmly established routine." Most of the programs consisted still of variety skits and other entertainment largely carried over from radio. But television was no such casual presence as radio. Demanding quiet and a semi-darkened room, the set dominated family life while it was on. One result was that the family spent more time together, though it also cut into the family's other joint activities. Something like one-sixth of the families had taken to eating before their TV sets, and almost as many more changed their supper hour for TV. Children watched three or four hours a day. But mothers were not troubled about adverse effect on their children's homework output. On the whole they felt that the TV set was a solver rather than a creator of tensions in the children. "It's much easier," Mrs. Maccoby was told. "It's just like putting them to sleep."[34]

So it seemed to many, and the commercialists were content that it seem so. From the time that the bluish glow of the television tube first lit up America's living rooms, the entertainments that held young and old in thrall featured lots of gunplay and other violence. Such programs commanded the biggest audiences, therefore the networks and their advertisers vied to supply them. Many surveys suggested that such excitements had harmful effects on the young but as with the link of cigarettes to lung cancer, there were contrary findings that the industry could always cite. Not until two decades later was scientific evidence finally amassed in a five-volume government report, and Surgeon General Jesse L. Steinfeld announced "a definite causal relationship between TV violence and antisocial behavior in children." What *The New York Times* called "the immunizing (of) children to violence" through the powerful imprint of this new medium was yet another legacy of the Cold War years.[35]

The consequences of this process took some time to unfold, but meanwhile what of their parents? What sort of citizens was this pastoralization of the bourgeoisie producing? Certainly not when the veterans of the Civil War homesteaded the West, and not even when Europe colonized South Boston, South Philadelphia, South Chicago and the Bronx at the turn of the century, had America witnessed a more sudden and sweeping relocation and reformation of an entire sector of its society. A whole group of interpreters, watching these young and middlish-young flock in such vast numbers to live such homogenized lives in such stupefyingly similar real-estate developments, rushed to identify new uniformities wrought by changes that must carry America beyond either the frontier or the melting pot.

Drawing for the most part on the new-fangled methods of the social sciences, these were the new categorizers. William H. Whyte, David Riesman, Vance Packard, A. C. Spectorsky, Daniel Bell, among others, saw in these suburbanites modifications in middle-class behavior patterns toward norms of conformity. To the types they identified they gave vivid, even haunting, names—the Organization Man bent on getting ahead by getting along, the Status Seeker craving outer evidences to shore up his inner identity, the Other-Directed Man looking to neighbors on his suburban block for clues to what he should want. Yet the suburbanites, though seemingly alike in age, size and plumage, flocking and alighting in flocks almost like swallows, eluded such typologies. About the only durable generality, applicable to them along with most of their generation everywhere in America, was that they seemed to carry a smaller baggage of traditionally received beliefs than either their parents or grandparents.

Engineers, middle-management men, young lawyers, salesmen, insurance agents, teachers, civil servants—innumerable white-collar types with an attaché case in their hand, a commuter's ticket in their hatband, and a promising place in some organizational hierarchy lived in these new neighborhoods. And much was made of their "upwardly mobile" wives who dashed about in Buick station-wagons from school and supermarket to golf and bridge at the country club. Leaving aside the corporate job transfers, which required families to pick up on short notice and move from Los Angeles or Philadelphia to a new residence near another company branch in Pittsburgh or Syracuse, something like a half-million families altogether made the step up from a smaller to a bigger house, usually in one of the long-established middle-class suburbs that had flourished before the Second or even First World War.[36]

But tract houses costing from $12,000 to $16,000 fell well within the purchasing range of large numbers of skilled and semiskilled workers in heavy industry. By the 1950s, moreover, something like a fifth of the new factory jobs being created were in industries started or moved outside the cities. So many of these blue-collar breadwinners moved to these outlying communities that *Fortune*, revising an earlier judgment about the uniformity of suburbanites, estimated that as many as a third of the middle-income families living in the new communities around America's cities were members of the working class. Oblivious to middle-class careerism, these family heads had no great expectations of getting ahead in their jobs as the men in the gray-flannel suits were said to. They measured their success instead by what they were able to buy—the new car standing in front of their house, the new single-unit washer-dryer, butterfly chairs in the rumpus room, the new TV. Under "every known technique of suasion and propaganda for turning luxuries into necessities," wrote Harvey Swados, the workers struggled to emulate a middle-class style of life by developing similar consumption habits. Among the rubber workers of Akron in 1957 he found twice as many taking second jobs as six years before, and a big rise in the number of working wives. "Even if he puts in fifty, sixty or seventy hours a week at one or two jobs," wrote Swados, "the skilled or semiskilled worker has to count on his wife's pay check, or his son's, his daughter's, his brother-in-law's, or on his mother's Social Security, or his father's veteran's pension," to hang on in "the great commodity scramble." The vast majority of such workers looked upon their new suburban homes as a paradise dearly gained, and sometimes outspent their white-collar neighbors furnishing out their power-mowed preserves.

The materialism of Americans, remarked on by visitors for two centuries, was far too widespread in such affluent times to be limited to a single class. By the mid-1950s two out of every three Americans owned and occupied their own home, and in consequence of a tripling of installment debt since 1948 some 75% of them were making monthly amortization payments on what they owed for their houses and for the "package" of appliances that American business had loaded them up with. "Where a man's treasure is, there will his heart be also," said the ancient scriptures. On this well-tested finding, the sheer inventory of American householders' possessions obtained with their "discretionary" dollars recorded like a cash-register slip the privatist craze of the free-spending 1950s.[37]

Ninety percent of these homeowners had bought refrigerators, 87% automatic washing machines, 76% had TV sets and 60% had telephones —the great proportion of them lately acquired. In 1956 Americans bought 3.7 million vacuum cleaners, 8.3 million electric irons, 1.9 million electric blankets, 5.4 million portable and clock radios, 3.6 million stoves, 3.9 million toasters, 590,000 garbage disposal units, and 975,000 home freezers. By that year they owned 8.2 million power mowers, 23 million electric shavers, 18.4 million electric coffee makers. In the same year Americans consumed 582 million pairs of shoes and slippers, 24 million mens' and boys' suits, 60 million mens' and boys' separate trousers, 1.75 billion pairs of stockings for men, women and children, 528 billion cigarettes, 6.6 billion cigars, 88 million bottles of ketchup, 648 million cans of peaches, and 1,102,000,000 tranquilizers. In that year Americans— 6.6% of the world's population—consumed more than half of everything made and sold on earth.[38]

This insatiable appetite for private consumption was hailed as the force building an endless prosperity for the America of the 1940s and 1950s. If this suburbia had critics, they mainly mocked the illusory rusticity of its jostling ranchhouses, or condemned the vulgarity of its monotonously-replicated "people cartons" and the garishness of the commercial strips that flourished along its highways. "Either America is a shopping center," wrote columnist Russell Baker of the suburban scene around him, "or the one shopping center in existence is moving around the country at the speed of light."[39]

In such circumstances a widening chasm opened between the public words of scowling determination and sacrifice of a country locked in Cold War and the private actions of a people at peace. When President Eisenhower prepared to go to the summit meeting with the Russians at Geneva in 1955, Secretary Dulles felt called upon to warn him to maintain "an austere countenance, when photographing together is inevitable," and to push hard in all his public statements for "satellite liberation." And when the President met the press in these years he often favored them with little speeches summoning America from its barbecue pits to the "long struggle" against "international Communism." Just how long this might be emerged in one such homily:

> We have just had some of our best educated men in America espouse Communism—or at least they have been supporters of Communism.
>
> I don't know why, but it does appeal to them. And as you go round the world, you find this kind of appeal, coupled with bribery, deceit, and corruption and profligate spending of money in some areas, on top of this [Communist] threat of force, of fear.
>
> You have not only a problem that is broad in scope but is great in depth. We must be strong in our beliefs, in our convictions in our hearts. We must be strong in our intellectual surety that this is the better system, we must prove it throughout the world, we must prove it to others. And finally, we must be strong militarily so that we may gain opportunity and time to do all this, these things . . . it might last forty years. . . .[40]

Among the business leaders whose opinion General Eisenhower so frequently sought, there was of course nothing but applause and approval for these solemnities. Yet there was a contradiction between the preachments of the Eisenhower leadership and the practices of corporate enterprise as they evolved in their free run through the 1950s. The basic virtues that Eisenhower and Dulles extolled out of their nineteenth century, small-town past, the old Progressive values of self-reliance, hard work and self-denying thrift got in the way of the galloping rush to cash in on the greatest consumer buying spree that had ever been seen. Put it this way:

the object of business is to make a profit, and the proprietor of the Abilene creamery or the family that owned the Muncie, Indiana, factory that was probably the typical form of American private enterprise up to 1939, were feeble and fitful pursuers of profit alongside the impersonally relentless profit-drive of the 500 or so supercorporations that dominated American economic life by the 1950s.

Mass production required mass markets, and rather than wait for mass demand the supercorporations went right out and created it. Designing goods to wear out in short order, persuading people that something new must replace the nearly new, inducing people to accept costly goods and then pay off the debt in installments over subsequent years, they forced the very prodigalities of waste in private budgeting that President Eisenhower denounced and deplored in public financing. In the face of insatiable drives for such "growth," the utterances of business leaders carried scant conviction. There was a loosening of the sense of a social responsibility, a falling away of the spirit of public community as instant gratification shouldered away not only forbearance and frugality but the citizenly habit of looking now and then to the common weal. The surge coursed through all of the instrumentalities of hired persuasion—for more elegant automobiles, more exotic goods, more erotic clothing, more opulent entertainment, appealing, as Kenneth Galbraith said, to "all of the modern range of sensuous, edifying and lethal desires."[41]

Ideology is the handmaiden of men's necessities, and ever more output of goods—or, as some said, the growth of productivity—became the indispensable and unquestionable remedy for all the discomforts, anxieties and privations associated with economic insecurity. More was better—this was the American way. "The democratic conception came first in politics, then in education and now in prosperity," proclaimed the president of the American Telephone and Telegraph Company, whose firm operated half of the world's telephones, all within the United States, by the 1950s. "Dig we must," said the signs on the Consolidated Edison trucks in Manhattan as if no further justification were needed to tear open the streets for expansion without limit. "From a dollar and cents point of view," said United States Steel Chairman Roger Blough, "it is quite obvious that over a period of years even those who find themselves at the short end of inequality have more to gain from faster growth than from any conceivable income redistribution."[42] Such was the gospel of growth, and hardly anybody stopped to ask: growth for what?

A first result of the thrusting, careering drive toward private enterprise in the 1950s was a neglect of all the aspects of American life that are carried on by community effort—notably the functions of government. The condition of social disrepair appeared all the more glaring by contrast with the private prosperity. The cult of consumption was fed, even artificially aroused, by the profit motive and the profit motive was regarded as its own justification because it generated production—the safeguard of full employment and prosperity unclouded by depression. The man set to watch over the state of the American economy, Chairman Raymond Saulnier of the President Eisenhower's Council of Economic Advisers, at one point stated that he considered his job was to seek "the maximizing of production."[43]

The outward signs of this grotesque disequilibrium were resolutely ignored by the nation through most of the Eisenhower years. Although the national income continued to rise, only a minute portion of the wealth was poured into the public services. Of the mere 20% of the Gross National Product diverted to public expenditures on the three levels of federal, state and local government, a much larger proportion went into defense and related expenses such as foreign aid than into the maintenance, expansion and qualitative improvements of essential public services. Without these services of course the private sector itself would have collapsed, and when the federal government began choking off funds for such purposes, state and local governments began almost involuntarily to expand their outlays to make up for Washington's niggardly ways in domestic spending. Yet the proportion of funds from all government sources for public services diminished in these years of phenomenal private prosperity—the ratio fell from 4.5% of national income in the late 1930s to 3% in the 1950s.[44]

By 1955 the schools of America were estimated to be short some 340,000 classrooms; there was a shortage of teachers estimated by the United States Office of Education at 150,000. At one point teachers with an average schooling of fifteen and one half years earned a salary of $3,725 whereas the average factory hand received $4,051; and it was a national joke that the janitor of the schoolhouse often got more money than the professional who taught in its classrooms. In 1955, Americans spent more on comic books than for textbooks for their schools .[45]

Over these years of extensive growth in the national income, the proportion spent for medical care fell behind by 10%. Despite the vast gains in income and a gradual aging of the population which intensified the nation's needs, the proportion of physicians in active practice declined and the shortage of hospitals grew acute. A ruthlessly effective doctor's lobby having defeated President Truman's comparatively modest health insurance proposals in 1949, the United States remained the only major country without a comprehensive national health plan. The Eisenhower administration's sole move on this front was to propose expenditure of $25 million for a reinsurance fund that might induce private health insurers to improve their coverage. As a way of dealing with a national problem that was already costing private citizens $25 billion a year, such a proposed government outlay could scarcely be—and was not—taken seriously. The absence of any comprehensive public health plan was particularly hard on people over sixty-five, whose numbers rose twice as fast as the population as a whole during the 1950s. Because of the revolution in family responsibilities that followed the twentieth century exodus from farms and small towns, no fewer than 8 million old people now lived alone (5 million of them without telephones), separated from and no longer cared for by their children.[46]

In every year in the Eisenhower decade more than a million new homes were built. Overwhelmingly, they were put up by private industry in the suburbs, which added some 14 million new inhabitants during this period. At the same time public housing, which got a start in the Depression to make jobs for construction workers and had been carried forward to help meet the emergency need for homes after the Second World War, was drastically cut back. From an outlay of some $425 million, expenditures sank to an average of $106 million between 1954 and 1959. Though the nation had an inventory of 10 million substandard units in these years, it built only 36,000 public housing units per year. The virtual suspension of the federal housing program was acutely felt in the cities, where blacks displaced by mechanization of Southern agriculture were arriving in record numbers. But when urban development bills were advanced by Congress, the President vetoed them on the ground that private enterprise should do the job. The decline of mass transit proceeded unchecked. While public funds (some of them provided by American foreign aid) were poured into the modernization of railroads in Europe and Japan, trains in the United States grew tardier, dirtier and more dangerous by the year.[47]

Such scandalous neglect of all of the public amenities—of schools, parks, streets, roads, garbage collection, slum clearance—when shops overflowed with gadgets and gimmicky consumer goods of ever-increasing ingenuity and luxuriance fairly drowned the private citizens—all this was the subject of intensive comment by visiting foreigners. "Sitting solemnly on [their] lawn chaises, overfed, oversatisfied, overbearing" (as the historian Eric Goldman wrote scathingly at the end of the 1950s), Americans in general seemed unaware of such contrasts. They were capable, while allowing law enforcement to be overworked and inadequate, of complaining about the growing problem of juvenile delinquency—and indeed juvenile crime tripled between 1948 and 1957.

As possibly such statistics hinted, the achievements of abundance were such as to carry within them the seeds of their own destruction.

Traffic jams created when so many private citizens drove their private vehicles into urban centers so poorly provided with public policing, public traffic regulations and adequate public thoroughfares made private ownership of cars pointless to the individual, ruinous to the community, and potentially murderous for all. Surveying the press of Manhattan's rush-hour traffic, Eric Sevareid wryly suggested "a plan for everybody on the West Side to shove cars into the Hudson River, and everybody on the East Side to shove them into the East River." *Time* magazine topped this with the idea that at the fast-approaching hour of complete jam-up, "the city lay boards across the tops of the sedans and start all over again." Visitors pointed out that the more goods consumed, the more wrappings and containers there were to be thrown away, the more essential was municipal garbage collection. Yet, they noted, municipal sanitary services were run with absurdly outmoded equipment. "If the appropriate sanitation services are not provided," said the German Herbert von Borch, "the counterpart of increasing opulence will be deepening filth."[48]

S O M E time in the middle of the Eisenhower years there occurred a souring of values. How long could Americans answer to the summons to sacrifice, work and self-restraint when they were daily turning ever more to private preoccupations and personal gratifications? How long could their leaders go on urging the morality of scarcity while practicing the profligacy of abundance? In the lower ranks of the corporations "new breeds" were observed "whose behavior can no longer be accounted for by the conventional rules of conduct." Such individuals found their authority not in any inner code of personal guidance but in what their group approved. They measured success in life by "how well a person sells himself on the market, how well he gets his personality across, how nice a 'package' he is." Arthur Miller's Willy Loman, portrayed on Broadway in *Death of a Salesman,* was such a figure who seemed to take his color from his social surroundings. All his life he strove to be popular and liked, forever dreaming that "personality always wins the day." His motto was: "Start big and you'll end big." His advice was to "get right down the field under the ball, and when you hit, hit low and hard." When someone asked people in Anaheim, California, in the heart of the California defense-industry belt, what they might do in a depression, one answered:

> No one is worried because there's a theory in town that if anything slips up the government will declare a moratorium on all debts. . . . Otherwise, this whole place might be a shambles overnight.

"We appear," wrote *David Riesman:*

> to be in a trap in which we may become weary of the goods we have
> learned to miss not having. We are a generation prepared for Paradise
> Lost, who do not know what to do with Paradise Found.

The discrepancy between what Americans said about the world and what
they did in it, identified by puzzled foreigners and disenchanted exiles
since Henry James' time as American "innocence," was beginning to
break down.[49]

The power of the old American ethic grew out of its roots in the
special American experience. In this far more was involved than the easy
confidence, exemplified in the American business creed, that for all problems there were practical solutions. Wilderness-born, yet child of Europe's
eighteenth century of enlightenment, America was the new land of
democracy. A free world in which a free man lives in a free society—this
was the American dream. Reinforced in this faith by the nation's achievements in law and social order in the nineteenth century, Americans took
for granted the existence of a rational universe that self-evidently ordained
democracy's advance from such beginnings throughout the entire world.

The second basic American assumption about this fundamentally
rational scheme for the universe was that it could be laid bare by the
methods of science and exploited by man through the technology of
industry. In the nineteenth century technology served man's needs in
mastering nature. But the further scientific investigations advanced, the
more they seemed to disclose that man himself was just another material
object determined by the regular operation of the universal scheme. By
the twentieth century, technologies based on these seeming regularities
were used to exploit human forces by the dominant elements in the
society. Man in the mass, man as a member of large organizations, could
be manipulated—and in the name of progress.

In America the faith of the Progressives prevailed longer than anywhere else. In Europe the doctrine of progress was dealt a blow by the
disruptions of the First World War and destroyed by the barbarities of
the Second. But the New World's optimism was such that it survived
America's failure to make the world safe for democracy in 1917. A sense
of guilt at having faltered and then pulled back reinforced the decision
of the 1940s to intervene a second time and do the job right, and led on
to the establishment on American soil of the United Nations and insistence that everybody else join it. Even after the demolition of Hitler, when
Europe collapsed and peace fled, the United States confidently assumed
that democratic progress awaited mankind and that America was privi-

leged to wage Cold War to ensure it.

In the Old World the decline of religion, the depersonalization of modern society, the limitations of science, the travail of the twentieth century, all had long since undermined the old certitudes, and the demonic powers of Hitlerism and fascism had completed their dethronement. With the breakdown of Europe in 1945 a powerful stream of revolt broke out. Had the Russians wanted a revolution just then, they might have had it: Communists were leaders of the Resistance, but with Moscow's overriding interest in consolidating its own position and taking all the reparations out of Germany it could get, the Communists only put a damper on political revolt in 1945. So the movement of 1945, unlike the upsurge of 1918 was not channeled into political revolution. For it was too broad to be political, and yet too diffuse to be called philosophical. Welling up from underground sources, converging and diverging, but flowing forward and carrying with it some of the most significant ethical, literary and cultural manifestations of the century, it was a kind of flooding, inchoate affirmation of life itself.

At the time many gave to this upwelling the name Existentialism. This was because the first strong voices heard rejected as discredited all notions of a universal order, and insisted that the one and only basis for the individual's life was his own existence. "Existence precedes essence," proclaimed Jean-Paul Sartre, like a man standing up to announce the new rules for a world beginning all over, "or, if you wish, you have to start with subjectivity." The central concern for contemporary man, he said, must be with the actually existing individual, caught up in a hopelessly absurd world, called upon to make something of himself as a free being, accepting responsibility for his own action. The challenge for any man alive was this: for the human situation there are no prescribed rules for existence.[50]

What Sartre and his contemporaries were saying reverberated with themes that had been sounding near the edges of Western consciousness for a long time. Kierkegaard, Nietzsche, Tolstoy—these were some of the nineteenth century voices whose existentialist overtones now resonated with urgent modernity. And though Sartre and his circle were unsparingly atheist, a major current of the movement, broad enough to comprehend such figures as Paul Tillich, Reinhold Niebuhr and Gabriel Marcel, was Christian. The stress on subjectivity caused many to warn that the new movement verged on the irrational. In primacy of influence the idea of life itself probably surpassed all others—in the struggle of life against form, in its fight against the machine. It demanded that each individual, thrust into the "here and now," without any help from God (said Sartre) or the world around him, must create in fear and trembling his own "human nature." The result was a turn inward, a dwelling upon the incurable isolation of the individual, an emphasis on the psychological tension in the human condition. Again, these themes had been signaled in art and literature.

If the century 1815–1914 was the Age of Confidence, the time that followed was, as Auden named it in 1944, the Age of Anxiety. An early prophet was Franz Kafka, whose heroes, designated some of them only by an initial, led the most marginal not to say precarious existence. Though they sought passionately to find out their individual place and responsibility in their world, Kafka's heroes could never learn it, and always died without finding out.[51]

The existentialism of Sartre was baffling to many, and simply inaccessible to Americans. When in his restless striving for personal meaning through involvement or "engagement," Sartre seemed to join forces with the Communists, Americans turned quickly aginst him. Young Americans preferred his old Resistance comrade Albert Camus, whose essays and novels of self-creating life in the face of an absurd existence were thought to be humanistically courageous. In Europe the mood was to set one's face against the confident individualism of former times and talk about 'anti-heroes' instead. Yet this struggle of life to create and expand its own authentic self was now in the mainstream of ideas, and raised the question of questions for the atomic age.

In the United States, where the existentalist movement was dismissed for dead by Norman Cousins in *The Saturday Review* in 1954, the question of how to create and widen the framework of living in the midst of the immobilized society was not a question widely faced. Norman Mailer had not yet begun, as he did later, to make his entire literary life a public and indeed exhibitionist series of frantic acts of self-creation.[52] As early as 1953, however, Robert Lowell confronted America's illusions with reality in an existentialist lament for General Eisenhower's inauguration day:

> Ice, ice; our wheels no longer move;
> Horseman, your sword is in the groove.
> Look, the fixed stars, itinerant,
> As lack-land atoms split apart,
> And the Republic summons Grant,
> The Mausoleum in her heart.[53]

For the most part amid standpat affirmations of the nineteenth century verities, it was left to the artists to see through to the core of American existence. When they did so, in this free society of free men, it was as if they were outside the scene entirely. Just as the most sterile years of the Stalinist terror brought forth inside the Soviet Union the great creative achievements of Pasternak and Solzhenitsyn when nobody else thought them possible, so the United States at the height of the Cold War harbored existentialist accomplishments of major importance to which prevailing attitudes were oblivious if not hostile.

When ideas have crossed the ocean in the past, Americans generally have had a way of putting their own stamp upon them. By and large the American transforming touch has been to turn them toward activism, activism beyond the scale experienced or dreamed of anywhere else. Thus between the World Wars the novel idea spread that when hard times befell a country its government could and should take measures to overcome them. When the Depression of the 1920s struck first in Europe, the nations there did something. The British devalued their money and put up their tariffs—and then carried on much as before. The French hardened their currency—and went on in their old ways. But when the United States met the Depression, there was a continental churning and an outpouring of action into every corner of the national life. Banks were closed, prices controlled, pigs ploughed under, rivers harnessed, a modern social-welfare base built amid prodigal expenditures of individual and national energies.

So it was with the idea of unbounded human freedom that took hold of Europe in 1945. Throughout the Cold War years, while the American society remained caught up in its illusions of omnipotence, certain artists in the United States saw through to the existential core of life and turned their insight into activism. Kept by the Depression nd the war from going to Europe, a handful of young American painters caught the fire of the new ideas when the Second World War exiled European painters to New York. The most gifted swiftly made Cubism and Surrealism their own, and by 1946 were launched on breath-stopping innovations such as art had never seen before. In a wild burst of creativity these young men began covering their canvases with powerful images of blazing violence and hidden order signalling the historic moment in transatlantic cultural traffic when the ideas are at the point of flowing the other way. The torchbearer of the abstract expressionists, as the New York School called themselves, was Jackson Pollock.

Born in Cody, Wyoming, and reared in a Los Angeles suburb in the same years as Richard Nixon, Jackson Pollock rode east to study with the regionalist painter Thomas Hart Benton in New York. There, fired by Surrealism, he took off like a Roman candle. He had heard how Max Ernst, to "force inspiration" for what he was about to paint, would sometimes tie a string to a tin can, punch a hole in the bottom, fill the can with paint and swing it across the blank canvas. What Ernst had toyed with as a kind of warming-up experience, Pollock turned into the ultimate act of creation. Tacking his canvas flat on the floor, he proceeded to paint his pictures by flicking streaks and gouts of pigment upon it with his outflung brush. "With the canvas on the floor, I feel nearer," he explained. "I can walk around it, work from the four sides and literally be in the painting." Hours might go by as he sat scowling at the blank canvas. But once started he "raced around it with pails, hurling gashes of violent hues to splash and flow, to gut and congeal . . . Then, his pails empty and fury spent, the painter squatted on his heels in a corner, trembling and exhausted."[54]

This was Action Painting. The gesture had been made the subject. His own unconscious impulses had been poured out through the violent act of painting. The canvas, said the critic Harold Rosenberg, had been seized upon as:

> an arena in which to act, rather than as a space in which to reproduce, re-design, analyze or 'express' an object, actual or imagined. What was to go on the canvas was not a picture but an event. . . . It is the artist's existence . . . he is living on the canvas. . . . What gives the canvas meaning is . . . the way the artist organized his emotional and intellectual energy as if he were in a living situation.

What could be more existential? "In the state of spiritual clarity," wrote the poet Frank O'Hara, "there are no secrets. The effort to achieve such a state is monumental and agonizing, and once achieved it is a harrowing state to maintain." Pollock was in analysis. He was tormented by doubts. He drank. But he painted with a volcanic intensity, covering giant canvases with convoluted traceries of intricate magnificence. His last huge canvas, SCENT, was studied with awe by his fellow abstractionists. On the night of August 11, 1956, he was killed when his small sports car veered off the road near his home in Easthampton, Long Island.[55]

The terrific discontinutiy between the artist's unbearable clarity and the complacencies around him went unremarked at the time, though Clement Greenberg in *The Nation* called Pollock the greatest artist America had produced and leader of a school that had showed the way for all modern art.

Much the same sort of perceptual gap yawned between his countrymen and another loner desperately hammering out his commitment to his own self during these years. This was David Smith, a brawny, hulking man born of pioneer stock at Decatur, Indiana who came to New York to become a painter about the same time that Pollock did. The spark of the exiles' ideas drove Smith to embody his abstract expressions in sculpture.

It was a task for herculean activism. Yet when Smith found his way he leaped right over an impediment that had stopped every sculptor since Phidias, the problem of a base for his figure. Smith set his Cubist composition, three-dimensional as ever, in a frame. With his endless ideas, his booming voice and his red rage at the society of trimmers around him, Smith was always re-creating himself. "Oh David," said Robert Motherwell, another leader of the New York School, "you are as delicate as Vivaldi and as strong as a Mack truck."

"The only creative substance in the work of art is the artist's identity," glowered Smith. Even fewer shared Smith's vision than Pollock's. Eleven years after Pollock's death Smith missed a curve near his home in the Adirondack foothills and was crushed to death inside his truck. He died, America's greatest sculptor, alone. By then, however, the powerful stream that had been flowing underground since the Second World War and in which Pollock and Smith were forcing influences had burst through.[56]

After the petrifying years of Cold War, American society's old flexibility and loose-jointed capacity for accommodation had dried out. As the walls went down with a shout at Berkeley in 1964, the rebellious students of the "free speech" movement set the American stamp on Sartre's life-affirming idea of 1945 and turned it into roiling action. Their avowed goal was to enlarge the framework of their existence. They wanted, they said, to "take a trip" to the frontiers of their sensibilities. Armed with the pill, pot, speed, hash, acid, meth, hair, gags, jokes, zen and obscenities, the New Left and the counterculture boiled out in a wave of furious activism. Sweeping through families, schools, campuses, churches, armed forces, corporations and political conventions and onto the universities and sidewalks of Europe and Asia and back, this wave became for a brief time the driving force in the life-affirming mainstream of twentieth century consciousness. America knew at last the measure of modern alienation and anguish.

THE IMPLAUSIBILITIES of American hammering on the hard line in the Cold War while piling up ever greater private gratifications on top of what was already the world's highest living standard were made all the more glaring by the signs of change in the Soviet Union during these same years. In August, 1953, the new Russian leader Georgi Malenkov delivered an address of the same order of importance as the election speech in which Stalin had announced Russia's intention to build Communist power to rival that of the United States nine years before.

Now, as if to announce that the policies proclaimed at the outset of the Cold War in 1946 had been fulfilled, Malenkov made known that the

Soviet Union had successfully tested an H-bomb. It should be possible, he added, now that both East and West possessed the bomb, to end the Cold War. These intimations alone—that the Soviet Union possessed new power to promote Communist expansion, and that it might also wish to negotiate with the West for mutual limitations on such power—laid down the main outlines for Soviet foreign policy for the duration of the Cold War.[57]

The reforming implications of Malenkov's speech—which was entitled "The New Course"—were strongest in what he proposed for the new regime's internal policies. Already there was a new air in Russia; Ilya Ehrenburg brought out a book titled *The Thaw*, which seemed to suggest the climatic change following the death of Stalin. The new premier, who after all had operated almost literally at Stalin's elbow since 1940, was enormously discreet about lending even a word of public approval to these movements among the country's intellectuals. Yet the fact was that the new regime in its first months quietly pardoned and released something like two million prisoners. The country was well on its way toward the liquidation of Stalin's police system. On top of this came the dismissal and arrest of Lavrenti Beria, the Presidium member controlling the police, shortly before Malenkov spoke.[58]

The execution of Beria, however, did not only bring about the end of mass terror in Soviet society. It also had the effect, in the inevitable competition for power among Stalin's successors, of removing the old element of physical violence. Thenceforth differences at the top—and increasingly at other levels—were settled by political processes, and the consequences were swift for the man who initiated the big change.

Did Winston Churchill sense this swing when he sent out his call for a meeting at the summit in the spring of 1953? Except for Anthony Eden's proposals for pulling back both Russian and Western military forces several hundred miles and thereby creating an extensive demilitarized zone in Central Europe, there were no positive Western manifestations of response to Malenkov's unmistakable signals for a Cold War letup in 1953. The American attitude was largely governed that year by Senator McCarthy. The Eisenhower administration, far from weighing a new chance for negotiations, was busy meeting the senator's demands to cut off the last remaining channels of trade with Russia.[59]

In such a glacial international atmosphere, the events of 1953 after the Stalinist ice age amounted to no more than a brief thaw. In his speech Malenkov had pledged more consumer goods for Russians:

> The Government and the Central Committee of the Party consider it necessary to increase significantly the investments in the development of the light, food and fishing industries, and in agriculture, and to

improve greatly the production of articles of popular consumption. . . . Our task is to make a sharp improvement in the production of consumer goods.

When Malenkov laid down these home policies for the new Russian government, there was no demur from any of his eight colleagues in the ruling Presidium, and all the organs of the Communist party and Soviet government gave forth a deafening roar of support.[60] Yet among the close associates of Stalin, competition within the collective leadership was not to be subdued. In the shift in rules, styles and stakes after the dictator's death, Nikita Khrushchev, who had been named party secretary as a counterpoise to Malenkov's power as premier, began to assert himself as Malenkov's rival for top leadership.[61]

At that point Khrushchev was sixty-one, no longer young. Unlike Malenkov and most of the other Presidium leaders, he was largely self-schooled. He was a peasant's son from Kalinkovka, and had worked in mines and metal shops in the Ukraine until the 1917 Revolution. Later he rose during Stalin's purges to become party boss first in Moscow and then in the Ukraine. Unlike most of Russia's top bureaucrats, in and out of the Kremlin, he had learned his Communism not out of a book but by contact in meeting halls, factories and tractor stations. Alone among Stalin's lieutenants, he lived and spoke as a man who had moved in Communism as a fish in water. He was the *muzhik* whom Stalin had commanded to dance the *gopak* at a Kremlin party. He was the earthy, proverb-quoting commissar of the cornfields at whom Beria had sneered as "our beloved chicken statesman" and "our potato politician." He seemed crude and he seemed too preoccupied with everyday operational affairs to pose a threat. It seems unlikely that when Stalin's successors installed this stubby, uncouth populist in the tyrant's key job as First Party Secretary, they thought such a clodhopper could fill such shoes.[62]

Yet that is what Khrushchev, operating from the same position from which Stalin rose to mastery over Russia, proceeded to do. Under Stalin Russia had been run from the Kremlin with the same sort of absolute monarchism by which Louis XIV's France was run from Versailles. The place of power was at the court, and Malenkov was a man of the court —the man, as it were, behind the monarch. Cool and intelligent, Malenkov placed himself deliberately at the head of the government ministries, which had emerged—almost like the supercorporations of America—as the dominant force in the Russian scene.

Ebullient and eager to infuse vitality into the party that had ceased to be the revolutionizing engine of Soviet change, Khrushchev went out in the country where Malenkov had never shown his face. He talked with people—party people and plain people. Making use of the powers vested in his position as party chief, he built up a core of supporters. Yet he never lost sight of the seat of final decision in the Presidium. In his surge for the top Khrushchev took up three issues—agricultural policy, industrial policy, and the maintenance of a hard ideological line in foreign affairs. These he developed in such a fashion that he managed to win over the Stalinist conservatives in the Presidium and topple Malenkov from command.[63]

The problem that Khrushchev first seized upon in his ceaseless traveling around the country was agriculture, Russia's Number 1 concern. Wherever he went, he talked to the party *apparatchiks* about the necessity of getting the country moving again. He seldom seemed to worry about what he said, who was listening, how it might diverge from Moscow's line. "You must plant potatoes in square clusters, you must grow cabbages as my grandmother did," he lectued cloth-capped peasants. He admitted that his plans for planting corn ("Cabbage on the stalk") had not panned out too well everywhere. "If you cannot catch the bird of paradise," he advised, "better take a wet hen."[64]

A month after Malenkov's big speech, Khrushchev addressed the party on the farm problem. The prime minister had remarked that Russian agriculture has turned the corner, was headed in the right direction and could supply what was needed. Khrushchev now took blunt exception to the premier's bland survey, and pointed out that it was based on the notoriously misleading estimate of "biological yield," or acreage planted, instead of the physical yield. Everybody knew, said Khrushchev, that physical yield—the amount actually harvested—was a lot lower, so much lower in fact that all complacency should be knocked out of estimates of Russian farm output. There was enough bread, all right, and there would be no shortage of bread grains, Khrushchev said, but there would be an intolerable shortage of everything else. The number of beef cattle, for instance, was down by 3,500,000 head from 1928, the year that collectivization began in Russia. In 1952 alone the number of all livestock had dropped by 2,100,000. After all the bureaucratic doubletalk of the Stalin years, this sounded like someone telling it more like it was.[65]

Virtually every twentieth century politician taking aim at supreme power over a nation sooner or later seeks to authenticate his capacities for leadership on the grand, bold scale by offering his countrymen a "Gallipoli." (This was the code name for the big plan that Winston Churchill conceived in 1915 to land an expeditionary force at Gallipoli on the Turkish flank of the Central Powers and thereby smash the Flanders stalemate and win the First World War by a single decisive stroke.) In schemes of such grandiloquent daring it is not even necessary that the bold stroke—Mao's "Great Leap Forward," Mussolini's mapping of Italy's Mediterranean "Mare Nostrum" in the 1930s—is ultimately successful. What matters—as when a Roosevelt summons America to become an arsenal of democracy and send a quarter of a million planes into the air, or when exiled Colonel De Gaulle (with Hitler in Paris) says "I am France" and calls on Frenchmen to hold on until freedom is restored— is that the conception is big enough to command individual sacrifice and common commitment by whole populations.

In his bid to take over Russia after Stalin, Khrushchev proposed such a big, bold plan. Instead of cosseting and chivvying and hectoring the hapless Russian peasants any longer, he proposed a total and breath-stopping switch. The entire weight of Russia's investment in agriculture, he said, should be taken away from the primordially stubborn *muzhiks* on their collectives and thrown into the opening up of vast tracts of grazing lands that for the most part had never been cultivated before—the Virgin Lands of Kazhakhstan and Siberia.[66]

The plan was to get the larger harvest needed by a rapidly industrializing and urbanizing Russia and get it fast by a heroically simple program: transport 250,000 "volunteers," mostly Young Communists, to the wide-open plains of Central Asia, let them build their own crude huts for a starter, then equip them with 120,000 tractors and put then to ploughing up and planting the grassy steppes. The scheme was so spectacular and gigantic and sudden that it carried all opposition before it. This was a plan to pour youthful energies into work for the party and the country—for bigger goals and on a greater scale than the Civilian Conservation Corps in which young Americans went out to repair the landscape in the Great Depression. It was a plan for subduing one of the great frontiers of the world, part of a national drive to the East as old in Russia as America's westward thrust.[67]

Whatever their objections in secret council, the Presidium conservatives stood aside to let Nikita Khrushchev lead the big trek to the Virgin Lands. He was the mobilizer, proselytizer, energizer, and the Party and the Young Communists operated as the immigration agents and land offices in the tremendous movement of people involved. A Malenkov man took the assignment as First Secretary in the Virgin Lands area, but Khrushchev sent in his own man as the party's second-in-command, and within six months he was officially in charge. Eyes, ears and good right arm on the job for the "potato politician," he was an official whom Khrushchev had brought from field work in Bessarabia to headquarters and then sent out to Kazakhstan—Leonid Brezhnev.[68]

The first year the young pioneers harvested 6,000,000 acres of spring wheat, and that was all the success that Khrushchev needed on his drive to the top. Later, since these Asian grasslands were semiarid, yields fell off sharply, and the whole venture lost its luster. But in 1954 and 1955 the total of new land plowed and planted in Central Asia rose to 32,-000,000 acres. The Young Communists spilled across the bare plains in whole towns and cities. The steppes were strung with power lines, dotted with tractor sheds, gashed by raw roads. In all Brezhnev could report that the pioneers were cultivating three times the total acreage tilled in all Russia when collectivization began in 1928—and as much as the total under cultivation in all of Britain, France and Spain together.[69]

To hear Khrushchev tell it, these were the party's achievements. The party and the Young Communists he said, were the driving force in all that was positive in Russian life. As for the government ministries, he never let up on his criticism of their obstruction, their lack of foresight, their lack of imagination. He blamed the Ministry of Agriculture for not planting corn, for leaving cattle on the range instead of fattening them near market on grain, for milking cows only twice a day. He blamed the industrial ministries for not providing tractors, combines, ploughs, spare parts. He blamed the Ministry of Housing for not rushing buildings materials to the Virgin Lands before winter set in. He blamed the Ministry of Transport for delivery foulups. Never once in his talks to party leaders, in his statements in the press, did he attack Malenkov. He simply went on and on about the ministries, all of them responsible to Malenkov as prime minister.[70]

As he traveled about making marathon speeches, wading nto cornfields, shaking hands with grizzled *kholkhoz* chairmen, Khrushchev displayed himself as the practical, downright man who knew how to get things done. Even more than his public harangues, the persuasiveness and authority of his private talk helped convince the party workers that he was the man to win. He succeeded in transferring a key Malenkov aide out of his central secretariat: after that, more and more Khrushchev men moved into provincial party posts. In this scene Khrushchev was fighting for the very careers of those who listened to him. In the neglect after the war years party cells had ceased to exist in most collectives in the countryside, and now Khrushchev, operating in fields where no Kremlin courtier had been seen before, planted and cultivated a new crop of *apparatchiks.*[71]

But it was still at the top in the Kremlin where Khrushchev had to gain adherents, and for this he needed an issue to bring over to his side Molotov and other conservatives. He was as brutal as the toughest old Stalinist in demanding strict party surveillance over artists and writers seeking freer expression as part of the cultural "thaw." He was in the forefront of the conservative drive to keep a hard line against the West in the Cold War, and with other Presidium members forced Malenkov in April, 1954, to retract his earlier statement that, since both Russia and America now had H-bombs, the outbreak of nuclear war would mean "the end of civilization." The doctrine was as Malenkov now agreed Molotov and Khrushchev had correctly stated: in a nuclear war, only capitalist countries could be destroyed, and Communism would come through the winner.[72]

Yet even with the toughest old Stalinists—Molotov, Kaganovich, Voroshilov—on his side along with his old friend and coruler of Moscow, Bulganin, Khrushchev could reckon with no more than a bare majority of the nine-man Presidium. The first signs of a workable anti-Malenkov majority appeared in the delegation that Khrushchev led to China in September, 1954. Neither the prime minister nor the foreign minister went on this supremely important mission, which was led by Khrushchev as chief of the Russian party. With him went Bulganin, the deputy premier, Dimitri Shepilov, the editor of *Pravda*, and Anastas Mikoyan, Russia's trade chief and a Presidium member who had hitherto sided with Malenkov. In Peking Khrushchev dealt in person with Mao Tse-tung and went to great lengths to win him over. Besides handing over Russia's remaining concessions in Manchuria, he negotiated an agreement to ship China such a quantity of capital goods that Malenkov's policy of diverting Russian production to consumer goods was knocked out then and there. Mikoyan, who was party to these decisions, thenceforth always appeared in Khrushchev's corner.[73]

This was the political issue—Malenkov's sponsoring of more consumer goods for the population—on which Khrushchev now moved to overthrow him. Since Malenkov's line involved little actual reduction of heavy industrial production, the issue was more a matter of doctrinal deviation than practical differences. But to the Presidium diehards, as Khrushchev reckoned, orthodoxy was everything. At the beginning of November Khrushchev and his man Shepilov opened fire in *Pravda*, the flagship of the party. Day after day for the next eight weeks *Izvestia*, the organ of the government, thundered back. From *Pravda* hurtled salvos about the overriding importance of heavy industry. The big guns of *Izvestia* boomed out in reply that consumer goods needed attention. Late in December *Pravda* shifted its ammunition and printed a broadside by Khrushchev himself calling heavy industry the very cornerstone of the Russian economy.

Then *Izvestia* fell silent, and a deadly torpedo was launched straight at Malenkov. As a sequel to the Beria case *Pravda* announced the trial and execution of Abakomov, ex-Minister of State Security, for his part in the "Leningrad Affair," the purge of Zhdanov followers carried out after

Zhdanov's death in 1949. Though the tie with Beria was still mentioned, it was well known that Malenkov had been advanced to Stalin's designated successor following the death of Zhdanov and the events in Leningrad. Publishing details of the case at this point obviously struck at Malenkov, and indeed implied a threat to implicate him still further as organizer and instigator of the affair.[74]

The cannonade for heavy industry went on. Past speeches of Stalin were wheeled up and fired off. The oldest of Stalinists, Voroshilov, unlimbered and let fly for heavy industry. Shepilov, who might have been described as Khrushchev's main battery, delivered the climactic barrage in a signed editorial on "The General Line of the Party and Some Vulgarizers of Marxism." Zeroing in on "bourgeois type" economists who "complained that heavy industrialization distracted from consumer-goods needs," he thundered: "It is difficult to think of a theory moe antiscientific, rotten and demoralizing for our people." By this time Malenkov was isolated and discredited. The party *apparatchiks* smarted under the dominance he had given to the state ministries. The industrial management feared his reforms. So did the military leadership, which carried new weight since the liquidation of the secret police. Early in 1955 the old-line Presidium majority swung behind Khrushchev. Malenkov resigned.[75]

On February 8 a deputy read his letter to the Supreme Soviet asking that "some comrade who possesses greater experience of government" take over. "I recognize clearly," Malenkov wrote, "my lack of experience in local work, and I see particularly my fault and responsibility for the unsatisfactory state of agriculture." He ended with a statement of faith in the primacy of heavy industry. Khrushchev at once rose and proposed Bulganin as the new prime minister. Malenkov became deputy premier, still with a seat in the ruling Presidium.[76]

The struggle for the succession was not ended, though Bulganin, an affable and ineffectual bureaucrat, at once acknowledged the primacy of the party over the government as Malenkov never did. But before Khrushchev could take control, it was necessary to smash the Stalinist legend.

This was not done at once, and when it was, Khrushchev's part in it was thoroughly pragmatic, operational and dictated by a dynamic that as a Stalinist himself he could ride but never ultimately control. Having bested the "softs," as Malenkov's group were known, he now swung back, skillfully preempting the center for himself, and began to isolate the "hards," of whom Molotov was by far the most outspoken. All practitioners of the Communist dialectic believe that change is the law of life, but Khrushchev far more than such a hard-shell Old Bolshevik as Molotov, lived the dialectic. Veering away from the "hards" in this new phase of the post-Stalin struggle, Khrushchev concentrated his drive successively in three interrelated issues: foreign policy, the problem of Stalinism and the question of economic reorganization.[77]

On this agenda the first move was to agree to a peace treaty with Austria. This Dulles had been demanding, in stalling off Russian demands for a summit meeting during the Cold War give-and-take of the past year or two, as a prior proof of Russia's sincere desire to negotiate with the West. Now suddenly Molotov, though he had been opposing such a treaty, was packed off to sign one. Both sides agreed to pull out their occupation troops, and let the Austrians form their own government. Freedom, Dulles proclaimed, had won another bastion. Yet since the new government could not take sides in the Cold War, it could also be said that a neutralist wedge had been driven across the Iron Curtain into the NATO bloc. "Well, I think we've had it," were Dulles' rueful words to Eisenhower in private: his stipulation for a prior Austrian treaty had been met and they would now have to attend the summit meeting at Geneva.[78]

A more important preliminary to the summit occurred in Eastern Europe. In a move bitterly opposed by Molotov, Khrushchev led a visit of friendship and reconciliation to Marshal Tito of Yugoslavia. Here, after the quarrel between Stalin and Tito, was a sensational change by the Russians. For Western newsmen it was a first chance to get a good look at the rising renovator of Soviet Russia, and some were so unprepared for his racy and pugnacious style that they reported him drunk. But Khrushchev was too precipitous for the Yugoslavs too. Almost before the engines of his TU-114 stopped, Khrushchev, with Bulganin and Mikoyan standing beside him on the airport runway, began to read a preposterous statement blaming Beria and his men for wrecking Russian-Yugoslav relations. Tito cut him short, and next day the Belgrade press said coolly that Yugoslavia would continue to pursue a policy independent of all blocs. Yet before the visit had ended Khrushchev had made his point that Stalin's successors desired to patch up the quarrel with the Yugoslavs and indeed hoped to create a healthier climate in the Eastern European bloc.[79]

Two weeks later at Geneva, the leaders of West and East met for the first time since the Potsdam Conference of the wartime allies just ten years before. As head of the government Bulganin spoke for Russia in the formal talks with Eisenhower and Eden. But when the Russians flew in everybody noticed that it was Khrushchev who climbed out of the plane first and Khrushchev, in his bell-bottomed suit, who got into cars ahead of his prime minister. Though at the state sessions Khrushchev would defer to Bulganin, when Eisenhower gave a dinner it was Khrushchev who answered the questions. Once Eisenhower took it upon himself to impress upon the Russians the gravity of any possible confrontation involving, as he said it must, nuclear weapons. "Yes," Khrushchev interrupted, "we'll get your dust and you'll get ours." It was one of the moments of truth in the Cold War—the brusque, face-to-face acknowledgment of the balance of terror and the mutual recognition that neither side could now much want to tilt the balance by more than a few hairsbreadths.[80]

It is now often said that the unspoken agreement reached at the 1955 Geneva summit was that the United States acknowledged Russia's dominant position in Eastern Europe. Nothing of the sort was said at the time, and indeed the United States not only pushed the rearmament of West Germany but stepped up its military, intelligence and propaganda operations throughout Germany, sending eastward agents and broadcasts aimed not only at the satellites but at the Ukrainians and other nationalities within the Soviet Union itself. When Dulles allowed himself to ask whether the Russian "maneuver" of easing tension "may in fact assume the force of an irreversible trend," Khrushchev, addressing East German party workers, made swift rejoinder:

> We are in favor of a détente but if anybody thinks that for this reason we shall forget about Marx, Engels and Lenin, he is mistaken. That will happen when shrimps learn to whistle.[81]

That summer the Central Committee upheld Khrushchev's policy of seeking friendship with Tito, though Molotov took the floor to speak openly against it. Voted down, the Old Bolshevik found himself compelled in October to publish an article in the journal *Kommunist* admitting that he had voiced "theoretically erroneous and politically harmful" views in an earlier speech before the Supreme Soviet. He had said, he explained, that the foundations of socialism had been laid in Russia when he should have said that socialism had already been built—a distinction that seemed academic but was not.[82]

This distinction was directly involved in the question of Stalinism, which was brought out into the open at the Twentieth Party Congress in February, 1956. The problem in any political state is the problem of reconciling freedom and order, and for the heirs of the tyrant it was clear that they must make a break with the past if they were to revitalize as well as stabilize the Soviet system. Three years after the death of Stalin, the moment had arrived. Khrushchev was the dominating figure at the Congress, consolidating his position from day to day. Of 133 Central Committee members elected, seventy-six had close career connections with the first secretary. Of five new candidate members of the Presidium and five new secretaries in the party Secretariat, every one was a Khrushchev protégé. In long speeches he used the occasion to impress upon the party and new elements in Soviet society—the experts, the intellectuals, the military, and the people in general—that he stood for a policy of change. Then, on the last day of Congress, he struck the blow.[83]

Speaking at a specially convened secret session he attacked Stalin for crimes committed during his twenty-seven years as ruler. The formal charge was that the dictator had fostered the "cult of the individual." It was not necessary to arraign him for thousands of murders to sustain this charge: the little group of men now in power could hardly have been innocent or ignorant of all of Stalin's crimes. Indeed, in a remarkable speech earlier in the Congress Mikoyan, criticizing excesses of the "cult of the individual," had cited the case of Stanislaw Kossior, party chief of the Ukraine purged in 1938 by Stalin's order. To those who had seen the Leningrad Affair used a year earlier as a bludgeon against Malenkov, the reference to Kossior's case could have been aimed only at Khrushchev, his successor as Ukrainian party secretary, and seemed at the least to have been intended to prod Khrushchev into delivering the speech he did.[84]

In that speech Khrushchev did not go into his part in the Ukrainian purge, any more than he went into the complicities of Malenkov or Molotov or Kaganovitch or any of the members of the Presidium except the dead Beria. But beginning with Stalin's scheming to hasten the death of the stricken Lenin and going on to the last uncompleted plot to do away with Molotov, Voroshilov and Mikoyan, he told such a tale of infamies as no high political leader has ever told in this century. The words fell like hammer blows.

Early in the 1930s Stalin grasped for absolute power, needed, he said, to intensify the class struggle. A majority in the Central Committee led by Sergei Kirov, the Leningrad party chief, resisted him. In 1934 Stalin ordered Kirov killed. Seizing upon the murder of Kirov as evidence of subversive forces at work, he directed the secret police to arrest thousands of party leaders as "enemies of the people." Thus his secret police carried through the "intensification of the class struggle." The great show trials of 1937, the purge of the Red Army generals, the execution of the famous Old Bolsheviks—all were carried through by forced confessions, torture and terror. The facts, said Khrushchev, had been brought to light by a special commission appointed to look into the trials of 1937–38. He read out extracts from case reports—"vile provocations, odious falsifications, criminal violations of revolutionary legality"—and as he read the pleas of the accused leaders and their fate—"Eikhe was shot," "sentence was pronounced in twenty minutes and Rudzutak was shot"—there were shouts and groans. The printed report was punctuated with notations of "commotion in the hall," "indignation in the hall." In all, 100 of the 123 members of the Central Committee elected at the Sixteenth Party Congress in 1934 were executed by Stalin.[85]

The net effect of this almost Dostoyevskian outpouring was to identify Krushchev as leader of a powerful current pushing for a general break with the Stalinist past. It also served to reassure the party workers that he was not another Stalin. Destroying Stalin's myth, he had rejected Stalin's mantle. Others, like Molotov, stood nearer in line as Stalin's successors; but by turning the contest into a test of anti-Stalinism and seizing its initiative, Khrushchev had gained the field for himself.[86]

After the Twentieth Party Congress, Khrushchev ruled for a relaxation on the literary and intellectual front in Russia in hopes that this might lead to voluntary attachment to his regime. The secret speech was read out at thousands of party meetings throughout the Soviet Union. For the first time a major leader had appealed outside the narrow structure of the party itself. The implications of the attack ranged Khrushchev with those forces in Russian society—the technocrats, the intellectuals, the military, the people in general—who wanted a break with terror, the concentration camps, the fear, the suspicion that had for as long as most people could remember kept ordinary political conversation out of Soviet life. If the message with which Khrushchev had shaken the thousands of Congress delegates meant anything to them as they went back to their home communities, it was that Khrushchev stood for change.[87]

And so it was in Eastern Europe. The secret speech was read in all the parties of the bloc, and indeed the copy which United States intelligence made public in June, 1956, was obtained through the Poles. In Poland, as elsewhere in the bloc, a New Course had been tried in the Malenkov period, and the party knew that trying to keep up a "war Communism atmosphere" was a liability. After Khrushchev's speech, the ferment bubbled to the top. In May Jacob Berman, the leader most identified with the police terror, was stripped of all his offices. Newspapers began openly criticizing the regime and demanding reforms. The ferment turned into a popular tide. In June it reached the working classes. Rioting broke out in Poznan, where workers besieged party and police headquarters and demanded an end to oppressive production rules and better pay. In three days' fighting fifty-three died, and the rising was only quelled by bringing in the Army.[88]

Convinced that a sharp break with the past was imperative, the party moved to bring back Wladislaw Gomulka into the leadership. Gomulka, imprisoned as too "nationalist" during the wave of purges following Stalin's quarrel with Tito, was opposed by Stalinists in the leadership. He had not yet been restored to office when the new group prepared to remove Marshal Rokossovsky, Polish-born Soviet army officer, as chief of the Polish armed forces. Alarmed that things had passed the point of no return, the Stalinists sent an urgent appeal to the Kremlin.[89]

Thereupon a powerful Russian delegation including Khrushchev, Kaganovich, Mikoyan and Molotov and a flock of senior generals, descended on Warsaw. Soviet armed forces in Poland began closing in on the capital. Even as the Russians arrived, the Polish Communists hastily co-opted Gomulka and two of his friends into the leadership. Khrushchev delivered a blistering speech against the Polish changes. Gomulka responded by threatening to call out the Polish people. The Poles, he went on, were bent on taking their own road to Socialism, but by no means disposed to weaken the protection against Germany that the alliance with Russia afforded. It was touch and go for Russian intervention. But Khrushchev decided to gamble on Gomulka. Ordering the troops back to base, the Russian leaders flew home. Next day Gomulka, reinstated as Poland's top Communist, announced his program for national recovery. Marshal Rokossovsky dropped out of sight. Overnight Gomulka won greater popularity than any Pole of this century. Intervention and revolt were alike averted.[90]

In Hungary the outcome was tragedy. There the country had already tasted national Communism when Imre Nagy briefly directed the country on a New Course during the Malenkov days. But afterwards the old Stalinist regime had been restored, the most unpopular in all Eastern Europe. During a visit to Moscow in 1956 Tito had urged Khrushchev to get rid of the hated and despised Hungarian leader Matyas Rakosi, but Khrushchev hesitated. In Budapest the same ferment was at work as in Warsaw. After the Poznan riots Hungarian intellectuals and students held meeting at which the Polish chiefs were publicly condemned for their handling of the workers. When there were cheers and calls for Imre Nagy, Rakosi drew up a list of 400 who had joined the criticism and called for their arrest. Thereupon Mikoyan flew to Budapest, and Rakosi was deposed and carried off to Moscow in a Russian plane in disgrace. But his successor was another hard-liner, Erno Gero.[91]

The Hungarian Revolution began when word spread through Budapest that Gomulka had regained power in Poland. Taking this to mean that the Russians were not willing to use force to prevent the return of an anti-Stalinist, students went to the center of the city on the evening of October 23 to demonstrate for the return of Nagy. Nagy, who had been professor of economics at the University of Budapest after his dismissal in 1955, had just been readmitted to the party. Amid excited expectancy, Gero went on the radio. In a brief, harsh speech he said there would be no change in the regime. The demonstrators marched to the radio building, where the secret police opened fire. By then workers were arriving in trucks from the ring of factories surrounding Budapest and they carried arms. Others broke into arsenals and took guns. The crowd surged on a giant statue of Stalin. Down it went amid yells of jubilation. Blowtorches cut it up, and the bronze head was carried to the center of the city. Throughout the night rifle fire went on. Red stars and other emblems were shot off buildings, and Hungarian flags were run up with holes in the center where the Communist insignia had been cut out.[92]

During the night Nagy was brought to the Parliament building and told that he had been restored to the Central Committee and appointed prime minister. But he was surrounded by secret police and by Stalinists who had already sent out a call for Russian aid against the "counterrevolution." Thus the intervention began, but with no clear notion against whom it was directed. The insurgents called a general strike, and idled workers in thousands turned into freedom-fighters. Small, local bands formed. When the Russians arrived, resistance was spontaneous, confused. The Russians rode in tanks, unsupported by infantry, and the crews seemed reluctant to open fire on the people.[93]

Next day the Russian leadership sent in Mikoyan and Suslov to look over the situation. It was confusing. The radio was still denouncing the rising as "counterrevolutionary," yet the Russian troops suppressing it were protecting the regime that the revolutionaries were fighting to bring into being.

After a night of nonstop conferences at party headquarters, a huge crowd of men and women began assembling in the bright sunshine. Waving flags and shouting "This is a peaceful demonstration" and "The radio is telling lies," they began marching toward Parliament Square. Along the way they fraternized with the Russian soldiers; a column of tanks moved up to accompany the marchers over the Danube bridge into the square, where most of the tanks were drawn up. Suddenly from the rooftops of surrounding buildings members of the AVH, the hated secret police, opened fire with machine guns. The demonstrators scattered. There was no place to hide. Bodies piled up, and were used as screens by the living. As many as 600 may have died.[94]

Within a half hour after the massacre the Russians had deposed Gero and replaced him as party chief with Janos Kadar. Kadar went on the air in a joint appeal with Nagy, promising magnanimity to the rebels and assuring the people that Hungarian-Russian relations would be "reviewed." While Mikoyan and Suslov returned to Moscow, Nagy repeated his calls for order. On October 28 he negotiated a ceasefire, and two days later Moscow issued a declaration acknowledging that Stalin's policy of interference in Eastern Europe had violated the "principle of full equality" and offering to reexamine economic relations between Russia and such countries as Poland and Hungary.[95]

But Imre Nagy, unlike Gomulka in Poland, was not the master of events. Although the Russians appeared to be withdrawing, there was still heavy fighting, especially at the Killian Barracks, where Colonel Pal Maleter had gone over to the insurgents and was directing a fierce resistance against pointblank fire from Russian tanks. Under pressure from the streets the new government added leading non-Communists to its cabinet, and began moving toward a multi-party system in which the Communists would have only a minority position. Nagy announced on October 30 the start of negotiations for Hungary's withdrawal from the Warsaw Pact. Finally he proclaimed that Hungary would be a neutral state.[96]

By then the Russians had made up their minds to intervene decisively. Unquestionably this decision was made easier by the announcement on October 30 of the Anglo-French ultimatum to Egypt and the uproar over their Suez invasion which followed. It was made even easier by the almost complete paralysis in the attitude of the United States government in the presence of the events in Hungary. Four years before John Foster Dulles had said "any revolt of free people in future would be supported by this country and Soviet intervention would be warned off with a clear threat that it would be met by United States reprisals." These claims were never sustained by the Eisenhower administration by anything more than propaganda balloons and broadcasts. When the Poles seemed on the point of taking arms against the Russians, Secretary Dulles hastened to the radio on October 21 to announce that in the event of Soviet intervention in Poland the United States would not move.

But as the Eastern European crisis rose to its peak in Hungary, more than the hollowness of American propaganda was exposed. A policy shaped by an unachievable goal of nuclear security and an ideology that barred negotiations with the Russians as unthinkable (in less than forty years), left the United States unprepared to take the lead when the hour for diplomatic initiative struck. Even when the embattled Hungarians wrung from *Pravda* the declaration on November 1 that "the Nagy government has won the support of the people," Washington hung back as if pinioned. More than a week passed between the first Soviet intervention in Hungary and the second. During those days Americans read in their newspapers the eyewitness reports of the increasingly successful fight by Hungarians for national independence. During those days their government limited itself to recommending to the United Nations on November 3 the "studying of 'suitable moves.'" No serious warning was sent to Moscow that its military intervention against Nagy, who was frantically appealing for help, would be viewed as a serious threat to world peace. The Hungarian question was repeatedly postponed in the United Nations, and when the Suez crisis broke the Russians were successful in great measure through their threats in making it the central issue. During a span of ten days no effort was made to fly United Nations observers into Hungary and so place it under some form of international supervision. The faith in an omnipotent America, fostered by the rhetoric of liberation and nurtured by smug boasts of American economic and military superiority, received a rude blow in the realization of the nation's abstention before the events in Budapest.[97]

The period of Soviet hesitation, unquestionably influenced by the policy of expediency adopted earlier toward Gomulka, now gave way to force in Hungary. Russian divisions poured into the country. Kadar left party headquarters in Budapest and joined the Russians in eastern Hungary. The freedom fighters fought and fell back. In Budapest the Russians tricked Maleter into negotiations, then arrested him. Nagy took refuge in the Yugoslav embassy, only to be seized by the Russians when he emerged under a safe-conduct. The last forty holdouts at the Killian Barracks, leaving under an amnesty, were mowed down to a man. So ended the revolution, and Kadar moved back into Budapest to rule with the AVH and the tanks. Nagy was shot in due course. "It was difficult," said Khrushchev later, "because part of the workers were on the side of the counterrevolution. . . . Bullets do not choose between striking class enemies or misguided workers. Believe me, my friends, we spent painful days and nights before coming to a decision."

The spectacle of the brutal way the Hungarian revolt was put down powerfully reinforced popular Polish backing for Gomulka, who had insisted that his country must pursue its own road to socialism but had never proposed throwing over the Russian alliance or introducing the multiparty system. Great crowds cheered his appearances, and Cardinal Wyszyinsky, primate of this Catholic country, lent his backing to the regime. The contrast with Hungary where Cardinal Mindszenty, the Catholic primate, had remained aloof from the regime, was instructive. Mindszenty took refuge in the United States embassy, emerging fourteen years later a broken man to go into exile in Austria.

Though the Soviet bloc emerged intact, the events of 1956 constituted a setback for Khrushchev's leadership. Within Russia itself his de-Stalinization produced such ferment that the party chief found himself telling a writers' meeting that "my hand would not tremble" if he had to shoot some young liberals. He conceded that he had gone too far in denouncing Stalin and said, "I am proud that we are Stalinists." It was at this time that the Central Committee met to consider a proposed economic reorganization, and the events reflected his diminished prestige. He did not speak at all, and the State Economic Commission thereupon constituted was given such powers that it became in effect the economic government of the Soviet Union.[98]

But by the next Central Committee session in February, Khrushchev was back on the attack and proposing his own sweeping plan for industrial reorganization. Decentralization was the goal of this program, which involved nothing less than the dismantling of the ministries and the transfer of the bureaucrats to the provinces where they would be responsible to local governments dominated by the party. When Khrushchev's program was launched, Molotov submitted his objections in writing to his fellow Presidium members at 3:00 A.M., and Malenkov and Kaganovich charged that the program would lead to anarchy. Yet Khrushchev was strong enough to obtain the sort of permissive approval he had won earlier for his Virgin Lands project, and following the publication on March 30 of "Theses on Comrade Khrushchev's Report," the program was widely publicized and discussed at innumerable party meetings before the May session of the Supreme Soviet. Party officials saw increased power to the party in the scheme, and Khrushchev won the military over by exempting the defense industry from the reorganization. But now both Malenkov and his group and the Old Stalinists were fighting for their positions as well as policies. They accused Khrushchev of trying to become another Stalin. The reforms were so sweeping that even Bulganin and Shepilov joined his old rivals. A coup was prepared. Upon his return from a trip to Finland in June, 1957, a Presidium majority of seven-to-four demanded Khrushchev's resignation.[99]

Khrushchev shouted that politics were not arithmetic. He had not been elected by the Presidium but by the Central Committee which since the Twentieth Party Congress was packed with his supporters. Marshall Zhukov now intervened to fly Khrushchev's committee supporters to the capital for the showdown. For four days Khrushchev held out while Bulganin's guards barred the doors to his supporters among the candidate members of the Presidium and the Central Committee. The majority also tried to prevent Khrushchev from communicating with his reinforcements, and there were bitter exchanges. But with the support of Zhukov and some younger members he managed to call together a Central Committee session. His very defiance shattered the confidence and solidarity of the majority. By the time the Central Committee had assembled on June 22 several of the original opponents had shifted sides. With overwhelming party backing, Khrushchev swept the Central Committee vote. Molotov, Malenkov, Kaganovich and Shepilov were stripped of their posts and expelled from the Central Committee. Molotov was shipped out to become Ambassador to Outer Mongolia. Malenkov was given charge of a power station in Siberia, Kaganovich of a cement factory in the Urals. Others were demoted. Bulganin and Voroshilov were not even affected for the moment, which suggests that they were the first Presidium members to shift back to Khrushchev. Nine new members, all Khrushchev supporters, were brought into the Presidium, which was now expanded to fifteen members.[100]

In due course all who had voted against Khrushchev lost their places in the Presidium, including his old partner Bulganin. But one other figure had to be purged swiftly. This was Marshal Zhukov, whose support had been *too* important in Khrushchev's success. Following the showdown, Zhukov was voted a full member of the Presidium, the first career Army man in the top leadership in Soviet history. Just four months later, while the victor of Stalingrad and Berlin was making a visit to Yugoslavia, Moscow announced that he had been dismissed from membership in the Presidium and Central Committee for permitting a "cult of personality" to grow up around him in the Soviet Army. Thus Khrushchev's monopoly of power had begun.[101]

What, amidst the raddled events of the mid-1950s, was to be said for the art of human communication by which the twentieth century, in both the technological and interpersonal senses, set such store? Was there no room left, between the threats of thermonuclear dust, for East-West diplomatic give-and-take? Must each side grow more unyielding, each seeming a monster to the other, with no means of communication? The Russian leadership, having boldly set out to accommodate their absolutist regime to certain long-denied private wants in their society, had found themselves in some very tight spots where diplomatic exchanges for relaxing international tensions might have seemed in order. But in these same years America had taken off on its flight of "studied lunacy," engineering a fabulous binge for the mindless requiting of the material wants of its private citizens, of the profit-greed of its private corporations, that left the nation's eye dulled to such opportunities. Lost in a sleazy materialism at home, paralyzed by a strategy of massive retaliation abroad, the American nation had nothing meaningful to say when "monolithic" Eastern Europe appeared to be cracking in 1956.

In such circumstances passivity is taken for powerlessness. The Russians, without letting up on their drive to renovate Soviet society, now began to expand their power and influence into places where they had never been felt before—into a vast new theater of the Cold War. This had spectacular results at Suez. In the longer run, however, the failure of American diplomacy to turn the events in East Germany in 1953 and in Poland and Hungary in 1956 to occasions for East-West negotiations led to new East-West crises climaxed by the placement of Russian missiles in Cuba in 1962.

CHAPTER 9

The Disintegration
of White Supremacy

THE SUEZ CRISIS AND THE EMERGENCE OF THE THIRD WORLD

As early as 1949, when President Truman was preparing to take the oath of office for his second term, many Americans felt that the United States should embark on a worldwide offensive against Communism. A State Department official, Robert Woodward, not only thought so but had some specific ideas about what the offensive should be. For a number of years the United States had been giving technical assistance to Latin American countries, with a view to speeding up industrialization. Why not expand this notion to all non-Communist undeveloped parts of the world?

Just when the State Department tabled the suggestion for further study, White House counselor Clark Clifford, telephoning around for ideas for the President's inaugural address, heard about Woodward's proposal and seized on it. When he prepared a draft of the inaugural address, the speech centered upon four points of foreign policy and Woodward's proposal was Number Four. High State Department officials argued that the passage was vague and premature. But Truman was enthusiastic, and it remained in the address.

On Inauguration Day the President spoke almost entirely about the Cold War. Near the end he said that America's foreign policy rested upon four props. The first was the United Nations, the second was the Marshall Plan, and the third was NATO. When he came to the fourth point his gravelly voice took on an emphatic edge. The United States, he said, should now embark upon:

> a bold new program for making the benefits of our scientific and industrial programs available for the improvement and growth of underdeveloped areas.

He did not spell out the program in detail because nobody quite knew what the details were, but the proposal that the mighty industrial superpower that produced more than a third of the world's goods should share its technical know-how made a big splash in the world's headlines. The newspapers dubbed the idea simply Point Four.[1]

The idea behind Point Four was this: that with American aid and self-help, non-Western nations could embark on programs of economic development that could ultimately deliver to them the kind of material well-being for their citizens that they could see being enjoyed by the people of America. Gradually and democratically achieved, the resulting economic advance would be seen to be self-evidently superior to lock-stepped, terror-driven progress in totalitarian Russia.

Despite some heady speeches about a "Marshall Plan for Asia" and a "TVA for the Yangtse," the new program began slowly and modestly. It was not until halfway through 1950 that Congress got round to voting the first $45 million. The United States was to supply the knowledge and the technicians—engineers, teachers, public health experts, economists, agronomists—and the recipient nations, possibly with the help of various international bodies, were to supply capital and workers for local improvement projects. By 1953 the Technical Cooperation Administration had a budget of $155.6 million and projects going in 33 countries. By then the United States found itself entering upon a new stage of the Cold War —the struggle for power and influence in what the French demographer Alfred Sauvy in 1952 first called the Third World.[2]

Seven years after the end of the Second World War the Cold War race to fill in the vacuum left by the defeat of Germany and Japan had ended at a kind of standoff in Berlin and Korea, and the competition now showed signs of turning into a scramble for the rest of the world. By and large these were the colonial lands of Asia and Africa long dominated by Europe. These new nations were made up of nonwhite peoples keenly sensitive to any signs of the white man's imperialism they had just cast off. Watch out, cried Franz Fanon, the Martinique-born Tom Paine of the awakening races, for "colonialism withdrawing its capital and technicians and setting up around the young State the apparatus of economic pressure."

To fight Communism the United States had already had to give up its cherished resistance to a large standing army and to entangling foreign alliances. To hold its own against the Communists among the emerging, postcolonial peoples of the Middle East, Asia and Africa, still other traditions and policies rooted deep in the country's past must give way. One was the doctrine of legal separation of blacks and whites. If the United States now judged security its supreme problem in a world that was two-thirds nonwhite, then for it to go on handling its race problem at home by official discrimination against blacks was untenable. Legal segregation of the races in modern America would have to go. Just as the Cold War drove the nation to put down its profoundly antimilitarist instincts and enact a peacetime draft, so the national interest of an America widely engaged in the world demanded that it overcome its rawest prejudices and get rid of the laws branding twenty million blacks second-class citizens.

The necessity of facing up to such a change, and the shocks and dislocations of trying to evade and accommodate to it, were probably the most wrenching effects wrought upon America by the Cold War. Not even waging all-out war upon a blatantly racist regime in Nazi Germany had seemingly altered the inveterate disposition of white Americans to think about their black countrymen, when they thought about them at all, as irresponsible and not readily educable, and to treat them, in law and in fact, more or less as children. But the meaning of the war against Hitlerite racism was not lost on blacks. There had been movements in the South that had been suppressed. Even before 1945, moving north where they could vote, blacks began to exert rising pressure against the white-supremacy system. During the Second World War, President Roosevelt reluctantly set up a Fair Employment Practices Commission that opened their way to jobs in wartime industries and government agencies.

The emergence of blacks in sports was an important ostwar change. What kind of a national pastime was baseball if it left out a fifth of all Americans, asked Branch Rickey, general manager of the Brooklyn Dodgers. One day in 1946 without announcement Rickey simply sent Jackie Robinson out to play second base for the Dodgers. Robinson had been an outstanding black athlete at the University of California in Los Angeles. He was picked for the taboo-smashing role not because he was the best player but because, Rickey had satisfied himself, he could take abuse and would not fight back. Helping win a pennant, he swiftly demonstrated that blacks could assimilate without posing a threat. Others followed who did not have to be so meek—Larry Doby, Joe Black, Roy Campanella, Willie Mays, and other stars in other sports.[3]

After the war another factor began to influence the mind of the South and its insistence upon embedding racial discrimination in law. On the wave of unprecedented prosperity after 1945 the big corporations expanded into the South. Something like one-fourth of the country's new plants were built there, where unions were weak or non-existent, and Southern communities competed to attract them with special tax concessions and gifts of factory sites. Around the new industries new middle-class elements grew up—lawyers, doctors, insurance and service suppliers, enginpers—who saw the South's future in terms of business growth. These people brought out the vote that carried four states for Eisenhower in 1952; they were the new Republicans of the South, conservatives in national issues, moderates on race. Many of the corporate executives, salesmen and investors who arrived from the North and West tended to be impatient with all local folkways that impeded the conforming dynamics of large-scale organization. In big business the prevailing view was that all its priorities converged in supporting the Marshall Plan and building up the defense establishment against international Communism. In 1947, the year that President Truman proclaimed these goals, he appointed a National Commission on Civil Rights under the former president of General Electric, Charles E. Wilson (sometimes referred to as "Electric Charlie" Wilson to distinguish him from "Engine Charlie" Wilson, president of General Motors). The commission reported racial discrimination in the South "intolerable" and urged measures to outlaw it.[4]

When Truman and his party endorsed the proposals in the 1948 campaign, new black voters in Illinois, Pennsylvania and Ohio helped him win reelection. But leading Southern Democrats in Congress bolted the party and carried four states against him. For years thereafter the Cold War abroad was complicated by an impasse in Washington. Southern legislators dominating all key committees bottled up civil rights measures, and talked to death by filibuster any bill that chanced to reach the Senate floor. Moreover, when General Eisenhower, as Chief of Staff, was asked his opinion about desegregating the armed forces, he opposed it.

> The human race . . . may finally grow up to the point where race will not be a problem. But if we attempt merely by passing a lot of laws to force someone to like someone else, we are just going to get into trouble.[5]

Largely because of the Korean War, in which black draftees were expected to fight against nonwhite Asians, Truman proceeded by executive order to desegregate the armed forces over a three-year period. Yet as the Cold War approached its peak, the normal processes and institutions of government seemed unable to concert the action against officially sanctioned segregation at home that America's international thrust demanded. In the event, however, that the usual instrumentalities of political action become hopelessly stalled, the machinery of American government provides a way to break the jam. When the executive and legislative branches prove unable to act on problems of overriding national importance, the judicial arm may sometimes intervene. This was what happened when Congress and President failed to deal with the race question in the 1950s.

Unable to obtain redress any other way, black leaders of the National Association for the Advancement of Colored People had brought suits in federal courts. A number of these cases appealed against local laws requiring racial segregation in public schools. It was their contention that segregated schools could not possibly provide equal educational opportunities for black children. Some Southern states spent three times as much per white pupil as they did for each black child. They were therefore unconstitutional. By 1953 several such cases (most memorably *Brown v. Board of Education of Topeka, Kansas*) had reached the Supreme Court, and shortly before he left office President Truman directed that the Justice Department lend a helping hand in the presentation of these cases. On behalf of the Executive, Secretary of State Acheson filed a formal declaration with the Court as follows:

> The segregation of school children on a racial basis is one of the practices in the United States which has been singled out for comment in the United Nations and elsewhere. Other peoples cannot understand how such a practice can exist in a country which professes to be a staunch supporter of freedom, justice and democracy. The sincerity of the United States in this respect will be judged by its deeds as well as its words.[6]

The cases were before the Court when the Eisenhower administration assumed office. Later that year, upon the death of Chief Justice Fred Vinson, President Eisenhower named Earl Warren, the Republican governor of California, to be head of the Supreme Court. The importance of this appointment was crucial. It was now the Republicans who were prosecuting the Cold War and no matter how indifferent its record with respect to black rights in the days of Hayes and McKinley, the Republican party was after all the party of Abraham Lincoln and the party that had placed guarantees of citizenship rights for blacks in Constitution.

In May 1954 the Supreme Court handed down its opinion, delivered by Chief Justice Warren and unanimous:

> We cannot turn back the clock. We must consider public education in the light of its full development and its present position in American

life ... today [as] perhaps the most important function of state and local governments. . . . In these days it is doubtful that any child may reasonably be expected to succeed in life if he is denied the opportunity of an education. Such an education, where the state has undertaken to provide it, is a right which must be available to all on equal terms. We come then to the question presented: Does segregation of children in public schools solely on the basis of race, even though the physical facilities and other 'tangible' factors may be equal, deprive the child of the minority group of equal educational opportunities? We believe that it does. . . .

To separate children in grade and high schools from others of similar age and qualifications solely because of their race generates a feeling of inferiority as to their status in the community that may affect their hearts and minds in a way unlikely ever to be undone. . . .

We conclude that in the field of public education the doctrine of 'separate but equal' has no place. Separate educational facilities are inherently unequal.[7]

On the day the Supreme Court declared segregation in the South unlawful, the Savannah, Georgia chapter of the Rotary was holding a luncheon meeting. When a news flash of the Court's decision was read to the group there was a burst of applause. Few of the members seemed much concerned. "Just what I expected," said one Rotarian. "It's a good thing," said another.[8] From the Deep South such might have been described as a Cold War reaction: in the kind of world contest the United States was then engaged in, the Supreme Court had made the consensus kind of decision that the national interest required. The decision, moveover, met the developing needs of big business—not only because an expanding economy was assured by the nation's international commitments, but also because Corporate America was growing to the continental size and scale where its structural efficiency was beginning to demand that members have interchangeable parts, North and South. For such large and rationally conceived organizations, it was a hindrance, an inconvenience, a kind of frictional dysfunction in the smoothly planned and managed corporate system, to meet up with these local idiosyncrasies about race. In the progress of the huge bureaucracies of American business, a racial reaction from the South was apt to seem a foot outthrust in their path.

For the management professional stepping out of a plane from the North it was a pain in the neck not to be able to move with unguarded ease in these Southern cities, having to take care in his speech, keep to the segregated channels, and put up with arbitrary local customs. The Southern salesman also knew that he could not expect to be promoted up the ladder to sales manager and sent north to the other rewards that belonged to membership in the large company if he had to be hobbled by the bonds of these eccentrically local ways. In every local Chamber of Commerce or Rotary Club it was known that Textron or Fine Foods or Rand McNally, Motorola or Westinghouse or Campbell Soup, all wanted to open plants to take advantage of the manpower and markets in Southern cities, and they would not want to be bothered with this cluttering racism.[9]

What went wrong? The effect of this Supreme Court decision, at first casually received, proved to be profoundly upsetting—at first to the South and ultimately to other parts of the country too. Both Presidents Eisenhower and Kennedy were later to say that they would have preferred that the blacks of the nation had made their bid for equality by going first for the vote in the South rather than for integration in the schools. *Brown v. Board of Education* held that the Constitution protected all Americans equally, regardless of race, and that was disturbing enough to those who thought the racial double standard part of the natural order. But the Court, citing "the findings of social science," had gone farther and declared that the black's inferiority was not congenital but induced. Thus in attacking segregated schools, the Court struck at the attitudes—those deep-seated assumptions that blacks were shiftless, lazy, irresponsible and deserving of inferior status—which had justified segregation. This shocked a great many people who still believed that the black's lesser role in society was due to his own shortcomings rather than anything the whites had done.

The effect of the Supreme Court decision was to challenge the Southern whites' assumption, shared by many Northerners, that black Americans were satisfied with the way things were, and were receiving all the opportunities they should expect. Although the citizens of the United States had probably ordained the decision the day they resolved to destroy a German regime founded on the master-race principle, the shock when its meaning struck home was profound. The decision forced white Americans to think about just where they stood on the race question and its implications in a way they had not thought about it since Reconstruction days nearly a century before.

Every sort of buried, banned, avoided, disregarded and decried question out of America's sorry racial past was brought uncomfortably up to date by the confronting impact of the Court's words: Whom—whites asked themselves—do you expect to see riding beside you on the bus or train? Whom would you be willing to see working in the office next to yours? Whom would you wish to see living in the house next door? Whom do you invite into your home after 5:00 P.M.? Whom do you expect your children to play with? Whom do you look for your daughter to date? In the black dramatist Lorraine Hansberry's Broadway play of 1959, *Raisin in the Sun,* the black family learns that when they try to move from a Chicago tenement to the suburbs their prospective white neighbors rush to buy the home to keep them out.

> BENEATHA, *the daughter:*   "What do they think we going to do—eat 'em?"
> HER MOTHER: "No, honey, marry 'em."[10]

Indeed the questions that came to be raised after 1954 asked Americans to make up their minds about all sorts of new questions that brooked no bland answers. Would you want to pay taxes to support not only your aged parents but *all* people who need public assistance? What do you think of the police when these officers seek to break up disturbances by people living in wretched, overcrowded urban ghettos? What do you think of the courts that bring such questions into the open? What do you think of the political system that permits these questions to be propounded in terms of whether black children shall be bussed into your local schools? In the next years and decades, the Supreme Court decision opened the door to criticism of the very institutions of the land.

One result of the Court's striking down the white supremacy principle in law at this moment was to give the radicals a legitimate reason to act radical again after the repressive times of McCarthyism. Not at once, but increasingly in the late 1950s, the old dissenters who had been driven out by the Grand Inquisition began to make their reappearance delivering speeches, writing leaflets and singing folk songs in a cause blessed by the highest judicial authority in the land—the civil rights movement. Cracking the Cold War mold of social impassivity, the court had opened the way to the activism that burst through in the 1960s.

Before the social wave set off by the 1954 decision passed its crest, there were signs along the highways, and not only in the South, saying —as if he were personally responsible—"Impeach Earl Warren." Before it ended, the violence used in the South to disrupt the lawful desegregation of the schools instructed the whole nation in how to be destructive about other issues later: the disruptions by students on the left in the 1960s were the product of disruptions by racists on the right in the 1950s.

Among the Southern Democratic elders of the United States Senate who had stonewalled against every move to uphold the Negro rights amendments enacted after the Civil War, the reaction was wrathful. For the diehard white supremacists Senator James Eastland of Mississippi rasped that "the South will not abide by or obey" the Court's "legislative decision." Senator Harry Byrd, bourbon boss of Virginia, vowed to fight back against "the most serious blow that has been struck against the rights of the states." Before long 111 Southern congressmen signed a Southern Manifesto for "massive resistance" against school integration. In a pivotal pronouncement Senator Richard Russell of Georgia, most influential of Southern leaders, noted General Eisenhower's stand against desegregation before his Armed Services Committee earlier, and confidently condemned the Court for "a flagrant abuse of judicial power."[11]

Behind these roars from the region's most responsible spokesmen, racism swung into action. The Georgia legislature rushed through a resolution revoking the license of any teacher who taught mixed classes. Rather than comply with the Court's ruling Prince Edward County, Virginia, abolished its public schools and set up a private system. The Ku Klux Klan sprang to life, and drew a crowd of 10,000 to a protest meeting in Spartansburg, South Carolina. Klaverns were organized, crosses burned. But the white-hooded Klan, with its propensity for lynchings, now had a bad name in the South; it was the White Citizens' Councils that took the lead in organizing defiance of the Court decision. The first such council was formed at Indianola, Mississippi, by a delta plantation manager and quickly signed up 100 members. Within weeks there were councils in seventeen counties, by October 80,000 members in Mississippi alone. The leading spirit was Judge Thomas P. Brady, a planter later elected to Mississippi's supreme court. His pamphlet *Black Monday*, dashed off the day after Earl Warren read the desegregation decision, affirmed that "the social, political, economic and religious preferences of the Negro remain close to the caterpillar and cockroach." For the next decade it was the handbook of the gun-toting, bomb-throwing white supremacists who patrolled the rural South in pickup trucks equipped with two-way radios.[12]

At this moment the President, had he thrown the power of the executive arm and the immense authority of his leadership behind the Court's ruling as vital to the national interest, might yet have swung his countrymen into line, and established the basis by which the party of Lincoln built up majorities needed in the urban North to consolidate control of Congress. That such considerations were present was to be seen in his prompt order to carry out desegregation in the Washington schools, and in the determination of Attorney General Brownell, the President's chief election strategist, to bring in a civil rights bill to enforce the Court's ruling before his 1956 campaign. But the President, born in Dennison, Texas, in the Old Confederacy, and persuaded moreover that he could hold himself above the battle, held back. He refused to express either "approbation or disapproval" of the Supreme Court's decision until the day he published his memoirs in 1965. Only then did he say: "There can be no question that the judgment of the Court was right."[13]

THE BATTLE for equal rights in the South was fought out on far wider fronts than any rednecks in pickup trucks could patrol and with weapons effective at far longer range than planters' shotguns. Nothing better exemplified the changing circumstances of Southern racial conflict than the events in Montgomery, Alabama, in 1955, when the moral force of the Third World—the militantly pacifist tactics by which Gandhi led India's fight for independence—was unexpectedly brought to bear by oppressed blacks standing up for dignity and common justice.

Like everything else in Montgomery, "Cradle of the American Confederacy," the public buses were still rigidly segregated a year after the Supreme Court had spoken. Then one evening in November after a hard day's work, Mrs. Rosa Parks, a black seamstress in the Alabama capital, boarded a bus and sat down in the first vacant seat. When the bus filled and the driver asked Mrs. Parks to move to the rear of the bus and give her seat to a white man, an unheard-of thing happened. Did the thought suddenly cross her consciousness just then of a Hitler lately brought low by the mustered might of the United States and most of mankind? Could she have been momentarily mindful of an Israel newly risen out of travail old as the Bible to stand free with the eager help of her country? She suddenly decided she was too tired to move. When she refused to give up her seat, she was arrested for disturbing the peace. Within hours word spread among Montgomery's blacks, and that night a group of twenty-five met to do something about it.

They not only raised bail to free Mrs. Parks. In a burst of indignation they voted on the spot to form the Montgomery Improvement Association, rally the community's 50,000 blacks, the principal patrons of the city's privately-owned busline, and boycott the buses until their facilities were open equally to all without discrimination because of race. As their president they elected the broad-browed young minister of the Dexter Avenue Baptist Church, Reverend Martin Luther King, Jr.[14]

In the South the churches were traditionally the areas of greatest autonomy for blacks. Dr. King was twenty-five. By birth and upbringing, by training and outlook, he was the man for the job. Born in Atlanta, he had grown up under the powerful influence of his father, pastor of Atlanta's leading black congregation and one of the most forthright and forceful of all black clergymen. On one memorable occasion in Atlanta's Jim Crow days, a shoe clerk had declined to serve Dr. King unless he and his small son moved to the rear of the store. "We'll either buy shoes sitting here or we won't buy any shoes at all," growled the minister, and marched his boy toward the door.

At Crozier Theological Seminary near Philadelphia, and at Boston University, Martin Luther King Jr. took his doctor's degree and mastered the revolutionary essence of Gandhi's pacifist "soul-force" techniques for eradicating evil by direct action. The Gandhian ideas were especially suited to the South, where the white majority held such a preponderance of force that violence by blacks would have been self-defeating. When King took the lead in Montgomery, probably no one else in the movement had heard of Gandhi. But they soon did. King was a preacher and teacher after his father's heart, steadfast and far-seeing, a leader of men.[15]

In their tense and painful struggle, the blacks of Montgomery endured arrests and insults and beatings. King told them to stand up for their rights but never to return violence for violence.

> Don't ever let anyone pull you so low as to hate them [he said]. We must use the weapon of love. We must have compassion and understanding for those who hate us. We must realize that so many people are taught to hate us that they are not totally responsible for their hate.

The maids and the cooks of Montgomery knew that they were part of a world affair. King was quick to make the link in his sermons and speeches with the struggle of the Egyptians, the Indians, the West Africans to free themselves from white colonialism. "The Red Sea has opened," he proclaimed. "The oppressed masses of Asia and Africa," having won their freedom as independent nonwhite countries, were now moving in concert with the oppressed of America toward the same "promised land of economic and cultural stability." The boycott went on for a year, and then was finally upheld by the courts. King was a hero, his jailing and the bombing of his home at the hands of the white supremacists reported along with his triumphant vindication in the South, the North and the Third World.[16]

W H E N President Eisenhower won reelection in 1956, one factor in the contest that caught the attention of Attorney General Herbert Brownell and other experts was the black vote. An examination of the results in big Northern cities persuaded many observers in both parties that with 3,500,000 blacks going to the polls and casting some 5.6% of the total turnout, the black vote was now substantial and that the traditional Northern black vote for the Democrats, very possibly because of the Supreme Court decision and the Administration's civil rights bill, showed signs of shifting toward the Republicans. In the South fewer than a million blacks voted in eleven states, but they swung heavily Republican and were credited with delivering Tennessee and Louisiana for the first time to the President. Eisenhower allowed Attorney General Brownell to resubmit his civil rights bill to Congress.[17]

Democrats controlled the new Congress, but some of them too read signs of change. In the Senate, Majority Leader Johnson made the move of his political life. A Texan who had never cast anything but a segregationist vote in his entire career, Johnson suddenly detached himself from the Southern bloc. With the argument that the Republican-Dixiecrat alliance was crumbling, he persuaded Senator Russell to head off a Southern filibuster for once. Meanwhile in cloakroom and committee he attended to the defanging of the Administration's bill. Out went any suggestion that the Congress of the United States uphold the Court's order for desegregation of the schools. Eisenhower had had the notion that the right to vote was a civil rights area less sensitive than schools, jobs or housing, and a good place to make the necessary moves against discrimination first. The Senate took out the bill's mild provisions for aiding the right to vote too. That left only the innocuous provisions for a Civil Rights division in the Justice Department and creation of a permanent Civil Rights Commission. Shorn to the last calculated millimeter to get the votes for passage, the first Civil Rights law since 1876 was shepherded through by Lyndon Johnson. But the process enforced by the Cold War was under way. Less than eight years later the same Lyndon Johnson would be pushing his fourth civil rights bill through Congress and proclaiming in a presidential address the words of the old cotton-picker's field song: "We shall overcome."[18]

In the maneuvering over the Civil Rights Act of 1957, however, segregationists began to believe that President Eisenhower had no heart for a showdown struggle on reinforcement. Some Southern governors talked of using their own police powers to block compliance with the Court's ruling. In July the general was telling his press conference, with astonishing lack of foresight: "I can't imagine any set of circumstances that would ever induce me to send federal troops into an area to enforce the orders of a federal court." When Martin Luther King wrote him asking him to visit the South and speak against segregation his comment was: "I don't know what good another speech would do right now." These were the days when the word went round that the President had called his appointment of Earl Warren to the Court "the worst mistake I ever made."[19]

In an amplification of its original ruling the Supreme Court had directed local authorities to prepare desegregation plans "with deliberate speed" and submit them to federal courts for approval. In the fall of 1957 the school board of Little Rock, Arkansas, put into effect its court-approved plan for gradual desegregation of the city's schools—high schools in 1957, junior high schools in 1960, elementary schools in 1963. To start with, just nine black pupils were to enter Central High, which had a hitherto all-white enrollment of 2000.

Unbeknownst to Little Rock, the governor of the state had other ideas. Orval Faubus had never been a race-baiter; in fact he had been elected as a moderate. He was born in 1910 in the little town of Combs in the Ozarks. Rising from humble beginnings, he made a creditable record as state highway commissioner, and as governor exemplified the generation of the New South that consciously sought to build up the region by bringing in industry from the North. An urbane and personable executive, he had accepted the the Supreme Court ruling. His was not a state of the Deep South. But two weeks before the schools opened Governor Marvin Griffin of Georgia, accompanied by Roy Harris, leader of the white-supremacist Citizens Council movement, swooped down on Little Rock. Addressing 350 members of the capital's Citizens Council about the "steadfast" resistance to school desegregation in his state, he proclaimed amid a chorus of rebel yells that to uphold racial discrimination he would "enlist every white man in Georgia." There was an uneasy stir in Little Rock, whose mayor, school board and representative in Congress were all strongly committed to the school plan. A state election was in the offing.

Under these circumstances, Governor Faubus came down on the side of the white supremacists. The night before schools were to open he made an unexpected appearance on television. In a speech that practically invited a riot the next day, the hitherto moderate governor asserted that it would "not be possible to restore or maintain order if forcible integration is carried out in the capital." He announced that he was directing the Arkansas National Guard to take station at the school. Next day 270 Guardsmen and a muttering crowd were at the schoolhouse door but not one black child appeared. Instead the school board went before Federal District Judge Ronald N. Davies—serving in Little Rock temporarily on assignment from North Dakota—and Judge Davies ordered the plan carried out "forthwith."

The following day the first of the nine black children approached the school. A Guardsman barred the door. Elizabeth Eckford, fifteen, then had to walk back down a long sidewalk lined by white adults screaming: "The niggers won't get in." She finally reached a bench at a bus stop and sat down. A white woman went over to comfort her. "What are you doing, you nigger-lover?" yelled a voice from the mob. The two finally got on a bus and left.

In Washington President Eisenhower repeated his statement that "you cannot change people's hearts merely by laws" and headed for his vacation at Newport. But the white-supremacist challenge had been accepted. On the basis of reports from FBI agents sent to the scene, the Justice Department asked Judge Davies to enjoin Governor Faubus from interfering with the court-approved plan. With the hearing set for ten days on, Faubus wired Eisenhower that he was being "investigated," his telephone tapped, and he was in danger of being taken "into custody, by force." Press Secretary Hagerty brought the telegram to Eisenhower at the Newport Country Club as the President holed out his putt on the first green. Sitting down in the golf cart with Hagerty, the general dictated a reply inviting Faubus to Newport. The governor duly appeared, Eisenhower talked to him, and afterward both issued complimentary statements. But Faubus did not remove the Guardsmen.

On September 20 Judge Davies granted the injunction against Governor Faubus. Next day, with the Guardsmen gone, the nine children slipped in a side door at Central High. But a crowd of a thousand white supremacists shouting "The niggers are in our school" and "Lynch them all" forced the authorities to call off classes by midday. By then there were fights inside the school as parents broke in to fetch their children. Newsmen were attacked and beaten.

The Governor's defiance had left the President with no other recourse than to act, and he now acted decisively. Flying to Washington, he went on nationwide television to condemn the "disgraceful occurrence" at Little Rock and to issue a proclamation calling upon those who had resisted federal law "to cease and desist." But next morning a crowd still milled around at Central High, and no black children entered the school. Thereupon the President took the ultimate action—one that he had two months before brushed aside as unimaginable. He ordered a thousand parachute troopers into Little Rock to put down the mob and at the same time placed all 10,000 members of the Arkansas National Guard on federal service.

For the first time since Reconstruction days, federal troops were thus sent into the South to protect the rights of blacks. The nine black children reentered Central High next day, this time escorted by 1,000 members of the 101st Airborne Division. For the remainder of the year desegregation went on at Central High with federal troops holding back jeering crowds. Following withdrawal of the troops Governor Faubus kept all high schools in Little Rock closed to prevent "impending violence and disaster." Then the mood seemed to shift. A federal court found the school-closing regulations unconstitutional, and on August 12, 1959, Elizabeth Eckford, who had walked so bravely through the mob two years before, made the trip to Central High again. Again there was a mob, but this time Little Rock police sternly maintained order. The crowds and the sidewalk insults gradually faded, and token desegregation of the Little Rock schools was peacefully accomplished. William P. Rogers, the new Attorney General, told Southern governors that desegregation was "inevitable." The entrenched opposition of Southern leaders in Congress staved off implementing legislation year after year, and legal segregation of schools was not substantially ended in the South until 1970.[20]

B U T   T H E   blacks of the South would not wait. Stirred by the "winds of change" that Prime Minister Macmillan reported sweeping Africa and the rest of the Third World, Martin Luther King cried out: "The whole world will be free before one of us can get a hamburger wherever he wants it." On February 1, 1960, four black freshmen at North Carolina Agricultural and Technical College in Greensboro used a device that had been tried many years earlier by black protesters. Taking seats at the local Woolworth's lunch counter, they simply sat there waiting for service until the store closed. This time the sit-in idea caught fire. Overnight it spread to fifty other Southern cities. At Nashville, Candie Anderson went to McClellan's variety store:

> We climbed over the rope. A policeman stood there and said quite clearly, 'Do not sit down,' and we sat down. . . . Young kids threw french fried potatoes at us, and gum and cigarette butts. The policemen simply lined up behind us and peeled us two by two off the stools. . . . The crowd in the store shouted out approval. Three paddy wagons were blinking at us from the street. Once more we have to walk through those crowds. Someone spit right in front of me. . . . The TV cameras took lots of pictures and we drove off to jail.

At Orangeburg, South Carolina a thousand students preparing to integrate lunch counters were schooled in nonviolence ("To prevent disfigurement of the face, bring the elbows together before the eyes"). Teargassed, drenched with firehoses, bludgeoned and locked up, the students sang like early Christian martyrs in their jails. It was a movement of the young. "We were not pleased with the acquiescent leadership of the adults," said Joseph McNeil, one of the Greensboro four. And as the fight to desegregate schools never did, the sit-ins brought out large numbers of blacks; an estimated 70,000 people sat in during 1960 in Southern restaurants and stores; 3,600 were arrested. Impatience was the mood. "The pace of social change is too slow," said James Lawson Jr., elected president of the Student Nonviolent Coordinating Committee at Raleigh in April. Everybody knew that 1960 was the year that a dozen African nations were gaining independence. "All of Africa will be free before we attain first-class citizenship," cried Lawson.[21]

Hailing the students Martin Luther King formed the Southern Christian Leadership Conference in their support. Late in 1960, near the end of the presidential election campaign, King and thirty-six others, mostly students, were arrested in Atlanta while trying to integrate a lunch counter. King was brought to court in handcuffs and sentenced to four months' hard labor in the state penitentiary.

As King was carried off to prison, telegrams deluged the White House demanding intervention. The President remained silent and Vice President Nixon, not sure whether a statement would do more electoral harm than good, declined to comment. Senator Kennedy however telephoned Mrs. King to say that he knew this was a trying period, and when his brother Robert telephoned the judge next day to ask whether bail would be allowed, the astonished judge consented to a plea by King's lawyer for his release. That Sunday Martin Luther King's father, a lifelong Republican who had already endorsed Nixon's candidacy, shouted from his pulpit: "I've got a suitcase of votes and I'm going to take them to Mr. Kennedy and drop them in his lap." Since Kennedy carried the election by a bare 112,881 votes there is little question that his "instinctive decision," as Theodore H. White wrote, "must be ranked among the most crucial" of the campaign. Said President Eisenhower's black White House aide, Frederick Morrow: "This won the election."[22]

Yet the very narrowness of Kennedy's victory fortified Southern resistance in Congress, cooled off the new President's civil rights ardor and ensured that racial segregation by law would not be terminated before the Cold War's end. When young black militants of the Congress of Racial Equality organized freedom rides to expose racial segregation in Southern bus terminals, Attorney General Robert Kennedy sought to dissuade them. When the riders went ahead,

> One bus halted at Anniston [Ala.] with a flat tire was attacked and burned by white men. Ten passengers were hospitalized. On Wednesday Birmingham police took into protective custody ten Tennessee college students, most of them Negro, when bus drivers refused to drive them to Montgomery on a regular bus. Seven were taken from jail in the middle of the night and were driven to the Tennessee line, but they soon returned. Yesterday morning after camping all night in the station amid rising tension they boarded a bus for Montgomery. Their arrival in the capital set off a two-hour melee. A mob of white men and women howling "Get them niggers" beat and kicked the white and Negro students, clubbed newsmen and severely injured a Justice Department representative who was trying to protect a girl from the mob.

Only after a mob threatened to overwhelm federal marshals sent in by the Justice Department to protect riders meeting with local blacks to hear a speech by Martin Luther King did Governor John Patterson order out the Alabama National Guard to head off any bloodshed. Next day,

> a convoy snaked across the gently rolling plain of the Alabama Black Belt like an armored battalion penetrating enemy territory. Motorized National Guard units scouted the road ahead and reconnaissance aircraft wheeled overhead. Well back in the column of forty-two vehicles a huge red-and-white Trailways bus purred smoothly along behind state highway patrol cruisers. The eleven freedom riders aboard, one white and ten Negroes, threw back their heads and sang with forced gaiety:

> > *"Hallelujah, I'm traveling*
> > *Hallelujah, ain't it fine,*
> > *Hallelujah, I'm traveling*
> > *Down Freedom's main line."*

Bruised and bandaged the Riders rolled on into Mississippi, and were promptly arrested as they tried to enter the white waiting room at Jackson. All summer long students kept arriving, and police kept arresting them. "The Negro is determined to push and push until segregation is ended," proclaimed Martin Luther King. That fall, in the annual United Nations debate on the admission of Communist China the Russian delegate said tartly: "If the way citizens are treated is a basis for membership in the United Nations, then the United States should be voted out of that body for her treatment of Negroes." On November 1, after Secretary of State Rusk had asked action in the national interest, the Interstate Commerce Commission banned segregation in all interstate buses, trains and terminals.[23]

The Kennedy administration, like its predecessor, favored voter registration over civil disobedience as the road to black freedom in the South —and to its own future there. With financial support from foundations, the young militants threw themselves into registering voters in the Deep South. Though forty-three per cent of Mississippi's population was black, only five per cent voted; not one held political office. In Waltham County John Hardy, a black college student from Nashville, set up a voters' school to help applicants bone up for interpreting the long and complicated state constitution to the satisfaction of the county registrar, John Q. Wood.

> On September 7, 1961, Hardy accompanied two Negro residents of the county, Mrs. Edith S. Peters and Lucius Wilson, down to Wood's office. Hardy waited outside while the two applicants went in. Wood flatly refused to let them apply. Hearing this Hardy walked in and introduced himself politely. But he was not able to say much more than his name.

Registrar Wood pulled a gun out of a desk drawer and ordered Hardy to leave. As Hardy turned around and started to walk out, Wood hit him on the back of the head with the gun, swore at him and told him never to come back. Mrs. Peters and Wilson, who had watched the whole episode, helped Hardy out of the courthouse. His head was bleeding profusely and he was staggering. After resting for a few minutes Hardy found the county sheriff Edd Craft and told him what had happened. Craft arrested Hardy for breach of the peace.[24]

In the spring of 1963 Martin Luther King decided that the time had come to make a strong effort to change the segregated pattern of life in Birmingham, the South's leading industrial city, numbering 150,000 blacks (forty per cent of the population). Birmingham was dominated by a huge complex of United States Steel plants and other big industrial and commercial establishments. The city government, just voted out in favor of more moderate leaders, responded to the first sit-ins with force. As a representative of diehard white-supremacist disintegration, Police Commissioner Eugene (Bull) Connor was all that King could have asked as an adversary. Using police dogs, cattle prods and firehoses against the black protesters, he arrested 150 and banned further marches without license. Thereupon King announced that kneel-ins would take place on the steps of all white churches on Easter Sunday. For this Bull Connor, with police dogs snapping in front of massed television cameras, subjected King to his twelfth arrest since he went to the aid of Mrs. Parks in Montgomery eight years before. Released on bail, King worked to keep the blacks united, the eyes of America trained on the scene and the moderates in the government moving toward a compromise. Each day there were minor demonstrations, and Bull Connor, refusing to relinquish his job, kept making arrests. King sent children to demonstrate saying: "Children face the stinging darts of segregation as well as adults." Soon Connor had arrested 3,000.

By May 2, 1963, things had turned ugly. Bricks and bottles were thrown, police dogs loosed on the marchers. Streams of water from firehoses bowled over black children. "We are ready to negotiate," said King, "but we intend to negotiate from strength. We want promises plus action." By now his words were addressed to Washington as much as to the officials of Birmingham. Deputy Attorney General Burke Marshall arrived, and a truce was called. Then there was another big march, and a thousand were arrested, nearly half of them juveniles held in a building at the state fair grounds. "All right," roared Bull Connor, "I've got plenty of room in jail."

Marshall found utter lack of communication. Local law enforcement officers said that the newly elected governor in Montgomery, George Wallace, might soon declare martial law. There was a growing realization on the part of many people, when they thought about it, that the blacks were demanding something that was not so unreasonable—to have a cup of coffee at a lunch counter, to get a decent job. Financial men began to fear economic effects on Birmingham of a real outbreak of violence. President Kennedy, Defense Secretary McNamara and Treasury Secretary Dillon put through telephone calls to such men as United States Steel Chairman Roger Blough who might help at a distance. "The city of Birmingham has reached an accord with its conscience," announced King. Civic leaders but not city officials pledged action: desegregation in ninety days of downtown lunch counters, hiring of black clerks in department stores, freeing of all arrested demonstrators, creation of a biracial commission as a 'channel of communication.' Thereupon outgoing Mayor Hanes denounced the white signers as "quislings, gutless traitors." Governor Wallace said: "I will not be a party to compromise on issues of segregation."

The calm endured just two days. Then early on the third morning two bombings shook the black quarter. One explosion demolished the house where King had been staying, a second a motel that had been his headquarters. At once rioting erupted. Blacks poured into the city, attacking police and firemen, wrecking scores of cars, burning small stores and an apartment house. Irregulars joined the police. Streets rang with the thud of clubs hitting heads. King rushed back from Atlanta, called upon blacks not to riot ("Violence has always been the tactic of the white man"), and said he did not feel the bombings nullified the agreement. Mayor Hanes said: "The nigger King ought to be investigated by the Attorney General."[25]

The lunch-counter sit-ins, the freedom rides, above all Birmingham —these events that millions saw on their TV roused the conscience of America. Up to this point the Kennedy administration's acts toward ending legal segregation had been limited to administrative steps. In the summer of 1963 President Kennedy moved for civil rights reform.

It came in a showdown with George Wallace, the former Golden Gloves bantamweight champion who had just won the governorship on a campaign pledge to "stand in the schoolhouse door" to prevent desegregation in Alabama. The issue was joined over the right of two black applicants to enroll in the University's summer session. The court issued orders, Wallace cried defiance. As registration day approached in Tuscaloosa, Washington alerted 3,000 troops, and the Governor brought 500 military police, 425 state troopers and 200 revenue agents into the university area. On the showdown day a kind of charade took place. As the two applicants approached the door, Wallace stepped forward and raised his hand in a stop signal. At this the federal law enforcement officers stepped back, and steered the two blacks to their dormitory. At word of Wallace's action, President Kennedy federalized the Alabama National Guard. When the Guardsmen arrived four hours later, the governor departed. Then the two black applicants entered to complete their registration. That night President Kennedy delivered a hard-hitting television address to the nation:

> We preach freedom round the world. Are we to say to the world—and much more importantly, to each other—that this is the land of the free, except for Negroes; that we have no second-class citizens, except for Negroes; that we have no class or caste system, no ghetto, no master race, except with respect to Negroes? . . . The time has come for this nation to fulfill its promise. . . .[26]

That summer white students from northern colleges and seminaries went South to help rebuild black churches and homes that had been burned by the segregationists. School teachers and university professors organized and trained civil rights workers. On August 28, 1963, in a mighty outpouring such as had never been seen before in the country's history, 200,000 Americans marched—blacks and whites together—to Washington's Lincoln Memorial to hear Mahalia Jackson's soaring songs and Martin Luther King's lyrical refrain: "I Have a Dream."

In the next years whites joined blacks in thousands to aid "direct action" by demonstrating in Florida, marching from Selma to Montgomery, enrolling black voters in the "Freedom Summer." In those years Congress passed not one but several civil rights bills, and by the end of the 1960s racial segregation by law had been abolished including—according to the Department of Health, Education and Welfare—segregation in Southern schools. The disintegration of white supremacy started—one of the unexpected but beneficial side-benefits of the Cold War—was thus completed, and in such diehard strongholds as Mississippi, blacks held local office and Charles Evers (brother of Medgar Evers, civil rights leader slain in 1963) contested the governorship as a major contender.[27]

The defeat of the white supremacists however had not opened the way for the racial integration dreamed of by Martin Luther King before his death by an assassin's bullet in 1968. On the contrary, at the very moment that President Lyndon Johnson proclaimed "We shall overcome," the white supremacists had already succeeded in exporting their racism to the nation in less blatantly overt form. The first form was called tokenism. The virtual abolition of legal segregation in the South, as consummated in congressional maneuvering over the Civil Rights Act of 1966, ensured that only token compliance would be required. At the end of the Cold War in 1963, only 12,868 of the 2,840,000 black school children of the eleven states of the old Confederacy had begun to attend public school with whites—a compliance rate of .004 %. In the state of Georgia, forty-four black children had been integrated into white schools. The announcement of the Department of Health, Education, and Welfare that legal segregation of public schools had virtually ended by the 1970s was to be read in terms of such "token" compliance with the Supreme Court order of fifteen years before.[28]

The second form that racism took after white supremacy crumbled was the *de facto* segregation of the races, and this far from covert form of racial discrimination, already flourishing in the North and West, was nationalized in the 1960s as the South fell back from separation of the races by law to separation in fact. By that time racial residential segregation had become universal in American cities, South and North: in 1971 the Chicago Board of Education reported that 94% of that city's black children were attending schools that were 90% or more black, up 4% from 1970.[29]

A L T H O U G H few involved would have said so at the time, the 1954 Supreme Court case, Montgomery, Little Rock, Birmingham—all were engagements fought in the Cold War struggle between East and West to prevail in the Third World. During the years of civil rights strife in the American South, this struggle intensified everywhere on earth. It erupted first in the Middle East and North Africa. Both Russia and the United States became involved, at first through other countries, in the end directly. The contest led to the Suez crisis of 1956.

Second only to "massive retaliation" among the repellent Cold War phrases for which Secretary Dulles had such a fatal gift was the threat of "agonizing reappraisal." Blurted out in Paris during one of his flying visits to shore up "free world" forces in Europe, the phrase was meant to convey that if the French did not support America's plans for European rearmament the United States might be obliged to reconsider its commitment to its allies. Though the rearmament problems were eventually smoothed out, an agonizing reappraisal by the Americans was precisely what awaited the French and indeed the British in the 1950s as the Cold War spread into colonial areas long dominated by those two allies. Between American interests and those of Britain and France there occurred a frontal clash that culminated in the Suez invasion and its failure followed by new shocks in Africa, Asia and Latin America.

Up to this point the British and to a lesser extent the French had been carrying out an orderly process of converting their overseas possessions into commonwealths of self-governing but associated nations. In Asia the British had set India free, in Africa they had made Kwame Nkrumah prime minister of the Gold Coast under a constitution granting self-government and, soon, independence (when it was renamed Ghana). Syria and Lebanon had become republics, and the French had also conceded autonomy to the Tunisians under Premier Habib Bourguiba.

What the British and French demanded of these new nations was continuing commercial ties; what Dulles wanted of them was allegiance to the West in the Cold War against international Communism. The testing point was Egypt. Upon taking office Dulles set out to erect across the entire Middle East a kind of eastward extension of NATO that— joined with SEATO on the eastern end—would form an unbroken wall of containment around Communism's southern flank. The general idea was to ring Russia and China with allies and bases that would cost so much less than large American forces stationed abroad that the administration could balance its budget back home and cut taxes. In Dulles' thinking this new anti-Communist alliance would draw together the "northern tier" countries of the region—Turkey, Iraq, Iran, Pakistan—which bordered directly upon the Soviet Union. Britain, with its bases in Iraq, might join this alliance. But the United States, while sponsoring and financing the whole arrangement, would stay out in deference to the nationalist sensibilities of Egypt and other Arab states.[30]

It was Dulles' judgment that if the United States would work out some sort of accord with the nationalist leaders of Egypt's 1953 revolution, then the Baghdad Pact, as the anti-Russian lineup was called, and other Western-oriented relationships within the region could still be made to prevail. This of course presupposed several things. One was that the Russians, whom the United States and its allies had successfully kept out of Iran back in 1946, would continue as they had under Stalin to refrain from pushing into the power vacuum left by British and French withdrawal from Asia and Africa. The second was that the leaders of the new Arab states would be no less cooperative than the turbaned pashas and camel-riding sheiks who had helped keep the region stabilized and the oil flowing as in the past.[31]

In the midst of these rather cavalier calculations in the West, a strapping young colonel with the profile of an ancient pharaoh emerged as the new strongman of Egypt. Here even more than the Cambridge-schooled Nehru or the American-educated Nkrumah was the new, post-colonial man, the personification of the vast nonwhite, non-Christian Third World. Gamal Abdel Nasser, the son of an assistant postmaster in the upper Nile valley, was the very antithesis of the robed and khafiyahed Arab on whom the British had so long relied to keep the Middle East in hand. Growing up in Cairo, he had organized schoolboy riots and shouted at RAF planes flying overhead: "O Almighty, may disaster take the British." A brave and efficient officer who detested greedy and porcine collaborators in terminal colonialism, Nasser fought to the bitter end in King Farouk's disastrous 1948 war against Israel. Returning, he personally recruited 700 members in the Free Officers' conspiracy, led the 1952 revolt that overthrew Farouk, and for a time wielded power through an older, pipe-smoking front man, General Mohamed Naguib. In 1954 at the age of thirty-six, he thrust Naguib aside and took over.[32]

The British, French and Americans alike were slow to grasp what was taking place in Cairo, the metropolis of the Middle East, the Arab world and all Islam. Young officers, students, clerks were astir with the ferment of an Arab nationalism impatient with frontiers fixed in Europe and impatient for a better life. An urban Arab who wore business suits and worked hard to improve the lot of city dwellers, Nasser knew how to use the radio like a Hitler or a Roosevelt, and whipped up a big following not only in Egyptian streets but in cities all over the Middle East and North Africa. In his book *Philosophy of Revolution*, the young colonel boldly described three circles of Egypt's destiny. The first circle was the Arab world united by its exploited past, its strategic present and its oil-rich future. In the second circle, the continent of Africa, "we cannot under any circumstances remain aloof," wrote Nasser, "from the struggle going on between 5 million whites and 200 million Africans for we are *in* Africa, their link with the outside world." Even in the third and widest circle, the far-flung domain of Islam, "we may realize (its) temendous potentialities, enabling its hundreds of millions united by a single creed to wield a power without limit." The French, faced with a spreading insurrection of Algerian Arabs, concluded that Nasser was at the center of their trouble. Claiming proof that the Egyptian strongman was training Algerian guerrilla fighters in Cairo, Premier Guy Mollet termed the book Nasser's *Mein Kampf*, a blueprint for conquest.[33]

To the imperious annoyance of Dulles, Nasser refused to accept the Baghdad Pact as anything other than a scheme to prevent self-determination among the Arabs. Radio Cairo, just as the French had feared, proclaimed that Egypt's new mission was the awakening and uniting of oppressed Arabs from the Atlantic to the Persian Gulf. The Americans, however they might protest their anticolonialism, were protectors of Israel. By the summer of 1955 Nasser had not only associated himself with the neutralism of India and the other Afro-Asian nations that met at Bandung and proclaimed their anticolonialist solidarity, he had also given

Washington and London to understand that he was looking for more arms than they would give him. Neither the Americans nor the British supposed that the Russians would be willing to deal with him.

In this they utterly misjudged Khrushchev, and indeed had been slow to draw the conclusion that the Geneva summit conference that same summer had mainly served to ratify the existing balance between East and West in Europe. With events at something of a standstill in the Far East, where might Stalin's restless successor better turn than southward to exploit the opportunities created by the departing armies of empire? The lines of the new Russian diplomacy had already been laid down in speeches offering discreet praise of neutralism and stressing the coexistence of nations above the insurrectionary mission of Third World Communist parties.

When the Russians arranged a deal to ship Nasser $155 million worth of arms from Czechoslovakia[34] in return for Egyptian cotton, the fat was in the fire. At first the Western allies were united in common embarrassment and chagrin. They were alarmed that the balance between the Arabs and the Israelis might be upset. Since 1950 they had been pledged by a Tripartite Declaration to defend whichever side became the victim of an aggression from the other, doling out arms warily to Arabs and Israelis alike, holding back on weapons of offense. Now the Russians had broken the monopoly of arms supply.[35]

In one quick leap the Russians had gained a toehold in the Middle East. Having accomplished what the czars had strained for in vain for centuries, they took off within days on yet another flanking jump into the postcolonial lands of south Asia. In November Premier Bulganin and First Secretary Khrushchev embarked on a good-will tour of India, Burma and Pakistan. There they proclaimed with brash insouciance: your Western enemies are our enemies too; we too are outraged by their imperialism; and we are the ones who can enable you, by training and material assistance, to dispense with their humiliating presence in your midst. Khrushchev bewailed the suffering of his Burmese hosts because the English "call you savages and barbarians." The English, he said, had "sat on the necks" of all South Asians and "robbed them of the last piece of bread." Before they left, the Russians entered into trade agreements with all three countries, and the beginning of a major new relationship with India. Like the arms deal with Egypt, it was part of a historic intrusion, extending the Cold War as it did on an entirely new front.[36]

In Washington, where President Eisenhower had been laid low for several months by a heart attack, the administration decided with British concurrence on an interim response to the startling Russian leap into the Third World. The response, confidently based as much on an estimate of Russian weakness as of American strength, was to accept the Soviet challenge on the economic front. The Egyptian government had announced a plan to build a huge dam at Aswan to harness the Nile's power, double the land under cultivation and lead the country triumphantly into the twentieth century. It was Nasser's bid to build up his country. Now the United States, Britain and the World Bank offered to put up the $400 million capital needed to start the immense project, and Eugene Black of the Bank traveled to Cairo to doublecheck whether Egypt would have funds enough to pay for the arms and for the $900 million in local expenditures that would be required to carry the Aswan project to completion.[37]

In February 1956 Nasser and Black reached agreement. But there the approach ended. Both the British and Americans cooled to the project and to the whole idea of trying to conciliate Nasser. Within Congress, for one thing, there was opposition to any aid for a foe of Israel in an election year, and for another strong resistance to financing the expansion of acreage to produce cotton that would compete with America's. In the highest councils of the Administration Secretary of the Treasury Humphrey, fighting jealously to defend his budget against any additions for foreign aid, boomed out questions as to whether Egypt had technicians to build or make use of a dam of such size. In the midst of these misgivings Egypt joined four other Arab nations in an anti-Israeli military alliance, and then outraged Dulles by establishing diplomatic relations with Communist China. By July a move was building up in Congress to ban all aid to Egypt, and with quick British concurrence Dulles prepared to tell Nasser that the deal was off.[38]

It is characteristic of the atmosphere of complacency and blunder in the West before the Suez crisis that Secretary Dulles conveyed the word to the Egyptians just three weeks after the last British soldier was withdrawn from Egypt. The word reached Nasser in Yugoslavia as he attended a much-publicized meeting with Tito and Nehru. All the world knew that one thing bound these three together, and that was neutralism, a doctrine Dulles was known to abhor. Doubtless Dulles welcomed the occasion to demonstrate conspicuously that neutralism in the mortal struggle between East and West was not only wrong but unrewarding.[39]

One week later, on July 26, Nasser counterpunched. He seized the Suez Canal by nationalizing the British-controlled Universal Suez Canal Company. "The canal is ours," he shouted to 250,000 followers in the Alexandria square. "We dug the canal with our lives, our skulls, our bones, our blood!" Nasser gave as his reason for acting the American abandonment of the Aswan project and the need for compensating money from canal revenues. The assertion thrilled Egyptians—"I could have kissed the colonel's feet," wrote the novelist Jaguih Ghali—and stirred citizens of all lands that had long been dominated by Western powers. But even if all of the canal's $25 million annual profit went for dam-building and not a cent for reimbursing the expropriated owners, the sum was far from sufficient to pay the bill.[40]

Taking over the canal and its revenues may or may not have been Nasser's real reason for acting. Quite possibly it was the American dislike for his arms deal—"Americans," he shouted, "may you choke in your fury!"—that drove him to seize the canal instead of turning first, as both the Americans and British seem to have expected, to the Russians for help. Eden, Dulles, Eisenhower—all had looked for this as Nasser's next move. For Eden, it was an unacceptable outrage and a call for all-out action. For Dulles, it was the shock of a lifetime.[41]

On his bedside table, as American newspaper readers had often been told, John Foster Dulles kept two books. The first was a well-thumbed Bible, from which he could quote long passages from memory since boyhood. The second, which he kept close at hand for years, was Stalin's *Problems of Communism*. Dulles dipped into it constantly. The chief argument of the book was that war would never involve the Soviet Union but would break out between and destroy capitalist nations because of the "inherent contradictions" in their suicidally competitive nature and notions. What thoughts passed through Secretary Dulles' head as he leafed through these pages amid the cries of the Allies in the year of Suez?[42]

Nasser's seizure of the canal, Eisenhower said later, "caused consternation in Britain" so great that thenceforth it was Washington's principal anxiety. Eden was livid with rage. For Britain Suez was an essential artery of trade, as it was for all Europe. Among the 16,000 ships a year that passed through were the tankers that carried a large part of Britain's vital oil supplies. For Englishmen, and especially for Tories like Eden, the canal signified empire, and for Nasser to grab for it but a few days after the last British troops had been withdrawn was an intolerable assault on Britain's still considerable power in the Middle East. This was violating treaties in the manner of Hitler and Mussolini twenty years before. To none did the parallel seem more striking than to the man who was Foreign Minister when Hitler invaded the Rhineland and when Mussolini took Abyssinia, and was now Britain's Prime Minister.[43]

Within a week the British cabinet had privately decided to restore Western control of the canal by force if necessary—that is to say, if negotiations did not achieve the purpose. As for Nasser, Eden shouted, "I want him destroyed. I want him removed."[44] The French were even more bent on striking down Nasser. For them the supreme objective was to win the war in Algeria. Premier Guy Mollet and others believed that the money, arms and revolutionary drive of the rebels came from Cairo. French opinion also stirred at the seizure of the Canal Company, founded by De Lesseps, builder of the canal. As for Nasser, Mollet had already identified him as a new Hitler. Within forty-eight hours Foreign Minister Christian Pineau was in London discussing with Eden the joint use of force; the French Defense Minister, Bourges-Manoury, was perhaps the strongest of all proponents of military action.[45] Word of the British determination was communicated to Eisenhower in a personal message from Eden: "We must be ready in the last resort to use force. I have this morning instructed our Chief of Staff to prepare a military plan accordingly."[46]

Eisenhower evidently was dumbstruck. For the United States the Suez Canal was neither lifeline nor symbol, nor was Nasser Public Enemy Number One. On top of that the general had just been nominated for a second term and was running for reelection in November on a platform of "peace" and "prosperity." It was well known moreover that the American people did not suffer other nations' imperialism gladly, especially not the British variety. Most important of all, Dulles' Middle East policy of building up anti-Communist alliances had launched the United States into a contest for influence in the Third World. In this contest, the Russians proclaimed pointedly that they were antiimperialists who did not have imperialist allies.[47]

As for Nasser he was an American problem too, but not for the same reasons as for the Allies. Washington intensely regretted that the Egyptian strongman had accepted Communist arms and let the Russians gain their first foothold in the Middle East. If Nasser's playing off the opposing parties of the Cold War were to lead other new nations to loosen their ties with the West, proclaim themselves neutral and invite Russian aid and influence, then the United States would experience a loss of authority and presence that could impair its vital interests. But for the Americans the use of force would simply not do at this point, especially when carried out by Egypt's former master. Force was only conceivable as a last resort dictated by some such necessity as averting general war. Nationalizing a property thirteen years before the lease ran out did not justify such extreme measures. Should the Egyptians mismanage the canal, or highhandedly interfere with its traffic, or oherwise affront the nations that used it, then perhaps the time would be at hand to intervene. All this was spelled out urgently if not clearly in Washington's messages to Eden over the next weeks.[48]

At the beginning of August Dulles was sent off to London to help the British while making sure that they did not resort to force. As Nasser had reckoned, the British lacked the means to retaliate at once. Both the

British and French military chieftains said they needed a month to mount an expedition against Suez. So at Eden's invitation a conference of twenty-two maritime nations met in London to discuss how to place the canal under an international management free from any one nation's control. It was Dulles' idea, and he took the lead in shaping the plan for a new international agency to run the canal for Egypt under United Nations control. By September the eighteen nations—Russia, India and two others dissenting—put the plan to Nasser, and he turned it down. Egypt, he said, would run the canal on the world's behalf, as impartially as the old company had done and as any new outfit could.[49]

Eden, the master diplomatist, still had one more diplomatic ploy before resorting to force—the United Nations. London and Paris could appeal to the Security Council, where they could lay their international rights issue clearly on the record before Russia imposed its veto. At the same time the old Suez Canal Company, in the absence of a legitimate "successor," could withdraw all non-Egyptian pilots, three-fourths of the lot, from the canal. In short order—in the British mind, "Egyptian" spelled "incompetent"—traffic would stop. Anglo-French forces would then land and take possession, incidentally knocking out Egyptian air-power and toppling Nasser. The eighteen-power scheme would be enforced on his successor, as the oil consortium had been imposed upon Mossadegh's three years before in Iran. The British authority would be preserved in the Middle East, the oil would be assured for Europe, and outside aid that presumably kept the Algerian rebels going would be totally cut off. One wrinkle in this overall plan was that Musketeer, the military operation, had to start ten days before its H-hour with embarkation of troops from Southampton. That meant in other words that a no from Nasser or a turn at the United Nations would have to be followed quickly. Otherwise there would be an extraordinary pause between a Soviet veto in New York and an Allied landing in Egypt.[50]

In early September, as Nasser turned down the eighteen-power plan, Eden and his cabinet called Parliament into session and prepared to take their appeal to the United Nations. In the very same days Dulles, trying frantically to forestall precisely this escalation toward the showdown that Eisenhower wished to avoid, whipped up still another plan, a scheme for a Suez Canal Users Association. Just as Mollet was arriving in London to firm up invasion schedules with Eden, Dulles' new scheme was decoded and placed before the prime minister. It was the hour for Eden to go before Parliament. Dulles got on the telephone. Could not the Users plan be given a trial before turning to the United Nations? In England, in the south of France, in the Mediterranean, the invasion forces were gathering. But at that moment the special relationship with the United States so prized by the British loomed in the prime minister's mind. If Nasser would repudiate this plan, then the United States would have a grievance to carry to the United Nations too.[51]

But no sooner had Eden agreed to delay and give the plan a try than from Washington came word that Dulles had said at a press conference that the United States had no intention of using force if the Egyptians should block the canal to the Users Association. On top of this the Egyptians had started running the canal when the company withdrew its pilots. Hiring pilots where they could find them, the Egyptians proved able to take the ships safely through. On the first day forty ships made the passage, in a week 254.[52] With the case for coercion evaporating, the British and French announced that they would take their grievances to the United Nations Security Council. Dulles, beside himself with anxiety lest London and Paris should be going to the United Nations, in Canadian Foreign Minister Lester Pearson's words, "as a cover for war," now besought all parties to seek agreement. The U.N. Secretary General, Dag Hammarskjold, brought the foreign ministers together with Nasser's representative.[53] A British statement of "six principles" was accepted by all sides. The night before the Security Council voted to leave the canal issue to direct negotiation, President Eisenhower told a television campaign audience: "It looks like here is a very great crisis . . . behind us."[54]

Quite the contrary and unbeknownst to Washington, the British cabinet nine days earlier had given up on diplomacy and instituted Plan II—that is, force. On October 3, Eden won approval from his colleagues to launch Musketeer as a "peace-keeping" operation should Israel attack Egypt. Here, in contrast with the plans that Dulles kept watering down at London, were grounds for going to war that the British and French could really control.

What they had entered into was in fact a conspiracy based on a secret alliance that the French, while all the palaver was going on, had struck up with Israel. For nearly a year Israel's Prime Minister David Ben-Gurion had been resolved to wage a preventive war against Egypt. He was intent upon wiping out once for all the threat of guerrilla raids across his borders; seizing the Eyptian shore of the Gulf of Aqaba and thus opening up Israel's own waterway to the East; and cutting down the Egyptian armed forces before they could use their Soviet-supplied arms to overpower Israel.[55]

Early in October Chancellor of the Exchequer Harold Macmillan returned to London after a chat with his old friend Eisenhower. "Ike will lie doggo" until the election, he told the cabinet. From that point on the British simply stopped telling the Americans anything. A document was said to have been drawn up pledging British as well as French coordination and support for an Israeli assault on the Sinai peninsula and the eastern flank of the Suez Canal.

By the plan worked out secretly with Ben-Gurion, the Israelis would attack Egypt through the Sinai peninsula, and next morning Britain and France would issue an ultimatum to both Israel and Egypt to pull back from the canal. Egypt would refuse, whereupon the British and French would start bombing Egyptian airfields and land their expedition to save world commerce. In order to fit the Israeli and Anglo-French moves together, it was necessary for the Israelis to land parachute troops a lot further west in Sinai than the Israelis needed to. But this was done because the British insisted that the canal must appear "threatened." In return the Israelis insisted that the British and French start air attacks to cover these forces much earlier than their Musketeer plan called for. Even so, because the Musketeer force was loaded on ships that needed at least six sailing days to reach Egyptian shores, there was bound to be a painfully long lapse of time between the Anglo-French ultimatum and the actual invasion of Egypt.

Perhaps the invaders thought to bull through while the United States was occupied in a presidential election. Perhaps, making the same erroneous assumption that President Kennedy did at the Cuban Bay of Pigs five years later, they expected the populace to rise and overthrow the strongman the moment the invaders went ashore. Perhaps they supposed that the simultaneous upheaval in Eastern Europe, a climactic moment in the Cold War, might distract and engage the attention of mankind.

At the moment the Hungarian revolutionary government announced it was abandoning the Warsaw Pact, the Israelis launched their blitz against Nasser. On the day that the Russian tanks returned to the Hungarian capital, British bombers struck Cairo airfields. In the hour when the freedom fighters were making their last stand in Budapest, Eden announced that Britain and France were intervening in the Egyptian-Israeli fighting, causing Opposition Leader Hugh Gaitskell to denounce the whole show as a "charade." In the incredibly drawn-out pause before the invasion ships arrived, the Egyptians sank ships to block the canal, the one thing the expedition was supposed to avert. Meanwhile pro-Nasser Arab nationalists in Syria dynamited the pipelines pumping oil to the Mediterranean from the Persian Gulf. To heighten the unreality of it all, the Israelis bowled over the Egyptian defenders in the Sinai and raced to all their objectives long before the invading fleet reached Egypt.[56]

At the White House barracks language exploded at the temerity of America's two chief allies in spurning official Cold War policy to attack a leading nation of the Third World. At this moment of maximum strain between the British and the man who had led them in some of their finest hours, his old comrade-in-arms, Marshal of the Air Force Sir John Slessor, happened to drop by. It was, Eisenhower told him, the worst day of his life. Dulles, who had only fragmentary reports of what had been brewing, told reporters he was convinced it was a case of collusion with Israel. The hour of agonizing reappraisal had come. Laid nakedly bare by the secretary's own acts as well as his colleagues' were the "inherent contradictions" in western amibitions so endlessly stressed in the book he kept by his bed. At this point the United States, to save its position in the Third World, turned on its two principal allies and introduced the resolution in the United Nations Security Council calling on all nations to refrain from force in the Middle East. Stiffly, the British and French representatives cast their countries' first vetoes in United Nations history.[57]

But now, having resorted to force, the British and French were unable to wield it. How could they now, Eisenhower demanded to know, be so preposterously slow about it? At the United Nations there was time to call a meeting of the General Assembly, the United States and Russia joining forces, to debate and vote a ceasefire. Still there was no invasion. The British and French had to ask the Israelis, who had already gained their objectives, to hold off complying in the ceasefire until they themselves could get into the act. By November 5, when the British and French troops finally appeared, supposedly to separate the combatants, Israel and Egypt were no longer fighting.[58]

By this time Election Day was dawning in the United States, events in Hungary had swept from rioting to revolution to brutal suppression, and, as the world looked from the White House, to the brink of events in which everything might fly out of control. Matters of still greater moment to Washington than the occupation of Suez were looming: a Kremlin tensed and beleaguered in an hour of upheaval posed the risk of world war by mutual miscalculation. At one point Washington had been trying to keep world attention riveted on Hungary, in hopes that Moscow might continue making concessions. The next minute Eisenhower had seen the British and French, oblivious to the momentous opening in Eastern Europe, attempting the most inept kind of Machiavellian tactics in the Middle East. "They did not tell me," he kept repeating. Yet Eden had said when Eisenhower was refusing to take seriously his talk of using armed force at Suez, that he hoped the United States, if the possibility of Russian intervention arose, would "take care of the bear." Now, just as Eisenhower moved to enforce the status quo against his allies in the eastern Mediterranean, the Russians threatened to intervene. Messages from Moscow went out to London, Paris and Tel Aviv reminding that Russia had rockets capable of stopping aggressors and threatening to dispatch "volunteers" to Egypt. A fourth message went to Washington proposing joint intervention by the United States and Russia. Eisenhower turned down the proposal, but Washington, in the ultimate act of the crisis, secretly placed its entire nuclear-bomber force on alert.[59]

In the upshot the unspoken accord of the 1955 summit was enforced, and in a new way. On the one side the United States stood aside while the Russians restored the existing order in its Eastern European zone of power. On the other side, the rigor of its actions doubtless reinforced by the implied Russian claim that they could police the aggressors, the United States took drastic measures against its allies to uphold the existing order in its zone of power in the Middle East. Unlike the Soviet declarations, which were published to the world even before they were delivered to the Western foreign offices, the American action took place behind the scenes, with the result that the Arabs of the Middle East came out of the Suez crisis believing that it was Russia's threats that saved them from the return of the colonialists.

Partly this was because Dulles was not the agent of this decision. He had been stricken on the eve of the Anglo-French landing, and underwent a three-hour operation for the removal of an intestinal cancer. In this hour it was Treasury Secretary Humphrey, strongman of the Eisenhower administration, to whom the President turned. Humphrey's method was brutally simple. He merely gave the British to understand, without bothering about any righteous reproaches, that he expected the British to accept the United Nations ceasefire—or face war on the pound and not so much as one dollar for oil supplies. Unless the British heeded the United Nations call by midnight of Election Day, Humphrey would withhold his consent, needed for any favorable action, should the British undertake to draw the large sum of dollars they were entitled to as members of the International Monetary Fund. He would moreover make no effort to line up American banking support for sterling, on which a run had already started that sent chills through the British cabinet.

Word of Humphrey's "ultimatum" reached London on the morning of America's election day. Macmillan, phoning to the Treasury on his way to a cabinet meeting, heard the message and arrived at the cabinet meeting a chastened man. Gone were the Chancellor's warlike accents, his resolve to fight to the end rather than "become another Netherlands." The formerly headlong Tory informed his colleagues that he could "not any more be responsible for Her Majesty's Exchequer" unless there was a ceasefire. It was a painful hour, but the British did as they were told. With their forces a third of the way down the canal, they passed the word of their decision to the French, who were horrified but helpless. All the advancing forces had British commanders and the British forces were in the van, leaving the French no chance to go on alone.[60]

Eisenhower was duly told that the invaders had accepted the cease-fire. He also heard that he had been comfortably reelected, though to his bitter disappointment he had failed to carry either house of Congress for his party. Very soon the general was talking again, and quite politely now, with Prime Minister Eden. But far from relaxing his pressure, he tightened the screws. Declining to let the British and French stay on at Suez, he backed Hammarskjold's plan for bringing the United Nations Emergency Force to post along the canal and clear it. Not until the British and French sailed away into the setting sun did the British get their International Monetary Fund loan and other aid for the battered pound sterling. By December, when Eden resigned in favor of Macmillan, the British had to resort to rationing gasoline.[61]

So perished the hegemony of Great Britain in the Middle East, and with it in the debacle went the Mollet government, the Fourth Republic, and what was left of the French empire. British forces did not entirely leave the area at once. But Macmillan, taking over after Suez, changed Britan's policy of orderly retreat from empire into a scramble in which practically every remaining colonial possession was freed or set irrevocably on course for freedom by the time the Conservative government left office eight years later.

The United States, when it intervened to frustrate the British and French at such painful cost, did not profit as expected by a rise in good will in the Arab part of the Third World. The Arab nationalists persisted in assigning the credit for forcing the British and French back from Suez to Russian threats rather than to American anticolonial rectitude. At the same time, Arab opinion of every stripe viewed the United States as the protector of Israel. Furthermore, the Suez affair dealt a heavy blow to the Baghdad Pact, and of all people it was Nasser, rebounding from his rescue to a stronger hold on his people and to high standing among Arab nationalists, who now sought to increase his power in the turbulent Middle East.

The response of the United States was a ponderous reassertion of old-fashioned Cold War formulas. As embodied in a joint congressional resolution, the Eisenhower Doctrine of 1957 pledged "to employ American military forces in the Middle East if any nation in that area requested help against Communist-instigated armed aggression." This had the ring of the Truman Doctrine and the form of the Eisenhower administration's Quemoy-Matsu resolution. It was tried just once. The following year another conspiracy of young Arab nationalist officers toppled the pro-Western government of Iraq. Shaken by strong pro-Nasser sentiment within, two nearby dominos, Lebanon and Jordan, tottered. At their governments' request the United States rushed Marines into Lebanon and Britain flew troops into Jordan. Both governments survived and the forces were soon withdrawn. But the new Iraqi regime pulled out of the Baghdad

Pact, tearing a big hole in the containing curtain across the Middle East that American policy had tried to build against "international Communism".[62]

The fact was that the Russians, having carried off their arms deal with Nasser, were in the Middle East and competing for influence in the Third World. Following the Suez crisis they entered into an agreement with Nasser to carry through the billion-dollar Aswan project. They also extended foreign-aid credits to Syria and Iraq even though this, as in Nasser's case, meant giving aid and support to a regime that was suppressing and jailing its native Communists. The Russian justification for such uncomradely tactics was that at this late-imperial stage of world affairs they were abetting movements of "national liberation."

The United States, throwing overboard its aversion to neutralism to keep up with this kind of competition, strove valiantly to defend its lead in a contest that, after all, was fought largely in terms of money. In terms of economic as opposed to military aid to the underdeveloped lands, the contest for the Third World was ultimately fought to a decisionless standoff, the United States spending $35.3 billion and the Russians $5 billion by 1965. Only Cuba moved over to the Communist camp. Neutralism, however, did well. Nasser, convening an assembly of African states in Cairo, was soon telling the new leaders of his "second circle" that the recipe for progress in his United Arab Republic was to keep a balance of one-third trade and credits with the Americans, one-third with the Russians, and one-third with the rest of the world.[63]

A STEADILY unfolding consequence of the spread of the Cold War into the Third World, and one seemingly unforeseen by the white Americans who led the way into the struggle against "international Communism," was a transformation in the racial consciousness of American blacks. A century of education, two decades of new experiences—military service abroad, mixed schools, television, above all the move to the cities —had primed the nation's blacks for it. And in the North they met with precisely what De Tocqueville had noted more than 100 years before the Cold War flight of Northern whites to the suburbs:

> I have remarked that the white inhabitants of the North avoid the Negro with increasing care in proportion as the legal barriers of separation are removed by the legislature.[64]

The goal of the vast majority of American blacks had always been integration into the American society, and this still tended to be so. But little by little the force of experience and new impressions combined to open to the American black a new perception not only of the world and of himself but—most important—of the white man. Up to this point he had so thoroughly absorbed the white man's way of looking at things that he exalted the white man's mystique and at the same time accepted with utmost sensitivity the white man's allegations of the savagery and immorality of blacks.

Suddenly in the 1940s blacks became aware that the Germans, supposedly among the most advanced of white men, had burned six million Jews. The savagery of the Germans was not lost on American blacks, who were not prone to make distinctions among white men and thought of white Americans as at most Germans once removed. Blacks also saw that America, the very citadel of democracy, had exploded not one but two atomic bombs, and furthermore that the bombs were not exploded against Germany, the principal enemy, but against a nonwhite country. Even the early defeats suffered by United States forces at Japanese hands left a lot of American blacks quietly glad seeing the white man get his pants kicked.

Stumbling into these new ways of looking at black and white in the world, some blacks were horrified to discover how thoroughly they had been taken in by the white man. Growing up they had played cowboys and Indians like everybody else, and not one of them had wanted to be "the dirty redskin." Shaken, they realized that they had missed the meaning of the white man's attempt to destroy the American Indian. All at once they saw, as the black sociologist, C. Eric Lincoln, put it, that "it was but a step from the white man trying to exterminate the Indians to his destroying the blacks," and the thought leaped to their minds that "the white man who had A-bombed Japan might try to destroy anybody who was nonwhite." On the strength of such searing suspicions, blacks looked at America's colonial past and America's identification with European imperialism, and saw the whole thrust of imperialism as directed toward the denigration of nonwhites everywhere on earth.

This, in ideas taking rudimentary shape among American blacks, was the meaning of how they began to look at the emerging Third World. And increasingly the spectacle of the destruction of the white man's empires, the satisfaction of seeing the sun set after all on British hegemony and the curtain fall on French empire, began to have some application in the American black's personal relations with whites. The old fear began to go. Assaults on whites by blacks became common, particularly in the South. Vituperation against whites began to be heard in the land. It became possible for blacks in America to say what was on their minds—and live.

The economic background for this transformation of black consciousness was mixed at best. Set against the standards of pay around the world, American black incomes during the Second World War rose to levels far above those of most countries and well above those prevailing in many countries of Europe. Yet in the only terms that mattered to him, the average black's income during the Korean War years, when he made his greatest gains, rose only from 53% to 57% of what the average white American earned.[65]

Unequal as this ratio was in 1952, it held out the promise of continuing improvement for the blacks as they moved increasingly into the productive centers of the American economy. Therefore the fact that in the Eisenhower years the average black share of the wealth actually declined stands out for its significance in the experience of all those American blacks who had begun to see the promise of American life. In each of the three recessions of the Eisenhower years blacks were the first to be fired—and the last to be hired when workers were taken on again. Nor was this all. In the 1950s the number of self-employed black businessmen fell from 42,500 to 32,400. At the end of the decade the infant mortality for blacks was 43.2 per thousand, for whites 22.9. Of the nation's 1,-500,000 hospital beds the vast majority were occupied by whites, and a large proportion were barred to blacks. In 1952, the same year that black Americans took eleven gold medals in the Helsinki Olympics, the American Red Cross maintained segregated blood banks.

And in Deerfield, Illinois, a middle-class Chicago suburb, a popular referendum halted an interracial housing project. "We're not bigoted," explained Mrs. William Walker. "I don't think we want to deny Negroes or anyone else the right to decent homes. But not next door." In one of four plants surveyed in the New York City suburbs a manager said: "You shouldn't hire them if it is going to destroy the atmosphere of the rest of the place. If they are at a minumum, all right." When blacks were hired, discrimination did not retreat much:

Q: Is there any kind of organized recreation here after hours?
A: We have bowling teams.
Q: Are there any Negroes who participate?
A: Oh no, the teams are only for us.[66]

Few other cultures have this problem. It was American society, dealing with its blacks, that held out the rewards—and barred the way. While the flood of black migrants into the urban North had risen to the point where blacks numbered 11% of the North's population, they occupied only 4% of the total areas of the Northern cities. In Chicago for instance 74% of the black population was jammed into six neighborhoods.

Had all the rest of America lived as close packed as New York's Harlem in 1959, the entire population of the country could have been contained in three of New York City's five boroughs. For all but the privileged few middle-class blacks, indeed, it was hard to survive, let alone win a better life.[67]

Caught up in the frustration and despair of their seeming powerlessness to claim simply the rights that white Americans already had, many blacks in the Northern ghettos began to react as members of their race had at other periods of disappointment and despondency in the past— they turned away from integration and looked inward upon their own resources and yearnings. Back in De Tocqueville's time American blacks had gone to Africa to colonize Liberia. Back in the 1920s the demagogue-dreamer Marcus Garvey had whipped up a considerable excitement in Harlem and other black communities for his "Back to Africa" movement. Now in the recession of the late 1950s when the number of unemployed blacks in Detroit rose to 39% of the city's black work force, a black leader named Elijah Muhammad began to command a large following for his Nation of Islam sect among the down-and-out blacks of Chicago and Detroit. These were the Black Muslims, and a television documentary in 1959 entitled "The Hate That Hate Produced" won them many new converts.[68]

Although the teachings of the Black Muslims also featured the bizarre visions and wild revelations common to extremist religious sects, their big message to the despairing young of the ghettos was a vituperatively aggressive denunciation of "the white devils." Blacks must separate themselves from the white man, they said: they must stop looking at themselves with the white man's destroying eyes, stop hating themselves:

> There is no such thing as a race of Negroes. This is a false name given to you during slavery by your slave master who after robbing you completely of your knowledge of your homeland, your parents and your culture, called you Negro or "nigger" because that word is "neuter." We are the *black* nation.

The way to become "fearless" said Elijah, was to repudiate everything having to do with the "white devils," and join instead the "725 million brothers and sisters of the world of Islam." In practice Elijah led his followers to live apart in small, sometimes armed congregations, and lacked the temper and capacity to spread these ideas widely. It was his chief convert, a spellbinding exconvict from Omaha named Malcolm X, who made America aware of the Black Muslims and set forth a new basis for black militancy just when the integrationist civil-rights movement began to lose its elan.[69]

Born Malcolm Little in Nebraska in 1925 and reared in Lansing, Michigan, Malcolm X was the son of a Baptist preacher who had been a strong backer of Marcus Garvey's Back-to-Africa movement. After his father's death in a streetcar accident, Malcolm dropped out of grade school, drifted to New York and, becoming a busboy in Small's Restaurant in Harlem, quickly fell in with an underworld life of racketeering and drug-pushing. Convicted of armed robbery, he was sent to prison where he became converted to the Black Muslims. After his release in 1952, he rose rapidly in the movement and became its chief spokesman. Here was a new kind of voice for black America. Martin Luther King was a black preacher whose gospel according to Gandhi traced from the Third World. But he was also a Christian standing on the same doctrines as white Americans. Malcolm's message exploded straight out of the Third World, and thudded into blacks and whites alike like flying shrapnel:

> The worst crime the white man has committed has been to teach us to hate ourselves.

Under Malcolm's tutelage Cassius Clay, the world's heavyweight boxing champion, embraced Islam and changed his name to Mohammed Ali.

In all that Malcolm had to say to desperate young urban blacks, the magic word was Africa. "We are an integral part," he would say, "of the nonwhite world of Islam that stretches from the China seas to the sunny shores of Africa." When Nasser took over the Suez Canal, he was hailed in Harlem by the Muslims. Nasser's picture went up on the walls of Muslim homes and temples in Chicago, Detroit and New York. Even in his bitterest attacks on the white man, Malcolm X kept bringing in the subject of Africa and its importance for black Americans:

> The same rebellion, the same impatience, the same anger that exists in the heart of the dark people of Africa and Asia is existing in the hearts and minds of 20 million black people in this country. But the black man in America has been mentally colonized, his mind has been destroyed. He is ashamed of what he is, because his culture has been destroyed, his identity has been destroyed; he has been made to hate the texture of his hair, he has been made to hate the features that God gave him.[70]

In the past times Africa for most American blacks was something to be ashamed of. "American Negroes," the former minister to Liberia observed in 1895, "are averse to a discussion of Africa." In a vague way they grew up knowing that they were descended from Africa, but from earliest times they had been made to feel that Africa was nothing. Margaret Brenman, a New Jersey schoolteacher, told in 1945 of a girl who after others had told where their people came from—Holland, Ireland, Poland, Puerto Rico—stood up and answered, "North Carolina." Other black children, drawing self-portraits in class, colored themselves white. "I opened a geography," one black has recalled, "and saw Africa represented by a native African with a headdress, some feathers round his middle and a spear. There was a handsome guy to represent the white, and then this black, kinky-haired spearman—that was me, that was the picture of what I came from . . . a savage, a cannibal, he was just the tail end of the human race, he was at the bottom."[71]

The change that stole over the outlook of American blacks can be traced to the years when the Cold War was spreading into the Third World. It began about the time Mrs. Parks refused to budge from her Montgomery bus seat, and in this change, as James Baldwin said, "the rise of Africa in world affairs" had "everything to do" with the black American's sharpening view of himself and his past.[72]

For a great many black Americans, it seems to have begun with Kwame Nkrumah. Winning prominence in the early 1950s as leader in the drive for an independent African nation of Ghana, Nkrumah emerged as a world figure, first as prime minister and then as president of the first West African country to win independence from the colonial powers. Pictures of Nkrumah getting off his airplane and being respectfully greeted by white dignitaries aroused new feelings for black Americans that "took a certain sting out of all those earlier pictures of the African savage." The African type now began to seem no longer quite so grotesque, or different. Nkrumah seemed a handsome man, dignified, with a strong face. Here was a chance for many to identify for the first time in a positive way with the continent of their black ancestors.

Nnamdi Azikiwe, the first African Governor General in Nigeria, made a similar strong impression when Nigeria took its place as an independent nation in 1960. The reappearance of Jomo Kenyatta in Kenya in 1959, the flow of front-page photographs, newsreels and movies from an Africa in which white power was falling and black men were acquiring dignity and taking command, the television interviews with distinguished African visitors—Mboya, Touré, Nyerere, Balewa, Senghor, Houphouet-Boigny—all of this in a flood dislodged a mass of old images of Africa that still filled most minds.

"It didn't come home to us," one Southern black leader said later, "until the Cold War came on and I realized that it would be a struggle for the loyalty of this two-thirds of the world and the winner would control the world. The United States couldn't be so dumb as to pass this leadership up just in order to keep the Negro down." Though many black Americans were still ashamed of being identified with Africa, men on

135th Street in Harlem were heard to say that they could hold their heads higher "since Nkrumah and Azikiwe came up." A woman standing at a bus stop was quoted as saying: "These Africans standing up in the United Nations, they make me proud."[73]

Early in 1961 after Patrice Lumumba, deposed premier of the Congo, was assassinated during intervention by United Nations forces, some fifty black intellectuals burst out in a wild demonstration at the General Assembly. Screaming "Vive Lumumba" they interrupted Adlai Stevenson's first speech as American representative. Since the United States had accused the Russians of backing Lumumba to get a foothold in Central Africa, many Americans supposed the riot Communist-inspired. To these black Americans, however, the murder of Lumumba was the African counterpart of immemorial American experience, "the international lynching of a black man on the altar of colonialism and white supremacy." The riot, the worst in United Nations history, signaled the new black American solidarity with Africa. When K. A. Gbedemah, Ghana's Minister of Finance in the late 1950s, was told by a Howard Johnson restaurant manager in Dover, Delaware, that he and his chauffeur would have to drink their orange juice outside ("Colored people are not allowed in here"), black Americans did a slow burn. By 1960 they were leading forays from the Northern cities to integrate restaurants along Route 40 and other highways outside Washington where such incidents had been common. "Embarrassed," the State Department formed a "special projects" section to integrate Washington property owners who refused to provide housing for diplomats arriving from twenty-two new African nations.[74]

In the South Martin Luther King had been one of the first to make the African tie in his sermons and speeches. Soon John Lewis, youthful leader of the sit-in movement exulted: "Something is happening to people in the southern Negro community. They're identifying with people because of color."[75] The day came in May, 1962, when the Harlem newspaper *Amsterdam News* reported in considerable excitement that "African trends" were heading into the neighborhood's beauty parlors:

Just the other evening on a TV recital, the new Metropolitan Opera tenor George Shirley appeared . . . wearing white tie and tails—with his hair quite long and natural, in a manner which has become identified with a number of leading diplomats from Africa.

Even more startling is a similar trend among the ladies. South African Miriam Makeba is said to have started the fashion . . . to transform straight or semistraight hair into tight, springy twists.[76]

The discovery of identity in Africa was proclaimed in many ways. In the forefront was Malcolm X. In a mocking speech after President Kennedy's assassination he spoke of the President's death as a case of "chickens coming home to roost." For this, Elijah Muhammad suspended him from the Black Muslims, and he went off to North Africa for a year. "These are our kind of people," he wrote from Cairo. "I haven't seen anybody here who wouldn't be jimcrowed in Virginia." In Islam he had felt the liberating force of a religion that unlike the Christianity of most black Americans was utterly untouched by white American influence. But he had already seen that the Black Muslim movement amounted to a strategic retreat for black America, and that to go forward blacks would have to define, assert and enforce their identity as a self-conscious, self-reliant group within the totality of American life. Not only building up their community by self-help was demanded, as Malcolm came to see it, but blacks must also defend themselves and fight for their rights in aggressive participation in everyday political life. On his return from Africa, Malcolm X founded the Organization of Afro-American Unity patterned on Nasser's Organization of African States, to work for these goals. As such, it did not go far. His murder—for which three followers of Elijah Muhammad were convicted and sentenced to life imprisonment —heightened the influence of his maturing ideas for black America. In the role of recreating black consciousness in America in these years, Malcolm X was a mediating figure of major importance.[77]

Many others who rushed to visit the continent found out what strangers they were, though in the days of tense racial confrontation in the later 1960s such men as Stokeley Carmichael, Robert Williams, and Eldridge Cleaver took sanctuary in Guinea, Ghana, and Algeria. On a march through Mississippi in 1964 with James Meredith, the new leaders of the Student NonViolent Coordinating Committee hit upon the slogan "Black Power."

It did not mean, as the more frantic of last-ditch white supremacists at once concluded, and the Black Panthers briefly asserted: "Black Firepower." It meant many things. It meant, as Martin Luther King said in a speech in Cleveland, that the American black had "come to a time," after 350 years, "when he can say to himself, I am somebody." It meant discovering, as Malcolm X had foretold, that "black is beautiful." It meant, as John Lewis of SNCC proclaimed:

> There's been a radical change in our people since 1960: the way they dress, the music they listen to, their natural hairdos. . . .

For many of the young it meant an impassioned turn to "Black Studies" and "African Studies." It meant, in short, what Malcolm X said Black

Power must be before it was. Ultimately black America could not take off as a separate state or nation—that was out of the question, and the great majority had said so by its rejection of the Muslims. Rather, Black Power was, in Stokeley Carmichael's words, "working to provide [the black] community with a position of strength to make its voice heard." [78]

Was there any question that "the black nation," searching for its identity, had begun to think of itself in some such fashion as one of the ethnic groups of America? Against the dogged resistance of white racism taking new forms to frustrate their drive for equal rights, blacks were seeking membership in the pluralism of late twentieth-century America. In 1952 the Tuskegee Institute recorded no lynchings for the first time in seventy-two years. In 1970 school segregation by law was ended in the land. Jim Crow was dead. Yet the odds against the blacks, in the face of the seemingly inextinguishable racism of the white majority, were great.

In the cyclical evolution of racial oppression in America, the Cold War years carried the struggle of blacks for dignity and justice to new ground. In the 1960s they achieved further economic and political gains and experienced a mighty consciousness-raising. But the President's Civil Rights Commission warned against a grim resettlement into "two nations," one black and urban, one white and suburban. And for their different reasons, many indeed in both races seemed to say that such an outcome would be all right with them.

Throughout the century from Lincoln to Lyndon Johnson three visceral urgencies had compelled the black man in America—to get food in his belly, to get a roof over his head, and to stay out of the white man's way and survive. The Southern experience had burned into his soul the sense that any brush with The Man, as he put it, could cost him his life at any hour on any day. The very education that enabled the fortunate black to teach or trade or preach only made him more visible, thus more vulnerable, to the irascible, unpredictable violence of the white man. In the years of the Cold War, when the black American came to see himself in the global scene, the old fear of The Man faded. But when he looked upon the white man with his new eyes, many an American black wanted less than ever any part of him. In such a mood, black separatism seemed beautiful.

Thus black ethnicity, delayed and usurped by other ethnicities that arrived later and brought less, proclaimed its right within the American pluralism of the Cold War years, and was authenticated as blacks stood up for what was theirs. With all its unparalleled wealth and diversity, it was clear, the America of the Cold War was very much an unfinished country. Yet the unfinished business to which the nation returned under stress of the Cold War was the issue that every Southerner knew in his heart had been settled on the dark and bloody ground of fratricidal strife long before. Black and white would live together in the United States; there was no other way.

But in the 1950s the issue of the 1850s was nationalized, and at last every great population center of the nation-state knew the torment of a tragic past as the Swedish sociologist Gunnar Myrdal had mildly entitled it a generation before: *An American Dilemma.* In the wavering impulses by which the nation seemed now to face up to and then evade this issue, prospects for more than a consolidation of positions won in the stormy decades of the Cold War seemed not auspicious. Very likely the very immensity of this nation-state might be most determinative of the outcome. America, Walter Lippmann said in 1970, would not fall under violence and totalitarian solutions—"the country's far too big for fascism on a national scale."[79]

CHAPTER 10

Sputnik and the Illusion of the Primacy of American Education

W HAT MADE the Cold War unique among the protracted great power confrontations of history was the frightfulness of the weapons that were brandished. For complexity and destructiveness of lethal armament, the United States led the way, and this was no accident.

The triumph of technological America—and its tragedy—was the consequence of a very special convergence. As heir to the history of Western science, the United States packed all the power accumulated over 400 years by the Baconian method. Quite as much as the scientists and engineers of Europe, American technologists had learned from the Galileos and Newtons how to probe the universe by taking nature apart, thus discovering and establishing its verifiable general laws. They too had every reason to know that:

> the unfolding of scientific thought between 1500 and 1700 outshines everything since the rise of Christianity, and reduces the Renaissance and the Reformation to the rank of mere episodes.[1]

But whereas the Baconians of Europe never doubted that man lives in and with nature, the Americans had quite a different conception. It was, as things turned out, their fateful contribution.

Americans not only arrived on their continent as immigrants but in an important way they remain so to this day. Sojourners still in a newfound land, they thought of the nature around them as a force to triumph over. They laid axe to the forests. They hacked through the mountains. They triumphed over the West—Theodore Roosevelt called his six-volume history of the United States *The Winning of the West*. They won victories over nature with their barbed wire and six-shooters, triumphing when they laid rails and killed Indians and varmints. The ability of Americans to win over nature hardened in time into one of the firmest articles of American faith.

When the expanding giant of the New World emerged into the twentieth century and was put to the test in two world wars, its people somehow knew that they could bend nature to their will and triumph by "know-how." And so they did. Victory was seen as a matter of posing the problems, and solving them.

In 1942, the problem was beating the Germans, and the engineers of Detroit, the Knudsens and the Fords, had the answer. They gutted the iron hills of Minnesota, produced a crushing weight of arms, and triumphed in every theater of war. The ultimate problem in the Second World War was the development of the atomic bomb, and it was in the handling of this problem that the scientific method of Western thought converged with the unique American conception of being outside and on top of nature, with fateful results. The problem was simply handed over to Vannevar Bush and his wizards to solve with two billion dollars.

Who else but Americans, never believing that they had to live with nature, would have supposed that building an atomic bomb was simply a matter of finding a technological solution? The Fermis and the Bohrs, Europeans who had never supposed other than that man is in nature, applied the verifiable general laws. Then the Americans, the Oppenheimers and the Comptons, the Bachers and the Allisons, brought the cosmic fire down to earth. The United States of America had triumphed over nature.

The scientific victory of the atomic bomb was thus the culmination of the American self-conception. It was technological apotheosis. The few theoretical physicists who accomplished it knew at once what they had done. "I am become death, the shatterer of the world," Oppenheimer quoted to himself from the *Bhagavad Gita* as the fireball went up.[2] At that moment, he *was* God.

From the peak of this apparent conquest over nature—and nations —there was only one way to go. It was all downhill for technological America, and it hit bottom with the ecological crisis a quarter of a century later. But that was not how it looked in Cold War times. In his victory address following the Japanese surrender in 1945, President Truman proclaimed that "a free people with free Allies who can develop an atomic bomb can . . . overcome all difficulties," and he affirmed that the achievement had shown the superiority of America's democratic system.[3] Even then, considering the extent of German wartime research into heavy-water nuclear reactions, it was an unwarranted boast.

Never as after Hiroshima was this unique American conception of a nature that had been conquered and ground under the heel so widely asserted and accepted. The problem-solvers of technological America went on to triumph over nature again and again. It was the age of plastics, when the very molecules of nature were rebonded into synthetic substitutes for the "natural" fibers and pelts thenceforth dismissed as inferior. It was the time of know-how, when industry, as never before, poisoned the air, earth and water to bring the step-saving benefits of its gadgetry to consumers who never doubted that nature need not be lived with.

If there were warnings, they were disregarded; if there were problems, they were "solved." After the Russians exploded an A-bomb the solution was to make a bomb a thousand times more destructive. After the Russians made an H-bomb almost as soon as the Americans, the solution was to ring Russia with so many Strategic Air Command bombers that one aggressive Russian move would rain overkill on every Soviet city.

R A I S I N G, inexorably raising, the price of war was the instinctive action of the world's richest nation, and indeed that was its unvarying Cold War doctrine from the time it was first formulated by Truman and Acheson until it was later extended by Dulles. But by the mid-1950s some of Dulles' old associates in the Eastern Republican Establishment thought it was becoming too crude. These men, who had held high government positions in the Cold War, now met as business leaders at the élite New York clubhouse of the Council on Foreign Relations to talk about such concerns. If balanced power had now become balanced terror, they asked, how could threats of massive retaliation stop the Russians from winning the Cold War by a series of little steps each too small to justify starting the holocaust?

This was just the kind of question being asked by the political scientists, who had become fascinated by power in the modern superstate. The more Cold War power tended to fall into balance, the more intently these analysts probed to find who held the power and how they made decisions. Out of such studies grew the curious Cold War subspecialty dedicated to unwrapping the riddle inside the enigma of Soviet power. It was the assumption of this variety of specialists, who were known as Kremlinologists, that commissars in medieval palaces tended as much as any other rulers to follow certain lines of rational behavior. Once the wielder of power had made a decision, the Kremlinologists held, certain goals and objectives could be discovered toward which such an action constituted "value-maximizing means." Accordingly they soaked up all the information obtainable about the decision-maker and his surroundings. Minute analysis of *Pravda* and the rest of the tightly-controlled Soviet press; amassing data about Soviet government workings down to the smallest city-block in Smolensk; sifting the banter of bibulous bureaucrats at Moscow embassy receptions; examining the rank-order of the ruling Presidium members in their published photographs—after enough of this sort of study certain Western experts began in these years to speak portentously of "knowing the other fellow's hand," and so predicting his next move. Inevitably, astonishments intruded on the game. When Molotov in 1957, having tried and failed to overthrow Khrushchev, was dispatched neither to death nor prison but by one of the Soviet leader's most exquisite inspirations was made ambassador to Outer Mongolia, Henry Roberts, the sage director of the Kremlin-watchers at Columbia University's Russian Institute, was heard to mutter, "It's a fool's game, a fool's game." But the Kremlinologists, some of whom were established in the universities and others in government-funded "think tanks" such as the Rand Corporation and the Hudson Institute, grew in number and in the weight of their publications as the Cold War wore on.[4]

The New York Establishment leaders called in a young political scientist from Harvard to help them review Cold War policy and write up the conclusions. Stocky, swift-witted, with a precise, Teutonic air about him, Henry Kissinger had just taken his Ph. D. in government after winning almost all the academic prizes Harvard had to offer. Born in the southwestern German city of Furth in 1923, he arrived in the United States with his parents as a refugee from Hitler's persecution of Jews. He attended George Washington High School in Manhattan, and then joined the Army, serving as an enlisted man in the counter-intelligence corps on the European front before being mustered out in 1946 to resume his studies at Harvard.[5]

After an eighteen-month searching review, the Council on Foreign Relations published a book by Kissinger which became one of the most talked-about books on the Cold War. Concealed within the jargon of "mutual deterrents," "risk manipulation" and "preemptive maneuver," *Nuclear War and Foreign Policy* contained a new thesis: limited warfare, especially with small nuclear arms, was a viable alternative to Dulles's dated diplomacy of massive retaliation. Strategy, said Kissinger, must direct the technology of weapons—and not the other way around. For Nelson Rockefeller, who left the Eisenhower administration in frustration at its combination of rigidity and complacency and then commissioned a series of foundation studies as a preliminary to running for elective office, Kissinger wrote another influential paper on Cold War strategy. The conclusions were deeply disturbing to Eisenhower: the United States would have to step up defense spending by at least three billion dollars annually for several years to to stay ahead of the Russians.[6]

By 1957, as these papers were being prepared, reports began arriving in Washington that the Russians were well on their way to developing a ballistic missile capable of striking targets in the United States from Soviet launching bases. President Eisenhower, well aware that the United States was several years away from developing an intercontinental ballistic missile, appointed a select committee to make a secret review of the military balance between the United States and Russia. Under the chairmanship of Rowan Gaither, president of the Ford Foundation, this group included such concerned members of the Eastern establishment as former Assistant Secretary of War John J. McCloy, former Undersecretary of Defense William Foster and former Defense Secretary Robert Lovett. The committee had just completed its review, and Premier Khrushchev had publicly announced successful testing of an ICBM with ranges of up to 5000 miles, when one of the most startling events of the Cold War occurred.[7]

On Saturday morning, October 4, 1957, the Soviet news agency Tass announced:

> The first artificial earth satellite in the world has now been created. The first satellite was launched in the USSR. . . . Artificial earth satellites will pave the way for space travel and it seems that the present generation will witness how the freed and conscious labor of the people of the new socialist society turn even the most daring of man's dreams into reality.

The announcement said that the satellite was twenty-two inches in diameter, weighed 184 pounds, and was circling the earth once every hour and thirty-five minutes at a speed of 18,000 miles per hour and at an altitude ranging from 170 to 570 miles.

Reporters rushed to Russian space experts who were in Washington to attend a conference of the sixty-four nations taking part in the 1957 International Geophysical Year. At a Russian embassy reception someone held out a portable radio. Professor A. A. Blagonrovov listened to the beep-beep signal transmitted from the satellite and relayed over an American newscast. "That is the voice," he cried. "I recognize it." The Russians called the satellite a *sputnik*, meaning an object that was traveling with a traveler—in other words, traveling with the earth, which in turn was traveling through space. By nightfall, the word sputnik, repeated with wonder and fascination, had a firm place in the American language.[8]

The first official American reaction was to appear unruffled. The president of the National Academy of Sciences cheered "a brilliant contribution to the furtherance of science." When reporters clamored for comment, Rear Admiral Rawson Bennett, chief of the Office of Naval Research, demanded to know why all the fuss over a "hunk of iron almost anybody could launch." Dr. John Hagen, his aide in charge of the Navy's IGY program, seemed chiefly put out by what he termed the Russians' "unethical conduct" in launching the satellite without first telling their IGY colleagues.

In every way Washington sought to minimize the achievement. Presidential Assistant Sherman Adams called the Russian satellite an "interplanetary basketball," and Clarence Randall, former steel executive on the White House staff, dismissed it as a "celestial bauble." Defense Secretary Charles E. Wilson, heard of the world's largest research program, appraised the orbiting of an artificial moon as "a scientific trick." When the public still appeared, as the *New York Herald Tribune* reported, "bewildered and bothered" by the news, President Eisenhower broke his silence to say that everything was all right. America's decision to separate research on space vehicles from work on ballistic missiles had been correct, he said, and its program was "all designed and properly executed." Secretary Dulles added more encouraging words. Not only did the country possess "a very marked superiority . . . in terms of actual military power," but it was "German scientists captured at the end of the Second World War [who] doubtless played a big part in the Soviet achievement."[9]

All this sounded hollow when on November 3, to the astonishment of both scientists and laymen everywhere, the Russians announced that they had launched a second Sputnik. Sputnik II weighed about half a ton, carried a living dog, and went into an orbit that at one point carried it a thousand miles from earth. In the United States, deprecation gave way to consternation. Senator Richard Russell, Democrat of Georgia, emerged from a briefing by Defense Department officials to say that he was shocked and appalled by what he had heard. What the Russians had achieved was an advance so great, he said, that it was not even in the planning stage in Washington. There was no hiding the evidence this time: Sputnik II could be seen, and was seen by millions of Americans who read the timetable of orbits in their newspapers and rushed to hilltops to watch it streak eerily across the December night sky.[10]

The shock of Sputnik was described by columnist Marquis Childs as "a second Pearl Harbor." But Pearl Harbor brought a simple, fighting response. Doubtless there were Americans who ran out of their houses to shake a frustrated fist at this insidious object that whizzed without let or hindrance across American skies. Yet how could they fight a vehicle of discovery that pierced the envelope of air and took man into a new era of space? Sputnik presented a far subtler and infinitely more subversive challenge. It set off a shock wave throughout the world. Gradually it dawned on Americans that a formidable advance in the art of missilery powered this peaceful traveler, that to fire such a load to such heights required rockets every bit capable of boosting nuclear-tipped missiles from Moscow all the way to Detroit, and that placing the satellite into such a high, planned orbit implied hairbreadth control capable of directing such rockets 6000 miles through the firmament and down to the River Rouge factory district of Detroit.[11]

In the mid-1950s, some Americans had become aware that with the equipping of Russian air force units with long-range Bison bombers, the frontier of destruction had moved at least in theory from the Rhine to the Mississippi. But the Russians had few such bombers, and, unlike the United States, few bases for them outside their own country. All bombers took hours to fly to their targets, and could be shot down before they got there. With ICBMs—Khrushchev's ICBMs—it was thirty minutes from launch to target, with an impossibly short fifteen minutes to defend against it.

As such unspeakable thoughts and fears began to penetrate day by day into American consciousness, the shaken country turned for reassurance to its own space-satellite program, which had been subject to a series of exasperating delays. After the launching of the second Sputnik, the new Secretary of Defense Neil McElroy stepped in to speed things up. Ending the policy of leaving the American satellite program in the care of the Navy while other service branches concentrated on long-range ballistic missiles, he ordered the Army, which had a well-tested Jupiter C rocket ready, to take over satellites and to get an artificial moon into orbit.[12]

With gaudy ballyhoo, the Defense Department published abroad that on December 4, the United States would put a satellite into orbit from its launching site at Cape Canaveral in northern Florida. Tens of thousands of spectators and hundreds of reporters gathered expectantly. The countdown started at 5:30 a.m., and was halted; a fuel valve was not working. The countdown began again, only to stop because of another mechanical failure. Somewhat after midday word went out that the launching would be delayed forty-eight hours until December 6. A chorus of jeers burst out in the European press. British newspapers vied at making up names for the American satellite—"Flopnick," "Stayputnick," "Kaputnick." The Communist East German newspapers made a play on the German word for late—spät—and sneered Spätnik. Washington had its own wry wisecrack as reported by The New York Times: "The American satellite ought to be called Civil Servant. It won't work, and you can't fire it."

At Cape Canaveral, December 6 dawned beautiful, and the crowd gathered. Everything seemed to be going well. Precisely on schedule at 11:45 a.m., the orange blaze of the blastoff seethed against the blue of the sky. Two seconds later the orange dissolved into a thick cloud of black brown smoke. The satellite, starting up, had exploded six feet off the ground and crashed back, burning on its pad.[13]

The Los *Angeles Herald and Examiner* headlined: "9-8-7-6-5-4-3-2-1-Pfft." "Oh dear," was the *New York Daily Mirror's* caption for the Vanguard pictured toppling into roiling flames on the Florida beach. "The Pearl Harbor of the Cold War," cried the *San Francisco Daily News.* "Alibis are worthless," commented the *Rocky Mountain News.* "One thing is sure, there was too much publicity. We always say too much." The *Des Moines Register* took the occasion to say that "Soviet newspapers have not told us whether any failures preceded the first success of the Sputniks. That's the difference between the free government of the people and the suppressive power of the police state." The *Waco News-Tribune* said: "The title that Friday's PFFT-nik deserves is: Washington goofed." And in Urbana, Illinois, a professor commented:

> The whole country suffers from a contempt for things intellectual. Everything has to serve some utilitarian purpose. They always give the experts a goal, cure cancer, and so on. To go further, to create something, one must be free and not tied to targets. One must be able to work for nothing but the beauty of the thing . . . What the Russians don't know is what a favor they've done us![14]

In Moscow, Premier Khrushchev said that the Russian satellites were "lonely, waiting for American satellites to join them in space." Then he asked, "Who wants to overtake whom in science? The United States would like to overtake the Soviet Union." Finally, on the last day of January, after frantic activity at Washington and Cape Canaveral, word was brought President Eisenhower at his vacation cottage in Georgia that the satellite would definitely be fired that night.

The blast-off was to come at 10:48 p.m. A special line was held open between Washington and Eisenhower's vacation headquarters in Augusta. General Andrew Goodpaster at the White House relayed the countdown.

> The firing command is given at 10:48. It takes sixteen seconds to start the rocket lifting off the ground.
>
> The main stage lifts off at 10:48:16.
>
> The program is starting OK.

They are putting it in the right attitude.

It is still going.

It is still going at fifty-five seconds.

It is still going and looks good at ninety seconds.

Jupiter is on the way.

It is through the jet stream.

115 seconds—it is going higher and higher.
Everything is going all right at 145 seconds.
[At 10:56] The second stage ignition has gone off OK.

"When will the announcement come that the satellite is in orbit?" asked the President.

It was to be at least an hour and a half after the satellite reached orbiting height before the instruments reported that it was making its first swing around the earth. To make sure the scientists waited until past midnight. At 12:44 A.M. came the word, "It's in orbit." The Eisenhower smile had never been more radiant. "That's wonderful, simply wonderful," the President replied.[15]

U P U N T I L October, 1957, it was unimaginable to most Americans that their ascendancy in matters of science and technology could be questioned. Now suddenly people caught a glimpse of themselves as they were reflected in the ironic eyes of the rest of the world—"a chain reaction of ridicule round the world," cried the *Oregon Journal*.[16] America had boasted it would be first. Instead the Russians had launched their Sputnik.

Only a few years before Vannevar Bush had said that Nazi Germany failed to develop the A-bomb because it was regimented and totalitarian whereas the wartime research of America, Britain and Canada was "on an essentially democratic basis." Of the Russians, America's head scientist in the Second World War had said:

the system with which we contend cannot possibly advance science with full effectiveness—it cannot even apply science to war in the forms it will take in the future without mistakes and waste and delay.[17]

Now whose were the mistakes, the delays? "I shrink a little inside," said Senator Majority Leader Lyndon Johnson, "when the United States announces a great event—and it blows up in our faces." At a tense session with senators, Secretary Dulles mumbled something about the abnormal Russian aerospace buildup having "warped their society" and brought out "weaknesses" such as consumer-goods shortages. The Russians produced only 100,000 cars a year, he noted. Senator Fulbright interrupted sharply, "You are describing Soviet strengths and calling them weaknesses," he snapped.[18]

The myth of superiority shattered, Americans fell back into an orgy of gloomy self-analysis. Clare Boothe Luce, a ranking Republican who had often voiced American self-satisfaction, now said, "The beep of the Russian sputniks is an outer-space raspberry to a decade of American pretensions that the American way of life is a gilt-edged guarantee of our national superiority." Editorialists denounced "the easy living in this country." "We spend one and a half billion on the annual change of our car models," said Dean John R. Dunning of Columbia University, "and they say we have better tailfins but they have better rockets."[19]

For a moment all the pentup frustration of the years welled up, and the distempers of economic slowdown, racial tension, unemployment and international mortification began to crowd on the American consciousness. Even before the Sputniks the big Eastern Republicans who brought Eisenhower to the White House had grown fearful that his administration had flagged in the arms race. Now the Democrats began to raise their cry of "missile gap" between the United States and Russia. The military-industrial elements centered in the Pentagon agitated for a "czar" to expedite production of more and better missiles than the Russians. At the White House the president struggled to deal with the new mood of fear and bewilderment. Putting all his prestige as soldier-president on the line, he managed to turn the challenge of Sputnik back on the people. Yet the stir of unrest that welled up could not long be put down, and in good measure it was the Russian moon in the sky of 1957 that elected Democrat John F. Kennedy president in November, 1960.[20]

General Eisenhower did not want to react strenuously to the explosion of the Red star into the firmament, but he became aware that Americans were upset as never before during his years in the White House. The shock of Sputnik had awakened him to the need of getting better technical advice about the new weaponry. He therefore called in a number of scientists, and he liked what they told him. What they said in effect was: America's scientific and technological superiority was still intact—but it could not long remain so unless something was done about the nation's schools. The attitude of America's parents and children toward the study of science must be turned around, and the best young people must be led into scientific careers in far greater numbers if the United States was, in the future, to stay ahead of the Russians in its general level of technological proficiency.[21]

In short, as Eisenhower heard this message, the answer to Sputnik was better education. What the general liked about this advice was that it would not require a heavy draft on the United States Treasury. He had already brushed aside the estimate that the Russians might have an operational ICBM within two years, and he assured the country that "long-range ballistic missiles, as they exist today, do not cancel the deterrent power of our Strategic Air Command." His deeper concern, as he told Emmet Hughes, was with "the economic strain over the long pull."

> If we let defense spending run wild, you get inflation . . . then controls.
> Then a garrison state . . . and *then* we've lost the very values we were
> trying to defend.[22]

But improving education was something in which all citizens could take a hand, and there was a sharp limit on how far the federal treasury could be used for the purpose. It could of course do something—indirectly. Such a course would suit President Eisenhower right down to the ground. A lot of people thought that the general had grown so fiscally conservative only in his late White House years. However, all the way back in 1949 when he was president of Columbia University, he had staked out his position against federal aid to the schools in a letter to a congressional committee:

> I would flatly oppose any grant by the Federal Government to all states
> of the Union for educational purposes, or education will become another
> vehicle by which the believer in paternalism, if not outright socialism,
> will gain still additional power for the Central Government.[23]

Ever since that time, at each succeeding session of Congress, other conservatives had fought and defeated measures for general federal aid to education. For some it was a principled resistance to the dangers of central and potentially tyrannical control. For many the real issue was racial—they were opposed to integrating blacks into the all-white schools of the South. For others the real issue was religious—they feared that any general federal aid to schools would extend to Catholic parochial schools and thus break down the traditional separation between church and state. Whatever the reason, Congress would not vote for general federal aid to the schools at this stage. It was therefore safe to say that if doing something about the schools was to be America's response to the challenge of Sputnik, whatever was done would not hit the United States Treasury very hard, and this was what mattered most just then in Eisenhower's mind. He well knew that if he was to call upon the nation to turn its schools around, he was really asking the people of America to do the job themselves—locally, and out of their own pockets.[24]

As his first public action after Sputnik Eisenhower announced in a nationwide broadcast that he was creating the post of Special Assistant to the President for Science and Technology, and named Dr. James R. Killian, Jr., president of the Massachusetts Institute of Technology, to the job.

The effect of this appointment, both on the bureaucratic warfare over missile development that had been raging around the president and on the recasting of American Cold War doctrine after Sputnik, was symbolic. It meant nothing less than that the eggheads, objects of hoots and jeers just a few years before, were being brought into the White House. Now the scientists at the universities, with whose studious researches Defense Secretary Wilson had had so little patience, were to be enlisted in the Cold War competition to outdo Russia. And now a whole range of expert opinion, and not just that of the overkill cultists of the Air Force doctrine, was to be made available to the White House.[25]

Dr. Killian himself was as stout a Cold Warrior as could be found in the land. Not a laboratory scientist at all, he belonged to the new breed of university administrators brought into prominence by their familiarity with the technological problems that were beginning to take hold of American government and society. Dr. Killian was a statesman of science.

In appearance and manner he was grave, mild, with pouchy cheeks, gray hair slicked back and a precise, quiet way of talking in a slightly southern accent. South Carolina-born, he had taken an undergraduate degree in engineering administration, and through the 1930s served as editor of MIT's excellent magazine *Tech Review*. Called upon to help run MIT during the war years when the place was almost an arm of the government, Killian had won the confidence alike of Cambridge scientists and Washington bureaucrats. In 1947 he became president, and exercised cool oversight in the large tasks of research and development that Washington assigned to MIT in the first years of the Cold War. He was equally adroit in aligning MIT in the forefront of the new industrial technology, and spoke easily of the "triple play of government to education to business." The proximity fuse, the early-warning net for continental air defense, the electronic controls for all the big bombers and missiles—these were among the major projects carried through for the Pentagon by the gifted scientists and engineers at the new kind of University of Technology run by Killian.[26]

In Washington Dr. Killian (the title was honorary, not earned) quickly formed the President's Science Advisory Committee and brought to the White House many of the top scientists who had been estranged from the government by the brutal Oppenheimer affair. It was not so much that such Oppenheimer foes as Lewis Strauss and Edward Teller now lost influence; on the contrary, Teller's advice remained as important with the Air Force as ever. Rather the effect was to introduce, backed by the prestige and authority of Killian's position at the White House, new voices and counsels. Long-haired or crewcut, the fifteen scientists of PSAC (called "P-sack") were full of ideas—about missilery, about disarmament, about test-ban proposals, and about education.[27]

"Our youth shuns science," cried Dr. Chauncey Leake of Ohio State medical school. "This must change or we perish." "The future belongs to the nation with the best technical brains," said Dean Dunning, one of the architects of the A-bomb and an old Columbia friend of Eisenhower's. "We are losing a war we have not yet fought. We have not entirely fallen behind but the Soviets have been producing scientists and engineers more than we." For at least six years, said Nicholas De Witt of Harvard, the Russians had been training more—no fewer than 1.7 million Russians were now studying at higher levels in science and engineering, two-thirds of all their students in higher education, in fact. Add to this that in a single generation they had by now trained up 3.6 million supporting technicians. By contrast, America was not even replacing the 18,000 scientists who left college teaching every year, and high school students, surveyed by Dr. H. J. Remmann of Purdue University expressed every intention of avoiding science like the plague. According to Dr. Remmann's sampling, 25% thought scientists "odd" and 14% thought them "evil."[28]

By November 1957, all these judgments had been funneled to the White House by Killian, and the President was ready to take this case to the country in a nationwide telecast from Oklahoma City. After defending his arms program and explaining how expensive new weapons systems were, General Eisenhower turned to what:

> incredibly, according to my science advisers, is for the American people the most critical problem of all, above all other tasks of producing missiles, of development of new techniques in the armed forces: we need scientists. In the ten years ahead, they say, we need them by the thousands more than we are now presently planning to have.

Then the President made his big pitch.

> This is National Education Week. No matter how good your school is, I wish that every school board member and every PTA would this week and this year make one single project their special order of business. This is to scrutinize your school curriculum and standards, then decide for

yourselves whether they meet the stern needs of the era we are now entering.

As you do this, my friends, remember that when a Russian graduates from high school he has five years of physics, four years of chemistry, one year of astronomy, five years of biology, ten years of mathematics and trigonometry and five years of a foreign language.[29]

The President had touched a chord. Here was something that the ordinary American could do about the Cold War. When President Truman had told people that international Communism was threatening them in Greece in 1947, they turned to stamp out Communists in their local schools and colleges. After Washington announced that the Russians had exploded an H-bomb in 1952, people volunteered to stand watch on shorelines and rooftops as airplane spotters. Now it seemed that every civil community, every club, every local chowder and marching society in the land wanted to do something about the schools.

> "We will look," said Susan.
> "Yes, yes," said all the children.
> "We will look and find it."
> So all the boys and girls looked.
> They looked and looked and looked for it.
> But they did not find it.

When the President of the United States told Americans at their TV sets to go out and find out what was going on at their schools, this was the sort of thing they found in the schools of the 1950s. Suddenly suburban America was reaching for a best-selling book by Dr. Rudolf Flesch called *Why Johnny Can't Read*, and all at once a pedagogical dispute that had been smoldering for years was being loudly aired at dinner tables, country club bars and PTA meetings from coast to coast. Could these parents want less for their children than that they should some day live in suburbs like their own? Of course not, and such hopes now required getting a college education so as to hold the job that enabled a person to live in a free-standing house with grass and trees around it. Such ambitions required that the children succeed in preparing for college in these competitive days, and gaining admission to a college whose name carried prestige. It gave such parents nightmares to think that their child might be falling behind in the absolutely primary skill of reading.

So these Americans demanded to know why the professional educators rejected "Phonics," as Flesch called the old-fashioned way of learning syllables instead of whole words. They were not satisfied when the perspiring principal protested that "research" showed Flesch's way not best for each child—and the schools had to educate all children. Why indeed could not their children learn to read the old way, and so discover at once the delights of such old favorites as Andersen's *Fairy Tales* and *Arabian Nights* and Mark Twain's stories? "The trouble," Flesch had told them,

> is that these have words like 'grieving' and 'serene' not in children's vocabularies. So instead Johnny gets these series of horrible, stupid, emasculated, pointless tasteless little readers, the stuff and guff about Dick and Jane, or Alice and Jerry visiting the farm and having birthday parties and seeing animals in the zoo, and going through dozens and dozens of totally unexciting, middleclass, middle-income, middle-IQ children's activities that offer opportunities for reading: "Look, look," or "Yes, yes," or "Come, come," or "see the funny, funny animals."

In frustration some parents took Flesch's book in hand, drilled their offspring nightly, and, egged on by approving articles in *Life*, led them lisping straight into Shakespeare and Homer. Amidst these alarms and confusions, blond, blue-eyed and empty-headed Dick and Jane disappeared from the "Language Arts" curriculum of America's schools.[30]

The call went out from Washington to devote special attention to the hunt for the brainiest, and this was quickly turned into a hunt for excellence—as if that were a discrete, definable attribute. In all the Lions clubs, League of Women Voters chapters and PTA meetings of America, excellence in education became the new watchword. The slogan was proclaimed by John Gardner, former professor of psychology at Stanford and now as head of the Carnegie Corporation the backer of many of the most interesting innovations in the schools. Considering the fact that an altogether unexpectedly large and growing postwar crop of children was just then flooding into the schools, this slogan was an audacious one. Considering the reality that to keep the Cold War economy prospering this mass of young people had to be kept off the job market in care of the schools, the slogan may have been a hopeless one. But Gardner threw down the challenge: so far, by assuming responsibility for the nurture of all children, the schools' achievement had been quantitative. Now the task was to produce quality too.

In a highly influential foundation report issued just as Sputnik spun into space Gardner wrote: "Too many of our school systems have fallen into a chronological lockstep under which equality means an exactly similar exposure to education regardless of variations of interest or capacity in the student." Equality of opportunity there must be, yes. But education was a sorting-out process, too, and "one of its most important goals is to identify and guide able students." The process of technological change—"and the times have grimly underscored the correctness of this view"—required "maximum development of individual potentials," above all in attaining "intellectual excellence."[31]

Since general federal aid to public-school education was blocked off all through the Cold War years by political inaction in Washington, the new thrust to improve education had to come from other institutions in American society. Now the big private foundations attained their peak influence. John Gardner at Carnegie, later to be Lyndon Johnson's Secretary of Health, Education and Welfare after the dam against large-scale aid to schools finally broke, played a leading role. Dean Rusk at the Rockefeller Foundation built up a huge program of international education. By far the biggest private force was Ford.

Endowed with the bulk of the founder's fortune after his death in 1947, the Ford Foundation set up shop in New York in 1950 at headquarters scarcely less grand than the parent company's in Detroit. As its first act to raise the level of higher education, it gave away $60,000,000 to a hundred colleges and universities. Its disbursements thereafter continued to be greater than those of many governments. Neither the family nor the company had a hand in its allocations. That was the job of its president, Paul Hoffman, former Marshall Plan chief and once head of the rival Studebaker Motor Corp., and a staff of pipe-smoking, tweed-jacketed professional money-spenders whom Dwight Macdonald dubbed "philanthropoids."[32]

One early Ford-funded effort that came into its own with Sputnik was the National Merit Scholarship program, which awarded four-year college scholarships to more than a thousand top achievers in highly publicized nationwide exams each year for the best high school seniors. Now another Ford-backed experiment also caught on—the Advanced Placement programs for talented and ambitious high school seniors. By the year after Sputnik, some 3,715 seniors who had taken college-level courses at their schools sat for special exams under the supervision of college professors and sixty percent won ratings of "creditable" or better. Fifty-three did well enough to be admitted to Harvard that fall with sophomore standing.[33]

On the crest of the post-Sputnik surge President Eisenhower sent Congress his recommendations for indirect federal action. "For long-term national security," he said, he was proposing a four-year, billion-dollar program to build up science training in the schools. Even that commitment, disappointing as it was to the education lobby, represented a larger outlay than General Eisenhower preferred. But Congress, while adamant against all general federal aid to education, was ready enough to accept federal responsibility in a national emergency such as it now perceived. In fear of possible Russian space supremacy foreshadowed by Sputnik, Congress passed what was the largest program of federal aid to education of the entire Cold War, and the most important since the GI Bill of Rights. This was the National Defense Education Act of 1958 for improving the teaching of science, mathematics and foreign languages at all levels of schooling.

Although the NDEA never remotely touched the whole fabric of American life as the GI Bill did, it exerted a substantial influence on the country's campuses and, to a lesser extent, its secondary schools. One provision of the new law put the federal government in the business of making loans to hundreds of thousands of college students. Such loans went by preference to those majoring in science and other fields favored by the new law, and if the teachers went on to teach, half the amount of the loan would be "forgiven," that is, canceled. A proviso was also inserted requiring the students to swear that they would not overthrow the government—a requirement that excited no opposition and little discussion at the time, although protests were raised in later years and the clause was eventually removed. The Federal Office of Education was also empowered by the new law to award some 5000 graduate fellowships for prospective teachers. Still other provisions of the act set up grants to states for teacher-training, for counseling and guidance programs to steer talented students into science, and for helping to buy science, mathematics and foreign language materials for the schools.[34]

The turn to the study of foreign languages was a telling measure of the shift in America's mood in the Cold War. At the end of the Second World War, when the very organ of world government established itself at the United Nations Plaza in New York City and everybody who wanted anything in international affairs had to speak the language of the Americans, many seemed to think it hardly worthwhile to learn other peoples' languages. English was ousting French as the language of diplomacy, had already supplanted German as the *lingua franca* of science, and was spoken by pilots and ground controllers on all radio approaches to the international airports of the world. It was the morning, as it seemed, of the American Century.

The assumptions of this all-conquering America took hold in the schools. The old urge in war to cease teaching the language of the enemy had brought a big drop in public-school German classes, and a country in the throes of McCarthyism was not about to replace the study of German with the study of Russian. The compulsion of second-generation Americans to turn their backs on what they perceived as the alien culture of their immigrant parents also reduced interest in foreign languages in general. By the time of Sputnik, four out of ten American high schools offered no foreign language instruction at all.[35]

But now there was a belated stir of concern. Under the duress of Russian competition in the Third World, for instance, some Americans began to urge that it might be good manners to converse in their native tongues with peoples whose goodwill America valued. In all the capitals of the Middle East and North Africa, Admiral Hyman Rickover pointed out, the United States had only two Arab-speaking ambassadors. "Such linguistic deficiencies cannot be found in the foreign service of any other leading country," said the irascible head of the country's nuclear submarine program.

America might also have something to learn, it was acknowledged, by familiarity with the tongue of its adversaries. "We have only one ambassador in a Communist country who speaks the language," cried Rickover. In one of his evening "editorials" during the Sputnik excitement the television commentator Eric Sevareid noted that the Russians kept a whole army of specialists busy in Moscow going through American technical publications. At the least, Sevareid suggested, the United States might expand the tiny staff assigned to translating articles from Russian scientific journals. With its customary capacity for excess, the United States not only began training more Russian translators but mobilized a sizable part of its computer industry in a costly and finally fruitless effort to devise a system of automatic machine translation that would have obviated the need for learning any foreign language at all and put mankind back where it was before the Tower of Babel.[36]

Meanwhile the National Defense Education Act set other Americans back to brushing up on their languages. Berlitz schools, phonograph-record lessons and other commercial aids to quick-study for prospective overseas travelers had a vogue. Television comedians tried out jokes with foreign phrases in them. A paean of purest melancholy called "Dead Leaves" but sung in French by the seventy-five-pound Paris nightclub entertainer Edith Piaf made its way up Tin Pan Alley's list of most popular recordings. And into the schools went some 8000 "language laboratories." Through these elaborate assemblages of electronic gadgetry linking a multi-track tape machine with ranks and ranks of speakers and earphones, a child could listen to the sound of a native speaker of a language, respond individually in the language—and then listen to the recording of his own pronunciation of it. Soon school boards were not only restoring language in the secondary schools but extending its study all the way down to the kindergarten. For a time Spanish or French was made compulsory in the second and third grades of the Anaheim, California, school system.[37]

Far deeper currents were running in American education at the time of Sputnik than were manifested in flashy gadgets for the schoolhouse or in a few catchy programs for the tiny élite at the very top. Outwardly the progressive educationists who had managed and shaped American public schooling according to the ideas of John Dewey held sway over American education. With their emphasis on the importance of getting along with other people and on accepting the American way of life, they had served the majority viewpoint well in the first years of the Cold War. The nation had prized conformity, and the "life adjustment" programs of Dewey's successors had provided it. Now, in the shock of Sputnik, many middle-class parents took a new look at their schools, and were troubled. Over the years the administrators had been fattening the curriculum with subjects like the social and physical sciences, art, music, the industrial arts. Now all this seemed an alarming departure from the reading, writing and arithmetic that these parents had known in their own classroom experiences.[38]

Such misgivings were voiced even before Sputnik, not only by specialists like Rudolf Flesch but by such professionals as Arthur Bestor of the University of Illinois. In earlier days Bestor had officiated as a professor at the holy of holies of the progressive education movement—Columbia University Teachers College. But now in widely publicized speeches and articles he asserted that "the persons running our public school system lost sight of the main purpose of education—namely, intellectual training." And when the Russians took first place in the heavens, Bestor was roused to impassioned denunciation. "We are paying the price," he cried. "In the light of the Sputnik, 'life adjustment education' turns out to have been perilously close to 'death adjustment' for our nation and our children."[39]

In this new mood Admiral Rickover, the testy atomic engineer who had won a great name with the public by building up a topnotch nuclear submarine program in the teeth of bureaucratic objections, went around the country winning cheers with his excoriations of the "softness" and "permissiveness" of American education. Parents nodded vigorously in agreement as he condemned them for becoming "so obsessed with 'democracy' and 'equality' that smart, industrious children have been denied praise and dull and lazy ones have escaped censure in the name of democracy in the classroom." What America needed, said the Austrian-born Rickover, was rigorous, toe-the-mark schooling like that enforced in the no-nonsense, subject-matter-oriented classrooms of France, Germany, Austria—and Russia. In and out of Congress there suddenly seemed to be a good many Americans ready to welcome a swing from permissiveness back to common sense—to discipline and dunce caps, to switches and multiplication tables and, said Dr. Margaret Mead tartly, toward those "highly satisfactory forms of torture which somebody (they themselves or at least their grandfathers) once suffered in the name of learning."[40]

The pendulum pushed by Sputnik was indeed swinging, and progressive education, which seemed to be much readier for it than anybody suggested, collapsed in a heap. The final blow that bowled over the professional life-adjusters was the sudden and imperious return to the realm of public education of the academics. Long years before, back in the days when the country took up progressive education and public-school education went professional, the scholars had loftily divorced themselves from the schoolmarms. Now, out of patience with the indifferent preparation of the high schoolers pouring into college lecture halls, the scholars turned vehemently upon progressive education as the principal cause of all classroom ills.[47]

First out of their ivory towers and back to the schools were the mathematicians. As early as 1951 faculty members at the University of Illinois began invading schools and rewriting elementary and secondary school courses. Along with their learning, they brought an imaginative touch. What cold have been more widely detested than the lowly rote-drills of elementary-school arithmetic? Men of grace and inspiration like Max Beberman and David Page dressed it up with sets, lattices and varying base-number systems as Mathmatics, queen of the sciences, and plugged it into the electronic computer. Thus was born what came to be known to millions as "the New Math." Before long elders at a national teachers meeting in Tulsa watched openmouthed as David Page in thirty minutes led a troop of ordinary third-graders with a fistful of Cuisenaire rods and different colors of chalk on a blackboard through a whole series of number systems on bases other than ten. And before long, as parents strained over the prodigious leaps plotted out in their children's "New Math" homework, a committee of the country's most redoubtable mathematicians met in Cambridge, Massachusetts, to demand that every college-bound high schooler be taught two years of calculus.[42]

It was not much different in the sciences. One day in 1955 the caustic eye of MIT Physics Professor Jerrold Zacharias came to rest on the budget of seventeenth-century mechanics that passed for physics in an American high school. Dr. Zacharias, the inventor of the atomic clock, was something of a near-critical energy-mass himself. He reacted. Calling together a team of the country's best physicists, including two Nobel Prize winners, he got them not only to help write new texts but also to act in movies of experiments and other demonstrations. Their new program looked expensive but Zacharias pointed out that education was a $25 billion business in America and far less was being spent on such "educational research and development," as he called it, than in private industry.

"We have brought physics up to 1927," said Zacharias. We have put subject-matter back into the curriculum, said others.[43]

When Dr. Killian went to Washington he took Zacharias and several of his fellow curriculum-reformers with him to serve on the White House Science Advisory Committee. They promptly set up a Course Content Improvement Program in the National Science Foundation, and barged into the schools to upgrade science instruction. They were a tough lot, scoffed at the emphasis on "the whole child," and demanded that the schools throw out the marmalade and concentrate strictly on the discipline in teaching physics, biology, chemistry, geology, and mathematics.

They also brought along their own educational psychologists. These were not teachers-college types who had gained their Ph.Ds with dissertations on "Public School Plumbing Equipment," "The Technique of Estimating School Equipment Costs," or "A Scale for Measuring Anterior-Posterior Postures of Ninth-Grade Boys." They were laboratory experimentalists who had probed deeply into the physiology of how children seem to learn. Of all these academics who took their place in the new roster of White House advisory committees, perhaps none spoke more directly to the country's new mood than Jerome Bruner. At his Center for Cognitive Studies at Harvard, Bruner had measured the eye movements of babies, analyzed the "cognitive styles" evidenced in young children, and come to some startling conclusions about the importance of "structure" in all learning. "Discovery," he said was what teachers should work for, and courses should be designed to abet "spiraling" from one discovery to the next. In a best-selling report from the reforming academics entitled *The Process of Education,* Bruner laid down a hypothesis that became the new movement's pioneering theme: "Any subject," he wrote, "can be taught effectively in some intellectually honest way to any child at any stage of development.[44]

Soon, bankrolled by $6,000,000 from the National Science Foundation, an uncompromisingly first-class "package" including an elegantly abstruse textbook, some sixty films and workbooks full of rigorous laboratory experiments, was being tried in a third of the country's physics classes and perused by dazed parents. The NSF helped the schools buy and equip laboratories so that they could perform the experiments as prescribed. The trouble was that few teachers, even with the best equipment, were up to teaching the course. So the National Science Foundation funded summer institutes at which teachers were initiated into the rigors. Zacharias himself bustled around to many of them, interrupting to tell the hapless teachers what they should be saying. It was a demanding discipline. Even the teachers that could handle the new materials protested. They said that the committee's "cookbook" experiments, however certified by the test kitchens of MIT, left them no leeway to adapt to meet the needs of on-the-spot learning situations.[45] The "New Physics" was too fancy for most high schools.

Backed by $12,000,000 from the National Science Foundation, the scholars of Biology converged in the Rocky Mountains the summer after Sputnik to grind out three different courses known, by the color of their textbook covers, as the Yellow, Green and Blue Biology, each with a dazzling panoply of four-color laboratory manuals and films. Four million of these books were used in the schools for a time, and thousands of teachers went to summer institutes to wrestle with their demanding complexities. In Chemistry the academics produced two programs, the best known of which was called CHEM study and sent textbooks into 1,200,000 homes in the 1960s. Other courses were devised for the Earth Sciences, and even for grade-school science. Commercial publishers, taking counsel with the bewildered teachers and battered principals, retitled their texts with voguish names like "Discovery" and "Learning Laboratory" and carefully left in enough of the old routines to keep the teachers from being put right out of business.[46]

Somewhere along the line the impetus to restore the old rigors flagged. The teaching of English and History proved all but impervious to the assaults of the reformers, whose priorities were in any case on the Science and Mathematics side of the curriculum. And after President Johnson took office, new urgencies arose in the land for meeting the long-neglected needs of black education, as a result of which courses in Cosmetics, Restaurant Arts and Home Budgeting began to look like anything but expendable "frills" for the training of thousands seeking a place in the Great Society. A monumental, statistics-packed report to the United States Commissioner of Education in 1964 also served to call into question the value and efficacy of the scholars' reforms. The finding brought in by Professor James Coleman, though subject to endless debate among specialists, seemed to say rather decidedly that in twentieth-century America the offerings of the schools appeared to make little difference in the development of the young. It was the home and the outside environment, not the schools and their lessons, that according to Coleman's tabulations exerted overwhelming influence in children's lives. Finally, even among the well-fed, the well-born and the fair-skinned outside the inner city, the heavy science injection they received after Sputnik generated their inevitable reaction.[47]

There is no question that in response to President Eisenhower's plea the nation's children received a dosage of science and mathematics. Between the years 1948 and 1963 the number of high school students taking these subjects more than doubled, rising well beyond the rate of population increase at the time. Moreover, wrote Professor Arthur Ross of Berkeley in 1964, "it is well established that an unusually high proportion of the more talented" were heading for scientific and engineering careers in answer to the Cold War call.[48]

But soon enough, and certainly after the Cold War ended in 1963, the educational evolution of these young people who scored high in College Entrance Examination Boards and other achievement tests underwent a change. Among members of this group, who were under heaviest parental pressure to excel academically and who therefore spent more time over the New Math, Zacharias's Physics course, and the assorted versions of the new Biology and Chemistry, there was a marked turning away from these subjects after they entered college. Dean Frederick Terman of Stanford, commenting in 1971 on what by then had been a widely observed "retreat from science and engineering among college men" observed that the falling off in interest set in soon after the post-Sputnik reforms were instituted. Looking back over trends in the career choices stated by top high school seniors in National Merit Scholarship competitions in the Cold War years, Dean Terman noted that the decline "began (with) the graduating classes of 1962 and 1963."[49]

By the time of Dean Terman's postmorten, of course, the shortage of engineers and scientists predicted in Cold War times had vanished. The beseeching advertisements of jobs with prepaid country-club memberships and free private swimming pools thrown in by aerospace contractors bidding for engineers had disappeared from the classified-ad sections of the newspapers. Indeed, for some of the young people who had been steered into the sciences after Sputnik and who had taken a few extra years to complete their training there was a shocking outcome: emerging from the graduate schools in the late 1960s they found themselves among the unwanted new Ph.D. physicists who took jobs as librarians—when they could get them. This dismaying outcome had a technical explanation: the experts back in Eisenhower's time and later had seriously underestimated the number of scientists who would pass up jobs in industry and defense work and go into teaching and training yet more scientists and engineers.[50] In a larger sense, like many of their generation, they were casualties of the Cold War.

For the impact of the Cold War upon the schools faithfully reflected the imperative needs as perceived through almost two decades by the Cold War society. In the opening stages it was the progressive educators who held responsibility for the socializing of the masses of idle young people, and the outcome of their life-adjusted program of schooling for American democracy through the early years of Red scares, Korean War and McCarthyism was a conforming and silenced generation the qualities of whose conduct as the organization men in the middle ranks of American business society in the intervening years gave small promise of vision, conviction or growth as the escalator lifted them to command level in the 1970s. In the perspective of these same years, the tough men who rushed in to decree their tough courses after Sputnik seemed—when they were followed by the Berkeley rising of 1964 and six years of rebellions in universities, colleges and high schools—only to have intensified the delayed fury of the frustrated young by imposing far heavier academic rigors on them.

On the playing fields of American education the Cold War had been fought by a variant of the two-platoon system of the college gridiron, the progressive educators team having made the running in the first half, and the Killians, the Zachariases and the other exponents of academic excellence taking the field from Sputnik until the final whistle in 1963. Conservative or liberal as either may be called, let there be no mistake about their common ends. Both of these squads played to the limit to win Ameria's Cold War against "international Communism." No doubt the followers of John Dewey who went so far beyond their leader in promoting the autonomy of the child that they turned their schools into playpens deserved, at the least, their name as progressive to an extreme. But it was also their life-adjustment doctrine that sanctioned and reinforced a conforming anti-Communist patriotism and a retributive antiintellectualism in the first half of the Cold War. When the country then found it self-defeating to denigrate intellect, the reforming eggheads of the scientific establishment remobilized America along the lines of an educationally select orientation for the concluding half of the Cold War. In the end, the influence of the reforming academics, like that of the life-adjustment professions before them, was repudiated when the students of America rose in rebellion as soon as the Cold War was over.

In 1970 Charles Silberman of *Fortune* magazine completed a reexamination of the schools for John Gardner's successor at the Carnegie Corporation. His report, *Crisis in the Classroom*, was first-rate and a best-seller. All too many of the classrooms he visited during his three-year study, said Silberman, seemed "joyless" and "oppressive." What afforded hope, however, were certain "informal" schools that were trying to break out of the prescriptive bounds of textbooks, grading, attendance-keeping and classroom policing. Was the pendulum swinging once again? It all sounded reminiscent of the emphasis back in the progressive schools of the 1920s and 1930s.[51]

"All fashions end in excess." This was the dictum of Paul Poiret, leader of Parisian haute couture in the 1920s, and it helps explain not only the cyclical turnabouts in education but much else in twentieth-century

American life. It is paucity of ideas that makes for the cyclical in human existence. There was still a shortage of ideas, not to speak of firm knowledge, in American education. The reforming academics had long since stalked back to their laboratories and studies, and nobody said anymore that Jerome Bruner talked with the accents of a new John Dewey. Indeed, nobody yet had any good notion of how children learn, or why. American education had grown to be a fifty-billion-dollar industry—and huge universities were hard at work on Research and Development in many fields. But little enough—less than one-half of one percent of educational funds —was spent on research into education.[52]

I T W A S in the realm of higher education that the policy of improving the schools and expanding science study to meet the challenge of Sputnik clashed most directly with the underlying educational doctrines formulated to wage and win the Cold War. To say this in these annals of American democracy is not to decry the spread of wisdom and knowledge. On the contrary, it is to point out that in this expansion of schooling, as in so many other instances, the well-intentioned acts of the Cold War had, by reason of such contradictions, unintended consequences. Thus it appears that from the earliest mobilization in the aftermath of the Second World War an American society intent on keeping the country prosperous and strong against the threat of "international Communism" persisted in holding its young people off the job market for the most prolonged span of adolescence ever attempted by any highly developed civilization. An endeavor so vast, so protracted and so fundamentally manipulative was bound to cause trouble for the institutions of education and society. It was also bound to submerge and roll right over the post-Sputnik campaign to raise national educational standards.

The drive to universalize and attenuate schooling had been the tidal force operating upon American education all through the twentieth century. As late as the year 1900 the proportion of American youth enrolled in secondary schools was still smaller than that in any western European nation except Italy. By the peak of the Cold War a half century later, 90% of all American young people aged 14 to 17 attended high school, and irresistible pressures were being exerted for the nation's children to go on to attend college as well.[53]

It was said that the colleges and universities of America had not been prepared for this. Expecting like everybody else a major depression after the Second World War, they had braced for a time of retrenching and contraction lest they turn loose masses of unemployed diploma-holders as the German universities did after the First World War. When the President's Commission on Higher Education in 1947 set a new goal of higher education for all, and the nation's birthrate simultaneously exploded, the colleges and the universities faced an ever-mounting tide of students that by the years after Sputnik fairly swamped them and threatened to sweep away the whole traditional system of higher education.

College for all—it was suddenly America's will. The thrust of technological innovation which powered the astonishing economic expansion of the Cold War period reinforced the need of the young for the college degree. As production grew ever more mechanized, fewer unskilled hands were needed at factories. The huge corporate organizations that now took the play completely away from the small business enterprisers in the economy were all of them structured bureaucracies—and they demanded credentials from anybody who applied for work. By writing tight entrance and apprenticeship requirements into labor contracts, trade unions fenced off many more good jobs from the casual applicant. The high school graduate, finding himself unwanted in the job market, faced a society all of whose most influential forces, not excepting his parents, seemed to be pressing him to get a college education. The diploma, the message said loud and clear, had great economic value. And his parents, such was the affluence of the times, often had the means to help him get it.

So it was that even before the exploding postwar birthrates began to be felt in burgeoning age-group pressures, college attendance shot up among young people coming of job-seeking age in the 1940s and 1950s. And it was a far more varied group of young people, of course, drawn from a wider segment of the whole society, that now filled the campuses to overflowing. The newcomers lacked, many of them, the common, largely upper-middle-class assumptions basic to the prewar Joe College life of the fraternity, the jocks, the pep meeting, the big dance. Lacking anything like secure prospects for the future, many of them were inordinately taken up with anxieties and ambitions for their careers. Yet if many students saw college as simply a business of getting themselves a sheepskin passport to a good job, the society's own intentions about the campus did little to suggest that there might be something more to higher education than that. For the social reality of this vast Cold War expansion of the college population, as Oscar Handlin has said, was "the existence of a large and growing age group which has no function but attendance at some kind of school."[54]

At this point the population explosion began to rumble and the walls of academe began to quake. Annual surges of awesome proportions all but flattened the doors of admissions offices. In the seven years between Sputnik and the end of the Cold War the number of young people attending college shot up by fifty percent, from 3 to 4.5 million, and by

1970 had more than doubled—to 7.6 million, considerably more than half of all members of their age group, and a proportion 1.5 times higher than that in any other nation on earth.[56]

The inundation strained America's higher education to the bursting point. The giant land-grant universities swelled to unprecedented size—the University of Minnesota, for instance, to 70,000 students, the University of Wisconsin to 68,000. Whole new chains of state universities mushroomed out of cornfields to make places for the hordes of young people. By 1970, just twenty-two years after its founding, the State University of New York, with 180,000 fulltime students on seventy campuses and a budget of $395 million, surpassed even California, oldest and most famous of the state multiversity systems with its 142,000 fulltime students and budget of only $350 million. Private four-year colleges, still admitting forty percent of all entering undergraduates, incurred huge deficits. In almost every town in the United States two-year community colleges sprang up to help meet the needs, and some two million young people took courses in such subjects as Accounting, Merchandising, Mathematics, Medical Office Practice, and Basic Baking while attending what educators—at least in California—called the thirteenth and fourteenth grades.[56]

Counterposed against these social, political and economic pressures engulfing the university was the academic reality. It was a formidable reality, based as it was upon the powerful facts of Cold War life. Unblinkable fact Number One was this: if society now wished to expand the facilities of higher education to an unprecedented degree, the professors would expect an appropriately greater price for their participation. But the price the scholars tended inevitably to ask was to pursue their own learned researches as fully and freely as possible. This meant that the members of the academic community on the campuses did not want, and would not ultimately accept, the job that their fellow countrymen were assigning them, to act as caretakers for America's youth.

Reinforcing this basic academic reality was a second unblinkable fact: the nation itself had made up its mind from the day of the atomic-bomb breakthrough during the Second World War, that the research which scholars preferred over teaching was in fact an activity vital to America's survival in the Cold War race. How else could the scientific discoveries be made without which America could not survive and surpass in the competition with Communist Russia?

America was therefore of two minds about higher education. In one part of its mind America wanted the university to remain off to one side as a kind of holding pen in which ever larger throngs of its youth should be retained, trained, socialized. In another part of its mind the country was summonng the university to the very center of its economic and political life—to supply the formulas that would solve the nation's problems, to perform the function as the 1947 President's Commission put it, of "a service station for the general public," and above all to keep making the discoveries that would keep the nation prospering, growing and always on top in the Cold War race for security. No wonder, in view of such schizoid ambivalence in the nation, that within the next decade the American university suffered a nervous breakdown.[57]

Confusion and contradiction were compounded by the ways in which trouble was for so long forestalled. How was it possible to cordon off an entire generation on what President Kingman Brewster of Yale was later to call "an involuntary campus"? With the launching of the Cold War as related in Chapter Two, a nationwide fear of Communism was generated that effectively cowed and silenced America's students during these years. And as the young of the 1950s perceived their lot, there was not much choice. Some few had not only switched off the science track but, in the new phrase, "dropped out" entirely. These were the "beats" who read Jack Kerouac's *On the Road* and headed down the highway to see if bumming around Denver was as great an experience as Dean Moriarty and Carlo Marx said it was. Under the unbelieving stares of the mass magazines, they huddled in San Francisco's coffeehouse, "the hungry i" to listen to the unbarbered poet Allen Ginsburg recite his poem, "Howl."[58]

But as practically everybody else saw it, there was just one way for the young to break out of their confinement all through these years, and that was to go after that parchment passport. The opening of the colleges to a far more varied and less homogeneously well-to-do swarm of young people led significant numbers of them to concentrate singlemindedly on getting the degree that seemed explicitly to promise both the security of a job and the prospect of favored access to the new society.

Institutional momentum also helped to keep things from breaking down sooner. The college presidents and deans who had often eagerly approved the plans for the tremendous expansion of their campuses and student bodies, hired anybody who had ever taught college subjects, kept on older professors and vied to sign up graduate students as auxiliary faculty to make up for the shortage of qualified academics. Besides it is not to be supposed that the faculties of higher learning across the nation laid down their teaching burdens in a body and turned wholly to research. By no means were all physical scientists with ideas sought after by the government and industry, or even social scientists trained, as the President's Commission bravely described them, to "apply at the point of social action" what they had "discovered concerning the laws of human behavior." But even in the Eisenhower years, when the nation supposed that its technological lead over Russia was so commanding that it could afford to hold back on university grants, the collective attitude of the academic community about its larger compact with American society was fairly clear. A survey taken in these years of more than 3000 faculty members showed that in American colleges as well as universities large and small, in all fields faculty of all ranks and ages wished to reduce their teaching still further, and all groups wished to increase the time devoted to graduate instruction and especially to research. In sum, the average number of classes taught by college professors during these years of unprecedented student population expansion declined by about one-third.[59]

The consequences were many, but taken as a whole they put a drastic distance between scholar and student. Of course the change in scale brought about by the vast increase in students affected the quality and dignity of instruction everywhere. Not only were the means of instruction simply not available, but the old network of personal appraisal by which faculty were recruited broke down. The rewards of the profession having increased, the motives for entering it grew more complex. No kind of professional system for ordering standards of responsibility, performance or even malpractice had ever existed among academics. Accordingly, deficiencies in faculty were not so easy to conceal as formerly. And they were almost impossible to correct. Professors were remote, lecturing to huge classes or leaving raw teaching assistants to take over most sessions. Even as their prima donnish perquisites and prerogatives grew, faculty absented themselves from university governance and other traditional functions. This was what Professor J. Kenneth Galbraith meant by his remark of self-criticism after the Harvard riots of 1969:

> There can be few who have more diligently avoided and evaded administrative responsibility in the university over a longer period of time than I.[60]

It was after Sputnik that such contradictions within American higher education ballooned out of all manageable proportions. The larger message that America received from the shock of the Soviet successes was that more education was needed—and people therefore sent even more of their children to college. But it was precisely at this time when the fear spread that the Russians might gain the upper hand in modern war technology that the nation turned to its talented academics and lavished upon them every reward to recoup America's Cold War supremacy. Coming at the moment when the scholars were successfully unloading their responsibility for teaching college students and devoting more time to pursue their research interests instead, the effect was to disorient the university and leave it in confusion as to its fundamental role in twentieth-century America.

The teaching, socializing and community-serving tasks of American higher education were not the only matters in question. Was the university to be a place for the disinterested search for truth, for conserving and transmitting the wisdom of the inherited past? In its inimitably split-level way, America only knew after Sputnik that it wanted from the university more of everything—but at that moment, more science and more scientists. For scientists ("It takes a long time to grow a scientist," President Eisenhower said), it must look to the reform of the whole system of education—in the schools and high schools, in the colleges and universities. For science, it must look to the pace-setting universities, the very seats of disinterested learning, the centers of research like Princeton.

Among the universities into which Washington pumped research and development money after Sputnik, Princeton with its traditions of independent and cloistered scholarship was far from the most prominent government partner. Yet a strong physical sciences faculty attracted government-sponsored grants early in the Cold War. Then a group of friends among whom Lewis Strauss and Allen Dulles were prominent helped the University acquire a large tract two miles outside Princeton as the James A. Forrestal Research Center, so named for the first Secretary of Defense, a Princeton alumnus. One of the advantages of the Center, President Harold Dodds explained, was that "security measures can be installed without appreciable interference with normal university activities." Behind its barbed wire, classified research multiplied. "In a class by itself" was the supersecret Project Matterhorn, which President Dodds proudly reported "played an important part in the development . . . of the hydrogen bomb."

Though Princeton's government contracts had grown through the mid-1950s at the rate of a million dollars a year, such gains were as nothing compared with the torrent of federal dollars that poured in after Sputnik. In his next annual report, President Robert Goheen reported that individual federal research projects had shot up by $7,000,000. Behind the Forrestal Center barriers a big particle accelerator was under construction and a jet-propulsion laboratory flourished. The Atomic Energy Commission alone spent $20,000,000 a year or more on highly classified work. In short order, Old Nassau was dependent on Washington for 30% of its annual income.[61]

It was the same story at all the great universities. Seventy-five per cent of MIT's support came from Washington, 50% of Columbia's, 40% of Stanford's, 30% of Harvard's. After Sputnik federal research grants to

SPUTNIK AND AMERICAN EDUCATION   365

universities in general grew at an annual rate of 21% until by 1968 they amounted to some $1.4 billion. Washington's money built and staffed huge military laboratories at MIT, Berkeley, Ann Arbor, Cal Tech, Johns Hopkins, and giant new hospitals alongside university medical centers from Pittsburgh to Houston. On the campuses the mighty monuments of federal funding presented their endless stark corridors, some without even doorknobs to reach for but instead an infinite perspective of sliding doors behind which professors could withdraw so that they could hardly be found—almost like the huge new federal post office people told about that opened for business without any windows to buy stamps at.[62]

Much of the time the professors were not there anyhow but airborne, flying to Washington to negotiate yet more grants. For the effect of Washington's policy of making contracts with the individual researcher was to turn faculty members into entrepreneurs. A new activity sprang up, called the art of grantsmanship. Undergraduates told of the adviser who could not be found because he was away in Timbuktu on a federal grant. Others went in for research so specialized that only a few individuals at other universities around the world could discuss it with them, necessitating grants to fly to congresses in Stockholm or Tokyo to keep abreast with the specialist colleagues of their so-called invisible colleges.

In this kind of world, about the only students the researcher saw were a few graduate students. In such circles, teaching was passé. Loyalties were to a man's specialty, not to his university, and when the scholar took off for a new post he took his grants with him. By 1961 no fewer than 49,000 of the 170,000 scientists and engineers employed in universities were taken up strictly with research and development. The university, Harvard President Pusey found himself saying, seemed to be a loose assemblage of enterprises held together by a common heating plant. California's President Clark Kerr, in the throes of constructing six new campuses, each to accommodate 27,000 more students, found nobody ready to say what kind of structure should be designed for the Biological Sciences because the subspecialties were so esoteric, so loose and so fast-changing.[63]

Some of the universities' federal activities were, as the phrase went, "spun off." On 9000 acres outside Palo Alto bequeathed by the founder, Leland Stanford University established the Stanford Research Institute, probably the most notable of the many government contract centers thus set up by universities. The Institute took on an astonishing variety of classified projects; by 1966 it had a payroll of 2000, a budget of $35,000,000. Stanford's own budget was not a great deal bigger, yet so large and multifarious had the university's noninstructional services grown that only 16% of its revenues came in from student fees and payments. An imposing array of private firms, drawn by the university's big electronic engineering division, took leases in the park, foremost among them Hewlett-Packard, started in 1947 by a pair of Stanford electronics men one of whom, David Packard, became President Nixon's Undersecretary of Defense in 1969.

Such Cold War collaboration, wrote sociologist Robert Nisbet, turned the university into "a religious monastery insisting upon all the affluence of freebooting capitalism." Only Harvard forbade clasified research through these years, and many a Harvard professor consulted for the government or found ways to join in indirectly. Often the government to be advised was in Asia or Africa, and there were substantial fees as well as junkets. At MIT it was understood that a professor could spend one day a week on his own affairs, and MIT faculty members used their time to start no fewer than 165 companies. Others accepted consultancies with private defense contractors. Three was the unofficial limit. Part-time consulting enabled such high-powered senior faculty as Jerome Wiesner and Jerrold Zacharias to live quite well, summering on Cape Cod and operating yacht-size sailboats.[64]

Always short of funds to meet the ever-rising costs of their fast-growing establishments, the university administrators readily fell in with policies of strong-minded academics who brought to the campus not only prestige but cash in the form of big grants from foundations and industry as well as government. The result in many departments and special institutes was to create islands of autonomous power in which so much of the university's real authority was wielded that the administrators lost real command. The further consequence was that when the pressure of undergraduate population on the campus finally grew too great for the professors and their deputies to perform their teaching functions with even minimal effectiveness, it was not the administrators of the universities who took action.

The action when it came took the form of a rebellion by students. The revolt started the year after the Cold War ended, in an inchoate rising at Berkeley in 1964. It spread thereafter across the country in a wave of sporadic explosions that did not stop erupting for the next six years. In the course of this upheaval, the whole stately edifice of higher education cracked, presidents toppled like ninepins, universities repudiated their alliances with the military, faculty and administrators loosened their ties with corporations and foundations, and the society itself ended up in a long drawn out crisis of confidence.

In time the American nation became confusedly aware that its young people were rising in protest at being kept so long out of the world of work and adult activity. This appeared to be the meaning of the demand, voiced over and over in the demonstrations, for "relevance" in their lives. It was at no time clear that the society knew how to deal with the root problem. In social terms it reacted by grudgingly letting down some of the bars of arbitrary restraint upon youthful conduct and according to youth the same code of conduct as adults. Politically, it reacted under the duress of having sent the young to fight its most unpopular war by extending in 1969 the right to vote to all aged eighteen or over. But the economic bind holding the young back from the job market remained.[65]

The question arises, how did it happen that the young people of America finally rose in 1964 to protest being kept for so long out of the mainstream of national life? The answer seems to be that the students who made the revolt of the 1960s were the first generation to have known nothing but the life of the Cold War. Born as the Cold War began in 1945, the first of them attained the age of eighteen and entered college as the Cold War was ending in 1963. Having thus grown up through all its years of omnipotence, they were also the first to see the Cold War in its overreaching, overweening entirety.

As long as they had lived, the world had been divided into two camps that were competing with each other ideologically and politically. As long as they could remember, the message had been dinned into their consciousness that it was only by more and yet more years of denying and sacrificing that America could win the battle against "international Communism." All the time that they had been growing up, they had been required to accept the larger assumption that young people should be kept out of the adult society of work and action. It was a member of the Students for a Democratic Society at Berkeley who blurted that, far from feeling privileged to be a member of a university with the largest concentration of Nobel Prize scholars on earth, he was there involuntarily. "Like don't give me that stuff about I'm here to learn," he said. "I'm here because I have to be, against my will."

In part he was there because of the draft—and guiltily unhappy about the exemption that the United States government vouchsafed him so long as he stayed on as a student. In part he was on campus because of the indiscriminate use being made by all of society's gatekeepers around him of college degrees as the passport for occupational entry. In part he was on campus because of the strong social pressure upon middle-class children to attend college and indeed graduate and professional school after that—and because of the opprobrium heaped upon students who broke off or dropped out.[66]

Such were the ones who were finally to see it all, the whole Cold War scene. They were the most permissively reared of all children, bred up on the bland behaviorism of Drs. Arnold Gesell and Frances Ilg, whose assurances that the most aberrant idiocies are "normal," set forth with charts and graphs in *The Infant and Child in the Culture of Today*, were cribside reading for parents in postwar years. "While baby naps, the mother should be preparing an interesting corner for baby's play when he wakes." These children were reared on the premise that they must never be bored. At Harvard in 1968 demonstrators dashed through corridors calling their fellows out "to root out the boredom of our daily lives."[67]

Having grown up in these years of television, these young people seemed to have a notably shortened attention span. Those who had come along before them had been as old as nine or ten when TV came in: though they had been given their chance to watch "Uncle Miltie" Berle Saturday nights on the ten-inch screens of their day, they had not been allowed to look at TV every night. Thereafter the parental resistance had worn down before the big living-room eye, and these were the first TV generation. They had been bombarded by sensation, surfeited with novelty, barraged by excitements: propeller caps on their heads, hula hoops in their hands, singing commercials in their ears, and everywhere the new —new designs for new cars, new modes for new gadgets, new motels and new jetports. Subjected to such a diverting clamor and above all such a pace of change, they could not stick the whole way to hold the line year after year against Communism, much less keep up with the demands of the Achesons and Dulleses and Rusks for yet more sacrifices.

From the time the Russians launched their satellite, the competition between the two camps had also become educational. The school system in which these rebelling students had grown up had emphasized the competitive acquisition of knowledge as a source of power and stability. By the time they had left high school they were better educated than any previous generation of students, but also more overworked.

All the emphasis on education and competition could not easily be sustained after the students entered the university. By then, the student was partly burned out. The personal benefits of intensive studying and searching for a profitable career began to appear less and less attractive in an affluent world—and even less so in a world that seemed to be making it difficult for a young person to become a part of the economic system. As the student came to view the implications of America's competition with Communism as a never-ending phenomenon, he began to question the social value of his efforts. Even if he were to maintain his enthusiasm for his undergraduate work through the impersonal and often perfunctory classes of the college years, by the time he reached graduate school he increasingly asked himself whether the competitive search for knowledge was worth it. At this point he began to view America's competition with the Communist world (and sometimes competition itself) as a form of mass paranoia, and he saw the university as an agent of the government that contributed to the perpetuation of the paranoid system. It was just such an evolution that underlay much of the protest at Berkeley.[68]

On top of this the rebellious student of the 1960s began to see America's mass society as unable to change. A pervasive and enveloping business orientation already, as he perceived it, so indoctrinated his elders into the role of credit-controlled consumers that Americans were beholden—all of them—to a way of life that may not have been in their own best interests. Indeed, government and education were seen as totally interdependent, and allied to ward off any reasonable attempts to change the society. Even protest seemed to be simply absorbed, and the bitterest of the young people pointed to the way hippies and protesters were institutionalized as part of the country's folklore and humor, and exploited by the advertising industry, which they had vowed on their bullhorns, in their posters and through their underground press, to destroy. In this kind of a culmination, the mobilization of the young ended in the helplessness of despair.[69]

The American campus on which these explosions erupted, however, would never be the same. There was a return to teaching—and to studying. Even at MIT it became hard to find a scholar who admitted to doing any more classified research. At Princeton, Project Matterhorn was rebaptized as the Plasma Physics Laboratory and where security men once stood guard at the Forrestal Research Center, students cycled freely on and off what was now known simply as the Forrestal campus. The drying up of federal research funds, and even more the discovery that the Cold War had trained up many more scientists than the country seemed to need, had worked wonders in recreating loyalty to their colleges and jobs in the freebooting faculty members who had a few years before so blithely deserted them for the high-salaried jobs elsewhere now suddenly in short supply.

But the scene that greeted the administrators as they crept out of their foxholes was not reassuring. The universities had grown accustomed after Sputnik to living in a style that could be sustained only by government subventions, and the scramble to get clear of federal defense work and the decisions in Washington to cut back research funds created huge deficits at some of the most famous private universities. The question for the 1970s, said President Pusey as he stepped down at Harvard, was whether such universities could survive without accepting government subsidy and thus becoming public institutions.[70]

A L T H O U G H   General Eisenhower's call to change the schools successfully diverted many in the country from demanding huge increases in defense spending after Sputnik, his authority as the repository of all wisdom in defense matters never went unquestioned thereafter. Democratic Majority Leader Lyndon Johnson opened Senate hearings to determine how the United States has "lost an important battle in technology" as demonstrated by "the satellites that are whistling over our heads." One by one the generals went before the committee to testify that the Russians had rockets "to which we have no response," and might surpass the United States in striking power by mid-1959. Soon not only the nation but the world was talking about the "missile gap" now being opened by the Russians, and at a meeting of the European allies in October a Dutch delegate openly charged that the United States "helped our enemy" by not straining hard enough to be first with the intercontinental ballistic missile.

In the end, Eisenhower succeeded neither in holding the line against the "spending spree" he feared nor in overcoming the Democratic charge that his administration was allowing the "missile gap" to open in the arms race with Russia. To allay Allied fears, he rushed to Paris ten days after suffering a stroke to promise intermediate-range missiles for NATO defense in Britain, Italy, Turkey. The record shows, moreover, that despite all of Eisenhower's dogged efforts to uphold fiscal conservatism, missile outlays rose steadily during the years he strove to hold them back. In fiscal 1955 missiles were already costing the federal government a sizeable $1.2 billion. By the year of the Sputniks outlays had more than doubled to $3 billion, and by 1958 they rose to $4.3 billion, by 1959 to $5.3 billion.[71]

It would seem that these expenditures kept rising despite the determined resistance of the President because the officials who worked for him prevailed against him. Of course it was extremely difficult for a Chief Executive who was absent from his desk for 120 days in a year, as Eisenhower was in 1957, and who took naps for several hours every afternoon, as Eisenhower did during his second term, to ride herd on the federal establishment. Yet even a Franklin Roosevelt, with all his might and guile at juggling bureaus and bypassing executives to keep tabs on what was really getting done, left this wry account of a president trying to impose his will on bureaucrats:

> The Treasury is so large and far-flung and ingrained in its practices that I find it almost impossible to get the action and results I want—even with Henry [Morgenthau] there. But the Treasury is not to be compared with the State Department. You should go through the experience of trying to get any changes in the thinking, policy and action of the career diplomats and then you'd know what a real problem was. But the Treasury and the State department put together are nothing compared

with the N-a-a-vy. The admirals are really something to cope with—and I should know. To change anything in the N-a-a-a-a-vy is like punching a feather bed. You punch it with your right and you punch it with your left until you are finally exhausted, and then you find the damn bed just as it was before you started punching.[72]

Eisenhower, bested in his efforts to hold down the Pentagon's space-and-missile spending, got in his last punch, and it was a good one even if it was too late to decide the fight, in his farewell speech to the country in 1961. It was his warning against the "military-industrial complex," and there can be little doubt that what the general had foremost in mind was the way the bureaucrats of the Pentagon helped to close the fancied missile gap even as the Democrats were persuading themselves and the nation of its existence.[73]

In the end, after gaining office in 1961 and examining the evidence, the Democrats themselves in the person of Defense Secretary Robert McNamara affirmed that there had been no missile gap. This outcome however was due not so much to the efforts of the Americans—Eisenhower included—to catch up. It was due largely to a decision made by the Russian leadership in the very moment of their 1957 breakthrough not to expand their lead in missilery.[74]

The decision was effectively concealed behind the boasts and threats of Khrushchev, the man who had to make it. The facts bore out its reality. Yet even in affirming its reality, the decision was ignored by the Kennedy administration, which proceeded to put through a huge expansion of the American missile program and of defense spending in general. The decision finally came to be recognized only years later after China's quarrel with Russia finally broke into the open and the Chinese wrathfully upbraided the Russians for making it. The import of the decision was this: notwithstanding Sputnik, and the successful tests of 1957, Russia would not build an elementary first-generation ICBM complex but would wait for the second and third-generation models. The result was a five-year delay in the establishment of an operational Soviet ICBM capability. Thanks to other decisions made in America, it did not slow up the arms race. But ultimately the decision spelled the end of the Cold War.[75]

The Russian action, which to Western eyes appeared to fly in the face of all the rules of Cold War strategy, grew out of the triangular relationship that from that time onward came to dominate Khrushchev's foreign policy. All during this time the Chinese factor was submerged, or perhaps one should say hidden from American eyes, by the ideological blinders that compelled them to look at the Communist world as monolithically indivisible. In truth, Khrushchev's problem from 1957 on was this: he found himself under pressure to reassert the policies of coexistence in order to minimize the chances of nuclear conflict with the Cold Warriors of the United States, while at the same time he was forced to conduct expansionist policies to prevent an open break with the Cold Warriors of China.[76]

In November of 1957, not long after the Russians had achieved their successful ICBM test and only days after they had sent Sputnik circling sensationally through space, all the world's Communist leaders assembled in Moscow to celebrate the fortieth anniversary of the Bolshevik Revolution. So great an occasion brought Mao Tse-tung himself to Moscow to salute the Soviet Union not simply as spiritual and ideological leader but as leader in the struggle against imperialism.

What glorious prospects for Communism Mao saw as he gazed upon the world from atop Lenin's tomb in Red Square where the movement had first caught fire only forty years before. Half of Europe now stood in the Socialist camp. China's Revolution was won. A Socialist moon glistened in the sky. And the Soviet Union, master of the hydrogen bomb, led America in intercontinental ballistic missiles. Under Soviet leadership, said Mao, the Socialist camp must now go on and show its military superiority in every way over the imperialists. "The East wind is prevailing over the West wind," he said. In short, enforced by Soviet arms, the Revolutions of 1917 and 1949 would now sweep over the unliberated remainder of the globe.[77]

That was not how Khrushchev saw it at all. Gratified as he was at Communism's spread and exhilarated at Sputnik's performance, Khrushchev looked upon the world with very different eyes as he stood beside Comrade Mao. Of course he felt the need within Soviet society for presenting Communist ideology as the wave of the future. He knew, and often said, that what the average Soviet citizen wanted after decades of deprivation was improvement of his everyday material well-being and some extension of his freedom. He was not unaware that the bracing Communist slogans that rang in the party newspapers and official speeches left the Russian masses indifferent and that patriotic pride in technological and economic achievements was taking the place of Communist ideology as the main cement of social cohesion. Yet what was to be the rationale for a totalitarian system unless it could somehow keep up the tensions that ideological mission engendered? Increasingly, the way in which Khrushchev and his associates kept up something of the old Marxist-Leninist élan was by turning outside the Soviet Union to the opportunities to score successes for Communism and inflict defeats on the West presented in the Middle East and other regions of the Third World.[78]

But this policy of militant expansionism was full of dangers. It was certain to multiply the chances of a confrontation with the United States and, by a miscalculation, of bringing on the last thing a great country that had built so much at such sacrifice in such short time could want—the unimaginable catastrophe of nuclear war. Mao in his fortieth anniversary speech had lightly observed that nuclear war would mean the end of capitalism but not of Communism: if 300 million Chinese were killed there would still be 300 million left alive. Khrushchev knew what thermonuclear war meant. He had a far more sophisticated appreciation of the capacities of the American deterrent, and he knew how much more was required than the orbiting of a Sputnik to prevail in a thermonuclear showdown. These were facts: first, the early big Russian rockets had been designed to carry the atom bomb, and for the hydrogen bomb much smaller types were appropriate; and second, the early rockets needed liquid fuel, which required laborious and hazardous loading at the last minute before firing, whereas solid-fueled American rockets were coming along in the 1950s that could be loaded and stored at the ready in almost invulnerable sunken concrete "silos" and fired at a moment's notice.[79]

Khrushchev, moreover, was building up the Soviet Union, not inviting its destruction. His ballistic missiles were instruments of the Russian state to be deployed with discretion in the interests of defending the power and wealth of forty years' sacrifice and struggle, not wantonly employed as the spearhead of the revolutionary struggle for the benefit of remote countries of which Russians knew nothing and for which they cared less.

Expansion and coexistence, then, were the two plunging horses that Khrushchev tried to ride in the hectic years after 1957 while Eisenhower was tussling with the "military-industrial complex" and parents were carrying their Cold War to the suburban PTAs. Galloping on for coexistence, the Soviet leader refused to rowel his people for the surrender of yet more consumer goods that might have paid for manufacture of the ICBMs for which the America of Secretary Charles Wilson's Pentagon-and-station-wagon economy had no match. Waving his hat for Communist expansion, Khrushchev promised before Mao left Moscow to give China an A-bomb—or so the Chinese have said. And as the First Secretary whooped and hollered, it became the deliberate policy of the Soviet Union to get all the propaganda mileage out of the "missile gap" exposed by Sputnik. One way Khrushchev did this was to have the Russian radio and newspapers quote back to the West the West's own exaggerated views of Soviet missile capacity, thereby reinforcing the exaggerations. When the Soviet Communist party laid down at the fortieth anniversary meeting the thesis that the strategic balance was changing in favor of the camp of socialism, the exaggerated statement became more menacing to the West because of its impact on the world in the wake of Sputnik.[80]

There was of course a contradiction between these two policies which Khrushchev pursued—the one a strategy of militant Communist expansion wherever opportunity offered, the other a strenuous search for accommodation with the United States. With a Communist's dialectical sense that change is the law of life, with insouciant bounce, peasant gusto and the nerves of a Bolshevik safecracker, the First Secretary held his clashing policies in rough harness by a common rhetoric of bluster. His course veered now one way and now another—first to Washington and then to Peking, into summit negotiations and out of them, into sending off ultimatums and recalling them. The addiction to improvisational moves and, even more, to a propaganda barrage so often and so heavily laden with menace courted unmistakable risks—and led in the end to the showdown crisis of the Cold War in the Cuban Missile affair of 1962.

In all fairness the age of bluster was not inaugurated by Khrushchev's spouting over Sputnik, nor even with the round of glowering diplomatic threats (known as "nuclear diplomacy") set off by the Kremlin after Russia acquired atomic and hydrogen weapons in the mid-1950s. It was that prophet of righteousness and pillar of the National Council of Churches, John Foster Dulles, who first made the public rattling of nuclear weapons a function of official Cold War strategy. In words that sent a palpable shiver through the world in 1954, the Secretary proclaimed "massive retaliation" as America's new slogan for the East-West contest, and shortly thereafter American policy was defined in a widely publicized interview as "brinkmanship."[81]

But the diplomatic notes with which the Soviet Union bombarded neighboring countries as soon as it had acquired a stockpile of nuclear weapons were, if possible, much more unsubtle. In the hours that troops were landing in Suez, the Russians reminded the British and French that they had such weapons close at hand with missiles ready to deliver them. After Sputnik, the reminders grew still cruder. In December 1957, a note from Bulganin to Prime Minister Macmillan asked:

> How can such NATO measures as, for instance, the round-the-clock flights over the British isles by British-based American bombers carrying atom and hydrogen bombs help to reassure people, to improve the situation? . . . I say frankly that we find it difficult to understand what, in taking part in such a policy, guides the government of such a country as Great Britain, which is not only in an extremely vulnerable position by force of its geographical situation but which according to the admission of its official representatives has no effective means of defense

against the effects of modern weapons. Nor can there, it is true, be any such defense.[82]

Within the Western alliance alarm over the decline of American prestige after Sputnik brought countermeasures that such fulminations did not deter. A special NATO meeting in December 1957 led to the installation of a large number of intermediate-range American missiles in England, Italy and Turkey in an effort to offset the extensive Russian intermediate-range ballistic program.

At no time did the prospects of ending the Cold War seem more bleak than in the aftermath of the Sputniks. This was the time when United States bombers were droning ceaselessly over their bases to ensure that some would escape surprise attack and strike back. It was the season when Khrushchev blurted to Westerners at a Moscow embassy reception: "We will bury you." In Syria the Russians actively backed a Communist plot to take power. In Asia, the Middle East and Africa they were offering arms and aid to the new, nonaligned nations. In Europe De Gaulle's return to power signaled new and major trouble for the unity of the Western alliance. And Khrushchev, detecting some timorousness in Bonn, informed the West Germans that at any time Russian rockets could turn their country into a "cemetery." In his dourest Cold War mood, Secretary Dulles summoned the Allies to stand fast "one year, five years, ten years, twenty years, I don't know"—until a change in the attitude of Russia's rulers should crown the "strategy of victory."[83]

But coexistence was also the name of the game—and coexistence in the most literal sense of the word requires the prevention of nuclear war. Abolition of nuclear arms was out of the question, and agreement on arms reduction always eluded the negotiators. Khrushchev as always bestrode the two horses. Aware of the terrible perils of the arms race, he was incongruously confident that Russia could outscore and outsmart the West. Eager to reduce the outlay on the nuclear and space races and channel the money to other sectors of the economy that badly needed it, he was at the same time filled with the ambition to score technological and military "firsts" that pushed a thumb in the eye of the United States and gave prestige to Russia and glory to Khrushchev's reign.[84]

To these fears and ambitions were added certain fears about the proliferation of nuclear weapons. The Russians never gave such arms to any Eastern European country—they might have been used against the Soviet Union; and after promising them the atom bomb, the Chinese say, Khrushchev went back on his word eighteen months later. The idea that West Germany might in one way or another acquire atomic weapons was the one possibility that produced unfeigned anxiety in the Russians. They could vividly imagine the political ends to which militarist elements in West Germany might put even a few nuclear weapons in dealing with the Soviet-bloc countries or even with Soviet Russia itself. The Americans, as their own failure to share nuclear warheads with anybody demonstrated, had misgivings quite as great. Yet mutual suspicions in the frozen positions of the Cold War kept the two superpowers backing stiffly away all through the 1950s.[85]

In the West, then, there was turmoil, gloom and widespread pangs of self-doubt in 1957, leading Eisenhower to bewail "the psychological vulnerability of our people" as disclosed by the Sputnik scare. In Britain a campaign for nuclear disarmament aroused wide and outspoken moral concern about the means through which Western purposes might be justifiably promoted. In America, however, a righteous enthusiasm for the end of opposing world Communism was strong enough to discourage much sensitivity about means. In the East, the state of affairs was obscured for all sides by the mighty cloud of smoke put out by Khrushchev as he consolidated the Russian hold on Eastern Europe, conciliated the Chinese, egged on the Arabs, and shouted that the Soviet Union, having surpassed the Americans in missilery, would soon catch up with and outdo them in the peaceful competition to produce the most butter.[86]

In this confused scene there was one area in which the mutual interests of the two superpowers might conceivably be so substantial as to be self-enforcing: the suspension of testing of atomic and hydrogen weapons. Well aware that his country had just finished a series of tests and that the United States and Britain were on the point of staging some important ones, Khrushchev on March 31, 1958, announced that the Soviet Union was voluntarily suspending all such tests. Six months later, the United States and Britain in turn proclaimed their willingness to suspend testing, and continued the suspension despite new Russian tests in November.[87]

CHAPTER 11

The U-2

THE SPLIT-LEVEL STYLE IN GOVERNMENT AND SOCIETY

Some time in the middle of the 1950s a perceptible change came over the suburban American landscape. Until then many of the millions who pushed into the open land around cities after the Second World War refused to live in anything but a ranchhouse. Bursting into the outlying areas from the confines of the cities, they thought of themselves as seeking peace and comfort in the openness of the countryside. The ranchhouse, with its low and rambling outlines, its picture window and gently-sloping peaked roof, its invitation to easy, indoor-outdoor, one-level living for all who could afford it, characterized the mood of the United States. The basic ideas in the ranchhouse mass-produced by builders after 1945—the land-hugging horizontality, the family-centered living, the big windows, the "utility core" at the center, the built-in furniture, the attached garage—all had been put forward by the great architect Frank Lloyd Wright in the Prairie Houses he built in and around Chicago between 1895 and 1904. The revolutionary concepts of Wright had thus materialized in the suburban building boom after 1945 in much the same way, and with much the same time-lag, as Einstein's equations took shape in the deadly artifacts of the post-Alamogordo world.[1]

But the ranchhouse, as built by the tract developers, did not present any sweeping view of broad rural acres from its picture-window. More often the scene was another ranch house a few feet away. Wide-openness to surroundings, moreover, turned out not to be what many migrants to the suburbs wanted. Contrary to Wright's concepts, these families wanted to turn inward, not outward. Thus some people thought of their picture windows as frontal display: a whole vernacular of show developed, of "picture window lamps," "picture window curtains," and so on. A third countering influence, and one of decisive importance, was the fact that in a growing number of suburban families more than one member began to take jobs, in consequence of which not just one but two cars became necessary.[2]

To add space for a full, two-car, twenty-four-foot-wide garage alongside a new ranchhouse would have hit the mass developer right where it hurts most. Making room for an extra car threatened to widen the lots out to 90 or 100 or even 110 feet—and it was on the land rather than the houses that speculative builders made their profits. At this point, when the developers were ready to shriek with pain, someone reached back to the ample Wright portfolio for his concepts about verticality—and simply slid the garage under the ranch house, sometimes under one side of the house or the other, sometimes under the middle, all on the same small plot as before. This grotesquely self-serving solution was the split-level house.[3]

The split-level—a dwelling defined as having at least three separate levels, two of them located one above the other and all of them a half-level apart in elevation—became an instant favorite on Long Island in 1954. Thereafter it spread widely, especially in the Eastern and North Central parts of the country. On level land where it was never meant to be it was ugly: rows of them, all presenting their high, or display, sides toward the street, looked like lines of sitting ducks. Yet the "split" was undeniably different, and thousands were looking for something different. It was bigger, or at least looked bigger. It was usually more costly, with its "family room"—another old Wright idea—on a lower, walk-in level and a third and often fourth bedroom on an upper level away from the living areas. It was an inward-looking house, having a strong appeal to the family preoccupied with itself and its security. And it was utterly automobile-oriented. If the car made the suburban ranchhouse possible, garaging the car or cars made the split-level necessary.[4]

The name was a giveaway. The split-level was a half-step house, a dwelling in which the open gave way to the secret, the face became a facade, and aspiration was separated from style, a half-story apart. Stairs, small stairways, were everywhere. "I'm always halfway up or halfway down, but never anywhere in particular," said one housewife. The style, said critic James Marston Fitch, was "all mixed up, the very reflection of the psychologically confused, mixed-up outlook of the 1950s, turning inward to get away from that hard, horrid reality."[5]

Truth to tell, the split-level house, reflecting the strain being put upon the nation as the old values gradually went sour and as other values were contending and working their way upward beneath the old ones, mirrored the discontinuities of the society around it. Do a society's moral imperatives take their shape in the stormy times of upheaval, in this case the Depression, the New Deal, the war years? Or were the values that impelled men in mid-century America more often worked out after they had achieved economic breakthrough—and were at leisure, so to speak, in the prosperous postwar years to justify their economic gains and collect new psychic and social rewards on the basis of them? Surely there was a widespread preoccupation with status, remarked by novelists, historians and behavioral scientists alike, in the Cold War years, and a heightened discrepancy between what people were and what they seemed, between what they did and what they said.[6]

No more prominent example of this split-level sort of outlook and conduct was to be seen than the changed views held by Americans in the 1950s about religion. On the face of things, Americans had never turned in such vast numbers to the institutions of worship and faith. From 1940 to 1962, the proportion of the population holding formal membership in churches rose from forty-nine percent to sixty-three percent, an all-time high. Yet during these same years the quality of religious feeling altered, became vaguer, less creed-committed, less denominational, more secular, more shallow. It declined in intensity, and indeed, as troubled churchmen attested, had probably been declining for some time.[7]

Because it took the fierce edge off old hates and prejudices, the new blandness in religious feeling facilitated social change. In the triumph of the New Deal coalition in the 1930s, important economic and political gains had been achieved by all minorities except the blacks. Foremost among these minorities to gain power were the Catholics and Jews. In the 1940s, first by the world war against Hitler and his racial doctrines, second by the electrifying victories of independent Israel, the Jews won a totally new acceptance among their countrymen. For Catholics, especially Irish and German Catholics, access to all the satisfactions of American life was complicated by unvoiced but deep-seated reservations about the war in Europe. Influenced, as Samuel Lubell's studies of Irish and German voting habits have shown, by their country's wartime alignment on the side of Britain and against Germany, these ethnic constraints within important elements of American Catholicism persisted until after V-E Day.

Then the Cold War removed them. Pitting the United States against Communism in Germany, in Italy and in the whole world, impelling the Eisenhower administration to call for "liberation" of the "captive nations" of Eastern Europe, the Cold War rallied, united and gave prominence as never before to American Catholics including such "new" immigrant elements from Eastern Europe as the Poles, Czechs, Slovaks and Hungarians, in the American confrontation with the godless ideologies in the Kremlin. On the crest of these powerfully converging currents Catholics rode at last the high flood of the American mainstream.[8]

Up to this point Protestantism had been the established national religion, no doubt about it. But in the years since the 1930s, as Will Herberg pointed out in his prescient work *Protestant, Catholic, Jew* (1955), Protestantism in America had insensibly given ground. Now, legislated by the New Deal majorities and ratified by the events of the Second World War and the Cold War, a new and considerably widened-out and watered-down version had been installed in its stead. The national religion for Americans henceforth was to be found in "the church of your choice"—indiscriminately Protestantism, Catholicism, Judaism. Any one of these three would do. This Cold War version, disestablishing Protestantism in America after 300 years, was proclaimed by President Eisenhower, as Herberg noted, in one of his inimitable press-conference homilies for the American people: "Our government makes no sense unless it is founded in a deeply religious faith—and I don't care what it is." On another occasion the general said: "I am the most religious man I know," and then added the new pluralist qualifier: "That does not mean I adhere to any sect. A democracy cannot exist without a religious base. I believe in democracy." A New York rabbi phrased it neatly in 1955: "The spiritual meaning of American democracy is realized in its three great faiths."[9]

Three centuries after their country's colonization amid the wars of these same religions, Americans were coming to feel that the choice among them was of little importance. From a fiery, bigoted, traditional belief in God, there was a retreat to believing in a belief in God, an outlook conducive to a secularization of the church in an ever more secularized society. Such was the split-level church pictured by the novelist Peter DeVries in *The Mackerel Plaza* (1957), whose propitiatory young pastor made his parishioners feel at home in church by complaining to the Zoning Board about a billboard that said: "Jesus Saves." The identification of militantly anti-Communist Catholicism with that form of national aspirations defined during the Cold War as "Americanism" completed the necessary conjuncture of national attitudes for the nomination and election in 1960 of John F. Kennedy as the first Catholic president of the United States. At the same time the trimmings and haulings of all the churches in the Cold War sped the decline of their authority, and set them up as highly vulnerable institutional targets for the waves of dissent and revolt that rolled through the society as the Cold War ended.[10]

IN SOCIAL LIFE the Eisenhower years more than most were a time of managed impressions. The strong element of idealization in American social conduct was never more pronounced. A glance back over the magazine illustrations of the late 1940s and 1950s and above all their advertisements, conveys a sense of a heavily cosmetized look about the American visage. Did these varnished males and veneered females really live? Doris Day and Rock Hudson, the box-office champions of the 1958–59 movie season, were touted by studio flacks as tops in that peculiarly American abstraction known as "sexiness." But when they went into a clinch, a reviewer remarked, "aglow from the sunlamp and agleam with hair lacquer," they looked "less like creatures of flesh and blood than a couple of 1960 Cadillacs that just happened to be parked in a suggestive position." Offscreen as well as on, the movie heroines of the day came off as dolls wrapped in cellophane. From the inflexible smiles of Hollywood it might have been supposed that what Americans saw in these years was Andy Hardy's vision of the happy life. The very family photographs on the nation's mantels were not only posed but retouched and for that matter, tinted.[11]

The preoccupation with social mobility—the efforts to move upward and the struggle to keep from plunging down a peg or two—led to an inordinate amount of attention to maintaining appearances in these years. The management of front, as scrutinized by Erving Goffman, the mordant morphologist of Eisenhower society, taxed the resources of an affluent America. It promoted a split-level way of life. These were years of raising everybody's title—vice president into group vice president, accountant into controller, secretary into administrative assistant, shipping clerk into traffic expediter, janitor into custodial engineer. In the same way certain hygienic accounterments of the scientific laboratory—glass, stainless steel, white tile, rubber gloves, laboratory coat—were taken over by such mundane callings as barbering, butchering, auto-repairing, pest-eradicating and street-sweeping, which thereby received the prestige of technology by seeming self-purification.

On the home front the decline in domestic services, as Goffman said, put the middle-class housewife in a particularly challenging situation. In serving dinner she had to, "manage the kitchen dirty work in such a way as to enable her to switch back and forth between the roles of domestic and hostess, altering her activity, manner and temper as she passed through the door to the dining room." The urge to present a front that could transcend such formidable dramatic demands led inevitably to the catered party. There the host and hostess could seem to have exactly the help which they did not have. For the fabrication of community standing a variety of artifacts became available in the 1950s: fake TV aerials were sold to people who had no television sets, packages of exotic travel labels for the suitcase for those who had not fared so far from home, wire-wheel hubcap attachments for motorists with ordinary, run-of-the-assembly-line cars.

In their drive for appearances that would exceed realities, people were not always content to own the biggest car on the block. Many in those years found that an even more impressive thrust of upward mobility could be mounted in a rented, chauffeur-driven Cadillac. Part of the performance was the wearing of rented jewelry, another phenomenon of these years that suggested the theater-going couple in the Cadillac seemed to have something which they did not. In such an ambiance of artificiality the very flowers worn were often plastic. The 1950s turned out to be the period of the toupée for men, falsies for women. It was the time when the concealment of grey hair came to be considered socially acceptable. In an era of heavily-inflected Americanism many thought it smart to Americanize their names and their noses.[12]

Of all the dualities rampant in these years of souring values, none occasioned such a buildup of day-by-day stresses as the American double standard in sexual conduct. The idea that premarital sex was acceptable for men but wrong and unacceptable for women underlay the implicitly patriarchal style of marital and family living that came down from Victorian times and won a new lease on life when the Cold War brought a sudden surge of domesticity to the American scene.

The glorification of domestic life was part and parcel of the big thrust for suburban living and consumer spending after 1945, and is commonly traced to the pent-up hunger for marriage, home and children created by the deprivations of the Second World War. This passion for homemaking seemed in no way dimmed by the high rate of mortality among American marriages (one in four), possibly because the society accepted divorce as the form of social insurance that had to be paid if domesticity was to be held in such high esteem. Far from abating, the double standard in American marriage may even have gained strength when the United States, a young country no longer, crossed the big demographic divide in 1950 and joined the other fifty of the world's eighty-four nations whose females outnumbered their males.[13]

The split-level style of the day—all "nice" girls aspiring to become homemakers, all boys aspiring to "make out" with them in the back seats of convertibles—survived even the shocking disclosures about everyday sex habits published by the Indiana hymenopterist Alfred Kinsey. On the basis of more than 100,000 interviews conducted over two decades, the so-called Kinsey reports—*The Sexual Behavior of the Human Male* (1948) and *The Sexual Behavior of the Human Female* (1953)—disclosed that about half the population engaged in premarital sex, a quarter in extramarital sex, and an estimated eight per cent of all males had experimented in the extraspeciate variety. But the most telling of all Kinsey's findings concerned changes in the nation's premarital sexual behavior. Once and only once in the twentieth century did these habits alter, and that was immediately after the First World War, it seemed. In that age of flappers, jazz and bathtub gin, the proportion of females who had sexual intercourse before first marriage shot up from twenty-five to about fifty per cent, and America shifted part of the way toward the standards of premarital permissiveness (especially with prospective spouse) that had prevailed for centuries in Europe.[14]

After the Second World War there appears to have been no such "revolution" in American sexual behavior as after the First. On the contrary the double standard gained ground as the nation girded for the Cold War while turning as never before to privatization in individual and family life. The American female became a consenting partner in the rush to marriage, the boom in babies and the proliferation of single-family homes. When the whole society including schools, churches, women's magazines and other organs of mass consumerism put out their messages about the wonderful world of feminine fulfillment in appliance-filled kitchens in children-filled homes amid flower-filled gardens, the woman of Middle America really believed them and gamely tried to carry out her mission. She bore three, four, five children. She surrounded herself with self-defrosting refrigerators, wall ovens and pushbutton dishwashers. She lived through her husband, who seemed to be going places. (And *he* was thought to regard her as not only bearer of his children but also attractive enough for display.) As *Look* magazine described her in 1956, she was both glamour-queen and housekeeper:

> The American woman [is] winning the battle of the sexes. . . . She is growing up and confounding her critics. . . . She works, rather casually, as a third of the U.S. labor force, less toward a 'big career' than as a way of filling a hope chest or buying a new home freezer. She gracefully concedes the top jobs to men. This wondrous creature marries younger than ever, bears more babies and looks and acts more feminine than the advanced 'emancipated' girl of the 1920s or even the '30s. Steelworker's wife and Junior Leaguer alike do their own housework. . . . Today, if she makes an old-fashioned choice and lovingly tends a garden and a bumper crop of children, she rates louder hosannas than ever before.[15]

In this kind of world, attitudes were all. In the teeth of Kinsey's findings on their own generation's sexual habits, American parents of the Cold War age took their stand on the new domesticity and demanded that their children behave differently from the way they themselves did as young adults (only seventeen per cent surveyed in 1963 would go along with premarital sex for sons with girls they intended to marry, and only five per cent endorsed this standard for daughters). Everybody's answer seemed to be early marriage, and the median marrying age for girls plunged from 21.5 in 1940 to 20.5 in 1966. Girls went to college not to find themselves but find a husband. "Dear Abby" counseled young females who wrote to her column that a "nice" girl must cultivate the arts of popularity and "go far enough to meet the boy to hold his interest without cheapening herself."

In the early Cold War years in particular, the mating game was often played out under conditions of stupefying make-believe. The girl sat around under the hair-dryer all weekend and then the young man arrived, bearing a flower for her. Duly dazzled, he fetched her away for the big evening date. Well into the 1950s many college girls played down their intelligence, skills and intentions when in the presence of datable boys, and allowed the young men to explain things to them tediously that they already knew. The idea, said Goffman unsparingly, was to make believe in the presence of the young man that they were the inessential other, the imaginary person desired for a consort, losing ping-pong games just before the end, and deliberately misspelling some of the longer words in their letters. One explained: "My boy friend seems to get a kick out of it, and writes back, Honey, you certainly don't know how to spell."[16]

Even though something like half the early marriages of the Cold War years broke up in quick divorce, the huntress tended to be the one entrapped by the pervading domesticity. By 1960 *The New York Times* reported: "Many young women whose education plunged them into a world of ideas feel stifled in their homes." CBS aired a much-talked-about TV show entitled *The Trapped Housewife,* and in 1963 Betty Friedan, a housewife in New York's suburban Rockland County, who had been a junior Phi Beta Kappa at Smith and then given her all to a husband and three children, published a piercing cry from the station-wagon and backyard swimming pool country. *The Feminine Mystique* was a book that had been written many times before without making such a stir—perhaps first by Mary Wollstonecraft 150 years before. The whole suburban bit about "the happy housewife heroine" radiant among hubby, kiddies and goodies, wrote Betty Friedan, was a fraud rigged by and for males.

The message resonated. All sort of individual women seemed to catch something from reading the book, and flocked to the best-selling author's lectures to tell her so. "Something is eating me," said one. Her conscience told her that she had all that a wife should want, yet what she wanted most of all—self-respect—she did not have. Husband faltering, children growing away, appliances palling, she found herself left with no identity as an individual.[17]

And the promises of domesticity *were* false. In the 1950s, when women were led to believe they had it so good, they actually lost ground in comparison to men. For all the bland claims about their exalted status issued by government and paeaned by women's magazines, the relative position of women with respect to occupational, economic and educational achievement slipped further back in the 1950s. The Department of Labor might clarion, as it did, that between 1950 and 1960 "nearly 2.75 million women had professional, technical or kindred positions—a 41% gain in ten years." What the announcement left out was that in the same years 4,500,000 men took similar jobs—an increase of 51%.

An examination of Census Bureau figures shows that in college and university faculties women held relatively fewer posts at the end of the Cold War than they held in 1940. In categories of lower status and pay, the trend went quite the other way. For "clerical and kindred" workers, the group that included sales and service, a substantial changeover from male to female workers—at least 10%—had taken place all along the line. In elementary and high school teaching, the one area where women had always held a strong position, they lost ground to men over the twenty-five-year span after 1940 notwithstanding the big demand for teachers. Between 1950 and 1960 the number of female teachers rose 43%, the number of male teachers 66%. In terms of income, men's gains outstripped those of women in all areas but one, the "professional, technical and kindred" category. Even there it would have been misleading to make much of the 5% margin of increase won by women because there were so few of them. The occasionally successful career girl of the Cold War years was no more representative than the all but mythical "self-made man" deified in the turn-of-the-century "American dream." More relevant was the fact that in the category of "clerical" workers where the bulk of women ended up, their average loss in income compared to that of comparably employed males, was greatest—fifteen per cent.

Finally, women suffered a big loss in the comparative educational superiority they had long enjoyed over men. By 1950 the female edge in average number of grades completed narrowed; by 1960 it all but disappeared. Among college-age Americans, notwithstanding military service, work responsibilities and other demands that interrupted male schooling, men had achieved just about the same levels of school years completed as women. Even though more girls went to college between 1940 and the end of the Cold War, the proportion of increase among males in the same years was three times as great.[18]

Such losses, along with such unsettling new forces as the huge peacetime military buildup, the threat of the bomb, and the growth of pollution, all added to the stresses as the Cold War broke up and the nation's institutions began to shake themselves loose from the immobilities of the postwar years. It would be going too far to say that there had been no change at all in the American family during the Cold War era. In a well-conducted survey among some 730 Detroit housewives in 1955, Robert Blood found evidence that although husbands held the preponderance of power and authority in most households, in almost none did they make all of the key decisions. In such matters as buying a house and deciding on vacations the wife had just as much say as the husband.[19]

All the same, in man-woman relationships as in almost everything else, there was a tremendous explosion in the 1960s, and the double standard itself seemed for a time to totter. With respect to sex, attitudes changed, if not behavior. The new trend was toward more equality between the sexes.

A decade after the end of the Cold War, parietal rules had been virtually scrapped by the colleges, and without even the mildest protests from Middle America. Abortion had been upheld as lawful. Faculty members could now live openly out of wedlock as only denizens of Greenwich Village could in the 1930s. An upper- or middle-class girl could without fuss go off for a ten-day trip with her boy friend, an act that a generation earlier would have meant the end of her. In the new and independent way such a girl thought about herself, it was simply not possible that anybody could own her—and suddenly the term "mistress," in the old sense of "setting a woman up" with a lot of elaborate arrangements, seemed not only dated but stupid.

None of this meant that the double standard had fallen. But options were open. After Kinsey, sex could be openly talked about, all the more so when the pill arrived to make contraception itself oral. Some, seeing the nation putting both Victorian and Freudian obsessions behind it, said that sex was becoming a form of play for the middle class, "a parallel to gourmet cooking."

The big change, the sociologist Ira Reiss said in 1966, was simply that:

> attitudes have consolidated with ehavior; what was done by a female in
> 1925 acting as a rebel and a deviant can be done by a female in 1965
> as a conformist. The major importance lies in the increased acceptance
> of premarital coital behavior rather than in increased performance of
> this behavior. Our young people are not less sure of their views, on the
> contrary they are more so.[20]

The fact that attitudes had at last caught up with behavior in sexual relations did not mean for a moment that the tension had gone out of them. In the new environment of accepted permissiveness, evidence existed that among college students, male as well as female, something like half or more had never had sexual intercourse. Relations were still fraught with terror, still the source of upset among adolescents. Though it might be understood that if boy and girl became intimate they slept together, that progression into an intimate relationship—the groping for commitment, establishing who loved whom, developing trust—consumed a lot of time and agonized energy.

The autonomy accorded the young, and the necessity for youth of having to turn inward for strength in the absence of a firmly organized universe around them that sent them strong signals on how to behave and what to believe and what to rely on, led them to assume more responsibility for their own sexual standards. Influence of parents progressively declined. The double standard, still powerful in lower-class and rural families, probably continued to command a majority. In the shift of standards Marilyn Monroe became the last of the sex symbols starred by Hollywood —the kind of woman men could want as a possession for conspicuous display to other males. Though Marilyn Monroe did not sleep like Jayne Mansfield, another voluptuous blonde movie queen of the Cold War era, on a heartshaped bed, she posed nude for calendar pictures, married Joe Di Maggio and drew storms of whistles and wolf-calls at all her publicity appearances. But she took her own life in 1962, and it came to be understood that she was in unhappy rebellion against the image of kittenish passivity that *Playboy*-readng males were thought to demand of her. A whole, heavily-cosmetized world of starlets, housewives and make-believe prom queens in doll's houses faded away. It would be easy to make a case that the girl of a decade or two later, with crumbs on her face, slouching about in jeans, inhabiting the same dormitory as the boy, and scornful of facade in feminine relations with men, was healthier, unburdened by such an overload of hypocrisy and sham.[21]

The Cold War years were the years of living it up on the expense account, the years when credit cards, launched with the first Diners Club card in 1950, ballooned until people began to use them to get credit not only at restaurants but at motels, hotels, airlines, resorts and wigmakers. To maintain the desired front, playing golf became important for many men of business, including those who had been reared playing handball or stickball on crowded city streets. Managing appearances loomed large for the father who remarked that his son had not got through Yale but had stayed there six months—"long enough to be in the Yale Club" downtown. In suburb or in town, the right club for meeting business prospects was deemed of great moment in these years. It was also thought to add style to the executive front to have an imported English secretary, a voice to answer the telephone with a Mayfair accent.

The management of front became a major preoccupation of institutions as well in the Eisenhower years. Trade unions, for example, maintained themselves in unprecedentedly elaborate settings, and staffed their marble palaces with academically trained experts who added to the other trappings of raw power an aura of thought and respectability. The penchant for horn-rimmed savants on the premises was not confined to United Auto Workers headquarters where Walter Reuther was forever talking of trade cycles, urban welfare and the Gross National Product. It was also exhibited among the grizzled ex-deckhands of Joe Curran's National Maritime Union, whose block-long establishment in Manhattan was built in the shape of a ship, and among the wheeler-dealer business agents of Jimmy Hoffa's Teamsters Union. There was also a tremendous enlargement of front in the "executive suites" of the big corporations, so extensive that it touched off the biggest office-building boom in thirty years in New York and other cities. Of course, as with the unions, many enterprises simply outgrew their old facilities and needed something better. But the growth of what an earlier generation called "side" was glaringly visible in their deep-carpeted front offices and oak-paneled boardrooms, in their jazzed-up reports to stockholders, in the inordinate care lavished by top executives on the corporation's public "image."[22]

A T   T H E   V E R Y   height of this national preoccupation with being one thing and looking like another, the most popular spectacle for Americans was watching some of their fellow citizens try to win instant wealth by answering questions on TV. The popularity of quiz shows was such that their idiom, like that of baseball and horse racing, had seeped into the national speech in the heyday of radio before the Second World War. The moment of suspense in those times had occurred when the contestant was shoved before the microphone and dared, after a correct answer had lifted his winnings to $32, to go for double-or-nothing by attempting the climactic answer to the $64 question. "The $64 question" entered the language, the phrase by which a suitor might describe his marriage proposal or a President his poser of whether to drop the A-bomb.

Like the giant networks that bestrode the new medium, quiz shows had simply moved over from radio to TV. But it tells something about the magnified scale of commercial TV, and the unbridled rapacity of the big networks, that the successor to CBS's prewar favorite went by the name of *The $64,000 Question*. By the late 1950s the networks, in their incessant battle for profits based on the rating of audience size for their competing programs, had launched more than twenty such shows and escalated them to the most elaborate scale and extravagance of money prizes. So expensive had the competition grown that the shows' sponsors watched their ratings week by week, and canceled if the audience rating slipped measurably at any time.

In such straits the producers took to rigging their programs to ensure maximum audience appeal. Very quickly the demand for personalities grew terrific. The TV audience did not simply watch a contestant win or lose, it reacted for or against him. The producers could readily see, studying the ups and downs of the weekly ratings, that some of the contestants came through as heroes, some as villains. They worked up plots in which the popular contestants won, and the others lost. The justification was that this was show business, not commerce or sport, hence there was nothing wrong with rigging the outcome. Anything less than a good show would have been depriving the audience of the fun.

Some of the techniques had been taken over from radio days. Each prospective contestant, for instance, took an exam. After that the quiz master could fix the show without even letting the contestant in on the secret. But as the front-office pressure mounted for bigger audiences and more profits, the quiz-show riggers asked for more. The shows needed emotion, and the poker-faced contestants who won or lost without registering any feelings were not nearly so interesting as the one who writhed under the strain before stammering out his answer. So the producers coached their contestants in nail-biting, and that did it. From that point the contestant was in on the fraud, it was only a matter of time before one would expose everybody.

In 1956 a disgruntled contestant complained publicly that a show called *The Big Surprise* was fixed. He was ignored. Next year the New York *World-Telegram and Sun* ran a series of front-page articles hinting at fakery in quiz-show programming. The Washington officials charged with policing the air evidently thought nothing of them. On April 22, 1957, *Time* published a much-discussed article that opened with the sentence: "Are the quiz-shows rigged?" *Look* carried a similar story. Again the authorities, not to mention the heads of the networks that took down $85,200,000 in profits that year, seemed to be looking the other way. It was not until the summer of 1959 when a sometime nightclub comic named Eddie Hilgesheimer blew the whistle on a show called *Dotto* that something happened. Hilgesheimer sold his story to the New York *Post.* The *Post,* hesitant about publishing, turned it over to the Manhattan District Attorney. Hearing this, the sponsor panicked and canceled the show, giving the *Post* excuse to print its story.[23]

In the ensuing outcry the TV industry might have stated publicly what its members said freely in private, that staging was simply a part of show business. But this was the split-level society, and its leaders put up a bold front. So did Charles Van Doren, by far the most famous of the personalities turned up in all the years of quiz-show competition. Tall, young and handsome, son of one of America's most celebrated intellectual families, a fledgling teacher of classics at Columbia University, Van Doren had become as fondly familiar as a member of their households to millions of Americans who had watched him in the isolation booth on NBC's program *Twenty-One.* When tough questions were hurled at him his face contorted, his brow beaded with sweat, his groans resounded in the living rooms of America as he parried and stalled until he could summon up answers from his astounding fund of knowledge. Each time during his fourteen-week climb toward his $129,000 earnings he had rallied, once reciting the lines from Milton that the ex-college president could not summon up, another time giving the name of Gentleman Jim Corbett's vanquisher after a corporation president drew a blank. When he finally lost, Van Doren was a kind of folk hero, and as such he took his place at the nation's breakfast table, a $50,000 a year commentator on Dave Garroway's *Today* show. Challenged by Herbert Stempel, a City College student who said he had been ordered by *Twenty-One*'s producers to "take a dive" rather than beat him, Van Doren told reporters: "At no time was I coached or tutored," and repeated his denial to the grand jury.

But in Washington the House Subcommittee on Legislative Oversight began an investigation, and soon the fat was in the fire. The producer of *Twenty-One* broke down, and admitted he had perjured himself before the grand jury. He told all—how he rigged the shows, how he coached the contestants, how he solicited a cover-up story from contestants once the District Attorney started his investigation. In New York the District Attorney said that of 150 members of the TV industry who had given evidence before the grand jury, at least 100 were lying.

Red-eyed and haggard, Van Doren appeared before the committee to say he had lied too. "I would give almost anything I have to reverse the course of my life in the last three years," he said. But the fraud had not been occasional, as his fans had hoped. It had been planned from the start, as carefully as a well-organized stock swindle. Van Doren testified that he had been foolish, naive, prideful, avaricious. To the bitter end he was an anguished soul, he said, torn by struggles of conscience. It was a sorry performance, and five hours later Columbia accepted his "resignation." The next morning NBC fired him. Three years later Van Doren and nine other contestants pleaded guilty to perjury charges in New York City and received suspended sentences.[24]

With their advertisers screaming, CBS banned all quiz shows and NBC bounced those which were admittedly corrupt. "Many a network official," said *Time*, "was trying frantically to prove [in the words of a popular commercial] that he was Mr. Clean." CBS President Frank Stanton went to the ludicrous extreme of telling the network's comedians that they could no longer use canned laughter. If absolute honesty were to prevail, said the *New York Herald Tribune*'s critic Marie Torre, TV men might have to use real bullets instead of blanks in Westerns. "This," she added deadpan, "we'd welcome." Somehow the industry—which added sixty minutes of nonsponsored, public programming a week in the flap and then cut it back drastically twelve months later—escaped any sort of sanctions. To a committee question Robert E. Kintner, president of NBC, answered that NBC got its "first established evidence of quiz-rigging" through the Washington hearings, and that he had not known about any kind of rigging until after Van Doren & Co. were long off the air.[25]

One night during this excitement one of CBS's programs presented *Judgment at Nuremberg*, a bitterly moving reminder of Nazi Germany's era of mass exterminations. After film clips of Belsen and Auschwitz with their crematoriums, the drama built up to its climax in which an American judge faced the Nazi whom he had just sentenced to life imprisonment. "How in the name of God," cried Claude Rains, playing the judge, "can you ask me to understand the extermination of men, women and innocent children by—." Suddenly the sound went off. Though Rains' lips spoke the words "gas ovens" they were not heard on the air. They had been cut off by CBS at the insistence of the program's sponsor, the American Gas Association, supplier of 95% of the gas used in American kitchen ranges.[26]

W H E N President Eisenhower assumed office he singled out the Tennessee Valley Authority as a prime example on the American scene of "creeping socialism." In the next four years the giant firms General Electric and Westinghouse advanced prices to TVA ten times on large turbines and six times on power generators. The more urgent problem seemed to be the creep of corporate capitalism, all the more so since sealed bids offered TVA by the two big competitors during this time had been identical or nearly identical on twenty-four occasions. Almost in self-defense TVA passed up the next almost identical sealed bids from the two supercorporations and awarded a turbine generator contract to a British firm that had underbid them by more than $5,000,000. Great was the outcry from General Electric and Westinghouse at an award that callously ignored, they said, the most elementary Cold War considerations of "national security." But amidst the disapproving clamor in the nation's press a Chattanooga newspaper picked up the item at the end of TVA's press release that the agency had been getting a lot of identical bids. It came to the attention of the most redoubtable congressional investigator of the day, who happened also to be a Tennessean and intensely interested in TVA. Senator Estes Kefauver threatened to start action if the government did not move.[27]

The government moved. By 1959 the Department of Justice had convened a grand jury in Philadelphia to look into charges that prices were fixed and bids rigged in the electrical equipment industry. For a time things went very slowly. Then in September word leaked that an officer of the Lapp Insulator Company, a minor electrical parts manufacturer in Philadelphia, was on the point of telling the truth to the government's antitrust lawyers: he and other company officials were part of a price-fixing conspiracy involving General Electric, Westinghouse and several lesser companies.

Just about everybody else in the land that September was following the progress of Nikita Khrushchev's barnstorming tour across the United States. But not the top management of General Electric and other big electrical firms who stood to be implicated in the largest fraud ever perpetrated in defiance of the Sherman Anti-Trust Act. After the Lapp disclosures others followed thick and fast. General Electric, Westinghouse and other firms were involved in violating the law in no fewer than nine different fields from the supplying of lowly $2.00 light-pole insulators to the sale of giant, multi-million-dollar dynamos. The question for General Electric Chairman Ralph Cordiner, who was chairman of President Eisenhower's Business Advisory Council as well as head of the nation's third largest manufacturing company, was the same as that posed for the leaders of the TV industry, and Cordiner came to the same split-level answer. Having had a number of run-ins with the authorities over antitrust law violations in the past, General Electric had issued a series of directives to its managers that it did not countenance meetings with competitors to curtail competition. Now it was Cordiner's position, fortified by the elaborate decentralization plan that he had put into operation a few years before, that neither he nor any of the dozen top executives at headquarters had been aware that the company's directives had been honored in the breach.[28]

Day by day, working first on the smaller companies where as in the case of Lapp Insulators many saw fit to tell the truth in hopes of winning immunity, the government's investigators built up their courtroom case. Surreptitious consultations in hotel rooms had been going on for so many years that practically no one with top responsibility for managing affairs could be unaware of the split between word and deed. The attendance roster was known as "the Christmas card list." Meetings were "choir practices." Companies had code numbers—General Electric was 1, Westinghouse was 2, Allis-Chalmers 3, Federal Pacific 7. Conspirators used first names on the telephone ("This is Bob, what is 7's bid?"). They covered tracks in expense accounts by charging fares not to the cities where they actually met but to others equally distant.

One apple-cheeked young executive of an Ohio firm who had often acted as secretary fetched up minutes from his cellar. There were neat copies of ground rules for the meetings (No breakfasting together, no registering at the hotels with company names, no calls to the office). Most revealing of all were piles of memos detailing "phases of the moon" schedules fixing the order and amount by which every two weeks each switch-gear manufacturer was to arrive at his bid. With this code-cracking information everything else became crystal-clear. Up to this moment of illumination the case had hung fire. Now, with his good friend Richard Nixon heading into a presidential campaign and in need of a presentable record of Republican antitrust enforcement, Attorney General William P. Rogers was suddenly armed to press a strong case. The Justice Department also had oil and drug cases going but these ran into Democratic as well as Republican resistance among congressional leaders. When Rogers passed the minutes of the switch-breaker cartel round the Cabinet table early in 1960, the die was cast. President Eisenhower glanced over the papers and commented: "The only thing these sons of bitches forgot to warn them about was, 'Don't take notes.' "[29]

The case went down to the wire a year later. Into court trooped 45 defendants, all well-groomed corporation executives in Ivy League suits, pillars of their communities and multimillion-dollar managers every one of them. Judge J. Cullen Ganey did not mince words:

> The real blame [he said] is to be laid at the doorsteps of the corporate defendants, for one would have to be naive indeed to believe that these violations involving so many millions upon millions of dollars were facts unknown to those responsible for the corporation.

Upon General Electric, Westinghouse and twenty-seven other companies with plants throughout the nation he levied fines totaling $1,900,000. In addition three General Electric, two Westinghouse and two other executives were sentenced to jail and fines of up to $12,500. In passing sentence Judge Ganey characterized these men as "torn between conscience and an approved corporate policy." They were caught on the stairs, that was to say, of the split-level society.

To this "shocking indictment of a vast section of our economy," as

Judge Ganey termed his finding, the reaction was scarcely pronounced. Of the top thirty American newspapers, about half shuffled off the story of the sentencing to their inside pages; a sizable proportion failed to carry the news at all. Westinghouse President Mark Cresap accepted the court's verdict and declared: "This is a management failure." At General Electric Chairman Cordiner dismissed all his men found guilty, including two $125,000-a-year vice presidents and insisted against their protests that nobody in his central office knew of any hanky-panky going on. None of the thirty newspapers emphasized that the corporations were guilty of commiting crimes. The opprobrium was shunted off on the convicted individuals. For the convicted corporations newspaper accounts used vague, neutral words like "proceedings," "antitrust suits," and "penalties," not "crimes."[30]

That same year Carrol Shanks, president of the giant Prudential Insurance Company, mentioned to his friend Owen Cheatham, Chairman of Georgia-Pacific, the leading American producer of plywood and a heavy Prudential borrower, that he "was looking for a deal where I could make a good capital gain, because I take such a plastering from taxes on my $250,000 salary." Owen Cheatham understood, and soon afterwards an arrangement was made for Shanks, who was also a Georgia-Pacific board member, to buy some timberland and immediately sell the timber on it to the plywood company. By putting in a little money of his own, at no risk to speak of, for the five years the contract was in force, Shanks could look forward to saving through capital gains, timber depletion allowances and a huge writeoff for interest payments to the bank that was financing him, some $400,000 after taxes.

Of course such practices in American business had been known in the past, but that was the point here. It was for almost precisely this kind of thing that Charles Evans Hughes had exposed the officers and directors of Equitable, Mutual and New York Life in his landmark insurance investigation of 1905, an investigation that led to sweeping reorganization of the entire life insurance industry and adoption of strict standards for the handling of policyholders' funds. When newspapers unearthed the facts, Shanks said he saw "not the slightest violation of ethics" in what he had done. Nonetheless his resignation was accepted and he retired on a pension of $100,000 a year. About the same time William Newberg, president of Chrysler Corporation, was found to have a half-interest in two firms whose sole customer was Chrysler. His profits over a six-year span were at least $450,000. Newberg resigned.[31]

The stern avowals of General Eisenhower in 1952 that members of his administration must be "clean as a hound's tooth" were most severely tested when in 1958 the House Committee on Legislative Oversight began to ask his top assistant Sherman Adams about his friendship with

Bernard Goldfine, a tireless name-dropper and influence-peddler. The committee ascertained that Goldfine's ventures brought him again and again before such agencies as the Federal Trade Commission (for mislabeling the product of his New England textile mills) and the Securities and Exchange Commission (for failure to file reports on one of his enterprises). It learned also that Goldfine had paid for the cost of a vicuna coat and of stays at Boston and New York hotels for Adams, who had interceded on Goldfine's behalf. The sort of man who bought his own stamps for the personal letters he mailed from the White House, Adams protested, "I have done nothing wrong." President Eisenhower said: "I need him," but with elections coming up was finally persuaded to let Adams go.[32]

FROM THE time the United States entered upon the Cold War against "international Communism," it was clear that there was to be more than one level to its activities in other lands. Below the level of diplomacy, of marshaling American political and economic power, was another, shadowy realm. When the Central Intelligence Agency was set up by the National Security Act of 1947, it may have appeared empowered simply to correlate, evaluate and coordinate the collection of intelligence about America's adversaries. But the Communist takeover of Czechoslovakia provoked fright in Washington. Defense Secretary Forrestal became convinced that the Communists might win the Italian elections in 1948. To prevent this he started a campaign to raise funds among his wealthy Wall Street friends to run a clandestine operation in Italy. Allen Dulles, the veteran of the wartime Office of Strategic Services who had helped draw up the blueprint for CIA, thought that the government must manage such activities itself.[33]

The National Security Council so ordered in the summer of 1948—with the understanding that all such operations must be secret and run in such a way that the government could plausibly deny any link with them. A special act of Congress empowered the director of the CIA (a military man in those days) to spend money "without regard to the provisions of the law . . . relating to the expenditure of government funds." Unmonitored by a congressional committee, the agency proceeded through its Plans Division to run "special operations" in utmost secrecy. Granted its crucial Cold War mission, granted its unprecedented freedom to spend, granted its director's place as member of the National Security Council itself, the CIA rose inevitably in the next fifteen years to become a powerful new institution with unanticipated influence in the direction and execution of America's foreign policy.

The individuals brought in to man and lead the agency were the kind to ensure and enlarge that influence. Many were from the Eastern Establishment, imbued like Forrestal and Lovett, McCloy and Bundy with the conviction that America was pitted against implacably aggressive Communism in a struggle that required the use of every resource. "It seemed that the Communists, unchecked, would win the allegiance of most of the world," said one later. The Third World War, already thought to have begun, might be lost long before any old-fashioned armed conflict in undercover warfare in propaganda, sabotage, espionage, subversion. Such struggles, urgently important, called for select talents. They also promised high excitement. So it was that gentlemen scholars from the best colleges —William Langer from Harvard, Sherman Kent from Yale—lent their learning to the CIA. So it was that genteel types from the Eastern seaboard's best-known families were recruited into the staff of the unmentionable agency. It was a chance to make boyhood last forever. From New Haven went Richard Bissell, a tall young economist and heir to a carpet-sweeper fortune who had helped get the Marshall Plan started. From a Back Bay mansion and the Harvard law school went Robert Amory Jr., brother of the society chronicler (*The Proper Bostonians*), Cleveland Amory. From New York went Frank Wisner, an old protege of Forrestal's.[34]

At once the nation that had always seen itself as the guardian and example of the open society was deeply engaged in the subterranean business of deception, bribery, gun-running and cutthroat intrigue. Some of the earliest CIA efforts were substantial. By all accounts the Kremlin's power to foment trouble anywhere through local Communist parties was unrivaled. But when Communists controlling the trade unions of France and Italy tried to disrupt the workings of the Marshall Plan in 1948 and 1949, the CIA's maneuvers more than matched their direst machinations. Sending funds and directives through AFL representatives in these countries, the American dirty-tricks department managed to split the French and Italian labor movements and build up for a brief but crucial period rival outfits that faithfully followed Washington's Cold War line.[35]

In propaganda warfare, though Russian efforts were characterized in the West as shamelessly subordinated to state direction, the CIA soon built up or bought up an ensemble of facades and mouthpieces for its propaganda line that rivaled Moscow's. Supplementing the politer niceties of the Voice of America, CIA-funded "private" groups sprang up to help Radio Free Europe and Radio Liberty transmit to the East the less inhibited inflections of Cold War ideology. If the Russians succeeded in organizing international assemblies of students, athletes, clerics, scientists and intellectuals as Soviet Cold War sounding-boards, the CIA dummied up rival "front" congresses (sometimes transmitting funds and directives through private foundations to spare their leaders' sensibilities) which denounced Soviet tyranny, oppression and concentration-camp terror in ways and at times that suited Washington's propaganda purposes. Where the claptrap rhetoric of the Communists insisted on "people" and "democracy" in all their front names, the cynics of the CIA strongly favored putting their money in fronts consecrated to "freedom" and "liberty."[36]

Whatever the obliquities of such CIA endeavors, and a good many of them could be charged off to the timeless practices of espionage, they were innocence itself alongside the agency's riskiest and, from the standpoint of national policy, potentially most influential activity. This was the subversion of foreign governments. The most secret of all CIA shenanigans, the "special operations" carried on by the supersecret Plans Division, reached their peak during the twelve years that Allen Dulles sat at the center of all the country's far-flung cloak-and-dagger business.

While his more famous brother was still senior partner in the firm, Allen Dulles was called from Sullivan and Cromwell during the Korean War and pressed into action by President Truman as General Walter Bedell Smith's second-in-command at CIA. When General Eisenhower took over in 1953 and brought John Foster Dulles to head the State Department, Allen Dulles was named head of the agency and chairman of the committee coordinating all American intelligence operations. Thereafter, in what were the climactic years of the Cold War, the role and power of the CIA rose to its zenith, and with reason. The policy of the United States laid down by the elder Dulles was "liberation" of "captive peoples" in the East and opposition to neutralism everywhere else as "an obsolete conception . . . immoral and short-sighted." And since President Eisenhower drew the line at outright war, this "victory-oriented strategy" had to be pursued by means short of war—by the subversive means, that is, devised and employed by the younger Dulles at CIA.

The Dulleses waged a two-level offensive. On the upper level the elder brother dashed round the world ringing "international Communism" with allies bound to the United States by treaties and hazing the waverers and neutrals. On the lower level the younger Dulles ran conspiracies and rigged plots to loosen the Communist hold on lands behind the Iron Curtain and topple regimes elsewhere if they seemed tempted to the immorality of not signing a mutual-assistance treaty with his brother. So intimate and easy was the split-level coordination when brothers worked together that at times the Secretary of State communicated directly with the CIA man in Cairo or personally interviewed its station chief in Saigon. A telephone call across Washington was enough to put a Central American government in jeopardy. A brotherly aside could divert cargoes anxiously awaited in a Far Eastern country. One brother carried the State Department, as it was said, in his hat; the other had the blackjack on his hip. Never in the history of foreign affairs was there such a team.

Though the stakes in Europe remained the highest, results in the days of the Dulles duumvirate were meagerest. A practiced hand at the old-style, upper-class sort of continental intrigue, Allen Dulles had subverted Germans at the highest level from his Swiss base in the early 1940s. Compared with the early successes achieved with major American trade-union participation in France and Italy, the Dulles network of subversion seemed to mesh indifferently with the proletariat in the Cold War ploys for Central and Eastern Europe. It centered around General Reinhard Gehlen, Hitler's old expert on the Russian military, who had been set up at the head of a big outfit operating stealthily out of Rudolf Hess' former Nazi headquarters near Munich. It was alleged to have infiltrated hundreds of agents into East Germany's ruling party, and possibly even a minister into the East German cabinet. By means of a tunnel boldly burrowed under a Berlin street it tapped every telephone call in and out of the Russian embassy. Every other trench-coated loiterer in Berlin was said to be in the CIA's pay. On the level of intelligence-gathering, Allen Dulles could tell his brother a lot. But on the level of providing the subversive shove that would help dislodge the Eastern European satellites from their Communist orbits, Allen Dulles' outfit was as helpless as his brother's when the showdown for "liberation" arrived suddenly in June, 1953.

East German workers, infuriated by harsh new work rules, rose in rebellion in the major cities. Fighting in East Berlin raged within a few feet of the American sector boundary. But the rebels went down before the Russian tanks with no sign of concerted insurgency and no help from across the border except encouraging broadcasts on the American radio station.[30] The push for "liberation" did not cease until 1956, when the United States again stood aside as Russian tanks moved into Hungary. Possibly the longest subversive reach attempted by the CIA was to give support to Ukrainian separatists. A series of savage assassinations in Munich put an end to the adventure. Russian-hired killers destroyed the exiled leaders by firing cyanide guns into their faces. In the end perhaps the CIA's most notable success on the East European front was not on the dirty tricks level but the intelligence-gathering feat of obtaining in Warsaw a copy of Khrushchev's secret de-Stalinization speech a few months after he delivered it in 1956.[37]

By then the CIA was part of the American presence everywhere. The Russians, whose photographing and microfilming of atomic secrets had so scandalized and outraged America a few years before, found themselves up against the full panoply of American technology arrayed in the secret war. Far beyond mere wiretapping and microfilming the CIA marshaled radios, cameras, computers, radars and long-range electronic gear that peeked and eavesdropped from vessels and planes along the remotest Communist borders. In Washington the agency took over an eight-story building in the woods across the Potomac and filled it with 10,000 employes and computer-run data systems of a costliness and complexity that not even the Pentagon thought it could afford. It had perhaps 100,000 operatives round the world, from spatted-and-caned boulevardiers in Paris to Pepsi-Cola distributors in Buenos Aires, from postdoctoral Sovietologists sifting dispatches in Bonn to cocktail waiters listening to tourists in Pnompenh. Its outlays, systematically concealed among other government accounts in much the same way as in Moscow, were estimated by Allen Dulles' opposite number, Soviet State Security Committee Chairman Alexander Shelepin at around $1.5 billion in 1959 and by some Americans at half that amount. Operating variously through the State-,Army, Navy, Air Force, Commerce and Labor departments, the foreign aid program, the Peace Corps, private corporations, foundations, unions and church bodies, it tipped over governments in Iran, Guatemala and Laos, and helped shake up others in Indonesia, Congo, Korea, Burma, Cambodia and Vietnam.[38]

As in Europe, the activities of the CIA on the Asian front helped polarize Cold War enmities. After the Chinese Communists had been brought to the peace table in Korea, the "liberation" doctrine spread to the Far East. It became the official assumption, proclaimed by Secretary Dulles, that the United States regarded the Chinese Communist regime as "a passing and not a permanent phase." Said Dulles, "We owe it to ourselves, our allies and the Chinese people to do all that we can to contribute to that passing."

While the Secretary negotiated a mutual defense treaty with the Nationalist regime on Taiwan, his younger brother at the CIA built up the island as an "unsinkable aircraft carrier" from which subversive activities could be mounted against the mainland and the whole Western Pacific area. Central to these operations was General Claire Chennault, former chief of the American Air Force in China and best-known American "China hand." The Taiwan-based Civil Air Transport Company that Chennault headed, ostensibly a Taiwanese commercial airline, "engaged in scheduled and nonscheduled air operations throughout the Far East," was in fact a CIA proprietary. Manned by old Flying Tigers who had free-lanced for Chiang Kai-shek against the Japanese before Pearl Harbor, the CAT ranged up and down Asia as one of the world's larger air services. In 1958, according to a CIA memo printed in *The Pentagon Papers*, it furnished "complete logistical and tactical support for the Indonesia operation"—an unsuccessful CIA attempt to overthrow President Sukarno through providing support to an army rebellion in Sumatra. It landed and supplied agents in North Vietnam at least a decade before Presidents Johnson and Nixon sent bombers there. By 1961 it carried out "more than 200 overflights of mainland China and Tibet"—missions that went 3000 miles inland and thus had to be staged through secret bases in Thailand. When at the height of a 1960 border row the Indian government protested "repeated flights by Chinese planes over India's Northeast Frontier Agency," Chou En-lai replied that investigation had established that these were not Chinese but American planes traveling across Thailand, Burma and the Indian frontier "to penetrate deep into China's interior where they parachuted weapons, supplies and wireless sets to secret agents."

In Southeast Asia the CIA reversed the so-called "domino" theory, not only embroiling the United States in propping up the domino in Vietnam but working undercover in nearby states to tip the dominos the other way. A leading figure in these intrigues was Edward Lansdale, a Madison Avenue-schooled Air Force colonel with close-set gray eyes and Gary Cooper jaw who had been at the forefront in aiding Ramon Magsaysay's successful campaign to put down the Communist Hukbalahap guerrillas in the Philippines. After Magsaysay crushed the Huks and became the hero-president of the islands, Lansdale moved on to Saigon. It was 1954. Dienbienphu had just fallen, the Geneva Conference had just sealed the end of French Indochina and the beginning of independent Laos, Cambodia and Vietnam. Many people, from President Eisenhower down, expected the Communists under Ho Chi Minh to win the election ordained at Geneva, and take over Vietnam.

Could America, in the sea-change of empire, roll back the Communists? Was not this the hour when the dauntless young agent of the Washington imperium could stride forward as his country's Clive of India, Rhodes of Africa or Roosevelt of San Juan Hill? Whatever the Dulles brothers may have hoped for as they sent their man into the mainland of Asia, Lansdale, battling the flooding tides of Asian nationalism, came out more like Lawrence of Arabia riding a Chevrolet instead of a camel.

In Saigon he got behind Ngo Dinh Diem, who had just returned from America to head a shaky regime. To some the free-steering Lansdale seemed a man who understood the people's problems; to others he was naive and less than sensitive to the desires of a nation that had already endured a dozen years of colonial warfare. Saluted as a builder in a best-selling book and movie *The Ugly American* (1958), damned as a destroyer in Graham Greene's mordant novel *The Quiet American* (1956), Lansdale, the CIA viceroy, gave Diem counsel and funds. In both North and South Vietnam the 1956 "free elections" went by the boards. All through the nine years (1954–1963) that Diem held increasingly arbitrary sway until his assassination in 1963, the CIA ran a separate operation in Saigon with Lansdale as station chief and a large staff rivaling that of the American ambassador.[39]

In Vietnam what the CIA began ended as war. In Laos, which lay closer to the actual border of China, the CIA's intervention also led to armed hostilities but in this case United States armed forces were never officially engaged and the CIA ran the show in the boondocks. In his lively novel about its birth at Geneva in 1954, *The Looking Glass Conference*, Godfrey Blunden retitled the country "Khaos." It was small, mainly jungle and mountains. Its chief export was opium. But it had Communists —the Pathet Lao—who persistently sought representation in the government, and the government's willowy neutrality affronted Washington's desire for vise-tight encirclement of the Communist bloc and weakened its official acceptance of Laos as a buffer state. Thus for years the United States bankrolled successive cabinets in Vientiane while the CIA secretly built airstrips, dropped supplies and trained anti-Pathet Lao forces in the hinterland. It was hard to tell where the activities of one Dulles brother let off and the other's began.

Yet even with such intimate topside liaison in Washington, an institution grown so large and complex, and so free from congressional constraints, generated a momentum not easily controlled. In 1958 Secretary Dulles died, and the unique dovetailing of diplomacy and subversion broke off. Allen Dulles stayed on until 1961, when the CIA-organized expedition to overthrow Castro came to grief in the Cuban swamps, roused America to the damage to the national interest that CIA skullduggery could do, and prompted the White House to clamp the lid on its filibustering Plans Division. Meanwhile, however, the CIA had gone overboard in Asia, prompting President Kennedy to say later, "Thank God the Bay of Pigs happened when it did. Otherwise we'd be in Laos by now—and that would be a hundred times worse."

In Laos, as in Vietnam, the agency intervened on the side of a rightwing strongman. By now CIA airpower had been expanded from CAT, renamed China Airlines, and included two other fronts—Air America and Air Asia. In September 1960 General Phoumi Nosavan formed a "Revolutionary Committee" and, supplied by a steady shuttle of the C.I.A.'s "civilian" air transports, occupied the capital. The American embassy in Vientiane however hedged on backing the CIA coup, and the premier, Prince Souvanna Phouma, did not resign. Instead his army supporters staged a comeback against the strongman's CIA-backed troops. The North Vietnamese stiffened and trained the Pathet Lao, and the diplomats were warning that the Chinese might react to pressure on their southern frontier as forcibly as they had to MacArthur's move to their Yalu border in the north a decade earlier. When General Phoumi made a stand at Nam Tha, fifteen miles from China, some bombs from the CIA's "civilian" aircraft dropped on Chinese towns, and the Russians began airdropping guns to the Pathet Lao guerrillas. The peace of the world hung in balance until Washington and Moscow found a formula for reneutralizing the little country in 1962. When war broke out in Southeast Asia, it was across the border in South Vietnam.[40]

The full extent of CIA "special operations" and the true extent to which they contributed over a period of more than two decades to the widespread American perception that the vital interests of the United States were being threatened by "international Communist" aggression in Southeast Asia is not likely to become known for many years. With the order to clamp down on the Plans Division after the Bay of Pigs, there was a general exodus of the more dashing clubmen and sporting types from the CIA. Whiting Willauer, Chennault's old fellow China hand who had helped him start CAT and then became ambassador to Honduras in 1953 to join in engineering the Guatemalan revolution, dropped out after the Bay of Pigs debacle. The "fun," it was said, had gone out of it after filibustering was frowned on.

Yet the scope and extent of the CIA's day-to-day activities in 120 countries remained secret, and the agency, large, costly, powerful and permanent, remained immune to congressional inquiry and proof against all but the most general statutory and fiscal controls. By law it worked only abroad, and all questions about it were brushed aside as endangering "national security." There did not seem to be much that the legislative branch could do about it. In 1972 the Senate Foreign Relations Committee was reduced to a roundabout way of getting information about its doings. Ray S. Cline, head of the State Department's Bureau of Intelligence and Research, appeared to testify on a $7,300,000 budget request for his office. The senators knew, however, that Cline had served earlier as deputy director of the CIA. How large a part of the nation's intelligence was covered by the sum requested, asked a senator. The United States, said Cline, spent "about $3 billion" yearly in collecting intelligence around the world—maybe more, depending upon what was considered "intelligence." Obviously the Cold War had brought as one of its unintended consequences a major new force, and with it a troublingly formidable new institution, into the conduct of the nation's affairs.[41]

C H A N G E , magnified and accelerated by technological thrust in the World War and Cold War, was the very condition of life through these years. The American approach to change in the 1950s was split-level— on the official level to stand immobilized against it, and on the next level below to drive for every technological innovation that could empower the United States by dint of the latest radar, maser, laser, or high-flying spy plane to win the Cold War against "international Communism."

In the dialectical world of the Marxist, change is the law of life, and as he scrambled for supreme power in the Communist world Nikita Khrushchev obeyed the law and at times seemed even to embody it. From outward appearances it was almost as if he began each day with no thought of where it might take him. His improvisations were dazzling. He seemed to be springing, like little 'Liza, across the ice-floes, keeping from falling in only because he kept racing on so recklessly. Later he confided, "You have no idea how hard it is to be a politician. It is the hardest job in the world." Yet Khrushchev ran so hard only to stay in place. He too was a leader made uneasy by change, a conservator, despite his outward style, in the world revolutionary Communist movement.[42]

Recognizing that a great nation could not continue to live with the Stalinist atmosphere of terror and lies, he broke the myth that had grown up round his iron predecessor. Fighting off palace conspiracies and satellite revolts, he began a search for a new formula of single-party government and another authority besides the knout to rule a superpower and its emerging "world Socialist system" of fourteen states and a billion people. At the same time, while smashing the cult of personality, Khrushchev was battling to bring Soviet ideology to terms with the facts of the nuclear age. No Western leader of his day—certainly not Eisenhower— so provoked and confronted change. Careening around blind dialectical corners, waving at the spectators even as he took the curves on two wheels, he shouted that war was not a fatal inevitability—and thereby revised a doctrine Communists had lived by for forty years. The new course along which Khrushchev led the insurrectionary proletariat was determined by the policy of peaceful coexistence. This policy implied not only that change would take a lot of time but that violent change in the world could be disastrous for existing Communist states and should be resisted.[43]

To Mao Tse-tung such attitudes to change had a counterrevolutionary sound about them. The aftermath of Sputnik was not the time to talk about the pitfalls of change. Revolutionary change had just liberated a fifth of mankind in China, and at this moment when it was spreading through an awakening Asia, the reactionary hostility to change of the United States prevented his occupation of China's last unreclaimed territories in Taiwan and the offshore islands. A prudent accommodation with the United States to reduce the chances of nuclear war at this point was just what China did not desire. To Mao at this time change meant the spread of revolutionary change by force—*Soviet* force—notwithstanding the risk—*Soviet* risk—that nuclear retaliation might be disastrously visited upon those who abetted the change. Mao did not shrink from the prospect, though he minimized it, because he welcomed a confrontation by which, he said, the forces of change—the rising peoples of the underdeveloped world—must prevail.

These attitudes to change came into sudden and brutal confrontation between the United States and Russia in 1960. The superficiality of any seemingly good relations between the two superpowers was abruptly laid bare. The Cold War between them was sharply stepped up. Only in later years was it seen that Khrushchev, the central figure in the U-2 affair, was caught and whipsawed between revolutionary China and counterrevolutionary America.

For an ideological movement such as world Communism, unity was the prior necessity for the victory ordained by history. Unity enforced by Stalinist terror was no longer judged possible, and Khrushchev, a man with immensely less power, operated as he said as a "politician." He kissed babies, patted nursemaids, addressed *kolkhozhniks* in cornfields, and generally behaved like a man running for office. Though he used every trick of bureaucratic squeeze, bluster and wile, every slippery device of "socialist legality," he always carried his programs by appeals to some Soviet precedent and ultimately by majority vote. Nothing quite like his performance had been seen since the Bolsheviks took over, and nothing remotely like it was seen thereafter. Yet behind the leaps and turns of the First Secretary's audacious improvisations, and the dimly decribed compromises of a Kremlin wheeler-dealer, a certain larger design could be discerned, though it would have taken a man of both greater power and greater powers to have carried the whole thing off as decisively as Khrushchev needed to, to stay on top in Soviet, in Communist, in world affairs.[44]

The heroic scheme of Khrushchev's grand policy, says Adam Ulam, the Harvard historian of Russian diplomacy, began to be made manifest after he became head of both the Soviet government and party in 1958. Peaceful coexistence was a very stretchable doctrine. Some days he blandished, other days he threatened, but always he sought to bring together and lead the contending and conflicting forces within Communism. Oversimplified, these contrary tendencies as expressed in international affairs could be stated thus: On the one side the Russians wanted to make the most of the inviting opportunities to expand their power and influence in the Third World following the collapse after Suez of British and French colonialism. On the other hand, well aware of the danger of nuclear holocaust, Khrushchev particularly wanted to secure a relaxation, a détente, in the nuclear arms race with the United States.

The Communist unity that Khrushchev commanded in the late 1950s by his leaps and jumps included, as far as the world could tell, the Olympian assent of Mao Tse-tung. Mao had journeyed to Moscow for the fortieth anniversary of the Bolshevik Revolution in 1957 and signed the Moscow Declaration of the fourteen ruling Communist parties upholding the policy of peaceful coexistence. Yet often, even when the Russians were most peremptorily laying down the line in, for example, Eastern European affairs, there was always a faint impression of an invisible Chinese presence behind Khrushchev's elbow of which he was continuously and often impatiently aware.

The improvement in Russian-American relations that Khrushchev sought at this stage of the Cold War turned on a number of things. The first was to get some agreement in the sterile talks on disarmament, particularly to find a way to end the nuclear tests and control the existing supply of nuclear weapons. Here the main obstacle, year after year, had been American insistence upon on-site inspection to make sure of detailed compliance, and Russian refusal to countenance any such invasion of their sovereign territory. The second was the still unsettled status of Berlin.

Khrushchev's standing proposition for settling these or almost any international difficulties was to call a summit meeting. President Eisenhower was leery. He had been none too happy about the 1955 Geneva summit, which gave the Russian leaders a matchless opening to make propaganda scores but yielded no lasting results. But pressure was building up for another meeting of the Big Four. Some of America's allies, particularly the Macmillan government in Britain, were outspokenly for it. Khrushchev went touring round the world presenting Russia as the true friend of peace because it was ready and eager for such a conference. Dulles doggedly resisted it. Then in the fall of 1958 Khrushchev sent a diplomatic note precipitating the second Berlin crisis.

He informed the Western powers that it was now thirteen years since the end of the war, that since then two Germanies had regrettably come into existence instead of just one, and that it was now high time to wind up the abnormal situation in West Berlin, where alone the powers still kept occupation forces. This should be done by some mutually agreed plan, by making it an international city or some such scheme, but it should be done within six months. Otherwise the Russians would turn over their part of Berlin to the East Germans and leave the other powers to negotiate with the East Germans their rights of access to West Berlin.[45]

The six-month deadline conveyed the air of an ultimatum. To the ailing Dulles the call for action was but another Russian exercise in blackmail. Eisenhower drew back. Later the American attitude softened, mainly in response to Macmillan's almost agitated pleas to explore what the Russians had in mind. But for the Americans to agree to recognize East Germany or clear out of Berlin was unthinkable. What, therefore, could the Russians be after?

No doubt Khrushchev needed foreign policy successes, and before the exchanges over Berlin ended Eisenhower was to volunteer that the situation in Berlin was in truth "abnormal." Khrushchev was looking for anything that he could pry loose from the West at this point. But the way he operated it was hard to tell whether he was serious. Dulles and Eisenhower were inclined to put it down as just one more barrage of rocket-rattling bombast like the threats over Suez in 1956 and the Lebanon landing in 1957. And when Macmillan persisted in flying to Moscow in midwinter to find out, Khrushchev took it for a grandstand play to the British voters and insulted him in session after session.

But the facts were presented in the Russian note. "The best way to solve the Berlin question," Khrushchev had said,

> would mean the withdrawal of the Federal German Republic from NATO, with the simultaneous withdrawal of the German Democratic Republic from the Warsaw Treaty Organization. . . . Neither of the two German states would have any armed forces in excess of those needed to maintain law and order at home and to guard the frontier.

To those not blinded by the sclerotic tunnel-vision of years and years of Cold War staring matches, this said that the Russians were looking for a way to an agreement that would make it impossible for West Germany to obtain nuclear weapons, a purpose by no means repugnant to the United States.[46]

In setting a time-limit, the Russians were not only playing to their post-Sputnik strength in missilery but were also influenced by the widening split in their own camp with China. Within a year or two this increasingly violent dispute might become public knowledge, and Russia's bargaining powers against the United States would shrink accordingly. But at this point a deal with the United States that banned Germany from the nuclear arms club might even be extended to include a tradeoff that America might welcome—elimination, at least for foreseeable years, of China as a possessor of nuclear weapons.

Here was the background: After Mao had visited Moscow to proclaim that "The East Wind is prevailing over the West Wind," the Russian leaders of the Eastern camp had agreed to advance the Chinese more economic and technical aid. But they were wholly unwilling to heed

Mao's demands that Russia, given its pronounced technological advantage over America after Sputnik, should engage in Dulles-style brinkmanship to advance Communism throughout the world even at the risk of nuclear war. Nor did they intend to build up Chinese forces for the purpose of overwhelming imperialism by force of arms. The costs of unforgotten foreign interventions in Bolshevik Russia, the twenty million dead of Hitler's invasion in the Second World War, had taught these revolutionaries that there were severe limits upon the militant approach to international affairs. The primarily economic strategy of peaceful coexistence laid down in the 1950s might be infuriatingly irrelevant to the problems of an economically backward China. But quite obviously it served Russia well in its contest with the United States. A military confrontation on the other hand could be disastrous. It could lead to the thermonuclear razing of America *and* Russia to the level of—China. In such an adventure there could be no profit for Moscow.[47]

Thus Russia refused to act in the late summer of 1958 when Mao Tse-tung wanted to unleash his troops upon the tiny, United States-protected offshore islands of Quemoy and Matsu. Khrushchev's letter to Eisenhower stating that "an attack upon the Chinese People's Republic, which is a great friend, ally and neighbor of our country, is an attack upon the Soviet Union," was wrung from the Russians, the Chinese later asserted, only after Mao's artillery bombardment of the islands had let up and the crisis had passed.[47]

Even before these all but unbending exchanges Khrushchev and other Russian leaders had begun to make guarded comment on Chinese affairs. To the astonishment of the world and the horror of the Russians, Mao had announced in early 1958 that China would bypass by a "great leap forward" the stages through which other Socialist states had passed. Marshaling all of China's incontrovertibly great manpower asset into one mighty mass effort, the country could overcome its industrial backwardness, double its steel output, vastly increase food production in new agrarian communes, and achieve the goals of fifteen years in one. To the Russians such a fantastic scheme promised an economic catastrophe for China and heavy new demands for Russian aid. But the Chinese claim that they were leaping right past socialism into communism also contained a covert criticism of Soviet society for insufficient ideological militancy, and a threat that China might try to compete with Russia within the Communist world by exporting its "purer" version of Communism and revolution.

By late 1958 however, it became apparent that the Russians were right about China's leap. In December the facts of disastrous shortages not only in industrial production but even in food-grain harvests became known, and Mao asked to be relieved of his position as chief of government (he kept his post as party chairman). The Russians saw their chance to bring the Chinese back under control.

Early in 1959 Chou En-lai traveled to Moscow and signed a deal whereby the Russians would ship seventy-eight more large industrial plants to China, bringing to 350 the number of such plants made available by the Soviet Union after 1950. Almost certainly, although the deal involved no new credits but was financed out of current production, the new program was dependent on China's own performance and upon the political and economic directions that would now be set out by Peking. The tutelary Russian position was underlined in a crucial sentence in Khrushchev's long speech that month to the Twenty-first Party Congress:

> One can and must construct in the Far East and the whole Pacific Ocean area a zone of peace and, first of all, a zone free of atomic weapons.

This open declaration that Russia would welcome a way by which Communist China might be prevented from ever acquiring atomic weapons was resolutely overlooked by an American government that shied away from any suggestion of disengagement as a Cold War sellout. But on June 20, as the world learned later, the Russians thought themselves sufficiently in control to cancel the 1957 agreement by which they had promised to provide the Chinese with the technical knowledge for the manufacture of atomic bombs. A month later the Russians extended to China's Asian rival India precisely the kind of aid they had withheld from China in January—a fresh $378,000,000 credit for economic development.[48]

For Chairman Mao only one more step was needed to conclude that Moscow had turned openly anti-Chinese. At a plenum of the Chinese Communist Central Committee in July-August 1959, Defense Minister Peng Liu-shai put down a memorandum attacking Mao's Great Leap policy, and it came out that he had shown it to Khrushchev and discussed it with the Soviet leader during a spring visit to Europe. The Russians themselves had hinted strongly that they wanted to be empowered to pledge that China would refrain from the production of nuclear weapons *if* the United States in return would make a similar pledge about West Germany. Had Marshal Peng and others been in favor of accepting the Russian proposals? Or, as was hinted later, were they at the prompting of the Russians even attempting to remove Mao and his group? Two things are clear. There was a violent secret dispute between the leaders of the Chinese and Russian Communist parties, and Mao successfully insisted on Peng's dismissal, installing Lin Piao as Defense Minister in his place.

This was not all. Following the uprising in Tibet and the flight of the Dalai Lama to India, Chinese forces crossed the Himalayan border and occupied an Indian outpost. It was then that Prime Minister Nehru told his parliament that the Chinse had already built a highway across the disputed frontier territory more than two years before, and secret negotiations thereafter had been fruitless. The action seemed contrary to China's 1955 Bandung pledge with other Asian countries not to use force in disputes among themselves. At this particular moment the action also seemed a challenge to Russian policy toward India. The Russian response, foreshadowing deeper differences with Peking, was to declare Moscow's neutrality in the dispute.[49]

Meanwhile, the other side of what Professor Ulam has called Khrushchev's grand design took shape. The summer of 1959 also saw Russia moving toward a summit meeting with the country against which Mao demanded that all Communists display unrelenting hostility. The United States sent a whole series of athletes, musicians, scholars, soldiers and political figures on visits to Russia. In June Vice President Nixon flew to Moscow where he stayed at Khrushchev's *dacha* and then went in the premier's company to tour the United States National Exhibition in Moscow. Somehow, surrounded by gleaming gadgets in the kitchen of an American model house, the two men got into a slambang argument that became a remembered milestone of the Cold War.

KHRUSHCHEV: You Americans think that the Russian people will be dumbfounded to see these things. The fact is that newly-built Russian houses have all this equipment now.

NIXON: We do not claim to astonish the Russian people. We hope to show our diversity and our right to choose. We do not wish to have decisions made for us at the top by government officials that all houses should be built the same way.

NIXON: Would it not be better to compete in washing machines than in rockets? Is this the kind of competition you want?

KHRUSHCHEV: Yes, this is the kind of competition we want. But your generals say, 'Let's compete in rockets. We are strong and we can beat you.' But in this we can also show you something, so that you will know the Russian spirit.

NIXON: You are strong and we are strong. In some ways you are stronger. We are both strong, not only in weapons but also in will and spirit. Neither should use that strength to put the other in a position where he faces an ultimatum.

KHRUSHCHEV: If all Americans agree with you, who don't we agree with?

NIXON: I hope the prime minister understood all the implications of what I said. What I mean is that the moment we place either one of these powerful nations in a position so that they have no choice but to accept dictation or fight, then you're playing with the most destructive force in the world.

KHRUSHCHEV: We too are giants. If you want to threaten, we will answer threat with threat.

NIXON: *(Tapping K's lapel)* We will never engage in threats.

KHRUSHCHEV: You wanted indirectly to threaten me. But we have the means to threaten you too. Ours are better than yours.

NIXON: Who wants to threaten?

KHRUSHCHEV: We want peace with all other nations, especially America.

NIXON: We want peace too.[50]

To millions of Americans witnessing it by specially relayed tapes on TV, the "kitchen debate" between Nixon and Khrushchev conveyed not only satisfaction at seeing an American standing up for his country against the foe. Through all the harshness of words ran a general air of joviality. Khrushchev at one point joshed Foreign Minister Andrei Gromyko standing nearby. Once, to underscore a point about all the benefits Soviet citizens had, he threw his arm around one of the Russian maintenance workers listening with obvious delight to the hassle. The scene brought shocked recognition that the foe, wagging a stubby finger, giving and taking blows, was a very human being, one you could do business with. The Gallup poll rating for Nixon shot up—and so did the percentage in America favoring a summit meeting. The next step followed soon. On August 3, 1959, President Eisenhower and Premier Khrushchev announced reciprocal visits, the first bringing the Russian leader to America the following month.[51]

The day before Khrushchev's arrival, Russia landed an 855-pound missile on the moon. The Premier swept into Washington in a giant white TU-114 jetliner and handed a model of the Lunik to President Eisenhower. The President, his aides, the crowds in the streets all were coolly polite. Allen Dulles, introduced at a reception, did not unbend when Khrushchev said, "I believe we get the same reports—and probably from the same people." Many Americans thought of the visitor as "the butcher of Hungary," and there was hostility on the part of the press as well as some Roman Catholic prelates. He was, moreover, a Soviet Communist, a man Americans had been conditioned to believe was a mortal enemy of the Republic.

In some ways Khrushchev's visit could be compared with President Nixon's visit to China thirteen years later. Nixon's too was an enigmatic overture that seemed to invite a new start in relationships. But Nixon's was remote and solemn, confined to honor-guard reviews, state banquets, cautious protocol, at the highest level, whereas Khrushchev's was brash, pushing, populist.

He barnstormed the country from coast to coast, appeared on television, engaged in off-the-cuff colloquies, complained loudly when Disneyland was taken off his itinerary because the police were worried about his safety ("Do you have launching pads there? Or have gangsters taken over the place?"), criticized a Hollywood filming of the cancan ("The face of mankind is more beautiful than his backside."), ate his first hot dog ("We have beaten you to the moon but you have beaten us in sausage making"), and waded admiringly into a field of Iowa's tall corn. Everywhere he went Khrushchev promoted the idea that "if the two biggest countries in the world" would develop friendly relations, "peace on earth will be more stable and durable." At the end of the tour Khrushchev spent three days with President Eisenhower at Camp David. Taking their meals together, strolling along the gravel pathways, the two men had plenty of opportunity to talk. Khrushchev agreed to remove his ultimatum on Berlin, and Eisenhower agreed eagerly to a summit meeting.[52]

But the bitter dispute with China that had erupted just before Khrushchev's visit wrecked the Soviet leader's hope of being able to speak for China in proposing worldwide nuclear limitations—and thus soured what otherwise would have been a crowning point of his career. Eisenhower himself has told how Khrushchev brought up the subject of China at Camp David and asked the President if he would like to discuss it. The reply represents another high mark in the frostbound annals of the Cold War. "I answered," the general wrote in his memoirs, "that I thought there was little use to do so for the simple reason that Red China had put herself beyond the pale as far as the United States was concerned."[53]

What if Khrushchev had unburdened himself to Eisenhower? What if the Americans had not been so conspicuously obtuse about not taking up the grandiose scheme for Pacific Ocean-Middle European limitations on nuclear arms that the Russian leader had been hinting at—by threat and by smile? What, indeed, if the summit had been held that fall instead of being put off, because General DeGaulle was wary lest the two superpowers settle affairs themselves, until the spring of 1960?

Whatever the answer to such questions Khrushchev, leaping across the crevasses of history, rushed from Washington to Peking. There he infuriated Chairman Mao by extolling the "spirit of Camp David" and warmly praising the statesmanlike qualities of President Eisenhower. Making no concession to Mao's view that socialism had become invincible, he said at the tenth anniversary celebrations of China's revolution:

We must and we shall defeat the capitalist countries in peaceful competition. . . . Socialism brings peace, that greatest of blessings to man. This is how the matter stands: either peaceful coexistence or war with catastrophic consequences.[54]

A man of Khrushchev's bounce and drive did not flag because half of his grand design was fading. Early in 1960 he proclaimed the largest Soviet disarmament program of modern times: the reduction of ground forces, because of the shift to reliance upon missiles, from 3,600,000 to 2,400,000 men over the next three years. In February Moscow revealed that the Russians would not provide nuclear arms to China—on the very day that Khrushchev was off in India signing a treaty granting a new $1.65 billion credit to India.[55]

It was at this point, when the three Western powers had finally fixed their summit date with Khrushchev in Paris for May, that the Chinese finally decided to go over to the attack. On April 16, 1960, the Peking journal *Red Flag* published an editorial entitled "Long Live Leninism!" a heavy onslaught by Mao Tse-tung himself. The article did not attack Khrushchev and the Russians by name, but its scathing dismissal of Yugoslav Communists and assorted revisionists was transparent enough. It was a public warning: if you Russians push through a détente with the West, we shall denounce you by name as being as vile as the Yugoslav revisionists.[56]

For Khrushchev this ended the last chance of producing at the 1960 summit any dramatic proposal to prohibit nuclear weapons in the Pacific in return for a similar ban in Germany. What was left was the increasingly dim prospect of wangling one-sided concessions out of the West. Shortly before the conference C. Douglas Dillon, the American Undersecretary of State, delivered a bristlingly unyielding speech in which he asked:

> Is the Soviet Union prepared to remove its forces from East Germany and the Eastern European countries on which they are imposed? Is it willing to grant self-determination to the East Germans and the peoples of the Soviet-dominated states in Eastern Europe?

Stung by questions to which all the answers would have to be "no," Khrushchev warned in a speech at Baku that the West would have to be more reasonable at Paris or the Russians would sign with the East Germans, and the Western powers would lose their entry rights—"land, water and air"—in Berlin.[57]

A M O N G the military jets crowding the United States base at the Turkish city of Adana in late April, 1960, the low black plane with the high tail looked out of place. Its wings were so wide and thin that they drooped. Its landing gear, like that of no other plane, was rigged bicycle-fashion—a wheel under the nose and another under the tail, with flimsy, wheeled "pogosticks" under the wingtips that could be dropped off as soon as the plane was airborne. The plane bore no identifying marks whatsoever. Its pilot—there was room for no other crewman beneath the glass canopy—seemed equally odd: he wore a special partial-pressure flying suit with oxygen tubes dangling from it at several points, and there was a revolver slung on his hip.

Francis Gary Powers was the senior pilot in the supersecret 10/10 squadron at Adana that was engaged in making reconnaissance flights at fantastically high altitudes over the Soviet Union. Like a handful of other former Air Force pilots, Lt. Powers had been hired in 1956 by the CIA at $1,800 a month to fly secret, "high-risk" missions. They were to carry out overflights of Russia in a special jet plane that Clarence (Kelly) Johnson, design chief at Lockheed and creator of the Air Force's F-104 Starfighter, had developed for this express purpose at the behest of Allen Dulles and Richard Bissell, head of the CIA's Plans Division. The jet had made its first flight in August, 1955, and it was given the designation "U-2." Besides the pilot, the jet carried heavy electronic gear and a battery of cameras that he could turn on at the flick of a button. The cameras recorded the photographic information which, when developed and inter-preted by experts, told the CIA what the directors of United States defense wanted perhaps more than anything else in the world to know: the location and activities of Soviet military elements, above all, of its missile forces.

Powers, a drawling, crew-cut ex-footballer from the hillbilly country of the Central Appalachians, had joined the operation because he liked the pay, which by the time he began flying from Turkey was $30,000 a year. From the time of the Suez crisis in 1956 and the Sputnik launchings in 1957, he carried out a number of "overflights," and many times flew over and successfully photographed the Tyuratam Cosmodrome, Russia's Cape Kennedy, which was located only a thousand miles north of his base near the Aral Sea.

On every mission his U-2 broke the world's official altitude record for airplanes of 65,669 feet, set in 1955 by the pilot of a British Canberra Mark II. Very probably he flew as high as 100,000 feet. At such levels his jet was not even visible from the ground. But that did not mean the Russians were unaware that he was up there. His jet carried electronic gear that picked up the indications of Russian radars tracking him, and Ameri-can radiomen south of the border could hear Russians excitedly barking messages of his course and speed.

Flying an airplane over another country's territory was not only a violation of international law, it was insulting to that nation and its prestige. Not only did it imply actual technological superiority but it spoke contempt for that nation's defenses. Never in all Powers's spy missions were Russian interceptor planes able to rise to the heights at which the U-2 flew, nor were Russian antiaircraft batteries able to fire that high. And since the conducting of such intelligence overflights could appear as the preliminary steps taken before going to war, they were matters of utmost political gravity. Indeed the United States government considered the sending of such U-2 missions over the Soviet Union an act essential to national survival in the Cold War days of the 1950s. Though Powers saw little of the pictures developed from his film and rushed off each time by special courier plane to Washington, it was evident enough from things said that "Operation Overflight" was a source of highly valued intelligence.[58]

Premier Khrushchev knew all about these secret flights, and had chafed at Russian helplessness to prevent them. At least once in 1956, immediately after an official visit to Moscow by General Nathan Twining, chief of the United States Air Force, an American plane flew clandestinely into Russia and penetrated as far as Kiev. "The question arose," Khrushchev said much later, "should we protest or not? I suggested not sending any protest. We learnt our lesson from the fact and stepped up our production of rockets and fighter planes." Later, in the intimate atmosphere of Camp David, Khrushchev had felt, he said, like asking Eisenhower why he was allowing U-2 flights over Russia, but decided it was too embarrassing.[59]

The President also said nothing, but by the following spring U-2 flights were few and far between. After a long pause one was carried out from Turkey on April 9. Then, late in the month, Gary Powers was alerted for the next flight. It was to start from a base in Pakistan, a favorable approach to the Soviet missile research center at Tyuratam. But for the first time in Operation Overflight's four years, the mission was to fly right across the face of Russia. After penetrating to the Cosmodrome, Powers was to fly northward over the big Soviet industrial center of Sverdlovsk behind the Ural mountains—and continue on over the Arctic cities of Archangel and Murmansk to terminate at the NATO air base of Bodo in far-northern Norway. This would entail a flight of at least 3,800 miles extending over nine hours, almost all of it over Soviet territory.

The flight was delayed two days because of weather. On the third morning Powers was kept perspiring in his pressurized flying suit past the scheduled 6:00 a.m. takeoff time until approval of the White House was belatedly received. Then Powers had a last word with the squadron colonel, locked his canopy shut, and took off. One remarkable thing about the U-2 was its forty-five degree angle of climb, so steep that the pilot had the feeling he was going to tip over on his back. In minutes, Powers was at 60,000 feet, transmitting the single-beep all's-well signal back to base before lapsing, by inflexible CIA rule, into radio silence.

The first leg of the flight was uneventful, with considerable cloud cover around the Cosmodrome. But between Chelyubinsk and Sverdlovsk, when the Urals were coming up snow-topped in sunlight on the left, Powers' automatic pilot went out of whack. He switched to manual, and pressed determinedly on. No U-2 had ever flown over Sverdlovsk before, and his cameras were working. About 30 to 40 miles northeast of Sverdlovsk he made a 90-degree turn and rolled into a flightline that would take him over the southwestern edge of the city. He was marking the time, altitude, speed, exhaust-gas temperature and engine-instrument readings in his log when "suddenly there was a dull thump, the aircraft jerked forward, and a tremendous orange flash lit the cockpit and sky."

For Powers there was just "time enough to think the explosion was external to the aircraft and, from the push, somewhat behind it." The plane fell away into an uncontrollable spin. Powers, thrown forward, did not use the ejection seat. Instead he reached over his head and unlocked the canopy, which sailed off into space. Without stopping to pull the switches that would have exploded the plane, he scrambled out, dangled frantically on his oxygen hoses till they snapped, and then fell free. At 15,000 ft. his parachute opened automatically. As he floated down he remembered a suicide device that the "agency" man had handed him before takeoff. It was a poison pin inside a hollowed-out silver dollar. He unscrewed the enclosing loop, slipped out the pin and put it in his pocket, and flung the dollar to the Siberian winds.

The moment Powers hit the ground less than a hundred yards from a village, citizens out for the May Day holiday gathered round him. Someone took his pistol. On the barrel were the inevitable words: "USA." In his seatpack was an American-flag poster with "I am an American" printed on it in fourteen languages. This spy in the sky, expecting to land in Norway, had also brought along his overnight kit. In it was his wallet with all his identification cards, his Social Security card, pictures of his wife Barbara. Flown to Moscow, Powers told the whole story of his spy flight from takeoff in Turkey to bailout over Sverdlovsk.[60]

The news that the U-2 had been shot down and its pilot captured was not long reaching Premier Khrushchev, who had been informed of the plane's incursion and had personally ordered Defense Minister Malinowski to bring it down. In his own curmudgeonly way Khrushchev passed the news on near the end of a three-and-one-half-hour address that day to the Supreme Soviet. He paused, glowered, then said: "I am in duty bound to report to you on the aggressive acts . . . by the United States of America." On May 1 the Soviet Union had shot down over Russian territory a plane "on a mission of aggressive provocation aimed at wrecking the Summit Conference" just seven days off. Eisenhower, the premier went on, seemed to want peace but he was surrounded by "imperialists" and "militarists."[61]

In announcing his sensation the Russian leader had elected to play a ruse by withholding the important details. The result surpassed his expectations, because Washington not only fell into the trap but issued version after floundering version until any remaining basis between Eisenhower and himself on which the summit conference could take place had been destroyed and Khrushchev was left with no alternative but to break it off.

First the National Space and Aeronautical Administration in Washington issued a statement that, yes, one of its high-flying U-2s on a routine weather reconnaissance flight over Turkey was missing after its pilot reported oxygen trouble and the plane, keeping on northward course after the pilot blacked out, strayed on over the Russian border. "There was absolutely no—N-O—no deliberate attempt to violate Soviet air space," added the State Department press officer. A little later NASA produced the name of the "weather" pilot as Francis G. Powers—and Khrushchev had the final detail needed to catch the United States government in a bald lie.[62]

Next day, with all his gusto, Khrushchev informed the Supreme Soviet that their government had captured Powers "alive and kicking," that he had been downed near Sverdlovsk over 1300 miles inside Russia, and that the pilot had confessed to being on a spy flight which began in Pakistan and was to end in Norway. "He told us, 'I think my flight was for the collection of information on Soviet guided missiles and radar stations,'" crowed Khrushchev.

It was not intended that the pilot should tell, Khrushchev went on. "He was equipped with a poison needle to kill himself before capture." Also in his luggage was "a pistol, a silver dagger, a penknife, two gold watches besides the one he wore, and seven golden rings for women." "Was he going to fly to Mars and seduce Martian women?" asked Khrushchev, and the Supreme Soviet exploded again in laughter. There was more, said the premier. "We have not only the instruments found on the aircraft but also developed film consisting of photographs of several places on our territory. Here, look at this," he cried, holding up the large glossy prints. "Here are the airfields," and his blunt finger stabbed at the evidence. Powers, he said, would be tried for espionage.[63]

"Like the successive shocks of an earthquake, each one worse than the one before," was the way *Newsweek* described the impact of the successive U-2 disclosures upon America and its allies. At first Americans might have taken some secret satisfaction in the accidental disclosure of their government's past alertness. But then came the revelation of confusion and ineptitude in handling the affair from day to dismaying day. The State Department admitted that the flight was one of "surveillance." It said that such flights had gone on ever since the Russians rejected the American "Open Skies" proposal at the 1955 Geneva conference for mutual aerial reconnaissance to reassure against possible surprise attacks.

In one of his most trenchant columns Walter Lippmann wrote that the only possible accounting for the dispatch of an American spy plane on the eve of a summit conference was that it had not been done with the President's knowledge. Khrushchev picked up and repeated the suggestion. The State Department seemed to go along with it by saying that "the authorities" had not authorized "any such flight as described by Mr. Khrushchev."[64]

But in Washington, where Secretary of State Christian Herter was receiving all sorts of signals, thoughts flew not only to the impending summit. They flew even faster to the presidential campaign and election to follow. Any version implying that the President was not aware of any important acts by his government would only lend substance to the cry that the Democrats were sure to raise on the hustings: that America was leaderless, slipping and stagnating, and it was time to vote Democratic and get the country moving again. Reached by telephone at his Gettysburg farm, Eisenhower chose not to follow the accepted practice whereby governments refrain from acknowledging their acts of espionage. As a good army commander, the general had been trained to accept responsibility for the actions of his command. Much more to the point, he was smarting under repeated charges that he was not in effective command of the government over which he presided.[65]

So by a last embarrassed lurch of what *Time* called "manly candor" Washington reversed itself, and Secretary Herter declared that the President had authorized the general program of spying though not specific missions. By taking this position Eisenhower betrayed his tacit alliance with Khrushchev, who was now deprived of any pretext for minimizing the incident. On top of all this at a press conference five days before the summit meeting Eisenhower justified the spy mission as "a distasteful but vital necessity," and left little doubt of an intention to send over more of them. With the rug pulled completely out from under him, Khrushchev had little choice after that but to react in outspoken and menacing tones.[66]

On the morning of May 16 the summit opened at the Élysée Palace in Paris without a single handshake. At once Khrushchev took the floor, curt, rude, defiant. As a precondition for going ahead with the conference, he demanded that the United States government "condemn the inadmissible and provocative actions of the U.S. Air Force with regard to the Soviet Union," that it commit itself to the discontinuance of such actions, and that it undertake to "punish those directly guilty of such actions." He accused President Eisenhower to his face of "treachery" and a "bandit" policy. He startled his listeners by saying that the U-2 incident "deeply involved" the "internal politics" of the Soviet Union, and by proposing that the summit be postponed for six to eight months in hopes that "another United States government will understand the futility of pursuing aggressive policies." Khrushchev had one more insult for the President of the United States, and this was that "conditions (having) now arisen which make us unable to welcome the President with proper warmth," his June visit to Russia in return for Khrushchev's 1959 trip to America should be indefinitely postponed. Eisenhower, in "complete disgust," at the Soviet leader's "antics," refused to accept his "ultimatum," charged him with "the sole intent of sabotaging this meeting," and the summit broke off.[67]

Thus the superficiality of the "friendly" relations that had been claimed between the two superpowers and their leaders was rudely exposed before all the world. Although Americans rallied to their president at the moment of Khrushchev's insults, the U-2 affair had profound effects on their outlook. The U-2 overflight with its train of fatuous lies out of Washington, ended for millions the innocent idea that the American government was somehow different from all those foreigners. The "credibility gap" of which so much came to be made in the Johnson and Nixon years was first opened in the hour when the Eisenhower administration was caught in a barefaced lie. The split-level character of public behavior and morality was openly exposed, so to speak, in the highest quarters. This may have been as telling a result of the Paris summit collapse as any of its international repercussions.

In the unchanging equation of international power, the revolutionaries of the East could be said to have balanced out once more against the reactionaries of the West. Eisenhower and Khrushchev had been deterred from détente. With the antagonists immobilized amidst the very tides of change, the Cold War remained in frozen deadlock. Premier Khrushchev, with his inseparable companion at Paris, Defense Minister Malinowski, still at his side, flew east in his big white TU-114 jet. General Eisenhower, with Khrushchev's bitter lame-duck label draped like an albatross round his neck, boarded his jet to close his career with a round of goodwill missions to the Third World and with a final denunciation of the American military-industrial complex whose enveloping power had thwarted his hopes of crowning his presidency by a relaxation of Cold War tensions with Russia.[68]

THE DEMANDS of American intelligence in the Cold War led not only to the U-2 but in due course to the spy satellite out of which developed the commmunications satellite and a new capacity to transmit telephone and TV signals simultaneously round the world. The military's requirement for an airplane large enough to carry the Bomb led to the first big jets, and out of this demand flowed one of the most interesting consequences of the Cold War: the jet age in commercial aviation. Specifically, the Eisenhower administration's policies had called for big troop-lift capability. To provide it Boeing designed the KC-135 for the Air Force, then gave it a facelifting and sold it to the airlines as the first big commercial jet.[69]

The British had led the way. They had put their turbojet Comet into service to Africa in the early 1950s, only to be forced to ground the plane after crashes traced to an eerie flaw brought out by the tremendous speeds at which it flew: "metal fatigue" in the skin which caused rupture of the pressurized cabin. Its outer surfaces burnished and flush-riveted to overcome this menace, the first Boeing 707 flew in 1954. But Civil Aeronautics Administration caution delayed its entry into airline service until late 1958. The following summer, when Pan American and British Overseas Airways put 707s into full operation on their transatlantic crossings, was the real start of the commercial jet age. Taking command despite the momentary crimp put in the American vacation rush to Europe by the U-2 and Berlin crises, the jetliner swiftly established its dominance in air travel. Within a decade jets were flying 93% of all passenger miles.[70]

The mass of Americans did not take very quickly to jet travel; in 1959 the great majority had still never been up in a plane of any kind. And the acceptance of jet speeds required some large changes in human assumptions. Thus when one of the first Pan American Boeings, laden with junketing travel agents and journalists, taxied to the end of the runway at New York's Idlewild airport in late 1958, a woman from Seattle peered out, then asked nervously: "Aren't they even going to use the propellers on the takeoff?" Compared to the propeller planes they displaced, the big jetliners shortened by half the time it took to get places. They were more comfortable because they flew above the weather at 30–40,000 feet and did away with the old vibration and pounding cabin noises. But they traveled so fast that the physiological rhythms of people on board were knocked out of kilter (a problem identified by jet-age medicine as "circadian disrhythmia") and the racket they made on takeoff was earsplitting for anyone on the ground. At Idlewild noise complaints from nearby residents shot up from two in July, 1958, to sixty-five twelve months later, and the congressman representing the district demanded that the jets be grounded.

All the same the plumes of black smoke in the sky, like the long clouds trailed by locomotive in an earlier day, were accounted necessary and even proud signs of progress and growth. The jetliners changed the patterns of travel. One big jet flashing back and forth in six-hour crossings could carry as many passengers as a *Queen Mary,* and by 1960 there were 480 Boeings and Douglas DC-8s on the North Atlantic run. By 1957 the planes had snatched the lead from the ocean liners, and within a decade drove them virtually out of the competition.

At first the fashionable people who had hitherto made their seasonal moves from Palm Beach and Newport to San Moritz and Antibes by ship greeted the jetliners enthusiastically. For the "jet set," as these people were instantly dubbed, the airlines cordoned off up to half the cabin space as "first class," and tried gamely to simulate the spacious elegance of the ocean liners by serving champagne and making customers comfortable with blankets and pillows as if they were in deckchairs. Air France offered meals "a thousand miles long." It became briefly chic to fly from New York to London for a weekend, and *The New Yorker* reported a young woman who before a ball at the Plaza flew to Paris to have her hair done. *Vogue* solemnly noted "the great change in the concept of travel dressing" without steamer and wardrobe trunks or even the clutter of train and piston-plane toiletry:

> The pale grey suit, its fresh white collar and cuffs, the white straw hat it's worn with, all such were impossible, or at least impractical, before the jets with their clean, unhectic swiftness.

In the nature of things however any service in such abundant supply could hardly maintain the trappings of exclusiveness, and anything that happened so fast as a jet crossing could hardly be thought of any more as America's grand tour, as some social achievement awarded only to the wealthy and those with beneficent uncles. In the style of travel made possible by the technology of the Cold War, opulence stood down in favor of mere affluence. A far larger proportion of Americans traveled to Europe in the 1950s than ever before, but they spent a considerably smaller proportion of total disposable income than those who went abroad in the luxury-liner heyday of 1929. Even after the arrival of the jet age those who persisted in traveling by ship were bigger spenders than those who went by air, accounting for an average outlay of $900 each for their European vacations in 1961 compared to $700 spent by each air traveler. Year by year the sum spent by each American visitor declined—to an average outlay of $470 by 1969. At the same time the duration of the average American's stay in Europe declined from forty-five days to twenty-seven. After the metabolic insult of the jet crossing followed the culture shock of the jet tour, summed up in the movie title of 1971: *If It's Tuesday, This Must be Belgium.*

The jets altered everyday as well as holiday patterns of life. From the outset businessmen flying at company expense were the keenest jet patrons. When Boeing and Douglas jetliners streaked from New York to San Francisco in five hours and from Chicago to New Orleans in an hour and a half, the smoking lounges of America's Pullman cars fell silent and the club-cars of the crack long-distance trains emptied. With the Twentieth Century Limited and the Santa Fe Superchief driven from the rails, the kind of itinerant male talk that Ring Lardner and John O'Hara had reported so faithfully from the sleeping-car smokers now had to be snatched on the gallop at the various Admiral's Clubs and President's Clubs set up by the airlines at all major airports where steady customers met and drank between flights.

The introduction of the big jets not only coincided with but to some extent made possible the huge overseas expansion of American corporations in the 1950s and early 1960s. And just as the airplane had made possible the large-scale migration of Puerto Ricans to the mainland after the Second World War, the ease of jet travel now created a two-directional flow in and out of San Juan as the demand for employment rose and fell with cycles of prosperity and recession in the United States. The big jets undoubtedly helped hasten the reality of statehood for both Alaska and Hawaii in 1959, binding them to the main forty-eight, expanding their trade, and delivering hordes of tourists and settlers. (By 1960 the island of Oahu had a density of population exceeding that of Belgium.)

The jets quickly entered the lives of the young, who felt none of the old hesitancies about taking to the skies. Between 1954 and 1960 the number of young people studying in Europe rose by 150%, and it soon became a commonplace for American students to know several continents first hand before they were twenty-one. Mass summer migrations of youth to Europe began with jets: 120,960 young Americans were recorded in 1960 as visiting foreign youth hostels, almost all of them in Europe. With almost any place on earth less than twenty-four hours away from any major American airport, office secretaries soon thought nothing of vacationing in Vienna, Delhi, or Lima.[71]

A striking instance of how jet travel could affect the life of a young American was afforded by the experience of a Sarah Lawrence student named Hope Cooke. Brought up by her uncle, the American ambassador in Teheran in the late 1950s, this college junior, traveling with other girls across Asia in the summer of 1959, flew into Darjeeling in northern India. There friends introduced her at a party to Prince Thondup, a handsome young widower from the tiny, independent Himalayan country of Sikkim. Two years later, she was invited back as a house guest in remote Sikkim, and from the Prince, heir to the country's throne, she received a large diamond ring. Early in 1963, at festive ceremonies attended by crowds of Nepalese, Tibetans, her American relatives and United States Ambassador to India J. Kenneth Galbraith, Hope Cooke, 23, became the bride of Prince Thondup and prospective queen of Sikkim.[72]

In 1959, when Mike Todd's film *Around the World in Eighty Days* was a tremendous hit, *The Saturday Review* predicted that a quarter of a million American tourists would soon be circumnavigating the earth each year by jet. *Mademoiselle* described an Arabian Nights outing— 1001 hours in Marrakech, Tangier and other North African pleasure-domes. Soon as many Americans were jetting to Japan as flew to all Europe in the early Cold War years. Spending overseas, at a time when people joked about America's uncountably vast gold hoard at Fort Knox, was encouraged by the $400 worth of goods that any traveler could bring back duty-free. The Harris-tweed suit made overnight in Hong Kong, the leather gloves bought in Paris, the elegant shoes brought back from Italy —all increased the appetite of the affluent society for imports. These were the years when the imported car was fashionable (by 1959 Volkswagen did business in all fifty states), when young couples filled their living rooms with trim Scandinavian furniture, when men sported Nehru jackets and took up "Mod" styles from Britain, when the children rode English racer bicycles, when backyard chefs grilled chicken in Japanese hibachis, when British ballet was a high cultural hit, when the young set flocked to French movies like *Hiroshima, Mon Amour*, when the still younger set discovered Dutch cassette tape-players, when every third woman's handbag was likely to have been mass-produced in Italy or France. In the summer of 1959 America learned to wear Madras sport shirts from India, West Coast specialty stores featured "Italian Festivals," and the makers of Campbell Soup sent tasters through Europe to import a continental flavor for some of their old red-labeled dependables. Japanese cameras, motorbikes, type-writers and transistor radios were on their way to capturing the American consumer society.

The jetliner also brought invisible imports—Zen, yoga, karate, exis-tential psychiatry, the Castroite slouch, beard, fatigues. James Bond, the

cool international counteragent created by the British novelist Ian Fleming, jetted across the Atlantic, borne along by the confirming implausibilities of contemporary CIA intrigue. Some 7,000,000 readers including
John F. Kennedy and uncounted collegians flew with him through eleven
thrillers. Displayed in such movies as *Dr. No* and *Goldfinger*, his late Cold
War style of downing vodka martinis before doing in Communists helped
displace the Bloody Mary as the drink of fashion. Up against a villainous
variety of Communist crypto-tycoons, Bond bested them all, some smoth-
ered by bird-droppings, some blown up by their own A-bomb, and one
"slowly sucked with a terrible whistling noise" out of the window of a
high-flying plane.

The day came when reexports became inevitable in the international
jet age. As such the Beatles topped all lists. Risen from the Liverpool
dockfront they took their best from the black culture of America and
rocked back across the ocean in accents that seemed to sway young people
everywhere. They appeared before 55,000 at New York's Shea Stadium.
They placed eleven platters atop America's hit parade (and took in $100
million, or more than the dollar earnings of some foreign countries). The
original dreamlike inanity ("I'd hate to have grown up where there we-
ren't any Beatles," said a girl in Iowa) persisted well after the Cold War
faded: John, Ringo, Paul, George commanded a world's affections elec-
tronically.

So far-reaching were the changes in habits of travel, living and
thinking wrought in a decade by jet flight that some began to compare
the effects with those brought about a generation earlier by the introduction of the automobile. And it was no longer thought fanciful to speak
of the world, as Marshall McLuhan did in 1963, as a "global village."
Meanwhile no more striking consequence of the jet was to be seen than
its impact upon international diplomacy. In the formal conduct of United
States foreign affairs, the jet plane did more than the depredations of
Senator Joe McCarthy to enforce the decline of the State Department.
In the age of Eisenhower it was the Secretary of State who seemed almost
continuously airborne as he flew endlessly round the Communist flanks
building up his Cold War garrisons and shoring up the resolve of his
wavering allies. "There's a trough of low pressure moving rapidly eastward
across the North Atlantic—and guess who's in it!" read the caption of a
British newspaper's cartoon of 1957 alerting its readers to hold on for yet
another visit from John Foster Dulles. Eisenhower's travels, though considerable, were mainly voyages of good will. It was later Presidents who
carried the diplomacy of the jet age to the logical extreme and conducted
their foreign relations in person. In a world where heads of state could turn
up almost anywhere in a few hours, the old channels of diplomatic agentry

began to lose their utility for all but humdrum routines. If war could be started without Congress, peace could be sought without ambassadors. On jet wings even the necessity of formal diplomatic relations fell away into inessentiality. In the 1970s President Nixon, dispensing with "recognition" altogether, flew to Peking to treat with leaders of the People's Republic of China face to face.[73] To the extent that the speed and range of the jetliner made it possible, this trip too had to be put down as an unintended consequence of the Cold War.

CHAPTER 12

The Cuban Missile Crisis

and the Rise

of the Military-Industrial Complex

A NY HISTORY of turn-of-the-century America takes note of the rise of the modern corporation, of the devouring combines and trusts thrown together by the robber barons as they muscled their way to dominance in American life. A history of the Depression and New Deal years lays stress in turn upon the sitdown strikes, coal-field starveouts and wrench-swinging, goon-slugging, Pinkerton-walloping donnybrooks at steel-mill gates by which organized labor kicked and clawed its way to power and perquisites in contemporary America. By the same token, any account of the Cold War years must record the arrival of a third force of formidable size and power at the center of the American scene—the military.

One big change sure to be noticed by a visitor returning to the United States in the midst of the Cold War after an absence of, say twenty-five years, was the emergence of the military as a major social institution. Officers of the armed forces, previously relegated in peacetime to the backwaters of American life, were pictured almost every day at the elbow of the President of the United States in conference and consultation. The military with their briefcases were constantly to be seen on Capitol Hill, in and out of government offices, hurrying to and from airplanes, arriving for negotiations and inspections at industrial installations across the land. Soldiers, sailors and airmen thronged the nation's bus and air terminals. At any family's festive Christmas dinner in these years, at least one member at the table was likely to be a serviceman home on leave. In the crowds that assembled to hail the New Year in New York's Times Square or San Francisco's Market Street, the olive drab of the Army, the slate blue of the Air Force and the dark blue of the Navy were apt to be the commonest colors. No weekend went by without the sight of long convoys of jeeps, trucks and weapons-carriers barreling, headlights lit, through crowded freeway traffic on the martial exercises of the Reservists. Again and again newspapers were filled with stories of these "weekend warriors" pulling out of their communities, leaving their wives, children and jobs, and rushing away on emergency orders, as many as 100,000 and for as long as six months at a time, to help man the outposts of Cold War in the recurrent crises of Cuba, Taiwan, Berlin. Scarcely a citizen asked a young doctor to feel his pulse or a young dentist to fill a tooth without being aware that any such young professional had probably just finished a service stint at some base hospital in Okinawa or some camp in Tennessee. Even after the Cold War ended and a new generation rebelled against the might of the military, so pervasive and omnipresent was the influence of the defense establishment that the very uniform donned for youthful protest was the GI jacket—military badge of pacifist protest.

The social transformation of which these changes were the visual manifestation was not accompanied by any such naked exploitation or caterwauling strife as were the shifts that brought big business and big labor to the fore in their time. Far less was the growth of the military imposed by any Hitlerite dictatorship of police and concentration camp. Yet the impact on American life was great and swift. In a few short years after the Second World War there was constituted the permanent military establishment feared and forbidden by the founders of the Republic. As it billowed up, established institutions were shouldered aside, cherished values were knocked reeling. Coming out on top at the very center of national power and policy, the military forced state, politicians, churches, education, industry and labor to obey its prescriptions, and sent its forming influence outward into almost every local community and every individual life.

Cold War required preparation for war, that was how it began. Patriotism, national defense, anti-Communism—these sacred impulses gave it impetus. Beneath them operated yet more powerful forces: the fears and the aggressive impulses energized by the development and utilization of nuclear energy as a war weapon and leading to an unprecedented arms race. Ever greater military strength, ever greater readiness became the ever advancing price the military placed on security. At no point could this movement of the United States toward a society influenced by the military establishment have been called the result of the deliberate choice of the American people. Rather, it was the outcome of an accumulation of military decisions, commitments and actions that built up over two decades amid a proliferating bureaucracy beyond the control of everyday democratic processes.[1]

With the coming of the Cold War each of the three services felt that it had to justify its existence in terms of its future importance in a general war with Russia. The Air Force believed that the coming war would be irretrievably won or lost in an initial air exchange between the United States and Russia. The Army held that any such match would be preliminary and inconclusive, the outcome awaiting the advance of ground forces and the occupation of territory. The Navy, equally sure that the Air Force's bombers were vulnerable, agreed with the Army that there must be balanced land, sea and air forces. In the contest for funds, doctrinal differences grew bitter. The services fought for all they could get, helped by interest groups among supporting industries, academic researchers, members of Congress. The Air Force, youngest and most aggressive of the services, gained the advantage.

To sway opinion and votes in their favor, political activities by military officers quickly came to seem justified: informing the public of the indispensability of sea, air or land power became the fulltime job by 1959 of 1,562 officers and 4,050 men operating out of the Pentagon as public-relations specialists. In 1952 the Army opened an office in Los Angeles to provide the right tanks and bazookas for the movies. "With Steve Canyon and Terry and the Pirates outstripping any competition," the Air Force gloried in packing the biggest martial wallop in the nation's comic strips. With Arthur Godfrey, the nation's leading TV entertainer, presiding over breakfast shows and evening spectaculars as a brigadier general of the Air Force reserve, the Air Force also felt that it held command of the air waves. The Navy, saving its salvos for the decisive closeup battles for funds, excelled in "leaking" stories to the press just before appropriations hearings in Washington.[2]

On Capitol Hill 330 officers and Defense Department employees, operating out of "legislative liaison" offices, lobbied and curried congressional favor. Whole task forces helped prepare and present bills, kept track of legislation, and primed service spokesmen before they testified at hearings. Others helped congressmen answer their mail, supplied information for their speeches, organized "inspection" junkets to Caribbean bases. It was not entirely uphill work. In 1960 the *Congressional Quarterly* reported no fewer than forty ranking Reserve officers in Congress, six of them generals. The Air Force rose to this challenge by setting up a congressional Reserve squadron—Brig. General Barry Goldwater commanding—which held weekly "drills" where they listened sympathetically to Pentagon propagandists.

And could a congressman be other than friendly and grateful to a branch of the armed forces that maintained large installations with multimillion-dollar payrolls in his district? By 1961 one or more such facilities had sprouted in 282 of the country's 437 congressional districts. With no exaggeration at all one naval officer referred to a prominent Cold Warrior and congressman from South Carolina as "Mendel Rivers of the Charleston Navy Yard."

The most binding ties of all were sought with the members of Congress who also had committee responsibilities bearing on the armed forces. Such men were asked constantly whether they needed jet airlift for weekend trips to their constituencies. When they fell ill or needed a checkup they were ushered into the biggest rooms and given the best doctors at service hospitals in Washington. The military did not wait to be asked. "You can look at some of our key people in the key places in Congress," remarked Representative Jamie Whitten, Democrat of Mississippi, "and go see how many military establishments there are in their districts." The most frequently cited example was Georgia, home for many years of the chairmen of both the Senate and House Armed Service committees. When another Air Force installation was proposed at the Pentagon for Georgia, a general remarked: "One more base would sink the state."[3]

If there was after all a limit to what serving officers could properly say about public issues, the armed forces could count during these years on lots of other voices. During the Cold War decades the United States was a nation of veterans, fully 15,000,000 of them. The most outspoken half million were organized in the American Legion and Veterans of Foreign Wars, sounding off dependably for defense spending especially for military pensions. Particularly useful to the military in promoting their interests in the Cold War years were the so-called "backstop" groups of civilians—the Association of the United States Army (63,000 members), the Navy League (32,000), the Air Force Association (60,000), the Aerospace Industries Association (79 member corporations) and the National Security Industrial Association formed during the Second World War by Secretary James Forrestal (502 member corporations). The great thing about these outfits was that they were not accountable to higherups in government and through their spokesmen and their advertisement-crammed magazines could push uninhibitedly for service causes. Although only the Aerospace Industries Association took the trouble to register under the lobby law, it would be difficult to find any occasion when any of these service associations took stands opposed by leaders of their service. More typically, when the Administration favored an Army of 870,000 and the Chief of Staff one of 925,000, the Army Association came out for an army of 1,000,000 to assure the nation's security.[4]

The support of the military provided by their arms suppliers was not only close, it derived from a relationship that was symbiotic. Peter J. Schenck, president of the Air Force Association and an official of Raytheon, a major Air Force contractor, described the basis for close military-industrial relations as follows:

> The day is past when the military requirement for a major weapons system is set up by the military and passed on to industry to build the hardware. Today it is more likely that the military requirement is the result of joint participation of military and industrial personnel, and it is not unusual for industry's contribution to be a key factor. Indeed there are highly placed military men who sincerely feel that industry is setting the pace in Research & Development of new weapons systems.[5]

Here the Air Force, which had come into existence without the long experience of research, development and even manufacture of weapons carried on by the Army in its arsenals and the Navy in its yards and shore stations, had a clear edge over the two senior services. The Air Force depended heavily upon the private aircraft companies that had mush-roomed to giant size in producing the hundreds of thousands warplanes demanded by the Second World War. Since this huge industry had little chance of keeping going without government orders, the aviation companies outdid themselves in campaigning for airpower and a bigger Air Force in the Cold War. Even after China had openly split with the Soviet Union and destroyed the whole assumption of a monolithic Communist threat on which the Cold War rested, Edward J. Lafebre, Washington representative of General Dynamics, told the Washington *Post:* "One must believe in the long-term threat." At the same time James J. Ling, head of Ling-Temco-Vought, a major Air Force supplier, was saying: "Defense spending has to increase, if we are not to be overtaken by the Soviets." Samuel F. Downer, one of Ling's vice presidents said: "We're going to increase defense budgets as long as those bastards are ahead of us."[6]

Small wonder that Senator Barry Goldwater believed that "the aircraft industry has probably done more to promote the Air Force than the Air Force itself." For as the statement of the Air Force Association president indicated, it had become hard to distinguish between the military and the industries supplying them. The men who comprised these organizations called each other on the telephone, met at committee hearings, served together on teams and task forces, and worked in neigh-boring offices whether in Washington or Seattle. The critical junction between the military establishment and defense industries was lubricated by a large number of retired officers who moved sideways off active aervice and into the higher ranks of the arms industry. According to a 1959 survey by a House Armed Services subcommittee, 1400 former officers of the rank of major or higher—including 261 generals and admirals—were working for the top 100 contractors. General Dynamics, which led in contracts in 1960, also employed the most retired officers—187.[7]

Though it heard talk of "booze, blondes and bashes" at some of the more convivial military-industrial get-togethers, the subcommittee ob-tained no evidence of outright crookedness. But something like half of all arms procurement was done with a relative handful of giant companies that did little other business. By 1960 ninety percent of all contracts were negotiated without competitive bidding and awarded on a cost-plus basis. Much of the plant of these specialized contractors was owned by the government. Most of their working capital was supplied by the govern-ment through progress payments—payments made in advance of comple-tion of the contracts. The government specified what the firm could and could not charge to the government. In this kind of association some proposals would come across the table from the government, some from the contractors. A General Dynamics man, John W. Bessire, said, "We try to foresee the requirements the military is going to have three years off. We work with their requirements people and therefore get new business." Richard Adams, of General Dynamics' Fort Worth office, told the Washington *Post:* "We know where the power is on Capitol Hill and among Executive departments. There's going to be a lot of defense busi-ness and we're going to get our share of it." Said John R. Moore of North American Rockwell: "A new system usually starts with a couple of military and industrial people getting together to discuss common problems." A high civilian in the Pentagon summed it up: "Pressures to spend more . . . in part come from the military here. Each military guy has his own pieces—tactical, antisubmarine, strategic. Each guy gets where he is by pushing his particular thing."[8]

What was good for the military, clearly, was good for its industrial suppliers, and it is a useful exercise to summarize just how good it became. For in addition to satisfying the Strangeloves of military technology and the Pentagon careerists, the military-industrial combine offered a liveli-hood to millions of Americans in and out of uniform whose primary concern was merely to earn a living for their families. To make a living off war in peacetime—that was the everyday complicity into which the participants in the military-industrial lashup were drawn by the incremen-tal dynamic of Cold War.

Professor Kenneth Boulding, calculating the scale of the world's war industry in 1963, reckoned that of the $120 billion expended that year for war purposes the United States accounted for a little over a third. (The Soviet Union, he said, accounted for a little less than a third, the rest of the world for the remaining third.)[9]

America's share at that date provided the livelihood for upwards of 8 million Americans. That was 10% of our labor force. To 3 million members of the armed forces and almost a million civilian Defense Department employees went $11.4 billion in pay. A million National Guard and other Reserve group members received a further $650 million. Three million Americans worked on war contracts in private industry—23% of all those employed in manufacturing jobs in Southern California, 28% of those in the state of Washington, 30% of the total in Kansas. In southern California more than half of the economic growth between 1947 and 1957 was attributable to defense work. In the San Diego area alone, war contracts were responsible for 70% of all gainful employment. When indirect as well as direct effects were measured, military spending accounted for more than half of all jobs in California, 59% of all employment in the Los Angeles area, and not quite half of all gainful work in the Seattle area.[10]

The $45 billion spent in 1963 made war the nation's leading industry, and so it had been for thirteen years. At no time during the final decade of the Cold War did spending consume less than half of the Federal budget, or less than 8% of America's Gross National Product. In the eight Eisenhower years alone, the armed forces spent $313 billion—$354 billion when the costs of military aid, atomic energy and strategic stockpiling were added in. The volume of this business, requiring no fewer than 38 million procurement transactions, surpassed all profits earned in the same years by the country's private enterprise.[11]

Though procurement ranged from aircraft ($7 billion) to musical instruments ($1.6 million), the bulk of these transactions were for major weapons sytems and were concentrated among a few suppliers. Of 160 awards totaling $21 billion, no less than $15.4 billion, or 73.4%, went to 100 companies of which sixty-five were engaged primarily in "research, development, testing and production of aircraft, missiles or electronics." Though there was a certain amount of subcontracting, a large and increasing proportion went to other big arms suppliers rather than to small business, that is, firms employing fewer than 500 workers. In 1960 five huge companies—General Dynamics, Lockheed, Boeing, General Electric, North American Aviation—did a quarter of the business, and twenty-one did half.[12]

By 1963 the military held first place in the country's real estate market, having acquired for its multifarious activities properties valued at more than $171 billion and exceeding the size of New England. By its strategic stockpiling policy the government had amassed $8 billion worth of minerals and other items, and become the main prop supporting the market for copper, lead, zinc, tin. The Defense Department had become the world's leading arms dealer, arranging overseas shipments by private industry to the tune of $2 billion a year. It ran the world's largest retail distribution operation through its PXes. The Pentagon was spending $4.6 billion yearly on one of the world's most expensive educational systems. With 350 stations and 1700 employees, its Armed Services Radio and Television Service was the world's largest broadcasting system. Not only did it have its own diplomatic corps but according to the scathing charges of Ralph Dungan, White House assistant to President Kennedy and Ambassador to Chile through most of the 1960s, the State Department "country desks are in the hip pocket of the Pentagon—lock, stock and barrel, ideologically owned by the Pentagon."[13] Such was the extent of the military establishment built up in the Cold War years.

The question may well be asked why the American people supported the vast military buildup through these years. The fundamental answer lies in the improvement in the standard of living afforded to millions and millions of people by reason of the enormous sums of money circulated around the defense plants and military posts across the nation. Between 1948 and 1963 the number of beauty shops shot up from 74,497 to 151,720, and the amount people spent in bowling alleys rose from $197 million to $433 million. In twelve years the number of supermarkets in the United States increased from 12,957 to 33,000 and the number of shopping centers from 1,100 to 11,200.[14]

Something of the meaning of what defense spending added to people's pocketbooks can be seen in the vacations that Americans began to take. The number of visitors to national parks—almost all of them located in the Far West—rose from 32,253,000 in 1950 to 86,663,000 a decade later. The number of Americans who took trips abroad zoomed from 435,000 in 1947 to 2 million in 1963. In the first six months of 1963 alone no fewer than 40 million Americans headed off, mostly by car, on vacation trips of a week or longer. By this time one in twelve California families had a boat too, so that presumably a good many of these holidays were spent on the water.[15]

Underneath the cranking up for military dominance, under all the calling of men to the colors, there was a strong push of general prosperity. These were the years in which the United States quadrupled the pollution of the atmosphere, a rate far exceeding the growth in population. The sootfall on New York City in 1958 reached a record of 107 tons per square mile. Such fouling of the urban air could hardly have been otherwise, granted the obsessive avidity with which Americans were buying and driving automobiles. In the late 1950s, the two-car garage had become a great selling-point for the new tract houses being put up. Everybody, it was assumed, owned a car, and more and more either had a second or were in the market for one. After twelve years of Cold War, twelve percent of American families owned a second car—three times as many as at the outset.[16]

IT IS SURELY ironic that the professional military man called to the Presidency because of his country's preoccupation with security amidst Cold War perils should end his eight years in office by warning against the unbridled power of the military. It is all the more ironic that the strong ideological bias of Eisenhower for private enterprise should have notably abetted the very military-industrial insurgence he inveighed against. And because the greatest impact of the rise of the military establishment during Eisenhower's years occurred in that part of the American economy engaged at the very forward edge of technological innovation, there was a third irony for General Eisenhower: his Administration's business orientation was to what might be called old business, not to the new.

Hardly had the general and his team of gray-haired business magnates been installed in office in 1953 than it became apparent with the hydrogen bomb breakthrough that it would now be possible to perfect much lighter warheads for missiles. At once the ultimate weapon of the Cold War became feasible—the intercontinental ballistic missile. With ICBMs the Russians could overcome the advantage of America's bomber bases around their borders. Intelligence suggested that the Russians might already be hard at work on such an undertaking. Alarm bells rang in the Pentagon.[17]

Ever since the end of the Second World War, the Army and Navy in particular had been carrying out work in their arsenals and laboratories on various kinds of rocketry. Even before V-E Day Army Ordnance men had rounded up Hitler's rocket wizard, Dr. Wernher von Braun, and a hundred or more of his experts who helped develop the V-2 ballistic rockets against England. Transporting them to the United States, the Army Ordnance people put them to work on Army projects. Most of them were short-range missiles. When President Truman brought K. T. Keller, president of Chrysler and one of the nation's most redoubtable automotive engineers, to oversee the infant American missile program, Keller lost no time getting such short-range Army rockets as the Corporal and Sergeant into field artillery units. The V-2 had already solved the major operational problems for what would later be called Intermediate-Range Ballistic Missiles—IRBMs. By 1953 the Redstone missile, named for the Alabama arsenal where von Braun and his experts worked, had already been successfully tested at ranges of up to 300 miles.[18]

The Air Force up to this point had not done a great deal of thinking about long-range missiles. Waging its ferocious fight to win first its independence and then its leading role in the defense of the United States, the Air Force had concentrated in the early Cold War years on building up the largest possible strategic bomber fleet. In the rocket area, almost its only activity had been work on guided missiles that could be launched from airplanes. But when the possibility loomed for creating a long-range weapon that could drop the hydrogen bomb on Moscow, the whole teeming, scheming, wheeling, dealing aggregate of singular ambitions and multiple interests that had grown up in the Air Force leadership and its industrial suppliers massed and surged into action. The Air Force had been assigned the mission of delivering the atom bomb, it was said, therefore the Air Force should develop all long-range missiles. In the early months of President Eisenhower's term when the new Administration was determining to close out the stalemated war in Korea and cut back most of all the size of the Army, the argument prevailed.[19]

So it was that the "flyboys," as the leaders of the youngest and most aggressive of the armed services styled themselves, wound up with responsibility for developing the weapon that was to dethrone the airplane at almost the moment it achieved supremacy. In this turnabout there was not only irony, but confusion. The Air Force, including many still imbued with the "wild blue yonder" zealotry that had helped outstrip the other fighting services, saw its overriding responsibility throughout the 1950s as conserving and enlarging the Strategic Air Command's huge complement of bombers. General Curtis LeMay, for example, kept insisting long after the Russian intercontinental ballistic missile had become a reality, that the main defense of national security rested in the big bombers. Inevitably, of course, the Air Force came to advocate all-out expansion of both bomber and missile forces.[20]

To have handed over the challenge of besting the Communists in space to the Army seems not to have been seriously considered by the United States. It was however what the Russians did. Traditionally stressing cannon power in their military doctrine, the Russians had long had autonomous armies of artillery. In 1957 Khrushchev created a separate rocket command under Marshal A. A. Grechko to develop Russia's military missiles. By that time the United States Air Force, with its snorting, swashbuckling zest and its doctrine of loosing coldblooded violence at a long and safe remove beyond the air-space of the isolated island-continent, had long since established seemingly unshakable claims on public opinion and Congress.[21]

Possibly giving the job to the Army also required overly direct acknowledgment of a debt to the Germans. As Secretary of State Dulles ceaselessly affirmed, the Americans had an affinity for the Germans, and made them their strongest ally in the Cold War. The Germans had invented the automobile, and the Americans had taken it from there. The Germans had split the atom, and the Americans had exploded it. The Germans had invented the V-2, and the Americans were now in the process of globalizing it. So, for that matter were the Russians, and before the contest reached its peak an English cartoonist would picture American and Russian missiles passing high in space and saying: "Hier können wir deutsch sprechen—Here we can speak German." At the mere thought of such nationally inadmissible attributions, Dr. von Braun became an albatross round the Army's neck.[22]

Whatever the force of such considerations, the argument with which the Air Force and its suppliers defeated the Army in the contest for the ICBM mission was a political one that had irresistible persuasiveness in the climate of 1953. The Army proposed to give the job to its Redstone arsenal whose 3600 people, including 500 scientists and engineers added to the original German team, constituted far and away the most experienced group of rocket technologists anywhere in the land. Among the services this was called "in-house" capability. Both the Army and Navy had built up such in-house capabilities at their own arsenals and Navy yards over the decades to develop and produce the weapons and munitions they needed. In the mighty expansion of the Second World War and its aftermath the only arsenal the Air Force had was the private aircraft industry.[23]

This struck the new Defense Secretary from Detroit as a far better arrangement. Having campaigned against creeping socialism, it was ideologically unsatisfying to Wilson and everybody else in the new, business-minded Eisenhower Administration to rely on Government facilities to do a job that could well be left up to private initiative. The government therefore turned to the Air Force and to industry. But the Army could not be utterly put down; it had powerful friends in Congress too. The Redstone arsenal was left with the assignment of working up a 1500-mile intermediate-range ballistic missile. The Air Force would take on the ICBM.

The decision was made by Wilson. In line with his pledge to "bring in some of those business brains" to help cut costs and establish a new equilibrium of "security with solvency," General Eisenhower had installed Wilson, the foremost motormaker and highest paid executive in the land, to enforce business efficiency and order at the Pentagon. For these ends, Wilson was a disappointment in office. Finally, after President Eisenhower stepped in, Wilson succeeded in reducing the Army's size to conform to its subordinate place in the "New Look" strategy. But he never got control of the Pentagon, and the Air Force not only eluded but baffled him. It achieved a great new expansion goal of 137 wings, and carried Congress with it year after year in its drive to win funds at the expense of the Army and Navy.[24]

In an air age, Wilson was an automobile man. In an age of rapid technological change, he personified at sixty-four a mature industry that had already standardized its product and now arrogantly resisted any but the cosmetic changes dreamed up by its stylists and market researchers. The standpat spirit of General Motors' kind of controlled and stabilized capitalism radiated from the highest government offices in these years. As exhibited even more forcefully in the steel industry's refusal until 1962 to accept the revolutionary economies introduced by the carbon furnace in Europe, it helped account for the slowing of America's economic growth from eight percent in 1950 to three percent in 1960.[25]

Laden with electronic circuitry and automated controls, the intercontinental bombers and supersonic fighters of the modern Air Force did not correspond to the wheels-and-engine procurement that the Middle West delivered in such quantity in the Second World War. They were not readily subject to the businesslike economies Wilson knew best. Neither did they lend themselves to quick and easy conversion to mass-market civilian production such as Wilson's assembly lines achieved after 1945. They were extravagantly specialized instruments of a new kind of warfare. They were prohibitively expensive. They were put together by teams of highly specialized technicians in plants that could make nothing else. They were produced for just one customer—the Air Force.[26]

It is not clear how long Eisenhower and Wilson thought of this kind of single-source procurement as "free private enterprise." But by assigning the job of building an ICBM to the Air Force they left to the airmen and their allies in the private sector the task of reorganizing the aviation armaments business so as to provide this drastically new kind of weapon. In early 1954 Wilson ordered Assistant Secretary of the Air Force Trevor Gardner, an electronics manufacturer from the West Coast, to form a committee "to eliminate interservice competition in development of guided missiles." Gardner's group wanted to steer the new business so far as they could to the big Air Force suppliers. But these giant companies still had huge contracts building airplanes, and besides it was not clear that among their help were the kind of people who could think in speeds of 18,000 m.p.h. and heights of 200 miles. The necessary across-the-board competence in the physical sciences had to be sought elsewhere.[27]

The committee turned to two of its own members, Simon Ramo and Dean Wooldridge, a pair of bright young scientist-executives who had just left Hughes Aircraft, a major Air Force supplier, to form their own tiny company in Los Angeles. Ramo and Wooldridge, one the son of a Salt Lake City storekeeper and the other the member of an Oklahoma oil broker's family, were both products of the California Institute of Technology. Ramo had coauthored a textbook: *Fields and Waves in Modern Radio*. Both had trained in the nation's top private-enterprise research centers (Ramo at General Electric, Wooldridge at Bell Laboratories), and were anxious to get into production rather than research. Offspring of the technological revolution, they were merchant scientists, men who brought blackboards into boardrooms and pioneered the business of aerospace.[28]

Only a free-swinging outfit like the Air Force, operating in the uninhibiting climate of southern California, where the only known tradition was change, could have hit upon such a solution to a problem often compared with development of the atomic bomb itself. Essentially, the Air Force's decision makers grasped that to provide the new weapons would require revamping the entire aviation armaments industry, using a lot of new corporations and the shells of some old ones. The first audacious move was to designate the infant Ramo-Wooldridge firm as its broker for aerospace to the entire industry. Obtaining top priority from President Eisenhower for the ICBM program in 1954, the Air Force dispatched a tall, solemn airman, General Bernard Adolf Schriever, to supervise the show from headquarters set up in the midst of the burgeoning Ramo-Wooldridge compound near the Los Angeles airport.[29]

Fittingly enough General Schriever was a German—that is, he had been born in Bremen forty years before and brought at the age of seven to Texas to join his father, an engineering officer for the Nord Deutsche Lloyd Line who had been interned there when his ship was caught in New York by the United States' declaration of war on Germany in 1917. Growing up in Texas, Ben Schriever attended Texas A&M, joined the Air Force as an aviation cadet at Kelly field, flew sixty-three missions over the Southwest Pacific as a B-17 pilot, and after the war took a master's degree in engineering at Stamford. As a rising young Pentagon planner, described by others as "insane" on the subject of missiles, Schriever leaped at the assignment, in the Air Force's freebooting military-industrial language, of "vice president in charge of getting things done" in the crash ICBM program.[30]

"Our whole philosophy is one of going to industry," proclaimed Schriever, handing over supervision of the Atlas, Thor, Titan and Minuteman missile programs to Ramo-Wooldridge, and cutting in North American and other aviation industry giants as "associate contractors." Basic plans for the Air Force Atlas owed much to von Braun and Company, and the Los Angeles missileers raided the Redstone arsenal for talent. With the kind of money Schriever was dispensing, they could hire scientists, mathematicians and space specialists all over the country.[31]

Electronics was basic to the new business. In the next three years some 470 plants mushroomed in the Los Angeles area. Another 500 sprang into existence in Massachusetts, so many of them along the new Route 128 outside Boston that it became known as Electronics Highway. By 1957 electronics was the fifth largest industry in the United States, doing $11.5 billion sales, the bulk of it (sixty percent) with the military. At Ramo-Wooldridge, gray-flanneled Ph.Ds chalked abstract formulas in their air-conditioned cubicles, and shot off charts, blueprints and contract changes to companies old and new. At every turn they demanded miniaturization. Not content with the tiniest transistors, they called for microminiaturization—printed-out circuitry. They pressed for computers cut to five-feet-by-five-feet in size for immediate development, computers in shoeboxes as soon as possible. New firms starting up in garages and warehouses around MIT, Caltech and Stanford won contracts to supply tiny servomechanisms that could aid missile control by sensing and correcting their own errors.[32]

Though Ramo-Wooldridge's fees shot up overnight to $40,000,000, these merchant-scientists were eager to get into the really big business of making the products they were now ordering. So was Thompson Products Company, a small, respectable Cleveland auto-parts maker that had entered the picture to help Ramo-Wooldridge finance its feverish expansion. Always ready to give its entrepreneurs a break, the Air Force encouraged Ramo-Wooldridge to pull together their consulting and managing functions in an entity called Space Technology Laboratories and then give this entity a corporate home by merging with Thompson Products. In the stock exchange Simon Ramo's and Dean Wooldridge's original shoestring of $6,750 each rocketed to a fortune of $3 million, the value of their new holdings. It was also their way of getting out of consulting and into producing aerospace hardware. In short order Space Technology Laboratories was "spun off" as a nonprofit corporation deciding, in Ramo's words:

> how big the missile should be, what warhead it carries, what accuracy it can be expected to have, how to get the optimum accuracy by the proper interaction between the rocket engines that produce the thrust and the gyros that hold direction. [It] decides how many tests one must call for to get the information required and hence how many test facilities are needed to provide these data on a timely basis.

Thompson-Ramo-Wooldridge went on by the end of the Cold War to become a $500,000,000 company, holding $127,000,000 in defense contracts in 1967, doing in Ramo's words "about one half government and one half commercial ventures."[33]

The line where Air Force left off and private industry began was not easy to discern. "We lived with these people every day," Schriever told a congressional committee later. A leading figure in Ramo-Wooldridge who left Hughes Aircraft and helped the young scientist-executives build their new empire was General Harold L. George, retired former commander of Air Force fighter planes in Europe. Chairman of Space Technology Laboratories when it was separated from Thompson-Ramo-Wooldridge was General James Doolittle, retired former commander of Air Force bomber planes in Europe. Members of the old decision-making Air Force leadership who had put the whole complex of military commands and weapons-supplying industries together, these retired generals continued to function in the "private" sector much as they had when they held their former jobs in the "public" sector, meeting at the same country clubs, and playing golf with the same industrialists and with the officers who now held their old titles but informally shared with them the decision-making. In such a world, as Professor H. L. Nieburg said, there could be little doubt "that Thompson-Ramo-Wooldridge was an Air Force entity, owned by the Air Force command in Washington." Ramo and Wooldridge, the once modestly paid aerospace scientist-enterprisers, were the multimillionaire beneficiaries of this order of grand-scale military-industrial manipulation.[34]

It was more than Congress could do to keep tabs on such maneuvers, and none the easier considering how many influential members of House and Senate were caught up in it. Dr. Ramo claimed that his outfit saved the government the equivalent of its $100 million fee by decisions made while getting Atlas and Thor into operation in less than forty-eight months. Since the first ICBM plans went back to 1948, not just to Ramo-Wooldridge's baptismal date in 1954, and the Air Force missiles grew out of these earlier designs, the claim was a dubious one. Besides, on Ramo-Wooldridge prompting, the Air Force went all out developing a special type of nosecone for its missiles before giving up and adopting the Army model—an "unnecessary and costly error," in the Army view, "involving the expenditure of $200 million or more." Without finding any instance of dishonesty, but with a strong implication that the taxpayer had not been well served, the House Government Operations committee judged that "government and private industry have become intermingled to the detriment of both."[35]

Waste and profiteering were rife. Two years later Government Accounting Office investigators, previously barred from examining missile-contract books by the Eisenhower Administration's orders, submitted first reports to Congress. The name of T-R-W kept cropping up:

COLONEL TREACY: I call your attention to item No. 11 up there. That is an armature.

MR. NORBLAD: Yes.

COLONEL TREACY: And this is an item that we bought from Thompson-Ramo-Wooldridge.

MR. HERBERT: Oh, they are our old friends.

COLONEL TREACY: I knew we would get into controversy.

MR. COURTNEY: There we go (*laughter*).

COLONEL TREACY: And they bought it from Westinghouse Electric Corporation, Small Motors division. And this item was charged to the government at $35.28. And the subcontractor's price, including about $3 of packaging, was $16.69.

MR. GAVIN: What did the government pay for it?

COLONEL TREACY: The government paid $35.28. And this is a markup of 111%.

MR. HEBERT: That is par for the course for Ramo-Wooldridge.[36]

By the time of this investigation in 1961 Thompson-Ramo-Wooldridge had long since turned into an outright aerospace contractor along with Varian, Litton, Thiokol and a whole roster of brand-new corporations wheeled into place alongside oldline airframe suppliers like Boeing, North American and General Dynamics. In the evolution the offspring of T-R-W, rechristened from Space Technology Laboratories as the Aerospace Corporation, with a $75,000-a-year president and hundreds of the high-paid former staff transferred to its rolls, grew into a $300 million giant, one of the Air Force's so-called nonprofit creatures used to escape Defense Department controls.[37]

The rampant machinations of the Air Force, now concerting with its industrial suppliers, now resorting to baffling bureaucratic ploys, now joining up with key members of Congress, proved endlessly frustrating to General Eisenhower. If there had been anything in his budgets he thought he could hold down, it was expenditures on the military, and the experts had told him that the potential of atomic weaponry, and for that matter of missilery, was relatively cheap. But he found that to cancel many of the programs required such huge cash drains in contract settlements that it was cheaper to carry them on at half-throttle than to close them out. It was easier that way, too, to avoid congressional uproar over terminations of bases and contracts. Before long the "frustrating, nonfunctional waste" of so much money running into military channels in a steady flow, wrote Eliot Janeway, "had taken on the proportions of a classified secret."[38]

In his second term Eisenhower tried fitfully to bring military costs under control. Faced once again after his 1956 reelection with a Democratic majority in Congress, the President tried his best to sway the Texan leadership in House and Senate toward his concept of "fiscal responsibility" by naming Robert Anderson of Dallas, former manager of the Waggoner oil, cattle and real estate empire and a dealer in the Texas political establishment, as his Secretary of the Treasury. The Adminstration plan, in the teeth of a recession, was to hold expenditures down to the level of the Treasury's actual day-to-day receipts. Military spending, said Anderson, was inching up at a rate that would wind up $2.4 billion over the year's estimates. The Air Force, even after allowing for every possible adjustment, was spending at a rate of at least a billion over its budget of $18 billion. Word accordingly went out to the Air Force's forty-two main suppliers: the department had no more money, and no plans for borrowing to continue making progress payments to them.[39]

The contractors had nowhere to turn. They had been relying on such payments for most of their working capital. Since even their plants were government-owned, they were in no position to borrow at the banks. They laid off workers—North American 19,000, Lockheed and Douglas 4,000 each, Republic 6,500, Boeing 1,250. By October, *Business Week* reported, the atmosphere was "near panicky." The stock marked dropped twenty percent. Then, just when Eisenhower's squeeze on the military-industrial combine was starting to hurt, the Russians launched their Sputnik. At this point amid the public outcry, Senate Majority Leader Johnson intervened. Hearings began on whether the United States was spending enough on "military needs." In short order the monetary squeeze eased off. The President, growling that "political and financial considerations" were interfering with "the strict military needs," broke off his plan for compelling the military to live within their means. The new Secretary of Defense, Robert McElroy, announced that the Army as well as the Air Force rocket programs would be expanded so that the United States could be safeguarded against any threat from space.[40] Clearly the big military was showing itself a force in the national life to rival big business and big labor.

Eisenhower's unhappiness at being unable to check its growth gave impetus after the Sputnik crisis to the creation of a civilian National Aeronautics and Space Agency to curb the Air Force ambitions and avoid the extension of the arms race into space. As a further step to control the Air Force empire-building, the Defense Department created its own Advanced Research Projects Agency to conduct research and development separate from the three services.[41]

Unable to prevent the creation of the new agencies, the Air Force and its contractors proceeded to try to take them over. The department entered into a virtual alliance with the Democrats in Congress, who were clamoring "missile gap" and demanding more funds for aerospace. In the act establishing NASA, the lines between military and peaceful uses of space were blurred. The new administrator of NASA, Keith Glennon, came to his office from the presidency of Case Institute of Technology in Cleveland where his sponsor, the chairman of the Case trustees, had been the board chairman of the ubiquitous Thompson-Ramo-Wooldridge.[42]

NASA contracts flowed to companies engaged in Air Force work, and Thompson-Ramo-Wooldridge's offspring, Aerospace Corporation, performed the same sort of high-level consulting for NASA that it had done for the Air Force. Before long 90% of NASA's budget was going to Air Force arms suppliers. The Advanced Research Projects Agency also, though funded to work for the Defense Department as a whole, spent 80% of its dollars for Air Force contracts within a year after its establishment. Then in late 1960, with the enthusiastic support of the Air Force, NASA swallowed the richest Army plum, the Redstone arsenal, complete with its team of German missileers. Thus at long last Dr. Wernher von Braun was brought officially into the mainstream of the American aerospace enterprise.[43]

MILITARY-INDUSTRIAL growth spurted to new heights in and after the years of President Kennedy. Up to this time the old men who had commanded the Second World War had led in waging the Cold War. Now, in the climactic phase of the confrontation with "international Communism" one who had been a front-line fighter in the Second World War took charge.

In a nation of veterans, John Fitzgerald Kennedy personified as no other political figure what for millions was the outstanding experience of their lives. Alice Roosevelt Longworth, watching him in casual banter among the dashing young campaign aides assembled round him at the White House, saw Kennedy as the "junior officer" of the Second World War. Unlike either Nixon or Johnson, Kennedy had tasted battle with the enemy, and all the world knew the story of how, after his PT-boat was holed and stranded in a night action in the Solomons, Lieutenant Kennedy swam seven miles to shore to get help to bring his wounded crew members to safety.[44]

Kennedy had also seen action, significant action, in another sense of that word. In London, where his father was ambassador from 1937 to 1941, he had come to adult awareness at precisely that moment of sea-change in Western history when the First World War's survivors, who had come home saying "goodbye to all that," gave way to those who like

Kennedy's older brother and brother-in-law rose against the Hitlerite tyranny and died fighting its onslaughts. His college thesis, published in 1941 as a book called *While England Slept,* was an account of this conversion by a true believer. Its hero, his hero, was Winston Churchill. Two decades later, the youngest President ever elected, Kennedy rode to the Capitol beside the oldest man ever to occupy the office. "Let the word go forth"—the voice crackled with youthful portent in the frosty January air—"from this time and place, to friend and foe alike, that the torch has been passed to a new generation of Americans. . . ."[45]

The idealism of that hour was translated into the Peace Corps, which sent 10,000 Americans aged 21 to 55 abroad in the 1960s; in the Alliance for Progress, which dispensed $9 billion in aid to Latin America; in the Development Loan Fund, which made $9 billion available on favorable terms to build up the new and underdeveloped countries of the Third World.[46]

Yet even on that inaugural day of high, youthful hopes, there was no thought but that the Cold War which had caught up America so obsessively that all other national goals were submerged in it, must go on. "Embattled we are," cried the new President in ringing tones, ready to "pay any price, bear any burden, meet any hardship" in "the role of defending freedom in its hour of maximum danger." The young President spoke the very words of the Cold War's founding grandfathers as he summoned his countrymen to "bear the burdens of a long twilight struggle, year in and year out." Once again, as it had been from Pearl Harbor to V-J Day, from Fulton, Missouri through all the turning points of the Cold War, the call was for "sacrifice" and "struggle." "Ask not what the country can do for you," was the impassioned cry, "Ask what you can do for your country."[47]

The very first thing Kennedy wanted to do was "get the country moving again." The recession in the closing Eisenhower months had continued to deepen in the weeks after the election. By February, 1961, unemployment had reached the dismaying level of 8.1% of the work force, the highest since the 1930s. Much had been made in the campaign of the need for economic growth in America. The resumption of economic progress, Kennedy had said, was "the number one domestic problem which the next President of the United States will have to meet." A growing economy was necessary not only to end the recession but also to provide for the staggering increase in the national population—nearly 30 million in the single decade of the 1950s alone. Just "to provide the 25,000 new jobs a week needed to keep you working and your children working" in the 1960s, he said, the economy had to expand at the rate of five per cent. The countries of Western Europe had been growing all through the decade at well above that figure while the rate of growth in the United States lagged behind at barely half as much.[48]

One significant difference helped to explain the discrepancy. In both the American and European systems the government's expenditures had been enormously enlarged so that they directly determined a large segment of each nation's economic activities. But the chief characteristic of the European countries which had maintained such strong and steady growth through the decade was the use of public funds on a rising scale for social welfare measures, especially for the education of the young and pensions for the old. In the United States, where votes could not be rallied for welfare measures during these years, the public funds went overwhelmingly instead for military measures.[49]

Urgent as were the needs in schools, health, housing and urban welfare, the essential American situation was not altered when the new adminstration took office in 1961. President Kennedy had won, but truth to tell he had barely won. He had been elected by 114,000 votes, the slimmest margin of any president in the twentieth century. The swing of fewer than 100,000 votes in eight states would have been enough to keep him from the White House. For example, he had carried the key state of Illinois by 8,800 votes, and polling-place hanky-panky in Cook County left some skeletons in the new Democratic administration's closet. Everett McKinley Dirksen, senior senator from Illinois and ranking conservative as well as Minority Leader of the United States Senate, knew where they were. Out of such considerations and many others, evident to a political eye as clear and cold as John Kennedy's, it behooved his Administration to start out with Republicans in the two central cabinet posts of Treasury and Defense, and to go as slow as the Eisenhower adminstration in attending to domestic needs. Though he had campaigned for civil rights, for instance, he made no move to press for them in office. Instead he turned to those causes that most nearly commanded consensus—the causes of the Cold War. If growth was indeed the ticket for the 1960s, it would be programmed in far greater outlays for the military. Listing the priorities for waging the conflict between "Freedom and Communism" in his first message to Congress, Kennedy said: "First, we must strengthen our military tools."[50]

As loudly as his rivals for the presidential nomination, Stuart Symington and Lyndon Johnson, Kennedy had trumpeted that a "missile gap" had been opening ever since Sputnik between the Russians and the lagging Americans. "For many years now we have been living on the edge of the crater," he said in 1958. In 1959 he had bemoaned that "in the years of the gap our exercises in brink-of-war diplomacy will be infinitely less successful." When Kennedy won the election, he intended nothing less than to win the Cold War and make America preeminent. For this, he was convinced, the strategy by which the United States had waged the Cold War through the 1950s needed total overhaul. Having cut back on all but its nuclear striking arm, he said, the United States could not stop the erosion of its security in small wars and by guerrilla-force encroachments "too small to muster massive retaliation with all its risks." The whole thrust of the Kennedy takeover in the field of defense, prefigured in the Gaither, Rockefeller and other studies in the preceding years, was to build up the military establishment yet further.[51]

In office Kennedy turned to his Republican Secretary of Defense, Robert McNamara, to devise new strategies and build new strength. Like Eisenhower, Kennedy had brought a businessman from Detroit to manage the Pentagon monster. Yet except for the fact that McNamara like Charles Wilson had been president of a giant automobile company, the two executives had little in common. McNamara was not primarily an automobile maker. He belonged to a breed new in big business, and wholly new in big government, where among the figures brought in from the private sector it had been lawyers and investment bankers rather than business executives who had shown a flair for public affairs.

McNamara was the most able and confident man ever to be Secretary of Defense. He had the energy, and some said the personality, of a locomotive. Ambitious, incisive, with a limitless capacity for work and an unconcealed impatience of pretense, McNamara was tough, trim—and a technocrat. He put things in order (Lyndon Johnson called him "the fellow with the Stacomb in his hair"). He believed that by subjecting any enterprise to a rigorous analysis based ultimately on the applications of mathematics to the insights of social science, not only its everyday problems but its larger direction could be brought under rational and purposeful control. From his days as a student and teacher of statistical analysis at the Harvard Business School and from his experience as a junior officer at the Pentagon during the war, McNamara had been fascinated by the intellectual problem of adminstering large organizations. As a member of a group of independent business analysts called the Whiz Kids, he was assigned after the war to the Ford Motor Company. The problems of Ford were such a challenge that—living among the university professors at nearby Ann Arbor rather than among the motormen in Grosse Pointe —he stayed on for fifteen years. In 1960 he became president, first man to hold the job from outside the Ford family.[52]

"This place is a jungle," he said soon after his arrival in Washington. To subdue it he placed the entire defense enterprise, in all its ramifications ancient and modern, under the new kind of systematic quantitative analysis he had been introducing into the workings of the Ford Motor Company. His basic tool was "operations research," first developed in the war in Britain where its practitioners were mostly physicists, mathematicians and engineers. After the war an invasion of economists gave operations research a new scope and validity. Where the scientists and engineers tended to accept the terms of the problems as presented to them, the economists, schooled in the search for the most efficient use of resources, accustomed to think in terms of such concepts as "marginal utility" and "opportunity cost," proved to be much quicker about widening the field and pursuing alternatives.[53]

In his drive to dominate the Pentagon McNamara insisted on two fundamentals: the use of analysis to force alternative programs to the surface; and the definition of "options" in quantitative terms in order to facilitate choice. To carry out this task he brought into the Pentagon young practitioners of the esoteric arts of systems-analysis, as operations research was more commonly called in America, and the electronic computer was established as the ultimate piece of machinery by which McNamara compelled precision in the choices put before him. The strain on the military professionals, whose mathematics had been confined to calculating artillery ranges, was something terrible. To be told that a rifle was not the infantryman's best friend but a component in a "weapons system" whose "cost effectiveness" had to be derived from a bewildering array of statistics for ammunition belts, bullets, training courses and arsenals, and then set off against even more farfetched statistics for rival BARs and mortars, was enough to make a Pentagon colonel put in for reassignment to Point Barrow.[54]

There was just time for McNamara to address ninety-six blunt questions to the three service departments in his first probe for "usable power" when the Kennedy administration, in full view of everybody, slipped on a banana peel and crashed heavily to earth. The embarrassing occasion was the preposterous Bay of Pigs filibuster of April, 1961. Apparently without having done the most elementary homework beforehand, the President had put his approval on CIA Director Allen Dulles' plan for overthrowing the radically anti-American government of the new Cuban strongman, Fidel Castro. On April 17 the Central Intelligence Agency's dirty-tricks department landed a force of 1,200 Cuban exiles on the island's south coast at a place called Bahia de Cochinos—Bay of Pigs. The landing beach was a bog. Castro's soldiers moved in fast. The expected popular uprising failed to take place. Within three days Castro had crushed the invasion in a disastrous blow to American prestige and to that of the young President. Kennedy was in a tizzy. He telephoned Presidents Eisenhower, Truman and Hoover for support. He rang up Nixon, Rockefeller and Goldwater to ask them to stand by their country. He set out to talk to every Republican leader. While newspapers had a field day reporting the blunders, he pleaded with their publishers to play down the story and "recognize the nature of our country's peril, which knows no precedent in history." Blaming himself for "depending on the experts," he took responsibility for the defeat upon himself, but before the year was out he replaced Allen Dulles at CIA and brought in General Maxwell Taylor as the new chairman of the Joint Chiefs of Staff.[55]

New presidents are traditionally accorded an early "honeymoon period" and there was little outward sign that the American people were ready to throw over their new leader when the wedding trip had scarcely begun. But Kennedys played even their touch football as if they could not afford to lose, and the young President who had promised to "get the country moving again" seemed to think that to win now he had to do something really big.

What else could this brave new world leader do to take off some of the pressures after this humiliating setback? During the campaign Kennedy had loudly proclaimed that America had better accept Russia's challenge in space. Then on the eve of the Bay of Pigs debacle, and just when his science advisors were telling him that the United States could not win the race to put a man in orbit, Moscow announced that the Cosmonaut Yuri Gagarin had successfully circled the earth in a two-hour flight. In twenty years of Cold War overreactions, what followed next probably took the prize. Kennedy asked his scientists to name a space goal beyond anything the Russians could be striving for, and, wrapping himself in the American flag, decided to go for it. The United States, vaulting grandly beyond the mere grasshopper jumps of the first orbiting Communists, would soar off beyond to the moon.

America, it was said, was rich, although by the time it got to the moon a decade later, it was learning it was not *that* rich. More hauntingly, what Kennedy did on the New Frontier in 1961 prepared the way for the deterioration and disruptions of the decade that followed. For in directing people's attention away from issues that embarrassed him toward the enemies which appeared to threaten their interests, he settled the priorities for the 1960s without even occasion for national debate. Mindless growth, trivial private consumption, urban neglect, environmental decay —all gained a free run as the New Frontier took America on new adventures in foreign intervention, yet more costly and sterile arms buildups, and the race in space.

The moon program was whipped together in one hectic weekend after the Gagarin triumph and the Bay of Pigs fiasco. From Friday afternoon McNamara, NASA Director James Webb and Vice President Johnson, the political godfather of aerospace, met around the clock until the crash program was handed to the President on Monday. "We were told," said one of the participants, "not to fool around." Going before Congress, Kennedy pledged that the United States would land a man on the moon and return him safely to earth "before this decade is out." By nearly unanimous vote, whipped along by the successful shot into space of Commander Alan Shepard that month, Congress in May backed the $20 billion Apollo lunar landing program that Kennedy proposed, and the first big budget breakthrough of the Kennedy Administration was chalked up by the aerospace industry.[56]

Named chairman of NASA's Space Policy Board, Vice President Johnson took a major hand in the shaping of the moon program. Already in his years as Senate Majority Leader, Johnson had operated as the key broker in the powerful coalition of the armed services, Congress and armament suppliers that pushed the arms race right into space. In alliance with such colleagues as Senator Robert Kerr, Clinton Anderson and Stuart Symington he had built up for himself political power, spreading the favor of plants, contracts and installations where they brought votes and support for his leadership, leaving to such others as his aide Bobby Baker[57] the exploiting of opportunities of political brokerage for personal wealth. Major new facilities sprang up at Houston in the vice president's home state, and at Cape Canaveral, Florida. The political configuration of the new contracting seemed shaped toward the West and the South.[58]

The development of NASA reflected fundamentally military priorities. Of Russian purposes in the space race Air Force Secretary Harold Brown said: "It is the same mixture that we ourselves have—I will put military goals reasonably high among them." But in the total design that McNamara was now assembling for the Kennedy Administration, space was only one of the "theaters" for which the American military establishment was to be prepared. In the grand strategy that now took shape, United States armed forces must be ready to fight three wars at once— a NATO war, a Southeast Asia war, and a smaller military engagement in Latin America.[59]

The new President took personal interest in the problem of Southeast Asia. Both in Laos and Vietnam the Communists were reported gaining fast. Kennedy felt that American nuclear power was irrelevant here, and it was necessary to build up capacity to fight limited war in jungles, wars in which nuclear weapons could not be used. The answer, touted by General Maxwell Taylor, the old parachute general, and by Walt Rostow, who wrote memos about guerrilla warfare as a feature of economic development, was called counterinsurgency. Kennedy, studying lists of equipment and quoting the sayings of Mao, ordered a buildup of the commandolike Special Forces, and over regular-army resistance restored their special badge of distinction—the green beret. With his computers and slide-rule geniuses, McNamara began to put through the realignment and costly expansion of forces that would take the United States down the trail of war on the Asian mainland.[60]

In the doctrine of "flexible response" that emerged, the capacity to fight guerrilla war, limited war of the conventional sort and limited nuclear war were all greatly expanded. But so was the strategic weapons arsenal for large-scale nuclear war, even though McNamara found out soon after assuming office that there was no missile gap after all. For though the Russians had left off making more liquid-fuel ICBMs, the United States kept right on deploying its own while pressing on with the rest of its program. McNamara increased by half the program for bringing along Polaris, the invulnerable undersea weapon of the nuclear submarines. He also ordered a 100 per cent boost in the production of solid-fuel Minuteman ICBMs. The number of nuclear bombers on fifteen-minute alert grew by 50 per cent. This brought the United States lead to the point where its power began to be measured in "overkill," the Cold Warriors' chilling term for the surplus of weapon-strength beyond that deemed sufficient to "kill" the adversary nation by nuclear assault.[61]

From the day Kennedy took office Russia's Premier Khrushchev had been pressing to see him, and Kennedy agreed to meet him in Vienna in early June. Already Khrushchev had fired off a blast ("Aggressive bandit acts cannot save your system") when the Cuban invasion fizzled, and at Vienna Khrushchev seemed intent on frightening the young American President. To Kennedy's polite observations about the need to avoid head-on collisions, Khrushchev answered with gruff and sarcastic diatribes. On the one big issue, the Soviet leader became almost menacing. If there was no agreement on a German treaty, he said, he would sign one with East Germany in December, West Berlin would become a free city, and further access for the West to Berlin would have to be negotiated with the East Germans. "I want peace," said Khrushchev at the end, "but if you want war, that is your problem." Kennedy said, "It is you, and not I, who wants to force a change."[62]

James Reston wrote that Kennedy was a shaken man after this encounter. The President's reaction, just three weeks after the Cuban debacle, was to accept Khrushchev's browbeating as a challenge to America—and to him personally. "The next President of the United States," he had said in one of his TV debates with Nixon, "in his first year is going to be confronted with . . . Berlin—there's going to be a test of our nerve and will." As the author of a book on the folly of the Munich pact, Kennedy had said over and over that on Berlin "we would have to make it cold—and mean it—that we would fight."

On July 26 Kennedy went before a national TV audience to proclaim defiance over Berlin as President Truman had proclaimed defiance in the first Berlin crisis a dozen years before. Then, Truman summoned and displayed American resolve to the Russians by demanding and getting peacetime conscription. Now Kennedy went Truman one better. Doubling draft calls, he announced that he was asking Congress for yet another $3.5 billion for his arms budget, an increase of 350,000 in strength of the armed forces, and authority to call 150,000 reservists to active duty. Then came the shocker.

Up to this point no President of the United States had ever brought out in public the subject of preparing the American people for a nuclear attack. Now Kennedy announced that he was asking Congress for $207 million to establish and stock with food, water and medical supplies fallout shelters in certain schools and office buildings, and to "improve our air-raid warning and fallout detection system, including a new household warning system which is now under development." This was alarming enough: nuclear war, obviously, was a real possibility. But the President had more to say:

> In the event of an attack, the lives of those families which are not hit in a nuclear blast and fire can still be saved—if they can be warned to take shelter and if their shelter is available. We owe that kind of insurance to our families—and to our country. The time to start is now. In the coming months I hope to let every citizen know what steps he can take without delay to protect his family in case of attack. I know that you will want me to do no less.

The announcement was hasty and ill-conceived. The Defense Department, to which the President assigned the project, had no real time to formulate a shelter policy. Alarmed, people leaped to the conclusion that nuclear war was an imminent possibility and rushed in panic to supermarkets to stock up on food. Get-rich-quick firms mushroomed in the shelter business. People seized upon the president's suggestion that fallout shelters were a personal as well as national responsibility. A debate broke out on TV, radio and in pulpits, triggered by a Jesuit priest's assertion that a man had a right to shoot a neighbor who tried to invade his family fallout shelter. Every citizen scuttling me-first for his funk-hole —was this the denouement of American individualism? Seldom had the country exhibited less of the instincts of true community. A civil defense official told Nevada businessmen to form a militia that could turn back refugees from California. An Idaho housing subdivision planned a shelter with armed guards to keep out nonmembers. The first slick Madison

Avenue brochure, whipped up in a frantic eight days at Pentagon crash-order, set forth how a family could escape fallout by going to sea in its cabin cruiser. A White House official, indignantly demanding how many people such advice would save, blew a last-minute whistle, and substituted another brochure. It was hoped that the Russians had been impressed, and in the end the whole shelter program was quietly dropped.[63]

But suddenly the East Germans began raising a wall along their border with West Berlin. Within days this crude barricade effectively plugged the flood of refugees from East Germany to the West. The impact, all the more so because the Western Powers could not unite to resist what was a flagrant violation of the Potsdam agreements, was that of another defeat for the West. Amid fears of an all-out war, a detachment of American tanks rolled up to the wall on one side, and a formation of Russian Tiger tanks took up a position facing them on the other. Yet the raising of the Berlin Wall could also be taken as signifying that the Russians were retreating from their intention of signing a peace treaty with the East Germans. So the crisis simmered on.[64]

By the end of 1961 the Kennedy administration was locked as totally in Cold War conflict and buildup as any of its predecessors. It had boosted appropriations for defense by 15%—or $5.9 billion beyond the $40.8 billion budget proposed by General Eisenhower—and launched a $20 billion space program besides. In all Congress appropriated $91 billion in 1961; Eisenhower had not asked for more than $83 billion. By the following year the country's outlays for defense and space had doubled the Eisenhower totals. The outlays, it was claimed, might have gone much higher but for the savings achieved by the new devices for cost-controls instituted at the Pentagon by Secretary McNamara for holding the military establishment from its more extravagant excesses.[65]

McNamara demanded that all fighting strength be organized in "program packages." This not only forced functional cost-analysis upon the services but, when Polaris submarines and the Air Force's B-52s, Skybolts and ICBMs all had to be considered as part of the same strategic package, it demonstrated clearly that many pet projects of the services—for which huge amounts had already been spent—were actually surplus to the nation's needs. It was by such criteria for instance that the atomic airplane project became unjustifiable, and in 1961, after outlays totaling $1 billion, was finally dropped. The $600 million Navajo project also fell by the wayside at the time. McNamara also sought to compel a return to more competitive methods of awarding contracts at the Pentagon, but here he never made more than a dent in the total sums granted by negotiation with "sole sources" and by "cost-plus-fixed-fee" awards.[66]

In terms of contract value, military procurement by open competitive bidding rose only from 11.9% in 1961 to 18.6% at McNamara's highwater mark four years later, and by then the Secretary was getting too embroiled in the Vietnam war to follow through in his drive to bring the military-industrial lashup to anything like a strict accounting. Far from giving ground in this war against waste, the armed services and their suppliers absorbed the shock of the Secretary's reforms like a pillow and puffed out in new places where the directives, rules and executive orders seemed not to apply. Resenting new methods, which they did not understand, the brass resorted to every form of inertial resistance known to the five concentric corridors of the Pentagon labyrinth. Contractors, bridling at any effort to yardstick their performance and meter their waste, worked overtime thwarting the Secretary's computerized bookkeeping and management techniques. Influential congressional committees kept intervening on behalf of the tender interests of their constituents, and Senators and Representatives (McNamara got 150 protesting phone calls from Capitol Hill the day he announced the closedown of 45 installations) snuffled for shares in the grubby provender of the pork barrel.[67]

In the end McNamara's reforms made little difference. He kept announcing fresh savings. The arms budget kept swallowing them up. Profiteering went on. The outcome was inevitable because when "more" was declared imperative, "how" was bound to be minimized, as Eisenhower had found out. The Kennedy administration thought it could make the military greater than ever, and yet more docilely submissive about accepting its rules for efficiency in style. Talent, drive, computer-based sophistication, all these were not enough when the overriding priorities kept handing the power to the military-industrial. McNamara was no more successful than Wilson before him. By 1964 a spokesman for the aerospace industry could affirm with confident cynicism:

> Waste can never be wholly eliminated from the Pentagon because the whole place is a waste . . . but waste or not, these military organizations and projects, and the industry which supports them, are absolutely necessary.

On this showing change, as Senator Fulbright was to say, would have to come "not from wisdom but from disaster."[68]

Yet even at this peak of insensate military buildup, countervailing forces were at work. In the Kennedy administration, as in those of Truman and Eisenhower, two tendencies sought expression. The one—dominant as a rooster-crow throughout—was aggressively globalist, affirming the United States purpose and power to intervene anywhere on earth to protect "freedom" against the spread of "international Communism."

The other was a prudential recognition and acceptance of the limits to which American power could push, the kind of self-restraint which overtook Truman in November 1950 when, having hazarded a stand and then countenanced a thrust north in Korea, he found himself suddenly looking China in the eye—and pulled back.

To have persisted in the interminable escalating, from the local scuffling and frontier scowling of the 1940s to the targeted space vehicles and Manned Orbiting Stations that were on the drawing boards of the 1960s, would have meant going the way of Dr. Strangelove. An alternative to Doomsday insanity was taking shape in the disarmament talks at Geneva from the mid-1950s onward and, quite explicitly, in the first nuclear test-ban discussions and the unofficial test moratorium that began in 1957. The Pugwash conferences kept such talk alive. These were annual meetings of international scientists convened originally in 1955 by Albert Einstein, Bertrand Russell and other Nobel Prize winners to "prevent a military contest of which the issue must be disastrous to all parties." They were named for the Nova Scotia estate of the Cleveland industrialist Cyrus Eaton where the scholars met when the United States government refused to grant visas to scientists from the Iron Curtain countries. In 1960 President-elect Kennedy sent a group of his advisers to the Pugwash conference held that year in Moscow. One was his old Boston friend Jerome Wiesner, who returned to the White House to become the President's Science Adviser and a steadfast advocate through the frantic military buildup and the plunge for a moon-race, of getting some arms-limitation agreement before it was too late.[69]

S U C H   W A S   the spectacle of the American society rushing head-down onward, and such were the circumstances of the new men who had come to direct it in Washington, immediately preceding the last big turning point of the Cold War. Looking back, one may see the Cuban missile crisis of 1962 as the decisive sequel to the long-accelerating processes gathering headway through years of Cold War in both capitalist and Communist societies. For the United States the Cuban showdown brought its uncertain young President to what he unquestionably thought was a judgment comparable to that which Truman thought he faced at the Yalu—and to his immense satisfaction and relief he deemed that he carried it off triumphantly. For the Russians this most direct and frontal of all confrontations between the two superpowers, climaxing Khrushchev's sometimes reckless zigzags between coexistance and aggressiveness, marked the high tide of Communism in the Cold War years.

The decision to emplace a Soviet missile base in Cuba was Khrushchev's ultimate gamble to tilt the international balance of power in Communism's favor. Had it succeeded it would also have relieved some strong domestic pressures on Khrushchev. For some years the Soviet premier had been cutting back on his country's conventional armed forces and, to impress the world in general but his restive generals in particular, had been bragging a lot about the power of Soviet missiles. The establishment now a few hundred miles from the United States of intermediate-range missiles, the one kind of missiles of which Russia had a plentiful supply, would in a single, swift, economical move have closed or narrowed the Soviet "missile gap" that his generals saw opening as Kennedy built up America's long-range nuclear-missile superiority—and do so without forcing Khrushchev to concentrate all available resources on a crash ICBM-building program.

On the international front, missiles in Cuba promised to give the Russians the leverage to get the West out of Berlin that they had lacked each of the three times they had tried before. The Cuban move promised also to lead on to further negotiations with the United States that might remove or effectively delay the two eventualities most feared by Russian diplomacy: the chance that Germany in the West or China in the East, the only two powers with important territorial claims against the Soviet Union, might come into possession of nuclear arms.

Both of these seemingly conflicting objectives stood a good chance of being achieved by the establishment of the Russian base in Cuba. It was not just that missiles on their flank could help persuade the Americans to pull back from Berlin and withhold nuclear arms from the West Germans. Looking beyond these goals, the strategic victories Khrushchev was driving for in Cuba and Berlin were precisely what he needed to squelch Mao Tse-tung's protestations that the Communist party of the Soviet Union was not leading the Communist world on a great offensive. With such triumphant evidences that the East Wind was indeed prevailing over the West Wind—and, as Khrushchev had insisted, by means short of suicidal war—Khrushchev could not only tell the Chinese that Russian missiles were more than sufficient to defend them and all other Communist countries. HE could go on to complete the "grand design" by pledging, in the same agreement by which the United States barred nuclear arms for the Germans, that China would not possess them either. With the signing of such a treaty for nonproliferation of nuclear weapons, quite possibly during the next United Nations General Assembly in New York, the Soviet Union would have achieved relaxation of tension in relations with the United States—and Communism would still be free to expand, as Khrushchev believed it inevitably must, into the beckoning power vacuums left in the Third World by the collapse of colonialism.[70]

Was all this farfetched? That Berlin was in the forefront of Khrushchev's thoughts as he thrust into Cuba is attested to by his many references to Berlin and the impending East German peace treaty in diplomatic messages to Kennedy and others during the secret buildup in the summer and early fall of 1962. For example, in early September his ambassador in Washington, Anatoli Dobrynin, summoned Kennedy's righthand man Theodore Sorensen to the Russian embassy and dictated a message for Kennedy. Russia, the Soviet leader promised, would do nothing "before the American congressional elections that could complicate the international situation or aggravate the tension between our two countries"—but after that the Berlin problem must be finally solved. Yet Berlin alone hardly justified the risks Khrushchev was taking. That the problem of China also figured in his plan is signaled by the Chinese statement published a year later when the split was past mending and the Chinese were spilling the beans.[71]

"On August 25, 1962," the Chinese said then, the Russians notified them that Secretary Rusk of the United States had proposed that the nuclear powers "refrain from transferring weapons to other powers" and that "countries not in possession of nuclear weapons should undertake to refrain from manufacturing them," and that the Soviet government "gave an affirmative reply." The Chinese government, the statement said, protested at once against any such deal, and indeed there is no record of Rusk having made such proposals or of the Russians agreeing to them. Such, presumably, were the lengths to which the Soviet government was prepared to go in the summer of 1962 to prevail over China's determination to become a nuclear power that Moscow was alleging to Peking a nonexistent understanding with the United States, in the expectation that once Russian missiles were emplaced in Cuba such a deal must follow and the Chinese could have no choice but to acquiesce in Moscow's arrangements for them.[72]

Though such pivotal maneuverings in advance of the October showdown are only to be inferred from the shadowy outlines looming through events, the facts of the Cuban missile crunch stand well out in the open.

Early in 1962 Kennedy cut off all trade to Cuba. Almost immediately Russia signed an agreement to provide $800 million worth of goods that year to Castro, who now openly proclaimed that he was a Marxist-Leninist. Thereafter, and at a rising rate through the summer, Russian arms poured into Cuba, and in early June Khrushchev acknowledged it in a speech to visiting young Cubans. The Russian decision to install missiles capable of carrying atomic warheads in Cuba appears to have been taken somewhere around the beginning of July, and may not have been communicated to the Cubans until the visit of former Minister of Industry

Che Guevara in late August. Well before that time the Chinese ambassador in Moscow, Liu Shao, was telling ambassadors from several neutral countries that Khrushchev had at last found the right way to solve the Berlin crisis.[73]

Once started, the Russian buildup went ahead with breathtaking speed. Everything depended on getting the sites established and the missiles operational before the Americans could do anything about them. To allay American suspicions Moscow put out a communiqué that to protect Cuba from "aggressive imperialist" threats, the Soviet government was sending arms and technical experts to train Cuban servicemen. At the same time Moscow launched a strong anti-U-2 drive, played up a U-2 crash in China, and wrung an apology from the United States when one strayed for nine minutes over Siberia on September 4. On September 7, when the poet Robert Frost visited the Kremlin, Khrushchev disparaged the spirit of the West and asserted that Americans were "too liberal to fight." Privately, he sent word by several channels to assure President Kennedy that all arms going to Cuba were for defensive purposes.[74]

In the United States there was an anxious stir. Cuban refugees were telling lurid stories of the island being converted into a Russian-armed camp. Republican politicians were calling for an invasion. To quiet rising public agitation, President Kennedy issued a statement on September 4. American intelligence sources, he said, had learned that the Russians were setting up in Cuba "antiaircraft defense missiles with a slant range of 25 miles," and had sent in some 3,500 military technicians to emplace these, radar and other installations. So far as was known, he stressed, no Soviet bases or "offensive ground-to-ground missiles" had been or were being installed. "Were it otherwise, the gravest issues would arise."[75]

Within the Kennedy administration the assessment was that the Russian buildup was "defensive." Intelligence from refugees arriving in Florida, reports from agents in Cuba, shipping intelligence (85 Russian shipments arrived by October 3), U-2 overflights—all supported this judgment. By September 19, when this estimate was reaffirmed by the Intelligence Board, 10,000 Russians were known to be in the country and no fewer than 15 SAM sites under construction had been photographed by U-2s. Bad weather, interservice disputes and Washington's concern not to precipitate another Powers incident combined to delay the next U-2 overflight until October 14.

On that day Major Rudolf Anderson Jr. flew over San Cristobal in western Cuba. Intelligence officers were stunned by what his photographs disclosed. In a field enclosed by a wood near San Cristobal the earth was scarred by a slash pattern that the photo-interpreters had seen nowhere outside the Soviet Union. Though there were no ballistic missiles in sight, a tent city appeared to be springing up near a group of trucks and construction equipment. Looking further, the photo analysts picked out missile erectors, launchers and transporters—all within a wider trapezoidal pattern observed at rocket sites in Russia, with a SAM site at each corner for protection. The evidence was all but conclusive: the Russians were rushing installation of large missiles in Cuba.[76]

The information was flashed to McGeorge Bundy, the president's special assistant for national security affairs, who had just finished saying on a nationwide television interview: "I know there is no present evidence, and I think there is no present likelihood, that the Cubans and the Soviet government would in combination attempt to install a major offensive capability." At approximately 9:00 A.M. on Tuesday morning, October 16, Bundy went to the President's living quarters with the message: "Mr. President, there is now hard photographic evidence that the Russians have offensive missiles in Cuba."

The President's reaction was startled anger. At considerable political cost on the home front, Kennedy had accepted Khrushchev's repeated protestations of unaggressive purposes and had publicly stated that only defensive missiles were being installed. The Chairman had lied to the President.

Kennedy said that the threat must be ended, the missiles removed. Mindful of the unhappy experience of "experts" in the first Cuban affair, he summoned a select group of fifteen top advisers that included his brother, Attorney General Robert Kennedy, and his speechwriter, Theodore Sorensen. Swearing all to total secrecy, he constituted them as the "Executive Committee" of the more formal National Security Council and ordered them to "set aside all other tasks to make a prompt and intensive survey of the dangers and all possible courses of action." For the next thirteen days, hermetically sealed off from the outside reality, speaking only to each other, sharing the same assumptions and values, and governed by abstract conceptions of will, power and prestige, this handful of "crisis managers" carried the "realism" of Cold War to its uttermost limits. In this atmosphere the ultimate resources of violence pushed mere diplomacy right out of the picture. If the final decision had rested with any six of the fifteen deliberators, Robert Kennedy said later, "I think the world might have been blown up."

The Excom, as the group was called, boiled the issue down to two and only two possible courses—take out the missiles by a swift air strike, or isolate them and compel their removal by a naval blockade of the island. To begin with, the President wanted the "clean, surgical air strike," and stunned Adlai Stevenson, who heard about the missiles from the President when he came down from the United Nations for a diplomatic lunch the first day, by saying so. Greatly troubled, Stevenson gave Kennedy a handwritten note early next morning warning that "to risk starting a nuclear war is bound to be divisive at best. . . . I confess I have many misgivings about the proposed course of action." But neither Stevenson nor his plea for diplomacy first carried much weight. What prevented the air strike was a fortuitous conjuncture of other factors that changed the President's mind.

First, Secretary McNamara, most highly regarded and trusted of the President's official counselors, fixed on blockade as the type of response least likely to bring on a suicidal nuclear engagement. Second, Robert Kennedy, the President's closest confidant, blurted out his objection to the air strike on moral grounds. At the first Excom meeting, he had scribbled a note to his brother: "Now I know how Tojo felt when he was planning Pearl Harbor." His impassioned insistence that it flew against all American tradition to launch an attack without warning struck a chord in the President. By the time Kennedy returned from keeping a campaign engagement in Connecticut, his brother and Sorensen had swung behind McNamara to form a pro-blockade coalition of the advisers he most trusted. That the Joint Chiefs and the CIA, the people who had brought him the Bay of Pigs, were now lined up in favor of the air strike gave Kennedy pause. Finally, the Air Force, prodded and questioned by Robert Kennedy and Sorensen, had declared that a surgical air strike limited solely to knocking out the missiles could not be carried out with high confidence. What the Air Force was preparing, the two advisers reported in a four-page memorandum handed the President as he stepped off the plane from Connecticut, was something different—a major attack by 500 planes on the missiles and on air bases and antiaircraft all around the island.

Either way, there was no time to lose. The Russians had managed to get some 40 strategic missiles ashore already, plus 42 Il-28 bombers for Castro. U-2 photographs showed nine missile sites being rushed to completion—six with four launchers each for 1100-mile medium-range ballistic missiles, and three fixed sites comprised of four launching sites each for the 2200-mile intermediate-range missiles that could be trained on targets as distant as Detroit and Chicago. Furthermore, the United States, under cover of previously announced naval maneuvers in the Caribbean, was massing military forces in the area, and sending U-2 reconnaissances over Cuba at a three-a-day clip that the Russians could hardly fail to notice.

In the Excom a majority now backed the blockade. As the President swung over from the air-strike camp, there were violent arguments. Former Secretary of State Dean Acheson, one of three outsiders called in, declared in no uncertain terms that the missiles constituted a direct threat to the nation's interests and must be taken out at once by bombing attack. Nettled, Sorensen protested, "We are not serving the President well." Robert Kennedy stated flatly that the President could not possibly order an air strike, and Acheson departed in a dudgeon while Sorensen began to write a blockade speech for the President.

Next day the options were reviewed with Kennedy present. Discussion turned at last to diplomatic moves that might accompany announcement of the blockade. Adlai Stevenson, who had been specifically summoned for this meeting by the President, proposed giving up the American base at Guantanamo or withdrawing the Jupiter missiles from Turkey and Italy in exchange for removal of all Russian missiles from Cuba. Former Defense Secretary Robert Lovett, CIA Director John McCone and others wanted no part of such ideas, and President Kennedy himself rejected them on the spot. Some thought that Kennedy had deliberately sacrificed Adlai to the hawks in order to give himself leeway to set a more moderate course. On Sunday morning Kennedy met with the Air Force bombing experts, and was told by General Sweeny, chief of the Tactical Command, that only 90% effectiveness could be guaranteed by a surgical air strike and that only the Air Force's big strike could do the job for sure. But such action meant killing large numbers of Russians, dismaying the Allies and the Latin Americans, and putting Khrushchev, with no advance warning, in a spot from which he might feel driven to reach for the nuclear pushbutton.[77]

Into this wrought-up, walled-in atmosphere of strictly martial preparations walked, of all people, the Russian foreign minister. By long-standing arrangement, Andrei Gromyko had an appointment October 19 for a courtesy call on the President while in the country to attend the United Nations Assembly meeting. Had Kennedy and his "Excom" the least thought of allowing Khrushchev a face-saving way out through secret communication of United States intentions, this was the moment for it. But Kennedy refused, and both sides smiled impassively through one of the most uncomfortable meetings of post-1945 diplomacy.

Thus the decision was made. Kennedy announced it to the world on Tuesday evening, October 22. The United States was instituting a "quarantine" of Cuban waters, and would search for and turn back all shipments of offensive weapons. "Within the past week," he said, "unmistakble evidence has established the fact that a series of offensive missile bases is now in preparation" in Cuba. Such an action by the Soviet Union "cannot be accepted by this country," the President said, and accordingly the United States was establishing a "quarantine" of Cuban waters as an initial step to secure withdrawal or elimination of the missiles from the Western Hemisphere. Any use of these missiles meanwhile would lead to a full retaliation by the United States against Russia, and unless the missiles were removed quickly the United States would take action against Cuba—invasion, air strike or both.

The first Russian response was to denounce the President's action as "piratical" and unacceptable. But behind the scenes Khrushchev dispatched two quick letters that Washington interpreted as "maneuvering." Meanwhile the Organization of American States met and voted, nineteen to one, to join the quarantine, thereby giving it some basis in international law. The Allies also lined up, not excepting General De Gaulle. When the Cubans appealed the matter to the United Nations, Adlai Stevenson presented large photographs of the missile sites and challenged the Russians to deny that they were theirs.

In Washington orders were now ostentatiously given to assemble troops in the southeastern states. The Strategic Air Command went on worldwide alert, and messages in plain English were flashed to the nine Polaris submarines at sea. At his brother's direction, Robert Kennedy summoned Ambassador Anatoli Dobrynin to his office that night to stress the gravity of the situation (and to say, Khrushchev claimed later, that if it went on much longer "the President is not sure that the military will not overthrow him").[78]

The violence of the atmosphere attending these determinations, in which not only Pearl Harbors but Doomsdays had been proposed, now communicated itself through Washington. The President tensed as he saw himself facing nuclear war. He talked at a tremendous pace, in machine gun bursts. His eyes were screwed up as if to shut out the vision of holocaust. The moment for interception of the first ship neared, and Secretary McNamara, entering the Navy's sacrosanct war-room to make sure the President's wishes were precisely fulfilled, was gruffly told by the Chief of Naval Operations, Admiral Anderson, to leave it to the Navy and, in effect, to mind his own business. The nervousness was almost insupportable. At this moment diplomacy's spokesman among the fifteen decision-makers, Dean Rusk, made his one memorable contribution to the discussions, "It's eyeball to eyeball, and I think the other fellow just blinked." A report was handed the Excom stating that a dozen of the Russian ships advancing toward Cuba had stopped dead in the water or begun to circle. Shortly afterwards the Americans stopped and boarded their first ship, the Lebanese freighter *Marucla*, carefully chosen because it was of non-Soviet registry though under Soviet charter; after a brief search of one hold, the boarding officer satisfied himself that there were no offensive weapons aboard, only trucks and newsprint, and allowed the *Marucla* to sail on.

At this Ambassador Averill Harriman, who had not been consulted, sent an urgent message to Kennedy: Khrushchev was desperately signaling a desire to cooperate for some peaceful solution. "We must give him an out," said Harriman. "If we do this shrewdly, we can downgrade the tough group in the Soviet Union which persuaded him to do this." At 1:30 on Friday afternoon Soviet Embassy Counselor Alexander Fomin phoned John Scali, Washington diplomatic correspondent of the American Broadcasting Company, and asked him to lunch. No sooner had they sat down than the Russian asked if the State Department would be interested in settling the crisis on these terms: the missiles would be dismantled and shipped back to Russia under United Nations supervision, and the United States would give a pledge not to invade Cuba. Scali dashed to the State Department, where Secretary Rusk promptly gave him a note for Fomin that the United States saw "real possibilities" in the suggestion. Before Scali could get to Fomin a long message came into the White House from Moscow that bore all the marks of having been written by Chairman Khrushchev himself. It dwelt on the drift to war and the necessity for stopping the drift before it was too late. Khrushchev had sent the missiles to Cuba, he said, only to save Castro from an invasion, and if Kennedy were now willing to give a no-invasion pledge, then there would be no further need to keep Russian military specialists in Cuba.

If there is no intention to tighten the knot [he wrote], and thereby doom the world to the catastrophe of nuclear war, then let us not only relax the forces pulling on the ends of the rope. Let us take measures to untie that knot. We are ready for this.[79]

But the crisis was not over. Next morning Radio Moscow began broadcasting a second Khrushchev letter addressed to Kennedy. This one was entirely different in tone and style. It bore the marks of Russian Foreign Office drafting. Almost as if the secret earlier message had never been sent, this one proposed to "remove from Cuba those weapons which you regard as offensive" if the United States would take its Jupiter missiles out of Turkey. Even as the message was on its way Russian missile batteries opened up on a U-2 over Cuba, and shot down Major Rudolf Anderson Jr., the pilot who had brought back first photographic evidence of the Soviet missile buildup. Thus notice was served that the first of the Russian missiles on Cuba had gone into action.

It was Robert Kennedy who after long debate suggested ignoring the broadcast letter and replying to the earlier letter as if it were a valid proposal. Accordingly a message went out from the president stating that he found "generally acceptable" Khrushchev's offer to remove the weapons from Cuba in return for an end to the quarantine and American assurances against an invasion of Cuba.[80]

Next morning, as intelligence reported no let-up in the feverish work on the missile sites and the Defense Department announced callup of twenty-four reserve troop-carrying squadrons that would be needed for invasion, the announcer in Moscow started reading another Khrushchev letter.

> In order to eliminate as rapidly as possible the conflict which endangers the cause of peace [said Khrushchev], and out of regard for the statement made in your message that there would be no attack, no invasion of Cuba . . . , the Soviet government has given a new order to dismantle the arms which you described as offensive and to crate and return them to the Soviet Union. . . . We are prepared to reach agreement to enable the United Nations representatives to verify the dismantling.[81]

Rather than wait for the official text, President Kennedy drafted a quick acceptance. "I welcome Chairman Khrushchev's statesmanlike decision—an important and constructive contribution to peace." After thirteen days the crisis was over. The whole world breathed easier. In Moscow, where presumably a Russian version of "Excom" had been meeting, Khrushchev's adviser Yuri Zhukov wrote: "We have lived through the most difficult week since the Second World War." In London Prime Minister Macmillan, veteran of Suez, gave thanks for the end of "the week of most strain I can remember in my life." At the White House, the president "walked with a different step." He gave out stern orders that no victory claims should be made. It proved anything but easy to get Fidel Castro, who was reported to have said that he would, if he could, have beaten up his Soviet benefactor, to go along with the Russian-American agreement. He never did permit the United Nations to send teams into Cuba to verify removal of the missiles, and it was only after Soviet Leader Anastas Mikoyan had spent a month of wheedling, cajoling and arm-twisting in Havana that Castro finally consented to relinquish the Il-28 bombers that the Russians had given him, and the Americans lifted their blockade.[82]

Having gained his goal, which was the removal of the missiles from Cuba, President Kennedy proceeded to execute in the aftermath of the showdown the withdrawal of Jupiter missiles from Turkey that he had declined to do under pressure. Ten years later, there seems little doubt that in an atmosphere of confrontation, attenuated to surrealist extremes of polarity by prolonged Cold War, Kennedy and his advisers overstressed the danger of nuclear war in the Cuban test. Simply by mustering overwhelming local superiority in conventional arms, and showing by their blockade and military buildup that they were fully prepared to use it, they persuaded the Russians to retreat. Thus after the first excited flush of hawkish bomb-lust, the nuclear option was posed almost exclusively for the Russians' decision. And one thing came clear in the crunch: Khrushchev, the rocket-rattler who had talked so freely for six years about his powers of missile destruction, was very far from carrying things to the point of nuclear engagement. Bold as had been his move to emplace missiles at America's front door, he was now compelled by the American ultimatum to appear before East, West and the Third World as never intending to unleash them in nuclear war, but only to bargain with them for Russian advantage.

To his own people, and possibly to some others, Khrushchev may well have appeared as the man who had saved the peace and avoided the catastrophe of nuclear war. But to many in the West the impression that emerged was that of an adversary quite evidently unable and even unwilling to act to anything like the unrelenting foe that Cold War ideologies demanded. This was a perception that Khrushchev in all his blustering campaigning for coexistence had never permitted, and one that would be intolerable to him at this juncture. And yet it carried a lesson about the actual nature of the adversary that had everything to do with the gradual decline of the Cold War from that time on in Western lands.[83]

In a larger sense Khrushchev's backdown amounted to acknowledgment on the part of the Soviet Union that it was No. 2 in the international political scene. In the world at large there was enormous relief at the Russian withdrawal. Moscow's drive into the Third World, which had seemed to gain momentum so long as Asians and Africans regarded it as the winning wave, slacked off. The Chinese began to work more openly against the Russian drive, and the Americans recouped, although this was largely because the competition with the Russians was henceforth reduced to terms measured in money.

Following the collapse of an elaborate policy design, the Russians now had to pick up the pieces and start all over again. The lesson of helplessness before the American sea blockade was not lost in Moscow, where among the generals and other dissidents the resolve grew to build a Soviet naval strength that would one day give Moscow its own capability of "flexible response." Meanwhile any hope of constraining China's nuclear armament was lost and the Chinese, having supported Khrushchev's moves into Cuba with flamboyant cries of approval, now filled the air with jeering questions and barely concealed rejoicing at the Russian leadership's discomfiture. The other part of the original design, the securing of the German peace treaty, had to be abandoned, and all the steam went out of the Russian push for Berlin.

For Khrushchev personally, it was a disaster from which he never recovered. There are grounds for believing that the Cuban missile outcome irretrievably undermined his position, though he held on to his leadership for two more years. When the day came in 1964 that he was finally retired by a conspiracy more successful than the "anti-Party plot" that he beat down in 1957, the Cuban missile crisis was duly alleged as a prime example of the "hare-brained schemes" for which he was then condemned.[84]

Though Acheson believed that President Kennedy was too anxious to make a deal with Khrushchev, chances are that the fault in American conduct lay instead in having overreacted, and that the United States had little cause for complacency over the chairman's downfall in 1964 and for satisfaction at starting him on the downgrade in 1962. The men who came after him held sterner views, and they pressed the arms race so relentlessly that by the 1970s they had attained parity with the United States and in some respects superiority. There was loss for America in the exchange.[85]

Once, when General Anastasio Somoza, dictator of Nicaragua, was about to pay a state visit to Washington, Sumner Welles sent President Roosevelt a long background memo. Roosevelt read it and sent it back with this note scrawled across the top: "I get it, Sumner. He's a son of a bitch but he's our son of a bitch." In the vituperative vernacular of the Cold War, what was so aptly unutterable among the Good Neighbors of the 1940s could easily pass for the language of moderation. But it is not recorded that this most American of appellations was ever bestowed, though as Russians went he deserved it, on the stubby chairman from Kalinovka. In the time of John Foster Dulles Americans were wont to picture Khrushchev as a Prince of Darkness and a worthy heir of Stalin. But though a brutal man (he could hardly have survived Stalin's regime had he been otherwise), the chairman pursued policies that Americans might have found more acceptable than they did. At home he stood for de-Stalinization. Abroad his version of coexistence was, toward America, a policy of détente. He let this be known at Geneva, though in 1955 not only Dulles but Molotov stood in the way. Later, after Russia developed the ICBM ahead of the Americans, he declined to dragoon the Soviet economy for an all-out drive to outproduce the United States in missiles. Instead he proclaimed a peaceful competition in producing butter and textiles, and unilaterally reduced his armed forces as if he meant it. For Khrushchev was an old-fashioned believer in the historically inevitable triumph of Socialism—and, as a defender of what Socialism had achieved in the Soviet Union, a believer that in an age when war was suicide the triumph would—must—be peaceful.

But strategic, or military, attitudes dominated the Cold War years and dictated that diplomatic methods, that is to say, negotiating, must always be unyielding. Khrushchev made his bid for an understanding with the United States by his trip to America in 1959. Eisenhower damaged him badly in the U–2 episode the next year. When the President elected publicly to accept responsibility for sending the spy plane over Russia on the eve of their meeting Khrushchev, who was working for rapprochement and had reportedly built a golf course in the Crimea in anticipation of Eisenhower's visit, was left with no way out other than to break up the summit session in Paris to save himself from critics in the Kremlin. In the Cuban affair, by exposing Khrushchev's rocket threats as not well founded and not even really meant, Kennedy gave the Chairman another push down his road to ruin.

In the light of the apocalyptic alternatives so freely urged on him at the time, Kennedy's handling of the crisis was thought to have been moderate. The sequel, however, suggested that he need not have been worried, if he had been more moderate. Somehow the menace of international Communism threatening the security of the United States from eighty miles off the Florida coast evaporated with the discovery, during the negotiations for the missile withdrawal, that the Soviet bases in Cuba had been manned by Russians to the total and forced exclusion of any and all Cubans. The popular American demand for rescuing the island from Communism simply faded away, and in November several senators who had been loudest in calling for the invasion of Cuba were retired to private life. But the huge military establishment that had grown under Kennedy to its greatest size was not to be denied. Martial capabilities, once ordered, funded and then brought into being, tend to find the mission for their fulfillment. Instead of a campaign in Cuba, the conventional forces that Kennedy and McNamara had built up to record peacetime levels in their first two years in office, now began to flow to Southeast Asia and the expanding war in Indochina.[86]

Thus the legacy of the Cold War, and the real sequel to the consolidation and triumph in Cuba in October, 1962, was embroilment and defeat in Vietnam a decade later. The links in this melancholy chain of events are to be traced in the next and concluding chapter.

The Nuclear Test Ban Treaty, the End of the Cold War, and the Strange Sequel in America and Vietnam

T HE COLD WAR pitted against each other not only the total industrial-military might of the world's two superpowers but also the rival value-systems they claimed to live by. At the height of the Cold War, when the chain of self-fulfilling prophecy had mustered each side to peak force short of battle, the concerting of national wills amounted to wartime mobilization of man's minds and wills. As prismatic transmitters of the collected signals of individual impulses, the schools, the churches, the unions, the press and TV seemed to amplify and relay in concentrated beams the hostility of all America to Russians and Communists. The very toys of the children took the shape of missiles, rockets and Red Army tanks. Even the comic strips joined the Cold War. Buzz Sawyer, flying for the Navy, was busy coping with "the sinister machinations of a World Power"; Terry left off fighting the pirates and warred on the Red Chinese; Joe Palooka outsmarted the Communists to rescue an American scientist in Austria; Li'l Abner helped liberate Lower Slobbovia; Winnie Winkle was locked up in a Russian jail; and Daddy Warbucks and his buddies blew up "enemy" planes carrying H-bombs.

The 1950s were a time when parents were doing the American thing, taking their children to see such historical restorations as Colonial Williamsburg and Sturbridge Village. Subscribing to *American Heritage*, visiting Concord's rude Bridge, touring the Natchez Trace, shopping for maple hutch furniture, flaunting Confederate flags—all this holding on to the past conveyed more than a little sense that the future was not there. In a time when Presidents and Secretaries of State engaged in global management, theatergoers flocked to a Broadway musical revue entitled *Stop the World I Want to Get Off.*[1]

In these years—Robert Lowell called them the "tranquilized Fifties" —the whole country was on drugs. Americans consumed tranquilizer pills at the rate of a billion a year. Sometimes it seemed as if the drug industry, proclaiming that everything from loss of appetite to sleep, back pain, dull teeth and "irregularity" could be cured by buying the fancy boxed product at the drug store, was sponsoring the Cold War. In September, 1955, Walter Cronkite brought his bulletins on President Eisenhower's heart attack. Immediately afterward followed the Bufferin commercial, the drug industry offering people the relief their nerves needed along with the unnerving news of the Cold War. Between 1945 and 1960 aspirin sales shot up 240%. A decade later, when the nation had roused to drug abuse among the young, research at a New Jersey high school indicated that a child's chances of shooting methedrine was five and one-half times greater if his father was on tranquilizers.

In 1959 Senator Estes Kefauver's Antitrust and Monopoly subcommittee reported that three drug companies topped the list of corporations (and eleven others were among the first fifty) making the highest rate of return on invested capital after taxes in the United States. The Kefauver investigation established that Americans were paying ten times as much as it cost in Mexico for the same drug—but without the American company's proprietary label. The drug boom grew out of the sensational development in the Second World War of penicillin. Since Sir Alexander Fleming had discovered his antibiotic in a common mold, the drug companies rushed to look into the possibilities of other molds. In 1945 Rutgers under a grant from the Merck Company found streptomycin, in 1947 Yale with funds from Parke Davis discovered chloramphenicol, in 1948 Lederle discovered chlorotyecycline, and in 1949 Pfizer discovered oxytetracycline. From these "wonder drugs" the firms reaped bumper profits and brought out yet newer drugs without waiting to ascertain whether they caused adverse side-effects in users.

So grasping were the monopolists and so unquestioning was America's drug acceptance that neither the Kefauver findings nor the election of a Democratic administration with a Democratic majority in Congress in 1960 sufficed to produce legislation regulating the loose practices and profiteering in pills and needles. As Congress shelved Kefauver's bill, the news burst out in Germany that babies without arms and legs were being born to mothers who had taken a drug not adequately tested. Shocked,

Americans next learned that the drug—thalidomide—would have gone on sale in the United States but for the personal efforts of Dr. Frances Kelsey of the Food and Drug Administration, who bent regulations to keep the industry from marketing it. In the ensuing outcry, Congress rediscovered and passed Kefauver's bill. Dr. Kelsey received a medal, and President Kennedy thanked Kefauver on behalf of the nation for his efforts.[2]

These were also the years that the computer began to emerge as a force in American life. Since the first electronic computer was not constructed until 1945, it is fair to say that this tremendous innovation arrived with the Cold War. Because of its importance in research and engineering, its spectacular advance exactly paralleled the arms race. By the 1960s the requirements of missilery has already dramatically reduced the computer's size and magnified its speed and storage power. Big computers calculated the astronauts' moon flights, small ones went along and programmed their communications, including the television pictures transmitted back to home TV screens. Computers were central to automation, first in laying out the plans, then in monitoring the machinery in steel mills, auto plants, textile factories and the like.

Such was the automating power of the computer that even in the 1950s, as the first big transformations were accomplished by General Motors and United States Steel, experts began to say that factory workers would soon be obsolete. Social scientists announced to their countrymen that they were already living in a postindustrial age, an age in which the number of factory workers might well decline to the number of farmers needed in the 1960s to produce the nation's food—not many more than five million. Although the number of jobs in the manufacturing sector ceased to grow by the late 1950s (the gains in employment were scored in the so-called "service" sector), no significant decline occurred during the Cold War years.

Yet if the computer was a *calculating* machine, ought not it to be a threat, or at least a competitor, to mankind's nonmanual employment? All the graveyard jokes about computers, in fact, concerned this potentiality. In the 1950s the experts were already programming computers to such tasks as storing and updating bank records, keeping track of inventories in large businesses, maintaining personnel files, allocating airline seat-reservations, and billing department-store customers. When people began to receive serial numbers that were then punched on a card by a computer, a good many accepted this as an inevitable and ultimately beneficial symbol of growth and progress. Much was made of the fact that the young were learning "the New Math" and already becoming adept at operating the computers as routinely as their elders had been with adding machines and typewriters. The largest new company to take its place among America's supercorporations during the Cold War years was the giant of the computer manufacturers, IBM, and it was an IBM plant at San Jose, California, to which Khruschev paid his visit in 1959 when he was to be shown American industry at its modern best. But the accelerating pressures and speeds of modern life embodied in a computerized society were among the forces against which people reacted once the Cold War ended. The young in particular were rebellious in asserting the overriding importance of personal relations despite the pressures of modern life, and in attacking the computerization of personal relations as inhuman. The technocrats scoffed and called them Luddites—after the nineteenth-century British factory workers who in blind protest went about with axes smashing their machines. For in an age of vast quantities and magnitudes, of huge numbers of people, there is no alternative to automation.[3]

If people were *not* to be turned into "things" and "numbers," and employment made intolerable, it was going to be necessary to make a new life of their leisure. Certainly the Cold War affected the changing uses of leisure. "Recreation in the present-day Western sense," said Arnold Toynbee, "has always seemed to me an unhealthy regression to childishness—in a creative life, there is no distinction between recreation and work." What was this Middle America that thronged to its playgrounds with cars and children and conforming ideology? It had been shaped, and its values established, in the Hollywood of the 1940s and 1950s when *Oklahoma!* played at the neighborhood movies, when John Wayne rode the range in his eagle-eyed prime, and the whole country went to the movies every week.

Authority flowed from these figures of the screen. Franklin Roosevelt brought movie stars around him in his birthday-party benefits for polio victims, and John Kennedy had a Hollywood tie in the family, through his brother-in-law Peter Lawford. Once, when the old movie star Adolphe Menjou wore a lapel watch in one of his films, the industry sold 8,000,000 lapel watches on the strength of his example. By the end of the 1950s television brought in some new style-setters—John Glenn, for instance, a Cold War figure who was just as handsome as the old-style movie stars and whose space helmet was widely copied and worn by juveniles as they watched him "live" on the living-room screen. Something of an entertainer as well as flier, ace, and astronaut, it was hard to tell just what he was. He appeared at parties where they threw people in swimming pools. Who, then, were the new—and nonpolitical—authorities to whom the public looked in the television years? They were people introduced to America first between the hours of eight and nine on Sunday evenings on the Ed Sullivan show—Leontyne Price, Dean Martin, the Rolling Stones, and the Beatles one memorable night in 1964.

Television gave instant national presence as well to stars of sport.

Great sports personalities had always tended to be All-American boy types —Bobby Jones, Red Grange, Joe DiMaggio. In the late Cold War years Arnold Palmer came on camera as such an All-American boy from Latrobe, Pennsylvania, charismatic victor in the Masters and National Open golf championships in 1960. Arnie, triumphing over all foes foreign and domestic, turned stardom into big business. His following was called an "army," like that of kings of old, or a chief of state. He had his own airplane, a Jet Commander. And he ruled over a commercial empire of sponsored goods—the Arnold Palmer boys' camps, pants, insurance, putting courses. When Arnie played on the tournament circuit, the Cold War subsidized his winnings. Some of the military-industrial complex profits fattened the prize money for the Pensacola Open (backed by Monsanto), the Greensboro Open (financed by Allied Chemical), and the San Diego Open (bankrolled by Convair).[4]

Though John Updike, the novelist, insisted that spectator sport was a degenerate form of play, it was the height of television entertainment. Like the senate hearing and the quiz show, the athletic contest was artificial but real, and not so endless as the one nor repetitive as the other. Sunday afternoon professional games were decisive, dramatic and free; they offered action, an outcome and displays of manly skill. For the average man they were a relief from the endless uncertainties of job and family. In contrast with so much else, the Cold War for example, they had a beginning, a middle and an end that left you knowing who won. What else was so sure, so interesting and so available at the flick of a TV switch? The best of Sundays heaped golf on top of football. As Bart Starr and Y. A. Tittle trotted off the field and America opened another can of beer, Arnie Palmer came on—curly-haired, tanned, trailed by a huge crowd. To the armchair army, there was even, when a birdie putt failed to drop, charisma in his wince.[5]

Have patience, work hard, make sacrifices—so went America's admonishments from Acheson and Dulles to Rusk. Was there not a rather cockeyed discrepancy between the stern facade and this settling back in Castro convertibles and inclining ever more to the hedonistic? A signal of approaching change was the appearance in 1961 of Joseph Heller's novel of the Second World War, *Catch-22*. At once farcical and an indignant denunciation of the stupidity and waste of warfare, *Catch-22* was a book that became possible only when a revulsion set in against the nonsense of war and the spectacle of a country led by its nose. As a description of one man's war with the Air Force, *Catch-22* came across as a marshaling of the facts from a bitter, later perspective. It was a story of the Second World War told with the hindsight of disillusionment with the Cold War.[6]

A T I T S P E A K the kind of mental mobilization against which *Catch-22* jeered—whether in a totalitarian society like Russia or in the United States defined as leader of the "free" world—tended to elevate ends to supreme importance and to display marked insensitivity about means. When the Cold War passed its peak, however, and wore on through the 1950s and into the 1960s, concern began to grow about the means by which it was waged. In this aspect of the conflict, no more striking example was to be seen than in changing attitudes, popular and official, toward nuclear testing.

When the United States emerged from the Second World War to find itself in contentious collision with the Communist ally almost everywhere in the world, the reaction was to thank God for entrusting the monopoly of the atomic bomb to the people of America. President Truman never made a more widely supported decision than when he made up his mind to withhold the secret of the A-bomb from the Russians and everybody else. And when the Armed Forces conducted the first tests in the Pacific after the war, about the only demur heard from anybody was the scientists' complaint that tests were not worth the trouble when only old wartime model bombs were used.

When native populations had to be uprooted from their living places on Bikini and Eniwetok atolls, the American public accepted these dislocations as unquestioned necessities of military operations with nary a whisper of popular disapproval. For the most part Americans seem to have regarded these first tests almost as martial displays or parades. The armed forces who staged them invited foreign representatives to witness them, not at all averse to giving Russians a firsthand scare. They also arranged to broadcast the first Bikini tests to the nation as a popular spectacle something like the Cleveland air show or the Kentucky Derby but also, since the taxpayers had footed the bill, a display of formidable weapons in which the country could take pride. After the 1946 tests the skimpy bathing suits girls wore were dubbed bikinis because they looked as if nothing were left.

By far the biggest controversy about the bomb was settled when Congress entrusted its manufacture and development to civilian rather than military authorities. Nobody questioned the provision of the 1946 Atomic Energy Act that charged the same agency that was to make the bomb with responsibility for determining whether its testing might be harmful to humans. The same unquestioning complacency prevailed after the government, finding the Pacific islands inconveniently remote, began detonating explosions in Nevada. By the end of 1952 no fewer than twenty separate tests had been carried out at Yucca Flats, seventy miles north of Las Vegas. An awed national TV audience of children and grownups viewed one such test, and saw the mushroom cloud as a pillar of American power.

Though the end of such attitudes was foreshadowed in 1949 when the Russians exploded their first A-bomb, for many Americans the Soviet success only redoubled the need for improving and testing American bombs. Even when in May, 1953, such a rain of radio. tive particles descended after one blast that the residents of St. George, Utah, had to stay indoors for most of the day, the event was scarcely noticed in the nation's press.

Except for scattered protests by Quakers and other pacifists, there was no outcry among Americans as the first ultrasecret thermonuclear explosions went off in the Pacific in the early 1950s. Then on April 1, 1954, the United States exploded its hydrogen bomb over Bikini atoll, and the cloud, bigger than any ever seen, dropped its radioactive particles on the Japanese fishing boat *Fortunate Dragon* 100 miles to the southwest, causing death to one crew member and inflicting radiation burns on the other twenty-two.'

That shocked and angered people everywhere. America's ambassador in Tokyo, without instructions and on his own initiative, issued an apology on behalf of his country. Prominent American biologists now challenged the Atomic Energy Commission's reassurances that radioactive materials thrown into the upper atmosphere had not reached levels dangerous to human health. Still, caught up in a race to the death, the United States pressed on with its weapons-testing program.

The *Fortunate Dragon* incident marked a turning point. The fishing boat's wireless operator was by no means the first Japanese to have been killed by an American nuclear bomb. The event starkly dramatized the danger to peoples not involved in the nuclear arms race. Apprehension spread that such innocent bystanders could at any time and place be poisoned by fallout from even distant tests by the Cold War rivals. On April 2 Prime Minister Nehru of India proposed a "standstill" in all nuclear testing. Nineteen Asian and African nations, meeting in 1955 at Bandung for the first conference of the uncommitted nations of the Third World, called for a moratorium in nuclear arms tests.

Out to win the Third World, Nikita Khrushchev announced in 1956 that if others would, Russia would support a nuclear test ban. For the United States, also pushing for the support and goodwill of the new, postcolonial countries, this was challnging pressure. American Cold War policy was not to negotiate except from "positions of strength," and with the Russians catching up fast in nuclear weapons and missiles America had to keep testing bigger and better weapons so as to build the positions of strength to negotiate from. For a time the Eisenhower Administration's propaganda sought to stress that American tests would achieve a "clean" bomb from which there would be little or no radioactive fallout. This only produced jokes about the dubious satisfaction of being killed by a "clean" bomb.[8]

More fundamental was the challenge to negotiate any disarmament at all. For this the rigidities of superpower rivalry, and the seemingly unbreakable deadlock of terror, imposed obstacles that East and West could not overcome. What by 1958 emerged from the proposals and counterproposals at the United Nations and elsewhere was this: if the Russians and Americans could not agree on any kind of disarmament, they might possibly come to some undetermined degree of arms control indirectly by means of an agreement to ban nuclear tests.

Distrust remained profound. Yet the clamor against poisoning from tests in the atmosphere spread from the uncommitted countries to the superpowers' allies and then to their own populace. In the interminable bargaining each of the superpowers satisfied itself that the other had not gained an unacceptable lead. In 1958 first the Russians and then the Americans announced that they would desist from atmospheric testing. The voluntary moratorium lasted three years.[9]

On the Russian side a key determinant of policy was the state of Moscow's relations with the Chinese. Ideological differences and state interests alike played their important part. At the same time that the Russians canceled their earlier pledge to help China build an A-bomb, refused to risk war to help Mao's push against Quemoy and Matsu, and pushed drives into the Third World literally at China's expense, Khrushchev was campaigning persistently to make an accommodation with the United States. As the Chinese saw it, Moscow was not only sacrificing world revolution to make a deal with the United States, but bent on uniting with the United States to keep Peking from becoming a nuclear power. By 1960 the Chinese had had enough. They had decided that their only course was to seize leadership of world communism from Moscow and set the movement back on the right revolutionary track.[10]

Americans at the time dismissed reports of such differences as devilish schemes to weaken Western vigilance. They held unshakably to the view that the Chinese massing across the Formosa Strait and the Russians menacing Berlin were indistinguishably manifestations of "international Communism" directed from Moscow. When therefore Eisenhower sent a U-2 spy plane over the Soviet Union on the eve of the Paris summit with Khrushchev, he not only made Khrushchev look ridiculous. He also played into Mao Tse-tung's hands. It became necessary for Khrushchev to tip over the tables at Paris, smash the summit conference, personally insult the President, and otherwise behave in a manner gratifying to those in

Peking and elsewhere who held that peaceful agreement with Americans was a sellout. Similarly, when President Kennedy after taking office put through a huge increase in the American military establishment, his action practically caused Quarterback Khrushchev to reverse his field and race back toward the Chinese side. The Soviet premier broke off his three-year test moratorium, and scheduled a series of superbomb blasts in the Arctic with a bellicosity that could only please the militant "hards" of Peking.[11]

Yet in judging the degree to which Khrushchev's field maneuvers during these years were actually swayed by the ideological fury of Mao and his circle in Peking, it is necessary to bear in mind that the Soviet leader's line left him more than simply two options. As Professor Marshall Shulman pointed out long ago, both the left and right syndrome of Russian behavior may be used for offensive and defensive purposes, and Khrushchev played it every way. Thus, the ending of the Cuban missile crisis showed how his style of quarterbacking could serve defensive as well as offensive purposes.

For this the subsequent revelations of the physicist Andrei Sakharov provided fascinating illustration. Like American scientists before them, some of those who perfected the Soviet nuclear weapon became profoundly convinced that it must not be used for war. In some sense Sakharov, father of the Soviet hydrogen bomb, thus combined in himself the roles of Teller and Oppenheimer. Having designed the big bomb, he vainly opposed Khrushchev's 1961 superblasts. Now he put before the Soviet hierarchy the idea that the Americans had offered as a fallback position in 1959: if East and West were hopelessly deadlocked on the need for on-site inspections, they could settle for a limited ban (on tests in the air, in space and under water)—and leave out underground tests that required close-up checking. This position now commended itself to the Russian leadership.

In consequence, Khrushchev's report to the Supreme Soviet in December claiming that the missiles had saved Castro from invasion and their withdrawal had "saved the peace," was more than a call for a breathing space. As never before the crisis over Cuba had demonstrated the need for nuclear coexistence. From that moment the nuclear test-ban treaty was foreordained. [12]

But when it came it had startling consequences.

LOOKING for a way to follow up his strong stand over Cuba in October, President Kennedy rightly concluded that the Russians might now reverse their previous position and agree on a nuclear test-ban treaty. American opinion had moved a long way from 1954, when a Gallup poll had disclosed no more than twenty percent of the public in favor of a suspension of nuclear testing. The United States had now completed its latest series of tests. Its experts had satisfied themselves not only that the country held a clear lead in nuclear weaponry. There had also been opportunity, as part of a $100 million expenditure on seismic research, to ascertain that not nearly so many on-site inspections might be needed after all to keep tabs on Russian compliance with a ban on underground testing.[13]

After many delays messages went back and forth between the governments, and the Americans and British prepared to send senior representatives to Moscow to discuss a treaty. At the same time, however, the Russians and Chinese exchanged letters vowing to find a basis for agreement between their viewpoints, and through the first half of 1963 something of a truce descended between the two Communist capitals. The Chinese prepared to send a strong delegation to Moscow. At the same time, according to their account, on June 4 their government warned the Russian rulers "against any agreement with the United States that would amount to depriving China of the right to equip itself with nuclear weapons." To this, the Chinese allege, Moscow responded three days later with the following reassurance: "The Western position on the suspension of nuclear testing does not at present provide any basis for the conclusion of an agreement."[14]

Then on June 8 the Soviet government announced to the world that it had agreed to American and British proposals to send senior representatives to discuss nuclear tests. The Westerners, the announcement said, would arrive in Moscow in July. This meant that they would be in town at the very same time the Chinese delegation was in Moscow to talk about patching up disagreements between China and Russia. It was all very reminiscent of another crowded summer in Soviet diplomatic history— the August days of 1939 when the Russians held talks in Moscow about a proposed anti-German alliance with the British and French at the same time that elsewhere in the city they secretly signed the nonaggression pact with Germany that partitioned Poland and brought on the Second World War.[15]

It is far from likely that Khrushchev saw the scene in any such light. Improvising to the last, he seemed to have thought that the likelihood of reaching an agreement with the West might make the Chinese more amenable. It did not. On June 19 they presented a bristlingly hostile, twenty-five-point reply to the Russian party's proposed agenda. This violent communication ripped away the truce that had prevailed since February. Assuming that the Russian leaders would never make it public, the Chinese began passing out copies in Moscow and elsewhere by every possible means. According to an indignant Soviet Foreign Office bulletin they even "scattered them from the car windows of the Peking-Moscow train, and read them over the public-address system between train stops." For such "unprecedented acts," Moscow expelled three Chinese diplomats. As Peking's retort, Chou En-lai met their plane, and the three were feted at a mass rally.[16]

When the two delegations finally began their talks, Moscow acknowledged publicly that it had received a "libelous" Chinese letter and would publish it with an "appropriate reply." On July 14, the day before the test-ban talks got under way in Khrushchev's office, the reply went out —a long and emotional "open letter" addressed not to the Chinese but to "all party organizations and all Communists of the Soviet Union." Such publication officially informed the world that there was indeed a rift between the Chinese and Russians. More than that, Moscow's action signified that having failed to swing Peking over to its coexistence line the Soviet Union was preparing to seek China's expulsion from the international Communist movement. Asserting that Mao was prepared to sacrifice millions in a nuclear war, the Russians protested that they could never "share the view of the Chinese leadership about creating a thousand times higher civilization on the corpses of hundreds of millions of people." Such views, they said, were "in crying contradiction to the ideas of Marxism-Leninism." The nuclear bomb, the Russians declared, "does not distinguish between imperialists and working people—it devastates entire areas."[17]

As the bilateral talks broke off in open ideological batttle the test-ban bargaining took center stage in Moscow. The Americans were led by Averill Harriman, who as ambassador to Russia in 1945 had been in on the Cold War from the start. Now he was to have a hand in ending it. Khrushchev began by saying that on-site inspection of someone else's country was espionage: you did not get the cat into the kitchen only to hunt the mice and not to drink the milk. With that, as Harriman and Kennedy had anticipated, the comprehensive test-ban that would have been so much harder to push through the Senate went out the window —and the limited test-ban was left on the table.

Such a treaty, Harriman said, could be negotiated in a few days. Actually the discussions, chiefly between Harriman for the West and Gromyko for the Russians, proved long and difficult. A clause permitting withdrawal and resumption of testing had to be inserted in anticipation of the Senate's insistence. Then a way had to be found for other countries —East Germany and China were the ones the Americans had in mind —to sign the treaty without thereby receiving implicit recognition. The solution was to set up multiple depositories, leaving each nation free to sign only in association with nations it approved of.

Finally the two sides initialed the treaty. Yet even at this hour when the talks with the Chinese had failed and the newspapers were filled with sensational reports of the dispute, the Soviet leadership made a last show of concern for China's interests in the agreement. Harriman put forward that the treaty should be supplemented by another forbidding transfer of nuclear weapons from one country to another. Khrushchev drew back, arguing that as other nations signed the test-ban treaty it would have the same effect. The Chinese were going to raise a storm, he could be sure, over the test-ban; to include a nonproliferation provision would drive them to a frenzy and to making the kind of revelations he feared. China, he said, was another socialist country, and he did not propose to discuss it with a capitalist. Harriman kept probing: "Suppose we get France to sign the treaty. Can you deliver China?" Khrushchev replied cryptically: "That is your problem." Harriman tried again: "Supposing their rockets are targeted against you?" The usually voluble Soviet leader was silent.[18]

In due course Khrushchev said: "Let us walk over to our dinner." They left the office and strolled through the Kremlin, once Stalin's gloomy fortress and now a public park, toward the Old Palace. Harriman remarked that he saw few security men around. "I don't like being surrounded by security men," Khrushchev said. "In Stalin's time we never knew whether they were protecting or watching us." As they walked a large crowd gathered behind them. Khrushchev turned and said: "This is Gospodin Garriman. We've just signed a test-ban treaty. I'm going to take him to dinner. Do you think he has earned his dinner?" The people applauded and applauded.[19]

In Washington, where the implications of the Russian-Chinese split sank in slowly, President Kennedy welcomed the treaty as "a shaft of light cut into the darkness." He quoted a Chinese proverb; "A journey of a thousand miles must begin with a single step." One after another the hard-liners of the Cold War came forward to urge the Senate to reject the pact. The "father of the hydrogen bomb," Edward Teller, predicted, "If you ratify this treaty you will have given away the future safety of the country." Admiral Arthur Radford, the man who almost brought "massive retaliation" to Indochina, voiced "deep concern" that ratification would "change the course of world history." "I'm not sure that the reduction of tensions is necessarily a good thing," testified Admiral Lewis Strauss, former Atomic Energy Commission chairman. For the Joint Chiefs of Staff General Maxwell Taylor said their "most serious reservation" was "the fear of a euphoria in the West which will eventually reduce our vigilance."

For their approval the Joint Chiefs had exacted a stiff price—commitment from the President that the United States would continue underground testing, a pledge that the government would be ready to resume atmospheric testing at short notice, more funds for strengthening of detection facilities, the promise of maintenance of the country's nuclear laboratories. The sum of all this, wrote Richard Rovere in *The New Yorker*, was that "an agreement intended to limit nuclear testing" had been turned into a "limited warrant for increased nuclear testing" underground.[20]

As the debate dragged on, the President was called upon to present a medal voted by Congress to Bob Hope for his trips to entertain the million Americans stationed abroad in the Cold War. Kennedy invited the entire membership of Congress to the White House rose garden for the ceremony. "This is the only bill we've gotten by lately," explained the President wryly, "so we would like to have them." Hope, professing apprehension at the sight of so many Senators and Representatives ("for a while it looked like a congressional investigation"), recalled that in the Second World War "I played in the South Pacific while the President was there—a very gay, carefree young man at the time. All he had to worry about then was the enemy."

Senator after senator placed it in the record that nothing in the treaty set any limit on the freedom of the United States to manufacture and stockpile all the bombs it wanted to, and that it said nothing to keep the United States from developing yet more powerful and destructive weapons. When some Senators wondered out loud whether it would be in the interests of the United States to stop atmospheric testing when the neutron bomb might be in the offing, Secretary Rusk responded that the neutron bomb would not be a substitute for the existing arsenal, since it was a weapon that killed only people. And does not destroy property, added Senator Humphrey quickly.[21]

Frank Lausche, Democrat of Ohio, read out eighteen cases of pledges broken by "Red Russia" and asked challengingly: "What can we expect?" But the retreat at Moscow to a ban merely on tests in the air, in space and under water, coupled with the assurance that the military could go on testing underground, overcame the fears that the United States Senate might be placing trust in Communists. On September 24, 1963, neither intending nor expecting to end the Cold War by their action, the senators voted 80-to-19 to ratify the Treaty of Moscow.[22]

ON THE OTHER SIDE of the world the explosion of the Chinese-Russian conflict into the public view as a result of the Treaty of Moscow was even more decisively disruptive than Khrushchev feared. The first shattering eruption was followed by a scandalously undisciplined airing of recriminations and charges. Gone was all pretense of the workers of the world uniting. In full view of the capitalists, Communists battled

Communists. Neither side would budge. In a different world, even a few of the grievances proclaimed would have led to war between the two countries. With such "fraternal" parties, it could be said, who needed bourgeois imperialists for foes?

In a series of nine lengthy articles published at intervals over the next year the Chinese Communists went back over every bitter row in a conflict that they now said had been steadily building up for seven years. No such violent, detailed and comprehensive attacks had been heard since Stalin turned on the Yugoslavs in 1949. The Chinese denounced the Soviet signature on the Treaty of Moscow as a "dirty fake," a "fraud," and a "sellout." They charged Khrushchev by name as a "traitor to Marxism-Leninism" who had forfeited any claim to be the lawful Soviet ruler. "He who claims to be the legitimate heir of Stalin," railed Peking, "now joins hands with the chieftains of imperialism."[23]

At intervals and in equally vicious language the Russians, always strongest in heavy artillery, thundered back. But in this recklessness and supposed madness in professing to welcome nuclear war, the correspondence showed Mao and his coworkers as shrewd analysts in foreign-policy matters. Almost pathological they might be about their crazy schemes for communizing 600,000,000 people in one fell swoop between seedtime and harvest; yet their nondomestic programs seemed founded on rational enough considerations.

They pitilessly dissected the selfish and nationalist motivations hidden beneath the Russians' language of international solidarity and devotion to Socialism. The Russians, they pointed out, were always ready with offers of help *after* an emergency, as in their statement of support for China in 1958 when Mao had just called off his push to take the offshore islands on which Chiang Kai-shek's remnants still held out under United States protection. Equally shrewd was their assessment of the Soviet government's predicament in the face of the "fraternal state"—it was more like a Frankenstein monster—that it had helped create on its Asian flank:

> The Soviet government is insolent enough to say that we are able to criticize them only because China enjoys the protection of Soviet nuclear weapons. Well, then, leaders of the Soviet Union, please continue to protect us awhile with your nuclear weapons. We shall continue to criticize you—and we hope you will have the courage to argue the matter out with us.[24]

The Russians on their side all too readily showed their fear of the Chinese. Over and over their arguments resolved into a single reiterated question: "Why do you need nuclear weapons when we are protecting you anyway?" It was a question that the Americans, for all their open society, had not yet had to debate with their German and Japanese allies. Taunted to the limits of fury by the Chinese on this count, the Russians went to strident lengths to prove how irresponsibly nonchalant the Chinese were about nuclear war. Over and over they recited Mao's famous words about 300 million Chinese surviving the holocaust when nobody at all would be left over in any other atomized land. They choked in apoplectic incoherence over "asides" dropped by Chinese officials that if "small nations" such as Czechoslovakia and Italy disappeared from the face of the earth, well, it would be in the interests of the socialist camp as a whole. The Chinese could retort, though they never quite went so far, that such statements were meant to unnerve the capitalists: had not Khrushchev often indulged in pretty much the same graveyard game? The Chinese argument at bottom was this: it paid to be tough when talking with the capitalists and to be unyielding about principles; this did not mean that it was not also well to be prudent in action and flexible on concrete problems. Altogether the Chinese had not taken great risks at all when they made their moves on the Indian border in 1959. Their activity—as apart from their words—in the Third World had not been so much revolutionary as cautious. Theirs was a caution which argued contrarily that they really did seek world revolution, that they were not striving recklessly for leadership in Communist parties in this country or that but working warily for the real thing—victory.[25]

The Russians, with some justice, accused the Chinese of giving a racist tinge to their variety of Communism. No doubt Peking's chief activities were most noticeable among the postcolonial peoples of Asia, Africa and Latin America where white was the color of oppression. And the Chinese always tried to portray Soviet Communism as "the rich man's Communism"—cautious, sedate, working hand-in-hand with imperialism; as against which Peking extended the helping hand to the *real* wretched and underprivileged of the world, or at least to the parties purporting to represent them, which had nothing to lose but Soviet subsidies and invitations to Moscow.[26]

Another aspect of the conflict brought to light by these violent exchanges was the matter of disorders and troubles along their common border. The Chinese alleged that in the spring of 1962:

> the leaders of the Russian party used their organs and personnel in Sinkiang China to carry out large scale subversive acts in the Ili region, and enticed tens of thousands of Chinese citizens into going into the Soviet Union.

This was a bit thick as any sort of explanation for what seems to have been a mass flight of Sinkiang Kazakhs to the Soviet Union. On their part the Russians alleged more than 5,000 border violations by the Chinese in 1962 alone. The implications of this aspect of the dispute grew even more obvious in later years.[27]

How far, then, when such forces thrust into view as the conflict became open, was this dispute ideological? It is alien to Communist habits of thought to allow major disagreements on policies to arise by pure accident or out of differing national interests. Thus in their fulminating polemics both sides groped for deeper explanations of what divided them. But the basic one was this: Russia was now highly industrialized whereas China was not—but had 600 million people. The Chinese saw Russia's intermittent efforts to reach an accommodation with the United States as expressing not only personal cowardice and treason on Khrushchev's part; it was also, in their view, a "revisionist" backsliding on the part of the Russian élite. Viewed in this way, the trouble went all the way back to the original denunciation of Stalin which, they now insisted, lowered the prestige of Communism in the international arena and opened the door to the evolution of Soviet society and policies on the pattern of Yugoslavia. The fact that Stalin would have been harder on the Chinese than his successors, and that in all likelihood he would not have confined himself to verbal attack, was conveniently overlooked.

The Russians, on their side, saw the Chinese grievances as an equal departure from the Marxist-Leninist orthodoxy. The Chinese experiment with communes, their stress on personal asceticism, their encouragement of farfetched revolutionary attempts in Iraq and elsewhere—all these were to the Russians manifestations of ultra-Trotskyite extremism. China's unwillingness to subordinate its policies to those of the Soviet Union was both evidence for and substance of a many-sided heresy.[28]

This proneness of practical, often cynical, men to rationalize a quarrel in terms of ideology was not without its uses. It enabled both sides to evade the nagging question: did Communism, or any universal ideology, make sense in the modern world? This sort of rushing for reassurance into the higher abstractions was not a vice limited to Communists. Ever since 1914 there had been a tendency of statesmen to universalize their aims and couch their objectives in ideological rhetoric. On this count the West, with its slogans of "making the world safe for democracy" and "preserving the free world," was caught in the same kind of dilemmas as Mao and Khrushchev.

The problem of China was too much for the men in Moscow. A Stalin might have been able to renounce the Chinese alliance and secure an official condemnation of China from the rest of the Communist parties of the world, thus casting the Chinese Communists outside the Moscow-controlled Communist bloc as Stalin in fact expelled the Yugoslavs in 1948. But when Khrushchev, and later his successors, moved to call a conference for this express purpose, the other Communist parties were able to frustrate any such action. From this time onward, the Soviet Union was no longer the sole center of international Communism, and it had to compete with China for the allegiance of Communist parties and national liberation movements everywhere.[29]

THOUGH it stopped the nuclear powers from further polluting the atmosphere, the Treaty of Moscow of itself carried little importance. It limited nothing that mattered significantly to the signers. It is true that among the hundred nations that adhered in the course of time was West Germany. But it placed no limit for instance on the manufacture and stockpiling of nuclear arms and missiles, and the arms race roared on (the United States alone piling up some 50,000 nuclear weapons) until the two superpowers agreed in 1972 at Helsinki to limit defensive missiles and to at least talk about placing the first curbs on their production of offensive missiles.

At the time the sole sequel to the signing of the treaty was joint support by the United States and Russia a month later for a United Nations Assembly resolution against orbiting nuclear weapons in space. In fact, after open eruption of the Russian-Chinese conflict a more far-reaching détente between Russia and America became less likely than before. A nonaggression treaty such as Khrushchev had proposed during the Moscow negotiations would have meant the West's implicit recognition of East Germany and of Poland's territorial gains under the Potsdam Declaration. It would have strengthened the Russian case against the Chinese charge that they were appeasing the United States without getting anything in return. As it was, Khrushchev had to give a warning on the eve of signing the treaty:

> This of course does not mean, comrades, that one should let oneself be prey to illusions that the dawn of new relations between us and the United States has already risen. No.

Measures of further détente would have strengthened Khrushchev's personal position but this was never the point. The United States now had less inducement to negotiate.[30]

For the Treaty of Moscow had a historical importance wholly incommensurate with its contents and utterly unintended and unexpected by its signers. It was the act that drove the Chinese Communists to a break with Russia so official and final that the United States government—even the United States government—could no longer doubt that the monolithic monster against which it had girded for nearly twenty years was no monolith at all. There was—the actions of the Chinese and Russian governments confirmed it—no such thing after all as the tentacled, conspiratorial, centrally controlled and coordinated "international Communism" against which the whole edifice of the "free" world's counterideology of anti-Communism had been erected. Instead of one vast spreading superpower of socialism, there were two—and none knew better than the Americans who had got tangled with it in North Korea that the contender in Peking had the makings of a second one.

It took an extremely long time for Americans to absorb this staggering information. The reports that a rift was in the making between Moscow and Peking had been officially dismissed again and again by their government as diabolical rumors put out by Communists to seduce Western hopes and weaken Western vigilance. America long ago had brushed off as traitors those China specialists in the State Department who had foreseen the divergence from the very beginning. The stertorous recoil from the frenzied shock of the Communists' victory in China followed by their even more traumatically unexpected onslaught in Korea had paralyzed the nation's senses and rendered the country incapable of perceiving or crediting the multiplying signs of the late 1950s that Peking was pressing its own destiny. It was hard enough for America to bring itself to the point of signing an agreement with Moscow, and only the brute fact of Moscow's capacity to unleash its own nuclear destruction on the country, coupled with a timely demonstration in Cuba that Moscow feared destruction even more, carried the United States finally to the negotiating table and to the all but noncommittal agreement embodied in the Treaty of Moscow.

And so, finally, it was done. The minor and elaborately marginal agreement, the treaty that skirted any limitation on armaments and steered clear of any curbs on sovereignty, capitalist or socialist, was signed. Instantly and shockingly, the indivisible, implacable, dictatorially regimented and demonically disciplined adversary against which the United States and its allies had stood cataleptically galvanized for twenty years—broke in two.

This was the end of the Cold War, of the eyeball-to-eyeball confrontation, as Dean Rusk called it, that dominated the history of the world and the life of America from the end of the Second World War. It was not marked by any speeches, it was not celebrated by any parades. It was not even, in the old fashioned sense, a victory. But the United States relaxed from the petrified, immobilized stance in which it had for so long stared at the transglobal adversary—all that time without much thought of anything else in the world except as it could be made to matter in this fixated confrontation.

F O R   T W E N T Y   Y E A R S   the United States had been up against a single adversary—international Communism managed from Moscow. Now there was a turn away from bipolarity. Through the very hour that Khrushchev signed the treaty, experts in the West could speculate about the possible "maturing" of Soviet society, about Kremlin decisions to turn away from futile expansionist adventures to more rewarding internal development tasks, about crafty Soviet stratagems of "two steps forward and one step back" in hopes that when the tension relaxed the West would slack up and Russia would gain time to reorient its economy and technology for the next go-around. To the end there was no doubt that the Russians would have expanded if the United States had not contained them.

But now, as it appeared, the Russians and Chinese were at each others' throats. Suddenly, they needed no American containing. They were containing each other. This was the tremendous new turn in world affairs that followed from the Treaty of Moscow.

For America, two consequences flowed from this drastically new assessment. The first was domestic, the second foreign. The first was a tremendous surge, after a preoccupation with stopping international Communism that had taken up all governmental energies for eighteen years, to attend to the neglected problems of education, health, welfare. The second, arising out of the thrust of anti-Communist ideology and the military-industrial buildup of the Cold War, but restrained till now by fear that international Communism would unite to stop it, was an American drive to intervene in force in Southeast Asia.

T H E   D E T E N T E   with Moscow brought a dramatic turn in the nation's attention to what Walter Lippmann called "the unfinished business of America," the pentup need for education, housing, health, welfare and aid for cities.

Very late in the Cold War America woke up to the fact that it had become an urban nation. The society's near obsession with "international Communism," the domestic turmoil over the Southern civil rights movement and the violence at Little Rock in 1957, all hindered this perception, and so did the overwhelmingly rural cast of mind in Congress and all the other lawmaking bodies of the republic. But the sheer weight of demographic numbers, coupled with the rising frustrations felt by individuals in a society whose institutions had ceased to correspond with reality, finally brought the country to awareness that it was not the same place any more. Thus the 1960 census showed that ninety-seven percent of the decade's growth in population—adding 28 million more Americans—had taken place in the nation's metropolitan areas. At the same time 11 of the 12 biggest cities, and 25 of the 50 biggest, lost population. Urban decay, crime, high taxes and deteriorating schools in the cities cried out to America so blatantly that something had to be done. By 1960 almost half the metropolitan population had moved out to the suburbs and all of these people had glaring problems too—poor transportation, overcrowded schools and recreational facilities, tightly circumscribed tax-bases. It was time, in short, to face the big change, and act.[31]

Up to this point the lawmaking organs of American society were not organized to act. They were in the hands of men opposed to such action. The problems were in the cities, and the legislatures represented the countryside. Basically this was because neither the executive nor the legislative branch of the government could bring itself to initiate and carry through the reapportionment of seats at the expense of sitting representatives that the population shift called for. Once again, therefore, as in the impasse over the race question after the Second World War, the judicial branch finally intervened to break the paralysis of representative government. The road to enforcing relief for the cities in the teeth of rural resistance led through the federal courts.

In 1959 four Tennessee cities joined to bring a suit against the apportionment system that left them grossly underrepresented in the state legislature. The four counties in which they were located held 38% of Tennessee's population, yet they had only 22% of the seats in the assembly and 20% of the seats in the senate. Not unnaturally, in such a misshapen legislature, the state wound up contributing $225 to the education of each child in rural school districts and only $90 for each pupil in the cities. This was the story in every one of the fifty states. In Georgia, Florida and California, the legislative imbalance was even worse. In none was there less than a two-to-one disparity between the most populated and least populated districts—in the case of Connecticut the disparity was 242-to-1. In Congress the imbalance between districts was substantial, and yet nobody seemed to be doing anything about it.

Finally the Supreme Court stepped in. In 1962, after the four Tenessee cities had appealed from an adverse lower-court ruling, the high court handed down the first of a series of major decisions that directed federal courts to enforce in all legislative apportionments the principle of "one man, one vote." The effect was to give the nation's metropolitan areas their due representation in all elected bodies including the House of

Representatives. The legislative ascendancy of rural America was dealt a rude blow; and with rising power among the lawmakers the cities pressed their new advantage as the Cold War drew to an end.[32]

As the nation turned to domestic reform a large part of its agenda for action lay ready and waiting, some of it pending since the Fair Dealing days of President Truman. Between old measures and new, a tremendous volume of social legislation poured through Congress in the first two years after the Cold War—more than at any time since the New Deal of 1933.

A startling shift occurred in the field of education. A coalition of conservative Southern Democrats and Republicans had long blocked all significant federal aid to schools except in the guise of Cold War measures. In the scrambling rush to attack poverty in the cities, the Administration overcame old fears of racial integration and federal control and momentarily stilled the violent dispute over whether Catholic schools should share in federal aid. Francis Keppel, who left the deanship of the Harvard Graduate School of Education to become Kennedy's and then Johnson's Commissioner of Education, helped persuade both sides in the fight to back a program that stressed aid for the child rather than the school. The Elementary and Secondary Education Act which Keppel steered to passage in 1965 opened the way. By authorizing aid for children attending both public and parochial schools but providing for control of expenditures by public agencies, the law broke the dam and sent a mighty flood of federal funds to the country's hard-pressed local school districts. In the next fifteen years 25,000 school districts would receive $60 billion from Washington for libraries, textbooks, supplementary services, research, teacher-training and special aid for low-income schools. This was not all. The Higher Education Act of 1965 doubled construction grants to colleges, created a federal program of "education opportunity" grants (worth an average $500 to each of 140,000 low-income students the first year), and created a National Teachers Corps to staff poverty-area schools.[33]

America finally entered the twentieth century in the field of government health insurance. Medicare, the federal program enacted in 1965, provided hospital and nursing home care under the Social Security system for all citizens over 65. The plan paid all hospital bills beyond the first $40 for sixty days, and paid all hospital charges above $10 a day for an additional 30 days after that. For elderly persons who paid a $3 monthly premium Medicare also offered a $50-deductible insurance on doctor bills. Best of all, by a little-noticed provision, states could obtain federal funds to fund another program, called Medicaid, that helped poor people not covered by Medicare.

In the rush to catch up on domestic change, Congress, brushing off a Southern filibuster, put through a sweeping Civil Rights law in 1964 and followed this up a year later with a voting rights bill that finally opened the way for blacks to exercise their franchise in the Deep South as freely as in the urban North. In the great outpouring of laws Congress also enacted a $1.1 billion measure for housing and urban renewal, appropriated $375 million for mass transportation, beefed up public works programs in the cities, and set up a permanent food-stamp program to give the urban needy direct benefit from federal purchasing of farm surpluses. In 1964, in a step reflecting the country's new concern for environmental protection Congress voted to establish a National Wilderness System including "wild rivers," Western timberlands, and beaches near cities.[34]

Every report of the President's Council of Economic Advisers since 1946 had stressed the overriding importance of business growth. In its first report after the Cold War ended the Council introduced a new priority for America:

> We cannot leave the further wearing away of poverty to the general progress of the economy. A faster reduction of poverty will require that the lower fifth of our families be able to earn a larger share of the national output.

In 1962, when President Kennedy was told that to bring unemployment down from 6% to 5% would require an outlay of $5 billion a year for five years, he dismissed the idea. After the Cold War, it was different. A few days after the Council of Economic Advisers issued its report President Johnson went before Congress to lead the nation in a new kind of war —a "war against poverty."

Of all the multitude of reforms started after the Treaty of Moscow, the war on poverty was the hardest to put across to the people of the nation. The job fell to Sargent Shriver, a personable Marylander who had married Kennedy's sister Eunice and had built up the Peace Corps of technically trained volunteers sent to aid underdeveloped countries in the last years of the Cold War. Shriver could see that the American people might be tired of waging wars and wars. The very success of America in other spheres, he acknowledged, made it hard to fight effectively against such a backyard foe as hunger or want. America had scored tremendous successes, he said, on its frontier, in the drama of immigration, by its technology; but—

> the frontier inspired a tradition of individualism that sometimes made the needed social action difficult to achieve . . . Immigration raised problems of discrimination against minorities. And the prosperity created by technological ingenuity often blinded Americans to the plight of the poor.

From his Office of Economic Opportunity Shriver mounted a staggering variety of programs in aid of the 35 million Americans shut out of the finger-licking abundance of the consumer society. Most of these programs served the cities, and many served blacks. The most urgent undertook to train and retrain men in skills the society needed. The Job Corps was started to take the 15% of the population aged 15 to 21 who were out of school and out of work (the proportion was 25% among young blacks) from their city and rural slum surroundings and give them useful work and basic schooling at Job Corps Training Centers. Other programs provided work-training for youths in their home towns, and a chance for children of the poor to go to college on "work-study" grants. When the "service" sector of the economy was growing faster than any other, it seemed to make sense that poor people should find jobs helping run social and educational agencies set up chiefly to meet their needs.

Shriver's office encouraged local groups to draw up blueprints for community action projects. "Community action," which at once came under fire from congressional conservatives, gave the neighborhood poor a chance to shape their own community-improvement projects. They started health clinics, programs for the aged, tutoring centers for dropouts, job-training for youths and adults, guidance and counseling centers for needy families, and day-care centers for children of working mothers. Shriver's OEO also took on the Head Start program, a scheme that had half a million teachers and volunteer workers running some 13,400 child-development centers where in eight summer weeks some 560,000 pre-school children from disadvantaged homes got close attention to help them on to a good start in first grade in the fall.[35]

The huge reform program of the two post-Cold War years swelled the federal budget by forty billion dollars. Imposing as this outlay was, it was too little and too late. Medicare was not a perfect measure. It helped only the old, and then only in a cumbersome and limited way. It gave physicians control over fees, which led to many scandals. And it was only a belated first step toward the day when, as in all other advanced countries, health care would be a matter of right to all citizens and serious illness need not be a passport to bankruptcy. By tying the educational reforms to its campaign against poverty, moreover, Washigton ran into trouble. The war against poverty did not go well. There was not enough money, and the funds were spread over too many programs, some of them hastily conceived and ill-run. The sociologist Herbert Gans has said that no numerical majority will ever tax itself or redistribute its wealth to make up income deficiencies for a minority. If millions of Americans resented WPA when the economy lay flat on its back in the 1930s, Congress, press and public proved dyspeptically critical of the antipoverty program in the overfed 1960s.

Faster than these programs could be enacted, and long before they would take effect, the forces pent up during the Cold War burst through the institutional constraints of the American society. In the early 1960s, when students from the north began trekking south to help blacks fight for their civil rights, the young began to come alive after the long sleep of the postwar years. "The Age of Complacency is ending," wrote C. Wright Mills. Youths from eleven campuses met at Port Huron, Michigan, to found Students for a Democratic Society and demanded "participatory democracy," starting at the colleges they came from. One of the thousand white volunteers who participated in the "Freedom Summer" voter-registration drive in Mississippi was a University of California graduate student named Mario Savio.

Back in Berkeley that fall Savio joined students defying a new rule ordering activists to remove their literature tables from the sidewalk outside Sather Gate. When police arrested a student, others surrounded a police car for thirty-three hours. Freed, the student proclaimed a new era: "You can't trust anyone over thirty." Savio, by now leader of what was called the Free Speech movement, was charged with having bitten a policeman in the thigh. Defiance mounted. The students took over the administration building, and started a free university. After Joan Baez sang "We Shall Overcome" Savio delivered a speech condemning the university as a machine that treated students as raw material:

> It becomes odious so we must put our bodies against the gears, against the wheels. . . . and make the machine stop until we're free.

When the police arrested 814 demonstrators, the students struck, and the faculty, in an uproarious meeting, upheld their right to free speech. Before it was over the chancellor was forced out, then President Clark Kerr, and the ferment spread right across America. At the University of Kansas authorities arrested 115 students for a sit-in protesting discrimination in fraternities and sororities. At Yale students demonstrated against the university for letting a popular professor go. At St. John's University in New York City, the largest Catholic university in the country, students denounced campus censorship and a ban on campus speakers. The campus unrest did not end for years.[36]

A year after the Cold War ended, the cities began to explode. Looting and rioting broke out in the Watts district of Los Angeles. Five days later 34 were dead, 1000 were under arrest and much of Watts was in ashes. City officials blamed civil rights workers and Communists for the uprising. But 30% of the adult males in the biggest black ghetto west of the Rockies were out of work. Later the violence burst out in Newark, where police beat up a black taxi-driver and 25 died, and in Detroit, where

32 died. Before the outburst ended in Detroit 7000 were arrested, and 5000 were made homeless by fires that burned out much of the center city. The violence erupted in Washington. President Johnson, who had proclaimed "We Shall Overcome" as he launched the war on poverty, watched helpless from a White House window as the fires of burning homes and stores reddened the capital sky.[37]

The assassination of President Kennedy in November, 1963, of Martin Luther King in 1967, of Robert Kennedy in 1968, like the rioting in the cities and the alienation of the young, were tragic sequels to the Cold War. The President's murderer, Lee Harvey Oswald, carried within his sick soul the contradictions of the whole era. Trained as a Marine, he had defected to Russia only to break away from that experience after three years, drifted with his Russian bride to Texas, involved himself briefly with Castro Cuba, and finally, at odds with his wife, his neighbors and himself, bought a mail-order rifle and vented all his frustrations by killing the President with a shot from a window as the motorcade rode by his place of employment. Resorting to much the same sort of sharp-shooter's stealthy ambush in Memphis, the twice-imprisoned criminal James Earl Ray, almost certainly a hireling, wreaked the wrath of a white supremacy that Martin Luther King had helped topple when the United States was forced to the conviction that legal segregation of the races was too high a price to pay in the Cold War competition with Russia. Sirhan Sirhan, the killer of Robert Kennedy, was a child of the Cold War. Reared in Palestinian refugee camps and brought to California by his family at the time of the Suez crisis, he shot Kennedy down in crazed protest at United States intervention in the Middle East. Political assassinations, large-scale rioting in the cities, and finally a national crisis of confidence—all were unhappy conditions tracing to origins in the Cold War era. Estrangement from authority and institutions of society, already widespread, was increased by the Cold War legacy of Vietnam.

The American involvement in Vietnam had Cold War roots. In the conviction that to save Europe from Communism the United States must support the French everywhere, the Truman administration delivered the first commitment to help defend Indochina in 1949. In the conviction that to save Southeast Asia from Communism the United States must hold South Vietnam, the Eisenhower administration established and propped up the Diem tyranny from 1954 to 1961. Still persuaded that Vietnam's fall would topple neighboring non-Communist states, the Kennedy administration sent in 25,000 military "advisers" to back up the next set of rulers in Vietnam. But it was the Johnson administration that two years after the Cold War made the fateful decision to commit "the sons and brothers of America" in war against Communism on the Asian mainland.[38]

Summation

LOOKING BACK over the pattern of Cold War developments in relation to what was taking place in the American society, certain things seem reasonably clear. Anything that happens affects the future. Within events some elements have more pervasive influence than others. In tracing the influence of the Cold War upon American life, at least seventeen causal relationships touched on in preceding chapters can be singled out.

§1.] When President Truman in April 1947 sought $400,000,-000 emergency aid for Greece and Turkey, he may have thought thereby to contain the spread of Russian influence in the Mediterranean and to demonstrate that Communism could not march unchecked out of Eastern Europe. But to get the votes in Congress for this measure he also took Senator Vandenberg's advice to "scare hell out of the American people." Promulgating the Truman Doctrine, he ended up in effect proclaiming America's Cold War. By the time he had finished removing all the qualifiers from his draft speech, he was telling Congress that it was "we or they" in a world where the forces of light, led by the United States, lined up against the forces of darkness.

Although the sinister instigators of evil against whom America was summoned to stand were not named in the speech, they were identified in every newspaper and radio account as world Communism led by Soviet Russia. And when President Truman in these circumstances proclaimed that "freedom was threatened around the world" and that the United States would "support" and "assist" any nation resisting "subjugation," the impact of his words rolled far beyond the point needed to get a favorable appropriation out of Congress. Indeed the President's aid program passed through Congress, and very likely the Truman Doctrine stopped the rise of Communism in Greece, even if Greece kept its place in the "free" world thereafter largely under militarist regimes that curbed the very freedom that Truman called threatened. In all likelihood the Truman Doctrine also had much to do with keeping major Russian influence out of the Middle East for another eight years. One might go farther and grant that the Truman Doctrine—along with other American policies —had some part in preventing Communists, perhaps even Russian Communists, from taking over parts of Europe west of the Elbe. Hence the declaration can be said generally to have accomplished the aims avowed by Truman and his advisers when the President came out with it in 1947.

But that was not the end of the affair. Ironically, the Truman Doctrine was promulgated just when (and no doubt because) mankind had acquired a weapon that could destroy any state. In the wake of the unforgotten Japanese sneak attack, and in the presence of the new military technology the A-bomb exemplified, many Americans sensed that their long era of what Historian Vann Woodward has called "free security" had ended. Even in the hour of great triumph they were not sure about the future, and some felt fear. "Confidence," said Ambrose Bierce "is being mistaken at the top of one's voice." In such moods, one result of the sweeping change proclaimed by Truman was to attach to the international policies of the United States such overriding precedence that, reversing the economic determinism of Marx, events and decisions involving American interests overseas began at times to sway events and decisions back in the homeland, instead of the other way around.

This is not to minimize the generally dynamic outthrust of the United States in the Cold War period. Many of the foregoing pages bear witness to the momentum of the nation's history, to the expansiveness of its institutions, to the enveloping zeal for the gospel of growth, to the aggressive drive above all of the American military to widen its influence and of American industry to enlarge its stake everywhere in the world. What turned out to carry large political, social and cultural importance, however, an importance that escaped the calculations of Truman and his internationalist-minded advisers, was the imponderable element of fear that came over people with respect to the nation's security as the President led it through such a swift and sweeping swing toward destinations and responsibilities unknown. Clutching the A-bomb but with Pearl Harbor seared fresh in memory, these Americans found themselves called less than two years after V-J Day to a new and worldwide confrontation with Communism.

The impact was swift and far-reaching. The response went far beyond the quickening of citizens' concern for "free institutions" and "guarantees of individual liberties" that the President had summoned them to defend. As America's press, radio, churches, schools, industries and unions led an ideological mobilization against Communism, there was no great rush of patriots to dedicate themselves to defense of the Bill of Rights. Instead, along with some well-intentioned complacencies about the Constitution and the dignity of man, dark forces of fear and hate were loosed in the land. Elements in the society that had long treated "American" as a proprietary word now loudly and aggressively defined it to exclude many of their fellow citizens. They formed vigilante groups and circulated lists of people who had been so "un-American" as to join with Communists in supporting the New Deal, Republican Spain or the Russian wartime alliance just ended.

As one government body after another endorsed or even added more names to these blacklists, the subordinates of the President who had proclaimed the Truman Doctrine commenced what Richard Hofstadter later called "the Grand Inquisition of the '50s." Although the Communist party was said by J. Edgar Hoover at the time to number 54,174, the Truman government arrested and secured the conviction of its twelve top leaders as leaders not of a party, but a "conspiracy." The government also dismissed employees who had shown any kind of "sympathetic association" with the listed subversive organizations. These actions had extensive and unintended consequences. One was to create conditions for a government service lacking in independent thought and hardly characterized by the courage to criticize. The impact was wide throughout the country. Government inquisitors cast their net so wide that over a span of ten years perhaps one in every four American families underwent the experience of a checkup on some member's loyalty.

Beyond Government itself, the employing agencies of the society took their cues from the aggressive band of list-makers, and began not only to dismiss the people named but fired or refrained from hiring others in fear of running afoul of the witch-hunters. Even among those never subjected to this kind of retributive publicity the effect was often to compel caution and compromise, trimming and punch-pulling. When parents, neighbors, teachers, preachers, employers and other community leaders complied with this conscriptive consensus, when school boards began decreeing that nothing "controversial" should be mentioned in classrooms, when newspapers and television programs imparted—along with news of atomic blasts—the same subduing signals, an inevitable result was that the very children growing up reflected the cowed conformity of the times. The outcome, so pronounced as to be remarked on widely by the mid-1960s, was a great crowd of safe, submissive children, a lot of guarded, noncommittal collegians looking to safe berths in the interior of large corporations. One of the scarifying results of the Cold War in America was its impact on the children. Put it down as an unintended consequence of the Truman Doctrine: the President had so far succeeded in scaring America that he silenced a whole generation of its young.

§2.] This was only the beginning. Other consequences unforeseen by the decision-makers of the Cold War followed upon the loss of China, the Soviet intrusion into ownership of the A-bomb, spy trials and the outbreak of the Korean War. The force of these unsettling events, which struck the United States one after the other in the late 1940s, was to raise fears of conspiracy and betrayal in the nation to a high pitch, and to send them coursing through the land in waves of hysteria and paranoia. What followed, as "loyalty" purges extended from Washington to state capitals and down to community and even office, shop and block levels, was one of the most shameful periods in the history of American democracy. Thus a consequence of the Cold War was to import into the United States the very spy mania and obsessions about conspiracy that had been among the most loathsome characteristics of its Soviet adversary.

§3.] Anti-Communism had been endemic to American life since 1917, and the stock in trade of certain rightwing politicians and newspaper owners for many years. But an important by-product of the Cold War mobilization was a new variety of anti-Communism imported in the earliest years of the East-West conflict. This was the version of the ex-Communists, and it gained great acceptance in the United States when the Grand Inquisition brought such ex-Communist intellectuals as Whittaker Chambers into the glare of publicity. This version identified Communism as a totalitarianism like the lately vanquished Nazism—and like Nazism bent irretrievably on world conquest and war. It made free with the "Munich analogy"—to negotiate with the Communists was to ap-

pease them and suffer the same disaster that befell the Western democracies after their Munich agreement with Hitler in 1938. Gaining currency as an unintended and largely fortuitous circumstance of the "loyalty" purge period, these perceptions crucially reinforced the
determination at this stage of the Cold War to form American policy in
a military mold.

On the crest of these anticipations, a bill to ban the Communist
party that had been brought up at the time of the Communist coup
against Czechoslovakia in 1948 was revived, and the prevailing mood
demanded repressive action. Truman resisted the proposed measure as
"worse than the Sedition Act of 1798." Years later almost every provision
of the 1950 McCarran-Nixon Act, passed by acclamation over Truman's
veto, was struck down by the Supreme Court as violative of constitutional
rights. The law placed severe limits on citizens' rights to travel, on freedom of entry into the United States. Although it did not in so many words
outlaw the Communist party, the measure required the party's officers to
register with the Justice Department and members to declare the names
of all clubs, societies and lodges they belonged to. A "concentration camp
clause" provided that all persons thought to be subversive should be
locked up as a menace to security whenever the President declared a
national emergency—and six installations in various parts of the country
were made ready to receive them. Here was another unintended consequence of the Cold War: for two decades (until Congress quietly repealed
the measure in 1972) the United States equipped itself with the same sort
of "slave" institution it abhorred as a hallmark of the totalitarian tyranny
it fought against.

§4.] The unintended consequence of this wild series of Cold
War events, which reached their peak after the Communist invasion of
Korea, was the rise to power of Senator Joseph McCarthy. In the midst
of its list-making purges, the government had just convicted Alger Hiss
of perjury and Klaus Fuchs had confessed in London to passing bomb
secrets to the Russians. On the issue of Communists in government,
McCarthy catapulted to the top, but for such a demagogue it was im-
material that he never ferreted out a Communist worth mentioning.
Waving "documents" and charging that large numbers of Communists
had infiltrated the State Department, he inaugurated "McCarthyism,"
the expression of the period's most violent, reckless mood. In McCarthy's
hands innuendo, threat and indiscriminate accusation, wielded with a flair
for publicity, indifference for truth and important support from embit-

tered Republican leaders, became blunt instruments for bludgeoning all who got in his way. He hazed bureaucrats, hounded senators and brazenly denounced the principal decision-makers of the Cold War as anti-Communist "traitors." Such was the power of McCarthyism that for a crucial four years of the Cold War it inhibited both Presidents Truman and Eisenhower from taking essential actions on both the international and home front.

Thus in consequence of the influence of McCarthyism, the entire State Department nucleus of trained, experienced China experts, comparable in every way with the group trained up to provide reporting and advice about Soviet Russia, was dispersed and its ablest members drummed out of the service just when the need for appraising and dealing with revolutionary changes in China cried out for their skills. In consequence of the influence of McCarthyism, the United States was enjoined from negotiating a relaxation of the Cold War in the "thaw" after Stalin's successors began ruling Russia. In consequence of McCarthyism, the State Department suffered a lasting decline in prestige and self-confidence and influence at the very time in the Cold War when stress on military strategy and spending demanded the ablest and most forceful assertion of the department's diplomatic, political and foreign-policy-shaping functions. In short, the mobilization of America for the Cold War had culminated in its immobilization by a virulently anti-Communist McCarthyism, with the unintended result that when circumstances changed and the interests of the United States might have called for certain action, Washington could not move.

In the recital of unintended consequences of the Cold War, no summary of the impact of McCarthyism can omit its effect upon the higher levels of government in Washington. In the frenzy of the 1950s the nation dealt ungenerously with some of its most useful public servants. The names of only two need be mentioned—General George C. Marshall, organizer of American fighting forces in their greatest war, who McCarthy said had "sold his country and would sell his own grandmother"; and Dr. Robert Oppenheimer, organizer of the wartime A-bomb project, who was publicly disgraced and stigmatized as a "security risk." In the Senate, where McCarthy was feared especially for his power at the polls, an atmosphere of threat and even blackmail led to the suicide of a senior member in the fear-filled spring of 1954.

Though McCarthyism receded by the mid-1950s, the ideological mobilization for the Cold War that gave rise to it persisted and in some respects intensified. Certain effects of McCarthyism, such as the paralysis imposed upon United States policy toward China, ramified unchecked for many years. The "loyalty" checkups of Truman, rebaptized as a "security" program by Eisenhower, lived on. After Korea came more showdowns with "international communism" in Indochina, Berlin, Suez. The overwhelming public response to the very fact of continuous Cold War precluded as virtually subversive any serious examination, let alone criticism, of the nation's institutions and purposes. The existence of Communist societies and widespread upheavals in many lands abroad appeared not as a reason for reconsidering—if only to reaffirm—the "American way of life." If anything, the division of the world into two camps seemed rather to many an irrefutable argument for accepting prevailing American values altogether and whole. Nowhere was this more evident than in the schools or even in the universities, supposedly the centers of skepticism and speculation. At times compliance in the 1950s seemed all but ubiquitous.

§5.] President Truman's decision to intervene in Korea to repel Communist invasion was a courageous and necessary act of the Cold War. But the manner of its making had unintended consequences that not only exacerbated the passions behind the Grand Inquistion at home but also had much to do with paralyzing United States diplomacy in the Far East until long after the Cold War. For the President did not consult with Congress about committing American soldiers in the Korean fighting. Instead he issued orders committing the United States to foreign war under the so-called inherent powers of the Executive. This course was chosen at the height of passions incited by the mobilization for Cold War and inflamed by anger and recriminations over the loss of China and the A-bomb monopoly. Acheson later said that he urged it because to consult Congress, let alone ask for a declaration of war, at this stage would have risked delay and the damage that the statements of "Jenner and the other wild men" in the Senate would have inflicted on the war effort. Truman's decision to bypass Congress facilitated the swift deployment of troops to Korea that enabled American forces to prevent the invaders from overrunning the entire peninsula. But the outcome at home ran far beyond the leaders' intentions. Truman's decision was the start of the credibility gap that widened disastrously in later years when Johnson and Nixon, relying on the Korean precedent of using inherent powers, shattered national confidence and incurred attacks for secrecy and evasion over their incursions into the lands of Southeast Asia. Not only Congress but the people lost confidence in Presidential responsibility, and the sense of powerlessness that many felt about American involvement evolved into a crisis of national confidence as the nation bogged down year after year in the Vietnam quagmire.

§6.] Even in the hungry 1930s Communist influence never amounted to much in the United States. As might be expected, the party's members exerted their greatest influence in the trade union movement, where by 1945 they held strong and even controlling positions in eleven of the smaller industrial unions affiliated with the CIO. Up to that time federal rules and regulations as well as the dynamic of organizing had favored the rise of the CIO, whose industrial unions were set up more along the lines of the big corporations than were the older craft unions of the AFL. After the Second World War the corporations and unions battled for power in a series of bitter strikes, the most crucial of which pitted the United Auto Workers against General Motors. Within the UAW the Communists were a gingery minority who hung on to their influence by discharging their union tasks ably and forming alliances with stronger elements. But the Communists were vulnerable to the charge that their final loyalty was to a foreign power. When Truman mobilized America in the Cold War against "international Communism," union leaders fighting for power within the labor movement seized upon anti-Communism as a weapon for clawing their way to the top. Though it meant throwing over old principles of working-class solidarity, almost all leaders of American labor lined up with the anti-Communists and drove out the Communists and their luckless allies in a short, fierce fight.

For the anti-Communist socialists and the liberals who purged the Reds from the CIO, however, it proved to be a brief victory. Out with the leftists went the organizing militancy of American labor. The Taft-Hartley Act and the regulating agencies stopped the trend toward industrial unions. Never recovering from the loss of its eleven Communist-led unions, the CIO lost membership. The solidarity of the workers became that of the AFL business unionists, who moved in as brokers in the special-interest politics of Cold War Washington and finally as partners in the military-industrial embroilment in Vietnam. Along with its militancy labor lost its underdog constituency, its potential for mass leadership, its mission of social transformation. The share of dollars that went to employees increased. But union membership did not increase. The unforeseen consequence of labor's joining the Cold War was its virtual emasculation as a mass movement.

§7.] The Marshall Plan was launched in the Cold War to restore the shattered economy of Western Europe. It in no way detracts from this declared aim that the Marshall Plan was also seen as a measure for propping up the American economy and providing markets for American exports. Thus when huge cotton purchases were made under the plan President Truman took credit for having prevented the disastrous return of five-cents-a-pound cotton prices that followed the First World War. But the influx of Marshall Plan dollars did more than relieve the financial worries of Southern cotton growers. Coinciding with the arrival in the delta of the cotton-picking machine, the Marshall money also financed the mechanization of the last remaining labor-intensive enclave within American agriculture. As fast as the delta planters acquired cotton-pickers and tractors with their export dollars they pushed out their black share-cropper families as redundant labor no longer needed on the plantation. The result was that the South's unwanted rural poor flooded north and west between 1945 and 1970 as never before and crowded into urban ghettos in one of the great migrations of history. The shift of Southern rural poverty to the inner cities of the North was an explosive, wholly unforeseen consequence of the Marshall Plan.

Almost all of the $13 billion that went for European recovery under the Marshall Plan was in fact spent right in the United States, a billion of it to pay for American coal for prostrated Europe. This huge sum underwrote much of the cost of mechanizing America's coal industry. In contrast with the hapless sharecroppers, the coal miners belonged to the country's most powerful and strongly led trade union. But the United Mine Workers could not and did not stop the transformation in the pits sparked by the Marshall Plan. In a series of violent strikes that more than once brought much of the nation's industry and transport close to a halt, John L. Lewis extracted wage rise after wage rise as labor's share. Once again, labor's victories were short-lived. By the time John L. Lewis died late in the Cold War, the United Mine Workers, once the most powerful of American unions, was a hollow shell. The number of miners actually at work had shrunk from 500,000 to 60,000—and large sections of the coal-rich states of Pennsylvania, Kentucky and Illinois and the whole state of West Virginia, had turned into disaster areas, outcomes certainly not foreseen when American labor cheered the adoption of the Marshall Plan.

§8.] The impact of the Cold War upon American schools did not end with the passivity and precocious careerism it enforced upon the young. After the Russians fired their Sputnik into the skies in 1957, the nation wheeled round on its schools, blamed them for stinting on the old American "know-how," demanded "excellence" instead of "life-adjust-ment" in their children's courses, and steered a high proportion of the most talented through demanding new programs in mathematics and physics to ensure theat the United States would be number one in science and engineering. Such sudden and unparalleled pressures upon schools and universities soon had serious consequences.

Beginning at Berkeley in 1964 the students of America broke out of their unprecedented spell of quiescence and exploded in rebellion against the much touted "multiversities" of which they were presumably the beneficiaries. Those who did so were the first to have lived all their life under the Cold War, the first to have seen it in its entirety. Born in 1945 as the Cold War began, they entered college in the fall of 1963, as it was ending. Demanding "free speech," they asserted life-styles different from their elders'. Demanding participation in the "real" world from which they felt fenced off, they condemned faculty upholders of "excellence" as servitors of Cold War society. The students' riots continued sporadically for six years, shattering the structure of the most famous universities in America, overturning their presidents, unmanning their professors and creating a generational conflict that spread through all the institutions of society. A consequence of this conflict was that the universities, after making substantial concessions to the students, experienced a drying up of funds which government and society had so lavishly provided. The large numbers of engineers and scientists trained to win the Cold War race with Russia were no longer needed. Suddenly there were too many Cold War technologists. A severe academic depression descended upon the campuses rent by nearly a decade of upheaval.

§9] In a rush to head off the challenge posed by Sputnik, the United States had poured huge sums into the universities in research grants and contracts. But at the same time that the government set highest priority on expanding university research for the Cold War, society was insisting that the universities also educate unprecedented numbers of students. Thus the universities were saddled with two contradictory tasks, and the strain was only intensified by the strong preference of most academics for research over teaching. The widespread neglect of masses of students under such circumstances contributed to the restiveness that finally boiled over at Berkeley in 1964. The outcome for the universities was doubly painful. As a consequence of accepting big government grants in the Cold War they had become dependent on Washington for a large part of their revenues. But rebellious students demanded that the universities cease working for the Pentagon. To stave off campus disturbances the universities divested themselves of defense contracts, only to plunge into deep financial crisis upon loss of these contracts, which declined anyway as a source of revenue as the Cold War urgency passed. Thus an unintended consequence of the Cold War was that such citadels of the Establishment as Harvard, Columbia and MIT found themselves so financially beleaguered that the price of their survival might finally be surrendering their private status for government subsidies.

§10] No one had to convert a nation nurtured on Manifest Destiny to the notion that America must grow to win the Cold War. When its leaders became convinced that the Russians were plotting to invade Western Europe and rule the world, the country's response was to quadruple its arms spending and enlarge its huge economic plant by a whole order of magnitude. In the process the idea of economic growth became an obsessive force that drove businessmen and pervaded the whole of society. The consequences were many, and extended far beyond the avowed goal of deterring Communist expansion.

In the Eisenhower years the impetus to growth was directed into the private sector. The mammoth buildup begun by Truman, while enormously enlarging land, sea and air forces of the United States, had also concentrated before all upon expanding the country's economic base—its capacity to produce electric power, aluminum, steel, oil. When Eisenhower's businessmen arrived in Washington to run the government, they let the military expansion taper off (they actually cut the ground forces). But following their profound conviction that the ultimate capacity of America to wage and win the Cold War lay in the power and vitality of its domestic economy, they removed Korean War controls, cut taxes and gave the private sector its free run.

One consequence of this was the national consumer binge that convulsed the society of the 1950s. The effect was to widen the gap between public demands for sacrifice in the collective effort of the Cold War and the private behavior of a nation requiting its every material whim in the pursuits of peace, and to bring on a gradual souring of values that traditionalists such as Eisenhower and Dulles could scarcely have intended. But "the overhang of traditional perspectives," as Harold Lasswell called it, nonetheless impelled the Eisenhower administration at the same time to cut down on federal spending. The unanticipated consequence of this was to open a glaring discrepancy between the recklessly indulged prosperity of the private sector and the decaying facilities and neglected services of the tax-starved public domain.

§11] A second consequence of directing the drive for growth in the Cold War toward the private sector was to fuel the race of American corporations to expand into markets abroad, especially Western Europe. Although the Marshall Plan was an enterprise run by businessmen, it was only after the European Common Market took shape behind the shelter of a militarized NATO that the biggest American companies, led by General Motors, began empire-building in the grand manner. Within a few years they controlled a sizable portion of the market in many countries, and dominated it in such fields as oil, photographic film and computers. Expanding into many countries, the supercorporations became multinational monsters, surpassing in wealth and income many of the nations in which they operated. By 1970 the gross value of production overseas of such companies amounted to twelve per cent of the Gross National Product of the United States.

The consequences for United States relations with other governments created by the rise of these large and self-propelled entities, were embarrassing enough. But the impact was soon felt in unforeseen ways on matters of fundamentally domestic concern. Government and union officials in Washington, office-holders and union members in Ohio, all were vitally concerned and affected when, by decision of the multinational corporation managers, jobs were sometimes created in Amsterdam—and abolished in Akron. It was a further outcome of the Cold War that decisions of these multinational managers to shift billions of dollars from one capital to another significantly affected the efforts of the government in Washington to avert a steady worsening in the country's international balance of payments from 1958 onward. At the least, the growth of private corporations overseas touched off in the 1950s had created a powerful new force in international affairs such as the decision-makers around Eisenhower never reckoned on.

When President Kennedy assumed command of the Cold War in 1961, growth became the official and uncontested aim of national policy. Thenceforth, the expansion broadened out into both the private sector and the military-space sphere. To encourage business growth, Kennedy put through a tax credit as a spur to investment, and followed this up with a tax cut. But even before these programs could get rolling, Kennedy boosted military outlays far beyond those of Eisenhower. Within a year of taking office he increased arms spending by nearly $6 billion and launched a $20 billion going-to-the-moon program. By this time the military expansion that Acheson had demanded in 1949 to build "positions of strength" in the Cold War had become the engine of economic growth. But waging the Cold War in 1961 had come to mean girding for three wars at once while outracing the Russians in space, and the gospel of growth called for even greater expenditures by consumers at home and by multinationals abroad. Because heightened economic activity boosted consumption of imported goods while decreasing the exports needed to pay for them, Kennedy's high-growth policies brought a further deterioration of the United States' international balance of payments. The day came when, though the gold remained stashed away at Fort Knox, actual ownership of most of it passed to others, mostly the one-time victims of the "dollar gap" in Western Europe. Not only that, $100 billion worth of dollars, the accumulated overhang of U.S. balance-of-payment deficits floated round the world pushing down the value of the American currency —the financial legacy of the Cold War. This fateful change was, of course, an unforeseen consequence of demands made upon America's resources by the Cold War.

After Lyndon Johnson became President, the nation gunned for growth full-throttle. Even as the Vietnam War loomed, the Great Society was proclaimed, hitching on to the engine of economic expansion the one part of the national budget—health, education, welfare—that had been left behind all through the Cold War ride. And as the Johnson "consensus" poured on the coal so that the express roared down the track even faster, the consequences of headlong growth began to explode on all sides. The dollar's strength plummeted in the international markets. Its domestic buying power began to be devoured by inflation. Finally, waking up among the shade trees and songbirds of the suburbs, the American public roused to belated ecological alarm. People became nervously aware that in endlessly expanding the output of factories and farms the day might dawn when the air, water and landscape in which they had to live might be poisoned. Impairment in the quality of life, inflation in the cost of living, devaluation of the dollar—all these enveloping ailments of the 1960s and 1970s were outcomes of the obsessive drive for growth sparked by the fleeting imperatives of the Cold War.

§12] Beneath these compulsions was an underlying irony. Though waged at all times in the presence of possible nuclear holocaust, America's Cold War required the preservation and indeed enlargement of the American way of life it was fought to uphold. From the very start the country's leader believed that the way to make the United States strong was to give full rein to its business economy. This doctrine did not only lead to runaway growth; it also fostered hypocrisy at all levels as from Truman to Kennedy ringing calls to sacrifice, work and self-restraint were received amid an atmosphere of consumer spending sprees and corporation stock-splits. An unintended consequence of the Cold War was to intensify the contradiction that had always existed within the American society between private interest and the common good.

Given the baby boom, the development of the automobile, government guarantees for home mortgages and the ingenuity of real-estate developers, there is no reason to suppose that America would not have expanded prodigiously into the suburbs after 1945 even if the United States and Russia had never quarreled. Yet, as Harold Lasswell showed long ago, "world politics and personal insecurity" are linked in modern times. The obsessive governmental concern with national safety that prevailed during years when people lived in fear of the nuclear nightmare reinforced the desire of millions of Americans after the Second World War to buy a house outside the crowded cities, see to the security of their families, and satisfy their appetite for consumer goods. In this way the Cold War abetted and accelerated a rush to the suburbs and a self-preoccupied privatism that led to some unexpected and unwanted outcomes.

Even more than national housing law, the administration of federal policy speeded the outward migration. While funneling cheap credit to the well-to-do in the suburbs, it set up all kinds of roadblocks for those seeking federal funds to buy or improve dwellings in any area that included older properties or slums. While Congress encouraged income-tax deductions for property taxes and home-mortgage interest that amounted to a further fifteen per cent subsidy on annual costs of private homeowning, it allowed public housing in the inner-city to grind to a virtual halt. If Washington's refusal to take up the problems of education, health and welfare made it hard for the suburbs to cope with their huge new populations, the plight of the cities was far worse. As whites moved out to the suburbs, masses of newcomers poured in from the rural South and Puerto Rico. Cut off from federal help while these crucial population changes took place, the cities struggled unaided. Blight spread, industry fled, and the tax-base shrank. Ironically, Washington had funds in these years only for expressway construction under the Interstate Highway and Defense Act, whose engineers, without thought of social planning, cut freeways that enabled suburbanites to get to their jobs but farther aggravated the plight of the cities, severing vital local arteries, creating still more slums, adding yet more reasons why those who could should abandon the cities for the security of suburban life. The end result of this enormous transplantation of people, wholly unanticipated when the Cold War began in the 1940s, was that America emerged from it split into two nations, one white and suburban, the other black and bottled up in inner-city ghettos.

§13] It was inevitable that the Cold War should have repercussions in an area of American life as central and as volatile as race. Having seen the United States wage all-out war to destroy a Hitlerite Germany dedicated to the master-race principle, the American black may already have decided the time had come to claim his rights as a first-class citizen. The unforeseen consequence of the Cold War was that it opened the way. At the peak of the Cold War in 1954, when the United States struggle with Russia was turning into a competition for the allegiance of the Third World, the Supreme Court handed down its order to desegregate the schools. Martin Luther King and others took it from there. Although the entrenched partisans of white supremacy in the Congress and the South battled to hold down the blacks, President Eisenhower had no alternative at Little Rock but to uphold the court rulings, and blacks went on to win their lawful civil rights. The retreat from white supremacy in the South was an unscheduled by-product of the Cold War.

A further outcome, sparked by the rise of free Africa and the Cold War competition, was that American blacks sharpened their sense of identity and ethnic pride in the rediscovery of their African inheritance. While four civil rights bills became law in less than ten years, more blacks won better jobs than before. But before the Cold War ended racial injustice, *de facto* now instead of *de jure,* was nationalized. The South's legacy was bequeathed to the nation. As whites scattered to the suburbs and blacks crowded into the inner cities, segregation was as total as before *Brown v. Board of Education,* even in the schools.

§14] Since the Cold War against the Russians was fought out short of open combat, the subterranean front became a major theater of operations. Only force stopped Communists and if Communists operated underground they must be stopped by underground force. Above ground or below, America did not do things by halves. The CIA, granted immunity from congressional and public scrutiny for its secret activities, soon grew to exercise formidable influence in national policy and even in cultural life. In the propaganda of "liberation" and "rollback" it became an instrument of provocation; in the slide toward intervention in Southeast Asia, it was the spearhead of commitment. By the time the unmentionable agency's U-2 was shot down over Russia, espionage had become central to America's Cold War and subversion a major part of it. Although Truman said he never dreamed in setting up the CIA that it would end up in such hanky-panky, the agency subverted American business enterprises, trade unions, religious organizations, and student and intellectual groups to its clandestine purposes. Apart from painful embarrassments for American summit policy in Cuba, Laos and elsewhere, the results of subterranean involvements spilled over into the conduct of American life. The habits of guerrilla warfare, espionage and sabotage, bugging and burglary did not cease with the Cold War but surfaced in the scene back home. In 1972 they introduced a new and sinister corruption into the style of American political campaigning. Veterans of the CIA's Bay of Pigs adventure were found rifling Democratic party headquarters and tapping its telephones in the pay of Republican campaigners. The intrusion of such practices in the elementary processes of democracy was an unforeseen consequence of the Cold War.

§15] Up to the beginning of the Cold War it was an article of American faith that the country must guard against the rise of a large permanent military establishment. All that changed when the nation decided that it faced a military threat from the Russians. In order to impress the Communists (and the people of the United States) with the seriousness of its resolve to oppose them at all costs, Congress in the midst of the Russian blockade of Berlin passed a bill for peacetime conscription. Setting aside as it did one of the nation's most cherished traditions, the action was termed a temporary one. But with the inevitable escalations in the Cold War, with the Communist invasion of Korea and the spread of American forces round the world, the draft was repeatedly extended.

As the temporary gradually became permanent, Pentagon planners made the draftee the mainstay of the American army. For the enhanced role of the ground forces in the strategy of flexible response adopted in the 1960s, conscription was essential. Then the United States became involved in large-scale fighting in Vietnam. Young Americans began to rebel at being conscripted to fight overseas in a war they wanted no part of. Older Americans had no patience with such attitudes, and Congress kept extending the draft. As the Vietnam involvement lengthened, conflict between young and old intensified, and raged in families, schools, all the institutions of the society. Essentially a Cold War leftover, the draft ripped the generations apart in the 1960s and early 1970s. Exacerbated by the persistence of the peacetime draft into the Vietnam years, the generational hostility that embittered American life in that period was thus an unforeseen consequence of the Cold War.

§16]   Obviously the power of the military to propose and to dispose in matters affecting how millions of Americans planned their lives had much to do with the generational conflicts that racked the society in the 1960s. Long before that time, thanks to the Cold War, the military had been raised to great power in Washington and indeed to a central place as an institution of American society. The military determined the forces needed to wage the Cold War, and lobbied in Congress for the funds. In short order the sums involved amounted to over half the national budget and a sizeable proportion of the total national product. When President Eisenhower attempted to put a lid on their growth, pressures from the Pentagon and its suppliers, constituting the largest single sector of the business economy, frustrated his efforts.

Though the Democrats' cry of a "missile gap" after Russia's early space feats proved false, the military-industrial complex did even better when Kennedy took office in 1961. Under his new strategy of flexible response, the new President expanded all the armed services and committed himself to a $20 billion space bonanza besides. As part of a military expansion costing nearly $6 billion, the Administration built up ground forces and created a new capacity for counter-insurgency in guerilla warfare. Large outlays on the nuclear striking force also played their part in the Cuban missile crisis. But when in 1963 Kennedy signed Khrushchev to the limited nuclear test band treaty, the military insistence on an under-ground testing program assured more heavy spending on missiles.

§17]   The unexpected outcome of the Treaty of Moscow was that the Chinese Communists split openly with the Russians, which brought about the end of the Cold War and its polarized confrontation between West and East. But this turn of events also brought the beginning of American intervention in Vietnam.

As the extent of the rupture between China and Russia became known in the West, it became evident that the United States no longer had to reckon with the deterring menace of a monolithically united Communist camp. With the Russians and Chinese at each other's throats and "international Communism" in open disarray, the United States could move with an impunity heretofore unimagined. The big risks for America of intervention on the Asian mainland suddenly no longer existed. It was only necessary to be persuaded that such intervention would be decisive and brief. This judgment was furnished in late 1964 by General Maxwell Taylor and Special Assistant for National Security Affairs Walt Rostow, after a trip to survey the situation in Saigon. The Kennedy

Administration had created the necessary forces, and the Peking-Moscow split left Washington free to use them. In the spring of 1965 President Johnson made his decision to commit American ground troops in force in South Vietnam.

The rise of the military-industrial complex in the 1950s and the formation of new land units and special forces were events in the Cold War that had unforeseen consequences subsequently in Southeast Asia. It was the last act of the Cold War, however, that decisively opened the way for America's war in Vietnam, and as such it was laden with irony. The Treaty of Moscow, leading at once to the Chinese-Russian split, brought as a second unintended consequence the collapse of the myth of monolithic international Communism; and this was followed soon after by a third unintended consequence of such compelling immediacy—the Vietnam war—that the triggering of the event by these antecedent factors was all but lost to view. The culminating irony of the Cold War was this: the Vietnam war was an unintended consequence not of the confrontation between the United States and Soviet Communism—but of its end.

W A S   T H I S   costly and long-drawn-out confrontation with the Communists worth it? At the time that Truman asked for his $400 million aid to Greece and Turkey to show the Russians that they could not barge into the Mediterranean or spread out unchecked into Western Europe, his doctrine of firmness and commitment seemed to make good sense for Americans. The United States had emerged victorious in 1945 from the greatest of all wars, at the peak of its power. It had a monopoly of the Bomb, a near-monopoly of the Gold, and an enormous, undamaged economic plant that worked best going full blast. By 1963 it was even stronger and richer, though it had lost forever its sovereign security and begun to transfer most of the gold, or title to it, to the rising conpetitors of Europe and Asia. Throughout the nearly two decades of the Cold War, the United States had kept war from its shores, preserved a fundamentally free society, and lived in unprecedented prosperity. It had met its basic goals as a twentieth-century nation-state: survival, liberty, economic well-being.

Yet the period of the Cold War was not a glorious period in United States history. It was not a time like Periclean Athens. It corresponded in significant ways with the period after the Civil War. In the realm of the spirit the Cold War years were not productive times, bringing nothing comparable for example, with the upwelling that poured out, in American letters in the years after the First World War. The best that could be said was that these years saw the United States accept its leading role in the world. The America of the Cold War years disbursed some $50 billion in aid to foreign countries, a record without parallel in history.

Yet this same America fomented a supercorporate imperialism, made the military a power of incalculable influence in the heart of government and abandoned the tradition of voluntary arms-bearing in peacetime for a garrison state. Spurning diplomacy for armed might, and relying overmuch on technical prowess, it exalted private security-seeking in the citizenry by its overriding obsession with building up national security in peacetime. The casualty in an age when urbanization and increasing population demanded human cooperation, was regard for the common weal. A prevailing hypocrisy abetted the decline in corporate and personal standards of conduct. Flouting individual rights in a paroxysm of anti-Communist hysteria the America of the Cold War enforced conformity on adults and silence on youth. It drove its blacks into urban ghettos, neglected the community services of government, and disastrously delayed major adjustments in the changing society.

The United States has long been one of the most dynamic of societies. Until recently—a mere fifty years ago—open and unrestricted immigration from the Old World kept its biological base in such constant change that the very composition of its nationality remained in process of formation. In all other respects it continued to be an open society, perhaps the most open in the world, accessible almost instantaneously by force of its high technology to all influences from without and within. This was the America that expanded in numbers, power and treasure almost uninterruptedly for two hundred years—over a continent, hemisphere, two oceans and finally, after 1945, on to the shores of the Eurasian landmass and to bases and warfronts beyond.

This America might have worked with the Russians except that in the two hundred years since its origin by revolution it had been overtaken by its wealth. History and geography shielded this America from the violence of the rest of the world's wars and upheavals, so that by 1945 the changes it had experienced were neither so wide nor so deep as those undergone by other, "older" societies. Even before the Second World War, Sir Denis Brogan liked to say that among the principal nations of the world the United States now had the longest-surviving, fundamentally unchanged form of government. Time, situation and interest all conspired in the world after 1945 to make this America a conservative, counterrevolutionary force.

So when Stalin, shrugging off America's A-bomb and its insistence on self-determination for all nations, moved unheeding to take over all Europe east of the Elbe, this America judged that Communist Russia was bent on world hegemony and took what it righteously assumed was "defensive" action. Its error was to have believed that ideology is more powerful in international affairs than national interest. From this obsessive perception—that the Russians were plotting military mastery of Europe and overthrow of non-Communist governments everywhere— flowed the succession of Cold War decisions and counter-decisions that kept reinforcing its seeming validity.

The Cold War, coming on the heels of the greatest of all wars, was too much even for America. Riding high—and mighty—the nation hurtled ahead to win it as it had won all its wars. President Truman said: "The whole world should adopt the American system." After him a whole generation of high-flying leaders came to look upon the world as an American preserve, organized and overseen by superior American wisdom and controlled, as needed, by American power. They positively believed they possessed both an understanding of events and a control over their flow. The academics and technocrats who eagerly served them offered a pretended objectivity that then helped justify their attempts to control the flow of events.

The main idea was to safeguard against mortal peril the sacred values of the American system. No doubt there was a Communist presence, and some Communist influence, in America during the Second World War. But nothing justified the assault on the most basic values of the Constitution and the Bill of Rights that followed. The obsession of anti-Communism spread until it pervaded the American consciousness. A whole canon of belief formed, almost like an unwritten constitution, with principles of anti-this and amendments of anti-that which were never codified. This set of assumptions was not spelled out in government policy, except in the negative sense of containing Russia, nor in educational policy, except in the black-listers' way of rooting Reds out of schoolhouses. It was a matrix pressed down upon our brow. We did not really know the code we were behaving by. America moved as instinctively as a school of fish.

If there was one idea around which this nay-saying ideology could have been said to form, it was the concept of national security. In the Cold War everything and everybody had to be subordinated to its overriding importance. America's Cold War was inaugurated with the National Security Act of 1947, managed thereafter by the National Security Council, and financed unquestioningly out of the enormous hunk of Washington's budget designated at the "national security component." Security was the national purpose. It was the watchword on all the frontiers of life —foreign, domestic and private. All segments of Cold War America, Adlai Stevenson along with Barry Goldwater, could be mobilized by an appeal to the interests of national security.

The myth was first pierced on the international front. From the start of the Cold War Americans had thought a Third World War would break out any day. "When the balloon goes up," was the popular phrase. Two fears reinforced these expectations—fear of the Bomb, and fear of another Pearl Harbor sneak attack. Government leaders acted as if such things might happen, and the imagined imminence justified everything. Yet the Third World War never did break out. The Cold War threw the nation into one big international crisis after another. But still each time the Bomb did not fall. Instead we had a series of little wars and, finally, Vietnam.

Somewhere along the line national security lost its intimidating, hypnotizing power. A general weakening occurred as some Americans thought national security was being threatened by imported Polish ham and still others feared collecting Soviet stamps. Oddly enough after appeals to national security in foreign relations lost its punch, "national security" became a catch-all issue in domestic politics. The government listened in on its own people's telephone conversations "in the name of national security." In the case of Daniel Ellsberg, charged with releasing the classified Pentagon Papers that backgrounded the Vietnam involvement, the government, in the name of national security, sought compromising evidence against the accused man by breaking into his psychiatrist's office. The Cold War carryover that national security justified anything became internalized in our society—and the Nixon Administration used the methods of the police-state to gain reelection.

Two things can be said: the Cold War has changed us—but we have overthrown the principles of the Cold War. By the time America's anti-Communist zeal had turned national security into a domestic political weapon, the nation was devoured by its own ideology. The myth of national security perverted American politics and corrupted all constitutional government. Yet Americans gained a belated opportunity to stop the rot when the Watergate scandal burst the skin of the body politic after Nixon's reelection victory.

Returning home after the 1973 Vietnam ceasefire, American prisoners of war, long held by Hanoi, discovered that the America they came back to had changed and no longer subscribed to the values for which it went into the Cold War. They were like men who had been sealed up in a time machine, like Rip Van Winkles coming out of caves. Doctors said they all felt traumatic strain. One, crying "I have missed so much," took his life. Another, quoted by *Newsweek*, said it all: "My God, the hippies have won!"

But if America had overthrown the old Cold War values, rancor and discord were the aftermath. There was also the POW colonel who said it was "great to see that so many Americans supported us in Vietnam." For many still reponded to the appeal of national security.

The old Cold War attitudes readily labeled those who did not support the flag in Vietnam as "effete snobs" and "media elitists." Such war-critics were thought to be traitorous, and by analogy in such a division, the question of loyalty comes up. But there was no single test. Who, it might be asked, troubled to wear American flags in their lapels during the Cold War? Nobody marched for peace in the Cold War years either. Then young America, shining with the purity of uncorrupted, unproved adolescence, followed the cheerleaders, and wore its crewcuts, bobby sox and Mickey Mouse grins.

The Cold War was over, and America would be long counting the cost. It took up to a trillion dollars, devoured America's export surpluses, ruinously unbalanced the country's economic payments, and forced repeated devaluations of the dollar. The Cold War placed material and moral demands on America for so long that constitutional government was corrupted and the seams of society itself cracked. The split-level, Victorian-like morality that the Cold War had fostered decayed in reverse into a sort of Regency wildness in which the absence of virtue was held a virtue and personal celebration was all. A fault line, rancorously symbolized in streets, families, campuses, all the institutions of society, by the peace-emblem versus the American flag, left the United States in a kind of societal schizophrenia. Long after its end, the Cold War's consequences in social disorder and spiritual malaise still beset the nation in the 1970s.

Bibliographical Essay

A s the Cold War recedes into history, much of what has been written about it takes on a preliminary appearance. Official versions, powerfully launched with Churchill's war memoirs, were succeeded by the works of "revisionists." Revisionism is in turn revised. In my own orientation perhaps a dozen books or so established the essential boundaries, facts and viewpoints of this much disputed period.

Early in the field, and founded on primary sources available, was William H. McNeill's *America, Britain and Russia, their Cooperation and Conflict* (1953). This volume in the chronological Chatham House *Surveys* originated by Arnold Toynbee and issued by the Royal Institute of International Affairs in London, is the work of an American scholar and largely sets the officially received version: that the Cold War originated because of the failure of the Russians to work with the Western Allies as the big war ended. I found the same message eloquently reinforced by Herbert Feis, the State Department scholar who talked intimately with high officials from Hull to Truman, had access to many documents and produced in *The China Tangle* (1953) and *Churchill, Roosevelt, Stalin* (1957) two volumes that were most useful. The official line was set forth with serene brevity in Charles B. Marshall's *The Cold War* (1966).

Actually the case against the containment policy was cogently argued at the very outset by Walter Lippmann in *The Cold War, a Study in U.S.*

Foreign Policy (1947). Later Norman Graebner in *Cold War Diplomacy* (1962), the Catholic scholar John A. L. Lukacs in *A New History of the Cold War* (1962) and the former State Department officer Louis Halle in *The Cold War as History* (1967), while holding the Russians mainly responsible, added increasingly critical analysis. For me the interpretation of foreigners repeatedly enhanced perspective and detachment: David Rees's *The Age of Containment* (1967), for instance, accented timeless balance-of-power elements from a British viewpoint, whereas Andre Fontaine's *History of the Cold War* (1965), written in Paris and tracing the origins to the Bolshevik Revolution and the twenty-year European civil war that followed, brought out the ideological component of the conflict. On the Russian side, the pervasiveness of ideology could be assessed in such a scholarly work as A. Gromyko's *History of Soviet Foreign Policy* (1969). The urbane recollections of the wartime envoy in London (Ivan Maisky, *Memoirs of a Soviet Ambassador*, 1968) are exceptional. If Foreign Minister Molotov wrote memoirs, they have escaped notice in East and West.

On the American side ideology loomed so large that revisionist writing, when it came along, mainly stood the official version on its end and attributed all responsibility for the Cold War to the United States. Most comprehensive of such writings are those of W. A. Williams, notably *The Tragedy of American Diplomacy* (1959) but also *The Contours of American History* (1965) and *The Great Evasion* (1964), tracing the Cold War back to the promulgation of the Open Door policy in 1901. With selected quotations from Acheson, Clayton and others Williams concluded that the trouble with Russia after 1945 began when the United States demanded the same open door for its trade in eastern Europe that it sought in China and, according to Williams's spirited argument, everywhere else. In *The Free World Colossus* (1965) David Horowitz carried this analysis to the point of a conspiratorial explanation of history. In *Atomic Diplomacy: Hiroshima and Potsdam* (1965), Gar Alperovitz deduced from 1945 events that American leaders rushed their A-bomb explosions to prevent the Russians from exerting as much postwar influence in Asia as in Europe.

Like the official doctrines enshrined in the memoirs and diaries of the Cold Warriors, such explanations ran up against what H.A.L. Fisher calls "the contingent and the unforeseen." The broad economic objectives of American foreign policy, however, were illuminated for me in the works of Williams, in Gabriel Kolko's *Politics of War* (1968) and *Limits of Power* (1971), in the essays in Barton J. Bernstein's *Policies and Politics of the Truman Administration* (1970), in Lloyd Gardner's *Architects of Illusion* (1970). Using the Dulles papers at Princeton, Walter LaFeber's *America, Russia and the Cold War* (1967) extended this analysis into the

1950s, and John Lewis Gaddis's careful *The United States and the Origins of the Cold War* (1972) marshaled strong evidence that American expansiveness, economic and military, left no room for diplomacy in these years.

Primary documentation of the Cold War remains meager. A single, seminal article that George Kennan wrote for *Foreign Affairs*, in July, 1947, entitled "The Sources of Soviet Conduct" and signed simply "X," defined the containment policy followed by every administration thereafter. But few such central papers have been published except in memoirs, and it is probably salutary to recall Hannah Arendt's judgment that memoirs are "in our century the most deceitful genre in literature." At the same time one should acknowledge Margaret Truman's reproach that historians tend to confuse remarks made in conversation or in private letters with settled policy. The three diaries of greatest value for the postwar years, tantalizing glimpses into history *wie es eigentlich gewesen*, are the *Private Papers of Senator Vandenberg* (1952), edited by his son Arthur Vandenberg Junior; the *Forrestal Diaries* (1951) edited by Walter Millis; and the *Journals of David Lilienthal* (1964). Weighty in judgment are the concluding pages of Henry L. Stimson's *On Active Duty in Peace and War* (1948), in which McGeorge Bundy assisted. Dean Acheson's *Present at the Creation* (1969), though it never doubts that the creation was infallible, is one of the best memoirs ever written by an American in high office; I have closely followed its account of the terminating of the Berlin blockade and in many other points. Neither Marshall, Dulles nor Rusk left such accounts; Stettinius' are inconsequential; and James. F. Byrnes's *Speaking Frankly* (1947) and *All in One Lifetime* (1958) never disclose just how peace slipped out the door while he was negotiating one treaty after another with the Russians.

President Truman's *Year of Decisions* (1955) and *Years of Trial and Hope* (1956) are breathtakingly selective and ex post facto, especially for the critical months of late 1945 and early 1946. Eisenhower's *Mandate for Change* (1963) and *Waging Peace* (1965) are with rare exceptions characteristically unrevealing. Winston Churchill's memoirs, excerpted in *Life* and published in four successive volumes from 1950 to 1953, may have had much to do with shaping American perceptions on the coming of the Cold War; but as history they can only be used with greatest care. The accounts of Anthony Eden and Harold Macmillan, Tories who really *did* preside over the liquidation of the British empire, are less than frank. Eden's *Full Circle* (1960), though quite informative about his postwar years at the Foreign Office, is unrevealing about his luckless year as prime minister. Macmillan's *Gathering Storm* (1971) is equally mum about Suez, and though it looses a few shafts at Dulles, is less than candid about the ins and outs of summitry with Kennedy.

Among general works dealing with international affairs of these times several can be enumerated: John W. Spanier's *American Foreign Policy Since World War II* (3rd ed. rev. 1968), Gaddis Smith's *American Diplomacy during the Second World War* (1965), Adam Ulam's *The Rivals: America and Russia Since World War II* (1971). In interpreting Russian foreign relations in the Khrushchev years, particularly with regard to disarmament, moves favoring détente with America and the snowballing China crisis culminating in the public excoriations of 1963, I have been greatly enlightened by Professor Ulam's history of Soviet foreign policy, *Expansion and Coexistence* (1968). There is no work of comparable authority and sweep in United States foreign relations.

But no one has written about the Cold War in America, and for this I have researched in both primary and secondary sources, often going back to materials first read and used twenty-five or more years ago. There is no general history of the years since 1945, and none covering the years 1945–63 treated in this book. But one work, Eric Goldman's *The Crucial Decade and After* (1960), I have drawn upon again and again through this volume. Though its lusty thesis of unabating economic and social revolutionary advance is hardly supported in these pages, its lively and incisive definition of men and events, its appraisal of incident, its choice of quotations have repeatedly influenced my later approach. I have also respectfully consulted Herbert Agar's troubled salute to the decade 1945–55, *The Unquiet Years* (1955). Of general treatises on America's past, many have been updated to include much or all of this period; John Garraty's *The American Nation* (1968) stands out for having been written from a contemporary vantage and for discerning sketches of such leaders as Kennedy and Dulles.

Here, by chapter, are some of the works I have used and notes on what they have meant to me.

CHAPTER 1.

It was Alan Bullock, citing the *Testament of Hitler* (1960) in a BBC talk, who pointed out that Hitler saw the inevitability of America's postwar predicament. How hard nevertheless America tried to say no to the Cold War is attested by the worrying and wrangling within Congress, within the administration, and within that man of supposedly instant decisions, President Truman himself. For all its international orientation Richard Gardner's expert *Sterling-Dollar Diplomacy* (1956) amply shows that getting the 1945 peacetime British loan through Congress was pulling teeth;

Cabell Phillips's *The Truman Presidency* (1966), while concentrating on the day to day chronicle of work done, records the hesitancies between the prewar traditionalism of Leo Crowley, John Snyder and Louis Johnson and the imperatives of global victory pressed by Leahy, Marshall, Forrestal, Acheson. As for the new president, Alfred Steinberg's *Man from Missouri*, (1962) picturing his father as a mule trader, provided rich evidence of Truman's sturdy Middle Western roots; Jonathan Daniels' racy *Man of Independence* (1950) showed on the other hand how leading Battery D prepared him to reverence Marshall and how early visits to Justice Brandeis swayed him in time toward an intellect like Acheson. William Hillman's *Mr. President* (1952), an extraordinary piece of Americana and the little volume *Truman Speaks* (1960), recording a visit to Columbia students, provided intimate revelations of the chief executive on the job.

Walter Johnson's admirable *Battle Against Isolation* (1944) sets the background for comparing William Allen White's Kansas pulpiteering for intervention in 1940 with the Truman-Churchill preaching mission to Missouri six years later. In neither case, of course, was conversion immediate. The *Private Papers of Senator Vandenberg* (1952), supported by H.B. Westerfield's *Foreign Policy and Party Politics* (1953), a scholarly work that is essentially Republican-oriented, portray the agony of the same tradition-shattering shift among the opposition in Congress. The leader of the Republican resistance, winning the domestic battle with the help of Southern Democratic votes but losing the

international war to the Administration's bipartisan strategy, is best seen in James Patterson's authoritative *Mr. Republican: Robert A. Taft* (1972). Though W. S. White's *The Taft Story* (1954) has telling anecdote and Ishbel Ross's discursive *An American Family, the Tafts* (1964) many homely details, this volume not only supersedes earlier studies but constitutes the most solid historical work so far on the postwar period. That the decision to seize world leadership would raise questions about the administration's reforming thrust at home was a theme of enlightening essays in Richard S. Kirkendall, ed. *The Truman Period as a Research Field* (1967). That the price of Cold War would be a basically conservative postwar government was the message provided by excellent studies founded on research in the Independence Library in Barton J. Bernstein ed. *Policies and Politics of the Truman Administration* (1970) and admirably supported by Barton J. Bernstein and Allen J. Matusow eds, *The Truman Administration, a Documentary History* (1966).

CHAPTER 2.

Truman himself tells (*Years of Trial and Hope*, 1956) how he changed the "shoulds" to "musts" in his speech for aid to Greece and Turkey. Concerning the emergence of the Truman Doctrine, I have not treated George Kennan's reticent *Memoirs I* (1967) as a major source because, though they provide firsthand details, by the time they appeared Kennan had disavowed the interpretation that Forrestal and Truman placed upon his powerful dispatches of 1945 and 1946 from Moscow. Joseph Jones's *Fifteen Weeks* (1955), the clear and careful report of a State Department officer who helped prepare the Truman speech, remains the best source on its evolution.

In tracing the spiritual mobilization of America that followed, I consulted S.M. Cavert's standard histories, *American Churches in the Ecumenical Movement*, 1969, and *Church Cooperation and Unity in America*, 1970, to compare the positions of American Protestantism after the two world wars. To establish the key role of

Reinhold Niebuhr in framing a world view hostile first to Hitler and then to Stalin, I read both his occasional postwar writings notably in *Christianity and Crisis* and *Christianity and Society*, and his systematic writings, such as *Children of Light and Children of Darkness* (1944), *Christian Realism and Political Problems* (1953), and *The Irony of American History* (1952). Articles by Arthur Schlesinger Jr. in Cushing Strout ed. *Intellectual History in America* (1968) and by Kenneth Thompson in Charles Kegley ed. *Reinhold Niebuhr, his Religious Social and Political Thought* (1956), were useful, as were the insights of Walter LaFeber in *America, Russia and the Cold War*, (1967). Ronald Stone's painstaking *Reinhold Niebuhr, Prophet to Politicians* (1972), which I read as a doctoral dissertation, helped bring it all together for me.

There is a major book to be written about American Catholicism in the Cold War. Monsignor Gannon's The *Cardinal Spellman Story* (1962), published at the peak of Spellman's career, is hardly a critical work, but I found it urbane and absorbing, a portrait of one of the most colorful and important Americans of his time, presenting much interesting and significant evidence of his national and international influence. The account of Spellman's dispute with Mrs. Roosevelt in Joseph Lash's excellently documented *Eleanor, the Years Alone* (1972) forcefully suggests his style and impact.

For the largely unexplored role of schools and universities in shaping the Cold War outlook, I found that the place to begin was in the sovereign analysis of the progressive movement's decline as set forth in Lawrence Cremin's authoritative *Transformation of the Schools* (1961). The issues were stated with passion by the acerb writings of Arthur Bestor (*The Restoration of Learning*, 1955). Robert W. Iversen's *Communism in the Schools* (1959) is a sensible, fact-filled study, funded by the Ford Foundation, that chronicles the firings and classroom muzzling, over a decade. Christopher Lasch's *The Agony of the American Left* (1968), the work of a professional historian with strong radical convictions, contains a critical essay on the Congress of Cultural Freedom that influenced my interpretation of the role of ex-Communists among the anti-Communist intellectuals of the time. Though no work pulls together the role of foreign area studies in the universities as a factor in Cold War mobilization, Dwight Macdonald's *Ford Foundation* (1956) trenchantly describes the part played by "philanthropoids." The subject of the silenced young is touched on in Fred J. Cook's indignant *Nightmare Decade* (1971) and John Brooks's dispassionately thoughtful *Great Leap* (1966), among other works I consulted.

CHAPTER 3.

Harry B. Price's straightforward study *The Marshall Plan and its Meaning* (1955) contains the standard official version, Joseph Jones's *The Fifteen Weeks* (1955) has excellent insider's detail on the technical shaping of the plan in Washington, and Kennan's and Acheson's memoirs as well as *Will Clayton, a Short Biography* (1958), by Ellen Clayton Garside, are important. The business orientation of the Marshall Plan is best seen in *The Private Papers of Senator Vandenberg* (1952), who planned it that way. My own interpretation of the Marshall plan is influenced by Thomas G. Patterson's telling documentation of the plan in Barton J. Bernstein ed. *Policies and Politics of the Truman Administration* (1970) as an instrumentality in support of American trade, and by Gabriel Kolko's assessment in *The Limits of Power* (1971) of the plan's failure to close the gap until the Korean war sent dollars chasing after European imports.

The impact of the Cold War on labor is not treated in Philip Taft's *Organized Labor in American History* (1964), the standard outline of the American labor movement, nor in the biographies of labor leaders. Among the books about Reuther I drew much information about his early life from Frank Cormier and William A. Watson *Walter Reuther* (1970). Of books by radicals about their battles in the union movement Len De Caux's *Labor Radical* (1970) is outstanding, Joseph Starobin's *American Communism in Crisis* (1972) equivocal, Wyndham Mortimer's *Organize!* (1971) of limited value. *Union Guy* (1949), by a Reuther stalwart, Clayton Fountain, is good on the period, and the writings of Irving Howe (*The American Communist Party, A Critical History*, 1959) and James Wechsler (*Reflections of a Middle-Aged Radical*, 1960) were useful. The most incisive analysis is to be found in B.J. Widick's *Labor Today* (1964), which soberly balances the financial gains won by Lewis and Reuther with decline in growth and zeal of their unions. E. Alton Lee's *Truman and Taft-Hartley* (1966) is a carefully researched study but does not go into the effect of the requirement of anti-Communist affidavits upon the shape and spirit of the union movement. Ronald Radosh *American Labor and U.S. Foreign Policy* (1971) was more useful for me than Alfred O. Hero and Emil Starr *The Reuther-Meany Foreign Policy Dispute* (1970); but the best account of the actions of the ex-Communist chieftain Jay Lovestone and his agents in aligning American labor in the Cold War I found in Joseph Goulden's *Meany* (1972), a work founded on extensive interviews with Meany and others. The interpretation of labor's later course owes little to Clark Mollenhoff's expose of Hoffa, *The Tentacles of Power* (1965), and less to the unrevealing autobiography *The Trials* of *Jimmy Hoffa* (1970); but R.C. and E.D. James's critical *Hoffa and the Teamsters* (1965) helpfully poses the complexity of the personality of the Teamster leader and his position in organized labor. It is a pleasure to acknowledge my debt to John Hutchinson *The Imperfect Union* (1970) for its careful sifting and annotating of the facts of Teamster malfeasance.

CHAPTER 4.

Though American policy in postwar Germany is treated at some length in John Gimbel *American Occupation of Germany* (1968), I drew my information from a scattering of sources. W.P. Davison's *The Berlin Blockade* (1958), the best work on the subject, expertly analyzes opinion including that of the Berliners and tends to view both Russian and Western attitudes as reflexive. Although these works are of decidedly different weight, style and intent, the memoirs of Robert D. Murphy (*Diplomat among Warriors*, 1964), Lucius D. Clay (*Decision in Germany*, 1950), Frank Howley (*Berlin Command*, 1950) Curtis LeMay (*Mission with LeMay*, 1965) and William H. Tunner (*Over the Hump*, 1964) all provided material of considerable value. On the Tito heresy Adam B. Ulam *Titoism and the Cominform* (1952) is the standard work. Lloyd C. Gardner's highly professional *Architects of Illusion* (1970) furnished strong criticism of Byrnes's policy, as did Kolko's *Limits of Power* (1971). For the negotiations to end the Berlin Blockade, my chief source was Acheson's *Present at the Creation* (1969).

The subject of military-civilian relationships in America's past is usefully reviewed from three points of view in Arthur A. Ekirch Jr. *The Civilian and the Military* (1956), John Swomley Jr. *The Military Establishment* (1964) and Samuel Huntington *The Soldier and the State* (1967), Jeffersonian, pacifist and conservative respectively. For historical background on the draft I used Jack Franklin Leach's *Conscription in the United States* (1952) and a sharply-argued work of constitutional analysis, J.R. Graham *Constitutional History of the Military Draft* (1971). The social history of the draft is reported in Thomas L. Hayes *Americans in Sweden* (1971), Jean Carper *Bitter Greetings* (1968), and a Quaker volume entitled *The Draft?* (1968). Proceedings of a University of Chicago conference that brought together a galaxy of experts, Sol Tax, ed. *The Draft, a Handbook of Facts and Alternatives* (1967) was helpful in places. The many Selective Service publications credited to Lewis B. Hershey furnished many facts, but the number of draftees serving and killed in Vietnam was elicited by correspondence directly with the Department of Defense.

CHAPTER 5.

Much has been written about the fear and suspicion that overtook Americans during the Cold War. Alan Barth's *The Loyalty of Free Men* (1951) is a work of distinction that still holds value; Robert Carr's *The House Committee on Un-American Activities* (1952) is a sturdily outspoken document; Eleanor Bontecou *The Federal Loyalty-Security Program* (1953), Ford-backed, assembles the facts of the Truman screening schemes; and Ralph S. Brown Jr. *Loyalty and Security* (1958), in the evidential tradition of legal research, authoritatively defines the wide impact of surveillance that I have cited. Alan D. Harper's *Politics of Loyalty* (1969) is a historian's analysis of inflamed domestic anti-Communism that is favorable to Truman; Richard Freeland's *Truman Doctrine and the Origins of McCarthyism*, documenting executive orders, lists, administrative actions and prosecutions, takes the extreme stand that the Truman administration was in effect the intellectual author of the McCarthy madness.

Of the confessional documents produced, Whittaker Chambers' *Witness* (1952) and *Cold Friday* (1964) were most revealing; those of Alger Hiss (*In the Court of Public Opinion*, 1957), Louis Budenz (*This is My Story*, 1947) and Elizabeth Bentley (*Out of Bondage*, 1951) close to worthless. Of the chronicles of the Hiss-Chambers trial I drew most, in the absence after so many years of new information, on Bert Andrews' eyewitness *A Tragedy of History* (1962). Leslie Fiedler's essay reprinted in *The End of Innocence* (1951), interpreting the trial as a debacle of the radicals on the left, seemed rather to demonstrate the polarizing of New York intellectuals in the Cold War. Arthur Schlesinger Jr.'s influential *The Vital Center* (1949), symbolizing this development even in its title, put the anti-Communist liberals over on the right, and R.H.S. Crossman ed. *The God that Failed* (1949) and Daniel Bell *The End of Ideology* (1959) tended to keep them there. Long afterward Eric Bentley ed. *Thirty Years of Treason* (1971) shows some still hurting from the brutality of the displacement: Walter Goodman's lively book *The Committee* (1968), though its wide perspective made it easier for me to frame my own judgments, struck me at times as so amused by the folly as not to be aware of the pain.

The dreaded arrival of the Russian A-bomb is traced out of the excellent official history of the Atomic Energy Commission, *The New World, I* (1962) by Richard G. Hewlett and Oscar Anderson, a model work of its kind and a mine of information and careful judgments; from the indispensable *Journals* (1964) of David Lilienthal; and from Joseph I. Liberman's competent *The Scorpion and the Tarantula* (1970).

A classic work in China affairs, a volume that may live as landmark in American scholarship, is Whitney Griswold *Far Eastern Policy of the U.S.* (1938). For the significance of American westering in the nineteenth and twentieth centuries I followed the thesis of Norman Graebner's well-judged *Empire on the Pacific* (1955).

For American experiences in the stormy years in and after the Second World War John K. Fairbank's *The United States and China* (1949) seems to me durable and useful. Tang Chou's *America's Failure in China* (1963) is a stern and unrelenting recital of the events; I made repeated use of it. Barbara Tuchman's graceful *Stilwell and the American Experience* (1970) usefully complements Theodore White, ed. *The Stilwell Papers* (1948) and the we-were-there jottings of Theodore White and Annalee Jacoby *Thunder Out of China* (1946). Don Lohbeck's *Patrick M. Hurley* (1956) is the general's position paper a dozen years later. *Wedemeyer Reports* (1958) is the story of another presidential emissary at sea in events. Stilwell, Hurley, Wedemeyer, Davies, Service, Marshall, Stuart—all are on record in *U.S. Relations with China* (1949), the still invaluable White Paper of which I made heavy use. More than any single account of these years I used Oliver Edmund Clubb *Twentieth Century China* (1965), which assimilates much of the earlier work and keeps a vigilant eye out for important detail. For treatment of Mao's rise I relied chiefly on the biography *Mao Tse Tung* (1970) by his leading Western interpreter, Stuart Schram.

Concerning the facts of McCarthy's life, especially the early times, I used Jack Anderson and Ronald May *McCarthy the Man, The Senator and the Ism* (1952), and of the Washington eyewitnesses who wrote about his days of glory I turned oftenest to Richard Rovere *Senator Joe McCarthy* (1959) as the most reliable and also the most discerning. But I found that early interpretations of McCarthyism, notably those embodied in Daniel Bell, ed. *The New American Right* (1955), which held that agrarian populism in the Middle West powered his rise, did not stand up. This interpretation was knocked down by vote analyses of Minnesota and North Dakota precincts offered by Michael Rogin in *The Intellectuals and McCarthy*, (1967). A second interpretation, holding that in turning toward McCarthyism a well-fed America was not voting its economic wants but its psychic needs, looked to the social scientists' notion of "status" as the key to McCarthy's support; but hard evidence for this intriguing explanation was also lacking, and in his contribution to the revised and expanded *The New American Right* (retitled *The Radical Right*, 1964). Richard Hofstadter backed away from it. Earl Latham's *The Communist Conspiracy in Washington* (1966) explained instead that the Republicans had been out of office so long that they were ready to try anything including McCarthyism; and Robert Griffith's carefully researched *The Politics of Fear* (1970), showed how entrenched

forces such as the Republican right, if angry enough, could exert an effective veto in America's two-party system. I found in Samuel Lubell's *The Future of American Politics* (1952) the decisive analysis that beyond these hard-shell Republicans McCarthyism gained its votes from ethnically German and Irish districts that in Wisconsin and elsewhere had tended to cast an anti-British and isolationist vote and now found their natural anti-Communism designated as patriotism.

CHAPTER 6.

Of the many works on the Korean War I used more than all others David Rees' *Korea, the Limited War*, (1964), a British work carefully founded on the documents and at home in both military and political issues. Among military writers S. L. A. Marshall's *The River and the Gauntlet* (1953), blunt and sparely written, best sets down the impact of the overwhelming of MacArthur by the Chinese. Concerning the prior United States approach to a treaty with Japan, no one has written more acutely than George Kennan (*Memoirs* I, 1967); I also consulted Frederick S. Dunn *Peacemaking and the Settlement With Japan* (1963), and took note of Walter LaFeber's comment on Dulles' "arm-twisting" role in *America, Russia and the Cold War* (1967), as well as Max Beloff's British perspective on *Soviet Policy in the Far East* (1953). Glenn Paige's minute-by-minute *The Korean Decision* (1968), product of the political scientist's fascination with presidential decision-making in crisis, furnished highly useful anatomizing of what went on in Washington in June, 1950. Of further analyses of unfolding events, the best is Allen. S. Whiting's lucidly argued *China Crosses the Yalu* (1960). Yet the missing element in this most openly military of Cold War confrontations is original Communist intent, and for this I turned, after reflection, to the Korean War chapter of Strobe Talbott ed. *Khrushchev Remembers* (1970). A work of high scholarship that bears in an important way on the Korean fighting is Richard M. Dalfiume, *Desegregation of the Armed Forces* (1969).

In the interpretation of McCarthyism after the Korean explosion, Richard Rovere's *Senator Joe McCarthy* (1959) proved as buoyant support as before. One of the intangible forces propelling the McCarthy wave was devastatingly defined in Richard Hofstadter's *Anti-Intellectualism in America* (1963). Continuously valuable was Robert Griffith's fastidiously researched *The Politics of Fear* (1970), whose solid data brought up from the private papers of senators and others showed the outlaw McCarthy political style. Yet even this firmly grounded and hard-hitting book, the best work so far on the politics of McCarthy, does not quite catch on to the terror of McCarthyism that drove a senator and a Voice of America official to suicide and two presidents to timorous compromise. Of a piece with these disgraceful events (McCarthy's part here is still confined to conjecture) was the simultaneous Oppenheimer proceeding. Philip M. Stern's *The Oppenheimer Case* (1969) is the best of published accounts.

I found invaluable background for the part that television assumed in politics in the Cold War years in the pertinent volumes of Eric Barnouw's standard history of broadcasting in the United States, vol. II *The Golden Web* (1968) and vol. III *The Image Empire* (1970). On the efforts at placing television in social context, Daniel Boorstin's learned ramble *The Image* (1964) seemed at least as suggestive and not so repetitive as Marshall MacLuhan's modish *The Medium is the Massage (1967)*. Gary Steiner's *The People Look at Television* (1963) chiefly said that TV is for entertainment. Martin Mayer's *About Television* (1972), like Stan Opotowsky's *TV, The Big Picture* (1961), remains a passing look. Fred Friendly's *Due to Circumstances Beyond our Control* (1967) seems hurried and unreflective. Although Theodore White's *The Making of a President 1960* provided insights into the Kennedy-Nixon debates, and Sig Mickelson's *The Electric Mirror* (1972) added more political facts, there is still no larger study of TV's political impact. The DuPont-backed annual *Surveys of Broadcast Journalism* give part of the picture. Yet television remains an unanalyzed medium. Herbert Alexander's works on campaign spending, which has come to mean spending for TV, are invaluable, especially as assembled and updated in *Money in Politics* (1972).

CHAPTER 7.

On the subject of economic growth, Simon Kuznets' authoritative *Postwar Economic Growth* (1964) and Herbert Stein's enlightening *Fiscal Revolution in America* (1969) furnished the most helpful insights. Of many treatments, the latest and liveliest is Peter Passell and Leonard Ross, *Retreat from Richness* (1973), which I read in proofs. That income distribution was an aching problem throughout these years was shown by Robert Lampman's work (*e.g., Share of Top Wealth Holders in National Wealth*, 1962) and further analyzed by Gabriel Kolko *Wealth and Power in the U.S.* (1962) and Michael Harrington *The Other America: Poverty in the U.S.* (1961). The American military-industrial buildup at the time of the Korean war is provocatively and trenchantly summarized by Eliot Janeway in *The Economics of Crisis* (1968), a work that combines insight and peremptory judgment while ranging over the entire postwar period. I found that the best technical summary and analysis of the strategic buildup is Warner Schilling, ed. *Strategy, Politics and Defense Budgets* (1962), especially Paul Y. Hammond's essay "NSC-68, Prologue to Rearmament." Although NSC-68 is a fundamental Cold War document never made public in more than two decades, a paraphrased version can be consulted in Cabell Phillips's valuable work *The Truman Presidency* (1966). Coral Bell's *Negotiation from Strength* (1963), researched from an Australian perspective, written with modest restraint and published by Chatham House, comes to two resounding conclusions: building strength by rearmament was an illusory goal, and neither Acheson nor Dulles, in consequence, was ever prepared to negotiate.

If the Truman years are only now coming under historical judgment, the literature of the Eisenhower period is much more tentative and incomplete. First papers made available in R.L. Branyan and L.A. Larsen, eds. *The Eisenhower Administration* (1971, 2 vols) have not yet suggested that the Eisenhower Library at Abilene is a treasure trove. Louis A. Gerson's *John Foster Dulles* (1957), in the series on American secretaries of state, is marred by a paucity of judgments. J.R. Beal's *John Foster Dulles* (1957) has intimate details but is uncritical. In Herman Finer's *Dulles over Suez* (1964), M. H. Guhin *John Foster Dulles, a Statesman and his Times* (1972) and Walter LaFeber *America, Russia and the Cold War* (1967), the critical reexamination that is sure to come has begun, and LaFeber, making incisive use of the Dulles papers in Princeton, has carried this task furthest. For assessment of Eisenhower I have had the advantage of the reinterpretation offered by Murray Kempton ("The Underestimation of Eisenhower", *Esquire*, Sept 1967), Richard Rhodes ("Eisenhower, Artist in Iron," *Harpers*, July 1970), and Arthur Larson *Eisenhower, the President Nobody Knew* (1968), all of which suggest that the general was far more in charge than contemporaries such as Marquis Childs (*Eisenhower, the Captive Hero*, 1958), Richard Rovere (*The Eisenhower Years*, 1956) and Walter Johnson (*1600 Pennsylvania Avenue*, 1960) believed. Harold Macmillan's *The Gathering Storm* (1971) brings in a contrary verdict. I found Melvin Gurtev's blow-by-blow account of *The First Vietnam Crisis* (1967) helpful, although *The New York Times* ed., *The Pentagon Papers* (1972) disclosed much that was new. Though Garry Wills's *Nixon Agonistes* (1970) is a game try, no biography of Richard Nixon has plumbed the depths of his character.

Emmet Hughes's well-phrased *Ordeal of Power* (1963) is the best insider book from the Eisenhower Administration. I also used Sherman Adams' *Firsthand Report* (1961) for background on Little Rock and much else, and Robert Donovan's *Eisenhower, the Inside Story* (1956), commissioned by Adams, because it drew on cabinet minutes. Robert Cutler *No Time for Rest* (1966) says little, Ezra Taft Benson *Crossfire* (1962) says less, Lewis Strauss *Men and Decisions* (1962) is tendentious —all in all, the Eisenhower literary brew is thin soup.

Concerning the economics of business expansion I found two monographic studies of the automobile industry most useful:

Lawrence White *The Automobile Industry since 1946* (1971) and Robert M. MacDonald *Collective Bargaining in the Automobile Industry* (1963). Of many works on the oil industry, none of them comparably critical, I made most frequent use of Robert Engler *The Politics of Oil* (1961). For the growth of American industry overseas since the war the basic work consulted was Raymond Vernon's comprehensive but analytical *Sovereignty at Bay* (1971). Kingman Brewster's lucid *Anti-Trust and American Business Abroad* (1958), Gilles Paquet ed., *The Multinational Corporation and the Nation-State* (1972) and Alvin J. Harman's monographic *The International Computer Industry* (1971) were useful for special aspects. Harry Magdoff's *Age of Imperialism* (1969) skilfully documents a Marxist interpretation.

CHAPTER 8.

In taking the measure of the lateral explosion of Americans after 1945 on their native ground, Robert C. Wood's problem-defining *Suburbia* (1959), the planning-oriented essays in William Dobriner ed. *The Suburban Community* (1958) and Scott Donaldson's thoughtful *The Suburban Myth* (1969), are basic. S. B. Warner's outspoken *The Private City* (1968) has important things to say about how Americans think about their countryside, and so have Bennett Berger in *Looking for America* (1971) and David Riesman in Walter McQuade ed. *Cities Fit to Live In* (1971). Though Richard O. Davies' solid and soundly-executed *Housing Reform during the Truman Administration* (1966) blocks out the fundamental legislation, my interpretation of dynamic forces operating within this framework stems more from Mark Gelfand's wide-ranging "A Nation of Cities," an unpublished Ph. D. dissertation (Columbia, 1972) and from Kenneth M. Jackson's pathfinding historical insights in "The Crabgrass Frontier, 160 Years of Suburban Growth in America," an essay in R.A. Mohl and J. F. Richardson, eds. *The Urban Experience* (1973, in press). Although I found the widely-circulated announcements about middle-class suburba-

nites in David Riesman's *The Lonely Crowd* (1955), W. H. Whyte's *The Organization Man* (1956) and A. C. Spectorsky's *The Exurbanites* (1955) valid up to a point, Herbert Gans's penetratingly observed *The Levittowners* (1966), Bennett Berger's essay in S. B. Warner ed. *Planning for a Nation of Cities* (1966) and Harvey Swados's early reports from assembly-liners in *A Radical's America* (1962) were of great importance in interpreting how everybody in these communities lived.

For measuring the consumer boom, I found Ben Wattenberg's chatty but informed passbook to the census, *This U.S.A.* (1965), John Brooks's spare, incisive *The Great Leap* (1966) and Bernard Nossiter's probing *The Mythmakers* (1964) repeatedly useful. Though their reports were uneven, I was grateful for the watchful eyes of the Australian Alan Ashbolt (*An American Experience*, 1967), the German Herbert von Borch (*The Unfinished Society*, 1962) and, for its British detachment, Andrew Shonfield's *Modern Capitalism*, (1965). Concurrent neglect of the public sector, scathingly identified in J. K. Galbraith's *The Affluent Society* (1958), I found voluminously documented in Seymour Harris's writings, notably *The Economics of the Po-*

litical Parties (1962), and those of Leon Keyserling (*Poverty and Deprivation in the U.S.,* 1962).

In tracing the transition from Stalin to Khrushchev in Russia, I followed most closely the careful writings of Robert Conquest, notably *Power and Policy in the U.S.S.R.* (1961), but paid attentive heed also to the work of Sovietologists such as Myron Rush (*Rise of Khrushchev,* 1958), Richard Lowenthal (*World Communism,* 1964) Robert C. Tucker (*The Soviet Political Mind,* 1963) and Edward Crankshaw (*Khrushchev,* 1966), and benefited by the work of such specialists as Sidney Ploss

(*Conflict and Decision-Making in Soviet Russia,* 1965) and Raymond Garthoff (*Soviet Military Policy,* 1966). Zbigniew Brzezinski's authoritative *The Soviet Bloc* (1960) is the standard work on East European events, and I followed it particularly in treating the Warsaw events of 1956. Melvin Lasky ed. *The Hungarian Revolution* (1957) brought together useful documentation, yet even as the West guards its Suez secrets, the East withholds the facts of Budapest: until the Soviet papers see the light of day accounts of the Hungarian rising remain incomplete.

CHAPTER 9.

Because it proved influential in the Supreme Court's 1954 desegregation decision, Gunnar Myrdal's weighty *An American Dilemma* (1944) was the starting point for exploring race in the Cold War. Along with Charles Silberman's level-headed *Crisis in Black and White* (1964), Samuel Lubell's brief *White and Black* (1964) provided insights as well as background. I made frequent use of Benjamin Muse's fact-filled *Ten Years of Prelude* (1964), and turned to Anthony Lewis's *Portrait of a Decade* (1964) as a well-chosen compilation of key *New York Times* reports. Of great value were the works of the indefatigable August Meier and Elliott Rudwick, notably the collection of documents *Black Protest in the 20th Century* (1971). I looked in vain for a record of Martin Luther King's countless speeches, found his *Stride Toward Freedom* (1958) important for the Montgomery boycott, and turned to David L. Lewis's indispensable *King, a Critical Biography* (1971) for many details. Of Louis Lomax's writings, I used his *When the World Is Given* (1963) for a report on Elijah Muhammad, on whom the early authoritative work is C. Eric Lincoln's judicious *Black Muslims in America* (1961). John Henrik Clarke's outspoken *Malcolm X, the Man and his Times* (1969) was excellent background for the *Autobiography of Malcolm X,* (1964), an American classic. Howard Zinn's book on the Freedom Riders (*SNCC, The New Abolitionists,* 1964) was useful, as was Frederick Morrow's

Black Man in the White House (1963), one of the more candid memoirs of the Eisenhower administration. Harold Isaacs's early work on the importance of Africa in black consciousness, *New World of the Negro Americans,* (1963), helped shape the theme linking the Cold War in the Third World with rising militancy among American blacks; I also drew on Peter I. Rose, ed. *Old Memories, New Moods, Americans from Africa* (1970) and R.L. Allen *Black Awakening in Capitalist America* (1969). I found Harold Cruse's searching, impassioned *Crisis of the Negro Intellectual* (1967) full of insights, and gained perspective on the strife-filled 1960s in Kenneth Clark's essay "Present Dilemma of the Negro," in the *Journal of Black History* (Jan 1968), C. Eric Lincoln's analysis in G.W. Shepherd Jr. ed. *Racial Influence on American Foreign Policy* (1970) and C. Vann Woodward's book *Civil Rights Movement Revisited* (1968).

As background for the Middle East and the Suez crisis of the Cold War, David A. Baldwin's standard *Economic Development and American Foreign Policy* traced the evolution from Point Four onward and Frantz Fanon's *The Wretched of the Earth* (1961) expressed the Third World's reaction thereto. Of memoirs about Suez, Anthony Nutting's uneven *No End of a Lesson* (1967) furnished one or two disclosures about Eden. Herman Finer's *Dulles over Suez,* a work of disciplined anger, marshals the facts and interprets them strongly against Dulles. Richard Goold-Adams' *John Foster Dulles Reappraised* (1962) is much less substantial. Andrew Beaufre's *The Suez Expedition* (1959) spills some French secrets. Hugh Thomas' *Suez* (1966) has all the facts available in Britain and must be read between the lines for the rest. Kennett Love's lengthy *Suez, the*

Twice-Fought War (1969) adds more information about CIA involvement, but I found Richard Neustadt's brief analysis in *Alliance Politics* (1970), bearing down on the decision-making in Washington, a far more penetrating interpretation, though wanting like the others with respect to the extent and impact of Russian involvement.

CHAPTER 10.

More than one of the Rockefeller Brothers Fund reports issued as Nelson Rockefeller's ambitions for elective office happened to coincide approximately with the Sputnik scare, has historic importance. That dealing with the state of education, largely written by John Gardner (his book *Excellence* (1961) came later), blew the bugle for higher academic performance. Admiral Hyman Rickover's raucous *Education and Freedom* (1960), another tract for the times, sounded the klaxon for more science and discipline in classrooms. Lawrence Cremin's elegantly balanced *Transformation of the Schools* (1961) explained why, inevitably, the Progressive movement in education should have collapsed just at this time. Slogans were minted out of Jerome Bruner's *The Process of Education,* (1961) a little book that packed a wallop and knocked open doors for the curriculum reformers. In a breathless book that made a big splash at the time but holds little substance for the later researcher, Martin Mayer's *The Schools* (1961) summarized the New Education. Places to look for post-Sputnik trends are Robert Heath ed. *New Curricula* (1964) and S. Willis Rudy *Schools in an Age of Mass Culture* (1965); John L. Goodlad's keenly informed *Changing School Curriculum* (1966) renders valuable critical judgments. Indispensable for recording progress and evaluation are the periodic reports of the respective course-content improvement projects—in Physics, Biology, Chemistry, Mathematics. The so-called Coleman Report, James Coleman *Equality of Educational Opportunity* (1965), is a work of formidable weight and influence, a landmark evaluation of performance and progress among public school students. The most important evaluation and forecast of outcomes in science-train-

ing and other new programs is to be found in Allen Cartter's contribution in C. T. Lee, ed. *Improving College Teaching,* 1967. Shrewd pointers on how these programs were put over are to be found in Francis Keppel's intensely felt but regrettably understated *Necessary Revolution in American Education* (1966). Charles Silberman's *Crisis in the Classroom* (1970) a work well grounded in the social sciences, sums up many of these developments, and singles out some new trends in their wake.

The specifications of postwar growth in colleges and universities were laid down in the influentially predictive report of the President's Commission *Higher Education for Democracy* (1947). Among critical assessments of what followed I found much to help form my own interpretation in the historical depth and social breadth of Oscar and Mary Handlin's overview for the Carnegie Corp's study of higher education, *The American College and American Culture* (1970). I also drew upon Robert Nisbet's wise and eloquent *Degradation of the Academic Dogma* (1971), Daniel Bell's eclectic *Reforming of General Education* (1966), Irving Horowitz and William M. Friedland's sardonically observed *The Knowledge Factory* (1970), Christopher Jencks and David Riesman's omnivorous *Academic Revolution* (1968) and upon two volumes edited by G. Kerry Smith, *Stress and Campus Response* (1968) and *Twenty-Five Years* (1970) that caught the unrest and turbulence of the times. Among other Carnegie project reports, I found Earl Cheit's *The New Depression in Higher Education* (1971) especially useful. James Ridgway's *The Closed Corporation* (1968) tellingly documented the onset of university dependence on Washington.

In interpreting the impact of Sputnik

on international rivalries, I benefited by the extra-American perspective of two valuable annual publications from London, *Documents on International Affairs* and *Survey, 1957–8*, both from Chatham House. As an analysis of Eisenhower administration strategic arrangements, Walt Rostow's bold and wide-ranging *The United States in the World Arena* (1960), I found, performed the kind of criticism for the Kennedy approach that Henry Kissinger's

more Europe-oriented *Nuclear Weapons and Foreign Policy* (1957) did earlier for the Rockefeller alternative. Zbigniew Brzezinski and Samuel Hungtington's *Political Power U.S.A./U.S.S.R.* (1963), though uneven, is an extremely provocative juxtaposing of East and West that I used with profit. In the main I followed Adam Ulan *Expansion and Coexistence* (1968) in trying to unravel Khrushchev's policy line.

CHAPTER 11.

Manners and morals of the Eisenhower years are fascinatingly touched on in Daniel Bell's topical *The End of Ideology* (1960). The thinning texture of American religious life is impressively observed and defined in Will Herberg *Protestant, Catholic, Jew* (1955), a work of lasting value. An audaciously original thesis to the contrary is to be found in Thomas Lachman *The Invisible Religion* (1966). Erving Goffman's unblinking *Presentation of Self in Everyday Life* (1959) constitutes a veritable camera-eye portrait of the times, and I have used it as such. In the same vein Daniel Boorstin's *The Image* (1962) mordantly takes apart the press conference and the incantatory style of public relations. The publications of Alfred Kinsey and his fellow investigators—*The Sexual Behavior of the Human Male* (1948) and *The Sexual Behavior of the Human Female* (1953)— are imposing works that belong to history. For an appraisal of what changed and what endured in American attitudes toward sex during the Cold War the best-balanced summation is to be found in the writings of Ira Reiss (*Premarital Sexual Standards in America,* (1960) and "Sexual Renaissance in America," *Journal of Social Issues,* April, 1966). These judgments are complemented by those of Robert O. Blood (*Husbands and Wives,* 1960) and Betty Friedan (*The Feminine Mystique,* 1963), pioneer of the women's liberation movement.

Various works record the slips in conduct of the Eisenhower years. Eric Barnouw's *The Image Empire* (1970) suggests the size of the financial stake in the TV quiz-show scandals, and Stan Opotowsky *TV, the Big Picture* (1961) acridly chroni-

cles the chicanery. The wrongdoing in the electrical industry is told best in John Herling's *The Great Price Conspiracy,* (1962), the source of General Eisenhower's quoted judgment on it all; John G. Fuller's *The Gentlemen's Conspiracy* (1962) presents a former businessman's cutting report on what the executives were up to. David A. Frier's *Conflict of Interest in the Eisenhower Administration* (1969) is scholarly but not penetrating enough for such a theme and subject. Though it lacks the apparatus of learning, I found myself much oftener consulting Walter Goodman's wide-ranging *All Honorable Men* (1965).

No one has begun to take the measure of the impact upon American policy—foreign or domestic—of that Cold War institution, the CIA. Allen Dulles' *The Craft of Intelligence* (1963) is immaculately reserved. H. H. Ransom's professional *Central Intelligence and National Security* (1958) accents theory, not facts. The partial revelations of Andrew Tully, *CIA, the Inside Story* (1962) and Sanche de Gramont *The Secret War* (1962) seem coy, foreign exposes uniformly unreliable, and even David B. Wise and Thomas B. Ross *The Invisible Government* (1964), a good early work, glaringly incomplete. In the Far East there is a little more to go on: Hugh Toye *Laos, Buffer State or Battleground* (1968) and George T. McKahin and John W. Lewis *The U.S. in Vietnam* (1967) are both outspoken and informed, and Neil Sheehan et al., eds., *The Pentagon Papers* (1972) opened a kind of window into CIA activities in Asia. Where possible I have used such knowledgable works as George Kennan *Memoirs II* (1972), Roger Hilsman

To Move a Nation (1967) and John Campbell The Foreign Affairs Fudge Factory (1972) for cross-checking.

For evaluating Russian policy in these years I relied on Ulam's Expansion and Coexistence (1967) and Marshall Shulman's judiciously balanced Beyond the Cold War (1966). For analysis of inner politics, Michel Tatu's ingenious Power in the Kremlin (1967) was indispensable. I also used Edward Crankshaw's The New Cold War (1969) and Thomas W. Wolfe Soviet Power and Europe 1945–70. For the crucial dispute with China, the analysis provided in Z. Brzezinski's introduction to A. Dallin and Brzezinski Diversity in International Communism (1963) was important, as were the writings of Richard Lowenthal (e.g. World Communism, 1964). I used Donald Zagoria's Sino-Soviet Conflict 1956–61 (1962) for the early years, John Gittings' Survey of the Sino-Soviet Dispute 1963–67 (1968) for the later period, and William E. Griffith The Sino-Soviet Rift (1964) throughout, both for interpretation and for documentation. From the Chinese side Oliver Edmund Clubb Twentieth Century China (1965) provides an authoritative outline; his China and Russia, the Great Game (1971) is a less successful effort to wind the skeins together. For the U-2 affair I drew a large part of the narrative from Powers' own account Operation Overflight (1970), and much of the Russian background from the analyses of Ulam and Tatu. On this phase Eisenhower's memoirs (Waging Peace, 1965) are for once quite revealing.

Cocerning jet travel John B. Lansing The Travel Market (1965) and Lansing and Dwight M. Blood The Changing Travel Market (1964) have both figures and trends. H. Peter Grey International Travel, International Trade (1970) provides analysis. But the literature is scant. John Burby's The Great American Motion Sickness (1971) makes a first try at bringing together the social aspects of the nation's addiction to speed and restlessness.

CHAPTER 12.

In interpreting the rise of the military as an enduring outcome of the Cold War I have taken from more than one viewpoint. Of such viewpoints The American Military Establishment (1971), put together by Adam Yarmolinsky, had too many to be of much help, though Ernest R. May's essay on military influence on diplomacy provided data and insights, Samuel Huntington's Common Defense (1961) and The Soldier and the State (1964) authoritatively demonstrate this growth from a conservative standpoint. Jack Raymond's Power at the Pentagon (1964) was valuable for its reporting rather than its analysis. James A. Donovan's Militarism U.S.A. (1970), though technical, is an extremely well documented and argued critique by a retired professional Marine officer. John Swomley Jr. The Military Establishment (1964) was helpful as a pacifist analysis, Seymour Melman's Pentagon Capitalism (1970) as a critical work from a business-engineering standpoint. Julius Duscha Men, Money and Politics (1965), Fred Cook The Warfare State (1962) and Richard J. Barnet The Economy of Death (1970) further documented the institutionalizing of the military within the society. George Thayer's hard-hitting The War Business (1969) demonstrated the palpable influence of Pentagon weapons-selling in American foreign policy.

Probably no single work set forth the facts and underlying import of the controversy over the military-industrial complex so trenchantly as H. L. Nieburg's solidly documented In the Name of Science (1966). Professor Nieburg's devastating demonstration of aerospace's budgetary dynamic not only underscored the obsolescence of Eisenhower's Pentagon leadership but influenced me to treat the arrival in Washington of the Kennedy Administration as yet another stage in the rise of the military. General John B. Medaris Countdown for Decision (1960), Michael Armacost The Politics of Weapons Innovation (1969) and C. W. Borklund Men of the Pentagon (1966) detail viewpoints within the military bureaucracy, and Ralph Lapp The Weapons Culture (1968) and Jerome

Wiesner *Where Science and Politics Meet* (1965) those of the bureaucracy's scientific members. Morton J. Peck and Frederick M. Scherer *The Weapons Acquisition Process* (1962) is an attempt to analyze costs in the labyrinthine processes of contract-letting. Some of the more extravagant instances of circumventing such attempts are caustically noted in J. K. Galbraith's tract *How to Control the Military* (1969), and clues to Eisenhower's vain struggle to fasten fiscal controls on the Air Force at the time of Sputnik, amply borne out upon investigation, were derived from Eliot Janeway's informed though declamatory *Economics of Crisis* (1968). Seymour Harris ed. *The Dollar in Crisis* (1962) documents the slippage in the international balance of payments. Rowland Evans and Robert Novak *Lyndon B. Johnson, the Exercise of Power* (1966), which is a source for information about Johnson's part in the form and timing of Senator McCarthy's censure in 1954, also furnishes evidence that the Senate Majority Leader operated effectively as the Air Force's ally. The interpretation of major military-industrial influence through the first Kennedy years, though it draws repeatedly on Theodore Sorensen's *Kennedy* (1965) and Arthur Schlesinger Jr.'s *A Thousand Days* (1965), much less so on David Halberstam's undocumented *The Best and the Brightest* (1972), fundamentally follows Nieburg. For the Vietnam sequel, which lies outside the scope of this book, an alternative version to Halber-

stam's is Walt Rostow *The Diffusion of Power* (1972).

Turning to the missile crisis of 1962, the great weight of information is from American sources. The best narrative of events based on Administration accounts is still Elie Abel *The Missile Crisis* (1966). Edward Weintal and Charles Bartlett *Facing the Brink* (1967), Henry Pachter *Collision Course* (1963) and David Larsen ed. *The Cuban Missile Crisis of 1962* (1963) are essentially Kennedy versions. Roger Hilsman *To Move a Nation* (1967) has further data, and Robert Kennedy *Thirteen Days* (1969) is a memoir of first importance and, brief as it is, adds substantially to the story. A historian's questions widen perspective: those Henry F. Graff's *The Tuesday Cabinet* (1970) asked about President Johnson's decisions threw light for me on President Kennedy's. I consulted the many decision-making analyses of the crisis, of which Graham Allison *Conceptual Models and the Cuban Missile Crisis* (1968) is a Byzantine example. To provide substance and engage in analysis of the Soviet side I found Ulam and particularly Tatu illuminating in piecing together motives and actions. W. E. Griffith *The Sino-Soviet Rift* (1964), T. W. Wolfe *Soviet Power in Europe* (1970) and Edward Crankshaw *The New Cold War, Moscow v. Pekin* (1963) also helped. Janos Radvanyi *Hungary and the Superpowers* (1972) has firsthand evidence from the time that Washington probably overreacted.

CHAPTER 13.

In *The Real Voice* (1964), Richard Harris has written the best account of Senator Kefauver's fight against drug profiteers. On the whole, computers seem to have arrived too precipitately to have claimed the attention of historians. Although I drew my information from many sources, Jeremy Bernstein *The Analytical Engine* (1964) was valuable for background. Joseph Becker and Robert M. Hayes *Information Storage and Retrieval* (1963), though technical, remains useful. Latter-day leisure is treated in essays in Philip Olson, ed. *America as a Mass Society* (1963) and in Lewis Mumford *The Myth of the Machine: The Penta-*

gon *of Power* (1970). I also consulted Reuel Denny *The Astonished Muse* (1957) and Hortense Powdermaker *The Hollywood Dream Factory* (1955), a small classic on movie impact on American culture.

For background of events leading up to the Treaty of Moscow I made repeated use of C.E. Zoppo, "The Test Ban," an unpublished Ph.D. thesis (1963) at Columbia University. The Chatham House *Surveys*, notably that for 1954 written by Coral Bell, were most helpful. and Jerome Wiesner's *Where Science and Politics Meet* (1965) had details about the Pugwash meetings. For the buildup of Russian-

Chinese tension I turned to Ulam and Tatu, though John Gittings *Survey of the Sino-Soviet Dispute* (1968), Morton Halperin and Dwight Perkins *Communist China and Arms Control* (1965) and L. C. Bloomfield et al. *Khrushchev and the Arms Race* (1966) were also valuable for assessing the Chinese component. Alan Whiting's narrative in C.J. Zablocki, ed. *Sino-Soviet Rivalry* (1966) also helped in places. Arthur Schlesinger Jr.'s *A Thousand Days* (1965) has a good account of Averill Harriman's dealings with Khrushchev in Moscow.

Although the imbalance in political power between rural and urban America that finally led to Supreme Court action may have contributed crucially to the violence of the 1960s, the subject of the reapportionment decisions has not yet attracted the attention of historians. Concerning the tumultuous sequel of the 1960s, William L. O'Neill's capsule of instant history *Coming Apart* (1971), though modishly participatory and far more endogenous than Eric Goldman's survey of the preceding years, has a great deal of informal anecdote and comment on student risings, urban firestorms and other dislocations of the decade. Presiding over *The Necessary Revolution in American Education* (1966) Francis Keppel grandly gives away credit for getting the huge appropriations through Washington to Khrushchev, John XXIII and the late Senator Taft. I found excellent background on urban problems after the Cold War in Mark Gelfand's unpublished Columbia University Ph.D., dissertation of 1972 entitled "A Nation of Cities." Professor Goldman's *The Tragedy of Lyndon Johnson* (1969) is replete with sharpened ironies. As a concluding irony Lyndon B. Johnson's *The Vantage Point* (1971) trudgingly retraces the enactment of his tremendous Great Society legislation even as, the Cold War over, the ground slipped under the nation's feet in the slide to Vietnam.

Notes

INTRODUCTION

1 J. Robert Oppenheimer, "International Control of Atomic Energy," *Foreign Affairs*, Jan. 1948, p. 239f.

2 Robert K. Merton, "Unanticipated Consequences of Purposive Social Action," *American Sociological Review*, pp. 894–904, Dec. 1936.

3 Robert K. Merton, *Social Theory and Social Structure*, (New York: Free Press, 1967, revised, orig. 1949), p. 421ff.

4 Ibid., p. 423.

CHAPTER 1.

1 Alan Bullock, *Hitler, a Study in Tyranny*, (New York: Harper Torchbook, revised, 1964), p. 765ff (Hitler's last days), p. 776 (Forster). Also Bullock, "Europe Since Hitler," *The Listener*, 29 Apr. 1971, p. 537ff. H.R. Trevor-Roper, introduction to Francois Benoud, ed. *The Testament of Adolf Hitler: the Hitler-Bormann Documents, Feb-Apr 1945.* (London: Cassell, 1960), passim.

2 Benoud, ed., *Testament of Adolf Hitler*, p. 107.

3 Charles B. MacDonald, *The Mighty Endeavor: American Armed Forces in the European Theatre in World War II*, (New York: Oxford, 1969), p. 497. Cornelius Ryan, *The Last Battle*, (New York: Simon and Schuster, 1966), p. 470 (Lt. Kotzebue et al.).

4 *The New York Times*, 28 Apr 1945, p. 1 (Truman) and 29 Apr 1945 (Torgau details, *Red Star*, Chicago *Sun* cartoon).

5 *St. Louis Post-Dispatch*, 1 Feb 1946, p. 1 (Miami sprees); 4 Feb 1946, p. 1 (idled strikes, *Egg and I*); 10 Feb 1946, P. 1 (teen-agers).

6 Elie Abel, "Decontrol Charlie," *The New York Times Magazine*, 14 Dec 1952 (Baruch). Frank Freidel, *America in the Twentieth Century* (New York: Knopf, 1960), 2nd ed., p. 486. *St. Louis Post-Dispatch*, 23 Apr 1946, p. 1 (housing). Kingsley Davis, "Urbanization of the Human Population," *Scientific American*, Sept 1965, p. 22. Benjamin Chinitz, "New York, a Metropolitan Region," *Scientific American*, Sept 1965, p. 134ff. Miles L. Colean, *Impact of Government on Real Estate Finance in the United States*, (New York: National Bureau of Economic Research, 1950), p. 107.

7 Colean, *Impact of Government*, p. 110. Glenn H. Beyer, *Housing: A Factual Analysis*, (New York: Macmillan, 1955), p. 127. Glenn H. Beyer, *Housing and Society*, (New York: Macmillan, 1965), p. 474. Saul B. Klaman, *Postwar Residential Mortgage Market*, (Princeton; Princeton University Press, 1961), p. 50. *The Fabulous Century*, Volume V, (New York: Time-Life Books, 1970), p. 210 (Benny Goodman). Harry S. Truman, *Memoirs*, I *(Year of Decisions)*, (Garden City: Doubleday, 1955), p. 514.

8 Truman, *Memoirs*, I, pp. 4–5. Arthur S. Link, *American Epoch*, (New York: Alfred A. Knopf, 1963), p. 667. Dean Acheson, *Sketches from Life*, (New York: Harper, 1960), p. 137. Cabell Phillips, *The Truman Presidency* (Baltimore; Penguin paperback 1969, orig. 1966), p. 6. *The New York Times*, 17 Apr 1945 (Truman). David Thomson, *HST, a pictorial biography*, (New York; Grosset & Dunlap, 1973), p. 70 (Truman-Early).

9 *The New York Times*, 24 Jun 1941, p. 7. See also George Seldes, *The People Don't Know*, (New York: Gaer, 1949), p. 89. Joyce and Gabriel Kolko, *The Limits of Power, the World and United States Foreign Policy, 1945–1954*, (New York: Harper & Row, 1972), pp. 481, 768 (Peter the Great's will). Phillips, *The Truman Presidency*, p. 9 ("gutsy little fighter"). George E. Mowry, *The Urban Nation, 1920–60*. (New York: Hill and Wang,

1965), p. 167ff. Jonathan Daniels, *Man of Independence*, (Philadelphia: Lippincott, 1950), p. 30ff. John A. Garraty, *The American Nation*, (New York: Harper, 1968), p. 805ff. Interview, Henry Graff, Sept 1970 ("Opinions like my barber's").

10 William Hillman, *Mr. President* (New York: Farrar Straus and Young, 1952), p. 33 (MacArthur).

11 *Public Papers of the President of the United States: Harry S. Truman 1952–3*. (Washington: Government Printing Office, 1955), p. 1202.

12 Alfred Steinberg, *Man from Missouri*, (New York: Putnam, 1962), p. 345 (120 steps a minute). Phillips, *The Truman Presidency*, p. 9ff. Daniels, *Man of Independence*, p. 89ff. Hillman, *Mr. President*, p. 179. Daniels, *op.cit.*, p. 186 ("I'm not used to meeting people like that").

13 Hillman, *Mr. President*, p. 137 (Adams et al.).

14 Merle Miller, *That Winter* (New York: Harper, 1946). *Time*, 19 Feb 1946, p. 80. Steinberg, *Man from Missouri*, p. 280. Daniels, *Man of Independence* p. 312. James Byrnes, *All in One Lifetime*, (New York: Harper & Row, 1958), p. 349. Barton J. Bernstein and Allen Matusow, eds. *The Truman Administration, a Documentary History*, (New York: Harper & Row, 1966), p. 217ff. Kolko, *Limits of Power*, p. 4.

15 *St. Louis Post-Dispatch*, 3–5 Mar 1946. *The New York Times*, 4–6 Mar, 1946. Steinberg, *Man from Missouri*, p. 281.

16 *The New York Times*, 6 Mar, 1946. *Time*, 18 Mar, 1946, p. 19. *Vital Speeches*, May 1946, p. 324ff (Churchill). Walter Johnson, *Battle against Isolation*, (Chicago: University of Chicago Press, 1944), p. 62 (White in Emporia, 1940). Francis Williams, *A Prime Minister Remembers, Memoirs of Earl Attlee*, (London: Heineman, 1961), p. 162.

17 *Public Opinion Quarterly*, X. 2, summer 1946, p. 264 (Gallup poll after Fulton speech. *The New York Times*, 7 Mar, 1946 (Shaw, French, Pearl Buck); 8 March 1946 (reader's letter);

10 Mar 1946 (*Wall Street Journal* quote).

18 *The New York Times*, 19 Mar 1946. *Time*, 25 Mar 1946, p. 26. Kenneth Ingram, *History of the Cold War*, (New York: Philosophical Library, 1955), p. 31.

19 Arthur S. Link, *Wilson, the Struggle for Neutrality, 1914–15*, (Princeton; Princeton University Press, 1960), p. 48 (statement by House).

20 J. McG. Burns, *Roosevelt the Soldier* (Boston: Houghton, Mifflin, 1970), pp. 186, 223. Dean Acheson, *Present at the Creation*, (New York: W. W. Norton, 1969), p. 4. W.S. Churchill, *The Grand Alliance*, (Boston: Houghton Mifflin, 1951), p. 373 (Stalin). H. B. Westerfield, *Foreign Policy and Party Politics*, (New Haven: Yale University Press, 1953), pp. 150, 196 (Asia Firsters). Robert Sherwood, *Roosevelt and Hopkins*, (New York: Harper, 1950). pp. 443, 557-576, 785-6, 792. Dept. of State, *Foreign Relations of the United States 1942*, Vol. III (Washington: Government Printing Office, 1960), p. 566ff. W.A. Williams, *Tragedy of American Diplomacy*, (New York: Dell paperback, 1962, orig. 1959), p. 202ff. *Correspondence between Chairman of the Council of Ministers of the U.S.S.R. and the President of the U.S. and the Prime Minister of Great Britain during the Great Patriotic War of 1941–45*, Vols I-III (Moscow: Foreign Language Publishing House, 1957), p. 314, 328. Ivan Maisky, *Memoirs of a Soviet Ambassador: the War: 1939–1943*, (New York: Scribner, 1968), pp. 251, 268, 282 (second front). Gabriel Kolko, *The Politics of War: the World and United States Foreign Policy, 1943–1945* (New York: Random House, 1968), p. 268. Dept of State, *Foreign Relations of the United States 1944*, II, pp. 627–28; *Foreign Relations of the United States, Teheran Conference*, pp. 530–31. Trygve Lie, *In the Cause of Peace*, (New York: Harper, 1954), pp. 18, 29. Herbert Feis, *Churchill, Roosevelt, Stalin* (Princeton: Princeton University Press, 1957), p. 39. Gaddis Smith, *American Diplomacy in the Second World War* (New York: Wiley, 1965) pp. 119, 173. Clement Attlee, *As It Happened*, (London: Heineman, 1954), p. 149.

21 *The New York Times*, 15 Jan 1946. *Time*, 12 Feb 1940, Oct 2, 1940 (statement by Vandenberg—"25 people"). Arthur Vandenberg Jr., ed, *Private Papers of Senator Vandenberg* (Boston; Houghton Mifflin, 1952), pp. 132–38, 140. See also *Vital Speeches*, 11, pp. 226–30 (Jan 1945 speech). Richard Rovere, *The American Establishment* (New York: Harcourt, 1962), p. 186 (1920 slogan). James Reston, "Events Spotlighting Vandenberg's Role," *The New York Times Magazine*, 28 Mar 1949, p. 10. Acheson, *Sketches from Life*, p. 123. *Time*, 30 Apr 1945. *Biographical Directory of the U.S. Congress, 1774–1971* (Washington: Government Printing Office, 1971), p. 1849 (Vandenberg). Cordell Hull, *Memoirs*, II, (New York: Macmillan, 1949), p. 1658. Sumner Welles, *Time for Decision* (New York: Harper, 1944), pp. 306, 388.

22 R.E. and T.N. Dupuy, *Encyclopedia of Military History* (New York: Harper, 1970), p. 1198 (Russian war casualties). Alexander Werth, *Russia at War, 1941–45*, (New York: Dutton, 1964), p. 1004 (Russian war damage). William Leahy, *I Was There* (New York: Harper, 1950); pp. 351–2. E.R. Stettinius, *Roosevelt and the Russians: The Yalta Conference*, (Garden City: Doubleday, 1949), pp. 300–335. Truman, *Memoirs*, I, p. 82. *The New York Times*, 25 Apr 1945. Dept of State, *Foreign Relations of the United States 1945*, V, p. 253. Diane S. Clemens, *Yalta*, (New York: Oxford, 1970), p. 283. Westerfield, *Foreign Policy and Party Politics*, p. 206 (House move against Communist party). Feis, *Churchill, Roosevelt, Stalin*, p. 518. Gaddis Smith, *American Diplomacy*, p. 137. *Public Opinion Quarterly*, X, 4, winter 1946–47, p. 608 (Gallup poll).

23 Eric Goldman, *The Crucial Decade and After*, (New York: Vintage paperback, 1960), p. 35. Arthur Link,

American Epoch, p. 683. Truman, *Memoirs* I, pp. 28, 547. Acheson, *Present at the Creation,* pp. 136, 163. Daniels, *Man of Independence,* p. 308. Steinberg, *Man from Missouri,* p. 279. James F. Byrnes, *Speaking Frankly,* (New York: Harper, 1947), p. 238. Sumner Welles, *Seven Decisions that Shaped History* (New York: Harper, 1950), p. 207.

24   Acheson, *Present at the Creation,* p. 191. Daniels, *Man of Independence,* p. 312. Truman, *Memoirs* I, p. 558. *Public Papers of the President, Harry S. Truman 1946,* pp. 426–28 (press conference exchange). Byrnes, *Speaking Frankly,* p. 240. Goldman, *Crucial Decade,* p. 40. *Vandenberg Papers,* p. 301.

25   *The New York Times,* 30 Mar 1946. Daniels, *Man of Independence,* p. 326. Goldman, *Crucial Decade,* p. 42 (quotes Cleveland *Plain Dealer).*

26   Friedrich Hayek, *The Road to Serfdom,* (Chicago: University of Chicago Press, 1944), pp. 10 ff.

27   Robert and Helen Lynd, *Middletown Revisited* (New York: Harcourt, 1973), p. 74ff. Goldman, *Crucial*

Decade, p. 54. James T. Patterson, *Mr. Republican* (Boston: Houghton Mifflin, 1972), p. 311ff. (Taft details).

28   Henry F. Pringle, *The Life and Times of William Howard Taft,* II (New York: Farrar and Rinehart, 1939), p. 128. (Letter to Helen H. Taft, July 8, 1894).

29   Walter Johnson, *1600 Pennsylvania Avenue,* (Boston: Little Brown, 1960), p. 226. Goldman, *Crucial Decade,* p. 56. W.H. White, *The Taft Story* (New York: Harper, 1954), p. 80. Freidel, *America in the Twentieth Century,* p. 493. Patterson, *Mr. Republican,* p. 335ff. Arthur Schlesinger Jr., "His Eyes Have Seen the Glory," *Colliers,* 22 Feb 1947, p. 12ff. Edward B. Lockett, "Big Two on Capitol Hill," *The New York Times Magazine,* 1 Jun 1947, p. 22. "Blunt Senator Taft", *Colliers,* 22 Nov 1947, p. 110. Richard H. Rovere, "What's Happened to Taft?" *Harper's,* April 1952, p. 38ff. *Time,* 20 Jan 1947; 15 Jun 1948. New York *Post,* 4 Mar 1948; 15 Jun 1948, p. 39. *The New York Times,* 1 Aug 1954, p. 1 (Taft quotes).

CHAPTER 2.

1   *The New York Times,* 11 Dec 1950 (Faulkner speech). See also R.G. Tugwell, *Chronicle of Jeopardy,* (Chicago: University of Chicago Press, 1955), p. 1.

2   *The New York Times,* 8 Oct 1945, p. 8 (Carruthersville speech), 7 May 1947 (Waco speech).

3   *The New York Times,* 10 Feb 1946, pp. 1, 30 (Stalin speech). *Izvestia,* 24 Jan 1962, p. 1 gives 1961 figures cited by Marshall Shulman, *Stalin's Foreign Policy Reappraised,* (New York: Atheneum paperback, 1969), p. 285.

4   *The New York Times,* 10 Feb 1946, pp. 1, 30.

5   A. Solzhenitsyn, *The First Circle,* (New York: Harper & Row, 1968), pp. 19–20, 326–7, 579. Shulman, *Stalin's Foreign Policy,* p. 25 (Blagonrovov). *Soviet Space Program: Organization, Plans, Goals and International Im-*

plications, Staff report, Senate Committee on Aeronautics and Space Sciences, 87th Congress, 2nd session, Washington: Government Printing Office, 1962), p. 64. Arnold Kramish, *Atomic Energy in the Soviet Union,* (Stanford: Stanford University Press, 1959), p. 97ff. (Soviet reactor).

6   M. Djilas, *Conversations with Stalin,* (New York: Harcourt Harvest paperback, 1962), p. 114. Walter Millis, ed. *The Forrestal Diaries,* (New York: Viking, 1951), p. 134 (Douglas statement). J.L. Gaddis, *The United States and the Origins of the Cold War,* (New York: Columbia University Press), 1972, p. 302.

7   Dept. of State, *Foreign Relations of the U.S. 1946,* VI, p. 696ff. (Kennan dispatch). See also Kennan, *Memoirs,* I, (Boston: Little Brown, 1967), pp. 294–5.

8   Robert Hector and Harold Steinberg, *The Chief Executive,* (New York: Crown, 1965), p. 268 (Roosevelt statement from First Inaugural, 4 March, 1933).

9   Forrest Pogue, *George C. Marshall,* I, (New York: Viking, 1963), p. xv. Thomas H. Ferrill, *George Marshall: American Secretaries of State,* XV, (New York: Cooper Square Publishing, 1965), pp. 74–83. Daniels, *Man of Independence,* p. 317. Acheson, *Present at the Creation,* p. 140 (Marshall),.

10 Stephen G. Xydis, *Greece and the Great Powers, 1944–47,* (Saloniki: Institute for Balkan Studies, 1963), p. 476ff. William H. McNeill, *America, Britain and Russia,* (New York: Oxford University Press, 1953), pp. 476–8. Winston Churchill, *Triumph and Tragedy,* (Boston: Houghton Mifflin, 1953), p. 311. Acheson, *Present at the Creation,* p. 219 (Vandenberg statement). Joseph Jones, *Fifteen Weeks,* (New York: Viking Harbinger paperback 1964, orig. 1951), Walter LaFeber, *America, Russia and the Cold War,* (New York: Wiley, 1967), p. 28. H.B. Price, *The Marshall Plan and its Meaning,* (Ithaca: Cornell University Press, 1955), p. 395. St. Louis *Post-Dispatch,* 2 Mar 1947. *The New York Times,* 2 and 5 Mar 1947.

11 *St. Louis Post-Dispatch,* 4 Mar 1946, p. 20. *The New York Times,* 12 & 13 1947 (St. Paul *Pioneer Press* quote). Goldman, *The Crucial Decade,* p. 59 (Vandenberg "scare hell" statement). Walter Johnson, *1600 Pennsylvania Avenue,* p. 206. *Vandenberg Papers,* p. 339. *Forrestal Diaries,* p. 251.

12 *Public Papers of the Presidents: H.S. Truman 1947,* pp. 178–9. Truman, *Memoirs,* II, p. 105ff. *The New York Times,* 13 Mar 1947. *Time,* 24 Mar 1947, p. 17ff.

13 St. Louis *Post-Dispatch,* 12, 13 Mar 1947. *The New York Times,* 12, 13 Mar 1947. Jones, *Fifteen Weeks,* p. 200. Acheson, *Present at the Creation,* p. 223 (U.N. and Vandenberg).

14 *The New York Times,* 14 March, 3–7 May 1947 (*Guardian,* Paris reports, French and Italian Communists).

H.G. Nicholas, *Britain and the United States,* (Baltimore: John Hopkins University Press, 1963), p. 22.

15 *Public Papers of the Presidents: H.S. Truman 1947,* p. 179

16 H.J. Morgenthau, *In Defense of the National Interest,* (New York: Alfred A. Knopf, 1951), p. 115ff. H.J. Morgenthau, *Purpose of American Politics,* (New York: Alfred A. Knopf, 1960), p. 158. Gabriel A. Almond, *American People and Foreign Policy,* (New York: Praeger, 1950), pp. 91, 130, 138–9, 228, 233. See also James Aronson, *The Press and the Cold War,* (Indianapolis: Bobbs-Merrill, 1970), p. 37 (National Opinion Research Center's successive polls).

17 *The New York Times,* 17 Apr 1947, p. 21. Goldman, *The Crucial Decade,* p. 60.

18 Allan Nevins, in *The New York Times Magazine,* 2 May 1948. Stephen King-Hall in *Readers' Digest,* Nov 1945, p. 14. Paul Hoffman, *Peace Can Be Won,* (Garden City: Doubleday, 1951), p. 116 (Vincent Sheean). Donald A. Schon, *Technology and Change,* (New York: Delacorte, 1967), p. 39. Victor C. Ferkiss, *Technological Man,* (New York: Braziller, 1969), p. 12.

19 In his earlier fantasy, *Animal Farm* (New York: Harcourt, 1946; Signet paperback, 1960), Orwell sketched a barnyard society that, especially in England, was taken as a Swiftian satire on the excesses of socialism. Socialist Prime Minister Clement Attlee was fond of quoting the dictum of Napoleon, the leader pig: "All animals are equal, but some are more equal than others." (p. 22).

20 George Orwell, *1984* (New York: Harcourt, 1949). Lionel Trilling in *The New Yorker,* 18 Jun 1949, p. 78ff. *Time,* 20 Jun 1949, p. 90. *Life,* 4 July 1949. *The New York Times Book Review,* 12 Jun 1949. *Atlantic Monthly,* July 1949, p. 83. *Commonweal,* 5 July 1949. *Catholic World,* August 1949, p. 76.

21 *Fortune,* Aug 1947 p. 165 (Taft quote).

22 S.M. Cavert, *Church Cooperation and*

Unity in America, (New York: Association Press, 1970), p. 29. S.M. Cavert, *American Churches in the Ecumenical Movement*, (New York: Association Press, 1969), p. 110. "The Churches and Economic Tensions," in Federal Council of Churches, *Biennial Report 1946*, p. 110. *Christianity and Crisis*, 13 May 1946.

23 *Biennial Report 1946*, p.135, and Cavert, *American Churches*, p. 191 (Dulles).

24 Ronald H. Stone, *Reinhold Niebuhr's Perspective on United States Foreign Policy*, unpublished Ph.D. dissertation, Columbia University, 1968, p.v. (Cf. R.H. Stone, *Reinhold Niebuhr, a Prophet to Politicians*, (Nashville; Abingdon, 1972) Arthur M. Schlesinger Jr., "Theology and Politics from the Social Gospel to the Cold War," in Cushing Stout, ed. *Intellectual History in America*, II, (New York; Harper, 1968), p. 158ff. Donald B. Meyer, *Protestant Search for Political Realism, 1919–41*, (Berkeley: University of California Press, 1961), pp. 360, 409. Gordon Harland, *Thought of Reinhold Niebuhr*, (New York: Oxford, 1960), p. 165. Kenneth Thompson, "Niebuhr's Political Realism," in Charles Kegley, ed. *Reinhold Niebuhr, His Religious, Social and Political Thought*, (New York: Mcmillan, 1956), p. 171ff. Kenneth Thompson, "Beyond National Interest: Reinhold Niebuhr's Theory of International Politics," *Review of Politics*, 19 April, 1965. R.Niebuhr, *Moral Man and Immoral Society*, (New York: Scribner, 1932). p.ix. R. Niebuhr, *Nature and Destiny of Man*, (New York: Scribner, 1940), p.x. R. Niebuhr, *Children of Light and Children of Darkness*, (New York: Scribner, 1944), p.10. Niebuhr, *Self and Dramas of History*, (New York: Scribner, 1955), p.85 (rationalism and sentimentality in the American liberal heritage). R. Niebuhr, *Christian Realism and Political Problems*, (New York: Scribner, 1953), pp.34, 36, 40 (evils of Communism).

25 Niebuhr articles: *Life*, 20 Sept 1948. "Editorial Notes," *Christianity and Crisis*, 5 Jun 1945, 1 Apr 1946, 15 Apr 1946, 8 July 1946. "Report on Germany," *Christianity and Crisis*, 6 Oct 1946, (hardening ideology after German visit). "Editorial Notes," *Christianity and Crisis*, 26 Oct 1946, 17 Feb 1947, 12 May 1947, 26 May 1947, 9 Jun 1947, 7 July 1947, 21 July 1947, 19 Jan 1948, 2 Feb 1948, 16 Feb 1948. "Amid Encircling Gloom," *Christianity and Crisis*, 12 April 1948. "Two Secular World Religions," *Christianity and Society*, Summer 1947. "Can We Avoid Catastrophe?" *Christian Century*, 26 May 1948.

26 *Chirstianity and Society*, Spring 1947 (U.D.A. background). Harland, *Thought of Reinhold Niebuhr*, p. 212 (names of followers). Kenneth Thompson, *Political Realism and Crisis in World Politics*, (Princeton: Princeton University Press, 1960), p. 50ff. LaFeber, *America, Russia and the Cold War*, p. 40. *Life*, 21 Oct 1946. *Life*, 20 Sept 1948. *Christianity and Crisis*, 4 Aug 1947. Stone, op. cit. p. 173. Jane Bingham, *The Courage to Be*, (New York: Scribner, 1961), p. 368 (statement by Kennan). Stout, *Intellectual History in America*, p. 368 (statement by Donegan). *The New York Times*, 2 Jun 1971.

27 Robert I. Gannon, *The Cardinal Spellman Story*, (Garden City: Doubleday, 1962), pp. 3ff, 115, 133, 168 (Spellman quotes). *Catholic Mind*, Jan 1968. *Catholic Action*, Jan 1946.

28 Francis Cardinal Spellman, *The Road to Victory*, (New York: Scribner, 1944), p. 390. Spellman, *The Risen Soldier*, (New York: Macmillan, 1944), p. 39. Spellman, *Action This Day*, (New York: Scribner, 1943), p. 22. Gannon, *Cardinal Spellman Story*, p. 389.

29 *The New York Times*, 18 Mar 1948 (St. Patrick's Day speech). Cf. Gannon, *Cardinal Spellman Story*, p. 247. *Newsweek*, 24 May, 1954, p. 54 ("richest see"). *See also* C.J.V. Murphy, "The Cardinal," *Fortune*, Feb 1960, pp. 151, 184. James Gallin, *Worldly Goods* (New York: Random House, 1971), pp. 139, 280. *The New York Times*, May 28, 1947; Jan 26,

1951; Jul 7, 1947, VIII, 1; Nov 16, 1970; Apr 5, 1972.

30 *The New York Times*, 3 Dec 1967. *America*, 16 Dec 1967 (Saigon speech). *Commonweal*, 15 Dec 1967, 13 Jan 1967. Robert Scheer, "Hang Down Your Head, Tom Dooley," *Ramparts*, Jan-Feb 1965, p. 27 (Spellman on Geneva conference).

31 Education in international affairs: Grayson Kirk, *Study of International Relations in American Colleges and Universities*, (New York: Council on Foreign Relations, 1947), p. 88. Irwin T. Sander and Jennifer Ward, *Bridges to Understanding*, (New York: McGraw Hill, 1970), p. 16 (Wisconsin survey). Charles Wagley, "Area Research and Training," Study No. 6 of Social Science Research Council, June 1948, p. 55. Howard E. Wilson, *Universities and World Affairs*, (New York: Carnegie Endowment for International Peace, 1951. Howard L. Nostrand and F.J. Brown, *Role of Colleges and Universities in International Understanding*, (Washington: American Council of Education, 1949), p. 1. William W. Marvel, *The University Looks Abroad*, (New York: Educational and World Affairs, 1966), p. 2. Quincy Wright, *Study of International Relations*, (New York: Appleton-Century-Crofts, 1955), p. ix. Wendell C. Bennett, *Area Study in American Universities*, (New York: Social Science Research Council, Jun 1951), p. 1. Jacques Barzun, *Teacher in America*, (Garden City: Doubleday Anchor paperback, 1954 (orig. 1945), p. 127ff.

32 H.E. Wilson, *American Higher Education and World Affairs*, (Washington: American Council on Education, 1963), p. 115. *University Centers of Foreign Affairs Research, A Selective Directory*, (Washington: Dept. of State, Office of External Research, 1968), pp. iii-ix, p. viii (statement by Nitze). *Report of the Committee on University and World Affairs*, (New York: Ford Foundation, 1960), pp. 2, 22. L. Gray Cowan, *History of the School of International Affairs*, (New York: Columbia University Press, 1954), p. 5. *Harvard Center for Inter-*

national Studies: the First Five Years, (Cambridge: 1963), p. 115. *Center for International Studies, A Description* MIT Center for International Studies, July 1955, p. 7. *The School of International Affairs*, (New York: Dienbienphu Family, 1971), mimeo, pp. 1-3. *Area Studies in American Universities*, (Washington: Dept of State Bureau of Intelligence and Research, 1959). p. 5. Maurice Harari, *Global Dimensions in U.S. Education: the University*, (New York: Center for War-Peace Studies, 1972), p. 4. *ICED Data Bank of International Programs of Higher Educational Institutions, Report for Year 1970-71*. (New York: International Council for Educational Development, Jun 1971), p. 20. Jacques Barzun, *The American University*, (New York: Harper, 1968), p. 51. Thomas Braden, "I'm Glad the CIA is Immoral," *Saturday Evening Post*, May 20, 1967. Christopher Rand, *Cambridge, USA*, (New York: Oxford, 1964), p. 73.

33 Schools: *Life Adjustment for Every Youth*, (Washington: Office of Education, 1948), p. 7ff. Also Bulletin #22 entitled *Life Adjustment for Every Youth*, (Washington, Government Printing Office, 1951). Arthur Bestor, "Life Adjustment Education, a Critique," in *Bulletin of American Association of University Professors*, Vol. 38, summer, 1952, p. 413ff. (Illinois details). John Dewey, "The Child and the Curriculum" (1902) in Martin Dworkin, ed. *Dewey on Education*, (New York: Teachers College paperback, 1959), p. 22. Harl R. Douglas, *Education for Life Adjustment*, (New York: Ronald Press, 1950), pp. 3, 168. Bernard Mehl, "Political and Social Cohesion of Secondary Education in the U.S." in Helen Heffernan, "Educational Explosion," in G.Z.F. Bereday et al., *World Yearbook of Education*, (New York: Harcourt, 1966), pp. 319, 324, 328-9. George Z.F. Bereday and J.A. Lauwerys, eds., "The Secondary School Curriculum" in *Yearbook of Education 1958*, (Yonkers: World Books Co. 1958), pp. 135-8. Hollis Caswell, "Speeding Curriculum

Change," *Teachers College Record,* Feb 1947, p. 306. Lawrence Cremin, *Transformation of the Schools,* (New York: Knopf, 1961), p. 300. Theodore Brameld, ed. *The Battle for Free Schools,* (Boston: Beacon, 1951), p. 26. *Vitalizing Secondary Education* (Washington: Federal Security Administration, Government Printing Office, 1951), pp. v, 75. Paul Jacobson, "How Can We Organize the High School Curriculum to Service Life Problems?" in *Bulletin of National Association of Secondary School Principals,* Vol. 23, 167, Jan 1950, p. 186. Edgar L. Hordon, in *Educational Outlook,* XXIV, 1949–50, p. 75 (Los Angeles). Dael Wolfle, *America's Resources of Specialized Talent,* (New York: Harper, 1954), pp. 1, 33. Robert W. Iversen, *The Communists in the Schools,* (New York: Harcourt, 1959), pp. 242–3.

34 John W. Studebaker, "Communism's Challenge to American Education," *School Life,* Feb 1948, p. 6ff. E.M. Dirksen, "Thrust of Communism Today," address to Chief State School Officers, *Bulletin of AAUP,* Vol. 38, Summer 1952, p. 220. Willis Moore, "Indoctrination in Education," *Bulletin of AAUP,* Vol. 38, Summer 1952, p. 220. Robert Havighurst, "Personal Freedom," *Bulletin of the AAUP,* Vol. 38, Summer 1952, p. 236. John W. Caughey, "In California," *Bulletin of the AAUP,* Vol. 38, Summer 1952, p. 254. Dwight Macdonald, *The Ford Foundation,* (New York: Reynal, 1956), p. 33. Martin Mayer, *The Schools,* (New York: Harper, 1961), p. 300. David Goslin, *The School in Contemporary Society,* (Chicago: Scott Foresman, 1965), p. 155. Alexander Meiklejohn, "Teaching of Intellectual Freedom," *Bulletin of the AAUP,* Spring 1952, p. 111. Iversen, *The Communists in the Schools* p. 260.

35 *School Life,* Feb 1948, p. 18 (Counts). *Not Guilty, Report of the Committee of Inquiry into Charges Made against Leon Trotsky,* (New York: Harper, 1938), p. vii (Dewey). George R. Geiger, *John Dewey in Per-* *spective,* (New York: Oxford University Press, 1958), p. 184. James T. Farrell, "Dewey in Mexico" and Jim Cork, "John Dewey and Karl Marx," in Sidney Hook, ed. *John Dewey, A Symposium,* (New York: Barnes and Noble reprint 1967 (orig. 1950), pp. 311, 331.

36 William F. Russell, "U.S.A. and U.S.S.R.," *Teachers College Record,* Vol. 48, No. 5, Feb 1947, p. 209.

37 *School Life,* Feb 1948, (CSSO resolution).

38 John K. Norton, "Should Members of the Communist Party be Employed as Teachers," *Teachers College Record,* Oct 1949. Mayer, *The Schools,* p. 74. Cremin, *The Transformation of the School,* p. 300.

39 Sidney Hook, ed. *John Dewey, A Symposium,* p. 214. Sidney Hook, "Heresy, Yes, but Conspiracy, No," *The New York Times Magazine,* 9 July 1950. *The New York Times,* 27 Jun 1950, p. 19 (Koestler and Congress for Cultural Freedom); 19 July 1953, IV, p. 10 (Hook, Counts); VI, p. 12 (Koestler). Christopher Lasch, *The Agony of the American Left,* (New York: Alfred A. Knopf, 1968), p. 63ff.

40 Hook, "Heresy, Yes, but Conspiracy, No."

41 Iversen, *The Communists in the Schools,* p. 285. *The New York Times,* 19 July 1953, IV, p. 10 (statements by Hook, Counts). See also Lasch, *Agony of the American Left,* p. 81.

42 *Congress and the Nation,* (Washington: Congressional Quarterly Service, 1965), p. 3. J. Frederick Dewhurst, *America's Needs and Resources,* (New York: Twentieth Century Fund, 1947), p. 316. *Americana Yearbook 1948,* (Chicago: Encyclopedia Americana, 1949), p. 333 (Hadley). John A. Garrity, *The American Nation,* (New York: Harper & Row, 1966), p. 860. Goldman, *The Crucial Decade,* pp. 13, 48.

43 *Education for Democracy,* (Boston: D.C. Heath, 1952), p. 18ff (Report of President's Commission on Higher Education, 1948). *Americana Yearbook 1948,* p. 333 (Gannon statement). John Brooks, *The Great Leap,*

(New York: Harper & Row, 1966), pp. 217, 232. Oscar and Mary Handlin, *The American College and American Culture*, (New York: McGraw-Hill, 1970), p. 73. *Current Population Reports*, Series P-20, No. 229, Table 1, (Washington: Bureau of the Census, 1971) (highest school-leaving age). Also, "Estimates of Median Age at High School and College Graduation, 1960 and 1950," Current Population Reports, Series P-23, No. 9 (Nov. 8, 1963). Communication from W. Vance Grant, Educational Statistics Division, U.S. Office of Education, 6 Sept 1972.

44 *The New York Times*, 24 Jan 1971, p. 1 (young maturing earlier).

45 *The New York Times*, 3 Feb 1971, p. 3 (education "gap" figures). Theodore Roszak, *The Making of the Counter Culture*, (Garden City: Doubleday, 1968), pp. xii-xiii. Kenneth Keniston, *The Young Radicals*, (New York: Harcourt, 1968), pp. 42-3.

46 Committee on Life Adjustment, *Vitalizing American Education*, (Washington: Government Printing Office, 1951), p. 75 (Junior Town Meeting of the Air, Houses of Tomorrow). "Youth Speaks for Democracy," *School Life*, Feb 1948, p. 23 (Dicksie Dillon et al.). Julius P. Eisendroth, "America's New 400," *Bulletin of National Association of Secondary School Principals*, Jan. 1950, p. 185, (no smoker meeting). *Columbia College Forum on Democracy*, 10 Feb 1949

(mimeo) and *Second Annual Columbia College Forum on Democracy*, 2-4 Mar 1950 (mimeo).

47 *The New York Times*, 1, 5, 27 Oct 1955 (Jimmy Dean). *Time*, 10 Oct 1955. *Newsweek*, 10 Oct 1955. "Dean of the One-Shooters," *Time*, 3 Sept 1956. "Moody New Star," *Life*, 7 Mar 1955, p. 125. Ezra Goodman, "Delirium over Dead Star," *Life*, 24 Sept 1956, p. 75. George Scullen, "James Dean, the Legend and the Facts," *Look*, 16 Oct 1956, p. 120. Hollis Alpert, "It's Dean, Dean, Dean," *The Saturday Review*, 13 Oct 1956, p. 28. Gerald Weales, "The Crazy, Mixed-up Kids Take Over," *The Reporter*, 13 Dec 1956, p. 40. Sam Astrakhan, "The New Lost Generation", *New Republic*, 4 Feb 1957, p. 17. Alain Bosquet, ed. *Les americains*, (Paris: Robert Delpire, 1958), p. 142.

48 *Newsweek*, 2 Nov 1953 and 11 Mar 1957, p. 102 (student quotes).

49 *The Nation*, 9 Mar 1957, p. 199ff ("silent generation"). "The Class of '58 Speaks Up," *The Nation*, 17 May 1958. Rose K. Goldsen, Morris Rosenberg, Robin Williams and Edward A. Suchman, *What College Students Think*, (New York: Van Nostrand, 1950), pp. xxii, 1-2, 75.

50 *Report of the President's Commission on Campus Unrest* (Scranton report), (Washington: Government Printing Office, 1970), pp. 20, 21.

CHAPTER 3.

1 *The New York Times*, 29 Apr 1947 (statement of Marshall after Moscow). Joseph Jones, *Fifteen Weeks*, p. 200. Acheson, *Present at the Creation*, p. 213. Harry Price, *The Marshall Plan and its Meaning*, p. 4.

2 *St. Louis Post-Dispatch*, 13 Mar 1947 (Lippmann). *The New York Times*, 12 Mar 1947, (Reston). Kennan, *Memoirs*, I, p. 326 ("trivia"). J.L. Gaddis, *The United States and the Origins of the Cold War*, p. 302ff.

3 *Forrestal Diaries* (New York: Viking,

1951), p. 136 (Kennan to Dept. of State. *Foreign Affairs* XXV, July 1947, pp. 566-582 (Mr. X).

4 *Dept of State Bulletin*, XVI, 18 May 1947, pp. 991-999 (Cleveland, Mississippi speech). Acheson, *Present at the Creation*, p. 229. Price, *The Marshall Plan and its Meaning*, p. 24. Jones, *Fifteen Weeks*, p. 210. Acheson, *Present at the Creation*, p. 230 (Vandenberg).

5 United Nations, *World Economic Report 1948*, p. 34. Kolko, *The*

Limits of Power (New York: Harper, 1972), p. 364ff. *Statistical Abstract of the United States 1949*, (Washington: Government Printing Office, 1949), p. 847 (contributions to UNRRA). U.S. lend-lease payments totalled $47.596 billion.

6 Jones, *Fifteen Weeks*, p. 210. Acheson, *Present at the Creation*, p. 231. Price, *The Marshall Plan and its Meaning*, p. 23.

7 *Dept of State Bulletin*, XVI, 15 Jun 1947, p. 1160.

8 *The New York Times*, 20 Jun 1947. Price, *The Marshall Plan and its Meaning*, p. 27. Acheson, *Present at the Creation*, p. 234.

9 Price, *The Marshall Plan and its Meaning*, p. 28. Acheson, *Present at the Creation*, p. 235. T.G. Paterson, "The Quest for Peace and Prosperity" in Barton Bernstein, ed. *Politics and Policies of the Truman Administration*, (Chicago: Quadrangle, 1970), p. 99.

10 Milovan Djilas, *Conversations with Stalin*, (New York: Harcourt Harvest paperback, 1962), p. 149f (Zhdanov description). Harrison Salisbury, *The 900 Days: the Siege of Leningrad* (New York: Harper & Row, 1969), pp. 133–39 (Zhdanov background). S.J. Zyzniewsky, "Soviet Foreign Policy," *Political Science Quarterly*, LXXIII (Jan 1958), pp. 216–19.

11 Salisbury, *The 900 Days*, pp. 580–81. LaFeber, *America, Russia and the Cold War*, p. 32. Zhdanov, whose son married Stalin's daughter Svetlana, was identified not only with the hard line against the West in 1939–41 and in 1946–47, but also with the "Zhdanovschina," the cultural purge of 1946–47 that swept far enough to affect culture heroes like the composers Shostakovich and Prokofiev. When Tito broke away from the bloc in 1948, Zhdanov was blamed. He died later that year, aged fifty-two, but the hard line was, if anything, intensified by Tito's defection, which set off a whole series of purges, corrective or preventive, of Titoist tendencies in other Eastern European countries that went on into the early 1950s. Svetlana

Alleluyeva, *Twenty Letters to a Friend* (New York: Harper, 1967), p. 192.

12 Zhdanov speech printed in Cominform newspaper *For a Lasting Peace, For a People's Democracy*, 10 Nov 1947, pp. 2–4. For Stalin on the two camps, see *Izvestia*, 28 July 1927, cited in Louis Fischer, *The Soviet in World Affairs, 1917–29*, (Princeton: Princeton University Press, 1951), p. 745.

13 *Vandenberg Papers*, pp. 379, 382.

14 Acheson, *Sketches from Life*, p. 130 (Vandenberg). *Vandenberg Papers*, p. 383 Westerfield, *Foreign Policy and Party Politics*, p. 279. Paterson, in Bernstein, ed., *Politics and Policies of the Truman Administration*, p. 98.

15 Kolko, *The Limits of Power*, p. 377 (Vandenberg). Richard J. Barnet, *The Roots of War* (New York: Atheneum, 1972), p. 152.

16 *Vandenberg Papers*, pp. 382, 391, 394, 471. *Forrestal Diaries*, p. 268. Price, *The Marshall Plan and its Meaning*, p. 21. *Time*, 7 Apr 1949, p. 31.

17 *Time*, 7 Apr 1949, p. 33–39. Price, *The Marshall Plan and its Meaning*, p. 41.

18 Paul Hoffman, *Peace Can Be Won*, (Garden City: Doubleday, 1951), p. 47. Interviews with Paul Douglas, Edward McMenemin, Hart Preston, March, 1971.

19 Paterson, "Quest for Peace and Prosperity," p. 60 (Council of Economic Advisers' statement). Price, *The Marshall Plan and its Meaning*, p. 40. Jones, *Fifteen Weeks*, p. 207. Walter LaFeber, *America, Russia and the Cold War*, p. 49.

20 Ellen Garwood Clayton, *Will Clayton, a Short Biography*, (Austin: University of Texas, 1958), pp. 119ff. "Spring Flower," *Time*, 3 Feb 1947, p. 18. "Will Clayton's Cotton," *Fortune*, Nov. and Dec. 1945. "Businessmen Making Policy," *U.S. News*, 23 Mar 1947, p. 20. Price, *The Marshall Plan and its Meaning*, p. 88 ($13.13 billion).

21 Harry C. Dillingham and David F. Sly, "The Mechanical Cotton Picker, Negro Migration and the Integration

Movement," in *Human Organization*, Vol. 25, No 4, Winter 1966, p. 345. T. Lynn Smith, "Redistribution of Negro Population in the U.S., 1910–1960," in *Journal of Negro History*, Vol. LI, No. 3, July 1966, p. 157.

22 Dillingham and Sly, "The Mechanical Cotton Picker," pp. 346, 349. John P. Davis, ed. *American Negro Reference Book*, (Englewood Cliffs: Prentice-Hall, 1966), p. 167. "Who Needs the Negro?" *Trans-Action*, 6 (Sept-Oct 1964), pp. 3–6. Charles Silberman in *Fortune*, Nov 1965. Commission on Technology, Automation and Economic Progress, *Technology and the American Economy*, I (Washington: Government Printing Office, Feb 1966), p. 21. Report of the Governor's Committee on the Los Angeles Riots, *Violence in the City: an End or a Beginning?* 2 Dec 1965, p. 71.

23 Allen J. Matusow, *Farm Policies and Politics in the Truman Administration*, (Cambridge: Harvard University Press, 1967), p. 22. Lauren Soth, *Farm Trouble*, (Princeton: Princeton University Press, 1957), p. 164. *Agricultural Statistics*, (Washington: Government Printing Office, 1950), p. 20. Murray L. Benedict, *Can We Solve the Farm Problem?* (New York: Twentieth Century Fund, 1955), p. 450. Lauren Soth, *Embarrassment of Plenty*, (New York: Crowell, 1965), p. 163ff.

24 Federal Trade Commission, *Report on the Fertilizer Industry* (9 Jan 1950), (Washington: Government Printing Office, 1950), p. 20. *Statistical Abstract 1960*, p. 632. "Fertilizer Use in the U.S. by Crops and Areas, 1964 Estimates," *Dept of Agriculture Statistical Bulletin No. 408*, (Washington: Government Printing Office, August 1967), p. 16.

25 Arthur Schlesinger Jr., *The Coming of the New Deal*, (Boston: Houghton Mifflin, 1959), p. 139ff. 387, 393 (1930s labor war). Charles A. Madison, *American Labor Leaders* (New York; Ungar, 1961, 2nd ed.), pp. 127ff, 308ff, 371. Sidney Lens, *Crisis of American Labor*, (New York: Sagamore Press, 1959), p. 158ff. Wynd-

ham Mortimer, *Organize!* (Boston: Beacon, 1971), pp. 103ff. Len De-Caux, *Labor Radical* (Boston: Beacon paperback, 1970), p. 248ff. Frank Cormier and William T. Watson, *Walter Reuther* (Englewood Cliffs: Prentice-Hall, 1970), pp. 97ff. Irving Howe and Lewis Coser, *The American Communist Party in the United States*, (Boston: Beacon, 1957), p. 465. James Wechsler, *Reflections of a Middle-Aged Radical*, (New York: Random House, 1960), p. 162. Irving Howe and B.J. Widick, *The UAW and Walter Reuther*, (New York: Random House, 1949), p. 150.

26 S.K. Bailey, *Congress Makes a Law* (New York: Columbia University Press, 1950), p. 106ff. Cormier, *Walter Reuther*, p. 218. Federated Press news release, 29 Sept 1945 (Moon Mullins meeting). Clayton W. Fountain, *Union Guy*, (New York: Viking, 1949), p. 160ff. *Christianity and Society*, Winter 1945, p. 8. B.J. Widick, *Labor Today*, (Boston: Houghton Mifflin, 1964), pp. 105, 181. H.A. Millis and E.C. Brown, *From Wagner Act to Taft-Hartley*, (Chicago: University of Chicago Press, 1950), p. 22.

27 Robert M. MacDonald, *Collective Bargaining in the Auto Industry* (New Haven: Yale University Press, 1963), p. 38. Lawrence White, *The Automobile Industry Since 1946*, (Cambridge: Harvard University Press, 1971), pp. 11, 253. Eliot Janeway, *The Economics of Crisis*, (New York: Weybright and Talley, 1968), p. 223. John Brooks, *The Great Leap*, p. 157. Goldman, *The Crucial Decade*, pp. 49, 269. Cormier, *Walter Reuther*, p. 83 ("sit down" song), p. 85 (Bulls Run, Overpass), p. 231. Fountain, *Union Guy*, p. 172. Federated Press news release, 28 Mar 1946. *United Auto Worker*, Sept 1945, p. 3. Irving Howe and B.J. Widick, *The UAW and Walter Reuther*, p. 187.

28 Cormier, *Walter Reuther*, pp. 241ff, 359 (CIA). Walter Reuther, "How to Beat the Communists," *Colliers*, 18 Feb 1948. "Threats to Human Freedom," *Columbia College Forum on Democracy*, 10–12 Feb 1949

(mimeo), p. 60 (statement by General Donovan). Joseph Goulden, *Meany*, (New York: Atheneum, 1972), p. 128ff. Alexander Werth, *France 1940–1955* (New York: Holt, 1956), pp. 384–85 (US unions' money in France). A significant aspect of the struggle for labor's support in Western Europe was that the miners who had to dig the coal for economic recovery in Britain and France belonged to Communist-led unions, and the same situation was feared in the Western zones of Occupied Germany. Up against the Communists' unassailable position in coal, the Marshall Planners turned to Saudi Arabian and other oil fields opening up in the Middle East. By contrast with coal, Persian Gulf oil was abundant and cheap, could be pumped virtually without human labor, piped and shipped over sealanes safeguarded by the Sixth Fleet and delivered at bargain prices to power plants and factories in Europe. An unintended consequence of the Marshall Plan for European recovery was that it helped finance the switch to oil that helped make Western Europe by 1956 dependent upon the Middle East for thirty per cent of its energy, and by 1970 for fifty-five per cent. R. Page Arnot, *The Miners III* (London: Allen and Unwin, 1961), p 180–2. United Nations, *Growth of World Industry, 1938–61* (New York, 1963), p 158 (coal, oil). Organization for Economic Cooperation and Development, *Energy Policy, Problems and Objectives* (Paris, 1966), p 160.

29 R. Alton Lee, *Truman and Taft-Hartley, a Question of Mandate*, (Lexington: University of Kentucky Press, 1966), p. 22. De Caux, *Labor Radical*, pp. 479, 491ff. Mortimer, *Organize!* p. 169. *United Auto Worker*, Sept 1949, p. 4. Benjamin Aaron, "Amending the Taft-Hartley Act: a Decade of Frustration," in *Industrial and Labor Relations Review*, Vol. 11, No. 3, Apr 1958, p. 327ff. Philip Taft, "International Affairs of Unions and the Taft-Hartley Act," in *Industrial and Labor Relations Review*, Apr 1958, p. 360.

James T. Patterson, *Mr. Republican*, pp. 356, 364. Fountain, *Union Guy*, p. 203. Federated Press news release, 3 Oct 1946. Howe and Widick, *The UAW and Walter Reuther*, pp. 160, 170, 183.

30 Aaron, "Amending the Taft-Hartley Act," p. 340. Madison, *American Labor Leaders*, p. 402. Lens, *Crisis of American Labor*, p. 168ff. DeCaux, *Labor Radical*, p. 526. Alfred O. Hero and Emil Starr, *Reuther-Meany Foreign Policy Dispute*, (Dobbs Ferry, N.Y.: Oceana Publications, 1970); pp. 37, 191f. Ronald Radosh, *American Labor and United States Foreign Policy*, (New York: Random House, 1969), p. 438. MacDonald, *Collective Bargaining*, p. 38ff (UAW pay). Bert G. Hickman, *Growth and Stability of the Postwar Economy* (Washington: Brookings, 1960), p. 159ff. *The New York Times*, 10 and 11 May 1970 (death of Reuther).

31 MacDonald, *Collective Bargaining*, p. 86 (wage rises of mid-1950s). White, *Automobile Industry since 1946*, p. 27 (Kefauver). Gardiner C. Means is credited with coining the phrase "administered prices". Daniel Bell, "The Subversion of Collective Bargaining," *Commentary*, March 1960, p. 195. John B. Rae, *The American Automobile*, (Chicago: University of Chicago Press, 1965), p. 211.

32 Aaron, "Amending the Taft-Hartley Act," p. 340. Madison, *American Labor Leaders*, p. 402. Lens, *Crisis of American Labor*, p. 168ff. DeCaux, *Labor Radical*, p. 526. Hero and Starr, *Reuther-Meany Foreign Policy Dispute*, pp. 37, 191ff. Radosh, *American Labor and U.S. Foreign Policy*, p. 438. Goulden, *Meany*, p. 324. *The New York Times*, 11 May 1970.

33 Roger F. Murray, *Economic Aspects of Pensions, a Summary Report*, (New York: National Bureau of Economic Research, 1968), p. 4. Joseph W. Garbarino, *Health Plans and Collective Bargaining* (Berkeley: University of Californis Press, 1960), p. 3. Floyd C. Mann and L.R. Hoffman, *Automation and the Worker*, (New York: Holt,

1960), p. 52f. G.F. Somers, ed. *Adjusting to Technological Change,* (New York: Harper, 1963), p. 134.

34 "The U.S. Labor Movement," *Fortune,* Feb 1951, p. 90ff. *The New York Times,* 20, 21 Nov 1948, p. 1. C.K. Brighthill, "Time to Consume," *Recreation,* Sept 1950, p. 199. "More than Half of all Shirts Sold Are Sports Shirts," *Good Housekeeping,* Feb 1953, p. 182. Max Gunther, *The Weekenders,* (Philadelphia: Lippincott, 1964), p. 26ff.

35 *The New York Times,* 18 Feb, 4, 12, 20 Apr 1948 (Lewis v. Taft). *Business Week,* 12 Nov 1949, p. 10. *Report of the Council of Economic Advisers,* (Washington: Government Printing Office, Dec 1949, p. 75. *Report of the Council of Economic Advisers,* (Washington: Government Printing Office, 6 Jan 1950, p. 36. D.M. Holland, *Private Pension Funds, Projected Growth,* (New York: National Bureau of Economic Research, 1966), p. 1. St. Louis *Post-Dispatch,* 29 May, 29 Sept 1949 (Ford pact); 14 Sept, 1 Oct, 11 Nov 1949 (steel pact). Murray, p. 15ff. Victor Christgau, "Social Security after Thirty Years," *Social Security Bulletin,* Aug 1955, p. 13. Wilbur Cohen and Robert Myers, "Social Security Act Amendments of 1950," *Social Security Bulletin,* Oct 1950, p. 3.

36 *Business Week,* 15 Oct 1949, p. 114. Holland, p. 1. Lenore Epstein et al. "Social Security After 30 Years," *Social Security Bulletin,* Aug 1955, p. 7. Charles Schottland, "Report," *Social Security Bulletin,* Feb 1955, p. 3. "The U.S. Labor Movement," *Fortune,* Feb 1951, p. 166.

37 Richard Ward, "Automation and Unemployment," in *New University Thought,* Vol. 2, No. 2, Winter 1962, p. 30ff (coal productivity figures). *Statistical Abstract of the U.S., 1964,* pp. 420, 432, 434, 439, 490, 560, 512, 716, 868 (coal output). *The New York Times,* May 30, 1954 (Lewis the banker). *Monthly Labor Review,* Oct 1961, p. 16 (coal output costs). *Report,* United Mineworkers of America Welfare and Retirement Fund, year

ending 30 June 1961, cited by Widick, *Labor Today,* p. 227 (UMW pension data). Solomon Barkin, "Decline of the Labor Movement," in Andrew Hacker, ed. *Corporate Takeover,* (New York: Harper & Row, 1964), p. 225.

38 Epstein, "Social Security After Thirty Years," p. 7. Murray, *Economic Aspects of Pensions,* p. 29. Holland, *Private Pension Funds,* p. 1. Victor Fuchs, *The Service Economy,* (New York: National Bureau of Economic Research, 1968), p. 14. *Statistical Abstract 1964,* pp. 285, 294 (private pensions). *Interim Report, Welfare and Pension Plan Investigation,* Subcommittee on Welfare and Pension Funds, Senate Committee on Labor and Public Welfare, 84th Congress, 1st session, (Washington: Government Printing Office, 1955), p. 42ff. (11,290,000 workers covered by pension plans, or 75% of the 15,000,000 covered by collective bargaining, with funds of $17 billion, a $2 billion increase over the preceding year.)

39 "Early Retirement," *Life,* 18 Feb 1957, p. 49ff. "Auto Union to Bargain for Retired Workers," *Business Week,* 1 Jun 1957, p. 130. "New Rentier Class," *Fortune,* Jun 1959, p. 159. Gertrude Samuels, "Inquiry into the Sunset Years," *The New York Times Magazine,* 20 Mar 1960. R. Weiner, "Retirement Village," *Travel,* Oct 1960. A. Herzog, "Portrait of our Senior Citizens," *The New York Times Magazine,* 4 Nov 1962. "Camping for Seniors," *Recreation,* May 1962, p. 236. *The New Yorker,* 4 Apr 1964, p. 120. "Doctor in the House," *Time,* 16 Feb 1962. "Retirement Cities," *Time,* 3 Aug 1962. "Old Folks at Home?" *Newsweek,* 25 Feb 1963. "Widening World of Retirement Towns," *Life,* 8 Nov 1963. P. Friggins, "Where Life Begins at 65," *Reader's Digest,* Jan 1966. "Life Begins at 52," *Fortune,* Sept 1966. J. Peter, "Retirement Country Club," *Look,* 15 Dec 1966. M.M. Glascock and E.A. Scholer, "Camping for Older Adults," *Camping,* Mar 1969. George Soule, *Longer Life,* (New York: Viking, 1958), p. 81.

Communications from Henry F. Patt, Office of Research and Statistics, Social Security Administration, and Paul Schmitt and Peg Vierebome, St. Petersburg *Times*, Oct 1972 (number of Social Security checks cashed in St. Petersburg).

40 Widick, *Labor Today*, p. 32 (statement by Reuther). *Statistical Abstract 1964*, p. 236 (wages, inflation, etc.).

41 *Statistical Abstract 1964*, p. 247 (union membership decline cited from *Handbook of Labor Statistics*). A.H. Raskin, "Labor's House Three Years After," *The New York Times Magazine*, 30 Nov 1958, p. 105. Murray Kempton, "Labor's Decline," *New York Post*, 28 Nov 1961. Widick, *Labor Today*, p. 31ff. Goulden, *Meany*, p. 324.

42 Daniel Bell, "The Racket Ridden Longshoremen," in Bell, *End of Ideology*, (New York: Free Press, 1960), p. 175ff. John Hutchinson, *The Imperfect Union*, (New York: Dutton, 1970), pp. 93ff., 141ff. *Interim Report, Welfare and Pension Plans Investigation*, p. 24 ff. (laundry workers). *The New York Times*, 11, 12, 21 May 1957.

43 *Interim Report*, Senate Committee on Government Operations, 85th Congress, 2nd session, (Washington: Government Printing Office, 1958), p. 11 (Leheney). Hutchinson, *The Imperfect Union*, p. 230ff.

44 *The New York Times*, 29 Mar; 3, 17 Apr, 1957. Goldman, *The Crucial Decade*, p. 315 (Teamster convention statements). Hutchinson, *The Imperfect Union*, p. 336 (Beck statement). James R. Hoffa, *Trials of Jimmy Hoffa*, (Chicago: Henry Regnery, 1970), p. 1ff. Widick, *Labor Today*, p. 145ff. Ralph C. and E.D. James, *Hoffa and the Teamsters*, (Princeton: Van Nostrand, 1965), p. 45ff. C.R. Mollen-

hoff, *Tentacles of Power*, (Cleveland: World Publishing, 1965), p. 66ff. Hutchinson, *op. cit.*, p. 253ff. (Hoffa).

45 *Violations or Nonenforcement of Government Laws and Regulations in the Labor Union Field*, Hearings of Permanent Subcommittee on Investigations, Senate Committee on Government Operations, 85th Congress, 1st session, 16–19 Jan 1957, (Washington: Government Printing Office, 1957), p. 216ff. J.L. McClellan, *Crime Without Punishment*, (New York: Duell Sloan, 1962), p. 40ff.

46 Goldman, *The Crucial Decade*, p. 316 (statement about Hoffa). Hutchinson, *The Imperfect Union*, p. 253ff.

47 *The New York Times*, 17, 25 July, 7, 14, 15, 19 Aug, 3, 4, 15 Sept 1959. (Landrum-Griffin Act). Widik, *Labor Today*, p. 73ff. *The New York Times*, 5 Mar, 27 July, 1964; 28 Feb, 5, 12, 19 Mar 1967; 26 Mar, 15 July 1969 (Hoffa conviction and sentencing).

48 "Papa Meany," *The New Republic*, 4 Mar 1968 (75,000 unionists in community boards, new income levels). Murray Kempton, *New York Post*, 28 Nov 1961 (Van Arsdale's Local 3 electricians).

49 Widick, *Labor Today*, p. 207ff. Daniel Bell, "The Subversion of Collective Bargaining," *Commentary*, Mar 1960, p. 195. Richard Dudman, "Agent Meany," *The New Republic*, 3 May 1969, p. 13. W.V. Shannon, "The Split in Labor," *Commonweal*, 24 Feb 1967, p. 584. John Corry, "The Many-sided Mr. Meany," *Harper's*, Mar 1970, p. 52. "Papa Meany," *The New Republic*, 4 May 1968. New York *Post*, 9 Sept 1955 (Meany living style details). Goulden, *Meany*, p. 370. C.L. Sulzberger, *A Long Row of Candles*, (New York: Macmillan, 1969), p. 694.

CHAPTER 4.

1 *The New York Times*, 22 May 1948, (SAC move to Offutt field, Nebraska); 10, 30 Mar, 16 April, 11 May, 25 July, 18 Sept, 1948; 21 Jan,

3 Mar 1949 (SAC world flights).

2 James Aronson, "The Press and the Cold War," p. 37 (National Opinion Research Center polls). Gabriel A. Al-

mond, *The American People and Foreign Policy,* (New York: Praeger, 1950,) p. 91 (1947 Gallup poll 54% expecting war within ten years).

3   John Studebaker speech in *School Life,* Feb 1948, pp. 1–7 ("Zeal for Democracy" issue). A.J. Liebling, *Mink and Red Herring* (Garden City: Doubleday, 1947), p. 9ff. Don Hollenbeck, "CBS Views the News" program, 1 Nov, 1947, also 4 Dec, 1947. A. J. Liebling, "The Wayward Press," *The New Yorker,* 1 Nov, 1947 (Rupert Hughes). Eric Bentley, "Bertholt Brecht before the Committee on Un-American Activities," *Folkway Record Notes,* Jun 1963 (with verbatim HUAC Hearings, 20–30 Oct 1947). Eric Bentley, ed. *Thirty Years of Treason, Excerpts from Hearings of HUAC, 1933–68,* (New York: Viking, 1971), p. 207.

4   Liebling, "The Wayward Press," 11 Oct 1947 (Winchell radio broadcast and State Dept ban on Pierre Courtade travel). Curtiss MacDougall, *The Press and its Problems,* (Dubuque: W.C. Brown, 1960), p. 5ff. Douglass Cater, *The Fourth Branch of Government* (Boston: Houghton, Mifflin, 1952), p. 8ff.

5   Severin Bialer, *Stalin and his Generals* (New York: Pegasus, 1969), pp. 516–17. Dwight Eisenhower, *Crusade in Europe,* (Garden City: Doubleday, 1948), p. 396. Truman, *Memoirs* I, pp. 303, 306. Hull, *Memoirs,* II, p. 1603ff. Robert D. Murphy, *Diplomat among Warriors* (Garden City: Doubleday, 1964), p. 253. Lucius D. Clay, *Decision in Germany* (Garden City: Doubleday, 1950), p. 26. Frank Howley, *Berlin Command* (New York: Putnam, 1950), p. 26. Dept of State, *Foreign Relations of the United States 1945,* III (Washington: Government Printing Office, 1960), p. 353ff.

6   Byrnes, *Speaking Frankly,* pp. 79, 105, 159. Murphy. *Diplomat among Warriors,* p. 250.

7   *Dept of State Bulletin,* XV, 15 Sept 1946, p. 499 (Byrnes's Stuttgart speech). Lloyd C. Gardner, *Architects of Illusion* (Chicago: Quadrangle, 1970), pp. 236, 254. Byrnes, *Speaking*

Frankly, p. 187ff. Clay, *Decision in Germany,* p. 78, Murphy, *Diplomat among Warriors,* p. 302. V.M. Molotov, *Problems of Foreign Policy,* (Moscow: 1949), p. 51. Kolko, *Limits of Power,* pp. 168–9. John Gimbel, *The American Occupation of Germany, 1945–49,* (Stanford: Stanford University Press, 1968), p. 117. *Time,* 12 July 1948, p. 17. *Current Biography,* Feb 1946, p. 60 and May 1963, p. 75. Drew Middleton, *The Struggle for Germany,* (Indianapolis: Bobbs-Merrill, 1949), p. 128.

8   N. Spykman, *The United States in World Affairs,* (New York: Harcourt, 1942), p. 43. Wright Mills, *The Causes of World War III,* (New York: Simon and Schuster, 1958), p. 10

9   *The New York Times,* 21 Mar 1948. *Time,* 17 May 1948, p. 30 and 28 June 1949, p. 16. Curtis LeMay, *Mission with LeMay* (Garden City: Doubleday, 1965), p. 425 (bomb tonnage dropped on Berlin).

10 *The New York Times,* 23 Mar 1948, p. 10. *Time,* 17 May 1948, p. 30.

11 Dept. of State, *Foreign Relations of the United States 1945,* III, p. 358ff. (Berlin agreement text). Clay, *Decision in Germany,* p. 25. Acheson, *Present at the Creation,* p. 260.

12 Gardner, *Architects of Illusion,* pp. 252, 256. Clay, *Decision in Germany,* pp. 160, 220. Herbert Feis, *From Trust to Terror: the Onset of the Cold War, 1945–50* (New York: W.W. Norton, 1970), p. 336. Manuel Gottlieb, *German Peace Settlement and the Berlin Crisis* (New York: Paine-Whitman, 1960), p. 186. C.M. Woodhouse, *British Foreign Policy Since the Second World War,* (New York: Praeger, 1962), p. 18.

13 Clay, *Decision in Germany,* pp. 199–201. Feis, *From Trust to Terror,* p. 336.

14 *The New York Times* reported (11 June 1948, p. 11): "The enabling act being passed by the Bizonal Economic Council, described as urgent in connection with currency reform, would permit Dr. Ludwig Erhard, Economics Minister, to assume 'economic dictatorship' right after the reform is put

through. Socialists and Communists in the Frankfurt assembly are opposed. He could release price controls, and certain commodity prices would go up, which they do not like." This was the beginning of Erhard's "Wirtschaftswunder"—the German economic miracle—that was to carry him to the Chancellorship a decade later.

15 Prague: Truman, *Memoirs*, II, p. 241. *Forrestal Diaries*, p. 387. Woodhouse, *British Foreign Policy*, p. 35. Feis, *From Trust to Terror*, pp. 291–4. LaFeber, *America, Russia and the Cold War*, pp. 68–9. Marshall Shulman, *Stalin's Foreign Policy Reappraised*, pp. 71–72. Adam B. Ulam, *Titoism and the Cominform*, (Cambridge: Harvard University Press, 1952), pp. 58–9. Gimbel, *American Occupation of Germany*, p. 172.

16 *The New York Times*, 26 and 27 Feb 1948. New York *Herald Tribune*, 17 Mar 1948, p. 25. (Alsop). *Forrestal Diaries*, p. 373. Clay, *Decision in Germany*, p. 354.

17 *The New York Times*, 17 Mar 1948. *Forrestal Diaries*, p. 387.

18 *Public Opinion Quarterly*, XII, 4, Winter 1948–9, p. 766 (Gallup poll).

19 *The New York Times*, 29 Jun 1948 (expulsion of Tito). LaFeber, *America, Russia and the Cold War*, p. 69. Ulam, *Titoism and the Cominform*, p. 62ff. Woodhouse, *British Foreign Policy*, p. 30. N.S. Khrushchev, *Crimes of the Stalin Era*, (ed. Boris Nikolaevsky), (New York: Praeger, 1956), p. 48. François Fejto, *Histoires des democraties populaires* (Paris: Editions de Seuil, 1952), p. 227.

20 *For a Lasting Peace, for a People's Democracy*, 10 Nov 1947 (Zhdanov speech), p. 1–4. Adam B. Ulam, *Expansion and Coexistence, Soviet Foreign Policy 1917–67* (New York: Praeger, 1967), p. 455. Kennan, *Memoirs* I, p. 400.

21 *The New York Times*, 21 Mar 1948. Clay, *Decision in Germany*, p. 357. Feis, *From Trust to Terror*, p. 333.

22 *The New York Times*, 18 Apr 1949, p. 10. Clay, *Decision in Germany*, p. 359. W.P. Davison, *The Berlin Block-ade*, (Princeton: Princeton University Press, 1958), p. 77.

23 *Dept of State Bulletin*, XVI, 6 May 1947, p. 994. Acheson, *Present at the Creation*, p. 261. Davison, *Berlin Blockade*, p. 77. *The New York Times*, 1, 10, 13, 16, 18, Jun 1948.

24 Truman, *Memoirs*, II, p. 125. *Forrestal Diaries*, p. 454. Clay, *Decision in Germany*, p. 374. Howley, *Berlin Command*, p. 196. Murphy, *Diplomat among Warriors*, p. 316. Acheson, *Present at the Creation*, p. 262.

25 *Time*, 12 July, 1948, p. 18 (airlift). Clay, *Decision in Germany*, p. 296. Murphy, *Diplomat among Warriors*, p. 251. LeMay, *Mission with LeMay*, p. 415. William H. Tunner, *Over the Hump*, (New York: Duell Sloan, 1964), p. 152. Byrnes, *Speaking Frankly*, p. 47. Gardner, *Architects of Illusion*, pp. 118–9. Link, *American Epoch*, pp. 714–5.

26 *The New York Times*, 25 Jun 1948, p. 28. *Time*, 28 Jun, 5, 19, 26 July, 2 Aug, 1948. Clay, *Decision in Germany*, p. 384. Crosby Maynard, *Flight Plan for Tomorrow: the Douglas Story*, (Los Angeles: Douglas Co., 1962), p. 2. Alvin Josephy, ed. *American Heritage History of Flight* (New York; American Heritage, 1958), pp. 176–7. "Special Study of Operation Vittles," *Aviation Operations*, II, No. 5, Apr 1949, pp. 9–110.

27 *Time*, 26 July 1948, p. 19. Clay, *Decision in Germany*, pp. 367 384. *Forrestal Diaries*, p. 480.

28 Clay, *Decision in Germany*, p. 367. Acheson, *Present at the Creation*, p. 261. *Time*, 26 July 1948, p. 19. "Special Study of Operation Vittles," p. 9.

29 *The New York Times*, 25 July 1948, p. 1 (statement by Dewey). Clay, *Decision in Germany*, pp. 381–82. "Good News from Europe," *Life*, 2 Aug 1948. LeMay, *Mission with LeMay*, pp. 416–42. Tunner, *Over the Hump*, pp. 212–24. Howley, *Berlin Command*, p. 202. Murphy, *Diplomat among Warriors*, p. 322. Bradford Westerfield, *Foreign Policy and Party Politics*, (New Haven: Yale University Press, 1955), pp. 307–8 (domestic im-

pact of airlift). Acheson, *Present at the Creation*, p. 261.

30 *Forrestal Diaries*, p. 487 (Truman's pledge he'd use the A-bomb).

31 *The New York Times*, 25 July 1948. See also Westerfield, *Foreign Policy and Party Politics*, p. 308.

32 LeMay, *Mission with LeMay*, p. 416–40. Clay, *Decision in Germany*, p. 382. Tunner, *Over the Hump*, p. 212–24. Howley, *Berlin Command*, p. 20. Murphy, *Diplomat among Warriors*, p. 322.

33 Dean Acheson, "On Dealing with Russia, an Inside View," *The New York Times Magazine*, 12 Apr 1959, pp. 27, 88–89. Acheson, *Present at the Creation*, pp. 267–274. Acheson said: "Negotiation is only a polite phrase for retreat." (*U.S. News*, 18 Nov 1959, p. 110) See also *The New York Times*, 26, 27, Apr, 5, 10, 11 May, 1949.

34 Murphy, *Diplomat among Warriors*, pp. 321–23. LaFeber, *America, Russia and the Cold War*, p. 223. Feis, *From Trust to Terror*, p. 358.

35 *Vandenberg Papers*, p. 406 (Vandenberg resolution).

36 Truman, *Memoirs* II, p. 240ff. Acheson, *Present at the Creation*, p. 286.

37 *Journal of the Continental Congress*, XXVII, Motion by Elbridge Gerry, resolved affirmative, 26 May 1784, p. 433. J.R. Graham, *Constitutional History of the Military Draft*, (Minneapolis: Ross and Haines, 1971), pp. 46, 49, 85. M.A. Kreidberg and M.G. Henry, *History of Military Mobilization in the United States Army, 1775–1945*, (Washington, 1945), p. 22.

38 Jack Franklin Leach, *Conscription in the United States: Historical Background*. (Rutland, Vt.: Charles A. Tuttle, 1952), p. 42 (Jefferson statement cited from *Writings of Thomas Jefferson*, XIII, p. 261). W.H. McNeill, "The Draft in the Light of History," in Sol Tax, ed. *The Draft, a Handbook of Facts and Alternatives*, (Chicago: University of Chicago Press, 1967), p. 117ff. American Friends Service Committee, *The Draft? A Report* (New York: Hill and Wang, 1968). p. 2–3 (Civil War resistance). *Congressional Record*, 65th Congress, Senate, pp. 955, 1082 (Reed); pp. 974, 1092, 25 April 1917 (Nicholls, Huddleston, Byrnes, Hayden). Arthur Ekirch, Jr., *The Civilian and the Military* (New York: Oxford, 1956), p. 271ff. Frederick M. Stern, *The Draft and the Military* (New York: St Martin's Press, 1957), p. 22. Lewis B. Hershey, *Outline of Historical Background of Selective Service*, Revised, (Washington: Selective Service, 1965, pp. 2–8, 12. Herman Beukema, "The Draft," *Americana Yearbook 1948*, pp. 45–46 (facts on armed forces strength after 1945). Jack Raymond, *Power at the Pentagon*, (New York: Harper & Row, 1964), p. 15.

39 *U.S. Budget for FY Ending June 30, 1951*, (Washington: Government Printing Office, 1950), p. 1165 ($1.077 billion for defense, 1939–40, $10.961 billion in FY 1948). Warren B. Schilling, et al., *Strategy, Politics and Defense Budgets*, (New York: Columbia University Press, 1962), pp. 10, 28, 41. John C. Ries, *Management of Defense*, (Baltimore: Johns Hopkins University Press), 1960, pp. 88–106. Walter Millis, Harvey Mansfield and Harold Stein, *Arms and the State*, (New York: Twentieth Century Fund, 1958), p. 40ff. Walter Millis, *Arms and the Men*, (New York: Putnam, 1950), p. 314. Demetrios Caraley, *Politics of Military Unification*, (New York: Columbia University Press), 1966, pp. 153–182. *Forrestal Diaries*, pp. 167, 409. Paul Y. Hammond, "Unification," in Gordon Turner, ed. *National Security in the Nuclear Age*, (New York: Praeger, 1950), p. 216. David Wise and Thomas B. Ross, *The Invisible Government*, (New York: Random House, 1964), p. 93ff. Samuel Huntington, *The Soldier and the State*, (Cambridge: Harvard University Press, 1967), pp. 345, 360. John Swomley, *The Military Establishment*, (Boston: Beacon, 1964), p. 140.

40 *The New York Times*, 17, 18 Mar 1948. *Forrestal Diaries*, p. 369.

41 *The New York Times*, 18 Mar 1948. *Forrestal Diaries*, pp. 373, 376, 377, 387, 392, 394, 395.

42 *The New York Times*, 18 Mar 1948. Truman *Memoirs*, II, p. 241.

43 *The New York Times*, 18 Mar 1948, p. 1 (statement by Neil). *The New York Times*, 21 Mar 1948 (stock market rise). *Time*, 29 Mar 1948, p. 24. *Christian Century*, 5 Apr 1948. *America*, 7 Apr 1948. *The New York Times*, 25 Mar 1948 (*Literary Gazette* quote).

44 *The New York Times*, 18 Jun 1948 (statement by Roberts). Fred J. Cook, *The Warfare State*, (New York: Macmillan, 1962), p. 108 (statement by Eisenhower). *Forrestal Diaries*, p. 400.

45 Cook, p. 108 (statements by generals). J. Lawton Collins, "National Security: the Military Viewpoint," in *Vital Speeches*, XIII, 1 Jun 1947, pp. 488–92.

46 Richard Gillam, "The Peacetime Draft, Voluntarism to Coercion," *Yale Review*, LVII, No. 4, Jun 1968, pp. 508, 509((statements by Gurney, Johnson). See also *Forrestal Diaries*, pp. 447–8. Swomley, *The Military Establishment*, p. 76.

47 Gillam, "The Peacetime Draft," pp. 511–12 (Price, Martin, Johnson, Radwan).

48 Leonard Wood, *The Military Obligation of Citizenship*, (Princeton: Princeton University Press, 1915), p. 56. Herman Hagedorn, *Leonard Wood*, (New York: Harper, 1931), II, pp. 159–60. E.W. Fisher, *Leonard Wood: Conservator of Americanism*, (New York: Doran, 1920), p. 292. Grenville Clark, *A Proposed National War Service Act*, (New York: pamphlet, 1942) p. 1.

49 Ekirch, *The Civilian and the Military*, pp. 151, 256–8. Huntington, *The Soldier and the State*, p. 271.

50 Harriet Douty, "Drawing the Line on Draft Evasion," *Congressional Digest*, 4 Apr 1968, p. 20. "Changing the U.S. Military Draft," *Congressional Digest*, Aug-Sept 1968, p. 193.

51 Harry A. Marmion, *Selective Service, Conflict and Compromises*, (New York: Wiley, 1968), p. 22. Sol Tax, ed., *The Draft*, p. 54. Raymond, *Power at the Pentagon*, p. 313.

52 Raymond, *Power at the Pentagon*, p. 313.

53 Gillam, "The Peacetime Draft, Voluntarism to Coercion."

54 On the basis of such behavioral patterns a professor of sociology termed the Kent State episode of May, 1970, in which young National Guardsmen fired into student demonstrators, "a case of working-class draft-dodgers shooting at middle-class draft-dodgers." Charles Moskos, "Attitudes of American Combat Soldiers toward the War in Vietnam," colloquium paper, Russell Sage Foundation, New York City, 26 May, 1970.

55 Marmion, *Selective Service*, p. 4. Jean Carper, *Bitter Greetings*, (New York: Grossman, 1968), p 66. (cites *Harvard Crimson*). Stewart Alsop, "American Youth in Canada," *Newsweek*, 20 July, 1970, p. 88; also *Newsweek*, 31 Aug, 1970, p. 80. Robert Fulford, "Our Newest Minority," *Saturday Night*, Nov 1968. Thomas L. Hayes, *Americans in Sweden*, (New York: Association Press, 1971), p 9. *Americana Yearbook 1971*, p. 272. Willard Gaylin, *In the Service of their Country: War Resisters in Prison*, (New York: Viking, 1970), p 277ff.

56 Marmion, *Selective Service*, pp. 88–97. American Friends Service Committee, *The Draft?* p. 24. Carper, *Bitter Greetings*, pp. 42–3. See also *United States v. Seager*, 380 US 163, 1965. Gary L. Walmsley, *Selective Service and Changing America*, (Columbus: Merrill, 1969), p. 40. Saul Braun, "From 1A to 4F and all Points in Between," *The New York Times Magazine*, 29 Nov, 1970, p. 34.

57 *The New York Times*, 6 May, 1967, p. 1 (statements by Rivers, Hebert). Bob Dylan's song is *Blowing in the Wind*, (1961). Edgar Z. Friedenberg, "The Draft and the Generation Gap," *Motive*, Oct 1967, p. 21ff. *American Legion Magazine*, Apr 1968. "Are Most in Vietnam Volunteers?" *U.S. News*, 14 Nov, 1966, p. 58. *The New York Times*, Aug 1966. (One-third of U.S. ground forces in Vietnam draftees). Office of Assistant Secretary of Defense (Systems Policy and Information), *Selective Service Calls, Induc-*

tions and Inductees on Active Duty, FYs 1949–51, unnumbered pages, Sept 1971. Communication from Robert C. Kovarik, Director for Information Operations, Dept of Defense, 1 Sept 1971, states: "In the period January 1961 through June 1971, U.S. military deaths from hostile action in connection with the war in Vietnam totaled 45,354. Of these 15,327 were draftees."

CHAPTER 5.

1 *Time*, 20 Aug, 1945, p. 19. "Dr. Einstein and the Atomic Bomb," *Reader's Digest*, Dec 1945. Nuel Pharr Davis, *Lawrence and Oppenheimer*, (New York; Simon and Schuster, 1968), p. 96.

2 Stimson and Bundy, *On Active Service in Peace and War*, (New York: Harper, 1947), p. 6, 644. Truman, *Memoirs*, II, pp. 524–5, 1011. Gaddis Smith, *Acheson*, pp. 160, 169.

3 Truman, *Memoirs*, II, pp. 87, 460. David E. Lilienthal, *Journals*, II, (New York: Harper, 1964), pp. 45–50. *Forrestal Diaries*, pp. 94–96. Byrnes, *Speaking Frankly*, pp. 269–76. Acheson, *Present at the Creation*, p. 151 ff. Morgan Thomas, *Atomic Energy and Congress*, (Ann Arbor: University of Michigan Press, 1956), pp. 39–40. Barton J. Bernstein, "American Foreign Policy and the Origins of the Cold War," in Bernstein, ed. *Policies and Politics of the Truman Administration*, (Chicago; Quadrangle, 1970), p. 46ff. *Time*, 22 and 29 Oct, 1945. *The New York Times*, 8 Oct, 1945, p. 8 and 11 Oct, 1945, p. 1 (speeches by Truman).

4 Membership of the Communist party declined from a high point of 100,000 in 1932. F.B.I. Chief J. Edgar Hoover, leading authority on the subject, estimated party strength in 1950 at 54,174 members, in 1953 at 24,796 members. Harold W. Chase, *Security and Liberty, the Problem of Native Communists, 1917–48*, (Garden City: Doubleday, 1955), p. 7.

5 *The New York Times*, 18, 26, 30, 31 Aug, 4, 11, 19, Sept 2, 16–30 Nov, 1945 (Pearl Harbor inquiry). *The New York Times*, 14 Feb, 1946 (Browder expulsion). *The New York Times*, 14 Oct, 1946 (Budenz speech). *The New York Times*, 18 Oct, 1946 (Eisler identified). *Hearings*, House Un-American Activities Committee, 80th Congress, 1st session, 24 Sept, 1947. (Washington: Government Printing Office, 1947), p. 14 (Budenz-Eisler testimony). *The New York Times*, 16, 17 Feb, 24, 26 Mar 16 July, 1946 (Canada spy trials). Truman, *Memoirs*, II, p. 51. *Forrestal Diaries*, p. 19. Samuel Huntington, *The Common Defense*, (New York: Columbia University Press, 1961), p. 125. Adam Yarmolinsky, *The Military Establishment* (New York: Harper, 1971), p. 29. Eric Bentley, ed. *Thirty Years of Treason* (New York: Viking, 1971), pp. 207–225.

6 Athan Theoharis, *Seeds of Repression* (Chicago: Quandrangle, 1971), p. 103. John W. Caughey, *In Clear and Present Danger*, (Chicago: University of Chicago Press, 1958), p. 41. Eleanor Bontecou, *The Federal Loyalty-Security Program*, (Ithaca: Cornell University Press, 1953), p. 21ff. Ralph S. Brown Jr., *Loyalty and Security* (New Haven: Yale University Press, 1958), p. 23ff. John H. Schaar, *Loyalty in America* (Berkeley: University of California Press, 1957), p. 138. Alan Barth, *The Loyalty of Free Men* (New York: Viking, 1951), p. 95f. Herbert Hyman, "England and America: Climates of Tolerance and Intolerance," in Daniel Bell, ed. *The Radical Right* (*The New American Right* expanded and updated), (Garden City: Doubleday, 1963, 2nd ed.), p. 227. Athan Theoharis, "Escalation of the Loyalty Program," in Bernstein, ed. *Politics and Policies of the Truman Administration*, p. 242. Christopher Lasch, *The New York Review of Books*, 6 Oct, 1967, p. 16. William C. Berman,

Politics of Civil Rights in the Truman Administration, (Columbus: Ohio State University Press, 1970), pp. 116ff. Richard M. Freeland, *The Truman Administration and the Origins of McCarthyism: Foreign Policy, Domestic Politics and Internal Security, 1946–48,* (New York: Alfred A. Knopf, 1971), pp. 207ff. Fred J. Cook, *The Nightmare Decade,* (New York: Random House, 1971), p. 62ff. Carey McWilliams, *Witch Hunt,* (Boston: Beacon, 1953), p. 22.

7 Brown, *Loyalty and Security,* p. 183 (estimate of numbers). Hyman, "England and America: Climates of Tolerance and Intolerance," p. 239. Bontecou, *Federal Loyalty-Security Program,* p. 25f.

8 *The New York Times,* 21 July, 1948 (Communist leaders). *Congressional Record* 18 Feb, 1947, p. 127 (Nixon maiden speech); 18 May, 1947, p. 6022 (other speeches). Robert Carr, *House Committee on Un-American Activities,* (Ithaca: Cornell University Press, 1952), p. 60. Alan D. Harper, *Politics of Loyalty,* (Westport, Conn.: Greenwood Publishing, 1969), p. 47ff. Louis Budenz, *This Is My Story,* (New York: McGraw-Hill, 1947), p. 234. Walter Goodman, *The Committee,* (New York: Farrar Straus), p. 190ff. Chase, *Security and Liberty,* p. 34.

9 New York *Daily News,* 1 Aug, 1948, p. 2. "Ghosts on the Roof," *Time,* 5 May, 1945. Elizabeth Bentley, *Out of Bondage,* (New York: Devin Adair, 1951), p. 308ff. Bert and Peter Andrews, *A Tragedy of History,* (Washington: Robert Luce, 1962), p. 4. Whittaker Chambers, *Witness,* (New York: Random House, 1952), pp. 3, 56, 60, 529. Hannah Arendt, *Crises of the Republic,* (New York: Harcourt, 1972), p. 39. Christopher Lasch, "Cultural Cold War," in *Agony of the American Left,* (New York: Alfred A. Knopf, 1969), p. 64. R.H.S. Crossman, ed. *The God That Failed,* (New York: Harper, 1947), passim.

10 New York *Daily News,* 4 Aug 1948, p. 3. Andrews, *A Tragedy,* p. 11. Chambers, *Witness,* p. 43. Ronald Seth, *The Sleeping Truth,* (New

York: Hart Publishing, 1968), p. 26.

11 New York *Daily News,* 4 Aug 1948. Andrews, *A Tragedy,* p. 13. Chambers, *Witness,* p. 430.

12 New York *Daily News,* 4 and 6 Aug, 1948. New York *Herald Tribune,* 4 and 6 Aug, 1948. Andrews, *A Tragedy,* p. 8. Goodman, *The Committee,* p. 245. Richard Nixon, *Six Crises,* (Garden City: Doubleday, 1962), p. 10. Arthur Schlesinger Jr., *The Coming of the New Deal,* (Boston: Houghton Mifflin, 1958), p. 77 (Hiss in AAA).

13 New York *Daily News,* 18, 19, 26, 31 Aug, 1948. New York *Herald Tribune,* 18 and 19 Aug, 1948. Andrews, *A Tragedy,* p. 77. Chambers, *Witness,* p. 605. Nixon, *Six Crises,* p. 41ff. Alger Hiss, *In the Court of Public Opinion* (New York: Alfred A. Knopf, 1957; p. 100. Goodman, *The Committee,* p. 255.

14 Andrews, *A Tragedy,* p. 78 (Washington *Daily News* headline). New York *Daily News,* 26 Aug, 28 Sept, 1948. New York *Herald Tribune,* 26 Aug, 1948. Chambers, *Witness,* pp. 1, 25, 705ff. Goodman, *The Committee,* p. 259. Andrews, *op. cit.,* p. 114, 170ff.

15 Whittaker Chambers, *Cold Friday* (New York: Random House, 1964), p. 45. Chambers, *Witness,* pp. 4, 626, 730ff. New York *Daily News,* 4 Dec, 1948. *The New York Times,* 7 Dec, 1948; 9 Jun, 1949. Goldman, *The Crucial Decade,* p. 103ff. Andrews, *A Tragedy,* p. 8. Goodman, *The Committee,* pp. 254, 267. Alistair Cooke, *A Generation on Trial,* (New York: Alfred A. Knopf, 1952), pp. 91ff, 142ff. Hiss, *In the Court of Public Opinion,* p. 318. Seth, *The Sleeping Truth,* p. 26f. Leslie Fiedler, "McCarthy and the Intellectuals," in *Commentary,* Aug 1951, p. 110ff. Cook, *Nightmare Decade,* p. 9.

16 Hannah Arendt, *The Origins of Totalitarianism* (New York: Harcourt, 1951), pp. 301, 314. Arthur Schlesinger Jr., *The Vital Center* (Boston: Houghton Mifflin, 1949, pp. 59–63. Klaus Knorr, *The War Potential of Nations,* (Princeton: Princeton University Press, 1956), p. 92ff. Crossman, *The God That Failed,* p. 1–11.

Robert Straus-Hupe et al. *Protracted Conflict* (New York: Harper, 1959), p. 1, 140, 200. Hayek, *The Road to Serfdom*, p. 181.

17 St Louis *Post-Dispatch*, 23 Sept, 1949, p. 1. Truman, *Memoirs*, II, p. 295. Lilienthal, *Journals*, II, p. 561ff. Richard G. Hewlett and Oscar E. Anderson Jr., *The New World 1939–46, History of the Atomic Energy Commission*, Vol. I, (University Park, Pa.: Penn State University Press, 1962), pp. 410, 621, 639. Morgan Thomas, *Atomic Energy and Congress* (Ann Arbor: University of Michigan Press, 1956), p. 67ff (Hickenlooper, Vandenberg statements).

18 St. Louis *Post-Dispatch*, 23 Sept 1949. Lilienthal, *Journals*, II, pp. 569, 570. Truman, *Memoirs*, II, p. 307. Goldman, *The Crucial Decade*, p. 100 (damaged stuffed deer).

19 Lilienthal, *Journals*, II, p. 573 ("near-panic"). St. Louis, *Post-Dispatch*, 24 Sept, 1949, pp. 2A, 2F (statement by Urey). LaFeber, *America, Russia and the Cold War*, p. 79 (statement by Vandenberg). Acheson, *Present at the Creation*, p. 345. Thomas, *Atomic Energy and Congress*, p. 67ff.

20 *The New York Times*, 26 Nov, 1949 (Johnson). *The New York Times*, 1 Feb 1950 (Truman H-bomb announcement). Truman, *Memoirs*, II, p. 309. Lilienthal, *Journals*, II, pp. 581, 613. Acheson, *Present at the Creation*, pp. 346, 349. Paul Y. Hammond, "NSC-68, Prologue to Rearmament," in Warner Schilling, ed., *Strategy, Politics and Defense Budgets*, (New York: Columbia University Press, 1962), p. 291ff.

21 *The New York Times*, 12 Jan, 1950 (statement by Taft): 8 Jan, 1950, p. 4 (Young Republican); 23 Sept, 1949, p. 21 (statement by MacArthur); 6 Nov, 1949, p. 19 (statement by Dewey). *The New York Times*, 20 Jun, 1952.W.S. Churchill, The Hinge of Fate, (Boston: Houghton Mifflin, 1950), p. 134 ("China," to Wavell). Norman Graebner, *Empire on the Pacific* (New York: Ronald, 1955), pp. v-vii, 228 ("flight of the eagle"). Whitney Griswold, *Far Eastern Policy of the United States*, (New York: Harcourt, 1938), p. 466. William Appleman Williams, *Tragedy of American Diplomacy*, (New York: Dell paperback, 1969), pp. 49, 50, 124. Walter Lippmann, *United States War Aims*, (Boston: Little Brown, 1944), p. 38. John K. Fairbank, *United States and China*, (Cambridge: Harvard University Press, 1949), p. 247. O. Edmund Clubb, *Twentieth Century China*, (New York: Columbia University Press paperback, 1965), p. 28. Max Ascoli, *The Reporter*, 8 Jan, 1952, p. 10.

22 Dept. of State, *United States Relations with China* (Washington: Government Printing Office, 1949), p. 57. *Forrestal Diaries*, p. 12. Theodore White, ed. *The Stilwell Papers* (New York: Duell Sloan, 1948), p. 323. Barbara W. Tuchman, *Stilwell and the American Experience in China, 1911–45*, (New York: Macmillan, 1970), p. 237. Theodore H. White and Annalee Jacoby, *Thunder Out of China*, (New York: Sloane, 1946), p. 256. Herbert Feis, *The China Tangle*, (Princeton: Princeton University Press, 1953), pp. 14, 216. C.P. Fitzgerald, *Revolution in China*, (New York: Praeger, 1952), pp. 87, 172. Clubb, *Twentieth Century China*, p. 187. Stuart Schram, *Mao Tse-tung* (Baltimore: Penguin paperback, 1970; orig. 1967), p. 227. Tang Tsou, *America's Failure in China, 1941–50*, (Chicago: University of Chicago Press, 1963), p. 350ff. Don Lohbeck, *Patrick H. Hurley*, (Chicago: Henry M. Regnery, 1956), p. 400. H.B. Westerfield, *Foreign Policy and Party Politics*, p. 251. Gaddis Smith, *Dean Acheson*, p. 157. Communication from Lillian Owens, Dec 1972 (Luce).

23 Schram, *Mao Tse-tung*, pp. 20, 26, 32, 41, 114, 126, 146, 203. Clubb, *Twentieth Century China*, pp. 87, 191, 202, 214.

24 Fairbank, *United States and China*, p. 265. Feis, *The China Tangle*, p. 244. Clubb, *Twentieth Century China*, p. 247.

25 Dept of State, *U.S. Relations with China*, p. 113. Feis, *The China Tangle*, p. 240.

26   Dept of State, *U.S, Relations with China*, p. 131ff. White, *Thunder out of China*, p. 279. Clubb, *Twentieth Century China*, p. 253. Fitzgerald, *Revolution in China*, pp. 90, 99. Albert Wedemeyer, *Wedemeyer Reports*, (New York: Holt, 1958), p. 348. Tang Tsou, *America's Failure in China*, p. 359. Feis, *The China Tangle*, p. 336. Hans Kohn in *Britannica Yearbook 1949* (Chicago, Encyclopedia Britannica, 1950), p. 201. Geraldine Fitch, *Blunder out of China* (New York: America-China Policy Association, 1947), p. 3. *The Chinese Communists as Agrarian Reformers*, (Los Angeles: Foundation for Special Research, Dec 1950), mimeo. Walter Judd, *Our Ally, China*, (Shanghai: International Publishers, 1945), p. 3. Fairbank, *United States and China*, p. 262. Gabriel Kolko, *The Politics of War* (New York: Random, 1968), p. 614. Joseph C. Grew, *The Turbulent Years*, (Boston: Houghton Mifflin, 1952), p. 464. *Forrestal Diaries*, pp. 103, 123. Truman, *Memoirs*, II, p. 66. Acheson, *Present at the Creation*, p. 133f. Lohbeck, *Patrick H. Hurley*, p. 428. Gar Alperovitz, *Atomic Diplomacy: Hiroshima and Potsdam-the Use of the Atomic Bomb and the American Confrontation with Soviet Power*, (New York: Vintage paperback, 1965), p. 93ff.

27   W. Lewisohn dispatch in *North China Daily News* (Shanghai) cited without date in *Yearbook of World Affairs 1949* (London: Institute of World Affairs, 1950), p. 135. Dept of State, *U.S. Relations with China*, pp. 148–151, 159, 180, 605–19, 969. Clubb, *Twentieth Century China*, pp. 269,

278. Tang Tsou, *America's Failure in China*, pp. 350ff, 424, 468. Charles Wertenbaker, "The China Lobby," *The Reporter*, 8 Jan, 1952, p. 16 (Chiang statement to Ambassador Stuart). Acheson, *Present at the Creation* pp. 143, 145. Feis, *The China Tangle*, p. 413ff. (Marshall notes on sessions with Byrnes-Truman). J.R. Beal, *Marshall in China*, (Garden City: Doubleday, 1970), pp. 1–2. Robert Payne, *The Marshall Story*, (Englewood Cliffs: Prentice-Hall, 1951, pp. 2, 53. John Melby, *The Mandate of Heaven*, (Toronto: University of Toronto Press, 1968), p. 167ff. Fairbank, *The United States and China*, p. 266. Westerfield. *Foreign Policy and Party Politics*, pp. 255, 268. John C. Campbell, *The United States in World Affairs 1948–49*, (New York: Harper) Council on Foreign Relations, 1949), p. 268.

28   Dept. of State, *U.S. Relations with China*, p. 315.

29   Ibid., p. 730, 770, 834. Clubb, *Twentieth Century China*, p. 282ff. Fitzgerald, *Revolution in China*, G.F. Efimov, *Borba dlya Demokratsii protiv Reaktsii v Kitae* (Leningrad, 1948), p. 8. and V. Maslennikov, *Mirovoe Khozyaistvo i Mirovaya Politika*, (Dec 1947), p. 19, cited in Campbell, *U.S. in World Affairs 1948–9*, p. 268, as Soviet historians' estimate of extent of Chinese land reform at that date. Chang Chia-ao, *The Inflationary Spiral: the Experience in China 1939–50*, (Cambridge; MIT Press, 1958) at p. 373 states the slide in the foreign exchange rate and the escalation in internal prices between January, 1946, and July, 1948, was as follows:

		Market rate for Chinese DOLLAR PER US $	Wholesale Price Index, Shanghai[30] JANUARY-JUNE, (1937 = 100)
1946	June	2,665	378,000
	December	6,063	681,000
1947	June	36,826	2,905,000
	December	149,615	10,063,000
1948	June	2,311,250	197,690,000
	August	8,683,000	558,900,000

30 Westerfield, *Foreign Policy and Party Politics*, p. 247 (statement by Vandenberg), p. 262 (statement by Acheson). *Vandenberg Papers*, p. 522. Tang Tsou, *America's Failure in China*, pp. 448, 467. A.T. Steele, *The American People and China*, (New York: McGraw/Council on Foreign Relations, 1966), p. 33. *The New York Times*, 12 Jan, 1947. William C. Bullitt, "Report on China," *Life*, 13 Oct, 1947. Campbell, *U.S. in World Affairs, 1948–9*, p. 276.

31 *Hearings on Emergency Foreign Aid*, House Committee on Foreign Affairs, 80th Congress, 1st session. (Washington: Government Printing Office, 1947), p. 23ff (statement by Judd). Westerfield, *Foreign Policy and Party Politics*, p. 262 (statement by Taft). Tang Tsou, *America's Failure in China*, p. 467.

32 Dept of State, *U.S. Relations with China*, pp. 267, 845. Fitzgerald, *Revolution in China*, p. 101.

33 Tang Tsou, *America's Failure in China*, p. 490. Fairbank, *America and China*, p. 270. Clubb, *Twentieth Century China*, pp. 286, 289ff. Peter Calvocoressi, *Survey of International Affairs 1949–50*, (London: Oxford University Press) Royal Institute of International Affairs, 1953), pp. 316, 319ff.

34 *The New York Times*, 24 and 25 Nov 1948. *China and Far Eastern Policy, 1945–67*, (Washington: Congressional Quarterly Service, 1967), p. 48f. Acheson, *Present at the Creation*, pp. 255, 406. Campbell, *U.S. in World Affairs 1948–9*, p. 276f. Westerfield, *Foreign Policy and Party Politics*, pp. 343ff, 354. Tang Tsou, *America's Failure in China*, p. 509ff. Steele, *American People and China*, p. 34.

35 *The New York Times*, 6 Aug 1949, p. 16. *The New York Times*, 29 July 1949. (Dewey statement on China failure). Campbell, *U.S. in World Affairs 1948–9*, p. 276f. Westerfield, *Foreign Policy and Party Politics*, p. 354. Steele, *American People and China*, p. 34. Calvocoressi, *Survey, 1949–50*, pp. 339, 499. *Dept of State Bulletin*, 15 Aug, 1949, p. 236 (statement by Acheson). Roderick MacFarquhar, ed. *Sino-American Relations, 1949–71* (New York: Praeger, 1972), pp. 65, 75, 78.

36 Richard Hofstadter, *Anti-Intellectualism in American Life* (New York: Vintage paperback, 1963), p. 41 ("Grand Inquisition of the 50s"). V.O. Key, *Politics, Parties and Pressure Groups*, (New York: Crowell, 1964), 5th ed.), p. 99. Earl Latham, *The Communist Conspiracy in Washington* (Cambridge: Harvard University Press, 1966), p. 417ff. Ronald J. Caridi, *The Korean War and American Politics* (Philadelphia: University of Pennsylvania Press, 1968), p. 3. Westerfield, *Foreign Policy and Party Politics*, p. 325. *Vandenberg Papers*, p. 466ff.

37 *Forrestal Diaries*, p. 404. Acheson, *Present at the Creation*, p. 216. Harper, *The Politics of Loyalty*, p. 78.

38 W.S. White, *The Taft Story* (New York: Harper, 1954), p. 80. Westerfield, *Foreign Policy and Party Politics*, p. 325. Norman Graebner, *The New Isolationism*, (New York: Ronald, 1956), p. 27. Caridi, *Korean War and American Politics*, p. 3. Samuel Lubell, *The Future of American Politics*, (Garden City: Doubleday Anchor paperback, 1956), p. 1. David Riesman and Nathan Glazer, "The Intellectual and the Discontented Classes-1955," in Daniel Bell, ed. *The Radical Right*, p. 87.

39 Westerfield, *Foreign Policy and Party Politics*, p. 162. Latham, *Communist Conspiracy*, p. 7. Barton Bernstein in Bernstein, ed. *Politics and Policies of the Truman Administration*, p. 292.

40 Robert Griffith, *The Politics of Fear* (Lexington: University of Kentucky Press, 1970), p. 3 ("Never saw him taking it easy"). Richard Rovere, *Senator Joe McCarthy*, (New York: Meridian paperback, 1959), p. 75ff. R.H. Luthian, "McCarthy as Demagogue," in Earl Latham, ed. *The Meaning of McCarthyism* (Boston: D.C. Heath, 1965), p. 1. William F. Buckley and L. Brent Bozell, *McCarthy and his Enemies*, (Chicago: Henry M. Regnery, 1954), p. 3.

[41] Griffith, *The Politics of Fear*, p. 29. Jack Anderson and Ronald May, *McCarthy, the Man, the Senator and the Ism*, (Boston: Beacon, 1952), p. 172. Goldman, *The Crucial Decade*, p. 140.

[42] Griffith, *Politics of Fear*, p. 40. *State Department Loyalty Investigation*, Senate Committee on Foreign Relations, 81st Congress, 2nd session, (Washington; Government Printing Office), p. 1771ff ("Lee list"). Rovere, *Senator Joe McCarthy*, pp. 22, 124.

[43] Griffith, *Politics of Fear*, p. 50. *Congressional Record*, 26 July 1946, p. A4892 (Byrnes letter). John Steinke and James Weinstein, "McCarthy and the Liberals," in James Weinstein and D.W. Eakins, *Studies on the Left*, (New York: Random House, 1970), p. 22. (Appleton, Wis. *Post-Crescent*, 9 Oct 1946: Byrnes' removal of the 105 shows "the Democratic national leadership sold the nation for its individual gain and put Benedict Arnolds as sentinels on the wall for a few thousand lousy votes in slum districts.").

[44] Rovere, *Senator Joe McCarthy*, pp. 81, 122, 125. Latham, *The Communist Conspiracy*, p. 270. Goldman, *The Crucial Decade*, p. 142. *Congressional Record*, 20 Feb, 1950, p. 1953 (McCarthy).

[45] Latham, *Communist Conspiracy*, p. 270. Rovere, *Senator Joe McCarthy*, p. 125. Booth Mooney, *The Politicians, 1945–60*, (Philadelphia: Lippincott, 1970), p. 102.

[46] *The New York Times*, 4, 5, 11 Feb, 1950. Acheson, *Present at the Creation*, p. 360. Alan Moorehead, *The Traitors*, (New York: Harper, 1963), p. 153. W.S. Schoenberger, *Decision of Destiny* (Athens: Ohio University Press, 1969), p. 264.

[47] Washington *Post*, 22 Feb, 1950. *Congressional Record*, 20 Feb, 1953, p. 1953. White, *The Taft Story*, p. 85. Rovere, *Senator Joe McCarthy*, p. 131. Acheson, *Present at the Creation*, p. 364.

[48] *Time*, 19 May, 1950, p. 20. Charles Wertenbaker, "The China Lobby," *The Reporter*, 15 Apr, 1952, p. 2. Latham, *The Communist Conspiracy*, p.

270ff. Rovere, *Senator Joe McCarthy*, p. 145f. Goldman, *The Crucial Decade*, p. 144. Eric Barnouw, *The Image Empire*, (New York: Oxford University Press, 1970), p. 10. *China and the U.S. Far Eastern Policy, 1945–67* (Washington: Congressional Quarterly Service, 1967), p. 1.

[49] *China and the U.S. Far Eastern Policy*, p. 4. *Time*, 19 May, 1950, p. 21. Goldman, *The Crucial Decade*, p. 152. Rovere, *Senator Joe McCarthy*, p. 152. Latham, *The Communist Conspiracy*, p. 283.

[50] Michael P. Rogin, *The Intellectuals and McCarthy*, (Cambridge: MIT Press, 1967), p. 261. Daniel Bell, *The End of Ideology* (New York: Free Press, 1960), p. 99. Richard Hofstadter, The Pseudo-Conservative Revolt," in Daniel Bell, ed. *The Radical Right*, p. 99. Bernstein and Matusow, eds. *The Truman Administration*, p. 403. Westerfield, *Foreign Policy and Party Politics*, p. 370f. Caridi, *The Korean War and American Politics*, p. 37.

[51] Hofstadter, "Psuedo-Conservative Revolt, p. 41.

[52] Rogin, *Intellectuals and McCarthy*, p. 220. E. Digby Baltzell, *The Protestant Establishment: Aristocracy and Caste in America* (New York: Random House, 1964), pp. 249, 277ff. Richard Hofstadter, *The Age of Reform* (New York: Vintage paperback, 1955), p. 9.

[53] Hofstadter, "Pseuedo-Conservative Revolt," p. 99.

[54] Lubell, *The Future of American Politics*, p. 140ff. Daniel Moynihan in *The New York Times*, 2 Mar, 1971, IV, p. 9. Rovere, *Senator Joe McCarthy*, p. 13. Talcott Parsons, "Social Strains in America, 1955," in Bell, ed. *Radical Right*, p. 175. Daniel Bell, "Status Politics and New Anxieties," in Latham, ed. *Meaning of McCarthyism*, p. 76.

[55] Lubell, *Future of American Politics*, p. 145. Rogin, *Intellectuals and McCarthy*, p. 220.

[56] Nathan Glazer and Daniel Moynihan, *Beyond the Melting Pot* (Cambridge: MIT Press, 1958), passim.

[57] Rovere, *Senator Joe McCarthy*, p. 5.

58 *The New York Times*, 26 Aug, 1950 (statement by Donahue); 27 Aug, 1950 (country ads); 23 Sept, 1950 (New Rochelle incident).

59 *The New York Times*, 25 Aug, 1950 (Matthews speech)

60 *The New York Times*, 12 Sept, 1950 (Johnson out). Acheson, *Present at the Creation*, pp. 373, 441.

61 Griffith, *Politics of Fear*, p. 118 (Truman statement). Thurman Arnold, *Fair Fights and Foul* (New York: Harcourt, 1965), p. 217. *The New York Times*, 30 Aug, 13 Sept, 1950.

62 *The New York Times*, 21, 23, 24 Sept, 1950. "If In Doubt, Don't Join," *U.S. News*, 22 Sept, 1950, p. 20. Griffith, *The Politics of Fear*, p. 121ff.

63 *The New York Times*, 23, 24 Sept, 1950; 23 Nov. 1950. Griffith, *The Politics of Fear*, p. 122. Truman, *Memoirs*, II, p. 284ff. Thomas Emerson and Norman Dorsen, *Political and Civil Rights in the United States*, I (Boston: Little Brown, 1967, 3rd ed.), pp. 192–5. Norman Dorsen, *The Rights of Americans* (New York: Pantheon, 1970), p. 238. *The New York Times*, 27 Dec, 1955 (concentration camps). *The New York Times*, 1 Jan, 1962 (history of camps). *American Civil Liberties Union Weekly Bulletin*, 11 Feb, 1963, p 3 (mimeo). *The New York Times*, 15 Sept, 1971. *U.S. Code, Title 50, Section 811*, dated-21 Sept, 1971 (repealing of Title II).

64 *Congressional Record*, 5 Sept, 1950, p. 14214 (statement by Malone). Barth, *The Loyalty of Free Men*, p. 45. Caridi, *Korean War and American Politics*, p. 55. Griffith, *The Politics of Fear*, p. 106.

65 David Rees, *Korea, the Limited War* (New York: St. Martin's Press, 1964), p. 198n (statement by Jonkel). Stanley Kelley, *Professional Public Relations and Political Power* (Baltimore: Johns Hopkins University Press, 1956), p. 107ff. Griffith, *The Politics of Fear*, p. 127.

66 Rovere, *Senator Joe McCarthy*, p. 169. Caridi, *The Korean War and American Politics*, p. 97. *China and Far Eastern Policy, 1945–67*, p. 4 lists three senatorial scalps. But opinions differ as to number—Cf. Griffith, *The Politics of Fear*, p. 125.

67 W.S. White, *The Professional, Lyndon B. Johnson* (Boston: Houghton Mifflin, 1964), p. 48 (statement by Johnson). Rovere, *Senator Joe McCarthy*, p. 82.

68 Goldman, *The Crucial Decade*, p. 142. (statements by McCarthy).

69 *The New York Times*, 9 Nov, 1950. Truman, *Memoirs*, II, p. 429. Westerfield, *Foreign Policy and Party Politics*, p. 380. Caridi, *The Korean War and American Politics*, p. 99. Harper, *The Politics of Loyalty*, p. 172. Spanier, *American Foreign Policy since World War II*, p. 153. *China and Far Eastern Foreign Policy, 1945–67*, p. 4. Shirley Hazard, *Defeat of an Ideal: a Study of the Self-Death of the United Nations* (Boston: Atlantic/Little Brown, 1972, pp. 14ff).

70 Truman, *Memoirs*, II, p. 256. Goldman, *The Crucial Decade*, p. 213. Rovere, *Senator Joe McCarthy*, p. 170ff. Joseph R. McCarthy, *America's Retreat from Victory*, (New York: Devin Adair, 1951), p. 171.

CHAPTER 6.

1 *The New York Times*, 7 Nov 1949 (Malenkov speech). Acheson, *Present at the Creation*, p. 449 (Rusk).

2 G.M. McCune, *Korea Today*, (London: Oxford University Press, 1950), p. 56ff. Max Beloff, *Soviet Policy in the Far East, 1944–51*, (New York: Oxford University Press, 1953), p. 157.

3 Truman, *Memoirs* II, p. 310. Dae-Sook Suh, *The Korean Communist Movement, 1918–48*, (Princeton: Princeton University Press, 1967), pp. 294–9.

4 Suh, *The Korean Communist Movement*, p. 256ff. *Current Biography 1951*, p. 222 (Kim).

5 Suh, *The Korean Communist Movement*, pp. 292–3.

6   *Dept. of State Bulletin,* XXII, 23 Jan
1950, pp. 111–6 (Acheson speech)
Suh, *The Korean Communist Move-
ment,* pp. 314, 319, 324–6. Beloff,
Soviet Policy in the Far East, p. 164.
John W. Spanier, *The Truman-
MacArthur Controversy and the Ko-
rean War,* (Cambridge: Harvard Uni-
versity Press, 1959), p. 24. Gaddis
Smith, *Dean Acheson,* p. 175.
LaFeber, *America, Russia and the
Cold War,* p. 95.

7   Acheson, *Present at the Creation,* p.
358. Truman, *Memoirs* II, p. 331.
Gardner, *Architects of Illusion,* p.
205. Herbert Agar, *The Unquiet
Years,* (London: Rupert Hart-Davis,
1957), p. 94ff. Henry S. Commager,
The New York Times Magazine, 29
Apr 1951, p. E-12. D.W. Brogan,
"The Illusion of American Omnipo-
tence," *Harper's,* Dec 1952.

8   *Congressional Record,* 5 Sept 1950, p.
14, 202 (Knowland) *U.S. News,* 13
Jan 1950. Douglass Cater, "Knowland, the Man who Wanted to be
Taft," *The Reporter,* 8 Mar 1956, p.
32. *Time,* 14 Jan 1957, p. 20. *Current
Biography 1951,* pp. 353–5 (Knowland).

9   Acheson, *Present at the Creation,* pp.
350, 432. Kennan, *Memoirs* I. p. 381.
Frederick S. Dunn, *Peacemaking and
the Settlement with Japan,* (Princeton:
Princeton University Press, 1963), p.
87. E.O. Reischauer, *The United
States and Japan,* (Cambridge: Har-
vard University Press, 1957), p. 49.
Glenn D. Paige, *The Korean Decision,*
(New York: Free Press, 1968), p. 64.
I.F. Stone, *The Hidden History of the
Korean War,* (New York: Monthly
Review, 1952), p. 40. Allen S. Whit-
ing, *China Crosses the Yalu,* (New
York: Macmillan, 1960), p. 34. Gaddis
Smith, *Dean Acheson,* p. 172ff.

10 Strobe Talbott, ed. *Khrushchev
Remembers* (Boston: Little Brown,
1970), pp. 367–68. The authenticity
of this source, consisting of some
thirty chapters pulled together from
taped interviews, is questioned. The
account of Korean events at least
seems reasonable, all the more so because here Khrushchev does not make

out the best case for the Communists.
He says he still thinks Stalin was
wrong when after saying, "Well, why
not?" and giving Kim the arms he
asked for invading South Korea, Stalin
pulled out all the Russian advisers and
line-of-supply people when the Americans' counterattack at Inchon made
things rough. Criticizing this decision,
Khrushchev still seems unable to understand the eminently sound reason
Stalin gave him: "If the Americans
pull it off I don't want any Russians in
PW camps."
At the time many Americans
were convinced that the Korean war
was part of a worldwide Moscow-
directed conspiracy. On April 5, 1951,
in sentencing Julius and Ethel Rosenberg for spying against the United
States, Judge Irving Kaufmann said:
"I believe your conduct . . . has already
caused the Communist aggression in
Korea. . . ." (quoted in Eric Bentley,
ed. *Thirty Years of Treason,* (New
York: Viking, 1971), p. 939).

11 Ernest R. May, "Military Involvement in Foreign Policy," in Adam
Yarmolinsky, The Military Establishment (New York: Harper & Row,
1971), p. 116. *Washington Post,* 5
Sept 1950 (Lippmann).

12 John McDermott, "The Crisis
Managers," in *The New York Review
of Books,* 14 Sept 1967, pp. 5–6.
Theodore Sorensen, *Kennedy,* (New
York: Bantam paperback, 1966), p.
765. Henry Graff, *The Tuesday Cabinet,* (Englewood Cliffs: Prentice-Hall,
1970), pp. 3, 96. Gaddis Smith, *Dean
Acheson,* p. 179.

13 Truman, *Memoirs* II, p. 332ff. Ache-
son, *Present at the Creation,* p. 402.
Spanier, *The Truman-MacArthur
Controversy,* p. 30. Paige, *The Korean
Decision,* p. 79ff. *The New York
Times,* 25–27 Jun 1950. *China
and U.S. Far East Policy, 1945–67,*
Congressional Quarterly Service,
p. 52.

14 Paige, *The Korean Decision,* p. 187.
Truman, *Memoirs* II, p. 333. W.H.
White, *The Taft Story,* (New York:
Harper, 1954), p. 97. *The New York
Times,* 28 Jun 1950, p. 4 (Taft said

however that he would have voted for a joint congressional resolution approving the president's action, signifying that his quarrel was solely with the legality of Truman's method.).

15 *The New York Times,* 28 Jun 1950. Truman, *Memoirs* II, p. 332ff. Acheson, *Present at the Creation,* p. 403. *Congressional Record,* 27 Jun 1950, p. 9229 (statement by Knowland).

16 The New York Times, 28 Jun 1950 (Truman's Indochina commitment). Gaddis Smith, *Dean Acheson,* p. 315.

17 *The New York Times,* 28 Jun 1950. *New York Herald Tribune,* 28 Jun 1950. The market dropped first in very heavy trading, then rose. *Congressional Record,* 27 Jun 1950, p. 9233 (statement by Humphrey). Truman, *Memoirs* II, pp. 340, 371 (Allied opinion). Paige, *The Korean Decision,* pp. 45, 270 (opinion poll). "Poll Notes," *Public Opinion Quarterly,* Mar 1950, p. 372.

18 Goldman, *The Crucial Decade,* p. 175 (Sgt. Kemp). Paige, *The Korean Decision,* p. 123. (Kim's speech, cited from *People's Daily* Peking, 28 Jun 1950). Trumbull Higgins, *Korea and the Fall of MacArthur,* (New York: Oxford University Press, 1960), p. 35. R.H. Rovere and Arthur Schlesinger, Jr., *The MacArthur Controversy and American Foreign Policy,* (New York: Farrar Straus, 1965), p. 118 (Dean). Charles Willoughby and John Chamberlain, *MacArthur, 1941–51,* (New York: McGraw-Hill, 1954), p. 365. Courtney Whitney, *MacArthur, His Rendezvous with History,* (New York: Alfred A. Knopf, 1956), p. 342 (Inchon). Robert D. Heindl, *Victory at High Tide* (Philadelphia: Lippincott, 1966), p. 20. Walt Sheldon, *Hell or High Water, MacArthur's Landing at Inchon* (New York: Macmillan, 1968), p. 20. Russell A. Cugeler, *Combat Action in Korea,* (Washington: Office of Chief of Military History, U.S. Army, rev. 1970), p. 70.

19 Rees, *Korea, the Limited War,* p. 99. Geoffrey Hudson, "Rise of Communist Power in the Far East," in Evan Luard, ed., *The Cold War Reappraised,* (New York: Praeger, 1964), p.

75f. Peter Calvocoressi, *Survey 1950– 51,* passim. Higgins, *Korea and the Fall of MacArthur,* p. 54. Truman, *Memoirs,* II, p. 360. Strobe Talbot, ed. *Khrushchev Remembers* (Boston: Little Brown, 1970), pp. 370–1.

20 Whiting, *China Crosses the Yalu,* p. 58ff. Stone, *Hidden History of the Korea War,* p. 126. Paige, *The Korean Decision,* p. 210f. K.M. Panikkar, *In Two Chinas,* (London: Allen and Unwin, 1955), p. 108. F. Williams, *A Prime Minister Remembers, Earl Attlee's Memoirs,* p. 235.

21 Whiting, *China Crosses the Yalu,* pp. 102, 117. LaFeber, *America, Russia and the Cold War,* p. 121. Rovere and Schlesinger, *The MacArthur Controversy,* p. 280. Talbot, ed. *Khruschev Remembers,* p. 372. Alvin J. Cottrell and James E. Dougherty, "Lessons of Korea—War, the Power of Man," *Orbis,* II, 1, Spring 1958, p. 39ff.

22 Rees, *Korea, the Limited War,* p. 147f. Higgins, *Korea and the Fall of MacArthur,* p. 79. Whiting, *China Crosses the Yalu,* p. 163. Whitney, *MacArthur,* p. 416. Goldman, *The Crucial Decade,* p. 180. John Dille, *Substitute for Victory,* (Garden City: Doubleday, 1954), p. 11.

23 Rees, *Korea, the Limited War,* pp. 155, 164 (shallow burial). Higgins, *Korea and the Fall of MacArthur,* p. 83. Spanier, *Truman-MacArthur Controversy,* p. 132. Goldman, *The Crucial Decade,* p. 180. S.L.A. Marshall, *The River and the Gauntlet* (New York: Time-Life Books paperback, 1963), pp. 16, 92, 163, 322.

24 *The Military Situation in the Far East,* Hearings before Senate Committee on Armed Forces and Committee on Foreign Relations. (Washington: Government Printing Office, 1951), pp. 19, 32, 67. Truman, *Memoirs,* II, p. 382. Rees, *Korea, the Limited War,* p. 166. Spanier, *Truman-MacArthur Controversy,* p. 137. Lukacs, *New History of the Cold War,* p. 99.

25 *Military Situation in the Far East,* p. 752. Rees, *Korea, the Limited War,* p. 178 (meat-grinder). M.B. Ridgway, *The Korean War* (Garden City: Doubleday, 1967), p. 113. Lawton J. Col-

lins, *War in Peacetime,* (Boston: Houghton Mifflin, 1969), p. 284.

26 Rees, *Korea, the Limited War,* p. 190. *Time,* Mar 5, 1950, p. 28.

27 Richard M. Dalfiume, *Desegregation of the Armed Forces* (Columbia: University of Missouri Press, 1969), p. 101. Truman, *Memoirs,* II, p. 182. Ridgway, *The Korean War,* p. 192. Collins, *War in Peacetime,* p. 77. Goldman, *The Crucial Decade,* p. 185. Communication from Robert C. Kovarik, Sept 1, 1971, and John L. Donnelly, Director for Information Operations, Office of Assistant Secretary of Defense, 13 Feb 1973 (total of 5,720,000 men served in the armed forces during the Korean war, whereas between Jan 1965 and Sept 1972, 2,-590,000 U.S. military served in Vietnam).

28 *The New York Times,* 11 Apr, 1951. Truman, *Memoirs,* II, p. 445. Acheson, *Present at the Creation,* p. 520.

29 *The New York Times,* 20 Apr 1951, p. 4. *Military Situation in the Far East,* p. 2558. Rovere and Schlesinger, *The MacArthur Controversy,* p. 8ff.

30 *The New York Times,* 4 May 1951, p. 9. *Military Situation in the Far East,* p. 1, 25. Rovere and Schlesinger, *The MacArthur Controversy,* p. 15.

31 *Military Situation in the Far East,* pp. 65, 732, 1717. Louis Morton, "The Twin Essentials of Limited War," *Army* magazine, Jan 1961, p. 47. S.L.A. Marshall, "A Big Little War," *Army,* Jun 1960, p. 20ff.

32 *The New York Times,* 16 Oct 1950, p. 1 (Leveiro). William Hillman, *Mr. President,* (New York: Farrar Straus, 1952), p. 33 (Truman on relief of MacArthur). Cabell Phillips, *The Truman Presidency,* p. 321.

33 LaFeber, *America, Russia and the Cold War,* p. 123. Spanier, *Truman-MacArthur Controversy,* p. 40. S.L.A. Marshall, *The River and the Gauntlet,* p. 20.

34 Acheson, *Present at the Creation,* p. 433. Kennan, *Memoirs,* I, p. 394. Dunn, *Peacemaking,* p. 98.

35 *Military Situation in the Far East,* p. 352 (statement by Marshall). Acheson, *Present at the Creation,* p. 533.

Spanier, *The Truman-MacArthur Controversy,* p. 275. LaFeber, *America, Russia and the Cold War,* p. 123.

36 R.H. Luthin, "McCarthy as a Demogogue," in Latham, ed. *The Meaning of McCarthyism,* p. 11. Latham, *The Communist Conspiracy,* pp. 322, 354. Rovere, *Senator Joe McCarthy,* pp. 5, 32. Emmet Hughes, *Ordeal of Power* (New York: Atheneum, 1963), p. 109. Goldman, *The Crucial Decade,* p. 250ff. Johnson, *1600 Pennsylvania Avenue,* p. 290.

37 Eisenhower, *Memoirs,* I, pp. 279, 320. Latham, *The Communist Conspiracy,* p. 347. Rovere, *Senator Joe McCarthy,* p. 199ff. Goldman, *The Crucial Decade,* p. 250ff.

38 *Special Senate Investigation of Charges and Countercharges involving Secretary of the Army Robert T. Stevens, John G. Adams, H. Struve Hensel and Senator Joe McCarthy, Roy M. Cohn and Francis C. Carr:* Hearings before Special Subcommittee on Investigations of the Senate Committee on Government Operations, 83rd Congress, 2nd session (Washington: Government Printing Office, 1954), p. 1785 (statement by McClellan). Also Eisenhower, *Memoirs,* I, p. 211. Hughes, *Ordeal of Power,* p. 93. Rovere, *Senator Joe McCarthy,* p. 33. W. S. White, *The Taft Story,* p. 230ff.

39 *Christian Century,* 15 July 1953, p. 811 (fear). *The New York Times,* 3 July 1953. Richard Hofstadter, *Anti-Intellectualism in American Life,* (New York: Vintage paperback, 1963), pp. 13, 222.

40 *The New York Times,* 17 Mar 1953.

41 J.B. Matthews in *American Mercury,* July 1953. Sherman Adams, *Firsthand Report,* (New York: Harper, 1961), p. 141. Robert Donovan, *Inside the Eisenhower Administration,* (New York: McGraw-Hill, 1956), p. 94. Hughes, *Ordeal of Power,* p. 94.

42 *The New York Times,* 9, 11, 19 July 1953. *Christian Century,* 22 July 1953, p. 838. *Time,* 20 July 1953, p. 15. Adams, *Firsthand Report,* p. 95. Donovan, *Inside the Eisenhower Administration,* p. 94. Hughes, *Ordeal of*

43 Michael Straight, *Trial By Television*, (Boston: Beacon, 1954), pp. 30, 57, 59. Latham, *The Communist Controversy*, p. 401. Rovere, *Senator Joe McCarthy*, pp. 30, 39, 206. Goldman, *The Crucial Decade*, p. 271.

44 *The New York Times*, 10 July 1953. Straight, *Trial by Television*, p. 170.

45 Fred W. Friendly, *Due to Circumstances Beyond our Control* (New York: Random House, 1967), p. 59ff. Barnouw, *The Image Empire*, p. 52.

46 Straight, *Trial by Television*, p. 60. Goldman, *The Crucial Decade*, p. 271.

47 *The New York Times*, 12 Jan 1954; 4, 5, 12 Apr 1954. Philip M. Stern, *The Oppenheimer Case* (New York: Harper & Row, 1969), p. 270.

48 *Special Senate Investigation*, p. 31. Griffith, *The Politics of Fear*, p. 257. *The New York Times*, 18, 24 Feb 11 Mar, 22 Apr 1954.

49 Washington *Post*, 10 Jun 1954 (Hunt). *The New York Times*, 10, 14 Jun 1954. *Time*, 21 Jun 1954, *The New Yorker*, 10 Apr 1954, p. 130.

50 John B. Oakes, "An Inquiry into McCarthy's Status," *The New York Times Magazine*, 12 Apr 1953, p. 28.

51 Washington *Post*, 20 ,21 Jun 1954 (Hunt suicide). *The New York Times*, 20 June 1954. Marquis Childs in *Washington Post*, 30 Jun 1954. Washington *Post*, 4 July, 5 and 7 Oct 1953. Drew Pearson in Laramie (Wyo) *Daily Bulletin*, 23 Jun 1954, p. 20. Frank E. Brandegee, Republican of Connecticut, took his life by inhaling gas in his Washington house 14 Oct 1924, His suicide was probably due to financial difficulties over real estate investments. *Dictionary of American Biography*, (New York: Scribner, 1943) II, p. 598.

52 *The New York Times*, 21 Jun 1954 (statement by McCarthy). Barnouw, *The Image Empire*, p. 26 (Steiger quote from Columbia Oral History project). Straight, *Trial by Television*, p. 146.

53 *Newsweek*, 7 Jun 1954, p. 27. *U.S. News*, 23 Apr 1954, p. 12.

54 *Special Senate Investigation*, p. 543, 2426, 2427, 2428. Goldman, *The Crucial Decade*, p. 274. Straight, *Trial by Television*, p. 247. Griffith, *The Politics of Fear*, p. 295. Rovere, *Senator Joe McCarthy*, p. 219. Latham, *Communist Conspiracy in Washington*, p. 401. Mooney, *The Politicians*, p. 203.

55 Rovere, *Senator Joe McCarthy*, p. 232ff. Eisenhower, *Memoirs* I, p. 329. Arthur Watkins, *Enough Rope*, (Englewood Cliffs: Prentice-Hall, 1969), p. 143.

56 Atomic Energy Commission, *In the Matter of J. Robert Oppenheimer, Transcript of Hearing before Personnel Security Board*, (Washington: Government Printing Office, 1954), *passim*. Stern, *The Oppenheimer Case*, p. 271. Thomas H. Wilson, Jr., *The Great Weapons Heresy*, (Boston: Houghton Mifflin, 1970), p. 152ff. John Major, *The Oppenheimer Hearing*, (New York: Stein and Day, 1971). pp. 15, 33ff. Warner B. Schilling, "The H-Bomb Decision," *Political Science Quarterly*, 71 (1961), p. 24ff. Lewis L. Strauss, *Men and Decisions*, (Garden City: Doubleday, 1962), p. 267ff.

57 *The New York Times*, 7 Jan 1951 (mutual fund data). *President's Economic Council of Economic Advisers*, (Washington: Government Printing Office, Jan 1951), p. 1. Henry Wallace, *60 Million Jobs*, (New York: Simon and Schuster, 1948), p. 202.

58 *President's Economic Report, Council of Economic Advisers*, p. 7 ("in the grip of inflation"). Bureau of Labor Statistics, *Consumer Prices in the U.S., 1949–52*, Bulletin #1165, (Washington: Government Printing Office, 1954), pp. 6, 9, 10, 11. *The New York Times*, 6 Jan 1951' (ten-cent phone calls). Goldman, *The Crucial Decade*, p. 187 (59.3¢ dollar).

59 *The New York Times*, 16 Aug 1949; 2 Jan 1950. Goldman, *The Crucial Decade*, p. 187. Phillips, *The Truman Presidency*, p. 406.

60 *The New York Times*, 30 Mar 1951 (tankers).

61 *The New York Times*, 2 Mar 1951. *Time*, 12 Mar 1951, pp. 21, 26.

Rovere, *Senator Joe McCarthy*, p. 38 (Strandlund). Phillips, *The Truman Presidency*, p. 409n (nine Truman men in jail).

62 *The New York Times*, 12 Aug 1951 (West Point). Goldman, *The Crucial Decade*, p. 189 (statement by Blaik).

63 *The New York Times*, 28 Mar 1951 (CCNY players).

64 *The New York Times*, 28 Mar 1951. *Congressional Record*, 27 Mar 1951, p. 2905 (Fulbright).

65 *The New York Times*, 24 Jun 1951. Eric Barnouw, *The Golden Web*, (New York: Oxford University Press, 1966), p. 244 (Zoomar lens). Harvey Wish, *Society and Thought in Modern America*, (New York: Longmans Green, 1953), p. 566. Joseph Bensman and Bernard Rosenberg, "Mass Media and Mass Culture," in Philip Olson, ed., *America as a Mass Society*, (New York: Free Press, 1963), p. 170 (Westinghouse report). Martin Mayer, *About Television*, (New York: Harper & Row, 1972), p. 31. Sig Mickelson, *The Electric Mirror*, (New York: Dodd Mead, 1972), p. 27. Leo Bogart, *The Age of Television*, (New York: Unger, 1958), p. 80. Harry J. Skornia, *Television and Society*, (New York: McGraw-Hill paperback, 1965), p. 81ff. Stan Opotowsky, *TV, the Big Picture*, (New York: Dutton, 1961), p. 185. Dwight Macdonald, *Against the American Grain*, (New York: Random House, 1962, p. 402.

66 *The New York Times*, 11, 12, 13, 14, 19, 27 May 1951 (Kefauver crime hearings). Barnouw, *The Image Empire*, p. 296. *Time*, 19, 26 Mar 1951. Goldman, *The Crucial Decade*, p. 191ff. *Newsweek*, 12 Mar 1951. Wish, *Society and Thought*, p. 566. Booth Mooney, *The Politicians*, p. 146.

67 Irwin Ross, *The Loneliest Campaign*, (New York: New American Library, 1968), p. 93. Frederick Bancroft, *Life of William H. Seward* I, (New York: Harper, 1899), p. 361 (telegraphing speech). Edwin Emery, *Introduction to Mass Media*, (New York: Dodd Mead, 1960), p. 56 (note on linotype newsprint). Mayer, *About Television*, p. 238 (FDR spoke twenty times on radio during first ten months in office). *Public Papers of the President: John F. Kennedy*, III, (Washington: Government Printing Office, (Washington: Government Printing Office, 1963), p. 315 (Churchill).

68 Truman, *Memoirs* II, p. 207. T.S. Settel, *The Quotable Harry Truman*, (Anderson, S.C.: Drake House, 1967), p. 133. Steinberg, *Man from Missouri*, p. 317. Barnouw, *The Image Empire*, p. 257. *The New York Times*, 15 July 1948 (Truman acceptance speech).

69 Barnouw, *The Image Empire*, p. 290. Hugh Sidey, *A Very Personal Presidency, Lyndon Johnson in the White House*, (New York: Atheneum, 1968), p. 119. Graff, *The Tuesday Cabinet*, pp. 104, 135, 160. Eric Goldman, *The Tragedy of Lyndon Johnson*, (New York: Alfred A. Knopf, 1969), p. 289. Daniel J. Boorstin, *The Image*, (New York: Harper Colophon paperback, 1964), p. 43. Joe McGinniss, *The Selling of the President*, (New York: Trident, 1969), p. 1.

70 Herbert E. Alexander and Harold B. Meyers, "A Financial Landslide for the GOP," *Fortune*, Mar 1970, p. 104. Alexander Heard, *The Costs of Democracy*, (Chapel Hill: University of North Carolina Press, 1960), pp. 7, 396. Barnouw, *The Image Empire*, p. 79 (1956 costs). Mickelson, *The Electric Mirror*, p. 45. Herbert E. Alexander, *Money in Politics*, (Washington: Public Affairs Press, 1972), pp. 53, 54, 79. Herbert E. Alexander, *Financing the 1960 Election*, Study #5, (Princeton: Citizens' Research Foundation, n.d.), p. 10.

71 Barnouw, *The Image Empire*, p. 165 (1960 costs). Mayer, *About Television*, pp. 246, 248. Mickelson, *The Electric Mirror*, pp. 58, 60, 62 (cost of spots), p. 243 (1970 costs). D.W. Brogan, *Government of the People*, (New York: Harper, 1933), p. 165. Alexander, *Money in Politics*, p. 140. E.W. Chester, *Radio, TV and American Politics*, (New York: Sheed and Ward, 1969), p. 22.

72 Earl Mazo, *Richard Nixon*, (New York: Harper & Row, 1959), pp. 4, 124, 130. Barnouw, *The Image Em-*

pire, p. 300. Eisenhower, *Memoirs* II, p. 68.

73 Theodore H. White, *The Making of the President—1960*, (New York: Atheneum, 1961), p. 289. Barnouw, *The Image Empire*, p. 164.

74 William Leuchtenburg, *Franklin Roosevelt and the New Deal*, (New York: Harper & Row, 1955), p. 169. Mayer, *About Television*, p. 248. Reuel Denney, *The Astonished Muse*, (Chicago: University of Chicago Press, 1957), pp. 30, 249. Brooks, *The Great Leap*, p. 161. David Riesman, Reuel Denney and Nathan Glazer, *The Lonely Crowd* (Garden City: Doubleday Anchor paperback, 1955, orig. 1950), p.

22. Rovere, *Senator Joe McCarthy*, p. 205. Barnouw, *The Image Empire*, p. 5. Foster Rhea Dulles, *A History of Recreation*, (New York: Appleton-Century-Crofts, 1965 (2nd ed)), p. 339. *The New York Times*, 4 May 1952 (Truman's TV White House tour reviewed; an estimated 30,000,-000 watched. Truman played Mozart's Ninth Sonata on the East Room piano. He said at one point, "We have a man who winds the clocks every Friday.") Max Frankel in *The New York Times*, 16 July 1972, IV, p. 1 (on new Presidential-candidate power bases and TV).

CHAPTER 7.

1 Charles Beard, *Economic Interpretation of the Constitution, (New York: Holt, 1913).* Arthur S. Link, "What Happened to the Progressive Movement in the 1920s?" *American Historical Review*, July 1959, p. 833ff. "Where are the Pre-war Radicals?" *The Survey*, LV, 1 Feb 1926, pp. 536–66. S.E. Morrison and Henry Commager, *Growth of the American Republic*, II, (New York: Oxford Univerisity Press, 1950), p. 549 ff. Hofstadter, *The Age of Reform*, p. 286. William Leuchtenburg, *The Perils of Prosperity*, (Chicago: University of Chicago Press paperback, 1958), p. 97ff. Walter Goodman, *The Committee*, (New York: Farrar, Straus, 1968), p. 24ff (House Un-American Activities Committee in 1938).

2 U.S. Department of Commerce, *Survey of Current Business*, XXVIII, Apr 1948, p. 21 (commodity export drop). U.S. Department of Commerce, *Foreign Trade, 1936–49*, p. 42. Joyce and Gabriel Kolko, *The Limits of Power*, (New York: Harper & Row 1972), p. 375. Thomas G. Paterson, "Quest for Peace and Prosperity," in Bernstein, ed. *Politics and Policies of the Truman Administration*, (Chicago, Quadrangle, 1970) p. 93.

3 *Report of the Council of Economic*

Advisers, 6 Jan 1950, p. 47. *Economic Report of the President*, (Washington: Government Printing Office, 6 Jan 1950, p. 1. Paterson in Bernstein, *Politics and Policies of the Truman Administration* p. 170. *Vandenberg Papers*, p. 385. Eliot Janeway, *The Economics of Crisis*, (New York: Weybright and Talley, 1968), p. 223. Herbert Stein, *Fiscal Revolution in America*, (Chicago: University of Chicago Press, 1969), p. 197ff.

4 Simon Kuznets, *Postwar Economic Growth*, (Cambridge: Harvard University Press, 1964), p. 41ff. Bert G. Hickman, *Growth and Stability in the Postwar Economy*, (Washington: Brookings, 1960), p. 159ff. Peter M. Gutman, ed. *Economic Growth, an American Problem*, (Englewood Cliffs: Prentice-Hall, 1964), p. 8. Edward F. Denison, "United States Economic Growth," p. 95. Robert M. Solow "Economic Growth," p. 105. Wilfred Lewis Jr., *Federal Fiscal Policy in Postwar Recessions*, (Washington: Brookings, 1962) Granville Hicks, "How We Live in America," *Commentary*, p. 182. Dec 1953, p. 509. Eli Ginzburg, ed. *Technology and Social Change*, (New York: Columbia University Press, 1964), p. 63. W.A. Lewis, *Theory of Economic Growth*, (London: Allen and Unwin,

1955), p. 226ff. Gabriel Kolko, "The American Income Revolution " in Philip Olson, ed. *America as a Mass Society*, (New York: Free Press, 1963), p. 105. Brooks, *Great Leap* pp. 80, 131. Gabriel Kolko, *Wealth and Power in the United States*, (New York: Praeger, 1962), p. 13. George Soule, *Planning USA*, (New York: Bantam paperback, 1967), p. 143. Leon Keyserling, *Poverty and Deprivation in the U.S.* (Washington: Conference on Economic Progress, 1962), p. 2. Eli Shapiro et al. "Decade of Corporate Capital Investment," in Ralph G. Freeman, ed. *Postwar Economic Trends*, (New York: Harper & Row, 1960), p. 317. Stein, *Fiscal Revolution* p. 220ff (role of Committee for Economic Development in growth doctrine).

5 *Dept of State Bulletin*, 29 Feb 1950, pp. 272–4. Acheson p. 344ff.

6 Phillips, *The Truman Presidency*, pp. 306–8 (paraphrase of NSC-68 a document still held secret twenty years later). Warner Schilling, "The Politics of National Defense, Fiscal 1950," in Schilling, ed. *Strategy, Politics and Defense Budgets*, p. 44. Paul Y. Hammond, "NSC-68, Prologue to Rearmament," in Schilling, *Strategy, Politics and Defense Budgets*, p. 291ff. Acheson, *Present at the Creation* pp. 371, 375, 439, 753. Kennan *Memoirs* I, p. 474. *Forrestal Diaries*, p. 432. LaFeber, *America, Russia and the Cold War*, p. 90. *Hearings on Assignment of Ground Forces of U.S. to Duty in European Theatres*, Senate Committees on Foreign Relations and Armed Services, 82nd Congress, 1st session, Washington: GPO, 1951). p. 77. Joseph Alsop in New York *Herald Tribune*, 3 Dec 1950, Sect. 2, p. 4 (leak of NSC-68). Paul Nitze, *U.S. Foreign Policy, 1945–55*, (New York: Foreign Policy Association Headline series, Mar-Apr 1956, p. 7ff. *The New York Times*, 8 Jun 1952 (Truman statement on big budget). Paul Nitze, "The Need for a National Strategy," address to War College, Carlisle Barracks, Pa. 27 Aug 1958 cited by Samuel Huntington, *The Common Defense*, p. 51. *Dept of State Bulletin*, 20

Feb 1950, p. 273 (Acheson on "positions of strength").

7 Truman, *Memoirs* II, p. 256. Acheson, *Present at the Creation* pp. 390, 437, 442, 492, 552. LaFeber, *America, Russia and the Cold War*, p. 124. Coral Bell, *Negotiation from Strength*, (New York: Knopf, 1963), p. 31ff. *The New York Times*, 21 Dec 1950. *Congressional Record*, 5 Jan 1951, p. 54 (Taft speech) Robert Taft, *A Foreign Policy for Americans*, (Garden City: Doubleday, 1951), p. 4. *Hearings on Assignment of Ground forces of U.S.*, op. cit. p. 6 (Eisenhower), p. 126 (Bradley), p. 526 (Dewey), p. 470 (Stassen), p. 745 (Clay).

8 Janeway, *Economics of Crisis* p. 254 (post-Korean figures).

9 New York *Herald Tribune*, 2 Jun 1952. *The New York Times*, 20 July 1952. Chicago *Daily News*, 20 July 1952. John Steele, James Shepley, interviews, Sept 1970. Paul T. David, Malcolm Moos and Ralph M. Goldman, *Presidential Nominating Politics in 1952*, IV, (Baltimore: John Hopkins, 1954), p. 53. Richard Rovere, *The Eisenhower Years*, (New York: Farrar Straus, 1956), p. 65. Richard Bolling, *Power in the House*, (New York: Dutton, 1965), p. 169. *Vandenberg Papers*, p. 573. Booth Mooney, *The Politicians* p. 144. Marquis Childs, *Eisenhower the Captive Hero*, (New York: Harcourt, 1958), p. 148. Sherman Adams, *First-hand Report*, (New York: Harper & Row, 1961), p. 18. Source of the anecdote is I. Jack Martin, asssistant to Taft, 1952. James T. Patterson, *Mr. Republican*, (Boston, Houghton, 1972), pp. 550, 572. Alexander Heard, *Costs of Democracy*, (Chapel Hill; University of North Carolina Press, 1960), p. 335n.

10 R. Niebuhr, *Christian Realism and Political Problems*, (New York: Scribner, 1953), p. 58. Eisenhower, *Memoirs* I, pp. 20ff, 85–7. Robert J. Donovan, *Inside the Eisenhower Administration*, (New York: McGraw, 1956), p. 200. Childs, *Eisenhower Captive Hero* p. 128.

11 *Time*, 12 May 1952. Eisenhower, *Memoirs* I, pp. 7, 18. Truman, *Mem-*

oirs II, p. 257. David B. Capitanchik, *The Eisenhower Presidency and American Foreign Policy*, (London: Routledge and Kegan Paul, 1969), p. 10. James A. Hagerty, interview, May 18, 1971. C.L. Sulzberger, *A Long Row of Candles*, (New York: Macmillan 1969), p. 699.

12 *Time*, 5, 12 July 1952. *Life*, 10 Jun 1952. Eisenhower, *Memoirs* I, pp. 21–2. Mooney, *The Politicians*, p. 132.

13 *The New York Times*, 26 Aug 1952. Patterson, *Mr. Republican* p. 575.

14 Henry Graff, interview, 4 Sept 1970. Prof. Alpenfels and Gen. Eisenhower were fellow members of the Educational Policies Commission, 1950–52. J.N. Kane, *Facts about the Presidents*, (New York: Wilson, 1968), p. 246.

15 *Time*, 4 Apr 1969, p. 19. Paul Hutchinson, "The President's Religious Faith," *Christian Century*, 25 Mar 1955. Walter Johnson, *1600 Pennyslvania Avenue*, (Boston: Little Brown, 1960), p. 317. Childs, *Eisenhower, Captive Hero* pp. 19, 287ff. Eisenhower, *Memoirs*, I, p. 32.

16 Hutchinson, "The President's Religious Faith". Robert E. Fitch, "Piety and Politics in President Eisenhower," *Antioch Review*, summer 1955, pp. 148–58. Merlin Gustafson, "The Religion of a President," *Christian Century*, 10 Apr 1969, pp. 610–3. Casper Nannes, "The President and his Pastor," *Colliers*, 11 Nov 1956, pp. 29–31. Edward L.R. Elson, *America's Spiritual Recovery*, (Westwood, N.J.: Revell, 1954), p. 28. *Christianity and Crisis*, editorial, 11 Apr 1969. Hughes, *Ordeal of Power* p. 150 (Luther anecdote) *Time*, 21 Dec 1953 (five of six bestsellers of 1953 religious).

17 Childs, *Eisenhower, Captive Hero* p. 23. Hughes, *Ordeal of Power* p. 149. Arthur Larson, *Eisenhower, the President Nobody Knew*, (New York: Scribner, 1968), p. 30. *The New York Times*, 30 May 1971 (statement by Hagerty). Interview, James A. Hagerty, 18 May 1971. Interview, Prof. Henry Graff, Sept 4, 1970.

18 Eisnhower, *Memoirs*, I, p. 172. Adams, *Firsthand Report* p. 355ff.

19 Fred Collins, "Our Omniscient Presi-dent, some forces of not-knowing," *New Republic*, Jun 1, 1959. Hughes, *Ordeal of Power* pp. 54, 92. Adams, *Firsthand Report* p. 47. Donovan, *Inside the Eisenhower Administration* p. 249. Larson, *Eisenhower* pp. 8, 21–2. Neustadt, *Presidential Power* p. 9 (statement by Truman).

20 Johnson, *1600 Pennsylvania Avenue*, p. 323. Hughes, *Ordeal of Power* p. 129. Childs, *Eisenhower, Captive Hero* p. 289. Adams, *Firsthand Report* p. 135ff. Donovan, *Inside the Eisenhower Administration* p. 83ff.

21 J.R. Beal, *John Foster Dulles*, (New York: Harper & Row, 1957), p. 309. Richard Goold Adams, *Dulles, a Reappraisal*, (New York: Appleton-Century-Crofts, 1962), p. 192. Louis A. Gerson, *John Foster Dulles*, (New York: Cooper Square, 1967), p. 9ff. M.H. Guhin, *John Foster Dulles, a Statesman and His Times*, (New York: Columbia University Press, 1972), p. 102. R.D. Challener and John Fenton, "Which Way America? Dulles Always Knew," *American Heritage*, July 1971, p. 15ff. *The New York Times*, 21 Jan, 1925, p. 4; 18 and 22Sept 1926, p. 10; 25 Mar 1928, p. 1; 30 Apr 1929, p. 1; 26 Oct 1930, p. 2; 21 Jun 1933 , p. 1.

22 S.M. Cavert, *American Churches in the Ecumenical Movement*, (New York: Association Press, 1969), p. 191. *Biennial Report*, Federal Council of Churches, 1946, p. 135. *Nomination of John Foster Dulles*, Senate Committee on Foreign Relations, 83rd Congress, 1st session, (Washington: Government Printing Office, 1953), p. 4. Gerson, *John Foster Dulles* p. 98. Adams, *Firsthand Report* p. 89. LaFeber, *America, Russia and the Cold War* p. 117 (Japanese peace treaty).

23 Harold Macmillan, *Riding the Storm*, (New York: Harper & Row, 1971), p. 178.

24 *The New York Times*, 6 Mar 1953, Eisenhower, *Memoirs* I, p. 142ff. Hughes, *Ordeal of Power* p. 100. Donovan, *Inside the Eisenhower Administration* p. 42. Beal, *John Foster Dulles* p. 309. Adams, *Firsthand Report* p. 96. Robert P. Cutler, *No Time for Rest*, Boston, Atlantic/Little

25 *Nomination of John Foster Dulles*, op cit., p. 10.

26 Stebbins, *U.S. in World Affairs 1953* p. 123. Rees, *Korea the Limited War* p. 406. Coral Bell, *Negotiation from Strength* p. 219.

27 Eisenhower, *Memoirs* I, p. 399. Stebbins, U.S. in World Affairs 1953 p. 132 (Churchill).

28 *The New York Times*, 12 and 15 May 1953. Hughes, *Ordeal of Power* p. 111. Macmillan, *Riding the Storm* p. 94 (personal communications).

29 Eisenhower, *Memoirs* I, p. 181. Adams, *Firsthand Report* p. 49. Beal *John Foster Dulles* p. 182. Rees, *Korea the Limited War* p. 429, 462 (Korean armistice).

30 Garraty, *The American Nation*, New York, Harper, 1966, p. 791. (statement by Dulles).

31 New York *Herald Tribune*, 18 May 1953. R.I. Branyan and L.H. Larsen, eds. *The Eisenhower Administration, 1953–61, a documentary history*, I, N.Y. Random, 1971, p. 32. Coral Bell, *Negotiation from Strength* p. 78. Childs, *Eisenhower, Captive Hero* p. 169. Mooney, *The Politicians* p. 171. Sidney Warren, *The President as World Leader*, (Philadelphia; Lippincott, 1964), p. 366. Capitanchik, *Eisenhower Presidency* p. 41. Coral Bell in *Survey of International Affairs 1954*, (London; Oxford/Royal Institute of International Affairs, 1957), p. 101 ('New Look' a Taft term). R.C. Snyder in Warner Schilling's *Strategy, Politics and Defense Budgets*, pp. 389, 468.

32 Snyder in Schilling, p. 390ff. Coral Bell, *Negotiation from Strength* p. 146. Charles Murphy in *Fortune*, Mar 1953, p. 111ff. Stebbins, *U.S. in World Affairs 1953* p. 84n.

33 Eisenhower *Memoirs* I, p. 128. Donovan, *Inside the Eisenhower Administration*, p. 58, 102ff. (statements by Taft). Adams, *Firsthand Report* p. 153. LaFeber, *America, Russia and the Cold War* p. 152 (statement by

Brown 1966, p. 320f. R.P. Stebbins, *U.S. in World Affairs 1953*, New York Harper/Council on Foreign Relations, 1955, p. 103.

Humphrey on pullout from Korea). Snyder in Schilling, p. 417, 426. Branyan and Larsen, *The Eisenhower Administration*, I, p. 38.

34 Snyder in Schilling. p. 444.

35 *Dept of State Bulletin*, 25 Jan 1954, p. 107 (Dulles speech). *The New York Times*, 13 Jan 1954. Snyder in Schilling, p. 463, 520. John Foster Dulles, *War or Peace*, (New York, Macmillan, 1950), p. 5.

36 Coral Bell in *Survey 1954*, p. 99 (statement by Stevenson). *The New York Times*, 7 Mar 1954, 9 Mar 1954 (Pearson), 13 and 14 Jan 1954.

37 Coral Bell in *Survey 1954*, p. 121, (statement by Churchill in Commons 23 Mar 1954).

38 *The New York Times*, 19 Apr 1954 (Pope), 3 April 1954 (Nehru), 11 Nov 1954 (New Zealand), 25 Mar 1954 (statement by Chet Holifield, Democrat of California, that test explosion "out of control), 17 and 24 Mar 1954, ("spying"), 25 Sept 1954 (death of *Fortunate Dragon* crew member).

39 J.R. Shepley, "How Dulles Averted War," *Life*, 16 Jan 1956.

40 Coral Bell in *Survey 1954*, p. 108n. See also Stebbins, *U.S. in World Affairs 1953*, p 348f.

41 Eisenhower *Memoirs* I, p. 123. Beal, *John Foster Dulles* p. 182.

42 *The New York Times*, 20 July and 5 Oct 1952. Gerson *John Foster Dulles* p. 86. *The New York Times*, 20 Jun 1953 (East Berlin). Stebbins, *U.S. in World Affairs 1953*, p. 140ff. James Reston, "An Enquiry into American Foreign Policy," *The New York Times Magazine*, 16 Jan 1955.

43 Dept of State, *Foreign Relations of the United States, Diplomatic Papers, The Conferences at Malta and Yalta, 1945*. (Washington, Government Printing Office, 1955), p. 770. Melvin Gurtov, *The First Vietnam Crisis*, (New York; Columbia University Press, 1967), p. 14, 21. James Reston, "The Agonizing Reappraisal Has Already Begun," *The New York Times*, IV, 2 May 1954, p. 8. Neil Sheehan et al, *The Pentagon Papers*, (New York; Bantam paperback, 1971), p. 26 (London dispatch to Washington from

Hanoi, 27 Feb 1946, about Ho's unanswered letters). Gaddis Smith, *Dean Acheson*, (New York; Cooper Square, 1972), p. 305, 315.

44 Gurtov, *First Vietnam Crisis*, p. 14, 22, 27. Dulles, *War or Peace*, p. 231.

45 Alsop in New York *Herald Tribune*, 13 Jun 1954. Whitney, *MacArthur* p. 509 (statement by MacArthur).

46 *The New York Times*, 7 May 1954. Gurtov, *First Vietnam Crisis*, p. 68, 78ff. LaFeber, *America, Russia and the Cold War*, p. 161 (Twining statement from *Dulles Oral History Project*, Princeton)

47 Hanson Baldwin, "New Look Reexamined in Light of Indochina," *The New York Times*, IV, 2 May 1954, p. 8. "What Ridgway Told Ike," *U.S. News and World Report*, 25 Jun 1954, p. 30. Ridgway in *Saturday Evening Post*, 28 Jan 1956. Gurtov, *First Vietnam Crisis* p. 125–6. LaFeber, *America, Russia and the Cold War*, p. 162. Ridgway, *Soldier*, (New York; Harper, 1956), p. 276–7. Roger Hilsman, *To Move a Nation*, (Garden City; Doubleday, 1967), p. 102.

48 Eisenhower, *Memoirs* I, p. 346–7. Gurtov, *First Vietnam Crisis*, p. 145. Hughes, *Ordeal of Power*, p. 344. Sheehan et al, *Pentagon Papers* p. 38–40 (3 cables between Dulles and Dillon, 5 Apr 1954; also narrative stating U.S. paying 74% of war costs in 1954, p. 11–12 congressional resolutions sought 3 Apr and 7 May 1954; also British participation); p. 40 (Cutler memo on Eisenhower-Dulles talk, 7 May 1954). Gerson, *John Foster Dulles* p. 160.

49 Sheehan et al, *Pentagon Papers*, p 40 (Dulles-Dillon cable to "prepare public"). Acheson, *Present at the Creation* p. 219.

50 *Public Papers of the President of the U.S.: Eisenhower 1954*, (Washington, Government Printing Office, 1955) p. 382 (Eisenhower statement about dominos). Coral Bell in *Survey 1954*, p 37. Stebbins, *U.S. in World Affairs 1953* p. 220. But did Eisenhower or Dulles invent the metaphor?

51 Sheehan et al. *Pentagon Papers*, p. 40 (Cutler memo). See also p. 12.

52 Gurtov, *First Vietnam Crisis*, p 106. Gerson, *John Foster Dulles* p. 168. Eisenhower, *Memoirs* I, p. 348. Stebbins, *U.S. in World Affairs 1953* p. 223. Coral Bell in *Survey 1954*, p. 37.

53 Sheehan et al, *Pentagon Papers*, p. 42 (Dulles cable to W.B. Smith at Geneva, 12 May 1954); p. 14 (National Security Council paper about "work with France only so far as necessary") p. 13 ("disaster" as term for Geneva accords). Branyan and Larsen, *The Eisenhower Administration*, I, p. 346, 350.

54 Sheehan, et al. *Pentagon Papers*, p. 22 (election delay). Gaddis Smith, *Dean Acheson* p. 305ff. Gurtov, *First Vietnam Crisis* p. 108, 114, 126. Stebbins, *US in World Affairs 1953* p. 223, 247. Bell in *Survey 1954*, p. 37, 39, 51, 54. Eisenhower, *Memoirs* I p. 370, 407. Anthony Eden, *Full Circle*, (Boston; Houghton, 1960), p. 259, 269.

55 *Time*, 1 Dec 1952 (Eisenhower statement about "business brains"). See also William Shannon, "Eisenhower as President," *Commentary*, 26, 5. Nov 1958, p. 393ff.

56 New York *Herald Tribune*, 24 May 1950 (29% of General Motors business with Dept of Defense). *The New York Times*, 17 Jan 1953. *Time*, 27 Jan 1953 (7.8% of Dept of Defense's grand total contracts).

57 *The New York Times*, 17, 18, 19 Jan 1953 (statements by Saltonstall et al). *Time*, 26 Jan 1953, p. 20.

58 General Motors Co., *Annual Reports, 1946–71* (yearly defense income). Cf. also Clark Mollenhoff, *The Pentagon*, (Garden City; Doubleday, 1965), p. 17, 160, 161. Richard J. Barnet, *Economy of Death*, (New York; Atheneum, 1969), p. 114.

59 *Time*, 2 Jan 1956, p. 54 (statement by Curtice, "Man of the Year"). *Time*, 2 Jan 1956, p. 47 (GM's billion earnings in 1956). *Time*, 31 Dec 1956, p. 56 (comparative automobile sales). Cf also Lawrence White, *Automobile Industry since 1946*, p. 14. John Brooks, *The Seven Fat Years*, (New York; Harper, 1958), p. 43, 80 (data on GM and Ford stock issues). Charles E. Edwards, *Dynamics of the U.S. Automo-*

bile Industry, (Columbia, University of South Carolina Press, 1965), p. 121 (growth of GM). By 1969 General Motors' gross income was $24.9 billion, and its operating costs exceeded the GNP of all but a dozen countries. Robert M. MacDonald, Collective Bargaining in the Automobile Industry, (New Haven, Yale, 1963), p. 86 (wage rises in 1950s). Kefauver in L. White, Automobile Industry since 1946. p. 127. Richard Barber, The American Corporation, its Power, Money and Politics, (New York: Dutton, 1970), p. 257. Robert A. Dahl, After the Revolution? (New Haven; Yale Univ Press, 1970), p. 120, 169.

60 T.R.B. in New Republic, 15 Dec 1952, p. 3. Dean Acheson, A Democrat Looks at his Party, (New York: Harper & Row, 1955), p. 28 (statement by Burgess). Rovere, The Eisenhower Years, p. 65 (car dealers in cabinet). Arthur Schlesinger, Jr. Kennedy or Nixon, Does it Make any Difference? (New York: Macmillan, 1960), p. 47 (statement by McKay). See also David A. Frier, Conflict of Interest in the Eisenhower Administration, (Ames; Iowa State University Press, 1969), p. 204.

61 Joseph and Stewart Alsop, "The Man Ike Trusts with the Cash," Saturday Evening Post, 23 May 1953. Sam Grafton, "Ike Counts on Mr. H." Colliers, 2 May 1953. W.H. Hessler, "George Humphrey, New Name on the Dollar," The Reporter, 17 Feb 1953. "Eisenhower's Righthand Man," U.S. News, 10 Apr 1953. "Secretary of the Treasury," Life, 16 Mar 1953. Donovan, Inside the Eisenhower Administration. p. 56. Mooney, The Politicians. p. 165. Childs, Eisenhower, Captive Hero p 165. LaFeber, America, Russia and the Cold War. p. 140. Hughes, Ordeal of Power, p. 71ff. Goldman, Crucial Decade. p. 240. Garraty, American Nation. p 807.

62 Donovan, Inside the Eisenhower Administration. p. 56.

63 Ibid., p. 141. Edmund S. Flash Jr. Economics in Action: the President's Council of Economic Advisers, (New York: Columbia University Press, 1965), p. 22.

64 The Reporter, 10 Jan 1954, p. 19 (Burns). Time, 15 Jun 1953. Time, 27 Jun 1955, p. 78. Newsweek, 23 Mar 1953. Vogue, Mar 1954, p. 103. Herbert Stein, p. 294-5.

65 The New York Times, 30 July 1954, p. 4 ($300 million figure). Branyan and Larsen, The Eisenhower Administration, I. p. 42f. Congressional Quarterly, Vol XI, No 40, week ending 2 Oct 1953 ($11 million campaign spending figure). "Ike's Minister for Prosperity," Colliers, 25 May 1956, p. 82. Donovan, Inside the Eisenhower Administration p. 165. Adams, Firsthand Report p. 156.

66 Interview, Henry Graff, 10 Sept 1970 (Eisenhower's liquid assets in 1949). William Hesseltine, U.S. Grant, Politician, (New York: Dodd, Mead, 1935), p. 146 (cites New York World, 9 Mar 1869, re Borie). Letter to The New York Times, 23 Jan 1953 (Grant-Stewart).

67 The New York Times, 29 Apr 24 May, 1953. Branyan and Larsen, The Eisenhower Administration, I, p. 123f. Robert Engler, The Politics of Oil, (Chicago; University of Chicago Phoenix paperback, 1961), p. 73, 86, 159, 230, 313. Oil and Gas Journal, 11 Oct 1954, cited by Engler, p. 94. Morton S. Mintz and Jerry S. Cohen, America Inc., (New York: Dial, Press 1971), p. 8 (cost of import quotas), p. 9. Drew Pearson and Jack Anderson, The Case Against Congress, (New York: Simon and Schuster, 1968), p. 432 (Eisenhower farm upkeep).

68 Paul Hoffman, Peace Can Be Won, (Garden City: Doubleday, 1951), p. 81. Caroline M. Miles, "The International Corporation," International Affairs, Jul 1967, p. 641. Leo Model, "The Politics of Foreign Investment," Foreign Affairs, Jul 1967, p. 641. Raymond Vernon, Sovereignty at Bay, (New York: Basic Books, 1971), p. 11f. Stephen Hymer and Robert Rowthorn in Charles Kindleberger, ed The International Corporation, (Cambridge: MIT Press, 1971), p. 88ff. Mira Wilkins, Emergence of Multinational Enterprise, (Cambridge; Har-

vard University Press, 1970). Mira Wilkins and F.E. Hill, *American Business Abroad*, (Detroit; Wayne State University Press, 1964), p. 393. Christopher Rand, *Cambridge USA*, (New York: Oxford Univ. Press, 1964), p. 87. "What U.S. Companies are Doing Abroad, a statistical summary," May 1969, p 13 (between 1961 and 1967 3,481 foreign manufacturing subsidiaries set up by U.S. companies). James W. Vaupel and J.D. Curban, *The Making of Multinational Enterprise*, (Boston; Harvard Graduate School of Business Administration, 1969), p. 3. Sidney E. Rolfe, *The International Corporation*, International Chamber of Commerce Background Report, 1969, p. vi, 18. Howe Martyn, *International Business Principles and Problems*, (New York: Free Press, 1964), p. 37, 44. Donald Schon, "The Future of American Industry," *The Listener*, 2 July 1970, p. 8f. Christopher Layton, *Transatlantic Investment*, (Boulogne; Atlantic Institute, 1966), p. 18 (20 U.S. corporations do 2/3 of U.S. business in Europe). J.J. Servan-Schreiber, *The American Challenge*, (New York: Atheneum, 1969), p. 3. Interviews, Paul Douglas, Edward McMenemin, Hart Preston, June 1971.

69 Servan-Schreiber, *American Challenge* p. 1. Vernon, *Sovereignty at Bay*, p. 91. Model, *"Politics of Foreign Investment,"* p. 641.

70 Vernon, p. 91. Alvin J. Harman, *The International Computer Industry*, (Cambridge; Harvard University Press, 1971), p. 12. T.A. Wise, "IBM's Five Billion Dollar Gamble," *Fortune*, Sep 1966, p. 118.

71 Gilles Bertin, *Foreign Investment in France*, p. 22, cited by Servan-Schreiber, p. 13 (size of U.S. share of French market). Harman, p. 36 *(force de frappe)*, p. 22 (GE-Bull). Vernon, *Sovereignty at Bay* p. 22. Gilles Paquet, ed. *The Multinational Firm and the National State*, (Don Mills, Onto.; Collier-Macmillan Canada, Ltd., 1972), p. 4.

72 Vernon *Sovereignty at Bay* p. 168 ($4 for every $1). Miles, "The International Corporation," p. 261 (Esso's home and overseas business compared). General Motors, *Annual Reports, 1945–71*.

73 Vernon, p. 108. Robert Heilbroner, "The Multinational Corporation and the Nation-State," *New York Review of Books*, 11 Feb 1971, p. 20.

74 Vernon, *Sovereignty at Bay*, p. 107 (global scanning examples), p. 18 ($110 billion figure). Harry Magdoff, *Age of Imperialism*, (New York: Monthly Review, 1969), p. 6of.

75 Courtney Brown, ed. *World Business*, (New York: Macmillan, 1969), p. 334 (statement by Ball). Vernon, *Sovereignty at Bay*. p. 27, 102, 180, 191.

76 Peter Passell in *The New York Times Book Review*, 23 Jan 1972, p. 23 (Smedley Butler statement). Vernon, *Sovereignty at Bay*, p. 88. Kingman Brewster Jr., *Antitrust and American Business Abroad*, (New York; McGraw, 1958), p. 3, 28, 36. Jeremy Main, "First Real International Bankers," *Fortune*, Dec 1967, p. 143f.

77 Frank Tannenbaum, "Survival of the Fittest," *Columbia Journal of World Business*, Vol III, No 2, Mar–Apr 1968, p. 17

CHAPTER 8.

1 D.W. Brogan, "The Illusion of American Omnipotence," *Harpers*, December, 1952. George Kennan, *Memoirs*, II, (Boston: Atlantic/Little Brown, 1972). The name "Udel-Ural" appears to have been invented in the Nazi propaganda ministry during the second World War. (p. 99).

2 *The New York Times* 23 and 26 Aug

1952 (Liberation Center). *The New York Times*, 1 Mar 1953, (Radio Liberation), *The New York Times*, 16 Mar, 13 Oct, 27 Dec 1952 (East European Fund), *The New York Times*, 28 April 1951, p. 49 (Kersten amendment). "For a Free Europe," *Life*, 16 July 1951.

3 *The New York Times*, 27 Aug 1953

(Dulles in Buffalo). *The New York Times*, 17 April, 26 June, and 6 July 1953, and 9 Feb and 19 May 1955 (Eisenhower on Eastern Europe). *The New York Times*, 9 Dec 1956 (Dulles "You can count on us."). *The New York Times*, 28, 30 July 1953 (Meany statements). *The New York Times*, 24, Nov 1954 (Catholic bishops' protesting oppression). *The New York Times*, 18 July 1953 (Reuther statement). *The New York Times*, 22 Oct 1953 (Spellman). *The New York Times*, 17 Feb 1954 (Douglas). *The New York Times*, 18 Mar 1954 (Kennedy). Athan G. Theoharis, *The Yalta Myths*, (Columbia; University of Missouri Press, 1970), p. 135. D.F. Fleming, *The Cold War and its Origins*, (Garden City: Doubleday, 1961), p. 740 (Nixon urging "rollback" cited from Alsop column in Nashville *Tennessean*, 20 May 1953).

4   "Yearend Business Review," *Time*, 31 Dec 1956, p. 57.

5   *Federal Reserve Bulletin*, XXXV, 1 (Feb 1949), p. 1, 4. *The Changing American Market*, (Garden City: Hanover House/*Fortune*, 1955), p. 52. Herman P. Miller, *Rich Man, Poor Man*, (New York: Crowell, 1971), p. 14.

6   Gilbert Burck and Sanford Parker, "The Changing American Market," *Fortune*, Aug 1953, p. 98. "A New Kind of Car Market," *Fortune*, Dept 1953, p. 98. "The Fabulous Market for Food," *Fortune*, Oct 1953, p. 135. "The Lush New Suburban Market," *Fortune*, Nov 1953, p. 98. Burck and Parker, "The Wonderful, Ordinary Luxury Market," *Fortune*, Dec 1953, p. 117. "Sixty-Six Million More Americans," *Fortune*, Jan 1954, p. 94. Burck and Parker, "The Insatiable Market for Houses, *Fortune*, Feb. 1954. Daniel Seligman and Sanford Parker, "Upheaval in Home Goods," *Fortune*, March, 1954, p. 97. D.A. Saunders and Sanford Parker, "The Sunny Outlook for Clothes," *Fortune*, April 1954, p. 133.

Brooks, *The Great Leap* p 132. Kolko, *Wealth and Power in America* p. 106.

Leon Keyserling, *Poverty and Deprivation in the U.S.*, (Washington; Conference on Economic Progress, 1962), p. 1.

7   Donald J. Bogue, "Urbanism and Metropolitanism" in William Dobriner, ed. *The Suburban Community*, (New York: Putnam, 1958), p. 24–25 (1940 census: 42. million (31.6%) in central cities, 26 million (19.5%) in suburbs; 1950 census: 50 million (32.-8%) in central cities, 35 million (24%) in suburbs; 1970 census: 63 million (31%) in central cities, 55 million (25%) in suburbs).

8   Ben Wattenberg, *This U.S.A.*, (Garden City: Doubleday, 1965), p. 18 (birth rate data). See also Brooks, *The Great Leap*, New York, Harper, 1966, p. 267ff.

9   Gurney Breckenfeld, "25th Anniversary of FHA," *House and Home*, Jun 1959, p. 105. "The Many-Fingered Puppeteer," *House and Home*, Jun 1963, p. 114. *Fact Book*, (Chicago; U.S. Savings and Loan League, 1971), p. 9f (wartime savings). *Changing American Market*, p. 76 (doubled-up families). Richard O. Davies, *Housing Reform during the Truman Administration*, (Columbia: University of Missouri Press, 1966), p. 41. Nathan Glazer, "The Renewal of Cities," *Scientific American*, Sept 1965, p. 195f. Mark I. Gelfand, *A Nation of Cities, the Federal Government's Response to the Challenge of Urban America, 1933–60*, unpublished Ph. D. dissertation in Political Science, Columbia University, 1972, p. 11, 19, 21 (This account draws heavily on this source.)

10   Scott Green, ed. *The New Urbanization*, (New York: St Martins Press, 1968), p. 145. See also Bennett M. Berger, "Suburbs, Subculture and the Urban Future," in S.B. Warner, *Planning for a Nation of Cities*, (Cambridge; M.I.T. Press, 1966), p. 147. *Fact Book*, p. 32. Davies, *Housing Reform*, p xi. David Riesman and Eric Larrabee, "Autos in America," *Encounter*, VIII (1957), p. 26–36. Walter McQuade, ed. *Cities Fit to Live In*, (New York: Macmillan, 1971), p. 11.

Robert C. Wood, *Suburbia*, (Boston; Houghton, 1959), p. 5.

11 Breckenfeld, "25th Anniversary of FHA," Davies, *Housing Reform* p. 24. Gelfand, *"A Nation of Cities,"* p. 325. Kenneth T. Jackson, "The Crabgrass Frontier, 150 Years of Suburban Growth in America," in R.A. Mohl and J.F. Richardson, eds. *The Urban Experience: Themes in American History*, (Belmont, Cal.: Wadsworth, 1973, in press).

12 "The Industry Capitalism Forgot," *Fortune*, August 1947. Berger, "Suburbs, Subculture and the Urban Future" p. 143. *House and Home*, June 1959. "FHA in Suburbia," *Architectural Forum*, Aug 1957, p. 160–1. Eric Hodgins, *Mr. Blandings Builds his Dream House*, (New York: Simon and Schuster, 1946) (from *Fortune*, April 1946).

13 Eric Larrabee, "The 6000 Houses that Levitt Built," *Harper's*, Sept 1947, p. 79f. Harry Henderson, "Mass Produced Suburbs," *Harper's*, Sept 1953, p. 25. F.L. Allen, "Big Change in Suburbia," *Harper's* June 1954, p. 21. "Levitt at Work," *Fortune*, Aug 1947. *Fortune*, Oct, 1952. Penn Kimball, "Dream Town Large Economy Size," *The New York Times Magazine*, 14 Dec 1952, p. 12. *The New York Times*, 18 Apr 1952, p. 52.

14 Charles Abrams, *Future of Housing*, (New York; Harper, 1946), p. 224ff. Nelson Foote, ed. *Housing Choices and Housing Constraints*, (New York: McGraw, 1960), p. 187ff. Gelfand, "A Nation of Cities" p. 329. Jackson, "Crabgrass Frontier,"

15 Richard Goode, *The Individual Income Tax*, (Washington: Brookings, 1966), p. 122 (15% tax savings). Alvin L. Schorr, "National Community and Housing Policy," *Social Service Review*, 39, Dec 1965, p. 433 (estimates $2–2.6 bil. subsidy annually to householders in late 1950s—calculation of $30 billion based on Schorr and Goode figures). Gelfand, "A Nation of Cities," p. 325.

16 *Fact Book 1971*, p. 32 (mortgage debt). Jackson, "Crabgrass Frontier," ("nearly half" of loans at peak made by FHA and VA). See also Bureau of Census, *Housing Inventory, Components of Change, 1950–56*, I, (Washington; GPO, 1968), p. 14, and *Financing of Owner-Occupied Residential Property*, II, p. 1, also *The Housing Situation, the Factual Background*, Housing and Home Finance Administration, (Washington; GPO, Jun 1949), p. 5. "The Many-Fingered Puppeteer," *House and Home*, Jun 1963, p. 114. Richard Hofstadter writes (Hofstadter and C.DeWitt Hardy, *Development and Scope of American Higher Education*, (New York: Columbia University Press, 1962); p. 104: "The influence of the real-estate speculator in fostering a kind of mandatory boasting and civic optimism in the U.S. is a profitable but neglected area for students of American culture.")

17 *Statistical Abstract of the U.S. 1964*, p. 758 (number of cars). Wattenberg, *This U.S.A.* p. 256. Brooks, *The Great Leap* p. 45. Herbert von Borch, *The Unfinished Society*, (New York; Hawthorn, 1962), p. 83.

18 Lawrence White, *The Automobile Industry since 1946*, (Cambridge; Harvard University Press, 1971), p. 3 (employment). John B. Rae, *The Road and the Car in American Life*, (Cambridge: M.I.T. Press, 1971), p. 230. Helen Leavitt, *Superhighway Superhoax*, (Garden City: Doubleday, 1970), p. 11. Wilfred Owen, *Current History*, Nov. 1970, p. 290. Wilfred Owen, "Dispersed Pattern of Urban Living," in McQuade, *Cities Fit to Live In* p. 31. Wilfred Owen, *Automotive Transportation Trends and Problems*, (Washington; Brookings, 1949), p. 6f. Riesman and Larrabee, "Autos in America" p. 26f. Edward Higbee, *The Squeeze: Cities without Space*, (New York: Morrow, 1960), p. 111, 136. Kenneth Jackson, "The Crabgrass Frontier" (20,000 shopping centers).

19 *Planning, Regulation and Competition—Automobile Industry*, Hearings, Subcommittee of Senate Select Committee on Small Business, 91st Congress, 2nd session, (Washington;

GPO, 1968), p. 147. Mintz and Cohen, *America Inc* p. 338. Philip Hillyer Smith, *Wheels within Wheels*, (New York; Funk and Wagnalls, 1968), p. 98, 158–9 (statement by Sloan). Subcommittee on Antitrust and Monopoly, Senate Committee on the Judiciary, 86th Congress, 1st session, (Washington; GPO, 1959), p. 1. White, *The Automobile Industry since 1946* p. 127ff (prices), p. 211, p. 248 (profits), p. 259, ("technological stagnation").

20 Alfred P. Sloan, *My Years with General Motors*, (Garden City: Doubleday, 1964), p. 5. *Planning, Regulation and Competition—Automobile Industry*, p. 964f. (windshields). White, *The Automobile Industry since 1946* p. 259 (oligopoly). John Burby, *The Great American Motion Sickness*, (Boston; Little Brown, 1971), p. 75. Bernard Nossiter, *The Mythmakers*, (Boston; Houghton, 1964), p. 85. Daniel P. Moynihan, "The War Against the Automobile," *Public Interest*, No 3, Spring 1966, p. 10f. White, *The Automobile Industry since 1946* p. 258 ($800 cost of annual model change). Burby, *The Great American Motion Sickness* p. 75 (estimate of $700 by Kaysen et al.) Robert M. MacDonald, *Collective Bargaining in the Automobile Industry*, (New Haven; Yale, 1963), p. 5.

21 *Time*, 2 June 1956. Brooks, *The Great Leap* p. 126. Dwight Robinson, "Fashion Theory and Product Design," *Harvard Business Review*, Nov–Dec 1958, p. 126 (cites paper by William Schmidt of Chrysler, "What Price Lowness," read at Passenger Car Activity Meeting of Detroit section, Society of Automotive Engineers, 5 May 1958.

22 James T. Flink, "Three Stages of American Automobile Consciousness," American History Association paper, New York City, 29 Dec 1971, p. 19ff. White, *The Automobile Industry since 1946*. p. 217 (horsepower, ads). Smith, *Wheels within Wheels* p. 160. Mintz and Cohen, p. 320. Edward Dahlberg, *Can These Bones Live*, (New York: New Directions,

1960), p. 84 ("flowerless and treeless plains of macadam").

23 Moynihan, "War Against the Automobile", p. 13. *Time*, 2 Jan 1956. Jackson, "The Crabgrass Frontier" (pre-Interstate net roadbuilding). Rae, *The Road and the Car in American Life*, p. 188. Leavitt, p. 8. Smith, *Wheels within Wheels* p. 150. Welby M. Frantz, chairman of American Trucking Association, in Karl M. Ruppenthal, ed. *Transportation Frontiers*, (Stanford: Stanford University Press, 1962), p. 106. Wilfred Owen, *Strategy for Mobility*, (Washington; Brookings, 1964), p. 137. William V. Shannon, "Untrustworthy Highway Fund," *The New York Times Magazine*, 15 Oct 1972. Eisenhower, *Memoirs* I, p. 501. *The New York Times*, 13 Jul 1954. Gelfand, "A Nation of Cities" p. 248. Jackson, "The Crabgrass Frontier," *Business Week*, 22 Jan 1955.

24 Leavitt, p. 1, 27f, 47 (Case, Buckley, president of State Highway Officials). Jackson, "The Crabgrass Frontier." Gelfand, "A Nation of Cities." p. 332ff.

25 K.M. Ruppenthal, *Challenge to Transportation*, (Stanford; Stanford University Press, 1961), p. 1 (Wilcox).

26 Leavitt, p. 29ff. Gelfand, "A Nation of Cities," p. 344. Jackson, "The Crabgrass Frontier." Ray J. Sampson and Martin T. Ferris, *Domestic Transportation*, (Boston; Houghton, 1966), p. 3. Philip H. Burch, *Highway Revenue and Expenditure Policy in the U.S.*, (New Brunswick: Rutgers, 1962), p. 165, 223. George M, Smerk, *Urban Transportation, the Federal Role*, (Bloomington: University of Indiana Press, 1965), p. 74. Wilfred Owen, *Metropolitan Transportation Problem*, (Washington; Brookings, 1966), p. 264f. Jane Jacobs, *Life and Death of Great American Cities*, (New York: Vintage paperback, 1964), p. 20. Burby, *The Great American Motion Sickness* p. 92. Rae, *Road and Car in American Life*, p. 109, 201. Denis Hayes, "Can We Bust the Highway Trust?" *The Saturday Re-*

view, 5 Jun 1971, p. 48. *The New York
Times,* 19 Aug 1971.

27 David Riesman in W. McQuade, *Cities Fit to Live In* p. 38. James Marston
Fitch, interview, 11 Feb 1972 (landscape of social peace).

28 *Fact Book 1971,* U.S. Savings and
Loan League, p. 19 (total private housing starts 1950: 1,908,000). Sources as
follows:

29 John Normile, "A Ranch House from
the Ranch Country," *Better Homes
and Gardens,* Dec 1947, p. 55. Mort
Reed, Jr. "One Story Plans can be
Compact," *Better Homes and Gardens,* Aug 1950, p. 46. "Low and Outside," *Harper's,* Oct 1952, p. 52 (Eastern ranch houses). Allen Gowans, *Images of American Living,* (Philadelphia;
Lippincott, 1964), p. 104. Douglas

	ALL PRIVATE STARTS[1]	1-FAMILY[2]	1-STORY[3]	SPLIT-LEVEL[4]
1945	325,000			
1946	1,015,000			
1947	1,265,000			
1948	1,340,000			
1949	1,430,000			
1950	1,908,000		992,000	
1951	1,420,000			
1952	1,446,000			
1953	1,402,000			
1954	1,532,000			
1955	1,627,000			
1956	1,325,000		861,000	59,000
1957	1,175,000			
1958	1,314,000			
1959	1,494,000	1,212,000		
1960	1,230,000	972,000		
1961	1,248,000	946,000		
1962	1,439,000	976,000		
1963	1,581,000	993,000		
1964	1,530,000	944,000	399,000	67,000
1965			385,000	72,000
1966			296,000	57,000
1967			307,000	61,000

[1] *Housing Construction Statistics, 1889 to 1964,* Bureau of Census, 1966, p. 20
[2] *Housing Construction Statistics, 1889 to 1964,* Bureau of Census, 1966, p. 43 (Table 11)
[3] *New One-Family Homes Sold and For Sale 1963 to 1967,* Bureau of Census and HUD, Construction Reports, p. 16. (Table I)
[4] *New One-Family Homes Sold and For Sale 1963 to 1967,* Bureau of Census and HUD, Construction Reports, p. 16.

See also: Bureau of the Census, *Construction Reports, Housing Starts,* Feb 1960.
Dept. of Labor, "New Housing and its Materials, 1940-56," Bull. 12-31, p. 27. "Characteristics of New One-Family Houses, Selected Characteristics, 1940, 1950, 1954, 1955, and
by selling price class, 1956."

PER CENT DISTRIB.	1940	1950	1954	1955	1956
One-story	67%	86%	n.a.	n.a.	87%
Split-level	n.a.	n.a.	n.a.	n.a.	6%
Other	33%	14%	n.a.	n.a.	6%
Unknown	—	—	n.a.	n.a.	1%

(pp 43, 45, 47 tables give breakdown of above percentages by 4 regions of U.S.)
See also: Bureau of Census, *National Housing Inventory, Components of Change, 1950-56,*
Vol I. Washington: GPO 1958, p. 14 (data on new construction, occupancy rate by race)

Haskell, interview, 13 Jun 1972 (1 of 10 houses architect-designed).

30   Interviews, Percival Goodman, Walter McQuade, Herbert I. Smith, James Marston Fitch, Feb–Jun, 1972. L.A. Cavitt, *Ranch Type Houses*, (Culver City, Cal.: Murray and Gee, 1947), p. 13. Tom Riley, *Build Yourself Ranch-Type House*, (New York: Popular Mehanics, 1951), p. 13, 19. R.B. Wills, *Better Homes for Budgeteers*, (New York: Architectural Book Publ. Co., 1946). William Ricciutti, "It's A Knockout," *Better Homes and Gardens*, Feb 1948, p, 41. John Normile, "$50,000 Worth of Ideas in a Lowcost House," *Better Homes and Gardens*, Apr 1949, p. 37 (Levitt). Elizabeth Gilrain, "Sunshine and Space," *Better Homes and Gardens*. Sept 1948, p. 49. Sam Bass Warner, *The Private City*, (Philadelphia; University of Pennsylvania Press, 1968), p. 200ff. Leonard Reissman and Thomas Ktsanes, "New Homes for Old Values," *Social Problems*, 7, Winter, 1959–60, p. 187ff. Morton and Lucia White, *Intellectual versus the City*, (Cambridge: Harvard University Press, 1962), p. 2, 235, 237. Oscar Handlin and John Burchard, eds. *Historian and the City*, (Cambridge: M.I.T. Press, 1963), p. 118. George R. Stewart, *American Ways of Life*, (Garden City: Doubleday, 1954), p. 165.

31   Vide supra, Figures extrapolated from data in Footnote 28.

32   Tracy B. Augur, of TVA, in *Planning*, 1948, p. 27. A.Caldwell, Philadelphia planner, in *Journal of Architecture*, Dec 1945, p. 298.

33   Chase, *Security and Liberty*, (Garden City: Doubleday, 1955), p. 2. Alan Barth, *Loyalty of Free Men*, New York, Viking, 1952, p. 213. *The New York Times*, 20 Apr 1948, p. 1. *Time*, 22 Mar 1948 (J. Barogni). *The New York Times*, 22 Feb, 21 May, 22 Jun, 28, 29 Nov, 1951; 12 Mar, 17, 18 Apr, 7, 15 May, 4 June, 6, 19, July, 5, 18 Oct, 1953 (civil defense). *Annual Report, 1951*, Federal Civil Defense, p. 15. *Annual Report 1952*, Federal Civil Defense, p. 2, 51. *Annual Report 1953*, Federal Civil Defense, p. 3, 5. *Federal Civil Defense Guide*, Part E, Ch. 12, Appendix 1, Annex 1, June 1967, p 2. Communication from William K. Chipman, Deputy Assistant Director of Civil Preparedness (Plans), 31 Jan 1973 (highway signs).

34   Kenneth Jackson, "The Crabgrass Frontier" ("escape" ads). John Keats, *Crack in the Picture Window*, (Boston: Houghton, 1957), p. 2. Berger, "Suburbs, Subculture and the Urban Future" p. 147. Paul Ylvisaker, "The Deserted City," *Journal of Architecture*, Dec 1954, p. 1. Lewis Mumford, *The Pentagon of Power*, (New York: Harcourt, 1970), p. 417. R.G. Tugwell, *Off Course from Truman to Nixon*, (New York: Praeger, 1971), p. 101. John Burby, *The Great American* p. 256f. Peter Blake, *God's Own Junkyard*, (New York: Holt, 1964), p. 1. Eleanor Maccoby, "TV, Its Impact on School Children," *Public Opinion Quarterly*, XV, 3, Fall 1951, p. 421ff. Harry J. Skornia, *Television and Society*, (New York; McGraw paperback, 1965), p. 143f. Brooks, *The Great Leap* p. 161f.

35   *The New York Times*, 11, 18, 20 Jan 1972 (TV violence). Marvin Barrett ed. *Survey of Broadcast Journalism, 1969–70, 1970–71, 1971–72*, (New York: Grosset), passim.

36   Wattenberg, *This USA*, p. 78ff. David Riesman, "The Suburban Dislocation," in Olson, *Mass Culture in America*, p. 283. Bennett M. Berger, *Looking for America*, (Englewood Cliffs: Prentice-Hall, 1971), p. 152. Brooks, *Great Leap*, p. 140. Editors of *Fortune, America in the Sixties*, (New York: Harper Torchbook paperback, 1960), p. 133f. William H. Whyte, *The Organization Man*, (New York: Simon and Schuster, 1956). David Riesman et al. *The Lonely Crowd*, (Garden City: Doubleday Anchor paperback, 1955). A. C. Spectorsky, *The Exurbanites*, (Philadelphia: Lippincott, 1955). Vance Packard, *The Status Seekers*, (New York: McKay, 1959); *Hidden Persuaders*, (New York: McKay 1957). Daniel Bell, *End*

of Ideology, (New York: Free Press, 1959).

37 Harvey Swados, "The Myth of the Happy Workers," *Nation*, 17 Aug 1957. Harvey Swados, "Less Work. Less Leisure," *Nation*, 22 Feb 1958. Harvey Swados, "The Miners, Men without Work," *Dissent*, Autumn 1959. (See also H. Sv ados, *A Radical's America*, (Boston: Little Brown, 1962), p. 14, 121.) Eli Chinoy, "Tradition of Opportunity and Aspirations of Automobile Workers," in Olson, ed. *Mass Culture in America*, p. 508. Berger, *Looking for America*, p. 164ff. *Changing American Market*, p. 95. *America in the Sixties*, p. 107. Kolko, *Wealth and Power in America*, p. 113. Riesman, *Abundance for What?* (Garden City: Doubleday, 1964) p. 107. (consumer "package"). Wattenberg, *This USA*, p. 241 (2/3 own their homes). *Fact Book 1971*, U.S.Savings and Loan League, p.32 *Statistical Abstract 1964*, p. 40. Paul M. Mazur, *Dynamics of Economic Growth*, (Englewood Cliffs: Prentice Hall, 1963), p. 121.

38 *Statistical Abstract, 1957*, p. 832 (refrigerators, washers, TVs, vacuums, electric blankets, radios, stoves, toasters, disposalls, freezers, mowers, shavers, coffee makers), p. 512 (telephones), p. 520 (TVs), p. 814–5 (clothes). See also 1964 ed p. 798, (suits), p. 804 (peaches, ketchup). Wattenberg, p. 258 (cigars, cigarets). Brooks, *The Great Leap* p. 141 (tranquilizers). *Time*, 31 Dec 1956 p. 54 (assertion that U.S. consumed 60% of world's goods).

39 K. Jackson, "Crabgrass Frontier," Peter Blake, *God's Own Junkyard*, p. 1.

40 *The N.Y. Times*, 1 May 1954 (Eisenhower). LaFeber, *America, Russia and the Cold War*, p. 184 (Dulles)

41 Simon Kuznets, *Postwar Economic Growth*, Cambridge: Harvard University Press, 1964), p. 111. Andrew Shonfeld, *Modern Capitalism*, (New York: Oxford, 1965), p. 11f. Paul M. Mazur, *The Standards We Raise*, (New York: Harper, 1953), p. 35. Francis Sutton, *American Business Creed*, (Cambridge: Harvard University Press, 1956), p. 152. Paul M. Mazur, *Dynamics of Economic Growth*, p. 116. J.K. Galbraith, *The Affluent Society*, (Boston: Houghton, 1958), p. 121 ("all of the modern range"). J.K. Galbraith, *Economic Development*, (Boston: Houghton, 1962), p. 4. Leonard Lecht, *Goals, Priorities and Dollars*, (New York: Free Press, 1966), p. 142. Russell Lynes, *A Surfeit of Honey*, (New York: Harper, 1953), p. 122. H.H. Remmers and D.H. Radler, *The American Teen-ager*, (Indianapolis: Bobbs Merrill, 1957), p. 64. Reece McGee, *Social Disorganization in America*, (San Francisco: Chandler, 1962), p. 159f. Arnold Toynbee, *America and the World Revolution*, (New York: Oxford, 1962), p. 103ff. Van Wyck Brooks, *America Comes of Age*, (New York: Huebsch, 1915), p. 103ff. Edward Dahlberg to Robert Hutchins, 5 Nov 1958 *(Epitaphs for Our Times*, (New York: Braziller, 1967), p. 29: "Change is the revenue of the cartel but the infamy and degradation of the people."

42 Galbraith, *The Affluent Society* p. 96 (statement by Blough). Sutton, *American Business Creed* p. 262 (statement by Gifford).

43 Allen Ashbolt, *An American Experience*, (New York: Paul S. Eriksson, 1967) p. 113 (statement by Saulnier).

44 H.S. Reuss, *The Critical Decade*, (New York: McGraw, 1964), p. 125f. Lecht, *Goals* p. 206. Ralph E. Freeman, ed. *Postwar Economic Trends in the U.S.*, (New York; Harper, 1960), p. 77ff. Rostow, "Dynamics of American Society," in Freeman, p. 3f. Galbraith, *The Affluent Society* p. 96. Riesman, *Abundance for What?* p. 105f. Edward Bliss, ed. *In Search of Light, the Broadcasts of Edward R. Murrow, 1938–61*, (New York: Knopf, 1969, p. 265, 305, ("Harvest of Shame"). Paul Goodman, *Growing Up Absurd*, (New York: Random, 1956), p. 95, 201. McGee, *Social Disorganization in America* p. 37. Harrington, *The Other America*, p. 10, 62, 103. *Congressional Quarterly*, XIII,

No 3, 21 Jan 1955 (Eisenhower economics). Eric Goldman, "Goodbye to the Fifties—and Good Riddance," *Harper's*, Jan 1960, p. 27. Arthur Schlesinger, Jr., "The Highbrow in Politics," *Partisan Review*, Mar-Apr 1953, p. 1. Agnes Meyer, "The Quest for a New America," *Antioch Review*, winter 1959–60, p 437f. Dwight Macdonald, "The Invisible Poor," *The New Yorker*, 19 Jan 1963. Paul Jacobs, "The Forgotten People," *The Reporter*, 22 Jan 1959, p 13. Rockefeller Brothers Fund, *Special Studies Project, Report of Panel IV*, (Garden City; Doubleday, 1958) p. 68, 71, 72 (public sector's share falls from 5 to 3%). Rostow, *U.S. in the World Arena* p. 20. Galbraith, *The Affluent Society* p 21. Robert Heilbroner, *The Future as History*, (New York; Grove Evergreen paperback 1961), p. 119. Robert M. Solow, "Income Inequality since the War," in Freeman, ed., *Postwar Economic Trends* p. 93f.

45 *The New York Times*, 24 Mar and 3 Nov 1957 (garbage collectors' v. teacher's pay). S.E. Harris, *Economics of the Political Parties*, (New York: Macmillan, 1962), p. 256f. Lecht, p. 20f. Myron Lieberman, *Education as a Profession*, (Englewood Cliffs; Prentice Hall, 1956), p. 386. Christopher Jencks, "Slums and Schools," *New Republic*, 10, 17 Sept 1962. Daniel Moynihan, "Second Look at the School Panic," *The Reporter*, 11 Jun 1959, p. 14.

46 Harris p. 264ff. Clark Tibbetts, ed. *Aging in Today's Society*, (Englewood Cliffs; Prentice Hall, 1960), p. 208. Leonard Engel, "Is the Salk Vaccine What Caused the Mess?" *Harper's*, Aug 1955. Edward T. Chase, Jr. "Can Blue Cross Survive its Own Success?" *The Reporter*, 29 Oct 1959, p. 15. Lucy Freeman, "Out of the Darkness," *Nation*, 31 Mar 1956. H. Azima, "Drugs for the Mind," *Nation*, 21 July 1956, p. 356. Harrington, *The Other America*, p. 103 (8 mil old folks, 5 mil without telephone). Dwight Macdonald, "The Invisible Poor" *The New York Times*, 28 July 1962, 28 July 1962 (day-care centers).

47 Harris, p. 281f. *Statistical Abstract 1964*, p. 750 (36,000 public housing starts annually out of million-plus total). Charles Abrams, "U.S. Housing," *New Leader*, 11 Jan 1958, p. 4. Bruce Bliven, "Golden Age of Buy Now, Pay Later," *The Reporter*, 3 May 1956. p. 19. Harvey Swados in *Esquire*, Sep 1959. Douglas Dowd, "Waiting for the Slump," *Nation*, 16 Jun 1956, p. 506. Harrington, p. 62. Leon Keyserling, *Poverty and Deprivation in the U.S.*, p. 4. Herman P. Miller in *The New York Times Magazine*, 11 Nov 1962. Gerald Burns, "Controlled Rents and Uncontrolled Slums," *The Reporter*, 12 Nov 1959, p. 16. William Hessler, "Refugees from Civic Progress," *The Reporter*, 9 July 1959, p. 27.

48 Virginia Held, "What Can We Do About Juvenile Delinquency?" *The Reporter*, 20 Aug 1959. Eric Goldman, *Harper's*, Jan 1960, op cit ("chaise longue"). Eric Sevareid, *The Reporter*, 5 Feb 1959, p. 6 (rush-hour). *Time*, The Last Traffic Jam," 15 Dec 1947, p. 28. Von Borch, *Unfinished Society* p. 83.

49 Andrew Hacker, ed. *The Corporation Takeover*, p. 10f. Brooks, *The Great Leap* p 58. David Riesman, "Abundance for What?" *Bulletin of the Atomic Scientists*, Apr 1958, p. 136 (Anaheim, "Paradise Found"). Whyte, *Organization Man*, p. 22. Arthur Miller, *Death of a Salesman*, (New York: Viking, 1947), p. 56, 64, 65. Fritz Pappenheim, *Alienation of Modern Man*, (New York: Modern Review, 1959), p. 199. Forrest J. Berghorn and G.H. Steere, "Are American Values Changing?" *American Quarterly*, Spring 1966, p. xviii, 521.

50 John Wild, *Challenge of Existentialism*, (Bloomington; University of Indiana Press, 1955) p. 10. J.P. Sartre, *Philosophy of Existentialism*, (New York; Philosophical Library, 1965) p. 427. J. Heinemann, *Existentialism and the Modern Predicament*, (New York: Harper Torchbook paperback, 1958), p. 9. R.D. Cumming, ed. *Philosophy of Jean-Paul Sartre*, (New York; Random, 1965), p. 185. Wil-

liam Barrett, *What is Existentialism?* (New York: Grove, 1964), p. 8. Ernest Breisach, *Introduction to Modern Existentialism*, (New York: Grove, 1962), p. 233. Maurice Friedman, ed. *Worlds of Existentialism*, (New York: Random, 1964), p. 3.

51 Jacques Barzun, in *American Scholar*, Oct 1946, p. 451. J.L. Brown in *The New York Times Magazine*, 2 Feb 1947. Joseph Barry in *The New York Times Magazine*, 24 Apr 1949. Bernard Frizell, "Existentialism," *Life*, 17 Jun 1946, p. 59. Charles Frankel in *The Saturday Review*, 11 Oct 1952, p. 14. 6 Sept 1953, p. 8. Pappenheim, *Alienation of Modern Man* p. 25. Erich Heller, *The Disinherited Mind*, (New York: Farrar Strauss, 1957), p. 157. Malcolm Cowley, *The Literary Situation*, (New York: Viking, 1954), p. 83.

52 Norman Cousins, "Decline and Fall of Existentialism," *The Saturday Review*, 10 July 1954. Norman Mailer, "The Existential Hero: Superman comes to the Supermarket," in *Presidential Papers*, (New York: Bantam paperback, 1964) p. 63f. William Barrett, *Irrational Man*, (Garden City: Doubleday Anchor paperback, 1962), p. 269.

53 Robert Lowell, in *Partisan Review*, Vol 20, Nov-Dec 1953. Dwight Macdonald, *Against the American Grain*, p. 155.

54 Harold Rosenberg, *Tradition of the New*, (New York; Horizon, 1959), p. 20. Frank O'Hara, *Jackson Pollock*, (New York; Braziller, 1959), p. 29, 32. Francis V. O'Connor, *Jackson Pollock*, (New York; Museum of Modern Art, 1967), p. 58, 59, 73. Rudi Blesch, *Modern Art USA*, (New York; Knopf, 1956), p. 22. Calvin Tompkins, *World of Marcel Duchamp*, (New York; Time-Life Books, 1966), p. 154, 174. C.L. Wysuph, *Jackson Pollock, Psychoanalytical Drawings*, (New York; Horizon, 1970), p. 10, 14, 19. Rosalind Krauss, "Jackson Pollock's Drawings," *Artforum*, Jan 1971, p. 58f.

55 Rosenberg, *Tradition of the New* (Action Painting) O'Hara, p. 29, 116. O'Connor, *Jackson Pollock*, p. 74. *Time*, 15 Dec 1955.

56 Clement Greenberg in *Nation*, 19 Feb 1949; in *Partisan Review*, Jan 1952 Cleve Gray ed. *David Smith* by David Smith (New York: Holt, Rinehart & Winston, 1967), p. 20ff (statements by Motherwell and Smith). Hilton Kramer, "David Smith," *Arts*, Feb 1960, p. 22, 31. *David Smith*, (New York: Solomon Guggenheim Museum, 1965), p. 10, 153. Gray, "Visit to David Smith," *Art in America*, Jan 1966. *Time*, 8 Nov 1968 11 Apr 1969. Rosalind Krauss, *Terminal Iron Works, the Sculpture of David Smith*, (Cambridge: MIT Press, 1971), pp. 2, 93, 145.

57 Robert Conquest, *The Great Terror*, (New York: Macmillan, 1968), p. 246. Robert Conquest, *Power and Policy in the USSR: the Struggle for Stalin's Succession*, (New York: Harper Torchbook paperback, 1967, orig. 1961), p. 260. Robert Conquest, ed. *The Soviet Police System*, (London: Bodley Head, 1968), p. 50. Harold Berman, "Soviet Law Reform," *Yale Law Journal*, Vol 66, No 8 (1957), p. 119. Robert Conquest, ed. *Justice and Legal System in the USSR*, (London; Bodley Head, 1968), p. 19. J.M. Mackintosh, *Strategy and Tactics of Soviet Foreign Policy*, (New York; Oxford, 1963), p. 74, 94. Coral Bell, *Negotiation from Strength*, p. 106. Z. Brzezinski and S. Huntington, *Political Power USA/USSR*, (New York: Viking, 1963) p. 244.

58 Conquest, *Power and Policy*, p. 516

59 Bell, *Survey 1954* (Churchill). Eden, p. 59.

60 *Vital Speeches*, XIX, No 22, 1 Sept 1953, p. 679 (Malenkov speech). Conquest, p. 249. Edward Crankshaw, *Khrushchev's Russia*, (London; Penguin paperback, 1959), p. 5.

61 Conquest *Power and Policy*, p. 228ff. Brzezinski-Huntington, *Political Power*, p 241ff. Crankshaw, *Khrushchev*, (New York: Viking, 1966) p. 188f.

62 *Time*, 6 Jan 1958, p. 17 (Beria). Conquest, *Power and Policy* p. 204, Crankshaw, *Khrushchev* p. 12ff. Brzezinski-Huntington, *Political Power* p. 135.

63 Brzezinski-Huntington, *Political*

Power p. 241f. Conquest, *Power and Policy* p. 228f.

64   *Time,* 6 Jan 1958, p. 17 (statements by Khrushchev). Crankshaw, *Khrushchev* p. 192.

65   Conquest, *Power and Policy* p. 114. Crankshaw, *Khrushchev* p. 192ff. Brzezinski-Huntington, *Political Power* p. 242.

66   Sidney Ploss, *Conflict and Decision-Making in Soviet Russia,* (Princeton; Princeton University Press, 1965), p. 12, 60. Crankshaw, *Khrushchev* p. 194. Conquest, *Power and Policy* p. 235. *The New York Times,* 14 Feb 1954, p. 17; 12 July 1954; 21 Sept 1954; 1 Nov 1954; 13 Sept 1955.

67   Ploss, *Conflict and Decision-Making* p. 60, 78, 86. Crankshaw, *Khrushchev* p. 194. Arthur Schlesinger Jr., *Coming of the New Deal,* (Boston; Houghton, 1959) p. 339 (CCC).

68   Ploss, *Conflict and Decision-Making* p. 168. Conquest, *Power and Policy* p. 242.

69   Conquest, *Power and Policy* p. 242. Crankshaw, *Khrushchev* p. 195.

70   Crankshaw, *Khrushchev* p. 196.

71   Conquest, *Power and Policy* p. 256. Crankshaw, *Khrushchev* p. 195f. Brzezinski-Huntington, *Political Power* p. 241f.

72   Brzezinski-Huntington, *Political Power* p. 242, Conquest, *Power and Policy* p. 260.

73   Conquest, *Power and Policy* p. 248. Crankshaw, *Khrushchev* p. 198.

74   Conquest, *Power and Policy* p. 252. Crankshaw, *Khrushchev* p. 199. Boris Nikolaevsky, ed. N.S. Khrushchev, "The Crimes of the Stalin Era," (New York: Columbia Russian Institute/Columbia University Press, 1956), p. 59. Bertram Wolfe, *Khrushchev and Stalin's Ghost,* (New York: Praeger, 1957), p. 60.

75   Conquest, *Power and Policy* p. 252. Brzezinski-Huntington, *Political Power* p. 245. Crankshaw, *Khrushchev* p. 200. Wolfgang Leonard, *The Kremlin since Stalin,* (New York: Praeger, 1962), pp. 120, 167.

76   Conquest, *Power and Policy* p. 255. Crankshaw, *Khrushchev* p. 201. A.J. Horelick and Myron Rush, *Strategic Power and Soviet Foreign Policy,* (Chicago: University of Chicago Press, 1965), p. 26. Thomas W. Wolfe, *Soviet Power and Europe,* (Baltimore: Johns Hopkins, 1970) p. 73.

77   Conquest, *Power and Policy* p. 256.

78   Brzezinski-Huntington, *Political Power* p. 246. Myron Rush, *The Rise of Khrushchev,* (Washington: Public Affairs Press, 1958), p. 2. Lazar Petrak, *The Grand Tactician,* (New York: Praeger, 1961), p. 3. Carl A. Linden, *Khrushchev and the Soviet Leadership,* (Baltimore; Johns Hopkins, 1966), p. 22. Robert C. Tucker, *The Soviet Political Mind,* (New York: Praeger, 1963), p. 91f. LaFeber, *America, Russia and the Cold War* p. 183.

79   *The New York Times,* 27 May 1955. H.W. Barber, *U.S. in World Affairs 1955,* (New York: Harper/Council on Foreign Relations, 1955), p. 53. Brzezinski, *The Soviet Bloc,* (Cambridge; Harvard University Press, 1960), p. 175. Conquest, *Power and Policy* p. 265. Crankshaw, *Khrushchev* p. 209. Hugh Seton Watson, *East European Revolution,* (New York: Praeger, 1956) p. 391. Richard Lowenthal, *World Communism,* (New York: Oxford, 1966), p. 14f.

80   Barber, *U.S. in World Affairs 1955* p. 39. Crankshaw, *Khrushchev* p. 214. Eden, *Full Circle* p. 327. Eisenhower, *Memoirs* II, p. 506. Interview, James A. Hagerty, 27 May 1971 (Khrushchev statement to Eisenhower).

81   *The New York Times,* 18 Sept 1955 (statement by Khrushchev). LaFeber, *America, Russia and the Cold War* p. 187 (statement by Dulles).

82   Conquest, *Power and Policy* p. 260, 280. Brzezinski-Huntington, *Political Power* p. 246.

83   Conquest, *Power and Policy* p. 268. Brzezinski, Huntington, *Political Power* p. 248. H. Rigby, "How Strong is the Leader?" *Problems of Communism,* Jul-Aug, 1959, p. 5. Roger Pethybridge, *A Key to Soviet Politics: the Crisis of the Anti-Party Group,* (New York: Praeger, 1962), p. 83.

84 Nikolevsky, "Crimes of the Stalin Era" p. S7, p. 82 (Kossior). Brzezinsky-Huntington *Political Power* p. 247. Crankshaw, *Khrushchev* p. 124. *Time*, 6 Jan 1958, 16 Sept 1957, p. 33.

85 Nikolaevsky, "Crimes of the Stalin Era," p. S22. Z. Brzezinski, *The Permanent Purge*, (Cambridge; Harvard University Press, 1956), p. 102. (1934 CC members).

86 Brzezinski-Huntington, *Political Power* p. 247. Conquest, *Power and Policy* p. 287. Crankshaw, *Khrushchev* p. 232. Pethybridge, *Key to Soviet Policy* p. 109.

87 Crankshaw, *Khrushchev* p. 235. Brzezinski-Huntington, *Political Power* p. 248. Conquest, *Power and Policy* p. 291. Pethybridge, *Key to Soviet Policy* p. 135.

88 Conquest, *Power and Policy* p. 292. Crankshaw, *Khrushchev* p. 230. Brzezinski, *The Soviet Bloc*, p. 310f. A. Korbinski, *Warsaw in Chains*, (New York; Praeger, 1957), p. 284.

89 *The New York Times*, 22 July 1956 ("separate ways to socialism"). Brzezinski, *Soviet Bloc*, p. 245. LaFeber, *America, Russia and the Cold War* p. 192. Edward Crankshaw, "Polarization of the Communist World," in Evan Luard, ed. *The Cold War, a Re-Appraisal*, p. 249. Louis Halle, *The Cold War as History*, p. 325. John Lukacs, *New History of the Cold War*, (Garden City: Doubleday Anchor paperback, 1966), p. 127, 137.

90 Brzezinski, *Soviet Bloc* p. 253. K. Syrop, *Spring in October*, (New York; Praeger, 1958), p. 132ff. Flora Lewis, *Case History of Hope*, (Garden City; Doubleday, 1958), p. 206, 209–22. *The New York Times*, 20, 21, 22, 24 Oct 1956.

91 Brzezinski, *Soviet Bloc* p. 207f. Lukacs, *New History of the Cold War* p. 140. Leslie B. Bain, *The Reluctant Satellites, Eyewitness Report*, (New York; Macmillan, 1960) p. 70. Raymond Garthoff, *Soviet Strategy in the Missile Age*, (New York; Praeger, 1958) p. 152. M. Lasky, ed. *The Hungarian Revolution*, (New York; Praeger, 1957), p. 177. Paul Kecskemeti, *The Unexpected Revolution*, (Stan-ford; Stanford University Press, 1961), p. 40ff.

92 Tibor Meray, *13 Days that Shook the Kremlin*, (New York; Praeger, 1959), p. 157. Paul Zinner, ed. *National Communism and Popular Revolution in Eastern Europe*, (New York, Columbia University Press, 1956) p. 398, 401–407. George Mikas, *The Hungarian Revolution*, (New York; Horizon, 1957), p. 3. David Pryce-Jones, *The Hungarian Revolution*, (New York; Horizon, 1970) p. 63. LaFeber, *America, Russia and the Cold War* p. 192.

93 Pryce-Jones, p. 66. Brzezinski, *Soviet Bloc* p. 214. Lasky, p. 187.

94 Lukacs, *New History of the Cold War* p. 143. Conquest, *Power and Policy* p. 291. Lasky, p. 209.

95 Brzezinski, *Soviet Bloc* p. 226. Lasky, p. 228. Interview, Dr. Bela Kiraly, 15 Sept 1971.

96 Brzezinski, *Soviet Bloc* p. 228. Halle, *Cold War as History* p. 329. Lasky, p. 249. Lukacs, *New History of the Cold War* p. 144. Pryce-Jones, p. 76.

97 Z. Brzezinski, "U.S. Foreign Policy in East Central Europe: a study in contradictions," *Journal of International Affairs*, Jan 1957, p. 6 ("studying of 'suitable moves' ") also statement by Dulles). Geoffrey Barraclough, *Survey of International Affairs 1956–7*, (London; Oxford/Royal Institute of International Affairs, 1958), p. 114 *(Pravda)*. D.F. Fleming, *Cold War and Its Origins*, p. 806ff. Wilbur Schramm, ed. *One Day in the World's Press*, (Stanford; Stanford University Press, 1959), *(Borba, Pravda, Le Monde, La Prensa, New York Times, Stockholm Dagens Nyheter)*. Janos Radvanyi, *Hungary and the Superpowers*, (Stanford; Hoover Institute Press, 1972) p. 12, 17f.

98 Crankshaw, *Khrushchev* p. 254 (statement by Khrushchev). Conquest, *Power and Policy* p. 293. Brzezinski-Huntington, *Political Power* p. 248. (statement by Khrushchev).

99 Brzezinski-Huntington, *Political Power* p. 205, 249. Crankshaw, *Khrushchev* p. 249f. Conquest, *Power and Policy* p. 292ff.

100 Brzezinski-Huntington, *Political Power* p. 248. Conquest, *Power and Policy* p. 309. Crankshaw, *Khrushchev* p. 250. *Time*, 6 Jan 1958, p. 17.

101 Conquest, *Power and Policy* p. 329ff. Crankshaw, *Khrushchev* p. 246. Brzezinski-Huntington, *Political Power* p. 252.

CHAPTER 9.

1 Louis M. Halle, *The Society of Man*, (New York; Harper, 1964) p. 21f. Patrick Anderson, *The President's Men*, (Garden City; Doubleday, 1968), p. 127. Eric Goldman, *Crucial Decade* p. 82. David A. Baldwin, *Foreign Aid and American Foreign Policy*, (New York; Praeger, 1966) p 60. Herbert Feis, *Foreign Aid and Foreign Policy*, (New York; Delta paperback, 1966) p. 52. Cabell Phillips, *The Truman Presidency*, p 202. David A. Baldwin, *Economic Development and American Foreign Policy*, (Chicago; University of Chicago Press, 1966), p 22. Herbert T. Schiller, "Uses of American Power in the Post-Colonial World," in Leonard Dinerstein and K.T. Jackson, eds. *American Vistas, 1877 to the Present*, (New York; Oxford paperback, 1971), p 215ff. *The New York Times*, Jan 21, 1949 (Point 4 speech).

2 Alfred Sauvy, *General Theory of Population*, (New York; Basic Books, 1964), p 52. Franco Nogueira, *The Third World*, (London; Johnson, 1967), p 30.

3 Frantz Fanon, *The Wretched of the Earth*, (New York; Grove paperback 1966), p. 97. Frank Tanenbaum, *From Slave to Citizen*, (New York; Knopf, 1946) p 127. Jackie Robinson, *I Never Had It Made*, (New York; Putnam, 1972) p. 50ff. Bill Roeder, *The Jackie Robinson Story*, (New York; Barnes, 1958), p 171. Arthur Mann, *The Jackie Robinson Story*, (New York; Grosset, 1949). *Adirondack Enterprise*, (Saranac Lake, N.Y.), June 9, 1969. Branch Rickey to Frank Tanenbaum, May 22, 1956 (File #11, Frank Tanenbaum Papers, Columbia University Library).

4 *To Secure these Rights*, Report of the President's Commission on Civil Rights, (New York; Simon and Schuster, 1947), p 139. Glazer and Moynihan, *Beyond the Melting Pot*, p 3. Michael Harrington, *The Other America*, p 61f. Charles Silberman, *Crisis in Black and White*, (New York; Random, 1964), p 22. Samuel Lubell, *White and Black: Test of a Nation*, (New York; Harper, 1964), p 69.

5 Richard Dalfiume, "Forgotten Years of the Negro Revolution," *Journal of American History*, June 1968, LI, p 90ff. Harvard Sitkoff, "Harry Truman and the Election of 1948: the Coming of Age of Civil Rights in American Politics," *Journal of Southern History*, 37: 597–616 (Nov 1971), W.E.B. Dubois, "Race Relations in the U.S., 1917–47," in Bernard Sternsher, ed. *Negro in Depression and War, Prelude to Revolution*, (Chicago; Quadrangle, 1969), p 31f. *Universal Military Training:* Senate Committee on Armed Forces, 80th Congress, 2nd session (Washington, GPO, 1958), p 995 (statement of Gen. Eisenhower).

6 Benjamin Muse, *Ten Years of Prelude*, (New York; Viking, 1964), p 12 (Acheson statement). Dalfiume, *Desegregation of the Armed Forces*, p 122. Harry S. Truman, "Progress in Civil Rights," *Vital Speeches*, July 15, 1952. William C. Berman, *Politics of Civil Rights in the Truman Administration*, (Columbus, Ohio State University Press, 1970), p 232.

7 *The New York Times*, May 12, 1954. Anthony Lewis, *Portrait of a Decade*, (New York; Random, 1964) p 15.

8 *The New York Times*, May 12, 1954, p 12 (Savannah).

9 Lubell, *White and Black* p 69. "Research Rebuilds the South," *Fortune*, March 1952, p 192. "Great New Fact," *Nation*, Sept 27, 1952, p 252. C.A. Chick, "Which Way?" *Vital Speeches*, Oct 1, 1952, p 764. "Enlightened Revolution," *Time*, Dec 10,

1951. "America's Third Migration," *Nation's Business*, March 1953, p 39.

10 Lorraine Hansberry, *Raisin in the Sun*, (New York; Random House, 1959), p 10.

11 *The New York Times*, May 12, 1954 (statements by Eastland, Byrd). Lewis, *Portrait* p 43 (Stanley). Muse, *Ten Years*, p 21.

12 Pat Watters and Reese Claghorn, *Climbing Jacob's Ladder*, New York, Harcourt, 1967, p 27. Ronald Segal, *The Race War*, (London; Cape, 1966) p 22. Lewis, *Portrait* p 6. Muse, *Ten Years*, p 42.

13 Eisenhower, *Memoirs*, I, p 229.

14 Martin Luther King, *Stride toward Freedom* in *A Martin Luther King Treasury*, (Yonkers; Educational Heritage Inc., 1964), p 32ff. Muse, *Ten Years*, p 52. Lewis, *Portrait* p 71, Segal, *Race War*, p 224. Earl E. Thorp, *Mind of the Negro: an Intellectual History of the Afro-Americans*, (Baton Rouge; Louisiana State University Press, 1961), p 43.

15 David L. Lewis, *King, a Critical Biography*, (New York, Praeger, 1970), p 7. Louis Lomax, *The Negro Revolt*, (New York; Harper, 1962), p 78.

16 August Meier, Elliott Rudwick and Francis Broderick, *Black Protest in the 20th Century*, (New York; Bobbs Merrill, 1971, 2nd ed.), p 300 (statement by King). Harold Isaacs, *New World of the Negro Americans*, (New York; John Day, 1963), p 51 (wider world).

17 Charles A.H. Thomson and Frances H. Shattuck, *The 1956 Presidential Campaign*, (Washington; Brookings, 1960) p 352. Rowland Evans and Robert Novak, *Lyndon B. Johnson*, p 160, 242. Adams, *First Hand Report*, p 338.

18 Evans and Novak, *Lyndon B. Johnson* p 124ff. Langston Hughes, *Fight for Freedom*, (New York; Norton, 1962), p 107. *Civil Rights in the U.S.* (Washington; Congressional Quarterly Service, 1963), p 7.

19 *The New York Times*, Sept 4, 1957. Lomax, *Negro Revolt*, p 113. Muse, *Ten Years* p 122. Lewis, *Portrait*, p 47f. Segal, *Race War*, p 226. Evans and Novak, *Lyndon B. Johnson*, p 122. Adams, *Firsthand Report*, p 335 (Eisenhower to King).

20 *The New York Times*, Sept 4, 6, 11, 12, 15, 20, 22, 23, 24, 25, 1957 (Little Rock), H. Frederick Morrow, *Black Man in the White House*. (New York; Coward-McCann, 1966) p 170. August Meier and Elliott Rudwick, *From Plantation to Ghetto*, (New York; Hill and Wang, 1966) p 228. Muse, *Ten Years* p 122f. Lewis, *Portrait*, p 47ff. Adams, *Firsthand Report* p 395f. Eisenhower, *Memoirs*, II, p 162ff.

21 Howard Zinn, *SNCC: the New Abolitionists*, (Boston; Beacon, 1964), p 21 (Candie Anderson), p 23 (Orangeburg). Lerone Bennett, *Confrontation Black and White*, (Chicago; Johnson, 1965) p 257. William L. O'Neill, *Coming Apart*, (Chicago; Quadrangle, 1971), p 159 (70,000 who sat in). James M. Lawson, Jr. "We are Trying to Raise the Moral Issue," Raleigh address in Memier, Rudwick, and Broderick, *Black Protest Thought*, p 334. Lomax, *Negro Revolt*, p 230. Congressional Quarterly Service, *Civil Rights in the U.S.*, p 10.

22 Lewis, *King*, p 126ff. Lewis, *Portrait of a Decade*, p 115f. Theodore H. White, *The Making of a President 1960*, New York, Pocket paperback, 1961, p 385. Morrow, *Black Man*, p 180.

23 Paul Good, "Odyssey of a Man and a Movement," *The New York Times Magazine*, Jun 21, 1967, p 252f. U.S. Commission of Human Rights, "The Struggle for Equal Service at Public Facilities," in Alan F. Westin ed. *Freedom Now!* (New York; Basic Books, 1964), p 155. Anthony Lewis, *Portrait* p 87ff. Zinn, *SNCC*, p 40ff. Watters and Claghorn, *Climbing Jacob's Ladder*, p 56f. Meier and Rudwick, *From Plantation to Ghetto*, p 229. Muse, *Ten Years*, p 206. James Farmer, *Freedom—When?* (New York; Random, 1965), p 11. Lomax, *Negro Revolt*, p 234. Meier and Rudwick, *Black Protest in the Sixties*, (Chicago; Quadrangle, 1970), p 4. Segal, *Race War*, p 234f. Victor S. Na-

vasky, *Kennedy Justice*, (New York; Atheneum, 1971) p 20f.

24 Muse, *Ten Years* p 240f. Lewis, *Portrait*, p 126ff.

25 *The New York Times*, May 1 through 12, 1963 (Birmingham). David Lewis, *King*, p 170ff. Anthony Lewis, *Portrait*, p 175ff. Muse, *Ten Years*, p 259. Meier and Rudwick, *From Plantation to Ghetto*, p 236f. Paul Good, "Birmingham Two Years Later," *The Reporter*, Dec 2, 1965. Arthur Waskow, *From Race Riot to Sit-In*, (Garden City; Doubleday, 1966) p 207. Navasky, *Kennedy Justice*, p 218f.

26 Navasky, *Kennedy Justice* p 241. Anthony Lewis, *Portrait* p 190ff. Muse, *Ten Years* p 267. *The New York Times*, June 12, 1963 p 20 (Kennedy).

27 Lester A. Sobel, ed. *Civil Rights 1960–66*, (New York; Facts on File, 1967), p 16, 18, 169, 244, 292. C. Vann Woodward, t al, *Civil Rights Movement Revisited*, (New York; A.P. Randolph Fund, 1968), p 12–14.

28 Watters and Claghorn, p 247. *Climbing Jacob's Ladder*, Alan F. Westin, "The Crawling Revolution," in Westin, ed. *Freedom Now!*, p 131 cites figures from *Southern School News*, spring 1963.

29 *The New York Times*, Nov 28, 1971.

30 H.G. Nicholas, *Britain and the U.S.*, (Baltimore; Johns Hopkins Press, 1963) p 41. Walter Z. Laqueur, *Soviet Union and the Middle East*, New York; Praeger, 1959), p 189. Paul Seabury, *Power, Freedom and Diplomacy*, (New York; Random, 1963), p 124. Chester Bowles, *Ambassador's Report*, (New York; Harper, 1954), p 22, 69. Ulam, *Expansion and Coexistence*, New York, Praeger, 1969, p 410. Richard Goold-Adams, *John Foster Dulles, a re-appraisal*, (New York, Appleton Century-Crofts, 1962) p 192. Eden, *Full Circle*, p 246. Herman Finer, *Dulles Over Suez*, (Chicago; Quadrangle, 1964) p 11. Elizabeth Monroe, "The Middle East," in Evan Luard, ed. *The Cold War Reappraised*, (New York; Praeger, 1964), p 147. Hugh Thomas, *Suez*, (New York; Harper, 1966), p 10. W.W. Rostow,

The United States in the World Arena, (New York; Harper, 1960) p 363.

31 Goold-Adams, *Dulles, a Re-Appraisal* p 196. Richard Neustadt, *Alliance Politics*, (New York; Columbia University Press, 1970) p 8.

32 *Time*, Aug 27, 1956, p 19. *Time*, July 28, 1958. p 19.

33 *Time*, Aug 27, 1956, p 19 (Nasser book)

34 At the time Kermit Roosevelt, the CIA operative who engineered the overthrow of Mossadegh in Iran in 1953, urged Nasser to soften the impact of his announcement by attributing the deal to one of the satellites rather than to Russia. The matter was decided when the British Ambassador Sir Humphrey Trevelyan telephoned Nasser to verify the deal. "Shall I say it's Czechoslovakia, Kim?" asked Nasser. That, according to Roosevelt's friend Miles Copeland, who says he was present, is when and how it was decided. Miles Copeland III, *The Game of Nations*, (London, Weidenfeld and Nicolson, 1969) p 135f. Kennett Love, *Suez, the Twice-Fought War*, (New York, McGraw, 1969), p 283.

35 Neustadt, *Alliance Politics*, p 12. Thomas, *Suez*, p 15.

36 *The New York Times*, Nov 20, 22, 25, 26, 27, Dec 3, 7, 14, 22, 1955. Louis Halle, *Cold War as History* p 337 (statements by Khrushchev).

37 Thomas, *Suez* p 17. Goold Adams, *Dulles, a Re-Appraisal*, p 195. LaFeber, *America, Russia and the Cold War*, p 199.

38 Finer, *Dulles over Suez* p 51. Thomas, *Suez* p 24.

39 *Time*, July 30, 1956. Love, *Suez, the Twice-Fought War*, p 220. Finer, *Dulles over Suez* p 45.

40 *The New York Times*, July 27, 1956. *Time*, Aug 6, 1956. Finer, *Dulles over Suez* p 56. Love, *Suez, the Twice-Fought War* p 347.

41 J.R. Beal, *John Foster Dulles*, p 258. Eden, *Full Circle* p 472. Finer, *Dulles over Suez* p 45. Anthony Nutting, *No End of a Lesson*, (New York; Clarkson Potter, 1967), p 22.

42 Beal, *J.F. Dulles* p 141.

43 Eisenhower, *Memoirs*, II, p 35. Eden,

44 *Full Circle*, p 470. Finer, *Dulles over Suez*, p 61. Thomas, *Suez*, p 33.

44 Eden, *Full Circle*, p 470. Nutting *No End of a Lesson* p 34 ("I want him destroyed").

45 Eden, *Full Circle*, p 470f. Finer, *Dulles over Suez*, p 66. Thomas, *Suez*, p 66. Andre Beaufre, *The Suez Expedition*, (New York; Praeger, 1959), p 37.

46 Eden, *Full Circle*, p 477.

47 Neustadt, *Alliance Politics*, p 33.

48 Eisenhower, *Memoirs* II, p 42f. Thomas, *Suez*, p 71.

49 *Time*, Sept 3, 1956. Finer, *Dulles over Suez*, p 142, 324. Love, *Suez the Twice Fought War* p 418. Thomas, *Suez*, p 106. Neustadt, *Alliance Politics*, p 14.

50 Eden, *Full Circle*, p 545. Neustadt, *Alliance Politics* p 19. Finer, *Dulles over Suez*, p 296.

51 *Time*, Oct 1, 1956. Eden, *Full Circle*, p 546, 556. Finer, *Dulles over Suez*, p 202. Neustadt, *Alliance Politics*, p 17.

52 Eden, *Full Circle*, p 345. Neustadt, *Alliance Politics*, p 18. Finer, *Dulles over Suez*, pp. 271, 296.

53 Eisenhower, *Memoirs* II, p 66. Neustadt, *Alliance Politics*, p 20.

54 Thomas, *Suez* p 121. Love, *Suez the Twice Fought War*, p 481.

55 Finer, *Dulles over Suez*, p 384. Thomas, *Suez*, pp 11, 121. Love, *Suez, the Twice-Fought War* p 440ff. Neustadt, *Alliance Politics* p 21ff.

56 Thomas, *Suez*, p 134. Finer, *Dulles over Suez*, p 388.

57 Finer, *Dulles over Suez* p 390. Thomas, *Suez* p 135.

58 LaFeber, *America, Russia and the Cold War*, p 193. Love *Suez, the Twice-Fought War*, p 225. Thomas, *Suez*, p 130.

59 Lafeber, *America, Russia and the Cold War* p 193. Love, *Suez, the Twice-Fought War*, p 625. Neustadt, *Alliance Politics*, p 26. Thomas, *Suez*, pp 134, 145.

60 Eisenhower, *Memoirs*, II, p 98. Eden, *Full Circle*, p 650.

61 Neustadt, *Alliance Politics*, p 28. Coral Bell, "The Diplomacy of Mr. Dulles," Canadian Institute of International Affairs *International Journal*, xx (winter 1964–5), p. 92.

62 *Time*, July 28, 1959. Eisenhower, *Memoirs*, II, p 77 (anti-colonial rectitude). Ulam, *The Rivals*, (New York; Viking, 1971), p 278f. Ulam, *Expansion and Coexistence*, p 618. LaFeber, *America, Russia and the Cold War*, p 198.

63 *Time*, July 28, 1959. Ulam, *The Rivals*, p 281. Leo Tansky, *U.S. and U.S.S.R. Aid to Developing Countries*, (New York; Praeger, 1965), p 18 (comparative figures).

64 DeTocqueville, (*Democracy in America* (1845), New York, Knopf, 1945), I, p 378.

65 C. Eric Lincoln, "The Race Problem and International Relations," in George W. Shepherd, Jr., *Racial Influence on American Foreign Policy*, (New York; Basic Books, 1970), p 39ff. Arthur M. Ross, "Negro in the American Economy," in Ross and Herbert Hill, eds. *Employment, Race and Poverty*, (New York; Harcourt, 1967), p 3. Herbert Hill, "Racial Discrimination in Nation's Apprenticeship Training," *Phylon*, fall 1962, p 217. Karl E. Taeuber and Alma Taeuber, *Negroes in Cities*, (Chicago; Aldine, 1965), p 59. *Economic and Social Status of the Negro in the U.S.*, (New York; Urban League, 1961), p 16–17. Andrew W. Lind, ed. *Race Relations in World Perspective*, (Honolulu; University of Hawaii Press, 1955), p 3. Arna Bontemps and Jack Conroy, *Any Place but Here*, (New York; Hill and Wang, 1966), p 227. Meier and Rudwick, *From Plantation to Ghetto*, p 234. Silberman, *Crisis in Black and White*, p 39. C.Eric Lincoln, interview, Apr 19 1972. Joseph D. Bibb: "It was a great day when the Anglo-Saxons lost their monopoly over instruments of war and terrorism . . . and of white imperialism . . ." (Oct 8, 1949 in Pittsburgh *Courier*, cited by Mark Solomon "Black Critics of Colonialism and the Cold War," in T.G. Patterson, ed. *Cold War Critics*, (Chicago; Quadrangle, 1971), p 227.)

66 Wallace Mendelson, *Discrimination*, (Englewood Cliffs; Prentice-Hall,

1962), p 143ff. p 116, p 136–7. Peter M. Bergman, *Chronological History of the Negro in America*, (New York; Harper, 1969); passim. John Griffin, *Black Like Me*, (Boston; Houghton, 1961), p. 54. Harry M and David H. Rosen, *But Not Next Door*, (New York; Obolensky, 1962), p 7. *To Secure these Rights*, p 70, 73. New York State Commission against Discrimination, *Discrimination and Low Incomes*, (New York; New School, 1959), (bowling).

67 Meier and Rudwick, *From Plantation to Ghetto*, p 234. Silberman, *Crisis in Black and White*, p 39. M.H. Scagliola, "Mental Health in the American Inner City," *The Lancet*, Dec 25, 1971, p 1415f.

68 C. Eric Lincoln, *Black Muslims in America*, (Boston; Beacon, 1961), p 68. Meier and Rudwick, *From Plantation to Ghetto* p 234. Rupert Emerson, "Race in Africa, U.S. Foreign Policy," in Shepherd, ed. *Racial Influence*, p 169f. *U.S. Commission on Civil Rights Report No. 3 Employment*. (Washington; Government Printing Office, 1961), p 1, 165 (Detroit jobless blacks).

69 Louis Lomax, *When the Word is Given*, (Cleveland; World, 1963), p 111 (statement by Elijah Muhammad, in Atlanta). Bontemps and Conroy, *Any Place but Here*, p 216. Lincoln, *Black Muslims* p 68f. O'Neill, *Coming Apart*, p 159 (TV program).

70 Lincoln, *Black Muslims* p 110. John Henrik Clark, *Malcolm X, the Man and his Times*, (New York; Macmillan, 1965), p xxii–xxiii, 210, 285. *Autobiography of Malcolm X*, (New York; Grove paperback, 1966, orig. 1964), pp 72, 152, 268, 300. Lomax, *When the Word Is Given*, p 130. Malcolm X, "Segregation v. Integration" and "Malcolm X Founds Organization of Afro-American Unity," in Meier, Rudwick and Broderick, *op cit.*, p 387ff. Nathan Wright, Jr. "The Crisis which Black Power Bred," in Peter I. Rose, ed., *Old Memories, New Moods, Americans from Africa*, (New York; Atherton, 1970), p 185.

71 Harold Isaacs, "American Negro and

Africa," *Phylon*, fall 1959, p 219 (statement by J.C. Smyth, former minister to Liberia), p 230 (geography lesson). Marguerite Cartwright, "Teaching the African Unit," *Phylon*, winter 1952, p 310. See also Isaacs, *New World of American Negroes*, p 135ff.

72 James Baldwin, *The New York Times Magazine*, Mar 12, 1961.

73 *Ibid.*

74 Isaacs "American Negro in Africa," p 231, Isaacs, *New World of American Negroes*, pp 142, 172, 288ff. Lewis, *Portrait*, p 239. Lincoln in Shepherd, *Racial Influence*, p 53. ["Most Embarrassing," *Time*, Apr 21, 1961, p 17. *U.S. News*, July 1, 1963. Rayford Logan in *Current History*, Jan 1962, p 28.

75 Isaacs, *New World*, p 51 (King's speeches). King, *Stride toward Freedom*, p 33, 51, 60. Lewis, *King*, p 71. John Lewis in *Dialog*, spring 1964, cited in Meier, Rudwick and Broderick, *Black Protest Thought* p 357.

76 *Amsterdam News*, May 5, 1962, cited by Isaacs, *New World*, p 96.

77 Malcolm X in *Dialog*, May 1962, cited in Meier, Rudwick and Broderick, *Black Protest Thought*, p 386. Lincoln in *Christian Century*, Apr 7, 1965. Bontemps and Conroy, *Any Place but Here*, p 244. M.A. Polsky and Ernest Kaiser, eds. *AFRO-USA*, (New York; Bellwether, 1971), p 39,-236.

78 Isaacs, *New World*, pp 54, 239 (King in Cleveland). Nathan Wright, "The Crisis which Bred Black Power," in Floyd Barbour, ed. *Black Power Revolt*, (Boston; Porter Sargent, 1969), p 103. Lerone Bennett, "What's in a Name?" *Ebony*, Nov 1967, quoted in Rose, ed., *Old Memories, New Moods*, p 383. John Lewis in *Dialog*, spring 1964, quoted in Meier, Rudwick and Broderick, p 357. Stokeley Carmichael, "What We Want," in *New York Review of Books*, Sept 22, 1965, p 5, quoted in Franklin Mitchel and Richard Davies, eds. *America's Recent Past*, (New York; Wiley, 1969), p 419.

79 Harold Cruse, *Crisis of the Negro In-*

tellectual, (New York; Morrow, 1967), p 3–10. Harold Cruse, *Rebellion or Revolution?* (New York; Morrow, 1968), p 74. Robert L. Allen, *Black Awakening in Capitalist America,* (Garden City; Doubleday, 1969), p 95, 132, 156. J.O. Killens, *Black Man's Burden,* (New York Trident, 1965), p 11ff. J. Saunders Redding, *On Being a Negro in America,* (New York; Charter paperback, 1951), p 1.. Ralph Ellison, *Invisible Man,* (New York; Random 1947), p 1. C. Vann Woodward, in *Civil Rights Movement Revisited,* p 17. *Urban America,*

Goals and Problems, Subcommittee on Urban Affairs of Joint Economic Committee 90th Congress, 1st session, (Washington; Government Printing Office, 1967), p 1. Kenneth Clark, "Present Dilemma of the Negro," *Journal of Black History,* Jan 1968, p 4. O'Neill, *Coming Apart,* p 193 (black 1964–68 income 52–63% of white average income). Kenneth Stampp, *The Peculiar Institution,* (New York; Knopf, 1956), p vii, 429. Lippmann, "The Presidents," interview in New York *Post,* Oct 23, 1971, p 24f.

CHAPTER 10.

1 Herbert Butterfield, *Origins of Modern Science,* (New York; Macmillan, 1952), p xiii.

2 Davis, *Lawrence and Oppenheimer,* New York, Simon and Schuster, 1968, p 240 (Oppenheimer statement).

3 Garrett Hardin, "The Tragedy of the Commons," *Science,* Dec 13, 1965, p 1243ff. *The New York Times,* Sept 2, 1945, p 4 (statement by Truman). Allan Nevins, "Assay of an Epochal Quarter-Century," *The New York Times Magazine,* Mar 30, 1958, p 14f.

4 Interview, Henry Graff, Sept 4, 1970 (statement by Roberts).

5 *Newsweek,* Jan 13, 1958 (Kissinger).

6 Henry Kissinger, *Nuclear Weapons and Foreign Policy,* (New York; Harper, 1957). Arthur Hertzog, *The War-Peace Establishment,* p 36.

7 Rockefeller Brothers Fund, *International Security, the Military Aspect, Report of Panel II of Social Studies Project,* (Garden City; Doubleday, 1958), p 6. *The Reporter,* Dec 26, 1957. *New York Herald Tribune,* Nov 23, 1957. Marton H. Halperin, "The Gaither Committee and the Policy Process," *World Politics,* April 1961, p 360. *Survey of International Affairs 1957–8,* (London; Oxford/Royal Institute of International Affairs, 1961), p 347f. Rostow, *The United States in the World Arena,* p. 368, 403. Childs, *Eisenhower the Captive Hero,* p 257.

Hertzog, *The War-Peace Establishment,* p 36. Paul Berman et al. "How to rule the empire without almost ever firing a shot," (New York; Nguyen Van Troi College, 1971), mimeo., p 8.

8 *The New York Times,* Oct 6, 7, 1957 (Sputnik). *Survey 1957–8,* p 347. Council on Foreign Relations, *United States in World Affairs 1957,* (New York; Harper, 1958), p 298. Goldman, *Crucial Decade,* p 307.

9 *The New York Times,* Oct 6 and 17, 1957 (reactions). *Time,* Jan 6, 1958, p 16 (Randall statement). *Survey 1957–8,* p 347 (Dulles, Eisenhower statements). *The New York Times,* Oct 9, 1957 (Bennett, Wilson statements). *The New York Times,* Nov 10, 1957 (Adams statement on Oct 15). *U.S. in World Affairs 1957,* p 300. "Sputnik," *New Republic,* Oct 14, 1957, Edward L. Katzenbach, "Sputnik," *The Reporter,* Oct 3, 1957. *Time,* Oct 18, 1957. Samuel Lubell, "Sputnik and American Public Opinion," *Columbia Forum,* winter 1957, p 18–19. Childs, *Eisenhower, Captive Hero* p 257. Goldman, *Crucial Decade* p 308.

10 *The New York Times,* Dec 4, 1957, p 4, and Dec 28, 1957, p 9 (sightings). "Grey Mood," *Time,* Dec 2, 1957. *New Republic,* Oct 14, 1957. *The Reporter,* Oct 3, 1957. *Survey 1957–8,* p 348. Goldman, *Crucial Decade* p 308.

11 *Survey, 1957–8,* p 349. *U.S. in World*

Affairs 1957, p 300. Childs, *Eisenhower, Captive Hero* p 260.

12 *New York Herald Tribune*, Oct 28, 1957 (McElroy). Eisenhower, *Memoirs*, II, p 224. Sherman Adams, *Inside Report*, p 415.

13 *The New York Times*, Dec 7 and 8, 1957 (U.S. launch). *Time*, Jan 6, 1958, p 16. New York *Herald Tribune*, Dec 7, 1957. Goldman, *Crucial Decade*, p 310.

14 Alain Bosquet, ed. *Les Americains*, (Paris; Robert Delpire, 1958), p 152 (American reactions, including Prof. Lindegren).

15 *The New York Times*, Nov 7, 1957 (statement by Khrushchev). Goldman, *Crucial Decade*, p 310 (second statement by Khruschchev). Eisenhower, *Memoirs*, II, p 258 (Canaveral log).

16 Kermit Lansner, ed. *Second-rate Brains*, (Garden City; Doubleday, 1958), p 8 *(Oregon Journal)*.

17 *The New York Times*, Oct 9, 1957 (cites Vannevar Bush *Modern Arms and Free Men*).

18 *The New York Times*, Dec 7, 1957 (statement by Lyndon Johnson), and Dec 8, 1957 (statements by Fulbright, Dulles).

19 New York *Herald Tribune*, Nov 8, 1957. *Life*, Mar 24, 1958, p 24. John R. Dunning, "If We Are to Catch Up in Science," *The New York Times Magazine*, Nov 10, 1957.

20 H.L. Nieburg, *In the Name of Science*, (Chicago; Quadrangle paperback, 1970), p 166. Daniel Greenberg, *Politics of Pure Science*, (New York; New American Library, 1967) p 139. Roger Hilsman, *To Move a Nation*, (Garden City; Doubleday, 1967), p 10. *The New York Times*, Oct 6, 1957 (statements by Symington, Jackson). New York *Herald Tribune*, Nov 8, 1957 (calls for a "czar").

21 Ralph Lapp, *The New Priesthood*, (New York; Harper, 1965), p 194. Nieburg, *In the Name of Science* p 159. Lansner, *Second-rate Brains* p 6.

22 Emmet Hughes, *Ordeal of Power*, p 250. *Survey 1957–8*, p 347

23 Congressional Quarterly Service, *Federal Role in Education*, (Washington; Congressional Quarterly Service, 1965), p 19 (statement by Eisenhower).

24 *Ibid*, p 19–20.

25 *Ibid*, p 8, 19. *The New York Times*, Dec 31, 1957.

26 *The New York Times*, Nov 18, 1957. New York *Herald Tribune*, Nov 8, 1957. Christopher Rand, *Cambridge USA*, (New York, Oxford, 1964) p 50.

27 Nieburg, *In the Name of Science*, p. 158f. Lloyd Berkner, "Earth Satellites and Foreign Policy," *Foreign Affairs*, Jan, 1958. Eugene Skolnikoff, *Science, Technology and American Foreign Policy*, (Cambridge, MIT Press, 1967), p 227. Jerome Wiesner, *Where Science and Politics Meet*, (New York; McGraw, 1965), p 45f. Harold K. Jacobs and Eric Stein, *Diplomats, Scientists and Politicians: the U.S. and the Nuclear Test Ban*, (Ann Arbor; University of Michigan Press, 1966), p 10.

28 Chauncey D. Leake, "We Don't Know What Hurts Us," *Saturday Review*, Jan 4, 1958. Dunning, "If We Are to Catch Up in Science." Lansner, *Second-rate Brains*, p 30 (statement by DeWitt). *The New York Times*, Nov 10, 1957 (survey by Remmann). *Life*, Mar 24, 1958.

29 *The New York Times*, Nov 14, 1957. New York *Herald Tribune*, Nov 8, 1957.

30 Rudolph Flesch, *Why Johnny Can't Read*, (New York; Harper, 1955), p 4, 25. *Elementary School Journal*, Oct 1955, p 56. *Time*, Jan 9, 1956. *Life*, April 21, 1958. "How the U.S. Wastes its Gifted Children," *Life*, Apr 7, 1958. Sloan Wilson, "It's Time to Close Our Carnival," *Life*, Mar 24, 1958. D.W. Brogan, "Unnoticed Changes in America," *Harper's*, Feb 1957, p 27. Franklin Folsom, "Why Russia's Scientists are so Good," *U.S. News*, Nov 15, 1957.

31 John W. Gardner, *Excellence*, (New York; Harper, 1961), p 26f.

32 *Rockefeller Brothers Fund Report, Panel V*, (Garden City; Doubleday, 1958), p 18, 25.

33 *The New York Times,* Sept 26, 1951,
    p 33. "New Elite," *Time,* Oct 15,
    1956. "Grades, Excellent," *News-
    week,* Oct 21, 1957. H.G. Spaulding,
    "Harnessing Our Brainpower," *Senior
    Scholastic,* Jan 24, 1958. Dwight
    Macdonald, *The Ford Foundation,*
    (New York; Reynal, 1956), p 9. Chris-
    topher Jencks and David Riesman,
    Academic Revolution, (Garden City;
    Doubleday, 1968), p 164 (National
    Merit). Daniel Bell, *The Reforming of
    General Education,* (New York; Co-
    lumbia University Press, 1966) p 125ff
    (advanced placement).

34 *The New York Times,* Dec 31, 1957
    (NDEA). Congressional Quarterly
    Service, *Federal Role in Education,* p
    8,19.

35 Howard Mumford Jones, *Our Great
    Society,* (New York; Harcourt, 1958),
    p 21. See also Charles G.Dobbins, ed.
    *Expanding Resources of College
    Teaching,* (Washington; American
    Council on Education, ser. I, No 60,
    Oct 1956), p 21.

36 Hyman Rickover, *Education and
    Freedom,* (Garden City; Doubleday
    paperback, 1960) p 109 (on ambassa-
    dors). New York *Herald Tribune,* Nov
    8, 1957 (Sevareid). *Thirteenth Annual
    Report,* National Science Foundation,
    (Washington, Government Printing
    Office, 1964), (language translation
    data).

37 Thomas J. Naughton, "Foreign Lan-
    guages the Easy Way," *Saturday Eve-
    ning Post,* Jan 24, 1959. Martin
    Mayer, *The Schools,* (New York;
    Harper, 1961), p 306. Francis Keppel,
    *The Necessary Revolution in Ameri-
    can Education,* (New York; Harper,
    1966), p 128. John L. Goodlad,
    Changing School Curriculum, (New
    York; Fund for Advancement of Edu-
    cation, 1966), p 81. J.B. Conant, *The
    American High School Today,* (New
    York; McGraw, 1959), p 22.

38 Lawrence Cremin, *Transformation of
    the School,* (New York; Knopf, 1961),
    p 325. Arthur Bestor, *Restoration of
    Learning,* (New York; Knopf, 1955), p
    22f. Arthur Bestor, "What Went
    Wrong with our Schools," *U.S. News,*

    Jan 24, 1958. Frank Jennings, "It
    Didn't Start with Sputnik," *The
    Saturday Review,* Sept 16, 1967, p 77.

39 *U.S. News,* Jan 24, 1958. Lansner,
    Second-rate Brains p 62. Cremin,
    Transformation of the School, p 344.
    S.Willis Rudy, *Schools in an Age of
    Mass Culture,* (Englewood Cliffs;
    Prentice Hall, 1965), p 325.

40 Margaret Mead, "Education is Ob-
    solete," *Harvard Business Review,*
    Nov-Dec 1958, p 24. Hyman Rick-
    over, *Education and Freedom,* p 109,
    154. Lansner, *Second-rate Brains,* p 43
    (Rickover). Cremin, *Transformation
    of the School,* p 348.

41 Cremin, *Transformation of the
    School,* p 325. Jennings, "It Didn't
    Start with Sputnik" p 96.

42 Evans Clinchy, "The New Cur-
    ricula," in Ronald Gross and Judith
    Murphy, eds. *The Revolution in the
    Schools,* (New York; Harcourt, 1964),
    p 220. Goodlad, *Changing School
    Curriculum,* p 11f. Robert W. Heath,
    ed. *New Curricula,* (New York;
    Harper paperback, 1964), p 9, 68, 82,
    94. *Innovation and Experiment in
    Education,* report of the Panel on Edu-
    cational Research and Development,
    n.d. p 3. Mayer, *The Schools,* pp 242,
    253, 263. Keppel, *Necessary Revolu-
    tion* p 114.

43 Rand, *Cambridge USA,* p 163f.
    Clinchy, "The New Curricula," p
    220.

44 Jerome S. Bruner, *Process of Educa-
    tion,* (New York; Vintage paperback,
    1960) p 33. Rickover, *Education and
    Freedom,* p 191 (dissertation topics).
    Innovation and Experiment, p 3ff Jen-
    nings, "It Didn't Start with Sputnik,"
    p 96.

45 Rand, *Cambridge USA,* p 163f.
    Goodlad, *Changing School Cur-
    riculum,* p 11f. *Annual Report 1968,*
    (Newton Mass.; Educational Develop-
    ment Center, 1968) p 67ff. Lawrence
    A. Cremin, "Curriculum-Making in
    the U.S.," *Teachers College Record,*
    Dec 1971, p 207ff.

46 Goodlad, *Changing School Cur-
    riculum,* p 41f.

47 James Coleman, *Equality of Educa-*

tional Opportunity, (Washington, Government Printing Office, 1965), p 4f. Goodlad, *Changing School Curriculum*, p 105. Jennings, "It Didn't Start with Sputnik" p 77. Heath, *New Curricula*, p 231.

48 Arthur M. Ross in F.H. Harbison and Charles A. Myers, *Education, Manpower and Economic Growth*, (New York; McGraw, 1964), p 87f.

49 Frederick E. Terman, "Supply of Scientific and Engineering Manpower: surplus or shortage?" *Science*, July 30, 1971, p 401. Also D.J. Watley and R.C. Nichols, "Career Choices of Talented Youth, Trends 1957–67," *Engineering Education*, April 1969, p 975ff.

50 Allen Cartter, "Future Faculty Needs and Resources," in C.B.T. Lee, ed. *Improving College Teaching*, (Washington; American Council on Education, 1967), p 111. R.J. Burke, *Politics of Research*, (Washington; Public Affairs Press, 1966), pp 146, 176. "Toward a Better Utilization of Science and Engineering Talents," (Washington; National Academy of Science, 1964), p. 33. F.H. Harbison and C.A. Myers, *Education, Manpower and Economic Growth*, p 66 (Harbison), p 93 (Ross). David G. Brown, *The Mobile Professors*, (Washington; American Council on Education, 1967), p 7. Gunnar Boalt and Herman Lantz, *Universities and Research*, (New York; Wiley, 1968), p 10. Frank J. Munger and Richard F. Fenno Jr. *National Politics and Federal Aid to Education*, (Syracuse; Syracuse University Press, 1962), p 15. *Science and Technical Manpower Supply, Demand and Utilization*, House Committee on Science and Astronautics staff study, 87th Congress, 2nd session, (Washington, Government Printing Office, 1963). *Basic Research and National Goals*, (Washington; National Academy of Science, no date). Burton R. Clark, *Educating the Expert Society*, (San Francisco; Chandler, 1962) p 28. *Federal Support of R & D at Universities and Colleges and Selected Nonprofit Institutions 1968*, National Science Foundation 69–33, (Wash-

ington; Government Printing Office, 1969). *Federal Funds for R & D and other Scientific Activities fiscal years 1969–71*, NSF 79–38, Vol XIX, (Washington; Government Printing Office, 1970). *Federal Funds for R & D and Other Activities 1965–67*, Vol XV, NSF 66–25, (Washington; Government Printing Office, 1966). Edward Alvey in *Americana Annual 1971*, (Chicago; Encyclopedia Americana, 1972), p 328. Dael Wolfle, ed. *America's Resources of Specialized Talent*, p 300.

51 Charles Silberman, *Crisis in the Classroom*, (New York; Atheneum, 1970), p 10.

52 Dwight E. Robinson, "Fashion Theory and Product Design," *Harvard Business Review*, Nov–Dec 1958, p 126 (statement by Poiret).

53 Bernard I. Bell, *Crisis in Education*, (New York; Whittlesey House, 1942) p 174. (comparison with Italy in 1900). Dept. of Health Education and Welfare, *Digest of Educational Statistics*, (Washington; Government Printing Office, 1969), (proportion of age-group now in school). Clarence D. Long, *Labor Force Under Changing Income and Employment*, (Princeton; Princeton University Press, 1958), Table A–2.

54 President's Commission on Higher Education, *Higher Education for American Democracy*, (Washington; Government Printing Office, 1947), passim. Fritz Machlup, *Production and Distribution of Knowledge in the U.S.*, (Princeton; Princeton University Press, 1962), p 78. Nevitt Sanford "Research and Policy in Higher Education," in Sanford, ed., *The American College*, (New York; Wiley, 1962), p 1014. David Riesman and Christopher Jencks, "The Viability of the American College," in Sanford, ed *The American College*, p 74. Theodore Schultz, "Capital Formation by Education," *Journal of Political Economy*, Dec 1960, p 571. Allan Cartter, "After Effects of Blind Eye to Telescope," *Educational Record*, 51, No 4, fall 1970, p 334f. Richard Hofstadter and C. DeWitt Hardy, *Devel-*

opment and Scope of American Higher Education, New York, Columbia University Press, 1952, p 107. Oscar and Mary Handlin, *American College and American Culture*, (New York; McGraw, 1970), p 73. Irving L. Horowitz and William M. Friedland, *The Knowledge Factory*, (Chicago; Aldine, 1970), p 42. Robert Nisbet, *The Degradation of the Academic Dogma*, (New York; Basic Books, 1971), p 72. G.Kerry Smith, ed. *Stress and Campus Response*, (San Francisco; Jossen-Bass, 1968) passim. S.L. Halleck, "Twelve Hypotheses of Student Unrest," in G.K. Smith, ed. *Twenty-five Years, 1945–70*, (San Francisco; Jossen-Bass, 1970), p 287ff. Boalt and Lantz, *Universities and Research*, p 4.

55 Seymour Harris, *How Shall We Pay for Education?"* (New York; Harper, 1947), p 44f. *Digest of Educational Statistics 1970*, p 64. *Unesco Statistical Yearbook 1970*, (New York; United Nations, 1971), p 304, 306. *Demographic Yearbook 1970*, (New York; United Nations, 1971), p 220, 250.

56 *Digest of Educational Statistics 1970*, p 61, 64. *New York Red Book 1970–1*, (Albany, 1971), p 683 (SUNY data). *The New York Times*, Jan 17, 1972 (SUNY data). Earl Cheit, *The New Depression in Higher Education*, (New York; McGraw, 1971), p. xi, 4. National Science Foundation, *Science Education Study Group*, Oct 1971, (Washington; Government Printing Office, 1971) (proportion of U.S. youth in college). Allan M. Cartter, ed. *American Universities and Colleges*, (Washington; American Council on Education, 1964, 9th ed.), p 242. S.K. Bailey, "Public Money and the Integrity of the Higher Academy," *Educational Record*, 50, No 2, spring 1969, p 149 (SUNY).

57 *Higher Education for American Democracy*, p 22. Handlin, *American College and American Culture* p 73.

58 Jack Kerouac, *On the Road*, (New York; Viking, 1957). Allen Ginsberg, *Howl and Other Poems*, (San Francisco; City Lights, 1956).

59 *Higher Education for American Democracy* p 23. Handlin, *American College and American Culture* p 73. R.M. Hutchins, "The Learning Society," in *Britannica Perspectives*, II, (Chicago; Encyclopedia Britannica, 1968), p 674 (survey of anti-teaching bias among professors). Allan Cartter "After Effects of Blind Eye," p 337.

60 J.K. Galbraith, "Case for Constitutional Reform at Harvard," *Harvard Alumni Bulletin*, Dec 23, 1968, p 13n. Students told the story of one great star at the University of Wisconsin who could not be bothered with appearing in his classes and put all his lectures on film for screening while he went off to Europe. Chancing to return just before the end of the term he strolled in to see himself in action. He found the amphitheatre empty, not a single student present. But down front a tape recorder turned. As one machine projected the lecture of the absent professor, the other recorded it for the absent students.

61 C.W. Dodds, *President's Report*, (Princeton University, annually 1947 through 1955). Robert Goheen, *President's Report*, (Princeton University, annually 1956 through 1968). Robert Goheen, *President's Report 1957–67*. (Princeton University, 1968).

62 Machlup, *Production and Distribution of Knowledge*, p 151ff. David Lilienthal, "Whatever Happened to the Peaceful Atom?" *Harper's*, Oct 1963. Ralph Lapp, *The New Priesthood*, pp 19, 21, 164. *National Science Policy;* Hearings before Subcommittee on Scientific R and D of House Committee on Science and Astronautics, 91st Congress, 2nd session, (July 12–Sept 17, 1970), p 61. *Federal Funds for R & D at Universities and Colleges f y 1968;* p 6f. *F. yrs 1969, 1970,1971*, p 6f. *F. yrs.1965, 1966, 1967, p 6f.*

63 Ross in Harbison, *Education, Manpower and Economic Growth*, p 90 (49,000 university men in research in 1961). Rand, *Cambridge USA*, p 35 (statement by Pusey). Don K. Price, "The Scientific Establishment," *Science*, Jun 19, 1962, p 1099ff.

64 *The New York Times*, Jan 17, 1960, p 127 (Packard). Burke, *Politics of Re-*

search, p 67 (SRI growth). Allan Cartter, ed. *American Colleges and Universities*, p 238. James Ridgeway, *The Closed Corporation*, (New York; Atheneum, 1968), p 16.

65 Nisbet, *Degradation of the Academic Dogma*, p 140. G.K. Smith ed., *Stress and Campus Response*, passim. Halleck "Twelve Hypotheses" in G.K. Smith, ed. *Twenty Five Years*, p 287ff. Lewis B. Mayhew, "And Now the Future," in G.K. Smith, ed. *Twenty Five Years*, p 306f.

66 Fritz Stern, "Reflections on the International Student Movement," *American Scholar*, Winter 1970, p 123 ("boredom of our lives"). Kingman Brewster, "The Involuntary Campus," *Educational Record*, 51, No 2, spring 1970, p 103 (statement by SDS student).

67 Halleck, "Twelve Hypotheses" p 287. Kenneth Keniston, "What's Bugging the Students," *Educational Record*, 51, No 2, spring 1970, p 118f.

68 Mayhew "And Now the Future," p 306f

69 Mayhew "And Now the Future," p 306f.

70 *President's Report, 1957–67*, Princeton University (renaming Plasma Physics lab). *President's Report 1970*, (Cambridge; Harvard University, 1971), p 3 (financial difficulties of private universities). Edward Alvey, *Americana Annual 1970*, p 970. Mayhew "And Now the Future," p 306f.

71 *The New York Times*, Nov 26, 27, and Dec 15, 17, 1957. Coral Bell, *Negotiation from Strength*, p 168. Eisenhower, *Memoirs*, II, p 205f. Hertzog, *War-Peace Establishment*, p 39. *Survey 1957–8*, p 34 (statement by Lyndon Johnson). *The New York Times*, Oct 11, 1957 (statement by Dutch delegate). Rostow, *U.S. in the World Arena*, p 402 (missile outlays). *The New York Times*, July 14, 1959.

72 Marriner Eccles, *Beckoning Frontiers*, (New York; Knopf, 1951), p 336 (statement by Roosevelt). Harold Macmillan, *Riding the Storm*, (diary reference to Eisenhower golf). p. 95.

73 Eisenhower, *Memoirs*, II, p 616. *The New York Times*, Jan 18, 1961.

74 Ulam, *Expansion and Coexistence*, p 609f. This analysis is in large part based on Prof. Ulam's treatment of Soviet policy.

75 William E. Griffiths *The Sino-Soviet Rift*, (Cambridge; MIT Press, 1964), p 17. D.S.Zagoria, *Sino-Soviet Conflict 1958–61*, (Princeton; Princeton University Press, 1962), p 160. Arnold Horelick and Myron Rush, *Political Succession in the USSR*, (New York, Columbia University Press, 1965), p 36. Walter Lafeber, *America Russia and the Cold War*, p 202. Arnold Horelick and Myron Rush, *Strategic Power and Soviet Foreign Policy*, (Chicago; University of Chicago Press, 1965), p 105.

76 Ulam, *Expansion and Coexistence*, p 613.

77 LaFeber, *America, Russia and the Cold War* p 203. Crankshaw, *Khrushchev*, p 268. Griffith, *Sino-Soviet Rift* p 17. Clubb, *Twentieth Century China*, p 352. Richard Lowenthal, *World Communism*, p 99f.

78 Ulam, *Expansion and Coexistence*, p 607. Crankshaw, *Khrushchev*, p 269.

79 Crankshaw, *Khrushchev* p 268. Griffith, *Sino-Soviet Rift*, p 17. Coral Bell, *Negotiation from Strength* p 177. Halle, *Cold War as History* p 347. Rostow, *U.S. in the World Arena* p 289. Thomas Schelling, *Arms and Influence*, (New Haven; Yale, paperback, 1967), p 272.

80 Crankshaw, *Khrushchev*, p 268. Griffith, *Sino-Soviet Rift* p 18. Brzezinski and Huntington, *Political Power*, p 424 (affluent Soviet society). Horelick and Rush, p 38. *Strategic Power*, Ulam, *Expansion and Coexistence* p 614.

81 Ulam, *Expansion and Coexistence* p 606. Halle, *Cold War as History*, pp 282, 301.

82 *Documents on International Affairs 1957*, (London; Oxford/Royal Institute of International Affairs, 1960), p 39 (Bulganin note).

83 *Survey 1957–8*, p 347ff. *The New York Times*, Dec 20, 1957 (statement by Dulles). *U.S. in World Affairs, 1957*, p 97 (statement by Khrushchev) Apr 27, 1957), p 300ff.

84 Ulam *Expansion and Coexistence,* p 610

85 Ulam, *Expansion and Coexistence* p 610

86 Eisenhower, *Memoirs,* II, 226. Coral Bell, *Negotiation from Strength,* p 186.

87 *Survey 1957–8,* p 356.

CHAPTER 11.

1 Peter Blake, *The Master Builders,* (New York; Knopf, 1960), p 296. Vincent Scully Jr., *Frank Lloyd Wright,* (New York; Braziller, 1960), p 21. Finis Farr, *Frank Lloyd Wright, a Biography,* (New York; Scribner, 1961), p 20. T.H. Robsjohn-Gibbings, *Homes of the Brave,* (New York; Knopf, 1954), p 11ff. John Keats, *The Crack in the Picture Window,* (Boston; Houghton, 1957), p 3. Cranston Jones, *Architecture Today and Tomorrow,* (New York; McGraw, 1961), p 96. Cranston Jones, ed. *Formgivers at Midcentury,* (New York; American Federation of Arts, 1959), p 14. *The New York Times,* April 10, 1959. *House and Home,* May 1959, p 95.

2 Ben Wattenberg, *This U.S.A.,* p 256 (cars-jobs). James Marston Fitch interview, May 15, 1972. Keats, *Crack in the Picture Window,* p 3ff.

3 "What's So Good about Splits?" *House and Home,* Feb 1955, p 144–55. Fitch interview, May 15, 1972. Percival Goodman, interview, Jun 15, 1972.

4 "What's Happening to Split-Levels," *Michigan Architect and Engineer,* May 1956, p 10. *House and Home,* April 1954, p 110–24. "Do Split Levels have to be so Ugly?" *House and Home,* Feb 1956, p 136–43. *House and Home,* Dec 1952, p 117–21. *House and Home,* April, 1955, p 104–115. *House and Home,* March 1955, p 139. *House and Home,* August 1956, p 120. "House by Mario Romanach," *Arts and Architecture,* April 1955, p 125–55.

5 *House and Home,* April 1954, p 111 (statement by housewife). James M. Fitch, interview, May 15, 1972.

6 Vance Packard, *The Status Seekers,* (New York; McKay, 1959), p 3. Hofstadter, p 63f., Lipset, p 26of. and Daniel Bell, p 39f., in Bell, *The Radical Right,* (Garden City; Doubleday, 1966).

7 Brooks, *Great Leap* p 351 (church membership rise). Max Gunther, *The Weekenders,* Philadelphia, Lippincott, 1964, p 154.

8 Lubell, *Future of American Politics,* p 133ff., and *Revolt of the Moderates,* p 64ff.

9 Will Herberg, *Protestant-Catholic-Jew,* (Garden City; Doubleday, 1955), p 3. Will Herberg, "Religion and Culture in Present day America," in Philip Olson, ed. *America as a Mass Society,* New York, Free Press, 1963, p 376ff. *The New York Times,* May 4, 1948 (Eisenhower "most religious man"), Dec 23, 1952 (Eisenhower "Our government makes no sense"), March 25, 1956 (Rabbi David J. Seligson "three great faiths").

10 Peter DeVries, *The Mackerel Plaza,* (Boston; Little Brown, 1954) p 209.

11 Dorothy Anne Robinson, "Yesterday and Today," *Ladies Home Journal,* August 1964, p 56. Maggie Angelo-glou, *History of Make-up,* (New York; Macmillan, 1970), p 129. Alan Ashbolt, *An American Experience,* p 179.

12 *The New York Times,* July 28 and Aug 24, 1959. Erving Goffman, *Presentation of Self in Everyday Life,* (Garden City; Doubleday Anchor paperback, 1959), p 37, 61, 66, 122, 246f. R.L. Duffus, *Nostalgia, U.S.A.* (New York; Norton, 1963), p 22.

13 Ernest Havemann, "Love and Marriage," *Life,* Sept 21, 1961, p 117 and Sept 28, 1961, p 122. Ira L. Reiss, "Sexual Renaissance in America," *Journal of Social Issues,* 22:2 (April 1966), p 123. Pearl Buck, "The Sexual Revolution," *Ladies Home Journal,* Sept 1964, p 43f. Christopher Lasch, "Divorce and the Family in America," *Atlantic,* Nov 1966, p 57, 65. William J. Goode, *Women in Divorce,* (New York, Free Press, 1958), p 43ff. *Demographic Yearbook 1955,* (New York;

U.N. Statistical Office, 1955), p 99ff.

14 A.C. Kinsey, *The Gall Wasp Genus*, (No. 58, Indiana University Studies series, Bloomington, 1923). A.C. Kinsey, W.B. Pomeroy and C.E. Martin, *Sexual Behavior in the Human Male*, (Philadelphia; Saunders, 1948), p 549, 585, 670. A.C.Kinsey, W.B.Pomeroy, C.E. Martin and P.H.Gebhard, *Sexual Behavior in the Human Female*, (Philadelphia; Saunders, 1953), p 286, 416. 298ff. Erwin O.Smigel and Rita Seiden, "The Decline and Fall of the Double Standard," in *Annals of American Academy of Political and Social Sciences*, Vol 376, March 1968, p 8. *The New York Times*, Jan 4, 1948. *The New Yorker*, Jan 3, 1948. *School and Society*, Aug 28, 1948. *The New Yorker*, Sept 19, 1953. Bruce Bliven, *New Republic*, Nov 9, 1953. William J. Goode, *World Revolution and Family Patterns*, (New York; Free Press, 1963), p 37. K. Robert L. Wikman, *Die Einleitung der Ehe*, (Abo, Abo Akademi, 1937), p. 113, 115, 264, 309.

15 *The New York Times*, Oct 22, 1967, p 80. Goode, *World Revolution and Family Patterns*, p 37. Smigel and Seiden, "Decline and Fall" p 6. Ira L. Reiss, *Premarital Sexual Standards in America*, (Glencoe, Ill.; Free Press, 1960), p 76f. "The 'New' American Woman," *Life*, Dec 26, 1956, p 6, 41, 65, 97. Gladys Taber, "Poet's Kitchen," *Ladies Home Journal*, Feb 1949, p 56. Shirley Jackson, "One Last Chance," *McCalls*, April 1956, p 22. "I'm Lucky! I'm Lucky! I'm So Glad to be a Woman," *Ladies Home Journal*, Feb 1960, p 63. Margaret Parton, "Whither Thou Goest," *Ladies Home Journal*, June 1959, p 139. Betty H.Hoffman, "Through All my Housework in an Hour," *Ladies Home Journal*, Oct 1960, p 184. "A New Look at the American Woman," *Look*, Oct 16, 1956, 1, 35, 41, Betty Friedan, *The Feminine Mystique*, (New York; Dell paperback, 1970), p 52.

16 Smigel and Seiden, "Decline and Fall" p 14 cites Ira Reiss, *The Social Context of Premarital Social Permissiveness*, (New York; Holt, 1967), ch vii. *Statistical Abstract of the U.S. 1967*, p 64. Goode, *World Revolution and Family Patterns*. p 40. Lasch, "Divorce and the Family" p 60 cites "Dear Abby" column. "Where There's a Man, Wear Red," *Mademoiselle*, August 1952, p 282. Goffman, *Presentation of Self* p 39. Mira Komarowsky, "Cultural Contradictions and Sex Roles," *American Journal of Sociology*, LII, (July 1946), p 184ff.

17 Haveman, in *Life*, Sept 21, 1961, p 117. Edward Sagarin, "Taking Stock of Sex," *Annals*, 378, Mar 1968, p 2. Peter Berger and Hansfried Kellner, "Marriage and the Construction of Reality," *Diogene*, 46:2 (1964), p 3f. Henry Anatole Grunwald, ed. *Sex in America*, (New York; Bantam, 1964), p 27. *The New York Times*, Jun 28, 1960. Friedan, *Feminine Mystique*, pp 18, 28, 62, 174.

18 Dean D. Knudsen, "The Declining Status of Women: Popular Myths and the Failure of Functionalist Thought," *Social Forces*, Vol 48, No 2, Dec 1969, p 183ff. Dept of Labor, Women's Bureau, *Job Horizons for College Women in the 1960s*, Bulletin 288, 1964, p 71. *Statistical Abstract of the U.S. 1967*, p 230.

19 Robert O. Blood and Donald M. Wolfe, *Husbands and Wives*, (Glencoe, Ill.; Free Press, 1960), p 19ff. William J. Lederer and Don D. Jackson, *Mirages of Marriage*, (New York; Norton, 1968), p 164.

20 Smigel and Seiden, "Decline and Fall" p 6. Reiss, "Sexual Renaissance" pp 123, 126. Bennett M. Berger, *Looking for America*, p 118ff. Robert E. Fitch in "The New Morality, What, Why—Why Not?" *Religion in Life*, XXXV, spring 1966, no. 2, p 180. John Gagnon and William Simon in Ailon Shiloh, ed. *Studies in Human Sexual Behavior: the American Scene*, (Springfield, Ill.; C.C. Thomas, 1970), p xix ("gourmet cooking").

21 "The Second Sexual Revolution," *Time*, Jan 24, 1964, p 54, 59. Bennett Berger, *Looking for America*, p 101. Mary Daly, *The Church and the Second Sex*, (New York; Harper, 1968), p 128. Reiss, in Grunwald, ed., *Sex in*

America, p 92. Paul and Emily Avery, "Some Notes on Wife-Swapping," in Grunwald, *Sex in America,* p 248. William and Jerry Breedlove, *Swap Clubs,* (Los Angeles; Sherbourne Press, 1964), p 18f. William and Jerry Breedlove, *The Swinging Set,* (Los Angeles, Sherbourne Press, 1965), p 41f. Charles and Rebecca Palson, "Swinging in Wedlock," *Society,* Feb 1972, p 28. Charles and Bonnie Remsberg, "Weird Harold and the First National Swingers Convention," *Esquire,* Dec 1970, p 189ff. "The American Way of Swinging," *Time,* Feb 8, 1971, p 51. Diana Trilling, "The Death of Marilyn Monroe," in Edward Wagenknecht, ed. *Marilyn Monroe, a Composite View,* Philadelphia; Chilton, 1969), p 125ff.

22 Brooks, *Great Leap,* p 139 (Diners club). Goffman, *Presentation of Self* p 246 (union staffs). Daniel J. Boorstin, *The Image,* (New York; Harper Colophon paperback, 1961), p 184f (corporate image). Spencer Klaw. "The New American Office," *Fortune,* Sept 1959, p 156.

23 *Quiz Shows,* Hearings before Subcommittee of House Committee on Interstate and Foreign Commerce, 86th Congress, 1st session (Washington, Government Printing Office 1960), p 4ff. *Time,* Oct 19, Nov 2, 9, 16, 1959. "Have We Gone Soft?" *New Republic,* Feb 16, 1960. Eric Barnouw, *The Image Empire,* p 122ff. Orville Klapp, *Heroes, Villains and Fools,* (Englewood Cliffs; Prentice-Hall, 1962), p 72. Robert McNeil, *The People Machine,* (New York; Harper, 1968), p 32. Goldman, *Crucial Decade,* p 316f. Ashbolt, *An American Experience,* p 55. Walter Goodman, *All Honorable Men,* (Boston; Little Brown, 1965), p 266

24 Ashbolt, *An American Experience,* p 56 (district attorney).

25 *Time,* Nov 2, 1959 (Torre) and Nov 9, 1959. Martin Mayer, *About Television,* p 122 (momentary increase in public programming after 1959).

26 "Moment of Silence," *Time,* April 27, 1959, (gas oven show).

27 R.A. Smith, "The Incredible Electrical Conspiracy," *Fortune,* April 1961.

Walter Goodman, *All Honorable Men,* p 16. John Herling, *The Great Price Conspiracy,* (Washington; Robert Luce, 1962), p 3ff. John G. Fuller, *The Gentlemen Conspirators,* (New York; Grove, 1962), p 21f.

28 R.A. Smith, "The Incredible Electrical Conspiracy II," *Fortune,* May, 1961. Goodman, p 22f. Herling, *Great Price Conspiracy,* p 48f. Fuller, *Gentlemen Conspirators,* p 34f.

29 Herling, *Great Price Conspiracy,* p 80 (Eisenhower statement). Goodman, *All Honorable Men,* p 41f. Fuller *Gentlemen Conspirators,* p 158f. Smith, in *Fortune,* April 1961, p 174.

30 Smith in *Fortune,* May 1961, p 99. Goodman, *All Honorable Men* p 20f. Fuller *Gentlemen Conspirators,* p 183f. Herling, *Great Price Conspiracy,* p 78 (oil, Salk drug cases), p 78, 193ff (Savage). *Yale Law Journal,* Dec 1961, p 288 (newspaper play).

31 *The New York Times,* Dec 24, 1960 (Shanks). *Time,* Aug 29, 1960, p 60. Goodman, *All Honorable Men,* p 64f. Robert F. Wasser, *Charles Evans Hughes, Politics and Reform in New York, 1905–10,* (Ithaca; Cornell, 1967), p 34. M.J. Pusey, *Charles Evans Hughes,* I, (New York; Macmillan, 1931), p 144, 160. *Time,* Aug 1, 1960, p 64 (Newberg).

32 *The New York Times,* Jun 19, 1958 (Eisenhower), *Time,* Jun 30, 1958. David A. Frier, *Conflict of Interest in the Eisenhower Administration,* (Ames: Iowa State University Press, 1969), p 11f. Goodman, *All Honorable Men,* p 194ff. Ashbolt, *An American Experience,* p 53f. Eric Goldman, *Crucial Decade,* p 315.

33 Lynn B. Kirkpatrick, *The Real CIA,* (New York: Macmillan, 1968), p 22. H.H. Ransom, *The Intelligence Establishment,* (Cambridge; Harvard University Press, 1970), p xiv, 22. David Wise and Thomas B. Ross, *The Invisible Government,* (New York; Random, 1954), p 95f. Sanche de Gramont, *The Secret War,* (New York; Putnam, 1962), p 28. Allen Dulles, *The Craft of Intelligence,* (New York; Harper, 1963), p 44f. Norman Cole, *CIA: Stranger than Fiction,* (Delhi;

Nam Yug, 1964), p 9f. Bruce Ladd, *Crisis in Credibility*, (New York; New American Library, 1968), p 2. Paul W. Blackstock, *Strategy of Subversion*, (Chicago; Quadrangle, 1964), p 116.

34 Unna Warren, "CIA: Who Watches the Watchman?" *Harpers*, April 1958, p 46ff. *The New York Times*, "CIA, Maker of Policy or Tool?" April 25, 1966. *The New York Times*, May 8, 1967 (statement by Braden). Wise, p 26 (Bissell), p 101 (Amery), p 172 (Wisner). *U.S.News*, May 1, 1961, p 24. (Bissell). James Burnham, *Coming Defeat of Communism*, (New York, John Day, 1950), p 23. Julius Mader, *Who's Who in the C.I.A.*, (East Berlin; no publisher, 1968). Alain Guerin, *Le general gris*, (Paris; Juillard, 1968), p 189 (Kent). Alain Guerin, *Qu'est ce qu c'est la C.I.A.?* (Paris; Editions Sociales, 1968), p 37. Miles Copeland, *The Game of Nations*, p 42ff.

35 *The New York Times*, May 8, 1969 (labor subversion). Thomas Braden, "I'm Glad the C.I.A. is Immoral," *Saturday Evening Post*, May 20, 1968. *The New York Times*, July 12, 1971, and Jan 23, 1972 (radio in cold war). John Swomley, *American Empire*, (New York; Macmillan, 1970), p 148. Ruth Shereff, "How the CIA Makes Friends and Influences Countries," *Viet Report*, Jan-Feb 1967, p 13.

36 *Ramparts*, April 1966, p 13. "The Silent Service," *Time*, Feb 24, 1967. Ransom, *Intelligence Establishment*, p 241.

37 Dulles, *Craft of Intelligence*, p 81 (obtaining Khrushchev secret speech). Wise and Ross, *Invisible Government*, p 99 (Dulles duality). Sanche de Gramont, *Secret War*, p 27, 31. Wise and Ross *Invisible Government* p 114 (Dulles to Cairo), p 156 (Lansdale), p 255 (Berlin tunnel). Guerin, *Le general gris*, p 173ff. Charles Whiting, *Gehlen, Master Spy*, (New York; Ballantine paperback, 1972), p 96ff. Guerin, *Qu'est ce que c'est la CIA?* p 27. Gilles Perrault, *Du service secret au gouvernement invisible*, (Paris; Le Pavillon paperback, 1971), p 70.

LaFeber, *America, Russia and the Cold War*, p 151. Blackstock, *Strategy of Subversion*, p 106, p 31 (Dulles statement). *Time*, Feb 24, 1967). (cabinet member), July 19, 1963 (Gehlen) *Newsweek*, May 6 1968, p 56 (Gehlen). Russell Baker, "The Other Mr. Dulles—of the C.I.A.", *The New York Times Magazine*, Mar 16, 1958, p 17ff. Dulles, p 87 (Ukrainians and cyanide). Wise and Ross, *Invisible Government* p 315–20 (cold war radio).

38 Guerin, *Qu'est ce qu c'est la CIA?* p 39. *Nation*, Jun 24, 1961 (10,000 agents). *The New York Times*, April 26, 1966, (statement by Shelypin at 21st Party Congress). Wise and Ross, *Invisible Government*, p 129ff (list of subverted governments, p 260 (McCone estimates). Enno Hobbing, "CIA—Hottest Role in Cold War," *Esquire*, Sept 1957, p 31f. Miles Copeland, *Game of Nations*, pp 42, 48. H.H. Ransom, *Intelligence Establishment*, p 88. Cf. J.F. Campbell, *The Foreign Affairs Fudge Factory*, (New York; Basic Books, 1971), p 147ff.

39 Allen S. Whiting, "What Nixon Must Do to Make Friends in Peking," *New York Review of Books*, Oct 7, 1971, p 10. Wise and Ross, *Invisible Government*, p 156f (Lansdale). William Lederer and Eugene Burdick, *The Ugly American*, (New York; Norton, 1958). Graham Greene, *The Quiet American*, (New York; Viking, 1956). Blackstock, *Strategy of Subversion*, p 203 (Richardson). George McT. Kahin and John W. Lewis, *U.S. in Vietnam*, (New York; Dial, 1967), p 66–7. *Ramparts*, April 1966, p 13. Edward G.Lansdale, *In the Midst of War, an American's Mission to Southeast Asia*, (New York; Harper, 1972), p 126, 154f.

40 Godfrey Blunden, *The Looking Glass Conference*, (New York; Vanguard, 1956). Schlesinger, *Thousand Days*, p 328. Sorensen, *Kennedy* p 726. Whiting, "What Nixon Must Do", p 10. Roger M. Smith, "Laos," in George McT. Kahin, ed. *Governments and Politics of Southeast Asia*, (Ithaca;

Cornell, 1964, 2nd ed.), p 538ff. Robert Shaplen, *The Lost Revolution*, (New York; Harper, 1965), p 359, 364. Robert Shaplen, *The Road from War*, (New York; Harper, 1970), p 349. Nina S.Adams and Alfred W.McCoy, *Laos, War and Revolution*, (New York; Harper, 1970), p xvii. Roger Hilsman, *To Move a Nation*, p 142ff. Peter D. Scott, "Air America: Flying the U.S. over Laos," *Ramparts*, VIII, p 39ff. *Time*, Mar 17, 1961 (Phoumi). Hugh Toye, *Laos, Buffer State or Battleground*, (London; Oxford, 1968), p 150. Bernard Fall, *Hell is a Very Small Place*, (Philadelphia; Lippincott, 1966), p 241. Bernard Fall, *Anatomy of a Crisis, the Laotian Crisis of 1960–1*, (Garden City; Doubleday, 1969), p 167. Blackstock, *Strategy of Subversion*, p 197. Marvin and Susan Gettleman and Lawrence and Carol Kaplan, *Conflict in Indonchina, a Reader on the Widening War*, (New York; Random, 1970), p 257. J. Mirsky and S.E. Stonefield, "The U.S. in Laos, 1945–62," in Edward Friedman and Mark Selden, *America's Asia, Dissenting Essays*, (New York; Pantheon, 1971), p 298ff. Arthur J. Dommen, *Conflict in Laos*, (New York; Praeger, 1964), p 128, David W. Conde, *CIA—Core of the Cancer*, (New Delhi; Entente Private Ltd., 1970) p 192.

41 Neil Sheehan et al. *The Pentagon Papers*, (New York; Bantam paperback, 1971), p 137. Hilsman, *To Move a Nation*, p 316ff. Allen Whiting, "What Nixon Must Do", p 10. Adams and McCoy, *Laos*, p 301ff. Peter B. Scott, "Air America," p 39ff. George Patterson, *Journey with Loshay*, (New York; Norton, 1954), p 41, 156. George Patterson, *Peking v. Delhi*, (London; Faber, 1963) , p 157. Neville Maxwell, *India's China War*, (New York; Pantheon, 1971), p 122. Wise, and Ross, *Invisible Government*, p 106. (China agents). *The New York Times*, Oct 21 and 24, 1954 (spy plane crash). *The New York Times*, Apr 7, 1960 (Indian protest) and Sept 18, 1960 (Chou's reply). *The New York Times*, July 28, 1958, p 1. *The New York Times*, July 14, 1964 (agents downed in North Vietnam). *The New York Times*, Apr 3, 1967 (CAT in Laos). *The New York Times*, Aug 3, 1971, (CIA in Laos). Adams and McCoy, *Laos* p 168. Hilsman, *To Move a Nation*, p 140 (Nam Tha). Wise and Ross, *Invisible Government*, p 234 (Cline). *The New York Times*, Mar 12, 1972, (Cline and senators).

42 *The New York Times*, Sept 12, 1971, p 77 (statement by Khrushchev).

43 Michel Tatu, *Power in the Kremlin, from Khrushchev to Kosygin*, (New York; Viking paperback 1970, orig. 1967), p 49. Edward Crankshaw, *The New Cold War, Moscow v. Pekin*, (Baltimore; Penguin paperback, 1969), p 29f. Thomas W. Wolfe, *Soviet Power and Europe, 1945–70*, (Baltimore; Johns Hopkins University Press, 1970), p 74f. Adam B. Ulam, *Expansion and Coexistence*, (New York: Praeger, 1968), p 572f. Marshall Shulman, "Recent Soviet Policy, some patterns in Retrospect," *Journal of International Affairs*, XXII, 1, p. 16f. Marshall Shulman, *Beyond the Cold War*, New Haven, Yale, 1966), p 50ff.

44 John Gittings, *Survey of the Sino-Soviet Dispute, 1963–67*, (London Oxford/Royal Institute of International Affairs, 1968), p 20f. Griffith *Sino-Soviet Rift* p 4f. Donald Zagoria, *Sino-Soviet Conflict, p. 49, 1956–61*, (Princeton; Princeton University Press, 1962) pp 49, 145f. Brzezinski, *The Soviet Bloc*, p 364f. Alexander Dallin and A. Brzezinski, *Diversity in International Communism*, (New York Columbia University Press, 1963), p xxv-xliv. David O. Levine, *The Rift*, (Jacksonville, Ill., Harris-Wolfe, 1968), p 88f. Richard Lowenthal, "Factors of Unity and Factors of Conflict, China and Russia," *Annals of the American Academy*, Sept 1963, Vol. 349, p. 106f. Edward Crankshaw, *Khrushchev, a Career*, (New York; Viking, 1966), p 227f.

45 Ulam, *Expansion and Coexistence* pp 572, 619–20, 632. Goldman, *Crucial Decade* p 328f. O.E. Clubb, *China and Russia: the Great Game*, New

York, Columbia University Press, 1971, p 413f. Wolfe, *Soviet Power and Europe*, p 90f. Crankshaw, *The New Cold War*, p 85. Halle, *The Cold War as History*, p 352. Horelick and Rush, *Strategic Power and Soviet Policy*, p 37f. *Documents on International Affairs 1958*, (London; Oxford/Royal Institute of International Affairs, 1962), p 146.

46 Ulam, *Expansion and Coexistence*, pp 618, 621. Richard Lowenthal, "Diplomacy and Revolution, Dialectics of a Dispute," from *China Quarterly*, reprinted in Roderick McFarquhar, ed. *China under Mao*, (Cambridge; MIT Press, 1966), p 425. Clubb, *Twentieth Century China*. p 352. Clubb, *China and Russia*, p 420f. Griffith, *Sino-Soviet Rift*, p 375.

47 *Documents on International Affairs 1958*, p 187. Clubb, *Twentieth Century China*, p 352f. Clubb, *China and Russia*, p 420f. Griffith, *Sino-Soviet Rift*, p 399.

48 *The New York Times*, Jan 28 1959 (Khrushchev speech). Ulam, *Expansion and Coexistence*. p 621. Gittings, *Survey of Sino-Soviet Dispute*, p 110f. Zagoria, *Sino-Soviet Dispute*, p 280.

49 David A. Charles, "The Dismissal of Marshal P'eng Teh-huai," *China Quarterly*, No 8, Oct–Dec 1961, p 63f. Jean Baby, *La grande controverse sino-sovietique, 1956–66*, (Paris; Grasset, 1966), p 67. William E. Griffith, "Sino-Soviet Relations, 1964–65," *China Quarterly*, No 25, Jan–Mar 1966, p 3. Clubb, *Twentieth Century China*, p 364. Clubb, *China and Russia*, p 428f. Griffith, *Sino-Soviet Rift*. p 18. Ulam, *Expansion and Coexistence*, pp 621, 624. R. Lowenthal, *World Communism*, p 220. Gittings, *Survey of Sino-Soviet Dispute*, p 110f.

50 *The New York Times*, July 25, 1959 (kitchen debate).

51 *The New York Times*, Aug 2, 1959 (Gallup report). Halle, *Cold War as History* p 365. Ulam, *Expansion and Coexistence*, p 624. Crankshaw, *Khrushchev*, p 274. Goldman, *Crucial Decade* p 329. *Panam Clipper*, (Atlantic Division), Vol 18, No 5, July 1959 (Nixon Moscow trip).

52 *The New York Times*, Sept 16 through 26, 1959 (Khrushchev visit). *The New York Times*, Sept 12, 1971. Goldman, *Crucial Decade*, p 330.

53 Eisenhower, *Memoirs*, II, p 445 (statement by Eisenhower). Ulam, *Expansion and Coexistence*, p 626.

54 *New York Times*, Oct 1, 1959 (Khrushchev Peking speech). Lowenthal, *World Communism*, p 425f. Clubb, *Russia and China*, p 436 Ulam, *Expansion and Coexistence* p 628. Griffith, *Sino-Soviet Rift*, p 400. Halle, *Cold War as History*, p 368.

55 Raymond Garthoff, *Soviet Military Policy*, (New York; Praeger, 1966), p 129. Wolfe, *Soviet Power and Europe*, p 164f. LaFeber, *America, Russia and the Cold War*, p 205. Tatu, *Power in the Kremlin* p 69.

56 *The New York Times*, April 28, 1960. Baby, *La grande controverse* p 71. Ulam, *Expansion and Coexistence* p 630. Clubb, *Twentieth Century China*, p 438. Tatu, *Power in the Kremlin* p 47. Griffith, *Sino-Soviet Rift* p 19.

57 *The New York, Times*, April 21, 1960 (Dillon). *The New York Times*, May 6, 7, 11, 1960 (U-2). *Time*, May 16, 1960. *The Reporter*, June 9, 1960. LaFeber, *America, Russia and the Cold War* p 206. R.P. Stebbins, *U.S. in World Affairs, 1960*, (New York; Harper, 1961), p 82. G.H. Hudson, *Survey of International Affairs 1959–60*, (London; Oxford/Royal Institute of International Relations, 1962), p 10f.

58 Francis G. Powers and Curt Gentry, *Operation Overflight*, (New York, Holt, 1970) pp 3, 13, 33, 43, 73, 80. Michel Bori and Jean Caumel, *Powers. ils ont tous menti*, (Paris; Galic, 1962), p 117. Allen Dulles, *Craft of Intelligence* p 67.

59 *The New York Times*, May 10, 1960, p 14 (Khrushchev statements). Eisenhower Memoirs, II, p 546. Adams, *Inside Report*, p 455. Ulam, *Expansion and Coexistence*, p 626. Tatu, *Power in the Kremlin*, p 55.

60 Powers, *Operation Overflight* pp 69, 77, 90. Borri and Caumel, *Powers*, p 117.

61 *The New York Times*, May 6, 1960.
Hudson in *Survey 1959–60*, p 60ff.
Tatu, *Power in the Kremlin*, p 55.
Goldman, *Crucial Decade*, p 335.

62 *Newsweek*, May 16, 1960. *Time*, May
16, 1960. Tatu, *Power in the Kremlin*,
p 55. Wolfe, *Soviet Power in Europe*,
p 86. Goldman, *Crucial Decade* p
336.

63 *The New York Times*, May 10, 1960.

64 *Newsweek*, May 16, 1960. *Survey
1959–60*, p 62f. *U.S. in World Affairs*,
1960, p 85ff.

65 *Survey 1959–60*, p 62f. *U.S. in World
Affairs 1960*, p 85ff. Goldman, *Crucial Decade*, p 337.

66 *Time*, May 16, 1960. *Survey 1959–60*,
p 62f. Adams, *Inside Report*, p 456.
Halle, *Cold War as History*, p 365.

67 *Public Papers of the Presidents of the
U.S., Dwight D. Eisenhower 1960–61*,
(Washington; Government Printing
Office, 1961), pp 427, 428, 436, 439.
The New York Times, May 17, 18, 26,
1960. *The Reporter*, Jun 9, 1960.
Ulam, *Expansion and Coexistence* p
633–4. Wolfe, *Soviet Power and
Europe*, p 92. Goldman, *Crucial
Decade* p 340. Eisenhower, *Memoirs*,
II, p 557. *Survey 1959–60*, p 62ff. *U.S.
in World Affairs, 1960*, p 85f. *Nation*,
Jun 4 1960. *Newsweek*, May 30, 1960.
Commonweal, June 17, 1960, p 302.

68 Ulam, *Expansion and Coexistence*, p
634, Wolfe, *Soviet Power in Europe* p
92. Eisenhower, *Memoirs*, II, p 557.
Tatu, *Power in the Kremlin*, p 77.

69 *The New York Times*, Mar 3, 9, 1965
(KC–135). Clay Blair Jr., "So You're
Flying to Europe," *Saturday Evening
Post*, Jan 10, 1959, p 15 (KC–119).

70 "The Jet Age," *Time*, Oct 24, 1955.
Aviation Week, July 6, 20, Aug 3, 10,
24, 31, Sept 14, Oct 12, Nov 9, Dec
7, 1959. *Pan American Clipper* (Atlantic Division), Vol. 18, January,
Spring, May, June, July, Sept, Nov,
Dec, 1959. *Pan American Clipper*
(Pacific Division), Feb, Oct, Dec,
1959. John B. Rae, *Climb to Greatness: the American Aircraft Industry,
1920–60*. (Cambridge, MIT Press,
1968), pp 206–7, 213. John Burby,
The Great American Motion Sickness,
Boston, Little Brown, 1971, p 189.

Brooks, *Great Leap*, p 270.

71 Willis Player, interview, July 1 1971
(Seattle passenger). "The Age of
Noise," *Time*, Mar 16, 1962, p 65f.
Time, Feb 22, 1960. Horace Sutton,
"From Magellan to Jets," *Saturday
Review*, Mar 14 1959. *Saturday Review*, Mar 7, 1959. Horace Sutton,
"Report from the Seven Seas," *Saturday Review*, Oct 17, 1959, p 28ff.
"The Small World of Jetliners,"
Readers Digest, July 1961, p 137.
"Europe by Air," *Mademoiselle*, Oct
1960, p 132. Jean Kerr, "Josephine in
Your Flying Machine," *McCalls*, Feb
1960. Samuel Grafton, "Are You Going to Fly?" *McCalls*, July 1960, p 87.
"The Vanishing American," *Newsweek*, Aug 21, 1961. "Too Clubby,"
Newsweek, Jun 19, 1961, p 76. *Look*,
Jan 6, 20, Mar 17, May 12, 26, Jun 9,
23, July 21, Aug 4, 18, Dec 8, 1959 (jet
travel). "New Shape for the Jet Age,"
Life, Jan 5 1962. "Jet Dressing,"
Vogue, Jan 1960. *American Heritage
History of Flight*, New York, American Heritage, 1962, p 369ff. John B.
Lansing, *The Travel Market, 1964–5*,
(Ann Arbor; Institute for Social Research, University of Michigan, 1965),
p 1, 34. John B. Lansing and Dwight
M. Blood, *The Changing Travel Market*, (Ann Arbor; Institute for Social
Research, University of Michigan,
1964), p 107. George F. Mott, ed.
Transportation Century, (Baton
Rouge; Louisiana State, University
Press, 1966), p 91ff. *Tourism in
OECD Countries*, (Paris; OECD
Tourist Committee, 1958 through
1970). H. Peter Gray, *International
Travel-International Trade*, (Lexington Mass.; Heath, 1970), p 3. Marion
Clawson and J.L. Knetsch, *Economics
of Outdoor Recreation*, (Baltimore;
John Hopkins University Press, 1966),
p 194. *Air Transport Facts and Figures, 1970*, (Washington; Air Transport Association, 1970). "Dog Fight
Over Charter Flights," *Business
Week*, Feb 28, 1970, p 128. *Aviation
Week*, Feb 16, Mar 9, 1970 and Aug
2, 1971. R.A. Smith, "Hawaii's A-
Poppin'," *Fortune*, June 1960. *Study
Abroad*, XVIII, 1970–72, (Paris;

Unesco, 1972), p 18. *Statistical Year-book 1970*, (Paris; Unesco, 1971) p 456. *Open Doors, 1970*, (New York; Institute of International Education, 1970), increase of American students in Europe.

72 Nancy Wilson Ross, "A Royal Princess," *Saturday Evening Post*, May 11, 1963. J.K. Galbraith, *Ambassador's Journal*, (New York; Signet paperback, 1969), p 483.

73 *The Saturday Review*, Mar 14, 1959, p 41 (Mike Todd show), p 28 (250,000 globe-girdlers a year forecast). "New Short Trips," *Mademoiselle*, Oct 1960, p 132 (North African excur-sions). *Annual Statistics of Immigration/Bureau*, (Tokyo; Japanese Ministry of Justice, 1971), U.S. air travel to Japan. *Statistical Abstract 1964*, p 211 (U.S. air travel to Europe in 1955). Herbert Prochnow, "Foreign Trade is a Two-way Street," *The Reporter*, Mar 20, 1958, p 16. *Time*, May 4, 1959, p 78 (imports). *Atlantic*, August 1957, p 64 (imports) *N.S. News*, June 27, 1960, p 62 (imports). "America Becomes a Trader," *Fortune*, Oct 1957, p 123. Osbert Lancaster, *Signs of the Times*, (Boston; Houghton, 1961), p 111 (Dulles cartoon). Brooks, *Great Leap*. p 272.

CHAPTER 12.

1 Samuel Huntington, *The Soldier and the State*, (Cambridge; Harvard University Press, 1964), p. 3. Jack Raymond, *Power at the Pentagon*, (New York; Harper, 1964), p. 14. James A. Donovan, *Militarism, U.S.A.*, (New York; Scribner, 1970), p 82ff. C.W. Borklund, *Men of the Pentagon*, (New York; Praeger, 1966), p 26f.

2 H.L. Nieburg, *In the Name of Science*, (Chicago; Quadrangle paperback, 2nd ed. 1970), p 40f. Huntington, *The Common Defense*, (New York, Columbia University Press, 1961), p 386. Samuel Huntington, "Interservice Competition and the Political Role of the Armed Forces," *American Political Science Review*, March 1961, p 40ff. Raymond, *Power at the Pentagon*, p 176.

3 V.K. Dibble, "The Garrison Society," *New University Thought*, V, 1–2 (spring, 1967), p. 106f. Samuel Huntington, "Defense Establishment: vested interests and the public interest," in Omar L. Carey, ed. *The Military Industrial Complex and U.S. Foreign Policy*, (Pullman; Washington State University Press; 1967), p 4. Huntington, *Common Defense*, p 387ff. Julius Duscha, *Men, Money and Politics*, (New York; Ives Washburn, 1965), p 50f. John M. Swomley Jr., *The Military Establishment*, (Boston; Beacon, 1964), p 113ff.

4 Huntington, "Interservice Competi-tion," supra, p. 40. Huntington, *Common Defense*, p 394ff. Donovan, *Militarism*, p 29f. "The Military Lobby, Its Impact on Congress, Nation," *Congressional Quarterly*, March 24, 1961, p 466 (Aerospace Industry Association).

5 Edgar M. Bottome, *The Missile Gap*, (Rutherford, N.J., Fairleigh Dickinson University Press, 1969), p 198 (Schenk).

6 Bernard Nossiter, in *Washington Post*, Dec 8, 1968. Cf. Nossiter, "Arms Firms See Postwar Spurt," in Seymour Melman, ed. *The War Economy of the U.S.*, (New York; St. Martin's, 1971), p 209, 212. J.K. Galbraith, *How to Control the Military*, (Garden City; Doubleday, 1969), p 22.

7 W.S. Fairfield, "PR for the Services—in Uniform and in Mufti," *The Reporter*, May 15, 1958, p 20. *Congressional Quarterly*, Mar 24, 1961, p 464.

8 Bernard Nossiter in Washington *Post*, Dec 8, 1968.

9 *U.S. News*, Aug 4, 1959. Kenneth Boulding, "The World War Industry as an Economic Problem," in Emile Benoit and Boulding, eds., *Disarmament and the Economy*, (New York; Harper, 1963), p 3. H.I. Schiller in Schiller and J.D. Phillips, eds., *Super-State: Readings in the Military-Industrial Complex*, (Urbana; University of

Illinois Press, 1970), p 2–3. Donovan, *Militarism* p 53.

10 James L. Clayton, ed. *Economic Impact of the Cold War*, (New York; Harcourt, 1970), p. 54. Duscha, *Men, Money and Politics*, p 62ff. Donovan, *Militarism*, p 45ff. Benoit, in Benoit and Boulding, p 36. Seymour Melman, *Pentagon Capitalism*, (New York; McGraw paperback, 1970), p 3f. Fred J. Cook, *The Warfare State*, (New York; Macmillan, 1962), p 23ff. Ralph Lapp, *The Weapons Culture*, (New York; Norton, 1968), p 21ff. Darcy Ribeiro, *The Americas and Communism*, (New York; Dutton, 1971), p 354.

11 Dibble, "The Garrison Society," p 106f. *Congressional Quarterly*, March 24, 1961, p 463 (Eisenhower defense spending, 38 million Defense dept. procurement transactions). Raymond, *Power at the Pentagon* p 294f. Nieburg, *In the Name of Science*, p 184f.

12 *Congressional Quarterly*, March 24, 1961, p 465. Donovan, *Militarism.* p 45. Duscha, *Men, Money and Politics*, p 62ff.

13 Eugene McCarthy, "The Limits of Power," *Atlantic Monthly*, Oct 1967. *Congressional Record* (Aug 15, 1967), p S11583. Walter Adams, "The Complex and the Industrial State," in Carey, *Military Industrial Complex and Foreign Policy* (McCarthy) p 22 (stockpiling). Duscha, *Men, Money and Politics*, p 63 (Pentagon real estate), 114 (stockpiling). George Thayer, *The War Business*, (New York; Simon and Schuster, 1969), p 179ff (Pentagon arms trade), p 200 (Ambassador Ralph Dungan). "Summary of Major Dept of Defense Educational Programs, fy 1971–2–3, Communication from John L. Donnelly, Director for Information Operations, Office of Assistant Secretary of Defense, June 6, 1973 (education).

14 Bureau of Census, *U.S. Census of Business 1948, Vol VII, Selected Services*, p 02, *1963, Vol. VII*, p 1–6 (beauty shops). *Statistical Abstract 1957*, p 863, 864, *Statistical Abstract 1964*, p 839 (bowling alleys). *Facts in Grocery Distribution*, (New York;

Progressive Grocers Magazine, 1961), p 11 (supermarkets). See also Godfrey M. Lebkor, *Chain Stores in America 1859–1959*, (New York; Chain Store Publishing Co., 1959), p 6. *U.S. Census of Business 1948, Vol II, Retail Trade-General Statistics* Pt 2, p 9. Interview, Jerry Scharnizon, Editor, *Supermarket* magazine, Jan 30, 1972.

15 *Statistical Abstract 1964*, p 202 (National Parks visits 1950, 1963); p 210 (travel overseas); 209 (trips in first six months 1963). Neil Morgan, *The California Syndrome*, (Englewood Cliffs; Prentice-Hall, 1969), p 202 (motorboats in California).

16 *Statistical Abstract 1962*, p 565 (cars, 1948 and 1960), Wattenberg, *This USA*, p 256, (multiple-car families). Barry Commoner, *The Closing Circle*, (New York; Harper, 1971), p 22 (pollution rise). Ashbolt, *An American Experience*, p 84 (New York sootfall).

17 *Time*, April 29, 1957. Raymond, *Power at the Pentagon*, p 237. Nieburg, *In the Name of Science*, p 203ff.

18 *Time*, Jan 30, 1950, p 55. *Time*, Feb 20, 1956. *Life*, "The Secret of Space, Nov, 1957, p 135.

19 Paul Jacobs, "Pilots, Missilemen, Robots," *The Reporter*, Feb 6, 1958, p 15. John B. Medaris, *Countdown for Decision*, (New York; Putnam, 1960), p 48ff (Redstone Missile). Michael Armacost, *The Politics of Weapons Innovation: the Thor-Jupiter Controversy*, (New York; Columbia University Press, 1969), p 113.

20 *The New York Times*, Nov 12, 13, 14, 1957 (LeMay to Argentina). Nieburg, *In the Name of Science*, p 40ff., 330. Armacost, *Politics of Weapons*, p 55f. Raymond, *Power at the Pentagon*, p 290. Ernest Schwiebert, *History of the Air Force Ballistic Missiles*, (New York; Praeger, 1965), p 57.

21 V.D. Sokolovsky, ed. *Soviet Military Strategy*, (Englewood Cliffs; Prentice-Hall, 1963), p 22. R.Y. Malinowski, "The Revolution in Military Affairs and the Task of the Military Press," in William R. Kintner ed. *Nuclear Revolution in Soviet Military Affairs*, (Norman; University of Oklahoma Press, 1968), p 35. R.L. Garthoff, *Soviet*

Military Policy, (New York; Praeger, 1966), p 22. T.W. Wolfe, *Soviet Strategy at the Crossroads*, (Cambridge; Harvard University Press, 1964), p 22. R.D. Crane, ed. *Soviet Nuclear Strategy*, (Washington, Georgetown Center for Strategic Studies, 1963), p 57, 62.

22   LaFeber, *America, Russia and the Cold War*, p 140. Albert N. Keim, "Ecumenical Protestantism and the Quest for International Peace," paper read at American Historical Convention, New York City, Dec 29, 1971.

23   Harold Martin, "Showdown in the Pentagon," *Saturday Evening Post*, Nov 9, 1957, p 114. Nieburg, *In the Name of Science*, pp 40f., 230. Armacost, *Politics of Weapons*, p 46. Medaris *Countdown*, p 100ff.

24   Raymond, *Power at the Pentagon*, p 246. Mollenhoff, *The Pentagon*, p 200. Richard J. Barnet, *Economy of Death*, (New York; Atheneum paperback, 1971), p 99.

25   James Flink, "Three Stages of American Automobile Consciousness" *Import Quota Legislation*, Hearings before Senate Committee on Finance, 90th Congress, 1st session, (Washington; Government Printing Office, 1966), Part 2, p 855 cited by Walter Adams in Carey, *Military Industrial Complex and Foreign Policy*, p 19.

26   Borklund, *Men of the Pentagon*, p 142. Nieburg, *In the Name of Science*, p 42. Bottome *Missile Gap*, p 43. Walter Adams in Carey, *Military-Industrial Complex and Foreign Policy*, p 19. Armacost *Politics of Weapons*, p 57. *11th Report, Organization and Management of Missile Program*, House Committee on Government Operations, 86th Congress, 1st session, Washington, Government Printing Office, 1959, p 69.

27   *Time*, April 29, 1957. *Life*, Nov 4, 25, 1957. *11th Report*, supra, p 70. Nieburg, *In the Name of Science*, p 200f.

28   Nieburg, *In the Name of Science*, p 45. Armacost, *Politics of Weapons*, p 55. Raymond, *Power at the Pentagon*, p 235. *11th Report*, p 74.

29   *Time*, Mar 4, April 1, 1957. *Life*, Apr 29, 1957. Nieburg, *In the Name of Science*, p 205. Raymond, *Power at the Pentagon*, p 237. *11th Report*, p 76.

30   *Time*, Jan 30, 1956 (Schriever); Apr 29, 1957 (electronics industry). Nieburg, *In the Name of Science*, p 200. *11th Report*, p 81.

31   *11th Report*, p 54 (Schriever statement). Nieburg, *In the Name of Science*, p 200f. Armacost, *Politics of Weapons*, p 157. Galbraith, *How to Control the Military*, p 20.

32   *Business Week*, Jan 15, 1955, p 66 (military share of electronics market).

33   *Business Week*, Dec 28, 1957. *Time*, Apr 29, 1957. Nieburg, *In the Name of Science*, p 200. Mollenhoff, p 213. *11th Report*, p 81 (Ramo cited from *Missiles Program*: Hearings before House Committee on Government Operations, 86th Congress, 1st session, (Washington; Government Printing Office, 1959), p 204. Morton J. Peck and Frederic M. Scherer, *The Weapons Acquisition Process*, (Boston; Harvard Business School, 1962), p 409.

34   *11th Report*, p 81 (George, Doolittle statements), p 93 (Schriever statement). *Business Week*, Jan 15, 1955, p 66 (George). *Business Week*, Jun 4, 1960 (Doolittle). Galbraith, *How to Control the Military*, p 24. Nieburg, *In the Name of Science*, p 205. Interview H.L. Nieburg, Aug 25, 1971.

35   *11th Report*, p 57, 93, 97. Nieburg, *In the Name of Science*, p 214.

36   *Sole-Source Procurement*, Pts. I, II, May-June 1961, Hearing before subcommittee for Special Investigations, House Armed Services Committee, 87th Congress, I, p 443, cited by Nieburg, *In the Name of Science*, p 213.

37   Armacost, *Politics of Weapons*, p 162. Peck and Scherer, *Weapons Acquisition*, pp 355, 408. *Business Week*, Jun 4, 1960. *Time*, Apr 29, 1957. Nieburg, *In the Name of Science*, p 209. Subcommittee for Special Investigations, (Aug 2, 1965), House Armed Services Committee, 89th Congress, 1st session, p 39, cited by Mollenhoff, p 214.

38   Janeway, *Economics of Crisis*, p 240.

Nieburg, *In the Name of Science*, p 45f.

39 *Business Week*, June 8, Oct 5, 19, 26, 1957. Janeway, *Economics of Crisis*, p 246. Nieburg, *In the Name of Science*, p 184ff. Eisenhower, *Memoirs*, II, p 215. Sherman Adams, *Inside Report*, pp 399, 411. Herbert Stein, *Fiscal Revolution*, pp. 318, 332.

40 *Business Week*, Oct 26, 1957 ("near panicky," layoff figures). Janeway, *Economics of Crisis*, p 254. Evans and Novak, *Lyndon B. Johnson*, p 166f. Nieburg, *In the Name of Science*, p 45.

41 *The New York Times*, Mar 30, 1958. Eisenhower, *Memoirs*, II, p 222. Raymond, *Power at the Pentagon*, p 224. Evans and Novak, *Lyndon B. Johnson*, p 194.

42 Nieburg, *In the Name of Science*, p 47f. Armacost, *Politics of Weapons*, p 238. Lapp, *Weapons Culture*, p 44. Donovan, *Militarism*, p 48. Duscha, *Men, Money and Politics*, p 177. Raymond, *Power at the Pentagon*, p 224. Melman, *Pentagon Capitalism*, p 75.

43 Nieburg, *In the Name of Science*, pp 211, 48 (ARPA's 80% Air Force work). *Investigations of Government Organization for Space Activities.* Hearings before Senate Committee on Aeronautics and Space Science, 86th Congress, 1st session, (Washington; Government Printing Office, 1959), p 413. Armacost, *Politics of Weapons*, p 238ff. Medaris, *Countdown*, p 257.

44 James McG. Burns, *John Kennedy, a Political Profile*, (New York; Harcourt, 1961), p 48ff. Schlesinger, *Thousand Days*, p 114. Sorensen, *Kennedy*, p 16.

45 Sorensen, *Kennedy*, p 240 (Kennedy), Schlesinger, *Thousand Days*, p 110f. Burns, *John Kennedy*, p vii ff.

46 *Congressional Quarterly Almanac 1960*, (Washington; Congressional Quarterly Service, 1961), p 64 (DLF figures). Schlesinger, *Thousand Days*, p 605 (Peace Corps), 106 (Alianza), 592 (DLF). O'Neill, *Coming Apart*, (Chicago; Quadrangle, 1961), p 416 (Alianza figures).

47 Sorensen, *Kennedy*, p 240–8 (Kennedy).

48 Richard Ward, "Automation and Unemployment," *New University Thought*, Vol 2, No 2 (Spring, 1962), p 43.

49 Shonfeld, *Modern Capitalism*, p 14, 66. Herbert Stein, *Fiscal Revolution*, p 351.

50 Schlesinger, *Thousand Days*, pp 118, 628. Sorensen, *Kennedy*, p 211f. Theodore Sorensen, *Decision-making in the White House*, (New York; Columbia University Press, 1963), p 44ff. *Public Papers of the Presidents, John F. Kennedy, 1961*, (Washington; Government Printing Offie 1962), p 23 (message to Congress). Mooney, p 351. *Congressional Quarterly Almanac 1960*, p 38.

51 Schlesinger, *Thousand Days*, p 307–11 (Kennedy statements). O'Neill, *Coming Apart*, p 31.

52 Schlesinger, *Thousand Days*, p 312. O'Neill, *Coming Apart*, p 30, Raymond, *Power at the Pentagon*, p 282. Borklund, *Men of the Pentagon*, p 206.

53 Schlesinger, *Thousand Days*, p 313–4 (McNamara, operations research).

54 Schlesinger, *Thousand Days*, p 315 (whiz kids). Raymond, *Power at the Pentagon*, p 288. Borklund, *Men of the Pentagon*, p 206.

55 Schlesinger, *Thousand Days*, p 315 ("usable power"). *Congressial Quarterly 1960*, p 39 (Bay of Pigs). Raymond Carr in Evan Luard, ed. *The Cold War: a reappraisal*, (New York; Praeger, 1964), p 232. Hilsman, *To Move a Nation*, p 285. Raymond, *Power at the Pentagon*, p 285. Schlesinger, *Thousand Days*, p 233ff. Elie Abel, *The Missile Crisis*, (New York; Bantam paperback, 1966), p 10.

56 Patrick Anderson, *The President's Men*, (Garden City; Doubleday, 1968), p 215. *Congressional Quarterly Almanac, 1960*, p 68. Hilsman, *To Move a Nation*, p 30f. Nieburg, *In the Name of Science*, pp 51, 159, 353. NASA reported spending $26.657 billion for the U.S. space program by 1972 (*The New York Times*, Dec 12, 1972).

57 In 1969 Baker was sentenced to five

years' imprisonment for fraudulently obtaining for a company he organized a contract to place vending machines in plants operated by the North American Aviation Cop., a leading defense contractor. *The New York Times,* Jan 30 and April 8, 1967, July 16, 1969.

58 Evans and Novak, *Lyndon B. Johnson, the Exercise of Power,* p 318. Nieburg, *In the Name of Science,* p 353. The Apollo program accounted for one-fourth of total U.S. research and development outlays Ralph Lapp, *The New Priesthood,* (New York; Harper, 1965), p 164.

59 Melman, *Pentagon Capitalism,* p 75 (Brown statement, 3-war strategy). Cf. Nieburg, *In the Name of Science,* p. 353.

60 Schlesinger, *Thousand Days,* p 316f. Robin Moore, *The Green Berets,* (New York, Crown, 1965), p 5. *Congressional Quarterly Almanac, 1960,* p 14.

61 Lapp, *The Weapons Culture,* p 20 (overkill). Schlesinger, *Thousand Days,* p 318, 348. O'Neill, *Coming Apart,* p 31. *Congressional Quarterly Almanac 1964,* p 64.

62 *The New York Times,* Jun 4 and 5, 1961 (Vienna). Schlesinger, *Thousand Days,* p 358f. *Congressional Quarterly Almanac 1960,* p 39. Ulam, *Expansion and Coexistence,* p 653. Tatu, *Power in the Kremlin,* p 170. Halle, *Cold War as History,* p 395.

63 *The New York Times,* July 26, 1961 (Kennedy speech). *The New York Times Magazine,* Nov 15, 1964. (Reston statement). O'Neill, *Coming Apart,* p 44–5.

64 Schlesinger, *Thousand Days,* p 358f.

65 Sorensen, *Kennedy,* p 543. Wolfe, *Soviet Power in Europe,* p 94. *Congressional Quarterly Almanac 1960,* p. 64. Tatu, *Power in the Kremlin,* p 171. *Aerospace Facts and Figures, 1964,* p 77, 81.

66 *Congressional Quarterly Almanac 1960,* p 64. Ulam, *Expansion and Coexistence,* p 654. Wolfe, *Soviet Power in Europe,* p 95. Edward Weintal and Charles Bartlett, *Facing the Brink,* (New York; Scribner, 1967), p 211.

67 Raymond, *Power at the Pentagon,* p 294. Nieburg, *In the Name of Science,* pp 54, 352. O'Neill, *Coming Apart,* p 33. *11th Report,* p 64. Peck and Scherer, *Weapons Acquisition,* p 47. Melman, *Pentagon Capitalism,* p 35ff. Duscha, *Men, Money and Politics,* p 70ff. Ben B. Seligman, *Business and Businessmen in American History,* (New York, Dial, 1971), p 359.

68 William J. Coughlin, "Alice in McNamaraland", *Missiles and Rockets,* August 3, 1964, p 46 cited by Nieburg, *In the Name of Science,* p 356. O'Neill, *Coming Apart,* p 34. J.W. Fulbright, "In Thrall to Fear," *The New Yorker,* Jan 8 1972, p 41.

69 "Scientists Report from Moscow," *War-Peace Report,* April 1961. Jerome Wiesner, *Where Science and Politics Meet,* (New York; McGraw, 1965), p 4, 169. Staff analysis, *The Pugwash Conferences,* Senate Committee on the Judiciary, Subcommittee to Investigate Administration of Internal Security Act and other internal security laws, 87th Congress, 1st session, (Washington, Government Printing Office, 1961), p 33–35, p 90. Nieburg, *In the Name of Science,* pp 155, 168.

70 Arnold Horelick and Myron Rush, "The Cuban Missile Crisis, an analysis of Soviet Behavior and Calculations," *World Politics,* April 1964. A. and R. Wohlstetter, "Controlling the Risks," *Foreign Affairs,* July 1965. Henry M. Pachter, *Collision Course,* (New York; Praeger, 1963), p 27. Graham T. Allison, "Conceptual Models and the Cuban Missile Crisis: rational policy, organization, progress and bureaucratic politics," n.d. p 11f. mimeo (cf. Graham Allison, *Essence of Decision: Explaining the Cuban Missile Crisis,* (Boston; Little Brown, 1971), passim.) Ulam, *Expansion and Coexistence,* p 654. Wolfe, *Soviet Power in Europe,* p. 94–5. Richard Lowenthal, *World Communism,* p 203f.

Philip Windsor "Berlin," in Evan Luard, ed. *The Cold War: A Reappraisal,* p. 136. Garthoff, *Soviet Military Policy,* p. 115. Smith, *Defense of Berlin,* p 235.

71 Horelick and Rush, "Cuban Missile Crisis," p 139. Sorensen, *Kennedy*, p 667. Ulam, *Expansion and Coexistence*, p 665.

72 Ulam, *Expansion and Coexistence*, p 665–6. Griffith, *Sino-Soviet Rift*, p. 351. Wolfe, *Soviet Power in Europe*, p 97.

73 Ulam, *Expansion and Coexistence*, p 650. Tatu, *Power in the Kremlin*, p 234. Hilsman, *To Move a Nation*, p 165f. *Congressional Quarterly Almanac 1960*, p 68f. Horelick and Rush, "Cuban Missile Crisis," p 142 f.

74 Tass, Sept 2, 1962 cited in Pachter, *Collision Course*, p 173. Tatu, *Power in the Kremlin*, p 240. Ulam, *Expansion and Co-existence*, p 667.

75 Hilsman, *To Move a Nation*, p 169. *Interim Report on Cuban Military Buildup*, Senate Committee on Armed Services, Preparedness investigation subcommittee 88th Congress, 1st session, 1963, p 2, 48. Sorensen, *Kennedy*, p 670 (Kennedy). Pachter, *Collision Course*, p 176.

76 *Cuban Military Buildup*, p. 6ff. Hilsman, *To Move a Nation*, p 190f. Allison (mimeo), p 47f. Abel, *Missile Crisis*, pp 17, 32. Sorensen, *Kennedy* p 672.

77 Abel, *Missile Crisis*, pp 32, 36, 79–80, (Sweeny) 84–5. Allison mimeo, p 50f. Neustadt, *Presidential Power*, p 203. Sorensen, *Kennedy*, pp 675 (Stevenson) 695, 686, 680, 692. Schlesinger *Thousand Days*, p 806ff. (Robert Kennedy). Robert Kennedy, *Thirteen Days*, (New York; Norton, 1969), p 4. Hilsman, *To Move a Nation*, p 170. Testimony of John Hughes, CIA, to subcommittee, House Committee on Appropriations, 88th Congress, 1st session, 1963, Part 1, p 7 cited in Horelick and Rush, "Cuban Missile Crisis," p 187.

78 *Dept of State Bulletin*, XLVII, 1220 (Nov 12, 1962) (Kennedy quarantine speech). David L. Larson, *Cuban Crisis of 1962, selected documents*, (Boston; Houghton, 1963), p 41, p 64 (O.A.S. resolution). Ulam, *Expansion*

and *Coexistence*, p 673. Tatu, *Power in the Kremlin*, p. 262. Hilsman, *To Move a Nation*, p 211. Abel, *Missile Crisis*, pp 96, 114. Sorensen, *Kennedy*, p 704. Schlesinger, *Thousand Days*, pp 809, 817. Robert Kennedy, *Thirteen Days*, p 65. Talbot, ed., *Khrushchev Remembers*, p 498 (Robert Kennedy—Menshikov).

79 Abel, *Missile Crisis*, pp 134 (Rusk), 137, 142, 152, 156, 158 (Khrushchev letter), 167. *The New York Times*, Oct 27, 1962. Hilsman, *To Move a Nation*, p 220. Schlesinger, *Thousand Days*, p 821 (Harriman) Raymond, *Power at the Pentagon*, p 286. Sorensen, *Kennedy*, pp 698, 712.

80 *Dept of State Bulletin*, XXVII, 1220, (Nov 12 1962), p 743 (Kennedy reply to Khrushchev). Larson, *Cuban Crisis*, p 159. Abel, *Missile Crisis*, p 176 (Robert Kennedy suggestion).

81 Larson, *Cuban Crisis*, p. 161.

82 *Dept of State Bulletin*, XLVII, 1220, (Nov 12 1962), p 745 (Kennedy reply). Larson, *Cuban Crisis*, p 165. Ulam, *Expansion and Coexistence*, p 675 (Zhukov, Castro). Abel, *Missile Crisis*, pp 95 (Macmillan), p 183 (Kennedy's "lighter step" noted by Don Wilson). Janos Radvanyi, *Hungary and the Superpowers*, (Stanford; Hoover Institute Press, 1972), p 138.

83 Weintal and Bartlett, *Facing the Brink*, p 54. Ulam, *Expansion and Coexistence*, p 676ff. Tatu, *Power in the Kremlin*, p 273.

84 Ulam, *Expansion and Coexistence*, p 677. Halle, *Cold War as History*, p 409f. Paul Seabury, *Rise and Decline of the Cold War*, (New York; Basic Books, 1967), p 126.

85 Weintal and Bartlett, *Facing the Brink*, p 66. *Congressional Quarterly Almanac, 1960*, p 90ff. *The New York Times*, Sept 12, 1971. Ulam, *Expansion and Coexistence*, p 676. O'Neill, *Coming Apart* p 72. *The Listener*, Oct 23, 1971 (Acheson-Kennedy).

86 *Expansion and Coexistence*, p 607, 676ff. O'Neill, *Coming Apart*, pp 31, 72, 80. Fulbright, p 45.

CHAPTER 13.

1 William Leuchtenburg, "Kennedy and the End of the Postwar World," in Aide Donald, ed. *John F. Kennedy and the New Frontier,* (New York; Hill and Wang, 1966), p. 133f. D.M. White and R. H. Abel, *The Funnies,* (New York; The Free Press, 1963), pp. 100, 122, 128, 281.

2 *The New York Times,* Jan 11, 28, Feb 25, Apr 21, 23, May 5, June 3, 16, Sept 8, 9, 10, Dec 19, 1960; Apr 13, 16, June 28, July 6, Aug 18, Oct 17, Nov 5, 1961; Feb 8, Mar 16, Jun 12, 13, 23, July 10, 13, Aug 10, 11, 12, 16, 24, Oct 12, 1962 (Kefauver drug inquiry). *New Republic,* Oct 14, 1957. *Milwaukee Journal,* Aug 29, 1972 (New Jersey survey). *Congressional Quarterly Almanac, 1961,* (Washington; Congressional Quarterly Service, 1961), p 290–292. Richard Harris, *The Real Voice,* (New York; Macmillan, 1964), passim. Joseph B. Gorman, *Kefauver, a political biography,* (New York; Oxford, 1971), p 354ff.

3 Jeremy Bernstein, "The Analytical Engine," *The New Yorker,* Oct 19, 1963, p 58f. and Oct 26, 1964, p 54f. "Boundless Age of the Computer," *Fortune,* Mar, Apr, June, Aug, Oct, 1964. "Electronic Business," *Fortune,* Oct 1957, p 138f. "Computer Age," *Business Week,* Apr 7, 1956, p 73ff. "Computers Start to Run the Plants," *Business Week,* Nov 5, 1960 p 50f. "Challenge of Automation," *Newsweek,* Jan 25, 1965, p 73ff. "Management by Computer," *Time,* Dec 21, 1962, p 67. R.R. Williamson, "Computer Key to Space Achievement," *Missiles and Rockets,* Feb 27, 1961, p 24ff. Richard Ward, "Automation and Unemployment," *New University Thought,* Vol 2, No. 2 (winter, 1962), p 30ff. Joseph Becker and Robert M. Hayes, *Information Storage and Retrieval,* (New York; Wiley, 1963), p 22. Fred Gruenberger, *Expanding Uses of Computers,* (Englewood Cliffs; Prentice-Hall, 1971), p 117. Donald G. Fink, *Computers and the Human Mind,* (Garden City; Anchor paperback, 1966), p 299. Automation note: quick-copying machines eased office routines and publishing methods. By 1970 15 million Xerox copies a year were being made at a single university (Communication from Michael Mannheim, Xerox Corp, Jun 1973

4 *New York Review of Books,* Jun 1, 1972, p 27–8. Arnold Toynbee, "Patterns and Predictions," *American Way,* Vol 5, No 8 (August 1972), p 19. Max Kaplan, *Leisure in America, a social inquiry,* (New York; Wiley, 1960), p 5. Hortense Powdermaker, *Hollywood, the Dream Factory,* (Boston; Little Brown, 1951), p 307, 325. Herbert Warren Wind, *Story of American Golf,* (New York; Simon and Schuster, 1956), p 524. "Tycoon on the Tee," *Dun's Review,* March 1964, p 39. Ernest Havemann, "Arnie's Business," *Sports Illustrated,* June 3, 1963, p 22–5. Roy Terrell, "Biggest Golf Hustler of them all," *Sports Illustrated,* Nov 12, 1962, p 28–32. "Chief," *Newsweek,* Apr 27, 1964, p 72. *The New Yorker,* May 16, 1964, p 178ff. Interviews with Gaquin, Bud Harvey, Joe Schedemann, Mark McCormick, Doc Giffin, March 1972 (Cold War sponsors). John Updike in *The New Yorker,* July 29, 1972, p 76. "Age of Willie Mays," *The Saturday Review,* May 8, 1971. Robert Lowell in *Life Studies,* (New York; Farrar Straus, 1967), p 85. *The New York Times,* Sept 29, 1969, p 95 (Jack Gould re Ed Sullivan). *The New York Times,* Mar 15, 1971, p. 95. Michael David Harris, *Always on Sunday,* (New York; Meredith, 1968), p 93.

5 *The New York Times,* Apr 14, 1972 (Reston). Gay Talese, "Grey Flannel Men at Bat," *The New York Times Magazine,* Mar 30, 1958.

6 Joseph Heller, *Catch-22,* (New York; Simon and Schuster, 1961), passim.

7 *The New York Times,* May 20, 21, 1953 (St. George, Utah); Los Angeles *Times,* Mar 17, May 20, 21, 1953. C.E. Zoppo, "The Test Ban," unpub-

lished Ph D dissertation, Columbia University, 1963, p 37ff. Harold K. Jacobson and Eric Stein, *Diplomats, Scientists, Politicians: the U.S. and the Nuclear Test Ban Negotiations*, (Ann Arbor; University of Michigan Press, 1966), p 9–12. Earl H. Voss, *Nuclear Ambush, the Test-Ban Trap*, (Chicago, Regnery, 1963), p 35. Arthur H. Dean, *Test Ban and Disarmament*, (New York, Harper/Council on Foreign Relations, 1966), p 91, 96–7. H. Peter Metzger, *The Atomic Establishment*, (New York; Simon and Schuster, 1972), p 104. Richard S. Lewis, *Nuclear Power Rebellion*, (New York; Viking, 1972), p 22. *Forrestal Diaries*, p 133. Truman, *Memoirs*, II, p 312. Paul Seabury, *Power, Freedom, and Diplomacy*, (New York; Random, 1963), p 160. Evan Luard, *Peace and Opinion*, (London; Oxford, 1962), p 22.

8 *The New York Times*, Mar 2, 18, 24, 25, 1954 (*Fortunate Dragon*); Apr 2, 1954 (Nehru); Apr 25, 1955 (Bandung); Apr 1, 1956 (Khruschev). C.J.V. Murphy, "Nuclear Inspection, a Near Miss," *Fortune*, Mar 1959, p 122f. C.J.V. Murphy, "The Case for Resuming Tests," *Fortune*, April 1960, p 148ff. Chalmers Roberts, "Hopes and Fears of an Atomic Test Ban," *The Reporter*, Apr 28, 1960, p 20. Thomas E. Murray, *Nuclear Power for War and Peace*, (Cleveland; World, 1960), p 86 (clean bomb). Voss, *Nuclear Ambush*, pp 41, 43. Coral Bell, *Survey 1954*, (London, Oxford, 1957), p 254ff.

9 Ralph Lapp, *The Weapons Culture*, (New York; Norton, 1968), p 35. Raymond, *Power at the Pentagon*, p 270. Dean, *Test Ban and Disarmament*, p 52. Ulam, *Expansion and Coexistence*, p 628f. Crankshaw, *Khrushchev*, p 235f. Marshall Shulman, *Beyond the Cold War*, (New Haven, Yale, 1966), p 64f. Herbert Schiller and Joseph D. Phillips, ed. *Super State*, (Urbana, University of Illinois Press, 1970), p 120 (Pauling protests). Jacobson and Stein, *Diplomats, Scientists* p 11.

10 Zagoria, *Sino-Soviet Conflict*, p 42. Griffith, *Sino-Soviet Rift*, p 164, p 421 (Khrushchev text). John Gittings, *Survey of the Sino-Soviet Dispute*, (London; Oxford, 1968), p 21. Alan Whiting, "A brief History," in C.J. Zablocki, ed, *Sino-Soviet Rivalry*, (New York; Praeger, 1966), p 9. Morton Halperin and Dwight H. Perkins, *Communist China and Arms Control*, (Cambridge, Harvard University Press, 1966) p 6, 19, 65. L.C. Bloomfield, W.C. Clemens Jr., and Franklyn Griffiths, *Khrushchev and the Arms Race*, (Cambridge; MIT Press, 1966), p 88f, 124f.

11 Zoppo, p 37f (Gallup poll). Bloomfield et al., *Khrushchev and the Arms Race*, p 90, 93. Ulam, *Expansion and Coexistence*, p 633, 666, 673, 677. Tatu, *Power in the Kremlin*, pp 59f, 303. Schlesinger, *Thousand Days*, p 844, 895. Crankshaw, *Khrushchev*, p 277. Hilsman, *To Move a Nation*, p 343. H.A. Dinerstein, *War and the Soviet Union*, p. xv. Garthoff, *Soviet Military Strategy*, p. ix. Whiting, "Brief History", p 9ff. Griffith, *Sino-Soviet Rift* p 351. Marshall Shulman, "Recent Soviet Foreign Policy, some patterns in retrospect," *Journal of International Affairs*, XXII, 1, p 32. *Test Ban Negotiations and Disarmament*, Hearings before Senate Committee on Foreign Relations, 88th Congress, 1st session, (Mar 11, 1963), (Washington, Government Printing Office, 1963), p 13 ($100 million for underground testing).

12 Ulam, *Expansion and Coexistence*, p 677.*New York Times*, Sep 10, 1973.

13 Schlesinger, *Thousand Days*, p 896. Tatu, *Power in the Kremlin*, p 353. Lukacs, *New History of the Cold War*, p 32. Jacobson and Stein, *Diplomats, Scientists* p 425.

14 Lowenthal, *World Communism*, p vi. Bloomfield et al. p 125. Whiting, "Brief History," p 9f. Ulam, *Expansion and Coexistence*, p 679. Tatu, *Power in the Kremlin*, pp 312, 241, 353. Arthur Hertzog, *War-Peace Establishment*, p 205.

15 *The New York Times*, Jun 11, 1963. Schlesinger, *Thousand Days*, p 902.

16 *The New York Times*, Jun 19, July 5, 6, 1963; June 30, p 6 (Chinese letter

text). *Izvestia*, July 5 1963 (Soviet Foreign Ministry statement) cited in Griffith, *Sino-Soviet Rift*, p 148. Ulam, *Expansion and Coexistence*, p 679.

17 *The New York Times*, July 14, 1963 (Russian reply text). Cf. Griffith, *Sino-Soviet Rift*, pp 156, 289. Tatu, *Power in the Kremlin*, p 353. Schlesinger, *Thousand Days*, p 902.

18 Jacobson and Stein, *Diplomats, Scientists*, p 454. Schlesinger, *Thousand Days*, p 908. Ulam, *Expansion and Coexistence*, p 680.

19 Schlesinger, *Thousand Days*, p 909.

20 *The New York Times*, Aug 15, 21, 22, 23, 21, 1963 (reactions to treaty). *Nuclear Test Ban Treaty*, Hearings before Senate Committee on Foreign Relations, (Aug 12–17, 1963), 88th Congress, 1st session, (Washington; Government Printing Office), p 275 (Taylor). Richard Rovere in *The New Yorker*, Oct 5, 1963, p 154–5 (Taylor). Richard Rovere in *The New Yorker*, Oct 5, 1963, p 154–5. Jacobson and Stein, *Diplomats, Scientists*, p 458f. Metzger, *Atomic Establishment*, p 68.

21 Hearings, p 11, 22, 73ff (Rusk, Humphrey, Aitken re neutron bomb). *Public Papers of the Presidents, John F. Kennedy, 1963*, (Washington, Government Printing Office, 1964), p 353 (Bob Hope).

22 Hearings, p 69 (Lausche). Schlesinger, *Thousand Days*, p 911.

23 "This is Betrayal of Soviet People," *People's Daily*, Aug 3, 1963 cited in Griffith, *Sino-Soviet Rift*, p 162, 163. Ulam, *Expansion and Coexistence*, p 684. Jacobson and Stein, *Diplomats, Scientists*, p 500.

24 Griffith, *Sino Soviet Rift*, p 371 ("Insolent enough to say", Sept 1, 1963). Ulam, *Expansion and Coexistence*, p 681

25 Lowenthal, *World Communism*, p viii. Bloomfield et al, *Khrushchev and the Arms Race*, p 123. Halperin and Perkins, *Communist China and Arms Control*, p 6f. Whiting, "Brief History", p 9f. Ulam, *Expansion and Coexistence*, p 682. Griffith, *Sino-Soviet Rift* p 165.

26 Griffith, *Sino-Soviet Rift*, p 388 (Ili),

p 426 (5000 violations). Ulam, *Expansion and Coexistence*, p 684.

27 Griffith, *Sino-Soviet Rift*, p 164, 289 (racism). Ulam, *Expansion and Coexistence*, p 683.

28 Gittings, *Survey of the Sino-Soviet Dispute* p 25. Ulam, *Expansion and Coexistence*, p 682. Whiting, "Brief History," p 9f. Bloomfield et al, *Khrushchev and the Arms Race*, p 88. Halperin and Perkins, *Communist China and Arms Control*, p 6. Griffith, *Sino-Soviet Rift*, p 171.

29 Shulman, *Beyond the Cold War*, p 34. Ulam, *Expansion and Coexistence*, p 685. Crankshaw, *Khrushchev*, p 284. Tatu, *Power in the Kremlin*, p 354.

30 *The New York Times*, June 20, 1963; Oct 17, 1963 (Assembly resolution). Khruschev at Plenum of Central Committee, Communist Party of the Soviet Union, Jun 18–21, 1963 (Moscow, 1964), p 266 cited in Ulam, *Expansion and Coexistence*, p 685.

31 *Statistical Abstract 1964*, (Washington; Government Printing Office, 1965), p 5 (U.S. population growth). Wattenberg, *This USA*, p 70 (decline in cities population). Gelfand, "A Nation of Cities," p 412.

32 *The New York Times*, Mar 27, 1962 (Tennessee apportionment); Feb 18, Mar 3, 1964 (One-man, one-vote). *Politics in America, 1945–66*, (Washington; Congressional Quarterly Service, 1967), p 77. Walter Lippmann, "One Man, One Vote Rule," *Newsweek*, May 19, 1965. J.E. Clayton, "Reapportionment Riddle," *The Reporter*, Feb 27, 1964. A.E. Hacker, "One Man, One Vote, Yes or No?" *The New York Times magazine*, Nov 8, 1964. J.N. Miller, "Our Horse and Buggy State Legislatures," *Readers Digest*, May 1965, p 49ff. D.H. Bieble, "Legislatures, the 100-year Lag," *Nation*, Nov 7, 1966, p 475f. Gelfand, "A Nation of Cities," p 422. Gene Graham, *One Man, One Vote*, (Boston; Atlantic/Little Brown, 1972), p 258.

33 *The New York Times*, Jan 13, March 27, Apr 2–12, 1965 (Elementary and Secondary Education Act). *Americana Annual 1966*, (New York; Grolier,

1967), p 247f. Keppel, *Necessary Revolution,* p 192.

34 *The New York Times,* Jan 5, July 22, 31, August 2, 1965 (Medicare). Gelfand, "A Nation of Cities" p 355f. "What the Doctor Ordered," *Time,* Aug 26, 1966, p 13. "Will it Work?" *Time,* June 10, 1966, p 33–4. O'Neill, *Coming Apart,* p 129.

35 *The New York Times,* Sept 10, 1965. Sargent Shriver, "Poverty," *Americana Annual 1965,* P 579ff. Sargent Shriver, "The War on Poverty is a Movement of Conscience," in 90th Congress, House Committee on Education and Labor, Hearings, Subcommittee on War on Poverty Program, April 1965, (Washington; Government Printing Office, 1965), pp 16f, 23f. Michael Harrington, "The Facts Are In," *Nation,* Jun 8, 1964. Douglass Cater, "Politics of Poverty," *The Reporter,* Feb 13, 1964, p 18–20. J.K. Galbraith, "Let Us Begin," *Harpers,* Mar 1964, p 16f. B. and P.C. Sexton, *Blue Collars and Hard Hats,* (New York; Random, 1971), p 142.

36 *The New York Times,* Oct 3, Nov 11, 15, 21, Dec 3, 4, 5, 8, 9, 10, 1964 (Berkeley riots). *The New York Times,* June 21, Aug 5, 20, 1964 (Freedom Summer). Sally Belfrage, *Freedom Summer,* (New York; Viking, 1965), p 9, 12, 87. Paul and Geoffrey Cowan, "Three Letters Home from Mississippi," in *Smiling Through the Apocalypse, Esquire's History of the Sixties,* (New York; McCall, 1970), p 583ff. Jack Newfield, *A Prophetic Minority,* (New York; Signet paperback, 1966), p 83f. (SDS). Mills cited in O'Neill, *Coming Apart,* p 276. Herbert Gans, "Majority Rule," *The New York Times Magazine,* Aug 3, 1969.

37 *The New York Times,* Aug 12, 13, 15, 1965 (Watts); July 20, 1966 (Hough); July 13, 14, 15, 18, 19, 1967 (Newark); July 24, 25, 26, 27, 28, 29, 1967 (Detroit); April 4, 5, 6, 7, 11, 1968 (Washington). U.S. Commission on Civil Rights, "Hearings, February 1965 regarding Mississippi Violence," in M.E. Gettleman and D. Mermelstein, *Great Society Reader,* (New York; Random, 1967), p 30f. Richard Hofstadter, "The Future of American Violence, *Harpers,* April 1970, p 47f.

38 Neil Sheehan et al, *The Pentagon Papers;* p. 113 (16, 732 men in Vietnam in Oct 1963). Lyndon B. Johnson, *The Vantage Point,* (New York; Holt, 1971), p. 232. Tom Wicker, *JFK and LBJ,* (New York; Morrow, 1968), p 244.

Index

A-bomb, 9, 45, 60, 63, 111, 126, 139, 145, 191, 214, 247, 250, 259, 336, 343, 423, 435, 437, 492, 511
American, 15, 18, 32–33, 44, 96, 97, 117, 127, 128, 173, 178, 187, 259, 471, 492, 508, 509, 514
Russian, 35, 163, 193, 209, 227, 337, 472, 494, 497, 521. *See also* U.S.S.R. first detected, 140
tactical, 193, 224, 230, 338, 449
Abel, Elie, 6, 529
Abilene, Kansas, 212, 215, 219, 265
Abakumov, Viktor S., 280
Abstract expressionism
New York school, 271–274
Acheson, Dean G., 16, 38, 53, 67, 68, 71, 112, 114, 135, 149, 162, 164, 168, 173–176, 180, 200, 209, 220, 230, 231, 337, 368, 464, 470, 497, 502, 514, 515
on Berlin blockade, 172
on China, Communist victory in, 148–150
Cleveland, Miss. speech, 68
on containment as military policy, 209
on Cuban missile crisis, 459
on Greece, Communist threat in, 38
on H-bomb program, 141
on Hiss, Alger, 155
on Marshall, George C., 37
National Press Club speech, 168
on school desegregation case, 296
on Soviets, 209
on Soviet A-bomb, 140
on Truman in retirement, 16
on U.S. foreign policy, 180
on Vandenberg, Arthur, 73
Adams, John G., 186
Adams, John Quincy, 15
Adams, Richard, 430
Adams, Sherman, 214, 218, 340, 394–395, 523
Adenauer, Konrad, 50
Adler, Julius Ochs, 121
Administered prices, 85, 235, 542
Adonis, Joe, 199
Advanced Research Projects Agency, 441, 442
Aerospace Corp., 440, 442
Aerospace Industries Association, 428
Africa, 8, 19, 22, 38, 230, 293, 294, 302, 306, 312, 313, 314, 325, 328–332, 366, 419, 472, 504, 525
and black Americans, 328–334
Agar, Herbert S., 516
Agriculture:
American, 157, 468, 487
mechanization of, 77–79, 267, 468, 499
Russian, 276–279
Agribusiness, 79
Agricultural Adjustment Administration, 133
Air Force Association, 428, 429

Airliners *See* jetliners
Alabama, 301, 434
  universities, 310–311, 333
Alaska, 421
Albania, 106
Alexander, Herbert E., 6, 522
Algeria, 314, 317, 319, 332
Ali, Muhammad (Cassius Clay), 329
Allen, George, 212, 238
Allen, R. L., 525
Alliance for Progress, 443
Allied Control Council (Germany), 107, 119
Allis-Chalmers Co., 393
Allison, Graham, 529
Almond, Gabriel A., 42–43
Alpenfels, Ethel, 215
Alperovitz, Gar, 514
Alsop, Joseph, 229
Alsop, Stewart, 105
Aluminum, 87, 211, 501
America, 119
American Association of State Highway Officials,
  256
American Automobile Association, 256
American Broadcasting Co., 461
American Committee for Cultural Freedom, 57,
  519
American Federation of Labor, 80, 82, 90, 91,
  94, 396, 499
American Federation of Labor-Congress of In-
  dustrial Organizations, 85, 90–95
American Gas Association, 391
American Legion, 57, 119, 125, 214, 428
American Liberation Center, 246
American Mercury, 184
American way of life, 57, 61, 120, 138, 142, 151,
  214, 248, 251, 256, 344, 353, 466, 497, 503
Americans for Democratic Action, 49
Amory, Cleveland, 396
Amory, Robert, Jr., 396
Amsterdam News, 331
Anderson, Arnold, 212
Anderson, Clinton P., 448
Anderson, Admiral George W., 460
Anderson, Jack (and May, Ronald), 521
Anderson, General Orville, 161
Anderson, Robert B., 441
Anderson, Major Rudolf Jr., 456, 461
Andrews, Bert, 133, 520
Antihere, 271
Antipoverty legislation, 487–490
Antitrust, 208, 234, 235, 243, 524
  and electrical manufacturing industry, 392
Apollo (moon) program, 448, 468, 502
Architecture, 257–259, 365, 377–379
Arendt, Hannah, 138, 515
Arizona, 89, 116, 163
Armacost, Michael, 528
Arms race, 5, 193, 226–227, 339, 344, 371, 375,
  405, 426, 431, 464, 468, 472, 482, 483, 501,
  502, 507

and Kennedy, 444, 447–451
and NSC-68, 209–210
Army General Classification Test, 59
Art (*See* Abstract expressionism; Motherwell,
  Robert; Pollock, Jackson; Rosenberg, Har-
  old; Smith, David; Surrealism)
"Asia Firsters," 21, 149, 174, 227, 229
Ashbolt, Alan, 524
Association of the U.S. Army, 428, 429
Aswan dam, 316, 317, 325
Assassinations, 2, 490
Atomic Energy Commission, 139, 140, 183, 193,
  364, 471, 477
Attlee, Clement, 65, 178, 535
Auden, W. H., 271
Austin, Warren, 148
Austria, 236, 353, 466
  peace treaty, 282
Automation, 84, 85, 88–89, 468–469, 602
Automobile, 61, 74, 75, 80, 84, 87, 90, 197, 234,
  260, 262, 382, 423, 436, 468, 469, 523–524
  horsepower, 255
  imported, 422
  invented by Germans, 435
  maiming power, 255
  and split-level houses, 378
  and suburbs, 253–257, 260, 378
  and styling, 254–255
  wide ownership of, 433
Azikiwe, Nnamdi, 330, 331

Bacher, Robert F., 140, 336
Baez, Joan, 489
Baghdad Pact, 313, 314, 324, 325
Baker, Bobby, 448, 598
Baker, Carlos H., 63
Baker, Russell, 264
Balance of payments, 243, 502, 503, 512, 528–
  529
Balance of terror, 282–283, 337, 473
Baldwin, David A., 525
Baldwin, James, 330
Ball, George W., 242
Bandung Conference, 314, 409, 472
Barkley, Alben W., 200
Barnet, Richard J., 528
Barnouw, Erik, 522, 527
Barth, Alan, 520
Baruch, Bernard M., 10, 36, 43
Bases, overseas, 210, 226, 337, 374. *See also* U.S.
  Dept. of Defense
B-29s in Britain, 111
Bay of Pigs invasion, 321, 401, 402, 446–447,
  458, 506
Beal, John Robinson, 523
Beard, Charles A., 205
Beatles, 423, 469
Beaufre, General Andre, 525
Beberman, Max, 354

Beck, Dave, 91–92
Becker, Joseph (and Hayes, Robert M.), 529
Behavioral scientists. *See* Social scientists
Belgium, 103, 114, 421
Bell, Coral, 523, 529
Bell, Daniel, 262, 521, 526, 527
    on business unionism, 94
Bell, Elliott V., 208
Bell Laboratories, 437
Beloff, Max, 522
Ben Gurion, David, 320
Benes, Edouard, 104, 106
Bennett, Admiral Rawson, 340
Benson, Ezra Taft, 523
Bentley, Elizabeth, 131, 520
Bentley, Eric, 521
Benton, Thomas Hart, 272
Beran, Cardinal, 51
Berger, Bennett, 524
Beria, Lavrenti P., 275, 280–282, 284
    on Khrushchev, 276
Berkeley, Calif., 54, 60, 169, 274, 358, 365–367,
    489, 500
Berle, Adolf A., 208
Berlin, 7, 18, 22, 32, 99, 100, 107, 119, 162, 171,
    228, 291, 293, 398, 405, 406, 411, 426, 450,
    454–6, 497
    blockade, 2, 107–115, 168, 170, 506, 515, 520
    East Berlin rising, 228, 398
    postwar status, 103
    Second Berlin crisis, 1958–1962, 114, 405,
        449, 450, 455, 456
    Wall, 451
Bernstein, Barton J., 514, 518, 519
Berman, Jacob, 285
Bernstein, Jeremy, 529
Bessire, John W., 430
Bestor, Arthur, 518, 535
Better Homes and Gardens, 258
Bevin, Ernest, 71, 101, 110
Bidault, Georges, 50, 71
Bikini, 97, 226, 227, 471, 472
Bipartisan foreign policy, 24, 67, 74, 75, 151–
    152, 206, 211, 221, 518
Birmingham riots, 309–310, 312
Bissell, Richard M. Jr., 396, 413
Bizonia, 103
Black, Eugene R., 316
Black, Joe, 294
Black Muslims, 328, 329, 332, 333
Black Panthers, 332
Black Power, 332
Black studies, 332
Blacks, 1, 77–79, 159, 178–179, 252, 267, 293–
    312, 325–334, 379, 423, 504, 509
Blagonravov, A.A., 35, 339
Blaik, Col. Earl H., 196
Blair House, 173, 204
Block, Herbert (Herblock), 156–157
Blood, Robert O., 386, 527
Bloomfield, Lincoln P., 529

Blough, Roger M., 310
    on economic growth, 265
Blue-collar workers, 90–91, 248–249, 262–263
Blunden, Godfrey, 401
Boeing Aircraft Co., 419, 421, 431, 440–441
Boer war, 123
Bohlen, Charles E., 113, 183
Bond, James, 422–423
Bontecou, Eleanor, 520
Boorstin, Daniel J., 522, 527
Borie, Adolph E., 238
Borkenau, Franz, 57, 132
Borklund, Clarence W., 528
Bormann, Martin, 8
Boston, 49, 116, 159, 160, 191, 301, 395, 453
Boulding, Kenneth E., 431
Bourges-Manoury, Maurice, 318
Bourguiba, Habib Ben Ali, 313
Bradley, General Omar C., 140, 180
Brady, Judge Thomas P., 300
Brandeis, Louis D. , 14, 517
Branyan, R. L. (and Larsen, L.A.), 523
Brecht, Bertholt, 98
Breech, Ernest R., 212
Brennan, Margaret, 329
Brewster, Kingman Jr., 362, 524
Brezhnev, Leonid I., 278–279
Bridges, Harry, 160, 218
Bridges, H. Styles, 87, 140, 156, 168, 182, 188,
    214
Brinkmanship, 1, 168, 227, 374
Britain, 9, 10, 17–18, 20, 22, 33, 37–40, 50, 71,
    105, 111, 115, 116, 123, 126, 142, 156, 178,
    204, 221, 223, 226, 239, 240, 242, 272, 326,
    343, 379, 391, 405, 406, 413, 419, 422, 433,
    469, 475, 542
    and B-29 bases, 111
    in European Recovery program, 69, 71
    in Germany, 99–113
    in Greece, 37–39
    and IRBMs, 370, 374–375
    in NATO, 114
    and nuclear disarmament, 376
    in Suez affair, 245, 288, 312–325, 374, 404
    as U.S. ally, 37, 39, 50, 111, 127, 175, 230,
        317, 321, 322
    U.S. 1946 loan to, 33, 38, 96, 517
Brogan, Sir Denis W., 202, 245, 509
Brooks, John, 519, 524
Broun, Heywood, 29
Browder, Earl, 129, 163
Brown, Harold, 448
Brown, Ralph S. Jr., 520
Brown, Walter, 206
Brown v. Board of Education, 296–297, 504
Brownell, Herbert, 300, 302
Bruce, David K.E., 75
Bruce, James, 75
Bruner, Jerome S., 355, 359, 526
Bryan, William Jennings, 179
Brzezinski, Zbygniew, 5, 524, 526, 527

Buck, Pearl S., 19
Buckley, Charles A., 256
Budapest, 18, 247, 286–9, 321, 525
Budenz, Louis F., 26, 520
  on Communist party as conspiracy, 129
Bulganin, Nikolai A., 280–2, 290, 315, 375
Bulgaria, 26, 69, 72, 106
Bullitt, William C., 148
Bullock, Alan, 517
Bundy, McGeorge, 53, 173, 395, 457, 515
Burby, John, 528
Burgess, W. Randolph, 235
Burma, 231, 315, 399, 400
Burns, Arthur F., 236–7
Bush, Vannevar, 336, 343
Business Advisory Council, 246, 398
Business overseas, 74, 238–244, 421, 492, 502.
  See also Multinational corporations
Business Week, 441
Butler, John Marshall, 162–3
Butler, General Smedley D., 243
Byelorussia, 246
Byers, B.B., 238
Byrd, Harry F., 184, 300
Byrnes, James F., 14, 17, 26–28, 31, 36, 100,
    109, 135, 155, 515, 520
  on the draft, 116
  Stuttgart speech, 100–101
  and Truman, 26–27
  on Wallace, 27

California, 78, 89, 131, 162, 163, 169, 268, 296,
    432, 450, 469, 490
  military-industrial complex and, 431
  universities, 59, 169, 294, 361, 365, 437
Cambodia, 231–232, 399–400
Camp David, 411, 414
Camp Doniphan, 13
Campanella, Roy, 294
Campbell, John Franklin, 527
Camus, Albert, 271
Canada, 114, 124, 226, 239, 242, 320, 343
  spy trial, 26, 129, 131
Cape Canaveral (Cape Kennedy), 341–343, 413,
    448
Carmichael, Stokeley, 332–3
Carnegie Corp., 53, 349–50
Carnegie Endowment for International Peace,
    133, 137
Carper, Jean, 520
Carr, Robert K., 520
Carruthersville, Mo., 33, 96, 128
Cartter, Allan M., 526
Case, Francis, 255–6
Case Institute of Technology, 442
Castro, Fidel, 401, 422, 446, 455, 458, 474,
    490
  relations with Khrushchev, 462
Catch-22, 470–1

Catholics, 49–52, 129, 158–60, 162, 216, 379,
    380, 410, 489, 518
  and federal aid to schools, 345, 486
Caudle, T. Lamar, 195
Central Committee of Communist Party,
    U.S.S.R. See U.S.S.R.
Central Intelligence Agency, 53–54, 82, 105,
    117, 183, 187, 246, 413, 415, 447, 504, 525,
    527
  and airlines, 399, 401–402
  and Bay of Pigs, 95, 446
  Cold War role, 395–402
  and Cuban missile crisis, 458–9
Central Treaty Organization (CENTO), 225
Chamberlain, Neville, 19
Chambers, Whittaker, 131–8, 494, 520
  on Communist underground, 132
  on Alger Hiss, 136
Change, engineering of, 138–9, 368
Changjon Reservoir, 177, 180
Chaplin, Charlie, 1, 131
Cheatham, Owen R., 394
Cheit, Earl F., 526
Chennault, General Claire, 399, 402
Chiang Kai-shek, Generalissimo, 141–50, 156,
    164, 168, 174, 214, 246, 399, 479
  "unleashing" of, 227
Chiang Kai-shek, Madame, 142
Chicago, 28, 37, 61, 79, 92, 127, 163, 212, 213,
    259, 327, 328, 329, 377, 420, 458
  school segregation in, 312
  housing segregation in, 327
Chicago Sun, on meeting of Allied armies, 9
Chicago Tribune, 152, 155, 157, 163, 206
Chief State School Officers, 56
Childs, Marquis W., 523
  on Hunt suicide, 189
  on Sputnik, 340
China, 22, 37–39, 67, 100, 109, 139, 141–150,
    154, 162–165, 166, 172, 181, 214, 239, 255,
    329, 494, 497, 514
  Civil war, 27, 141–150
  Communist party, 141–150
    articles opposing Moscow, 479
    Long March, 144
    Mao article opposing Khrushchev, 412
    reply to Russians, 475–476
    split with Moscow, 429, 478–482
  Nationalist, 141–150, 228, 229, 399, 552
  People's Republic of, 149–150, 223, 313, 372,
    401–403, 406, 411, 424, 453, 455, 456,
    473, 476–477, 507, 515
    and CIA, 400
    "Great Leap Forward," 407–408
    and Khrushchev, 411–412
    in Korea, 164, 176–178
    Nixon visit to, 411, 424
    and nuclear weapons, 406, 408, 454, 463,
      475, 479
    recognition of, 173, 308, 316, 476
    and Russia, 106, 150

warns against advance to Yalu, 177
China lobby, 156
China White Paper *(U.S. Relations with China)*, 150, 156, 521
Chinese Eastern railroad, 145
Chou En-lai, 145–150, 164, 176, 223, 408
  meets diplomats expelled by Moscow, 476
  protests CIA overflights, 400
  signs economic pact in Moscow, 408
Christian Century, 119
Christian Herald, 46
Christian realism, 47–48. *See also* Niebuhr, Reinhold.
Chrysler Corp., 233, 255, 394, 433
Churchill, Winston S., 2, 8, 16–25, 33, 37, 65, 66, 73, 97, 99, 107, 200, 204, 223, 230, 231, 275, 277, 513, 515, 517
  on German invasion of Russia, 21
  on H-bomb test results, 226
  Iron Curtain speech, 17–18, 33, 97, 99, 128, 245
  as Kennedy hero, 443
  on 1954 Indochina crisis, 230
  on summit in 1953, 223
  on U.S. and China, 141–142
"Circadian dysrhythmia," 420
City College basketball scandal, 198
Civil Aeronautics Administration, 419
Civil Air Transport Co. (China Air Line), 399
Civil Rights Commission, 303, 333
Civil Rights Act:
  of 1957, 300, 303, 308–309
  of 1964, 486
  of 1965, 487
  of 1966, 312
Civil rights movement, 299, 300, 311, 484, 489, 504
  and Kennedy, 310–311, 444
Civilian Conservation Corps, 278
Civilian Defense (air), 259–260, 348, 450
Clark, Grenville, 121
Clark, Kenneth B., 525
Clark, General Mark W., 66
Clark, Tom C., 129
Clarke, John Henrik, 525
Clay, Henry, 100
Clay, General Lucius D., 66, 100, 107–115, 117–118, 212–213, 520
  on Berlin blockade preliminaries, 107
  and Eisenhower campaign, 212
  and interstate highway plan, 256
  on "possibility of war" in 1948, 105
  on stand at Berlin, 110
Clayton, William, 66, 74, 77, 514, 519
  on European economic crisis, 69
"Clean" bomb, 472–473
Cleaver, Eldridge, 332
Clemenceau, Georges, 65
Cleveland, Grover, 200
Cleveland Plain Dealer, 28
Clifford, Clark, 292

Cline, Ray S., 402
Clubb, Oliver Edmund, 521, 528
Coal, 28, 69, 87, 499, 542
  and Berlin blockade, 8, 108–110
  mechanization, 88–89
  strip-mining, 88
Coexistence, policy of, 315, 372, 475, 403–404, 407, 453, 463, 464, 473, 474
Cohn, Roy M., 182, 183, 185, 188
Coleman, James S., 356, 526
Collins, General J. Lawton, 178
  on nuclear war, 120
Collisson, Norman H., 75
Columbia Broadcasting System
  and quiz shows, 391
  Trapped Housewife show, 384
Columbia University, 5, 53, 58, 66, 132, 212, 215, 236, 237, 345, 347, 364, 390, 501, 517, 529
  College Forum on Democracy, 61
  Institute of Russian Affairs, 53, 337
  Teachers College, 55, 56, 353
COMECON (Council of Mutual Economic Assistance), 72
Comic strips, 427, 466
Commission for a Just and Durable Peace, 47
Committee to Defend America by Aiding the Allies, 17
Committee on Academic Freedom, 57
Communist Party, U.S.A. 25–26, 129, 121, 161–162, 190–191, 493, 495, 498, 510, 529
Communist Party, U.S.S.R. *See* U.S.S.R.
Cominform (International Communist Information Bureau), 72–73, 106
Comintern (Communist International), 72
Community action programs, 488
Community colleges, 361
Communism, international, 4, 43, 49, 51, 54, 55, 57, 60, 64, 85, 95, 98, 99, 171, 172, 207, 209, 210, 213, 224, 239, 264, 295, 313, 325, 348, 358–359, 367, 395, 397, 402, 403, 442, 452, 465, 473, 483, 484, 493, 497, 498, 507, 508, 556
  Acheson on, 38, 180
  and American Committee for Cultural Freedom, 57
  Chinese-Russian split and, 483–484
  and domino analogy, 38, 231
  educators on, 55–57
  and Munich analogy, 138
  Niebuhr analysis and ADA, 47–48
  Spellman on, 50
  Truman on, 40–41, 493
  Vaudenberg on, 73
Communist movement, international, 167, 222, 372–373, 476, 479, 480–482
  and China, 144, 479–482
  Cominform of 1940s, 72–73
  Comintern of 1920s, 72
  and Cuba, 454–456, 463

and Eastern Europe, 17–18, 72–73, 106, 285, 289, 405
and France, 38, 72–73, 76
and Germany, 100, 107, 113, 406, 451
and Italy, 38, 72–73, 76
and Korea, 166, 170, 176–7, 181, 224
and Laos, 402
1919 Bolshevik revolution, 20, 33
"specter" of 1848, 20
and U.S., 129, 131, 453–454, 458
Computers, 240, 468–469, 502, 529
in automatic language translation, 352
chief invention in Cold War, 197
in CIA, 398
in missiles, 438
in Pentagon, 446, 449
Conant, James B., 141
Concentration camp bill, 162, 495
Condon, Edward U., 131
CONELRAD (Control of Electromagnetic Radiation), 260
Conference on Faith and Order (1937), 221
Confidence, crisis of, 490, 497
Congress of Industrial Organizations (CIO), 80–87, 95, 498
Congress of Cultural Freedom (*See* American Committee for Cultural Freedom)
Congress of Racial Equality (CORE), 307
Congressional Quarterly on reservists in Congress, 427
Connally, Tom, 24, 100, 114
Connelly, Matthew H., 195
Connor, Eugene (Bull), 309
Conquest, Robert, 524
Constitution, federal, 23, 30, 48, 206, 250, 493, 510
Consumer goods:
in America, 209, 234, 237, 251, 255, 369, 383, 422, 501, 503–504
record spending on, 248
in Russia,
Khrushchev goals for, 373, 376
Malenkov drive for, 275, 280
Containment, policy of, 35–36, 48–49, 67, 209, 515
Continental Congress, on standing armies, 115
Cook, Fred J., 519, 528
Cooke, Hope, 422
Coolidge, Calvin, 28, 65, 143, 172
Cordiner, Ralph J., 392
on electrical industry price-fixing, 394
Cordon sanitaire
around Russia, 20, 126
Cormier, Frank (and Watson, William A.), 519
Corporations, 3, 74, 233, 4, 259, 264, 467–468, 503–504
and aerospace contracting, 436–439
and automation, 84–85
image preoccupation with, 388
overseas expansion of, 74, 238–244, 421, 502, 509.

and price-fixing, 235
and race, 295, 297–298
supplant family-owned small-town industries, 157, 360
and youth, 59–60, 360–361
See also Administered prices; Business overseas; Growth, economic and business; Marshall Plan; Multinational corporations.
Corruption, political, 201–202, 213
under Truman, 194–196
under Eisenhower, 394–395. *See also* Television, campaign spending.
Costello, Frank, 199
Cotton, 67, 69, 76, 316, 499. *See also* Marshall Plan.
Council of Economic Advisers, 76, 208, 236, 266
on 1950 inflation, 194
on poverty, 487
Council of Foreign Ministers, 26, 39, 67, 99, 100, 113, 167
Council of Soviet-American Friendship, 184
Council on Foreign Relations, 26, 39, 42–43, 67, 99–100, 167, 337, 338
Dulles speech to, 225–226
Counterculture of youth, 60, 86, 89, 274, 266–269, 469
Counter-insurgency, 448, 507
Counts, George S., 55–57
Courtade, Pierre, 99
Courtship and dating, 384, 386, 387
Cousins, Norman, 271
Crankshaw, Edward, 524, 527, 529
Credibility gap:
in Korean war, 174, 497
in U-2 affair, 418
Credit cards, 387
Cremin, Lawrence A., 5, 518, 526
Cresap, Mark W. Jr., 394
Crisis managers, 173–4, 457
Cronkite, Walter, 202, 469
Crossman, Richard H. S., 521
Crowley, Leo T., 517
Cruse, Harold, 525
Cuba, 95, 121, 243, 325, 401, 449, 455, 465, 490, 506
missile crisis of 1962, 2, 173, 291, 374, 452–465, 474, 407
San Cristobal photos, 456–457
Cummings, E.E., 65
Curran, Joseph E., 388
Curtice, Harlow, 212, 234
Cutler, Robert, 523
Czechoslovakia, 51, 71–72, 108, 169, 181, 246, 480
arms for Egypt, 315, 579
1948 coup, 104–105, 107, 114, 118–119, 131, 246–247, 395, 495

Daily Worker, 26, 129
Dalai Lama, 409
D'Alessandro, Thomas, 201
Dalfiume, Richard M., 522
Daniels, Jonathan, 517
Davies, John Paton, 150, 521
Davies, Richard O., 524
Davies, Judge Ronald N., 304
Davison, W. Phillips, 5, 520
Day, Doris, 381
Dean, James, 62
Dean, General William F., 176
De Caux, Len, 83, 519
De Gasperi, Alcide, 41, 50
De Gaulle, Charles, 66, 241, 242, 278
    backs Kennedy in Cuba, 460
    delays summit, 411
    returns to power, 375
De Gramont, Sanche, 527
De Tocqueville, Alexis, 325, 328
De Vries, Peter, 380
De Witt, Nicholas, 347
Denney, Reuel, 529
Depression, 3, 29, 36, 47, 58, 79–80, 151, 236,
    249, 250, 272, 379
    fear of another, 76, 79, 86, 89, 126, 193, 259
Des Moines Register, 342
Detroit, 28, 47, 74, 79–81, 88, 90, 93, 129, 211,
    225, 235, 236, 242, 255, 328, 329, 336, 340,
    350, 435, 445, 458
Development Loan Fund, 443
Denver, Paul A., 159
Dewey, John, 54, 55, 206, 353, 358, 359
Dewey, Thomas E., 136, 149, 151–152, 201,
    211–214, 220
    on Berlin blockade, 111
    on Communist victory in China, 141
    on Russian A-bomb, 140
Diamond, Sigmund, 5
Diem, Ngo Dinh, 51, 95, 232, 400, 401, 490
Dienbienphu, 186, 229, 230, 231, 400
Dillon, C. Douglas, 310, 412
DiMaggio, Joe, 387, 470
Dirksen, Everett McK., 163, 188, 444
Disarmament, 128, 376, 405, 412, 453–4, 473,
    515.
    See also Testing, suspension of nuclear.
Disneyland, 411
Divorce statistics, 382
Djilas, Milovan, 35
Dobriner, William, 524
Dobrynin, Anatoly F., 455, 460
Doby, Larry, 294
Dodds, Harold W., 364
Dodge, Joseph M., 225, 235
Dollar gap, 76, 210, 503
Dollar, devaluation of, 503–512
Domino theory, 231, 400
Donaldson, Scott, 524
Donegan, Rt. Rev. Horace W.B., 49

Donohue, Joseph, 160
Donovan, James A., 528
Donovan, Robert J., 523
Donovan, General William J., 82
Doolittle, General James H., 439
Douglas, Helen Gahagan, 163
Douglas, Paul H., 161
    on Churchill summit call, 223
Douglas, William O.
    on Stalin postwar speech, 35
Downer, Samuel F., 429
Draft, the, 2, 23, 115–125, 292, 367, 450, 506,
    520, 548
    and Vietnam, 549
Drug industry, 529
    and antitrust, 393
    expansion of, 467–468
    investigation of, 467
    "wonder" drugs, 467–468
Drugs, 274, 467
Drury, Allen S., 189
Dubinsky, David, 49
Dulles, Allen W., 221, 364, 397–402, 447, 527
    and Bay of Pigs, 446
    and beginning of CIA, 395
    and Guatemala, 187
    heads all intelligence, 397
    and Khrushchev, 410
    and U-2, 413
Dulles, Foster Rhea, 182
Dulles, John Foster, 1, 47, 51, 111, 133, 134,
    168, 182, 187, 212, 213, 220, 221–231, 264,
    282, 312–323, 337, 338, 343, 368, 374, 397,
    399, 405–407, 423, 435, 464, 470, 501,
    514–516, 523, 525
    on Asian strategy, 229
    on Austrian treaty, 282
    and brinkmanship, 227
    on China
        Communist victory in, 141
        liberation of, 399
    on Communist bloc trends, 283
    crusading aims, 224
    on Eastern Europe, 246
    and Eisenhower, 221
    Hungarian revolt and liberation policy, 288
    on Indochina
        Geneva conference, 232
        U.S. intervention, 230
    on "liberation," 228
    massive retaliation speech, 225–226
    1955 summit meeting, 264
    on Sputnik, 340
    and Suez, 312–323
    and U.S.S.R.
        on nature of Soviet Communism, 222
        on postwar relations, 47
        on struggle with, 375
    on "unleashing" Chiang Kai-shek, 227
Dungan, Ralph A., 432
Dunn, Frederick S., 522

Dunning, John R., 344, 347
Durkin, Martin, 235
Duscha, Julius, 528
Dylan, Bob, 125

Eastern Europe, 18, 24, 33, 36, 51, 98, 154, 245, 246, 282, 283, 285, 375, 398, 412, 492, 514
  Chinese influence in, 405
  peace treaties, 26–27
  rebellion, 228, 245, 285, 321, 323
  Russian dominance, 24–25, 36, 72, 97, 106
Eastland, James O., 299–300
Eaton, Cyrus S., 453
Eckford, Elizabeth, 304, 305
Ecological alarm, 79, 336, 337, 487, 503
Economic Cooperation Administration, 75, 76.
  See also European Recovery plan; Marshall Plan.
Economy of abundance, 209–210
Eddy, Mary Baker, 208
Eden, Anthony, 65, 231–232, 275, 282, 318, 317–324, 515, 525
Educational Policies Commission, 56
Edwards, Jonathan, 47
Edwards, Willard, 155
Egg and I, The, 9
Egypt, 38, 230, 255, 288, 302, 313–322
Ehrenburg, Ilya, 275
Einstein, Albert, 127, 377, 453
Eisenhower, Dwight D., 1, 15, 27, 37, 46, 64–67, 84, 85, 95, 99, 100, 117, 119, 122, 157, 164, 182, 187, 188, 198, 202, 204, 211, 212–219, 223–237, 242, 246–248, 254, 255, 257, 264–268, 271, 282, 283, 296, 298, 300, 302, 304, 305, 307, 315, 317–324, 327, 338, 339, 342–7, 350, 356, 357, 362–364, 369–371, 373, 379–382, 391, 392, 394, 400, 403, 405, 406, 410, 411, 414–419, 423, 431–441, 444–446, 451, 452, 465, 473, 496, 497, 501, 502, 504, 507, 515, 523, 525, 527, 528
  on Adams, Sherman, 395
  American Legion speech, 214
  attack on clergy, 184–185
  on book-burners, 183
  on Brown v. Board of Education, 300
  on businessmen in Washington, 232–233
  Camp David and U-2, 411
  on China, to Khrushchev, 411
  on Churchill's summit call, 223
  corrects Stassen on McCarthy, 182
  on "creeping socialism," 391
  on defense spending, 345
  on electrical industry price-fixing, 393
  on federal aid to education, 345
  on FDR, 218
  on Indochina as domino, 231
  on informing citizens outside cities, 203
  on interstate highways, 255, 257
  on Korean peace, 223–224
  Little Rock speech, 217
  on McCarthy, 218
  modest means, 237–238
  1952 campaign aims, 213–214
  on nonintervention in South, 303
  Oklahoma City speech on schools, 347–348
  origins, 216
  personal ambitions, 215
  refuses to accept "ultimatum," 418
  religion, 217, 380
  on Russia, long struggle with, 264
  on segregation in armed forces, 295
  on Sputnik, 340
  on Stalin's death, 222
  on TV campaign commercials, 201
  on U-2 flights, 417
  on U.S. satellite, 343
Eisenhower Doctrine, 324–325
Eisler, Gerhart, 129, 131
Ekirch, Arthur A. Jr., 520
Elections:
  1946, 28–30, 36, 68, 129, 151
  1948, 14, 15, 49, 83, 111, 135–137, 151–152
  1950, 162–164
  1952, 211–212
  1954, 184, 188–190, 192
  1956, 247, 321–324
  1960, 307, 417, 467
  1962, 458, 465
Electric power, 211, 391–392, 501
Electronics, 364–365, 399, 413, 422, 431, 436, 438, 468
  Boston Route 128, 438
  in Southern California, 438
Elementary and Secondary Education Act (1965), 486
Eliot, T.S., 65
Ellsberg, Daniel, 511
Elson, Rev. Edward L. R., 216
Ely, General Paul, 229
Employment, 194, 266, 468, 488, 502, 504
  in arms industry, 431
  of women (See Women)
Employment Act of 1945, 15, 80, 194, 207
Engler Robert, 524
Eniwetok, 97, 226, 471
Episcopal church, 49, 136
Erhard, Ludwig, 545
Erickson, Frank, 199
Ernst, Max, 272
Estonia, 72, 106
European Coal and Steel Community, 239
European Defense Community Treaty, 222, 232
European Economic Community (Common Market), 239, 502
European Recovery program (Marshall Plan), 71, 74, 75
Evans, Rowland (and Novak, Robert), 529
Evers, Charles, 311
Executive Committee (Excom), 173, 458–461
Executive Order 9835, 129–30

Existentialism, 270–274
Expansion attic, 260–261
Exports, U.S., 67, 71, 76, 88, 208, 242, 243, 498, 503

Fairbank, John K., 521
Fair Deal program, 15, 152, 154, 235, 486
Fair Employment Practices Commission, 294
Fallout shelters, 450–451
Family, the, 89, 250, 267, 378, 381–387
Fanon, Frantz, 293, 525
Farley, James J., 50
Farouk I, King, 314
Fast, Howard, 131
Faubus, Orval E., 304, 305
Faulkner, William, 1, 32
Federal aid to education, 350–352, 486
Federal Bureau of Investigation (FBI), 137, 154, 164, 183, 204, 304
Federal Communications Commission (FCC), 197
Federal (National) Council of Churches, 45–47, 183–184, 221, 370
Federal Highway Fund, 256–257
Federal Housing Administration (National Housing Administration), 249–251
Federal Pacific Co., 393
Federal Reserve system, 237, 248
Federal Trade Commission (FTC), 395
Feis, Herbert, 513
Fellowship of Reconciliation, 47
Fertilizers, chemical, 78–79
Fiedler, Leslie A., 520–521
Fifth Amendment, 93, 185
Finer, Herman, 523, 525
Finland, 20, 21, 39, 72, 290
    relations with Russia, 104, 105, 119
Finletter, Thomas K., 75
Fischetti, Charlie, 199
Fisher, Frederick G., 190–191
Fisher, H. A. L., 514
Fitch, James Marston, 5, 378
Five-per-centers, 194–196
Flanders, Ralph E., 186, 192
Fleming, Sir Alexander, 467
Fleming, Ian, 423
Flemming, Arthur S., 46, 423
Flesch, Rudolf, 348–349, 353
Flexible response, policy of, 123, 449, 506
Florida, 9, 16, 89, 93, 162, 311, 341, 465
Flying saucers, 44
Foch, Marshal Ferdinand, 65
Fomin, Alexander S., 461
Foner, Eric, 5
Fontaine, Andre, 514
Food and Drug Administration (FDA), 468
Ford, Henry, 81, 254
Ford, Henry II, 212
Ford Foundation, 53, 339, 350, 518, 520

Ford Motor Co., 84, 212, 234, 240, 242, 254, 445
Fordham University, 50, 59
Foreign aid, 76, 157–158, 164, 210, 246, 266, 267, 325, 509
Foreign ministers' conference (See Council of Foreign Ministers)
Foreign Policy Association, 43
Formosa (See Taiwan)
Forrestal, James V., 35, 39, 98, 108, 111, 138, 151, 161, 173, 239, 364, 395, 396, 428, 515, 517, 518
Forster, Rudolf, 8
Fort Knox gold, 422, 503, 508
Fort Monmouth, 186
Fortunate Dragon, 226–227, 472
Fortune, 248, 251, 262, 358
Fosdick, Dorothy, 49
Foster, William C., 339
Fountain, Clayton, 519
Fox, William T. R., 5
France, 13, 20, 21, 33, 38, 40, 46, 54, 65, 66, 69, 71, 75, 99, 100, 103, 107, 108, 116, 126, 171, 207, 222, 228, 230–231, 240, 272, 278, 326, 353, 422, 475, 477
    Communist party in, 38, 72, 73, 76, 82–83, 95, 106, 396, 398, 542
    in Indochina, 143, 174, 186, 228–232, 490
    and NATO, 114–115
    postwar recovery, 239
    at Suez, 245, 288, 312–325, 274, 404
    as U.S. ally, 175, 317, 321, 322
Frankensteen, Richard, 81
"Free speech" movement, 274, 489, 500
Freedom riders, 307–308, 310, 525
Freedom summer, 311, 489
Freeland, Richard, 520
Friedan, Betty, 384, 527
Friedenberg, Edgar Z.
    on the draft, 125
Friendly, Fred W., 522
Frier, David A., 527
Frost, Robert, 218, 456
Fuchs, Klaus, 155, 495
Fulbright, J. William, 67, 196–197, 344, 452
Fuller, John G., 527
Fulton, Mo., 16–18, 129, 223, 443
Futurology, 44

Gabrielson, Guy G., 156
Gaddis, John Lewis, 515
Gagarin, Yuri, 447
Gaither, Rowan, 339, 445
Gaitskell, Hugh, 321
Galbraith, John Kenneth, 122, 265, 363, 422, 524, 528
Gandhi, Mohandas K., 301–302
Ganey, Judge J. Cullen, 393
Gannon, Robert I., 59, 518

Gans, Herbert J., 5, 488, 524
Gardner, John W., 349–350, 358, 526
Gardner, Lloyd C., 514, 520
Gardner, Richard N., 517
Gardner, Trevor, 436
Garraty, John A., 5, 516
Garroway, Dave, 390
Garside, Ellen Clayton, 519
Garthoff, Raymond L., 524
Garvey, Marcus, 328, 329
Gary, Elbert, 45
Gbedemah, K.A., 331
Gehlen, General Reinhard, 398
Gelfand, Mark, 6, 524, 530
General Dynamics Corp., 429, 430, 440
  in top five arms contractors, 431
General Electric Co., 241, 295, 437
  and price-fixing case, 391–394
  in top five arms contractors, 431
General Motors Corp., 10, 81, 84, 211, 233–235,
  240, 254, 256, 295, 436, 468, 498, 502
  decline in arms contracting, 234
  leads consumer boom, 234
  leads multinational expansion, 240–241
  Wilson confirmation hearings, 233
Generation gap, 60, 89, 125, 500, 506
Geneva conference on Far East (1954), 51, 231–
  232, 400, 401
  U.S. role, 232
Geneva summit conference (1955), 264, 282–
  283, 315, 405, 417, 464
George, General Harold L., 439
George, Walter, 40
Georgia, 28, 180, 213, 233, 304, 312, 428
  Savannah and desegregation decision, 297
  Atlanta and Martin Luther King, 301, 306–
  307
German-Americans, 47, 379
  and McCarthy, 159–160, 521
Germany, 3, 4, 7–10, 12, 18, 20, 32, 48, 50, 67,
  69, 96, 116, 126, 169, 176, 181, 192, 220,
  270, 286, 293–4, 338, 340, 353, 379, 391,
  435, 467, 475, 504
  occupation of, 69
    currency reform, 104, 107, 112, 170, 545
    U.S.-Russian rivalry in, 4, 25, 67, 99–115,
    542
  in World War II, 17, 72, 326, 337, 398, 494
    East Germany (German Democratic
    Republic), 113, 341, 405, 449, 451,
    476, 482
      East Berlin rising (1953), 228, 291, 398
      and CIA, 398
      peace treaty abandoned by Khrushchev,
      463
      and second Berlin crisis, 406, 412, 449,
      454–455
    West Germany (Democratic Republic of)
    112–114, 170, 240, 242, 375, 405–406,
    430
      economic recovery, 239

rearmament, 176, 223, 229, 232, 282,
  312
Russians demand withdrawal from
  NATO, 406
Soviet fears of German A-bomb, 375–
  376, 454
strongest Cold War ally, 435
test-ban treaty, adheres to, 482
Gero, Erno, 286–287
Gerson, Louis A., 523
Gesell, Arnold (and Ilg, Frances L.), 367
Ghali, Jaguih, 317
Ghana, 313, 330–332
G.I. Bill of Rights (Servicemen's Readjustment
  Act of 1944) 57–60, 80, 86, 89, 194, 250–
  257, 351
Gimbel, John, 520
Ginsburg, Allen, 362
Gittings, John, 528, 529
Glazer, Nathan, 159
Glenn, John, 469
Glennon, T. Keith, 442
Godfrey, Arthur, 248, 427
Goebbels, Josef, 107
Goffman, Erving, 381–382, 384, 387–388, 527
Goheen, Robert F., 364
Goldfine, Bernard, 395
Goldman, Eric F., 5, 139, 267, 516, 530
Goldwater, Barry M., 219, 428, 429, 446, 510
Gomulka, Wladislaw, 106, 286–287, 289
Good Housekeeping, 50
Goodlad, John L., 526
Goodman, Benny, 10
Goodman, Percival, 5
Goodman, Walter, 521, 527
Goodpaster, Andrew J., 342
Goold-Adams, Richard, 525
Gottwald, Klement, 72, 104
Goulden, Joseph, 519
Graebner, Norman A., 514, 521
Graff, Henry F., 5, 529
Graham, Frank P., 131
Graham, J.R., 520
Grant, Ulysses S., 192, 215, 238, 271
"Great debate" (1951), 210
"Great Leap Forward", 479
Great Society programs, 484–489, 503
Grechko, General A.A., 434
Greece, 38, 50, 119, 348
  shipping interests and McCarthy, 182
  and Tito, 107
  U.S. aid to, 37–41, 67–69, 171, 230, 492, 508,
  518
Greenberg, Clement
  on Jackson Pollock, 273
Greene, Grahame, 401
Grey, H. Peter, 528
Griffin, Marvin, 304
Griffith, Robert, 5, 521, 522
Griffith, William E., 528, 529
Griswold, A. Whitney, 521

Gromyko, A., 514
Gromyko, Andrei, 410, 459, 476
Gross national product, 210–211, 234, 242, 266, 388, 431, 502
Ground Control Approach system, 112
Groves, General Leslie R., 120, 192
Guaranteed annual wage, 84
Guatemala, 247, 402
  and CIA, 187, 221, 399
Guevara, Che, 455–456
Guhin, Michael H., 523
Gurney, J. Chandler
  on the draft, 120
Gurtev, Melvin, 523

Hadley, Loren H.
  on G.I. Bill students, 58
Hagen, John
  on Sputnik, 340
Hagerty, James A., 215, 217, 305
Hagerty, Thomas, 93
Hahn, Otto, 127
Halle, Louis J., 6, 49, 514
Halley, Rudolph, 198–189
Halberstam, David, 529
Halperin, Morton H. (and Perkins, Dwight), 529
Hammarskjold, Dag, 222, 320, 324
Hammond, Paul Y., 523
Handlin, Oscar, 360, 526
Hanes, Arthur, 310
Hansberry, Lorraine, 299
Harding, Warren G., 23, 28, 65, 143, 172
Hardy, Andy, 381
Hardy, John, 308–309
Harman, Alvin J., 524
Harper, Alan D., 520
Harper's, 258
Harriman, W. Averill, 33, 75, 461, 476–477, 529
Harrington, Michael, 523
Harris, Roy, 304
Harris, Richard, 529
Harris, Seymour E., 524, 528
Harvard University, 53, 70, 121, 133, 139, 190, 330, 350, 355, 364–366, 368, 369, 395, 396, 404, 445, 486, 501
Hawaii, 172, 421
Hay, John, 142, 143
Hayek, Friedrich, 29
Hayes, Rutherford B., 296
Hayes, Thomas L., 520
Hayden, Carl T., 116
Head Start program, 488
Health-care programs. See Medical insurance
Hearst newspapers, 98, 131, 206
Heath, Robert, 526
Hebert, F. Edward, 125
Heller, Joseph, 470
Hemingway, Ernest, 65
Herberg, Will, 380, 527

Herling, John, 527
Hero, Alfred O. (and Starr, Emil), 519
Hershey, General Lewis B., 122, 520
Herter, Christian A., 417
Hess, Rudolf, 398
Hewlett, Richard G. (and Oscar Anderson), 521
Hickenlooper, Bourke B., 139
Hicks, Granville, 208
Higher Education Act (1965), 486
Hilgesheimer, Eddie, 389
Hill, Virginia, 199
Hillenkoetter, Admiral Roscoe H., 117
Hillman, William, 517
Hilsman, Roger, 5, 527, 529
Hirohito, Emperor, 80, 230
Hiroshima, 96–97, 192, 226, 259, 337
Hiss, Alger, 132–138, 155–156, 164, 183, 495, 520
Hitler, Adolf, 4, 7–10, 12, 18–21, 23, 41, 47, 72, 80, 100, 107, 116, 119, 145, 169, 171, 192, 221, 230, 269, 270, 278, 294, 301, 314, 317, 318, 338, 398, 426, 433, 442, 495, 504, 517, 518
Ho Chi Minh, 171, 228, 229, 232, 400
Hodge, General Courtney, 9
Hodgins, Eric, 251
Hoffa, James R., 92, 388, 519
Hoffman, Paul G., 46, 75, 76, 148, 211, 212, 350
Hofstadter, Richard, 129, 493, 521, 522
Hollywood, as lifestyle-setter, 98, 381, 469
  Dean, James cult, 62
  gives way to TV, 469–470
  lacquered look, 381
  Monroe, Marilyn as sex-symbol, 387
  Wayne, John influence, 469
Holmes, Oliver Wendell Jr., 133
Home mortgages, 3, 87, 250–257
Hook, Sidney, 56–57
Hoover, Herbert C., 28, 69, 127, 143, 151, 172, 206, 236, 446
Hoover, J. Edgar, 55, 206, 493, 549
Hope, Bob, 478
Hopkins, Harry L., 35
Horowitz, David, 514
Horowitz, Irving L. (and Friedland, William M.), 526
House, Col. Edward M., 20
House and Home, 251
House Armed Services subcommittee, 430
House Subcommittee on Legislative Oversight, 390, 394
House Government Operations committee, 439
House Un-American Activities committee, 98, 131, 136, 137, 154, 183, 520, 521
Housing:
  Great Society legislation, 487, 503
  postwar fiasco, 10
  private, 249–261, 267, 504
  public, 267, 444, 504
  segregation in, 252, 327, 333
Howard, Roy W., 148

Howe, Irving, 519
Howley, Frank, 520
Huddleston, George, 116
Hudson, Rock, 381
Hudson Institute, 337
Hughes, Charles Evans, 394
Hughes, Emmet John, 345, 523
Hughes, Rupert, 98
Hughes Aircraft Co., 437, 439
Hula hoops, 1, 368
Hull, Cordell, 24, 74, 513
Humphrey, George M., 225, 235, 316, 323
Humphrey, Hubert H., 162, 175, 478
Hungary, 20, 51, 106, 181, 246, 410
　in Cominform, 72
　revolt, 245, 246, 286–289, 291, 321, 322, 398
Hunt, Haroldson R., 158
Hunt, Lester C., 188–190
Huntington, Samuel P., 117–118, 520, 526, 528
Hurley, General Patrick J., 143–145, 521
Hutchinson, John, 519
Hydrogen bomb:
　American, 141, 193, 226, 280, 337, 466, 472
　leads to ICBM race, 433
　Russian, 274–275, 280, 337, 348, 372, 474

Ickes, Harold L., 206
Immigration, 161, 159, 204, 206, 250, 351, 487, 509
Imports, U.S., 67, 76, 210, 503
Inchon, 176, 556
Income, distribution of, 29, 84, 248–249, 487–488, 523
　by race, 327
India, 19, 37, 38, 177, 223, 231, 301, 302, 313, 314, 319, 407, 422, 472
　and border war with China, 400, 409, 480
　and Russian aid, 408, 412
Indochina, 174–175, 247, 400, 465, 477, 497
　crisis of 1954, 186, 228–232.
　See also Cambodia; France; Geneva; Laos; Vietnam.
Indonesia, 231, 243, 399
Inflation, 28–29, 503
　in Korean war, 194, 210, 211
Installment debt, 263, 265
Institute of Advanced Study, 193
Institute of Pacific Relations, 164
Intercontinental ballistic missile, 339
　American ICBM program, 339, 370, 373, 433, 435–442, 449, 451, 453
　Russian ICBM program, 339–341, 345, 371–373, 413, 416, 433, 434, 449, 464
　U-2 surveillance of sites, 413–415
Intermediate range ballistic missile:
　American IRBMs, 370, 375, 434, 435, 459, 461
　　Redstone, 434, 435
　　Jupiter for NATO, 370

　removed from Turkey, 462
　Russian IRBMs, 375
　　in Cuba, 454–458
International Bank for Reconstruction and Development (World Bank), 316
International Brotherhood of Teamsters, 80, 91–94, 388, 519. See also Hoffa, James.
International Business Machines Corp., 241, 242, 469
International Geophysical Year, 339–340
International Ladies Garment Workers Union, 49, 80
International Longshoremen's Association, 91
International Monetary Fund, 323, 324
International Typographers Union, 83
International Union of Electrical and Radio and Machine Workers, 83
Interstate Commerce Commission, 308
Interstate Highway and Defense system, 255–257, 504
Iowa, 139, 190, 411, 423
Iran, 38, 40, 97, 100, 157, 230, 247, 313, 319, 399
Iraq, 313, 324, 325, 481
Irish-Americans, 49–52, 94, 161, 379, 521
　and McCarthy, 158–160
Iron Curtain, 18, 73, 99, 104, 105, 181, 246, 282, 397, 453
Isaacs, Harold, 525
Islam, 314, 328, 332
　See also Black Muslims
Isolationism, 17, 23, 39, 41–42, 73–74, 211, 213, 221
Israel, 105, 243, 301, 314–316, 320–324
Italian-Americans, 50, 105, 159–160
Italy, 18, 21, 38, 41, 51, 66, 69, 171, 230, 359, 379, 422, 480
　Communist party, 38, 72, 73, 82, 83, 95, 106, 119, 396, 398
　missile bases in, 370, 375, 459
　1948 elections, 52, 105, 395
Iversen, Robert W., 518
Izvestia, 280

Jackson, Charles, 182
Jackson, Donald, 184
Jackson, Henry M., 188
Jackson, Kenneth M., 5, 524
Jackson, Mahalia, 311
Jackson State College, 63
Jacobsen, Eddie, 13, 14
James, Henry, 268
James, R.C. and E.D., 519
Janeway, Eliot, 440, 523, 528
Japan, 20, 140, 142, 166, 167, 168, 172, 176, 181, 226, 228, 231, 239, 242, 267, 293, 336, 399, 472, 480, 492, 522
　occupation of, 32, 67, 117, 145–146, 169–170
　peace treaty with, 169, 181, 203, 221

trains in, 267
in World War II, 9, 10, 21, 32, 33, 128, 144–146, 166, 170, 175, 326, 422
Japanese-Americans, 161–162
Jehovah's Witnesses, 215
Jencks, Christopher, 526
Jefferson, Thomas, 79, 115, 206
Jenner, William E., 175, 497
Jessup, Philip C., 53, 113, 156, 162, 164
Jet age, 419–424, 428
    jetliners, 139, 197, 410, 418, 419–421
    "jet set", 420
    main innovation of Cold War years, 197
Jewish-Americans, 28, 29, 49, 159, 237, 338, 379
Job Corps, 488
John XXIII, Pope, 530
Johns Hopkins University, 133, 156, 365
Johnson, Andrew, 14
Johnson, Clarence L., 413
Johnson, Edwin C., 40, 120, 141
Johnson, Hiram, 169
Johnson, General Hugh S., 36
Johnson, Leroy, 120
Johnson, Louis A., 141, 161, 517
Johnson, Lyndon B., 2, 13, 138, 172, 173, 193, 204, 215, 219, 303, 311, 333, 350, 356, 400, 418, 441, 442, 444, 445, 447, 448, 486, 487, 490, 497, 503, 508, 529, 530
    on civil rights, 303
    Great Society program, 487
    on McCarthy, Joseph, 163, 184
    on McNamara, Robert, 445
    as president, 486–487
    as presidential candidate, 219
    as Senate majority leader, 303
    and space race, 447
    on Sputnik, 370
    on Vanguard, 343
    as Westerner, 13
Johnson, Walter, 517, 523
Johnston, Eric, 208
Joint chiefs of staff, 108, 117, 120, 229, 230, 447, 458
    and test-ban treaty, 477–478
Joint Congressional Committee on Atomic Energy, 139, 141, 226
Jones, Alton (Pete), 212, 238
Jones, Galen, 54
Jones, Joseph, 518, 519
Jonkel, Jon, 163
Judd, Walter C., 148–149
Juvenile delinquency, 62, 267

Kadar, Janos, 287–289
Kafka, Franz, 271
Kaganovich, Lazar M., 280, 284, 286, 290
Kansas, 17, 129, 236, 431, 489
Kazakhstan, 278–279
    See also Virgin lands.

Kefauver, Estes, 85, 162, 198, 235
    crime hearings on TV, 198–200
    drug investigation, 467–468
    and electrical price-fixing, 392
Kegley, Charles W., 518
Keller, K.T., 233, 433
Kelsey, Frances C., 468
Kempton, Murray, 523
Kennan, George A., 49, 53, 67–9, 209, 515, 518, 519, 527
    cable on Soviet conduct, 85–86
    on Japan, 169–170, 522.
    on Niebuhr, 49
    on U.S. and Tito, 107
Kennedy, Joseph P., 49, 50
Kennedy, John F., 1, 51, 64, 122, 123, 173, 193, 194, 201, 202, 204, 215, 298, 307, 308, 310, 321, 332, 344, 372, 380, 423, 432, 442–443, 444, 453–461, 465, 468, 469, 474, 476–484, 486, 487, 490, 502, 503, 507, 515, 516, 528, 529
    assassination, 490
    on Bay of Pigs aftermath, 447
    on Berlin, 449–450
    and Bond, James, 423
    Catholic president, first, 52
    on Churchill, 200
    on counter-insurgency, 448
    Cuban blockade speech, 459
    on fallout shelters
    and Hollywood and TV personages, 469
    ignores Soviet ICBM cutback, 450
    inaugural speech, 443
    on Laos, 401
    on missile gap, 444
    on need for economic growth, 443
    Nixon debates, 202
    on space race, 194
    speech on sending troops to Alabama, 311
    Sputnik assists to presidency, 344
    on Treaty of Moscow, 477
    Turkish base trade-off, rejects, 461
Kennedy, Robert F., 2, 91–94, 307, 457–459, 461, 529
    assassination, 490
    and civil rights, 444, 307–311
    on comparing self with Tojo, 458
    talks to Dobrynin in Cuban crisis, 460
Kent, Sherman, 395
Kent State University, 63, 548
Kenyatta, Jomo, 330
Kenyon, Dorothy, 156
Keppel, Francis, 486, 526, 530
Kerouac, Jack, 362
Kerr, Clark, 365, 489
Kerr, Robert M., 448
Kersten, Charles, 246
Key, V. O., 151
Keynes, John Maynard, 65, 207
Keyserling, Leon H., 208, 209, 524
Khrushchev, Nikita S., 114, 276–277, 278–291,

315, 339, 341, 371–375, 392, 398, 403–412,
449, 453–462, 472–474, 481–482, 484–
507, 515, 524, 529, 530
on atom-free Pacific zone, 408
on balance of terror, 282–283
on Berlin demands, 407
on Communist aims, 283
and Cuban missile crisis, 453–462
on farm problems, 276–277
on Hungarian revolt, 289
ICBM cutback, 371–372
ICBM tests, 339
meets Kennedy at Vienna, 449
Khrushchev Remembers, 170, 176, 276, 460,
522, 556
nuclear test suspension, 473
Peking speech on peaceful coexistence, 411–
412
as politician, 403
on Quemoy-Matsu, 407
Secret speech against Stalin, 284, 398
on shooting dissidents, 289
on Sputnik, 342
as Stalinist, 289
Treaty of Moscow negotiations, 476, 478,
482
and U-2 crisis, 414, 415–416, 418
on U.S. satellite tests, 342
"We will bury you," 375
on West's need to be "reasonable on Berlin,"
412
Kierkegaard, Sören, 270
Kilgore, Harley, 161
Killian, James R. Jr., 346–347, 355, 358
Kim Il-sung, 166, 167–168, 176, 190–191, 556
King, Coretta, 307
King, Martin Luther Jr., 2, 301–302, 303, 306–
311, 329, 331, 332, 504, 525
assassination, 490
Lincoln Memorial speech, 311
on nonviolence, 302
King, Martin Luther Sr., 302, 307
Kinsey, Alfred C., 382–384, 527
Kintner, Robert E., 391
Kiraly, Bela K., 5
Kirkendall, Richard S., 518
Kirov, Sergei N., 284
Kissinger, Henry A., 173, 338, 339, 526
on limited nuclear war, 338
Kitchen debate (*See* Richard M. Nixon)
Know-how, 293, 336, 337, 499
Knowland, William F., 168, 169, 174, 184, 214,
223, 232
Koestler, Arthur, 57, 132
Kohlberg, Alfred, 156
Kolko, Gabriel, 5, 514, 519, 520, 523
Kommunist, 283
Konev, Marshal Ivan S., 9, 99
Korea, 100, 162, 163, 165, 204, 211, 293, 453
North Korea (Democratic People's Republic
of Korea), 166–181, 483

South Korea (Republic of Korea), 166–181,
399
Korean war, 76, 122, 151, 158, 160, 162, 164,
166–181, 194, 195, 197, 210, 219, 223, 224,
229, 230, 232, 234, 239, 245, 248, 295, 327,
357, 397, 434, 494, 497, 501, 506, 519, 522,
556
allies in, 175, 178
as police action, 120, 122, 174, 229
stalemated, 181–182
truce, 223
Kossior, Stanislaw, 283
Kostov, Traicho, 106
Kravchenko, Victor, 138
Krieger, Leonard, 5
Krock, Arthur, 164
Krug, Julius A., 76
Ku Klux Klan, 300
Kurile Islands, 145
Kuznets, Simon S., 523

Labor, organized, 79–95, 98, 208, 256, 360,
388, 493, 498
productivity, 79, 84, 88, 265
share in Gross National Product, 84, 388
status of, 80, 388
and youth, 59–60, 89, 360
Lachmann, Thomas, 527
La Feber, Walter, 514, 518, 522, 523
Lafebre, Edward J., 429
La Follette, Robert Jr., 54
La Follette, Robert Sr., 206
Lampman, Robert J., 523
Landon, Alfred M., 206
Landrum-Griffin act, 93
Langer, Prof. William L., 396
Langer, Sen. William, 165
Language laboratories, 352
Lansdale, General Edward, 400–401
Lansing, John B. (and Blood, Dwight M.), 528
Lansing, Robert, 220
Laos, 231–232, 399, 400–402, 448, 502
Lapp, Ralph E., 528
Lapp Insulator Co., 392
Lardner, Ring, 421
Larsen, David L., 529
Larson, Arthur, 218, 523
Lasch, Christopher, 518
Lash, Joseph, 518
Lasky, Melvin, 525
Lasswell, Harold, 501, 504
Latham, Earl, 521
Lattimore, Owen, 156, 164
Latvia, 72, 246
Lausche, Frank, 478
Lawford, Peter, 369
Lawson, James Jr., 306
Lawyers Guild, 191
Leach, Jack Franklin, 520

League of Nations, 22–23
Leahy, Admiral William D., 17, 173, 517
Leake, Chauncey D., 347
Lebanon, 313, 324, 406, 460
Leber, Annadore, 110
Lee, E. Alton, 519
Lee, Robert E., 154
Leheney, Ray, 92
Lehigh University, 58
Le May, General Curtis E., 109, 112, 434, 520
Lend-lease, 10, 23, 96
Lenin, V. I., 7, 20, 131, 166, 169, 283, 284, 372
Leuchtenburg, William E., 5, 202
Leveiro, Anthony, 180
Levine, Nathan, 137
Levitt, Abraham, 251
Lewis, Anthony, 525
Lewis, David L., 525
Lewis, John, 331, 332
Lewis, John L., 15, 28, 80, 82, 87–90, 91, 499, 519
Lewis, Sinclair, 44–45
L'Humanité, 99
Liberal party, 49
Liberation policy, 51, 214, 228, 245–247, 264, 289, 379, 397–399, 504
Liberia, 328, 329
Liberman, Joseph I., 521
Lie, Trygve, 19, 22, 164
Life-adjustment education, 54, 353, 357, 358, 499
Life, 48, 49, 148, 227, 248, 349, 515
Lilienthal, David E., 139–141, 208, 515, 521
Limited war, 45, 180, 338, 448, 449
Lin Piao, 145, 408
Lincoln, Abraham, 151, 192, 200, 213, 217, 296, 300, 333
Lincoln, C. Eric, 5, 326, 525
Ling, James J., 429
Lippmann, Walter, 43, 67, 142, 172, 334, 417, 484, 513
Literary Gazette (Moscow), 119
Lithuania, 72, 246
Little Rock, 183, 217, 303–306, 312, 484, 504, 523
Liu Shao, 456
Lloyd George, David, 64
Lockheed Aircraft Co., 413, 431, 441
Lodge, Henry Cabot, 159, 212–214
Lohbeck, Don, 521
Lomax, Louis E., 525
Long, Clarence D. Jr., 201
Long, Huey P., 157
Longworth, Alice Roosevelt, 442
Look, 383, 389
Los Angeles, 9, 262, 272, 427, 431, 437, 438
Los Angeles Herald and Examiner, 432
Love, Kennett, 525
Lovestone, Jay, 519
Lovett, Robert M., 66, 74, 114, 173, 339, 395, 459

Lowell, Robert, 271, 467
Lowenthal, Max, 14
Loyalty-security programs, 154, 494–496, 520
    under Eisenhower, 182, 193
    registration of Communists in New Rochelle, New York, 160
    under Truman, 129, 154
Lubell, Samuel, 379, 521, 525
Lucas, Scott, 156, 163
Luce, Clare Boothe, 348
Luce, Henry R., 49, 143, 148, 251
Ludden, Ray, 150
Lukacs, John A.L., 514
Lumumba, Patrice, 331
Luxemburg, 114, 241
Lynd, Robert and Mary, 29

MacArthur, General Douglas, 13, 32, 66, 117, 148, 164, 174–182, 214, 227–228, 229, 402, 522
    on Communist victory in China, 141
    on ending war by Christmas, 177
    "entirely new war," 177
    on improbability of Chinese entry in Korea, 177
    on Indochina, 229
    on Korean truce, 229
    "no substitute for victory," 179
    Senate hearings on relief of, 180
    speech to Congress, 179
Maccoby, Eleanor, 261
Mad magazine, 1
Mademoiselle, 422
Magdoff, Harry, 524
Magsaysay, Ramon, 400
Mailer, Norman, 271
Maisky, Ivan M, 514
Malaya, 231
Makeba, Miriam, 331
Malcolm X, 328–329, 332, 525
Malenkov, Georgi M., 166, 222, 223, 274–281, 283–284, 290
Maleter, General Pal, 288, 289
Malik, Jacob A., 113
Malone, George W., 162
Malraux, Andre, 193
Manchester Guardian, 40
Manchuria, 143, 145–146, 149–150, 162, 167, 177, 280
Manifest destiny, 37, 64, 142, 149, 501
Manned orbiting stations, 453
Mansfield, Jayne, 387
Mao Tse-tung, 5, 138, 143–145, 146–150, 166–170, 174–177, 181, 229, 278, 280, 372, 373, 403, 405–412, 448, 454, 473, 476, 479–481, 521
Macdonald, Dwight, 59, 350
MacDonald, Robert M., 524

Macmillan, Harold, 144, 170, 306, 320, 323–325, 372, 405, 406, 461, 515, 523
Marcel, Gabriel, 270
Maritime Commission, 195
Marshall, Burke, 309–310
Marshall, Charles B., 49, 513
Marshall, General George C., 13, 27, 36–37, 38, 39, 49, 67–71, 74, 75, 82, 95, 101, 105, 117, 146–148, 151, 161, 164–165, 172, 181, 200, 214, 496, 515, 517, 521
  on aid as nonpartisan, 68
  on Berlin blockade, 110
  on European economic crisis, 67
  Harvard speech on aid, 70
  on Korean fighting, 181
  on "putting out fires," 118
  on universal military training, 118
Marshall, S.L.A., 522
Marshall Plan, 39, 46, 49, 61, 69, 72, 73, 76, 79, 85, 86, 97, 98, 101, 105, 106, 114, 119, 148, 194, 203, 209–211, 239, 292, 294, 350, 395, 498, 502, 519
  and businessmen, 75–76
  and labor, 81–89
  and U.S. cotton economy, 77–79
  and U.S. coal industry, 88–89
Martin, Dean, 469
Martin, Edward, 120
Martin, Homer, 81
Martin, Joseph W. Jr., 38, 39, 105, 179
Marucla, 460
Marx, Karl, 7, 20, 206, 283, 492
Masaryk, Jan, 72, 104–105, 106
Massachusetts Institute of Technology, 54, 346, 354, 356, 364–366, 438, 501
  Center for International Studies, 54
  and government, 54, 365–366, 369
  and industry, 366
Massive retaliation policy, 224, 228, 312, 337, 338, 374
  called out of date, 338
  Dulles speech, 235–236
  Indochina, tested in, 232
  not followed in 1956 crises, 245
Matthews, Francis, 160–161
Matthews, J.B., 184–185
Matusow, Allen J., 518
May, Ernest R., 528
Mayer, Martin, 522, 526
Mays, Willie, 294
Mazey, Emil, 92
McCarran, Pat, 140, 161
McCarran Act (1950), 161–162, 495
McCarthy, Joseph R., 1, 153–155, 156–165, 182–193, 195, 200, 204, 214, 217, 219–224, 232, 275, 423, 495, 521, 529
  on Acheson, Dean, 163–164
  on Fisher, Fred, 191
  on Jessup, Philip, 156, 163–164
  on Kenyon, Dorothy, 156
  on MacArthur dismissal, 164

  on Marshall, George C., 165
  on methods, 190
  on Peress, Irving, 186
  speeches, 155
  on State Department, 163–164
  "twenty-one years of treason," 188
  on Zwicker, Ralph, 186
McCarthyism, 157–165, 182–193, 213, 299, 357, 495, 520, 522
  and "concentration camp" bill, 162
  economic components, 157–158
  ethnic components, 158–159
  and Hunt suicide, 189
  named, 157
  and McCarran-Nixon Act, 161
  named, 157
  and Oppenheimer affair, 192
  Republican diehard component, 156–157
McClellan, John L., 91, 93, 183, 184, 188
McCloy, John J., 16, 53, 66, 173, 339, 395
McCluer, Franc B., 16–17
McCone, John A., 459
McCormack, General James, 140
McCormick, Robert, 131, 163
McDonald, David J., 84
McElroy, Neil H., 341, 441
McKahin, George T. (and Lewis, John W.), 527
McKay, Douglas, 235
McKinley, William, 121, 202, 203, 296
MacLean, General Raymond S., 120
McLeod, Scott, 182
McLuhan, Marshall, 203, 423, 522
McNamara, Robert S., 310, 445–446, 447–452, 465
  during Cuban crisis, 460
  and the draft, 123
  fails to halt noncompetitive contracting, 452
  favors blockade in Cuban crisis, 458
  finds no missile gap, 449
  flexible response policy, 449
  and space race, 447
McNeil, Joseph
  on sit-ins, 306
McNeill, William H., 513
McQuade, Walter, 524
Mead, Margaret, 353–354
Medaris, General John B., 528
Medical insurance
  lack of, 89, 266–267, 444
  Medicaid, 486, 503
  Medicare, 486, 488
Meet the Press, 135, 141
Meier, August, 525
Mellon, Andrew W., 75
Melman, Seymour, 5, 528
Mendès-France, Pierre, 231
Menjou, Adolphe, 88, 469
Meredith, James, 332
Merton, Robert K., 3, 5
Mexico, 55, 243, 467

Michigan, 23–24, 74, 93, 184, 211, 212, 214, 328
  universities, 63, 365
Mickelson, Sig, 522
Middle East, 86, 105, 243, 294, 312–325, 490, 492
  oil, 38, 313, 314, 317, 319, 321, 542
Mikoyan, Anastas I., 280, 282–284, 286, 462
Miles, Leland, 62
Military aid, 209–210, 431
Military establishment, 5, 116–117, 123, 224, 225, 425–453, 465, 501, 502, 509
  bases and congressional districts, 428
  labor force, 431
  lobbying, 427–428
  1957 spending showdown, 440–441, 507
  permanent, 117, 506
  public relations, 427
  retired officers on arms-suppliers' payrolls, 430
  rise of, 2, 425–428, 492, 528
  in Southeast Asia, 465
Military-industrial complex, 95, 100, 210, 233, 344, 366, 373, 419, 428–453, 484, 490, 507, 508, 523
  cost-plus contracting, 439–440
  creates prosperity, 432
  defined by Eisenhower, 371, 433
  few firms dominating, 431
  greatest U.S. industry, 432
  noncompetitive bidding, waste 451–452
  regional importance, 95
  in Southeast Asia, 465
Military Security act (1948), 117
Miller, Arthur, 268
Miller, Ruth McCormick, 163
Millis, Walter, 515
Mills, C. Wright, 102, 489
Mindzenty, Joseph Cardinal, 51, 246, 289
Minnesota, 175, 213, 336, 521
Missiles (See Intercontinental Ballistic Missile; Intermediate Range Ballistic Missile)
Missile gap, 344, 370, 371, 442, 444, 449, 507
  Dutch NATO delegate on, 370
  Kennedy on, 444
  Khrushchev and, 373–374, 454
  McNamara on, 371
Mississippi, 67, 299, 308, 309, 311, 332, 489
Missouri, 13, 16–18, 20, 116, 172, 179, 212, 517
Mitchell, James P., 218
Mitchell, Wesley Clair, 236
Moch, Jules, 76
Mohl, R.A. (and Richardson, J.F.), 524
Mollenhoff, Clark, 519
Mollet, Guy, 314, 317, 319, 324
Molotov, Vyacheslav M., 21, 71, 96, 143, 280, 281, 284, 286, 290, 464, 514
  Austrian treaty, 282
  confesses error, 283
  and Marshall Plan, 71
  to Outer Mongolia, 290, 337
  Tito visit, 282

and Truman, 25
Mongolia, Outer, 144, 337
Monroe, Marilyn, 387
Monroe Doctrine, 40–41
Montgomery, Ala., 301–302, 309, 310, 312, 330, 525
Moody, Dwight L., 215
Moore, John R., 430
Morley, James William, 5
Morrow, E. Frederick, 307, 525
Morse, Wayne L., 188
Mortimer, Wyndham, 519
Mossadegh, Mohammed, 319, 580
Moscow declaration (1957), 405
Moscow, Treaty of (See Testing, suspension of nuclear)
Motherwell, Robert, 274
Moynihan, Daniel Patrick, 255
Mudd, Roger, 198
Muhammad, Elijah, 328, 332, 525
Multinational corporations 241–244, 502, 503, 524.
  See also Business overseas
Mumford, Lewis, 529
Mundt, Karl E., 134, 140, 161, 187, 189
Munich agreement (1938), 4, 138, 169, 223, 449, 494–495
Murphy, Robert D., 108, 112, 520
Murray, Philip, 80, 82–85
Murrow, Edward R., 186
Muse, Benjamin, 525
Music, 1, 60, 62
Mussolini, Benito, 80, 230, 278, 317
Mutual Security act (1951), 182, 246
Myrdal, Gunnar, 334, 525

Nagasaki, 97, 141, 192, 226, 259
Naguib, General Mohammed, 314
Nagy, Imre, 286–289
Nassau County, Long Island, 258
Nasser, Gamal Abdel, 313–314, 315–319, 324, 329, 580
Nathan, Robert R., 208
Nation, The, 48, 62–63, 273
National Academy of Sciences, 340
National Association for Advancement of Colored People (NAACP), 296
National Association of Secondary Education, 54
National Association of Student Counselors, 61
National Broadcasting Co., 390, 391
National Commission on Civil Rights, 295
National Council of Christians and Jews, 184
National Defense Education Act (1958), 351, 352
National Education Association, 56
National Guard, 63, 116, 123, 124, 304–305, 308, 311, 431, 548
National Labor Relations Board, 87

National Maritime Union, 388
National Merit scholarships, 350, 357
National Recovery Administration, 36, 79, 206
National Science Foundation, 355, 356
National security, idea of, 54, 128, 392, 402, 509, 510
National Security Act (1947), 124, 395, 510
National Security Council, 117, 118, 128, 172, 210, 218, 510
  establishes CIA, 395
  Excom, 457
  on Geneva conference as "disaster," 232
  Tuesday cabinet, 529
NSC-68, 210, 523
National Security Industrial Association, 428
National Space and Aeronautical Administration (NASA), 416, 441, 442, 447, 448
Navy League, 428
Nebraska, 47, 97, 154
Nehru, Jawaharlal, 227, 313, 316, 409, 422, 472
Neil, Edward F., 119
Neo-isolationism, 160, 210, 219, 224
Netherlands, 69, 103, 114, 143, 240, 242, 323, 370
Neustadt, Richard E., 525
Neutralism, 315, 316, 318, 325, 397
Neutron bomb, 478
Nevins, Allan, 44
Newberg, William, 394
New Deal, 14–15, 29, 31, 48, 59, 71, 75, 76, 80, 81, 85, 86, 87, 92, 98, 133, 136, 139, 152, 154, 157, 158, 164, 206, 207, 208, 235, 236, 250, 379, 380, 486, 493
New Hampshire, 213, 214
  universities, 183
New Left, 274
New math, 354, 468
New Mexico, 156
New Republic, 235
New York, State University of, 361
New York Daily Mirror, 98, 342
New York Herald, 142
New York Herald Tribune, 139, 340, 391
New York Post, 389
New York State Crime Commission, 91
New York Times, The, 19, 67, 90, 121, 148, 164, 180, 189, 525
  breaks Oppenheimer story, 187
  on Communist victory in China, 149–150
  on dissatisfied housewives, 384
  on Kefauver crime hearings, 198
  on Sputnik, 341
  on TV impact on children, 261
  on tidelands oil bill, 238
  on Truman-Molotov encounter, 25
  on U.S. "concentration camps," 162
New York University, 215
New York World Telegram and Sun, 131, 389
New Yorker, The, 420, 477
New Zealand, 227
Newsweek, 62, 417, 511

Nicholls, John, 116
Niebuhr, Reinhold, 47–49, 206, 212, 270, 518
Nieburg, H.L., 5, 439, 528, 529
Nietzsche, Friedrich, 270
Nisbet, Robert A., 366, 526
Nitze, Paul H., 49, 54, 210
Nixon, Richard M., 5, 63, 131, 161, 163, 173, 184, 201, 217, 229, 242, 273, 306, 393, 400, 409, 410, 411, 418, 442, 446, 449, 497, 511, 523
  Checkers speech, 201
  China visit, 424
  Communists, bill outlawing, 131
  on Eastern European rollback, 246
  and Hiss, Alger, 132–138
  debates John Kennedy, 449
  and Khrushchev kitchen debate, 409–410
  liaison with McCarthy, 183
Nkrumah, Kwame, 313, 330, 331
Nobel prizes, 140, 240, 354, 367, 453
North American Aviation Co. (North American Rockwell), 430–431, 437, 440, 441
North Atlantic Treaty Organization, 49, 114, 209, 212, 213, 219, 226, 247, 282, 292, 313, 448, 502
  in Berlin crisis, 406
  France withdraws from, 375
  gets missiles, 370, 375
  organized, 114–115
  and U-2, 414, 415
North Carolina, 116, 246, 330
  universities, 131, 306
North China Daily News, 146
North Dakota, 165, 304, 521
Norton, John A., 56
Norway, 19, 20, 105, 414–416
Nosavan, General Phoumi, 401
Nossiter, Bernard, 524
Nuclear Test Ban treaty, 5, 51, 96, 474–484.
Nutting, Anthony, 525
Nye, Gerald P., 133

Oakland Tribune, 169
Oder-Neisse border, 101
Office of Economic Opportunity, 488
Office of Strategic Services, 395
Office of War Mobilization, 100
O'Hara, Frank, 273
O'Hara, John, 421
Ohio, 61, 116, 235, 295, 393, 478, 502
Oil, 79, 86, 158, 238, 241–243, 501, 502, 524, 542
  and antitrust, 393
  and cars, 254, 256.
  See also Middle East; Texas
Oil and Gas Journal
  on tidelands oil, 238
Oklahoma, 162, 432
Old age, 89–90, 266–267. See also Pensions

Oligopoly, 234, 240, 254
Olson, Philip, 529
O'Neill, William L., 530
Open Door policy, 24, 33, 142–143, 145, 149, 172, 514
Opium war (1838–40), 177
Opotosky, Stan, 522, 527
Oppenheimer, J. Robert, 2, 140, 141, 183, 187, 189, 190, 192–193, 336, 347, 474, 496, 522
Orange County, California, 258
Oregon Journal, 343
Organization of American States, 460
Organization of African States, 332
Organization of Afro-American Unity, 332
Orwell, George, 44–45, 535
Oswald, Lee Harvey, 490
Overkill, 337, 449
Oxnam, G. Bromley, 184

Pachter, Henry M., 529
Pacifists, 47–48, 472, 520
Packard, David, 366
Packard, Vance O., 262
Page, David, 354
Paige, Glenn, 522
Pakistan, 313, 315, 414, 416
Palmer, A. Mitchell, 33, 206
Palmer, Arnold, 470
Panama, 221
Pan American World Airways, 419
Paquet, Gilles, 524
Paris summit conference (1960), 418–419, 465, 473
Parks, Mrs. Rosa, 301, 309, 330
Passell, Peter (and Ross, Leonard) 5, 523
Pasternak, Boris, 272
Pathet Lao, 401–402
Patio, 258
Patterson, James T., 518
Patterson, John M., 308
Patterson, Robert, 121
Patterson, Thomas J., 519
Pauker, Ana, 106
Paul VI, Pope, 50
Peace Corps, 443, 487
Pearl Harbor, 10, 21, 117, 119, 126, 128, 143, 173, 193, 259, 340, 342, 399, 443, 458, 460, 492, 493, 511
Pearson, Lester B., 226, 320
Peck, Morton J. (and Scherer, Frederick M.), 528
Peking, 5, 144, 146–149, 169, 280, 374, 411, 412, 424, 473, 474, 476, 479, 480, 483, 508
Pendergast, Tom, 14
Peng, Liu-shai, Marshal, 408
Peng, Ti-huai, General, 177
Pensions, old-age, 87–90, 93
  private, 89–90, 543
  public (*See* Social Security)

Pentagon Papers, 399–400, 511, 523, 527
Peress, Irving, 185
Perry, Commodore Oliver H., 142
Philadelphia, 92, 132, 200, 251, 259, 262, 301, 392
Philippines, 121, 168, 174, 228, 239, 400
Phillips, Cabell, 517, 523
Piaf, Edith, 352
Pierce, Franklin, 15
Pike, Sumner T., 16
Pineau, Christian, 318
Pius XII, Pope, 50–51, 227
Plattsburgh, New York, 121
Playboy, 387
Ploss, Sidney, 524
Pluralism, 159–160, 333, 380
Point Four, 194, 292–293, 525
Poiret, Paul, 358
Poland, 21, 24–25, 69, 99, 101, 106, 108, 329, 475, 482
  1956 revolt, 247, 285, 288, 291
  and Russia, 72–73
Polaris submarines, 449, 451, 460
Polk, James K., 15
Polish-Americans, 246, 380
Politburo (*See* U.S.S.R., Communist Party)
Pollock, Jackson, 272–273
Pollution, 79, 432, 447, 482, 503
Population, 89, 382
  and employment, 443
  movement to cities from South, 77–79, 327, 499, 504
  movement to suburbs, 249–250, 504
  postwar rise, 59, 237, 360, 484–485
Potsdam conference (1945), 32, 96, 103, 282, 451, 482
Potter, Charles E., 184
Powdermaker, Hortense, 529
Powers, Francis G., 412–419, 528
Poznan riots (1956), 285
Prague, 18, 104–105, 131, 246
Pravda, 20, 45, 280, 288, 337
Presbyterian church, 216, 220, 236
President's Commission on Campus Unrest (1970), 63, 64
President's Commission on Higher Education (1948), 59, 360, 362, 526
President's Scientific Advisory Committee, 346–347, 355–356, 453
Presidium (*See* U.S.S.R., Communist party)
Presley, Elvis, 1, 61
Press
  and the cold war, 97–99, 246, 493, 494
Price, Harry B., 519
Price, Leontyne, 469
Price, Melvin
  on the draft, 120
Prince Edward County, Virginia, 300
Princeton University, 62, 63, 220, 514, 523
  federal grants to, 364, 365, 369
Progressive Citizens of America, 49

Progressive education, 54, 58, 352, 354, 357, 358, 518, 526
Prokoviev, Dmitri, 540
Prosser, William L., 54
Protestant churches, 46, 47, 49, 157, 183, 380, 518
Public schools (See Schools)
Puerto Ricans, 421, 504
Pugwash conferences, 453, 529
Pusey, Nathan M., 365, 369

Quemoy-Matsu, 324, 407
Quiz-show scandals (See Television)

Racial discrimination, 3, 28–29, 252, 293, 312, 325–334, 345, 505
Radford, Admiral Arthur W., 229, 477
Radio, 61, 98, 111, 179, 200, 201, 203, 228, 246, 261, 300, 314, 388–389, 436, 450, 461, 493. See also Conelrad.
Radio Free Europe, 246, 283, 396
Radio Liberation, 246, 283
Radio Liberty, 396
Radio Cairo, 314
Radosh, Ronald, 519
Radvanyi, Janos, 529
Radwan, Edward, 121
Railroads, 28, 254, 267, 421
Rains, Claude, 391
Rajk, Laszlo, 106
Rakosi, Matyas, 286
Ramadier, Paul, 65
Ramo, Simon, 437, 438
Ranch house, 258–264, 377, 571
Rand Corp., 42, 337
Randall, Clarence B., 340
Ransom, Harry Howe, 527
Raskin, Abraham H., 90
Ray, James Earl, 490
Rayburn, Sam, 11, 15
Raymond, Jack, 528
Reapportionment, legislative, 485–486, 530
Recession:
    of 1949, 87, 89, 208, 237, 249, 251
    of 1953–1954, 237
    of 1957–1958, 85
    of 1960, 443
Reconstruction Finance Corp., 195–196
Reconversion, postwar, 9–11, 15, 74, 117, 207
Red Flag (Peking), 412
Red Star (Moscow), 9
Reed, James A., 116
Rees, David, 514, 522
Reiss, Ira L., 386, 527
Religion, 216, 379, 380, 527
    decline of power of, 45, 270, 379
    secularization in, 46, 380

Remarque, Erich Maria, 65
Remmann, H.J., 347
Reparations, postwar, 33, 100, 103, 221, 270
Research and development, 240–241, 359, 361, 429, 431, 468, 500
Reservists, 123, 124, 425–426, 431
    callups, 122, 426, 450, 462
    numbers in Congress, 427
Reston, James B., 67, 449
Reuter, Ernst, 110, 111
Reuther, Victor G., 81
Reuther, Walter P., 81–85, 92, 206, 235, 246, 388, 579
    on Communists as puppets, 83
Revisionist historians, 2, 513, 514
Rhee, Syngman, 168, 176
Rhodes, Richard, 523
Richardson, Sid, 158, 238
Rice, Eugene F. Jr., 5
Richberg, Donald, 206
Rickey, Branch, 294
Rickover, Admiral Hyman G., 352, 353, 526
Ridgeway, James, 526
Ridgway, General Matthew B., 178–179, 181, 230
Riesman, David, 262, 269, 524
Rio de Janeiro, treaty of (1942), 114
Rivers, L. Mendel, 428
Roberts, Clifford, 212
Roberts, Henry L., 337
Roberts, Owen J., 119
Robeson, Paul, 1
Robinson, Jackie, 294
Rockefeller, Nelson A., 214, 338, 445, 446, 526
Rockefeller Foundation, 53, 350
Rock'n'roll, 1, 61, 423
Rocky Mountain News, 342
Rogers, William P., 184, 305, 393
Rogin, Michael P., 521
Rokossovsky, Marshal Konstantin, 285, 286
Rolling Stones, 469
Romains, Jules, 65
Roosevelt, Eleanor, 11, 518
Roosevelt, Franklin D., 8, 11, 12, 14, 19, 21, 23–5, 35–37, 50, 79, 80, 97, 98, 121, 126, 128, 131, 133, 136, 143, 151, 164, 173, 200, 202, 203, 206, 207, 211, 215, 218, 219, 222, 228, 278, 294, 314, 370–371, 464, 469
Roosevelt, Kermit, 580
Roosevelt, Theodore, 121, 143, 206, 213, 221, 222, 336, 400
Root, Elihu, 121
Rose, Peter I., 525
Rosenberg, Harold, 273
Rosenberg, Julius, and Ethel, 186, 556
Ross, Arthur M., 357
Ross, Charles, 140
Ross, Ishbel, 518
Rostow, Walt W., 54, 173, 448, 507, 526, 529
Rothschild, Joseph, 5
Rovere, Richard H., 160, 478, 521, 522, 523

Rowe, James H. Jr., 104
Royal Institute of International Affairs (Chatham House), 513, 523, 526, 529
Rubber, 231, 254, 256
Rudwick, Elliott, 525
Rudy, S. Willis, 526
Ruhr, 99, 103
Rumania, 26, 72
Rush, Myron, 524
Rusk, Dean, 53, 105, 138, 166, 171, 177, 308, 350, 368, 455, 460, 461, 470, 478, 483, 515
Russell, Bertrand, 453
Russell, Richard B., 15, 122, 123, 180, 233, 300, 303, 340
Russell, William F., 56

St. Clair, James D., 191
St. George, Utah, 472
St. John's University, 489
St. Louis Post-Dispatch, 39
St. Paul Pioneer Press, 39
St. Petersburg, Fla., 89
Sakharov, Andrei D., 474
Saltonstall, Leverett, 186, 233
San Francisco, 22–25, 128, 132, 133, 142, 160, 179, 203, 218, 239, 362, 421
San Francisco Daily News, 342
Sartre, Jean-Paul, 270–271, 274
Saturday Evening Post, 250
Saturday Review, 271, 422
Saulnier, Raymond J., 266
Sauvy, Alfred, 293
Savio, Mario, 489
Sayre, Francis B., 133
Scali, John, 461
Schenck, Peter J., 429
Schilling, Warner R., 523
Schine, G. David, 182–183, 185–187
Schlesinger, Arthur Jr., 5, 518, 520, 529
Schmidt, William M., 255
Schools, 45, 52, 60, 64, 444, 493, 497, 499, 518
    Cold War ideology in, 52–64, 98
    desegregation in, 296–312, 345, 504
    and economic growth, 59–60, 359
    reorienting goals after Sputnik, 344–359
    post-Cold War legislation, 486, 488, 503
    shortage of, 266
Schottland, Charles I.
    on mechanization and early retirement, 88
Schram, Stuart R., 521
Schriever, General Bernard A., 327, 437–438
Science, 48, 140, 192, 240–241, 269, 270, 339–340, 343, 344, 346–347, 447, 474
    and education after Sputnik, 344–345, 351, 356–358, 359–369
    and status, 381. See also Technology.
Scientific Advisory Committee to Atomic Energy Commission, 140, 193
Seattle, 91, 419, 430, 431

Securities and Exchange Commission (SEC), 233, 395
Seager, J.B. Allan
    on "silent generation", 63
Selective Service system, 115–25, 520. See also Draft, the.
Senate Armed Services committee, 186, 300, 428
Senate Foreign Relations committee, 211, 402
Senate Special Committee to Investigate Organized Crime, 198
Senior citizens, 89–90, 266–267
Servan-Schreiber, Jean-Jacques, 240
Service, John S., 150, 521
Servicemen's Readjustment act (1944). See GI Bill of Rights.
Sevareid, A. Eric, 268, 352
Seventh Army (Germany), 247
Seventh Fleet (Far East), 174, 176, 227
Seward, William H., 200, 203
Sex, 61
    abortion reform after Cold War, 386
    double standard, 382–384
    marriage, early, 384
    marriage, open, accepted after Cold War, 386
    the pill, effect on, 386–387
    premarital, 382, 384, 386, 387
Shanghai, 144, 146
Shanks, Carrol M., 394
Sharecroppers, southern, 77–79
Shaw, George Bernard, 19
Sheehan, Neil, 527
Shelepin, Alexander N., 399
Shenton, James P., 5
Shepard, Alan B. Jr., 448
Shepilov, Dmitri T., 280, 281, 290
Shirley, George, 331
Shonfield, Andrew, 524
Shopping centers, 254, 264, 432
Short, Dewey, 179
Shostakovich, Dmitri, 540
Shriver, R. Sargent Jr., 487–488
Shulman, Marshall D., 5, 474, 527
Siberia, 33, 206, 290, 456
Siegel, Benjamin (Buggsy), 199
Sikkim, 422
Silberman, Charles E., 78, 358, 525, 526
Silent generation, 2, 60–63, 123, 203, 494
Sinclair, Upton, 206
Singer Co., 242
Sirhan, Sirhan, 490
Slessor, Sir John, 322
Sloan, Alfred P. Jr., 254
Smith, David, 273–274
Smith, Gaddis, 5, 515
Smith, G. Kerry, 526
Smith, Kingsbury, 112
Smith, General Walter Bedell, 117, 232, 397
Snyder, John W., 517
Social scientists, 42–43, 236–237, 262, 269, 468, 521

and desegregation decision, 298
and higher education, 362–363
and Pentagon planning, 445–446
and postindustrial society, 468
and Soviet behavior, 337–338
Social Security, 87, 157, 237, 486
Socialism, 48, 76, 80, 81, 100, 131, 158
Sokolovsky, General Vasily D., 107, 110, 119
Solzhenitsyn, Alexander, 34, 272
Somoza, General Anastasio, 464
Sorensen, Theodore C., 455, 457, 458, 529
Southeast Asia Treaty Organization (SEATO), 225, 313
Southern Christian Leadership Conference (SCLC), 306
Southern Manifesto, 300
Souvanna Phouma, 401
Spaatz, General Carl A., 120
Space race, 194, 375, 434, 441, 447, 502, 507
Space Technology Laboratories, 438, 440
Spain, 20, 192, 493
Spanier, John W., 516
Spectorsky, A.C., 262, 524
Spellman, Francis J. Cardinal, 49–52, 246, 518
Split-level houses, 377–379
Sports, 387
    baseball, integration of, 294
    basketball, cheating in, 196
    Olympics, blacks in, 327
    Palmer and Tittle on TV, 470
    viewing, as TV pastime, 470
Sputniks, 35, 339–344, 350, 352–356, 372, 413, 441, 444, 499, 526
Stalin, Josef V., 1, 4, 8, 12, 19, 20, 21, 24–25, 32–35, 45, 48, 51, 67, 72, 96–99, 104, 106, 107, 112, 119, 132, 138, 143, 166, 168, 170, 171, 176, 177, 207, 213, 222–224, 246, 247, 274–277, 281–289, 313, 315, 317, 403, 404, 464, 472, 479, 481, 482, 496, 509, 518, 524, 556
    on Berlin, capture of, 99
    on Churchill Iron Curtain speech, 20
    death of, 222
    Khrushchev speech denouncing, 284
    postwar buildup speech, 33
    on postwar expectations, 35
    on risk of U.S. intervention in Korea, 170
    on Tito, 106
Stalin, Svetlana, 540
Standard Oil Co. of New Jersey, 240, 241
Stanford Research Institute, 365–366
Stanford University, 63, 357, 364, 365, 437, 438
Stanton, Frank M., 391
Starobin, Joseph, 519
Starr, Bart, 470
Stassen, Harold E., 182, 213
Steel, 87, 211, 254, 436, 468, 501
Stefan, Karl, 154
Stegner, Wallace, 63
Steiger, Rod, 190
Stein, Herbert, 523

Steinberg, Alfred, 517
Steiner, Gary, 522
Steinfeld, Jesse L., 261
Stempel, Herbert, 390
Stepinac, Archbishop Aloysius, 51
Stern, Fritz R., 5
Stettinius, Edward R. Jr., 195, 515
Stevens, Robert T., 185–187
Stevenson, Adlai E., 186, 213, 226, 331, 457–460, 510
Stewart, Alexander T., 238
Stilwell, General Joseph, 521
Stimson, Henry L., 53, 119, 121, 127–128, 164, 239, 515
Stone, Ronald H., 518
Strandlund, Charles, 195
Strategic Air Command (SAC), 97, 193, 337, 345, 375, 434, 460. See also U.S. Air Force
Strategic stockpiling, 431, 432
Strauss, Lewis L., 140, 193, 347, 364, 477, 523
Strikes, 9, 28, 46, 79–80, 499
Strout, Cushing, 518
Stuart, J. Leighton, 148–149, 521
Studebaker, John W., 55
Studebaker Corp., 75, 211, 212, 350
Students, 1, 52–64, 348–369, 499–500
    revolts, 54, 60, 299, 366–369, 489, 501
    school-leaving age, 3, 59.
Student deferments (See Draft, the)
Students for a Democratic Society (SDS), 367, 489
Students Nonviolent Coordinating Committee (SNCC), 306, 332
Stuttgart, 100–101
Subversive Activities Control Board, 161–162
Suez crisis, 220, 221, 245, 288, 291, 312–325, 374, 406, 413, 461, 490, 497, 515, 525
Sukarno, 399
Sullivan, Ed, 98, 469
Sullivan and Cromwell, 221, 399
Summerfield, Arthur E., 211–212, 214, 235
Sun Yat-sen, 144
Survey of Broadcast Journalism, 522
Surrealism, 272–273
Suslov, Mikhail A., 287
Sverdlovsk, 414–416
Swados, Harvey, 524, 263, 524
Sweden, 3, 124, 222
Sweeney, General Walter C., 459
Swomley, John Jr., 520, 528
Swope, Herbert Bayard, 43
Symington, Stuart, 188, 444, 448
Syria, 313, 321, 325, 375

Taber, John, 31
Taft, Charles Phelps, 46–47
Taft, Philip, 519
Taft, Robert A., 15, 30–31, 46, 87, 148, 152,

156, 169, 175, 210–213, 214, 219, 224, 225, 235–238, 246, 518, 530
on brother Charles, 46
on Communist victory in China, 141
on Eisenhower spending, 225
on European aid, 148
on facts, 30
on McCarthy, 156
on meat prices, 31
"no more Bohlens," 183
on tact, 31
on Truman "usurpation" of Congress on Korea, 174
Taft, William Howard, 30, 46, 127, 143
Taft-Hartley Act, 46, 82, 87, 98, 498
Taiwan, 168, 176, 178, 228, 229, 242, 399, 403, 426
Talbott, Nelson Strobridge III, 522
Tang Chou, 521
Tannenbaum, Frank, 244
Tarr, Curtis, 124
Tass, 339
Tatu, Michel, 527, 528, 529
Tax, Sol, 520
Taylor, General Maxwell D., 173, 447–448, 507
Taylor, Robert, 98
Tech Review, 346
Technical Cooperation Administration, 293
Teheran conference, 22, 24, 97
Television, 98, 179, 187–204, 246, 247, 261, 331, 368, 411, 419, 426, 449, 450, 468, 469, 494, 522, 527
A-tests on, 471–472
aerials, fake, 381
and attention span, 368
in campaigns, 200–202
and civil rights, 309, 310, 325
and crime hearings, 198–200
Eisenhower Little Rock speech on, 217
and the home, 258, 261
major innovation of Cold War years, 197
and McCarthy, 153, 186–192
Moscow kitchen debate on, 410
quiz-show scandals, 388–391
shelter debate on, 450
from space, 419
and sports, 197, 469
Truman's White House tour, 204
and violence, 260–261
Teller, Edward, 347, 474, 477
Tennessee Valley Authority (TVA), 139, 259, 391
Terman, Frederick E., 357
Testing, suspension of nuclear, 405, 453, 471–478, 507, 508, 529
atmospheric, 376, 473, 474, 476
in space, 474, 482
limited test-ban treaty (Treaty of Moscow), 474–478, 482–483, 484, 487, 507, 508
underground, 474, 475, 507
Texas, 62, 78, 213, 238, 300, 303, 437, 441, 490
Thailand, 231, 400

Thalidomide, 468
Thaw, the, 223, 275, 279, 496
Thayer, George, 528
Thirty-eighth parallel, 166, 176–177, 179
Thomas, Hugh, 525
Thomas, J. Parnell, 131
Thomas, R.J., 82
Thompson, Kenneth W., 518
Thompson-Ramo-Wooldridge Co. (TRW), 438–440, 442
Thondup, Prince, 422
Tibet, 400, 408
Tillich, Paul, 270
Time, 5, 45, 75, 119, 131, 132, 137, 188, 248, 268, 389, 391, 417
Tito, Josip Broz, 35, 105–107, 282, 285, 286, 316, 520
Tittle, Y.A., 470
Todd, Mike, 422
Tokyo, 32, 108, 167, 172, 174
Tolstoy, Leo, 270
Torre, Marie, 391
Totalitarianism, 41, 43, 45, 48, 138, 171, 222, 293, 343, 372, 471, 494–495
Tourism, new, 420–422, 432. *See also* Jetliners.
Toye, Hugh, 527
Toynbee, Arnold J., 469, 513
Treaty of Moscow (*See* Testing, suspension of nuclear)
Trevelyan, Sir Humphrey, 579
Trilling, Lionel, 45
Trotsky, Leon, 55
Trotskyites, 56, 80
Trout, Bob, 198
Truman, Bess, 12, 15
Truman, Harry S., 2, 9, 10, 11–16, 17–18, 25–28, 32–39, 43, 44, 46, 49, 51, 55, 59, 65, 67, 70, 73, 74, 80, 82, 86, 87, 96, 97, 101, 105, 108, 111, 114–120, 127–129, 134, 137, 138, 141, 148, 151–152, 156, 157, 160–164, 168, 169, 172, 177–181, 195, 200, 204, 206, 207, 209, 212, 213, 215–220, 224, 239, 246, 292–293, 337, 348, 397, 433, 446, 450, 452, 453, 471, 486, 490–498, 501, 503, 504, 513, 515, 517, 518, 520, 523, 524
on A-bomb in Berlin crisis, 111
on A-bomb and Russians, 128
announces Soviet A-bomb, 140
on "babying" Russia, 26
becomes president, 16
on Brandeis, 14
cancels lend-lease, 10
on Eisenhower in office, 218
on German invasion of Russia, 12
invites Churchill to Fulton, 16
Korean decision, 172
on loyalty-security program, 130
meets Allied armies, 12
1948 acceptance speech, 200
on Peter the Great's "will," 11
Point Four speech, 292–293
on postwar "cooperation" to Molotov, 25

on predecessors, 15
becomes president, 16
relieves MacArthur, 13, 179
St. Patrick's Day speech, 118–119
on 1798 mood of Congress, 161
on technological supremacy, 337
Truman Doctrine speech, 39–41
on U.S. Berlin stand, 108
on U.S. postwar economic power (Waco), 32–33
on U.S. as postwar leader (Carruthersville), 33
on Wallace speech, 27
Truman, Margaret, 515
Truman Doctrine, 2, 39–41, 49, 64, 67, 72, 79, 97, 107, 118, 151, 173, 324, 492–494, 518. *See also* Britain; Greece; Turkey.
Tuchman, Barbara W., 521
Tucker, Robert C., 524
Tully, Andrew, 527
Tunner, General William H., 109, 520
Turkey, 37–41, 67–69, 171, 222, 230, 313, 370, 375, 412–416, 459, 461, 462, 497, 508, 518
Tuskegee Institute, 333
Twentieth Party Congress (*See* U.S.S.R.)
Twining, General Nathan F., 230, 415
Tyuratam cosmodrome, 413, 414, 415
Tydings, Millard E., 156, 162–163

U-2, 404, 412–419, 456–458, 461, 465, 473, 504, 528
Ukraine, 246, 284, 398
Ulam, Adam B., 404, 409, 515, 520, 527, 528, 529
Unemployment insurance, 87, 157, 237, 487
Unilever Ltd., 242
Union for Democratic Action, 49
Union of Soviet Socialist Republics, 2, 81, 96, 126, 232, 402
A-bomb and H-bomb, 35, 226, 227, 274–275
agricultural policies, 276–279
Bolshevik revolution, 20, 33, 166, 205, 206, 372, 405
China, relations with, 150, 371–373, 403–404
A-bomb promise withdrawn, 375, 408, 412, 473
aid in 1957, 373, 406–407
charge heresy, 481–482
Chinese diplomats expelled, 476
in civil war, 141, 150
impact of Cuban crisis, 454, 455, 463, 464
Khruschev visit to Peking, 411
in Korean war, 170, 176
negotiations in 1963, 475–476
"open letter" on dispute, 476
split, 476–482
tardy Quemoy-Matsu support, 407, 473, 479
trade pact of 1954, 280
trade pact of 1959, 408
Communist party, 276, 454

Central Committee, 283–284, 289–290
Congresses:
16th, 284
19th, 222
20th, 283–285, 290
21st, 408
Politburo, 24
Presidium, 276–278, 280–284, 290–291, 337
consumer policies
under Khrushchev, 373, 376
under Malenkov, 275, 280
Destalinization, 283–285, 289
Eastern Europe, relations with, 4, 18
Budapest revolt, 286–289
Czech coup, 104–105
as economic bloc, 72–73
New Course and Hungary, 286
New Course and Poland, 285
post-Tito purges, 106–107
postwar, 24, 26, 33–34, 97
Warsaw crisis, 285–289
Yugoslav expulsion, 105–107
and Finland, 104, 105
Five-Year plans, 34–35
Khrushchev foreign policy, 372–376, 462–464
Khrushchev premier and party chief, 403
leadership struggle, 272–282
missile development, 35, 340–341, 371–372
police terror, 34, 138, 275, 283–285, 403
post-Stalin New Course, 222, 274–280
prison camps, 34, 275
Stalin's postwar expansion plan, 34–35, 72
Supreme Soviet, 281, 283, 290, 415–416, 474
technological and scientific development, 34, 347, 348, 353
Third world, relations with, 372, 375, 463, 472, 473
with Egypt, 315
with India, 315, 408, 412
U.S., relations with,
and A-bomb, 126–129, 375, 406, 408
consolidates Eastern Europe hold, 104–107
Cuban missile crisis, 452–465
in Germany, 99–107
Berlin blockade, 107–115
East Berlin riots, 228, 291, 398
Western zone currency reform, 104
Second Berlin crisis and Eisenhower, 405–408, 411, 463
Second Berlin crisis and Kennedy, 449–450
the Wall, 451
and Greece, 37–40
in Japan, 21, 169–170
Kennan's analysis, 35–36
in Korea, 170
Marshall Plan, opposition to, 71–73
in Middle East, 37–39, 105, 315, 324–325, 372, 375
postwar aid and reparations, 33–34
test-ban treaty, 471–478
U.S. intervention in Russia, 20, 33

as World War II allies, 8–9, 10, 20–21, 23–25, 44, 128, 132, 239, 493
World War II, 12, 21–25, 72, 99, 100, 407
Union Theological Seminary, 47, 49
Union welfare funds, 91–94. *See also* Pensions, private.
United Auto Workers, 81–85, 98, 235, 388, 498
United Department Store Workers, 94
United Fruit Co., 221, 243
United Mine Workers, 15, 28, 83–85, 87–90, 499
United Nations, 15, 18–25, 37, 40, 45, 48, 68, 71, 98, 99, 105, 111, 114, 128, 132, 133, 136, 156, 164, 179, 200, 222, 292, 296, 308, 319, 323, 331, 351, 454, 458, 460, 462
and blacks, 296
founded in U.S., 269
General Assembly, 322, 454, 459, 482
and Hungary, 288–289
and Korea, 173, 177–179, 228
and nuclear ban in space, 482
Security Council, 113, 173, 319, 322, 331
and Suez, 288, 319, 320
United Nations Emergency Force, 324
United Nations Relief and Rehabilitation Administration (UNRRA), 25, 68–69
U.S. Air Force, 23, 42, 44, 97, 109, 120, 139, 161, 178, 193, 224, 225, 230, 246–247, 399, 412, 414, 418, 419, 426, 428, 436, 501, 502, 529
Cold War, mission of, 97, 427
in comic strips, 427
in Cuban missile crisis, 458, 459
ICBM mission, 435
missiles, late start in, 434
and private industry, 429, 435
rise and expansion, 210
spending squeeze of 1957, 441
in World War II, 96, 435
U.S. Army, 36, 123, 124, 204, 225, 230, 305, 338, 399, 426, 434, 501, 502, 508
in Europe, 210, 247
"in-house" technical capability, 429, 435
integration of, 178, 295–296
in Korea, 175–180
in Little Rock, 305
and McCarthy, 183–193
missile program with von Braun, 341, 433, 435
postwar reduction, 115
Redstone arsenal, 434, 435, 442
in World War II, 8–9, 96
U.S. Chamber of Commerce, 95
U.S. Department of Defense, 35, 53–54, 95, 128, 161, 173, 210, 225, 340, 341, 427–453, 462, 501, 502, 520
arms dealing, 432
broadcast system, 436
created 1947, 117
diplomatic service, 436
educational system, 432
employment by, 431

Korean intervention, 173
real estate, 432–433
retail market system, 432
spending, 436
U.S. Department of Health, Education and Welfare, 350
U.S. Department of Justice, 125, 136–137, 162, 206, 235, 238, 303, 304, 307, 392, 393, 495
U.S. Department of Labor, 399
on women in professional jobs, 385
U.S. Department of State, 35, 53, 67, 74, 98, 117, 132, 133, 136, 138, 140, 141–150, 154, 155, 156, 162, 164, 169, 182, 183, 209, 222, 241, 243, 331, 397, 398, 399, 402, 416, 417, 423, 461, 483, 495, 496, 513, 514, 518
as bureaucracy, 370
and Dept. of Defense, 118, 432
and jets, 423–424
and McCarthy, 154–165
Point Four, 292
Policy Planning staff, 49, 67
U.S. Navy, 53, 54, 96, 174, 176, 210, 225, 227, 341, 399, 426, 433, 449, 451, 460, 501, 502
as bureaucracy, 370
Cold War mission of, 427
Navy yards as "in-house" technical capability, 429
U.S. Steel Corp., 45, 84, 265, 309, 310
and automation, 468
U.S. Supreme Court, 124, 253, 495, 504, 525, 529
desegregation decisions, 297–305, 312
reapportionment decisions, 485–486
United Steel Workers, 80, 84
Universal Military Training, 118, 120, 121
Universities and colleges, 42, 52–59, 240–241, 359, 369, 486, 497, 500, 518, 587
government contracts, 54, 364–369, 500
parietal rules changed, 367, 386
population growth, 59, 86, 360–361
sports scandals, 96–97
student unrest, 366–369, 500
Updike, John, 470
Urban decay, 252–253, 444, 447, 485
crowding, 267, 499
delay of Federal action, 266–268
Great Society programs, 486–488, 503
housing and freeways, 255–257, 504
mass transit, lack of, 267, 268
public housing, lack of, 252–253, 267, 444
Urban riots, 489, 490
Urey, Harold C., 140

Valentine, Alan, 75
Van Arsdale, Harry, 94
Van Buren, Martin, 198
Vandenberg, Arthur Jr., 515
Vandenberg, Arthur Sr., 23–24, 26, 40, 67, 100,

111, 114, 115, 118, 152, 211, 221, 492, 515, 517, 519
on businessmen for Marshall Plan, 74, 75
on China policy, 148
on Clayton, Will, 74
on German invasion of Poland, 23
on Greek-Turkish crisis, 38, 39
on Hoffman, Paul, 75
on Lilenthal, David, 139
on Marshall Plan, 73
Senate speech on collective security, 24
on Wallace, Henry, 28
Vandenberg Resolution, for NATO, 114
Vandenberg, General Hoyt S., 23
Van Doren, Charles, 390
Vanguard missile, 341–342
Van Zandt, James, on Truman Doctrine, 40
Varga, Eugene, 76
Vatican, 50–52, 66
Vaughn, General Harry H., 16–17, 195
Veblen, Thorstein, 47, 206
Velde, Harold, 183
Venezuela, 242
Vernon, Raymond, 524
Veterans Administration, 57–60, 250–257
Veterans Emergency Housing program, 10
Vietnam, 51, 95, 123, 125, 173, 204, 219, 231, 400, 448, 465, 490, 507, 511
    North Vietnam, 400, 401, 402
    South Vietnam, 399, 401, 490
    war, 5, 124, 125, 178, 452, 498, 503, 508, 512, 520, 529, 530
Vincent, John Carter, 164
Vinson, Fred M., 296
Virgin lands, 278–279, 290
Virginia, 37, 164, 165, 300, 332
Vishinsky, Andrei, 45, 98
Vogeler, Robert, 246
Voice of America, 396
Von Borch, Herbert, 268, 524
Von Braun, Wernher, 433–437
Voroshilov, Kliment, 280, 281, 284, 290

Wagner Act, 79
Wake Island, 97, 177, 180
Wallace, George C., 310, 312
Wallace, Henry A., 12, 14, 27–28, 31, 49, 51, 83, 111, 151, 194, 206
Walsh, Rev. Edmund, 154
Warner, Sam Bass, 524
Warren, Earl, 296, 299, 300, 303
Warsaw Pact, 288, 321, 406
Washington Daily News, 135
Washington Post, 156, 189, 215, 429, 430
Washington Times-Herald, 156
Wattenberg, Ben, 524
Wayne, John, 469
Webb, James E., 447
Wechsler, James A., 519

Wedemeyer, General Albert C., 521
Weintal, Edward (and Bartlett, Charles), 529
Welch, Joseph M., 90–91
Welles, Sumner, 464
Westerfield, H. Bradford, 517
Westinghouse Corp., 75, 197, 391–394, 440
Westminster College, 16–18
Westmoreland, General William C., 230
West Point (U.S. Military Academy) 37, 100, 185, 198–199
Wheeler, General Earle G., 173
Wherry. Kenneth S., 40, 156
White Citizens' Councils, 300, 304
White, Harry Dexter, 137
White, Lawrence, 254, 523
White, Theodore H., 307, 521, 522
White, William Allen, 17, 517
White, William S., 152, 518
Whiting, Allen S., 522, 529
Whitney, Alexander F., 28
Whitten, Jamie L., 428
Whiz kids, 445
Whyte, William H., 262, 524
Widick, B. Jack, 5, 519
Wiesner, Jerome B., 366, 453, 528, 529
Wilbur, C. Martin, 5
Wilcox, Howard, 256
Wiley, Alexander, 140
Willauer, Whiting, 402
Williams, Robert, 332
Williams, William Appleman, 514
Wills, Gary, 523
Wilson, Charles Edward, 295
Wilson, Charles Erwin, 10, 81, 84, 211, 225, 233–238, 295, 346, 373, 435, 436, 445, 451
    on America and General Motors, 233
    McNamara, compared to, 445
    prefers private missile procurement, 435
    on Sputnik, 340
Wilson, Woodrow, 20, 22–23, 65, 128, 133, 169, 217, 220
Winchell, Walter, 98–99
Wisconsin, 153, 159, 186, 214, 246, 521
    universities, 53, 153, 361, 587
Wise, David B. (and Ross, Thomas B.), 527
Wisner, Frank, 396
Wolfe, Thomas W., 527, 529
Women, 382–88
    and Cold War domesticity, 249–250, 382–384
    and employment, 383, 385
Wood, General Leonard, 121
Wood, Robert C., 524
Woodcock, Leonard, 92
Woodward, C. Vann, 259, 492, 525
Woodward, Robert F., 292
Wooldridge, Dean E., 437
World War I, 13–14, 20, 36, 45, 65, 69, 77, 116, 117, 206, 221, 240, 245, 262, 269, 272, 407, 442, 499, 508

sexual revolution following, 383
World War II, 1, 2, 12, 14, 19–22, 37, 46, 50,
    54, 59, 65–67, 72, 74, 76, 81, 85, 101, 105,
    117, 122, 141–142, 143–146, 161, 172, 176,
    177, 181, 200, 206, 212, 219, 234, 245, 259,
    262, 269, 294, 327, 336, 361, 407, 429, 436,
    442, 467, 470, 475, 478, 509, 510
    Allied relationships, 2, 19–22, 24–25
    end of, 4, 7, 32, 41, 52–53, 57, 60, 65, 77, 79,
        80, 109, 115, 117, 150, 159, 169, 175,
        193, 207, 209, 238, 239, 251, 255, 293,
        340, 351, 359, 377, 421, 433, 461, 471,
        483, 485, 498, 504
    second front, 21
World War III, 35, 97, 105, 120, 149, 247, 396,
    511
Wouk, Herman, 53
Wriggins, W. Howard, 5
Wright, Frank Lloyd, 377–378
Wyoming, 188–189
Wyszinsky, Stepan Cardinal, 289

Xoxo, Kochi, 106

Yale University, 42, 46, 47, 121, 173, 362, 387,
    395, 467, 489

Yalta conference, 24–26, 97, 103, 132, 164, 228,
    246
Yalu River, 177, 402, 453
Yarmolinsky, Adam, 528
Yenan, 143–145
Young, E. Merl, 195
Young Communists, 278–279
Young Republicans, 141, 156, 191
Yucca Flats, Nev., 471
Yugoslavia, 35, 51, 72, 107, 246, 291, 412, 481,
    482
    in Cominform, 72–73
    defection, 4, 105–106
    Khrushchev visit, 282
    Nasser visit, 316
    rift compared to 1963 Chinese split, 479
    and UNRRA, 69

Zacharias, Jerrold R., 354–356, 358, 366
Zagoria, Donald S., 528
Zellerbach, James D., 75–76
Zoppo, C.E., 529
Zhdanov, Andrei A., 72–73, 106–107, 280–281,
    540
Zhukov, Marshal Georgei K., 99, 290, 291
Zhukov, Yuri, 461
Zinn, Howard, 525
Zwicker, General Ralph W., 186